# Smart Technology Applications in Business Environments

Tomayess Issa
*Curtin University, Australia*

Piet Kommers
*University of Twente, The Netherlands*

Theodora Issa
*Curtin University, Australia*

Pedro Isaías
*Portuguese Open University, Portugal*

Touma B. Issa
*Murdoch University, Australia*

A volume in the Advances in Business Information
Systems and Analytics (ABISA) Book Series

www.igi-global.com

Published in the United States of America by
    IGI Global
    Business Science Reference (an imprint of IGI Global)
    701 E. Chocolate Avenue
    Hershey PA, USA 17033
    Tel: 717-533-8845
    Fax:  717-533-8661
    E-mail: cust@igi-global.com
    Web site: http://www.igi-global.com

Library of Congress Cataloging-in-Publication Data

Names: Issa, Tomayess, editor. I Kommers, Piet A. M., editor. I Issa,
    Theodora, 1958- editor.
Title: Smart technology applications in business environments / Tomayess
    Issa, Piet Kommers, Theodora Issa, Pedro Isaias, and Touma B. Issa,
    editors.
Description: Hershey : Business Science Reference, [2017]
Identifiers: LCCN 2017003790I ISBN 9781522524922 (hardcover) I ISBN
    9781522524939 (ebook)
Subjects: LCSH: Business enterprises--Computer networks. I Green technology.
    I Technological innovations--Economic aspects.
Classification: LCC HD30.37 .S638 2017 I DDC 658/.05--dc23 LC record available at https://lccn.loc.gov/2017003790

This book is published in the IGI Global book series Advances in Business Information Systems and Analytics (ABISA) (ISSN: 2327-3275; eISSN: 2327-3283)

# Advances in Business Information Systems and Analytics (ABISA) Book Series

Madjid Tavana
La Salle University, USA

ISSN:2327-3275
EISSN:2327-3283

## MISSION

The successful development and management of information systems and business analytics is crucial to the success of an organization. New technological developments and methods for data analysis have allowed organizations to not only improve their processes and allow for greater productivity, but have also provided businesses with a venue through which to cut costs, plan for the future, and maintain competitive advantage in the information age.

The **Advances in Business Information Systems and Analytics (ABISA) Book Series** aims to present diverse and timely research in the development, deployment, and management of business information systems and business analytics for continued organizational development and improved business value.

## COVERAGE

- Data Management
- Legal information systems
- Business Models
- Business Process Management
- Management information systems
- Geo-BIS
- Business Systems Engineering
- Decision Support Systems
- Statistics
- Performance Metrics

IGI Global is currently accepting manuscripts for publication within this series. To submit a proposal for a volume in this series, please contact our Acquisition Editors at Acquisitions@igi-global.com or visit: http://www.igi-global.com/publish/.

# Titles in this Series

*For a list of additional titles in this series, please visit: www.igi-global.com/book-series*

*Handbook of Research on Advanced Data Mining Techniques and Applications for Business Intelligence*
Shrawan Kumar Trivedi (BML Munjal University, India) Shubhamoy Dey (Indian Institute of Management Indore,
India) Anil Kumar (BML Munjal University, India) and Tapan Kumar Panda (Jindal Global Business School, India)
Business Science Reference • copyright 2017 • 438pp • H/C (ISBN: 9781522520313) • US $260.00 (our price)

*Exploring Enterprise Service Bus in the Service-Oriented Architecture Paradigm*
Robin Singh Bhadoria (Indian Institute of Technology Indore, India) Narendra Chaudhari (Visvesvaraya National
Institute of Technology, Nagpur, India) Geetam Singh Tomar (Machine Intelligence Research (MIR) Labs, India)
and Shailendra Singh (National Institute of Technical Teachers' Training and Research, India)
Business Science Reference • copyright 2017 • 378pp • H/C (ISBN: 9781522521570) • US $200.00 (our price)

*Applying Predictive Analytics Within the Service Sector*
Rajendra Sahu (ABV-Indian Institute of Information Technology and Management, India) Manoj Dash (ABV-Indian
Institute of Information Technology and Management, India) and Anil Kumar (BML Munjal University, India)
Business Science Reference • copyright 2017 • 294pp • H/C (ISBN: 9781522521488) • US $195.00 (our price)

*Enterprise Information Systems and the Digitalization of Business Functions*
Madjid Tavana (La Salle University, USA)
Business Science Reference • copyright 2017 • 497pp • H/C (ISBN: 9781522523826) • US $215.00 (our price)

*Strategic Information Systems and Technologies in Modern Organizations*
Caroline Howard (HC Consulting, USA) and Kathleen Hargiss (Colorado Technical University, USA)
Information Science Reference • copyright 2017 • 366pp • H/C (ISBN: 9781522516804) • US $205.00 (our price)

*Business Analytics and Cyber Security Management in Organizations*
Rajagopal (EGADE Business School, Tecnologico de Monterrey, Mexico City, Mexico & Boston University, USA)
and Ramesh Behl (International Management Institute, Bhubaneswar, India)
Business Science Reference • copyright 2017 • 346pp • H/C (ISBN: 9781522509028) • US $215.00 (our price)

*Handbook of Research on Intelligent Techniques and Modeling Applications in Marketing Analytics*
Anil Kumar (BML Munjal University, India) Manoj Kumar Dash (ABV-Indian Institute of Information Technol-
ogy and Management, India) Shrawan Kumar Trivedi (BML Munjal University, India) and Tapan Kumar Panda
(BML Munjal University, India)
Business Science Reference • copyright 2017 • 428pp • H/C (ISBN: 9781522509974) • US $275.00 (our price)

www.igi-global.com

701 East Chocolate Avenue, Hershey, PA 17033, USA
Tel: 717-533-8845 x100 • Fax: 717-533-8661
E-Mail: cust@igi-global.com • www.igi-global.com

# Table of Contents

## Section 1
## Smart Technology and Design

## Section 2
## Smart Technology and Health

## Section 3
## Smart Technology and Education

## Section 4
## Smart Technology in the Information Society

# Detailed Table of Contents

### Section 1
### Smart Technology and Design

Recently, computer vision is playing an important role in many essential human-computer interactive applications, these applications are subject to a "real-time" constraint, and therefore it requires a fast and reliable computational system. Edge Detection is the most used approach for segmenting images based on changes in intensity. There are various kernels used to perform edge detection, such as: Sobel, Robert, and Prewitt, upon which, the most commonly used is Sobel. In this research a novel type of operator cells that perform addition is introduced to achieve computational acceleration. The novel operator cells have been employed in the chosen FPGA Zedboard which is well-suited for real-time image and video processing. Accelerating the Sobel edge detection technique is exploited using different tools such as the High-Level Synthesis tools provided by Vivado. This enhancement shows a significant improvement as it decreases the computational time by 26% compared to the conventional adder cells.

The chapter shows the evolution of virtual reality interfaces and technologies to the current moment and verifies what led them to an alleged decline in early 1990. Due to the development of the industry of digital games, new forms of interaction have being researched and presented to the public. It will also be shown the application of virtual reality in different contexts of digital games, in addition to reporting a brief experience of the research group in art, science and technology, Lab|Front (Laboratório de Poéticas Fronteiriças - CNPq/UEMG).

**Chapter 3**

*Ayodeji Opeyemi Abioye, University of Southampton, UK*
*Stephen D Prior, University of Southampton, UK*
*Glyn T Thomas, University of Southampton, UK*
*Peter Saddington, Tekever Ltd., UK*
*Sarvapali D Ramchurn, University of Southampton, UK*

This chapter discusses HCI interfaces used in controlling aerial robotic systems (otherwise known as aerobots). The autonomy control level of aerobot is also discussed. However, due to the limitations of existing models, a novel classification model of autonomy, specifically designed for multirotor aerial robots, called the navigation control autonomy (nCA) model is also developed. Unlike the existing models such as the AFRL and ONR, this model is presented in tiers and has a two-dimensional pyramidal structure. This model is able to identify the control void existing beyond tier-one autonomy components modes and to map the upper and lower limits of control interfaces. Two solutions are suggested for dealing with the existing control void and the limitations of the RC joystick controller –the multimodal HHI-like interface and the unimodal BCI interface. In addition to these, some human factors based performance measurement is recommended, and the plans for further works presented.

**Chapter 4**

*Marcos Levano, Universidad Catolica de Temuco, Chile*

The following chapter shows the development of a learning methodology used to validate self-directed learning generic competences and knowledge management in a competence-based model in the engineering computer science program of the Universidad Católica Temuco (UCT). The design of the methodology shows the steps and activities of the learning-by-doing process, as shown gradually in the learning results of the competence. The designed methodological process allows creating working schemes for theory-based teaching and learning, and also for practicing and experimenting. The problematology as controlled scenarios is integrated in order to answer problems in engineering, allowing the process of validation in the self-learning and knowledge management competences. Thus, the achievements in the results have allowed helping the teachers to use their learning instruments.

**Section 2**
**Smart Technology and Health**

**Chapter 5**

*Garden Tabacchi, University of Palermo, Italy*
*Monèm Jemni, Qatar University, Qatar*
*Joao L Viana, University Institute of Maia (ISMAI), Portugal*
*Antonino Bianco, University of Palermo, Italy*

Adolescents' obesity is a major concern in our modern life that could lead to significant increase in the rate of obese future generations and consequently in the health budget. The ASSO (Adolescence

Surveillance System for Obesity prevention) project in Italy is tackling this new pandemic using the new e-technology through a multi facets monitoring system on life style including food consumptions, meal patterns and habits, alcohol, smoking, physical activity, fitness and sedentariness, and biological/genetic, and socio-cultural/environmental characteristics of adolescents. The project has been recently piloted in the South of the country. This chapter summarizes the design and structure of the ASSO system, its implementation and the results of an evaluation process for its possible extension to the whole Italian territory and to other European realities as a national surveillance system.

The term Autism Spectrum Disorders (ASDs) covers conditions such as autism, childhood disintegrative disorder and Asperger syndrome. In this line, the World Health Organization (WHO) points that core symptoms of ASD are: a mixture of impaired capacity for reciprocal socio-communicative interaction and a restricted, stereotyped repetitive repertoire of interests and activities. Therefore, it is fundamental for a person with ASD to develop skills to communicate with his/her peers, share ideas, and express feelings. On those grounds, this chapter presents an intelligent ecosystem to support the development of social communication skills in children with ASD. The ecosystem uses a knowledge model that relies on ontologies, and defines the main elements that will be used for psychological intervention process. The different activities that will be carried out during the therapeutic intervention can be done using a robotic assistant or a Multi-Sensory Stimulation Room. This proposal has been tested with 47 children of regular schools, 9 specialists on ASD, and 36 children with ASD.

# Chapter 7

The study presents an adaptation of the Mastermind game for blind users called MasterBlind. The game mechanics were simplified and auditory feedback introduced. The research object was to understand what kind of sounds would work better to help blind people play the game. Three versions were presented to the subjects - pentatonic notes, animal sounds and vowels - to help users recall previous steps in the game. The main hypothesis predicted that blind users would consciously benefit from the auditory feedback provided. The second hypothesis predicted that users would benefit less from the feedback that doesn't provide semantic information- auditory icons versus earcons. The results were congruent with the hypothesis. MasterBlind can be a usable, enjoyable and a challenging experience for blind users as long as it provides semantically significant feedback. However, new developments are in progress to prove our ideas having in mind the inclusion of blind people.

# Chapter 8

This chapter discusses challenges related to studying the use and usefulness of research products (robust, high fidelity prototypes placed in real use contexts for research purposes). Methods and methodologies for studying use and usefulness of such research products embedded in users' everyday lives are still lacking and need to be better established. By presenting a case of such research product in use, a robot avatar, we wish to illustrate how new knowledge of relevance for both designers and users can be gained. The robot avatar was designed to represent chronically ill adolescents at school, improving his/hers learning opportunities, as well as helping maintain social connections with peers. The chapter shows how methods were adapted and tools designed to work with this user group and learn about the role of avatars in education and reduction of social isolation. The value of using the avatar, and similar research products, is considered.

# Chapter 9

In this chapter, we focus on an emerging strand of IT-oriented research, namely Human-Data Interaction (HDI) and on how this can be applied to healthcare. HDI regards both how humans create and use data by means of interactive systems, which can both assist and constrain them and the operational level of data work, which is both work on data and by data. Healthcare is a challenging arena where to test the potential of HDI towards a new, user-centered perspective on how to support and assess "data work". This is especially true in current times where data are becoming increasingly big and many tools are available for the lay people, including doctors and nurses, to interact with health-related data. This chapter is a contribution in the direction of considering health-related data through the lens of HDI, and of framing data visualization tools in this strand of research. The intended aim is to let the subtler peculiarities among different kind of data and of their use emerge and be addressed adequately. Our point is that doing so can promote the design of more usable tools that can support data work from a user-centered and data quality perspective and the evidence-based validation of these tools.

## Section 3
## Smart Technology and Education

### Chapter 10

*Katharine Jones, AUT University, New Zealand*
*Mark S. Glynn, AUT University, New Zealand*

Children's use of social media affects their interactions with consumer brands. Because children's social media use is a part of people's increasing use of social platforms to communicate and share content with each other, it is important to understand how children are using such platforms as sources of market-related information. This is because children's socialisation as consumers depends upon their accessing a range of market-related information sources, and social media platforms are envisaged to facilitate such access. Children's interactions with consumer brands are governed by interaction processes, and such processes shape the relationships that children may form with brands. Understanding these interaction processes will provide insights for parents, educators, and business marketers seeking information as to how the next generation of consumers use social media for market-related activities.

### Chapter 11

*Nataliia V. Morze, Borys Grinchenko Kiev University, Ukraine*
*Eugenia Smyrnova-Trybulska, University of Silesia in Katowice, Poland*
*Olena Glazunova, National University of Life and Environmental Sciences of Ukraine,*
*  Ukraine*

This chapter discusses theoretical, methodological and practical aspects of a design of a university learning environment for SMART education. Smart technology is analyzed against university background. The authors consider a process of transformation from e-learning to smart education, in particular the VLE objective according to the concept of smart education, formation of individual learning trajectories in a smart environment and a quality university educational environment for smart education. In the second part of chapter, the authors look at the development of teacher ICT competence of teachers in the system of smart education and present their conclusions. The references include more than thirty items: articles, books, chapters, conference proceedings on SMART education, university learning environment, virtual learning environment (VLE).

### Chapter 12

*María Soledad Ibarra-Sáiz, University of Cadiz, Spain*
*Gregorio Rodríguez-Gómez, University of Cadiz, Spain*

The increasing use of technological tools to support the process of participation in assessment is explained, firstly, by the current tendencies in assessment and learning in Higher Education which encourage the active participation of students as a means to improve their learning; secondly, by the universal presence of technology that makes it impossible to conceive of any educational process that does not contemplate its use and that is leading to ever more courses that are either virtual or require minimal attendance;

and, finally, an environment in which there are ever greater numbers of students per class. This chapter presents the results of using the web-based EvalCOMIX® programme in the context of a number of Higher Education training courses. Data has been collected through questionnaires and interviews applied to students, lecturers and academic coordinators. The results illustrate the ease of implementation of EvalCOMIX®, its usefulness in creating and sharing assessment instruments and the opportunity it provides to facilitate student participation in assessment.

## Chapter 13

In a dynamically changing higher education environment, a deep understanding and facilitation of relevant and flexible academic development is vitally important organisationally. A qualitative case study methodology was employed to analyse the organisational positioning and design of academic development as a means of gaining insights into the needs, challenges and evolutionary trends occurring at one university. A non-linear organisational-level data analysis based on triangulation from document study, direct observation, and experiential and reflective knowledge, provided theoretical and practical insights into how academic development is embodied institutionally. A design perspective revealed the characterisation of an expanded remit, as complex, contradictory and complementary. The study concluded that new configurations in the practice of academic development are convergent in nature, integrating a transformative agenda representational of professional learning trends globally. An important implication this study raises is the mounting influence the application of smart technologies can play in the area of training and development within business organisations.

## Chapter 14

This chapter discussed the results of a study that explored students' perceptions of personal mobile devices in the classroom and suggestions for policies. Thirty-four students enrolled in two undergraduate courses taught at a Brazilian higher education institution took part in the study. Data collection consisted of a survey and focus group interview. Quantitative data suggested an overall tendency to rare use of the devices for content and non-content activities. Qualitative results, however, showed that students may have used more often their devices in class. The results discussed several policies recommended by the students ranging from allowing the devices for content and emergency to not using social media for off- task activities. The study suggested that inappropriate use of mobile technology in the classroom may be minimized if students participate in the development of policies, and instructors integrate the devices in class to promote engagement and interest among students. Recommendations for practice and future research are discussed.

## Section 4
## Smart Technology in the Information Society

### Chapter 15

*Tânia Isabel Gregório, University of Lisbon, Portugal*
*Pedro Isaías, The University of Queensland, Australia*

Companies are becoming more focused on customers and on new ways to approach them individually. Mobile technologies and Web 2.0 have been pushing companies to evolve in this area. This research is focused on the way Customer Relationship Management (CRM) systems are used, on a European level, by recruiting companies to assist candidates in finding a satisfactory job. A framework is presented to identify how CRM 2.0 and mCRM (mobile CRM) can help candidates to find jobs in a personalized way. A set of four hypotheses have been defined. To gain a better understanding of these CRM systems, the methodology used in the exploratory study was quantitative, employing a non-probabilistic sampling technique, with 35 recruiting agencies being studied. Results showed that the use of software in recruiting agencies is quite common and that CRM 2.0 is present in the vast majority of the studied companies. When it comes to mobile CRM, there's still much to be explored in this channel, as agencies focus their resources on Web 2.0, leaving this channel's great potential of mobile CRM unused.

### Chapter 16

*Peter Gobel, Kyoto Sangyo University, Japan*
*Makimi Kano, Kyoto Sangyo University, Japan*

This chapter describes a pair of studies investigating factors involved in task-based learning using digital storytelling. In Study 1, the stories were analyzed using the factors of topic, time, medium, and reported technological proficiency. Student attitudes towards the tasks were gauged using a questionnaire that measured perceived task cost and value, engagement with the task, and expectancy for success on future tasks. In Study 2, three mid-task planning conditions were introduced and a questionnaire was administered to see student attitudes towards various modes of mid-task planning. The results of Study 1 suggest that digital storytelling can be incorporated into EFL classes to reduce foreign language anxiety, to provide greater opportunities to use English, and to foster ICT skills. The results of Study 2 suggest that students favor a teacher-led planning condition, and that this planning condition had a positive effect on student attitudes towards the project (value and cost).

We live in an ever-changing world. Despite that many new and excellent reforms are achieved, this period of time is also very confusing when many things that were regarded as concrete are becoming virtual. In spite of all this incompleteness, our common goal should be a good information society and the purpose of this chapter is to find out some factors that reveal the steps toward it. The question we ask is how to find a balance between a good life and eServices from the human point of view. The key findings pointed to issues in the needs of structural changes in the society. Another challenge that can be observed and which will be in the most essential role in the future, is the ownership and control over My Data. Agreements are a common practice in the business and when the subject is eServices in the future, we cannot avoid discussion of the end-user agreements, too.

# Foreword

The concept of Smart Technology has acquired importance in last years and is usually associated with the use of technology innovatively and strategically in a business context. This approach could be included in a large perspective of "smartness" as a sustainable development model, usually associated with the concept of smart city or smart regions. Giffinger et al. (2007, p.11) correlated smart cities with six characteristics, built on the smart combinations of endowments (a smart economy; smart mobility; smart environment; smart people; smart living; and, smart governance).

Smart cities are supported by Smart Technologies. Subsequently, Smart Technology could facilitate knowledge and learning dissemination mainly though the use of digital infrastructures for communication and knowledge management. In this way, Smart Technology could provide granted interactive business solutions for industry. The technological solutions such as apps, dashboards or optimization algorithms, videoconferences, e-learning, etc are actually usual tools used by manufacturing 4.0 and are part of a smart tech revolution.

The key words of this smart tech revolution could be: "instrumented, interconnected and intelligent". "Instrumented" refers to the capability of capturing and integrating real world live data through the use of sensors, meters, appliances, personal devices, and other similar sensors to an entrepreneurial use. "Interconnected" means the integration of these data into a computing platform that allows the communication of such information among the various firms or into an entrepreneurial ecosystem. "Intelligent" refers to the inclusion of complex analytics, modelling, optimization, and visualization services to make better operational decisions.

Smart technologies, such as mobile management apps, big data or artificial intelligence, could bring advantages for small business improving flexibility and performance. Mobile management apps facilitate the management and gives to the business owners' flexibility and visibility in some operational process with a lower cost. Big data could provide information to more informed business decisions (before just available to large firms), with for instance some reporting tools like Crunchboards or Microsoft Power BI. Small businesses can now create tailored dashboards and reports more focuses on the business in less time and with fewer resources. And artificial intelligence can offer intuitive solutions suitable with their customers needs.

Finally, Smart Technology has the potential to change the face of business, allowing: "think bigger" (detecting opportunities); "rethink marketing" (using less expensive digital tools; "make smarter" (providing connected and tailored products and services); "security top level" (improving security precautions); "Intelligent workforce" (requiring more qualified and creative people).

This book aims to become the reference edition for all those interested in Smart Technologies in Business Environments. The subject area is a combination of Business Environments with Smart Technologies. The emphasis on Smart Technologies in Business Environments provides a particular value proposition and allows characteristics of flexibility and adoption to diverse audiences.

This multi-disciplinary book contributes from several researches, considering the field of Smart Technologies in Business Environments. Nowadays Smart Technology becomes a basic instrument for economies and people. Encouraging smart technologies could simultaneous provide friendly environments to business and enhance quality of life worldwide.

*Luisa Carvalho*
*Universidade Aberta (Portuguese Open University), Portugal*

## REFERENCES

Giffinger, R. (2007). *Smart Cities: Ranking of European Medium Sized Cities*. Retrieved from http://www.smart-cities.eu/download/smart_cities_final_report.pdf

# Preface

In the 21ˢᵗ century, smart technology becomes a fundamental instrument for businesses, education and individuals worldwide to enhance job performance and productivity and to ensure the job is efficient and effective. Additionally, smart technology can improve communication, collaboration, cooperation, connection, job efficiency and proficiency between employees vs. employers, employees vs. stakeholders, students vs. students, and students vs. teachers locally and globally. Using smart technology can improve data management, support availability of Internet mobility, stimulate creativity and innovation, encourage factor of globalization phenomena, enhance customers' and students' satisfaction via communication, collaboration, cooperation and connection. Furthermore, using smart technology can reduce utility cost; more sustainable and saving energy among businesses, education and individuals.

Conversely, employing this technology can cause massive risks to our society locally and globally from increasing carbon emission, raw materials, life spans of smart technology and recycling. Furthermore, this technology can cause further risks to human begin attitudes and behaviour namely; cognitive, social and physical developments, as well as security risks. To tackle these risks, designers, businesses and education should and must take some responsibility to raise the awareness in relation to smart technology risks and designers and HCI specialists should add to their notions of design the concept of "green" technologies, since the current technologies are adversely affected and causing major problems to the environment, as the smart technology recycling is causing enormous problems to the environment and planet. Finally, some of the current materials belong to our seventh generation; therefore, we need to keep this notion in our design now as well in the future. The purpose of this book is to examine the risks and opportunities of smart technology adoption in various sectors from a global perspective. This book will cover enormous topics in relation to the journey of Smart technology and ICT particularly: Technology Opportunities; Technology Risks; Technology and Sustainability; Technology, learning and teaching; Technology and Businesses; and Technology and Education. This book will assist various sectors of Smart Technology adoption, since this tool will improve their job performance and productivity. Furthermore, this book aims to support researchers and academics' work and sharing the latest research to Smart Technology adoption among their students nationally and internationally in various sectors especially in the higher-education sector.

Chapter 1 is "Acceleration Sobel Edge Detection Using Compressor Cells Over FPGAS," and created by Ahmed Abouelfarag, Marwa Ali Elshenawy, Esraa, and Alaaeldin Khattab. This chapter discusses the recent discussion about computer vision which is playing an important role in many essential human-computer interactive applications, these applications are subject to a "real-time" constraint, and therefore it requires a fast and reliable computational system. Edge Detection is the most used approach for segmenting images based on changes in intensity. There are various kernels used to perform edge detection, such as:

Sobel, Robert, and Prewitt, upon which, the most commonly used is Sobel. In this research a novel type of operator cells that perform addition is introduced to achieve computational acceleration. The novel operator cells have been employed in the chosen FPGA Zedboard which is well-suited for real-time image and video processing. Accelerating the Sobel edge detection technique is exploited using different tools such as the High-Level Synthesis tools provided by Vivado. This enhancement shows a significant improvement as it decreases the computational time by 26% compared to the conventional adder cells.

Chapter 2 is called "Expansion of Uses and Applications of Virtual Reality" written by Pablo Gobira and Antônio Mozelli. This chapter shows the evolution of virtual reality interfaces and technologies to the current moment and verifies what led them to an alleged decline in early 1990. Due to the development of the industry of digital games, new forms of interaction have being researched and presented to the public. It will also be shown the application of virtual reality in different contexts of digital games, in addition to reporting a brief experience of the research group in art, science and technology, Lab|Front (Laboratório de Poéticas Fronteiriças - CNPq/UEMG).

Chapter 3 is titled "Multimodal Human Aerobotic Interaction" and authored by Ayodeji Opeyemi Abioye, Stephen D Prior, University of Southampton, Glyn T Thomas, Peter Saddington and Sarvapali D Ramchurn. This chapter discusses HCI interfaces used in controlling aerial robotic systems (otherwise known as aerobots). The autonomy control level of aerobot is also discussed. However, due to the limitations of existing models, a novel classification model of autonomy, specifically designed for multirotor aerial robots, called the navigation control autonomy (nCA) model is also developed. Unlike the existing models such as the AFRL and ONR, this model is presented in tiers and has a two-dimensional pyramidal structure. This model is able to identify the control void existing beyond tier-one autonomy components modes and to map the upper and lower limits of control interfaces. Two solutions are suggested for dealing with the existing control void and the limitations of the RC joystick controller –the multimodal HHI-like interface and the unimodal BCI interface. In addition to these, some human factors based performance measurement is recommended, and the plans for further works presented.

Chapter 4 is titled "Methodology for Knowledge Management and Self-Directed, Science Program Engineering Computing" and written by Marcos Levano, Universidad Catolica de Temuco, Chile. This chapter shows the development of a learning methodology used to validate self-directed learning generic competences and knowledge management in a competence-based model in the engineering computer science program of the Universidad Católica Temuco (UCT). The design of the methlogy shows the steps and activities of the learning-by-doing process, as shown gradually in the learning results of the competence. The designed methodological process allows creating working schemes for theory-based teaching and learning, and also for practicing and experimenting. The problematology as controlled scenarios is integrated in order to answer problems in engineering, allowing the process of validation in the self-learning and knowledge management competences. Thus, the achievements in the results have allowed helping the teachers to use their learning instruments.

Chapter 5 is titled "Adolescence Surveillance System for Obesity Prevention (ASSO) in Europe: A Pioneering Project to Prevent Obesity Using E-Technology" and authored by Garden Tabacchi,; Monèm Jemni, Joao L Viana, and Antonino Bianco. This chapter aims to discuss the ASSO. Adolescents' obesity is a major concern in our modern life that could lead to significant increase in the rate of obese future generations and consequently in the health budget. The ASSO (Adolescence Surveillance System for Obesity prevention) project in Italy is tackling this new pandemic using the new e-technology through a multi facets monitoring system on life style including food consumptions, meal patterns and habits, alcohol, smoking, physical activity, fitness and sedentariness, and biological/genetic, and socio-cultural/

environmental characteristics of adolescents. The project has been recently piloted in the South of the country. This chapter summarizes the design and structure of the ASSO system, its implementation and the results of an evaluation process for its possible extension to the whole Italian territory and to other European realities as a national surveillance system.

Chapter 6 is titled "An Intelligent Ecosystem to Support the Development of Communication Skills in Children With Autism: An Experience Based on Ontologies, Multi-Sensory Stimulation Rooms, and Robotic Assistants" and authored by Vladimir Robles-Bykbaev, Martín López-Nores, Jorge Andrés Galán-Mena, Verónica Cevallos León Wong, Diego Quisi-Peralta, Diego Lima-Juma, Carlos Andrés Arévalo Fernández, and José Pazos-Arias, University of Vigo. This chapter aims to discuss the ASDs. The term Autism Spectrum Disorders (ASDs) covers conditions such as autism, childhood disintegrative disorder and Asperger syndrome. In this line, the World Health Organization (WHO) points that core symptoms of ASD are: a mixture of impaired capacity for reciprocal socio-communicative interaction and a restricted, stereotyped repetitive repertoire of interests and activities. Therefore, it is fundamental for a person with ASD to develop skills to communicate with his/her peers, share ideas, and express feelings. On those grounds, this chapter presents an intelligent ecosystem to support the development of social communication skills in children with ASD. The ecosystem uses a knowledge model that relies on ontologies, and defines the main elements that will be used for psychological intervention process. The different activities that will be carried out during the therapeutic intervention can be done using a robotic assistant or a Multi-Sensory Stimulation Room. This proposal has been tested with 47 children of regular schools, 9 specialists on ASD, and 36 children with ASD.

Chapter 7 is titled "Auditory Feedback in a Computer Game for Blind People" and authored by Ana Teixeira, Anabella Gomes, and Joao Gilberto Orvalho. The study presents an adaptation of the Mastermind game for blind users called MasterBlind. The game mechanics were simplified and auditory feedback introduced. The research object was to understand what kind of sounds would work better to help blind people play the game. Three versions were presented to the subjects - pentatonic notes, animal sounds and vowels - to help users recall previous steps in the game. The main hypothesis predicted that blind users would consciously benefit from the auditory feedback provided. The second hypothesis predicted that users would benefit less from the feedback that does not provide semantic information- auditory icons versus earcons. The results were congruent with the hypothesis. MasterBlind can be a usable, enjoyable and a challenging experience for blind users as long as it provides semantically significant feedback. However, new developments are in progress to prove our ideas having in mind the inclusion of blind people.

Chapter 8 is titled "Experiences With a Research Product: A Robot Avatar for Chronically Ill Adolescents" and written by Jorun Børsting and Alma Leora Culén. This chapter discusses challenges related to studying the use and usefulness of research products (robust, high fidelity prototypes placed in real use contexts for research purposes). Methods and methodologies for studying use and usefulness of such research products embedded in users' everyday lives are still lacking and need to be better established. By presenting a case of such research product in use, a robot avatar, we wish to illustrate how new knowledge of relevance for both designers and users can be gained. The robot avatar was designed to represent chronically ill adolescents at school, improving his/hers learning opportunities, as well as helping maintain social connections with peers. The chapter shows how methods were adapted and tools designed to work with this user group and learn about the role of avatars in education and reduction of social isolation. The value of using the avatar, and similar research products, is considered.

Chapter 9 is titled "Human-Data Interaction in Healthcare" and created by Federico Cabitza and Angela Locoro. In this chapter, we focus on an emerging strand of IT-oriented research, namely Human-Data Interaction (HDI) and on how this can be applied to healthcare. HDI regards both how humans create and use data by means of interactive systems. Healthcare is a challenging arena where to test the potential of HDI towards a new, user-centered perspective on how to support and assess "data work". This is especially true in current times where data are becoming increasingly big and many tools are available for the lay people, including doctors and nurses, to interact with health-related data. This chapter is a contribution in the direction of considering health-related data through the lens of HDI, and of framing data visualization tools in this strand of research. The intended aim is to let the subtler peculiarities among different kind of data and of their use emerge and be addressed adequately. Our point is that doing so can promote the design of more usable tools that can support data work from a user-centered and data quality perspective and the evidence-based validation of these tools.

Chapter 10 is called "Children Using Social Media to Connect With Others and With Consumer Brands" and authored by Katharine Jones and Mark S Glynn. This chapter aims to discuss social media usage via children. Children's use of social media affects their interactions with consumer brands. Because children's social media use is a part of people's increasing use of social platforms to communicate and share content with each other, it is important to understand how children are using such platforms as sources of market-related information. This is because children's socialisation as consumers depends upon their accessing a range of market-related information sources, and social media platforms are envisaged to facilitate such access. Children's interactions with consumer brands are governed by interaction processes, and such processes shape the relationships that children may form with brands. Understanding these interaction processes will provide insights for parents, educators, and business marketers seeking information as to how the next generation of consumers uses social media for market-related activities.

Chapter 11 is called "Design of a University Learning Environment for SMART Education" and authored by Nataliia V. Morze, Eugenia Smyrnova-Trybulska, and Olena Glazunova. This chapter discusses theoretical, methodological and practical aspects of a design of a university learning environment for SMART education. Smart technology is analyzed against university background. The authors consider a process of transformation from e-learning to smart education, in particular the VLE objective according to the concept of smart education, formation of individual learning trajectories in a smart environment and a quality university educational environment for smart education. In the second part of chapter, the authors look at the development of teacher ICT competence of teachers in the system of smart education and present their conclusions. The references include more than thirty items: articles, books, chapters, conference proceedings on SMART education, university learning environment, virtual learning environment (VLE).

Chapter 12 is named "EvalCOMIX®: A Web-Based Programme to Support Collaboration in Assessment" and created by María Soledad Ibarra-Sáiz and Gregorio Rodríguez-Gómez. This chapter aims to examine the web based programme in assessments. The increasing use of technological tools to support the process of participation in assessment is explained, firstly, by the current tendencies in assessment and learning in Higher Education which encourage the active participation of students as a means to improve their learning; secondly, by the universal presence of technology that makes it impossible to conceive of any educational process that does not contemplate its use and that is leading to ever more courses that are either virtual or require minimal attendance; and, finally, an environment in which there are ever greater numbers of students per class. This chapter presents the results of using the web-based EvalCOMIX® programme in the context of a number of Higher Education training courses. Data has been collected through questionnaires and interviews applied to students, lecturers and academic coordinators. The results illustrate the ease of implementation of EvalCOMIX®, its usefulness in creating and sharing assessment instruments and the opportunity it provides to facilitate student participation in assessment.

Chapter 13 is called "Transformative Academic Development: A Complexity of Converging Features" and written by Kuki Singh. This chapter aims to examine and discuss the new configurations in the practice of academic development. In a dynamically changing higher education environment, a deep understanding and facilitation of relevant and flexible academic development is vitally important organisationally. A qualitative case study methodology was employed to analyse the organisational positioning and design of academic development as a means of gaining insights into the needs, challenges and evolutionary trends occurring at one university. A non-linear organisational-level data analysis based on triangulation from document study, direct observation, and experiential and reflective knowledge, provided theoretical and practical insights into how academic development is embodied institutionally. A design perspective revealed the characterisation of an expanded remit, as complex, contradictory and complementary. The study concluded that new configurations in the practice of academic development are convergent in nature, integrating a transformative agenda representational of professional learning trends globally.

Chapter 14 is titled "University Students' Perceptions of Personal Mobile Devices in the Classroom and Policies" and written by Ieda M. Santos and Otávio Bocheco. This chapter discussed the results of a study that explored students' perceptions of personal mobile devices in the classroom and suggestions for policies. Thirty-four students enrolled in two undergraduate courses taught at a Brazilian higher education institution took part in the study. Data collection consisted of a survey and focus group interview. Quantitative data suggested an overall tendency to rare use of the devices for content and non-content activities. Qualitative results, however, showed that students may have used more often their devices in class. The results discussed several policies recommended by the students ranging from allowing the devices for content and emergency to not using social media for off- task activities. The study suggested that inappropriate use of mobile technology in the classroom may be minimized if students participate in the development of policies, and instructors integrate the devices in class to promote engagement and interest among students. Recommendations for practice and future research are discussed.

Chapter 15, "CRM 2.0 and Mobile CRM: A Framework Proposal and Study in European Recruitment Agencies," is written by Tânia Isabel Gregório and Pedro Isaías. This chapter aims to examine how companies are becoming more focused on customers and on new ways to approach them individually. Mobile technologies and Web 2.0 have been pushing companies to evolve in this area. This research is focused on the way Customer Relationship Management (CRM) systems are used, on a European level, by recruiting companies to assist candidates in finding a satisfactory job. A framework is presented to identify how CRM 2.0 and mCRM (mobile CRM) can help candidates to find jobs in a personalized way. A set of four hypotheses have been defined. To gain a better understanding of these CRM systems, the methodology used in the exploratory study was quantitative, employing a non-probabilistic sampling technique, with 35 recruiting agencies being studied. Results showed that the use of software in recruiting agencies is quite common and that CRM 2.0 is present in the vast majority of the studied companies. When it comes to mobile CRM, there's still much to be explored in this channel, as agencies focus their resources on Web 2.0, leaving this channel's great potential of mobile CRM unused.

Chapter 16 is called "The Complexities of Digital Storytelling: Factors Affecting Performance, Production, and Project Completion" and created by Peter Gobel and Makimi Kano. This chapter describes a pair of studies investigating factors involved in task-based learning using digital storytelling.

In Study 1, the stories were analyzed using the factors of topic, time, medium, and reported technological proficiency. Student attitudes towards the tasks were gauged using a questionnaire that measured perceived task cost and value, engagement with the task, and expectancy for success on future tasks. In Study 2, three mid-task planning conditions were introduced and a questionnaire was administered to see student attitudes towards various modes of mid-task planning. The results of Study 1 suggest that digital storytelling can be incorporated into EFL classes to reduce foreign language anxiety, to provide greater opportunities to use English, and to foster ICT skills. The results of Study 2 suggest that students favor a teacher-led planning condition, and that this planning condition had a positive effect on student attitudes towards the project (value and cost).

Chapter 17 is titled "Our Future: With the Good, the Bad, or the Ugly eServices? Case Finland" and written by Maija R Korhonen. We live in an ever-changing world. Despite that many new and excellent reforms are achieved; this period of time is also very confusing when many things that were regarded as concrete are becoming virtual. In spite of all this incompleteness, our common goal should be a good information society and the purpose of this chapter is to find out some factors that reveal the steps toward it. The question we ask is how to find a balance between a good life and eServices from the human point of view. The key findings pointed to issues in the needs of structural changes in the society. Another challenge that can be observed and which will be in the most essential role in the future is the ownership and control over My Data. Agreements are a common practice in the business and when the subject is eServices in the future, we cannot avoid discussion of the end-user agreements, too.

Finally, this book is mainly intended to support various business sectors, an academic audience (academics, university teachers, researchers, and post-graduate students – both Master and Doctorate levels). In addition, this book will be beneficial for public and private universities, IS developers and researchers, education managers, Professionals related to the information society, ICT, education, sustainability and green IT sectors.

*Tomayess Issa*
*Curtin University, Australia*

*Piet Kommers*
*University of Twente, The Netherlands*

*Theodora Issa*
*Curtin University, Australia*

*Pedro Isaias*
*The University of Queensland, Australia*

*Touma B. Issa*
*Murdoch University, Australia*

# Section 1
# Smart Technology and Design

# Chapter 1
# Accelerating Sobel Edge Detection Using Compressor Cells Over FPGAs

**Ahmed Abouelfarag**
*AASTMT, Egypt*

**Marwa Ali Elshenawy**
*AASTMT, Egypt*

**Esraa Alaaeldin Khattab**
*AASTMT, Egypt*

## ABSTRACT

*Recently, computer vision is playing an important role in many essential human-computer interactive applications, these applications are subject to a "real-time" constraint, and therefore it requires a fast and reliable computational system. Edge Detection is the most used approach for segmenting images based on changes in intensity. There are various kernels used to perform edge detection, such as: Sobel, Robert, and Prewitt, upon which, the most commonly used is Sobel. In this research a novel type of operator cells that perform addition is introduced to achieve computational acceleration. The novel operator cells have been employed in the chosen FPGA Zedboard which is well-suited for real-time image and video processing. Accelerating the Sobel edge detection technique is exploited using different tools such as the High-Level Synthesis tools provided by Vivado. This enhancement shows a significant improvement as it decreases the computational time by 26% compared to the conventional adder cells.*

## INTRODUCTION

Nowadays computer vision, which includes acquiring, processing, analyzing, and understanding of digital images to attain certain numerical information from the captured frames, is a weighty center of attraction for a lot of researchers; one of the reasons is that human-computer interaction has become an increasingly important part of our daily lives. It expanded from desktop applications to include games,

DOI: 10.4018/978-1-5225-2492-2.ch001

learning and education, commerce, health and medical applications, emergency planning and response, and systems that support collaboration and community. Computer vision is currently being used in many applications such as: augmented reality, automated optical inspection, automatic number plate recognition, etc. With the remarkable elaboration of information technology in our society, it is expected that computer vision systems will be embedded in many aspects of the environment.

Computer vision is a challenging operation due to its strict time requirements in order to be able to process in real time because most of the computer vision applications require immediate response within tight time frames. Real-time systems are widely used for human-computer interactive applications. Therefore, it must meet real-world requirements and consequently be able to control and respond effectively to them. Moreover, a real-time application program is an application program that should function and produce an output within a time frame that the user senses as immediate or current. Computational time must be less than a defined value, usually measured in a few milliseconds depending on the throughput rate and the frame sizes.

When building any system, the main objective is to achieve its required functionality with the highest achievable performance levels. However, there is no optimal solution; therefore any solution is a trade-off between power, time, silicon area, accuracy and many other less critical factors. Recently, computing algorithms have no longer been able to boost performance by continuously escalating the clock speed of the processors they run on. This prompted using processors with thousands of cores on them, which were principally designed for highly parallel operations.

Real-time processing -especially video processing- requires high computational demands along with the requirements of low power and low cost. In the recent years, many approaches have been devoted to develop architectures that could tackle these demands. Application-Specific Integrated Circuits (ASICs) yield the best performance regarding the computational throughput at low power consumption, on the other hand ASICs lack flexibility and also require high development time (Saponara, Casula, & Fanicci, 2008). The next thought would be the general purpose Digital Signal Processors (DSPs), which grant proficient programmability. However, the higher the complexity of the system, the worse its performance gets (Kumar, et al., 2015).

In the recent years, Graphics Processing Units (GPUs) have taken over the field of multimedia processing due to its massively parallel architecture (Mccool, 2008), but at the same time, GPUs are not able to exploit low-level parallelism and they also occupy bigger silicon area compared to ASICs.

Moreover, the insatiable demand for high-speed and accurate response requires a corresponding enhancement in computation speed and performance. That is why FPGAs are used in the presented work. FPGA devices boost abundant resources with which components that are responsible for accelerating signal, image and data processing can be provided, because of its massively parallel structure and also because currently developed FPGAs offer better performance regarding the computational speed, resource capacity and power consumption.

In order to accelerate a specific algorithm on an FPGA board, High Level Synthesis (HLS) is required, which is an automated hardware design process which interprets the algorithmic description of a desired behavior and creates its digital hardware design. The first step in the synthesis process is defining the high-level specification of the problem, at which: the code is analyzed, architecturally constrained, and scheduled to create Register-Transfer Level (RTL) HDL. The goal of HLS is to give a better control over optimization of the design architecture, and to accelerate the IP creation by enabling C, C++ and System-C specifications such that they can be targeted into Xilinx All Programmable devices without the need to manually create RTL.

The majority of computer vision applications require finding certain feature points throughout the frames of the input real-time videos. Many features could be extracted to distinguish interest regions in images such as: corners, blobs, ridges, illumination differences, etc. Among these features, edges are one of the most widely used features. Edge detection is an image processing operation that is responsible for finding the boundaries of objects within images. It works by detecting discontinuities in brightness. Moreover, edge detection is used for image segmentation and data extraction.

During the early stages of image processing, many image features must be identified in order to evaluate and estimate the structure of objects in images (Jain, Kasturi, & Schunck, 1995). Edges are one of the important features as most objects' information are enclosed by their edges. An edge in an image can be identified as the points at which sudden changes in intensities of the neighboring pixels occur. Techniques that use larger convolutional kernels give better results, but on the same time they are computationally more complex (Sujatha & Sudha, 2015).

This research outlines an enhanced operator cell that can be used over FPGAs, it makes use of compressor cells instead of using the conventional adders. The basis of this enhancement in the architecture is the Sobel edge kernels as they are the most suitable kernels due to their separability and lack of multiplications; in Sobel, multiplication delays can be avoided because multiplications by 0 or 1 are not considered as computational burden, and also multiplication by 2 is a 0ne-bit shift that needs only one clock cycle (Schiel & Bainbridge-Smith, 2015). Therefore; the main enhancement would be in improving the performance of the addition operation.

## BACKGROUND

### Dwarf Selection

The Berkley Dwarves are defined as "algorithmic methods that capture a pattern of computation and communication" which "present a method for capturing the common requirements of classes of applications while being reasonably divorced from individual implementations (Asanovic, et al., 2006).

The most compatible dwarf with video and image processing is dense linear algebra, which exploits vector-vector, matrix-matrix, and matrix-vector operations. Any frame/image is considered as a 2D-array on which many different operations could be done, such as: pre-processing, segmentation, feature extraction, etc. Real-time processing requires doing the same aimed image processing operations on all pixels or pixel windows per second, which leaves only a few nanoseconds to process each individual pixel (Johnston, Bailey, & Gribbon, 2004).

### Edge Detection

Edge detection is a primary operation in image processing and computer vision, especially in object detection applications. Edge detection aims at identifying the points of sharp changes in brightness or, in other words, the points having discontinuities. (Sujatha & Sudha, 2015)

Edge detection is normally performed using 2-D convolutions. Intensity values of edge pixels is evaluated by calculating the dot-product of the convolution kernel with the corresponding area of the image. There are various edge detection techniques such as Sobel and Canny edge detection methods. Canny detector has many advantages as it enhances signal-to-noise ratio of images and has a smoothing effect. On the other hand, Sobel operator is simple, less time consuming and also easier to implement. In this proposed work, Sobel edge detection technique is exploited, as it is more suitable for real-time video processing which requires high-speed operations to be performed. The Sobel operator has two 3X3 kernels, as shown below:

$$G_x = \begin{bmatrix} -1 & -2 & -1 \\ 0 & 0 & 0 \\ 1 & 2 & 1 \end{bmatrix}$$

$$G_y = \begin{bmatrix} -1 & 0 & 1 \\ -2 & 0 & 2 \\ -1 & 0 & 1 \end{bmatrix}$$

These kernels are applied separately to the image and produce separate horizontal and vertical gradients (Gx and Gy). Next, Gx and Gy can be combined together to calculate the magnitude of the gradient using:

$$G = \sqrt{G_x^2 + G_y^2}$$

Typically the magnitude could be calculated using:

$$|G| = |G_x| + |G_y|$$

## Application Selection

Any video is composed of successive sequence of frames that are played straightly after each other within a certain frame rate (frames per second "fps"). Eventually, in order not to increase time latency, a system which can perform data stream processing without going through a costly storage operation during its critical processing path must be developed. Accordingly, frames must be processed "in-stream" as they fly-by (Johnston, Bailey, & Gribbon, 2004). The architectural features that should be met are explained below:

- **Single Instruction Multiple Data (SIMD):** It encompasses broadcasting an individual instruction to multiple processors, which concurrently executes the instruction on different partitions of the data at the same time, thus allowing a bigger number of computations to be performed in a shorter time. SIMD also plays an important role in speeding up vector operations. That is why SIMD is thought of as a method to exploit Data-Level Parallelism (DLP).
- **Very Long Instruction Word (VLIW):** It speeds up high-level operations by providing the ability to perform multiple instructions in one cycle all at one time. This allows the instructions to be software-pipelined by the programmer. It must be put into consideration that for the VLIW to work

properly, data operated on must have no dependencies among them VLIW exploits Instruction-Level Parallelism (ILP).

- **Efficient Memory Subsystem:** If there doesn't exist an efficient way of transferring the data streams between the system components, any other speeding up techniques would be completely wasted.

Consequently an efficient hardware architecture should be chosen such that it is well-suited for real-time video and image processing in order to be able to meet the real time constraints required by the target application. In this research the Sobel edge detector is accelerated by offloading it on the FPGA board while introducing a novel operator cell that enhances and accelerates the addition operation.

## Computation Pattern

Generally image and video operations can be implemented on either of these four implementations: a software running on general purpose Central Processing Unit (CPUs) or microprocessors, a software running on a specialized Graphics Processing Unit (GPU) or a Digital Signal Processor (DSP), a hardware implementation on a dedicated FPGA, or a hardware implementation on an Application Specific Integrated Circuits (ASICs).

- General purpose CPUs are generally serial/sequential (e.g. they run a code), even multi-core or multi-threaded processors will not fully utilize or exploit all parallelism due to memory and input/output sharing and threads communication overheads due to the serial nature of individual threads.
- GPUs are faster that CPUs because they are mainly designed for graphics purposes; however, they are still slower than dedicate image/video hardware because they need to support a big number of general graphics processing functions.
- ASICs are considered dedicated hardware implementations, designers can make use of all kinds of optimizations before the fabrication process; however, they are more complex and expensive than FPGAs.
- FPGAs have many advantages over the previously mentioned implementations: they are re-programmable, its design can be easily fixed. Moreover, current FPGAs are improving in terms of speed, power consumption, functionality and capacity. FPGAs' performance is well suited to real-time High-Definition (HD) image and video processing because of its massively parallel structure. That is why FPGAs have been chosen as a hardware implementation for the proposed model.

## OpenCV

Open Source Computer Vision Library (OpenCV) has been chosen as the main library to be used in this research because of its various advantages over many other computer vision libraries and platforms such as: libCVD (Cambridge Video Dynamics), Matrox Imaging Library from Matrox, VXL, NI Vision from National Instruments, Open eVision, Adaptive Vision Library, Common Vision Blox, FastCV Computer Vision SDK, etc. For example, Matrox Imaging Library is not object oriented which makes it more difficult to maintain and debug the codes. VXL can handle very large images, but it has many disadvantage: it has not been recently updated, it comes with its own core libraries that replace standard C++, and also it is not licensed and badly documented. Moreover, most of the previously mentioned computer vision libraries are either badly documented, unfinished, not recently updated, or not open source.

OpenCV an open source computer vision and machine learning library of functions written in C/C++. It gets more image processing done for the computers processing cycles, and not more interpreting because it is closer to directly providing machine language code to the computer to get executed. Moreover, typical OpenCV programs only require ~70 MB of RAM to run in real-time. Additionally, OpenCV offers higher portability; any device that can run C, can also run OpenCV. It is also not constrained with a certain development environment, it can work on any C-programming IDE depending on which operating system used. For example, Microsoft Visual Studio or NetBeans are the typical IDE used for OpenCV. In Linux, it is Eclipse or NetBeans, and in OSX, Apple's Xcode can be used.

OpenCV was mainly built to provide a common infrastructure for computer vision applications and to accelerate the use of human-computer interactive applications. In addition OpenCV is a BSD-licensed product therefore OpenCV makes it easy for businesses to utilize and modify the code (OpenCV | OpenCV, 2016)

The library has more than 2500 upgraded and optimized calculations, which incorporate comprehensive set of computer vision and machine learning algorithms. These algorithms can be utilized to distinguish and perceive faces, recognize objects, classify human actions in videos, track camera movements, track moving articles, extract 3D models of items, deliver 3D point clouds from stereo cameras, and so forth. OpenCV has more than 47 thousand individuals of user community and evaluated number of downloads surpassing 7 million. The library is utilized broadly in companies, organizations, research groups and by governmental bodies (Bradski & Kaehler, 2008).

Alongside entrenched organizations like Google, Yahoo, Microsoft, Intel, IBM, Sony, Honda, Toyota that utilize the library, there are numerous new businesses, for example Applied minds, VideoSurf, and Zeitera, that make broad utilization of OpenCV.

OpenCV has C++, C, Python, Java and MATLAB interfaces and backings Windows, Linux, Android and MAC OS. OpenCV inclines generally towards real-time applications and exploits MMX and Streaming SIMD Extension (SSE) instructions when accessible. A full-included CUDA and OpenCL interfaces are by and large effectively grown right at this point. There are more than 500 algorithms and around 10 times as many functions that compose or bolster those algorithms. OpenCV is written natively in C++ and has a layout interface that works seamlessly and consistently with STL containers (Bradski & Kaehler, 2008).

## Zedboard

In the presented work, Xilinx's Zynq-7000 All programmable SoC Zedboard has been used as the target device, it is shown in Figure 1. The board contains all the necessary interfaces and supporting functions to enable a wide range of applications. The expandability features provided by the board idealize it for speedy prototyping and proof-of-concept development.

The Xilinx Zynq 7Z020 device is in the center of the board, to its left there is a 512 MB Micron DDR3. The Xilinx JTAG connector is in the upper side. It is powered via a 12 volts power jack. It also provides an on/off switch to control its operation.Zedboard enables embedded computing capability by using DDR3 memory, Flash memory, gigabit Ethernet, general purpose I/O, and UART technologies. Zedboard's key features:

*Figure 1. Plan View for Zedboard*
ZedBoard \ Zedboard, 2016.

- Zynq-7000 AP SoC XC7Z020-CLG484-1 processor.
- 512 MB DDR3.
- 256 MB Quad-SPI Flash memory.
- 4 GB SD card.
- Onboard USB-JTAG programming.
- 10/100/1000 Ethernet.
- USB OTG 2.0 and USB-UART.
- Expansion connector:
  - FMC-LPC connector (68 single-ended or 34 differential I/Os).
  - 5 Pmod compatible headers (2 × 6).
  - Agile Mixed Signaling (AMS) header.
- For the clocking, it has a 33.3333 MHz clock source for PS and a 100 MHz oscillator for PL.
- Display:
  - HDMI output supporting 1080p60 with 16-bit YCbCr 4:2:2 mode color.
  - VGA output (12-bit resolution color).
  - 128 × 32 OLED display.
- Configuration and Debug
  - Onboard USB-JTAG interface.
  - Xilinx platform Cable JTAG connector.

- General purposes:
  - 8 user LEDs.
  - 7 push buttons.
  - 8 DIP switches.

## HIGH-LEVEL SYNTHESIS

Xilinx Inc. offered a new mainstream technology called Vivado HLS. The main objective of using Vivado HLS is to speed up the process of transforming the algorithm from C or C++ or System -C into a VHDL/ VERILOG IP core inside the used FPGA board. HLS tools parse an existing high-level programming language as an input and generate its corresponding HDL design. Xilinx integrated HLS tools into their Vivado tool chain at a more mainstream price point compared to other tools such as: CatapaultC from Mentor Graphics and Mathworks Matlab HDL code.

The Vivado High-Level Synthesis compiler enables C, C++ and System-C programs to be directly targeted into Xilinx devices without passing through the steps of manually creating RTL. Vivado HLS is a widely searched tool used to increase the hardware designer's productivity, and it is confirmed that HLS tool support C++ classes, templates, functions and operator overloading. Vivado HLS has been included as a no cost upgrade in all Vivado HLx Editions. (Vivado High Level Synthesis, 2016). Supporting both the ISE and Vivado design environments Vivado HLS provides system and hardware designer alike with a faster path to IP creation by:

- Abstraction of algorithmic description, data type specification (integer, fixed-point or floating point) and interfaces (FIFO, AXI4, AXI4-Lite, AXI4-Stream).
- Extensive libraries for arbitrary precision data types, video DSP and more.
- Directives driven architecture-aware synthesis that delivers the best possible QoR.
- Accelerated verification using C/C++ test bench simulation, automatic VHDL or Verilog simulation and test bench generation.
- Multi-language support and the broadest language coverage in the industry.
- Automatic use of Xilinx on-chip memories, DSP elements and floating-point library.

## LITERATURE REVIEW

Anusha, Prasad, & Narayana (Anusha, Prasad, & Narayana, 2012) proposed an FPGA-based architecture for edge detection using Sobel edge detector. Anusha et al. chose to implement the Sobel edge detector because it yield less blurring and deterioration in high levels of noise. The authors' main concern was that the data involved with the edge detection operation is very large and therefore it affects the speed of image processing. Anusha et al. used a 3 × 3 convolutional kernels processing images of size 640 × 480 pixels. The hardware implementation that has been used was implemented on an Altera FPGA board, it has been coded using Verilog and simulated using Modelsim 6.5e. The execution time for the entire program of edge detection is found to be a few seconds.

Nayak, Pujari, & Dash (Nayak, Pujari, & Dash, 2014) described the implementation of SOBEL and PREWITT approach for edge detection in video and image processing using FPGA boards and Model Based Approach. The FPGA implementation has been done on Cyclone II FPGA board using Altera DE2 FPGA kit. The presented design worked at 27 MHz clock at VGA resolution of 640 × 480 pixels.

Khidhir & Abdullah (Khidhir & Abdullah, 2013) presented an FPGA-based architecture for Sobel edge detection using Virtex-5 ML506 board on gay-scale images. The Sobel operator has been modified in order to be able to find the edges in images with noise reduction. The presented modified Sobel operator achieved better results with better and sharper edges.

Abouelfarag, Elshenawy, & Khattab (Abouelfarag, Elshenawy, & Khattab, 2016) presented an enhanced operator cell that can be used in the RSDA. The novel operator cells make use of the compressor cells instead of using the conventional adders.

## Problem Statement

Working on real-time video requires operating abiding by tight deadlines within which results must be guaranteed. Each incoming frame must be processed, and multiple computationally intensive operations are done on each one of the frames. The main objective of the presented work is to accelerate the addition operations that are most widely used in edge detection operations.

An enhancement to the addition operation on the FPGA has been introduced, it makes use of the compressor cells. Compressors are logic circuits that can add multiple bits at a time and that is why it is called "Column Compressors". Compressors significantly enhance the carry propagation delays (Jones, Powell, Bouganis, & Cheung, 2010). Compressors are a basic component for multipliers and large-input adders, therefore it will obtain higher performance cells 3-to-2, 4-to-2, 5-to-2 and 9-to-2. It compresses multiple input bits that need to be added to two outputs, that is why it is called a compressor".

Using the conventional ripple carry adders will add each two values together. Therefore, multiple adders will be used. The main disadvantage of ripple carry adders is that they produce high carry propagation delays. When analyzing the timing constraints using Xilinx, the time taken to add two 8-bit numbers was 9.774 nanoseconds, which is considered a very high delay for rea-time applications. This delay is due to the carry propagation delay.

Implementing Sobel edge detection method would need a mapping computation as shown in Figure 2.

In Figure 2, the numbers on the right represent the numbering of the image pixels what will be operated and the letters from 'a' to 'i' are corresponding to the values in the Sobel kernels, and are numbered as shown in Figure 3.

After multiplying each pixel to its corresponding value in the kernel, all the values need to be added together afterwards. Using the operator cells on the FPGA board, only two numbers would be added at a time. In this work, an enhanced operator cell is introduced that will speed up the addition processes and improve resources usage. In Sobel technique, multiplications are not considered a burden because its kernels only has the values 0, 1, and 2. Multiplication by 0 and 1 are not considered an operation while multiplication by 2 can be performed by a logical 1-bit shift operation. Therefore, the main concern in this work is to enhance the addition-responsible operator cells.

*Figure 2. Computation mapping using Ripple Carry Adders*

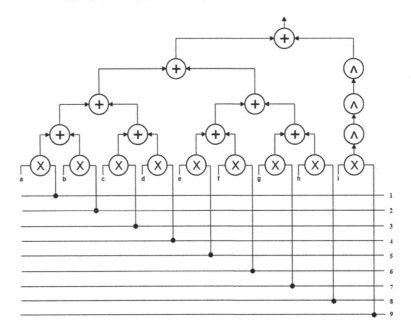

*Figure 3. Numbering of image pixels*

| a | b | c |
|---|---|---|
| d | e | f |
| g | h | i |

## SOLUTIONS AND RECOMMENDATIONS

This work introduces a novel operator cell to the FPGA architecture which makes use of compressors. Compressors are logic circuits that can add multiple bits at a time ad that is why it is called "Column Compressors". Compressors significantly enhance the carry propagation delays (Jones, Powell, Bouganis, & Cheung, 2010).

Using the conventional ripple carry adders will add each two values together. Therefore, multiple adders will be used. The main disadvantage of ripple carry adders is that they produce high carry propagation delays. When analyzing the timing constraints using Xilinx the time taken to add two 8-bit

*Figure 4. 8-bit addition using full adders*

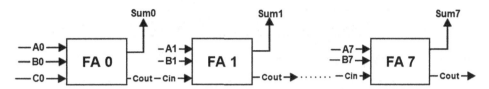

numbers was 9.774 nanoseconds, which is considered a very high delay for a real-time application. This delay is due to the carry propagation delay. Figure 4 shows how the 8-bit addition operations are dependent on each other.

In addition, the Zedboard has been used and the Sobel edge detection has been implemented on it using different tools provided by Xilinx such as the High-Level Synthesis which raises the abstraction level from the Register Transfer Level (RTL) to the algorithmic level, which adds flexibility and ease of design for the hardware designer.

## 3:2 Compressors

The mapping computation of Sobel edge detection technique using 3:2 compressors is shown in Figure 5. Four 3:2 compressor operator cells are utilized, each cell is composed of 8 compressors in order to add 8-bit numbers. The delay of 3:2 was found to be much less than that of the ripple carry adders adding the 8-bits. For adding nine values, addition will be performed on two levels with each level having a delay of 5.144 nanoseconds. Therefore, the addition delay for the two stages would be 10.288 nanoseconds.

*Figure 5. Computation mapping of Sobel using 3:2 compressors*

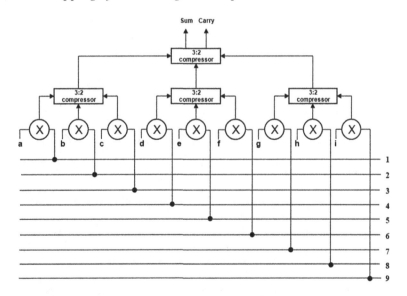

*Figure 6. Resources required when 3:2 compressors are used*

| Site type | Required |
|-----------|----------|
| LUTs | 160 |
| SLICEL | 40 |
| SLICEM | 40 |

## 4:2 Compressors

Using compressors will enable the architecture to add more numbers per cell, but on the other hand it will increase the delay, due to the carry dependencies and it will also need two-level addition in order to be able to add nine numbers, as shown in Figure 7.

When introducing the 4:2 compressor cells to the architecture, a pass through cell will be used (annotated by a "^") which passes data to the next level. The addition level using the 4:2 compressor cells produces a delay of 5.806 nanoseconds in addition to the delay of the next stage of the 3:2 compressor cells.

## 9:2 Compressors

As shown in Figure 8, when using 9:2 compressor cells, addition could be done on one stage. But, each compressor cell would produce a relatively high delay. Using eight 9:2 compressor cells would produce a delay of 10.478 nanoseconds.

*Figure 7. Computation mapping of Sobel when using 4:2 compressors*

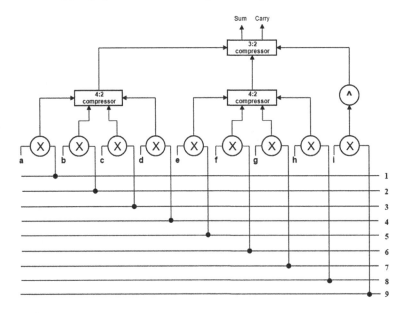

*Figure 8. Computation mapping of Sobel when using 9:2 compressors*

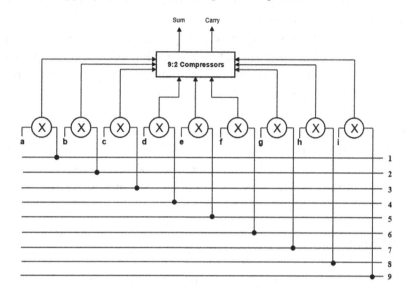

## Hardware Implementation for Edge Detection

While the required output of any real-time application is concerned about time constraints, it can be beneficial to take advantage and make use of the parallelism, low cost, and low power consumption offered by FPGAs. Many image processing applications require that redundant massively-parallel operations be performed on each pixel in the image resulting in a tremendous number of operations to be performed per second. Thus the perfect alternative is to make use of an FPGA board. Continual growth in the size and functionality of FPGAs over the recent years has resulted in an increasing interest in their use for image processing applications. The main advantage of using FPGAs for the hardware implementation of image processing applications is because of their massively parallel structure that is able to exploit spatial and temporal parallelism.

Video and image processing operations can be implemented using either one of these implementations:

- Software running on general purpose CPU or microprocessor.
- Software running on a specialized DSP or GPU.
- Hardware implementation on a dedicated Application Specific Integrated Circuit (ASIC)
- Hardware implementation on an FPGA board.

General Purpose CPUs are generally serial or sequential, in other words, they run a code. Therefore, they face multithreading overheads. Even multi-core or multithreaded processors will not fully utilize nor exploit all parallelism due to memory and input/output sharing and threads, and threads communication overhead (serial nature of individual threads). However; GPUs are faster than CPUs because they are designed mainly for graphics but they are still slower than dedicated image/video hardware implementations because they need to support a large set of general graphics processing functions. Moreover, implementing the algorithm on a dedicated ASIC board is complex and expensive and after the implementation, no further debugging or optimization can be done. Therefore, FPGAs are considered the optimal approach for real-time HD video and image processing.

FPGAs' elementary building blocks are relatively simple and dependent on the manufacturer and on the model. Typical elementary blocks that can be found inside FPGA devices are small logical functions (usually the locations inside those memories are just a dew bits wide), small multiplexers, and carry-chain devices. FPGAs which are oriented to high-end performance also have dedicated components such as: entire multipliers and adders.

The presented work targets offloading the Sobel edge detection algorithm from Processing Systems (PS) to Programmable Logic (PL) taking the advantage of HLS tool flow to accelerate the implementation on Zynq platform. In this way, pixel-based image processing and feature extraction are processed in hardware domain as hardware accelerators, while frame-based processing and decisions are done in software domain.

## High Level Synthesis

Vivado HLS, is a new mainstream technology offered by Xilinx Inc. The main objective of using Vivado HLS is to accelerate the process of transforming the algorithm from C or C++ or System -C into a VHDL/VERILOG IP core inside the used FPGA. HLS tools parse an existing high-level programming language as an input and generate the corresponding HDL. Some of these tools are quite popular in the Electronic Design Automation (EDA) industry such as CatapultC from Mentor Graphics and Mathworks Matlab HDL coder, but are very expensive. Xilinx recently integrated the support of HLS into their Vivado tool chain at a more mainstream price point.

HLS raises the abstraction layer from RTL to the algorithmic/behavioral level, allowing designers to focus on what needs to be done instead of the specifics of how to implement on a particular target. The stepping to HLS appears to be analogous to software designers moving to use high-level programming languages (C/C++) instead of assembly language.

A basic HLS tool flow is shown in Figure 9, as illustrated, the source code is first compiled into a representation called a Control and Data Flow Graph (CDFG). This generated CDFG is optimized based on automatic or manual algorithms for allocation (allocation of computing and storage resources), scheduling (clocking and timing), and binding (mapping operations to allocated computational or storage resources). After optimization is complete, then HDL RTL is generated. The HLS solution was generated with the Xilinx HLS tool suite version documented in Figure 10.

There are a few limitations that must be taken into consideration when building Vivado HLS projects:

- No dynamic memory (all need to be static): the IP of the C code that needs to be generated cannot have dynamic memory allocations.
- No system calls.
- Avoid recursive functions.

## HLS and OpenCV

All OpenCV processing can be done on a standard microprocessor, but real-time applications require a processing rate that exceeds the ability of microprocessors. Therefore, using FPGAs is a favorable choice. Zynq All programmable SoC family provides an ideal platform for implementing OpenCV-based designs.

*Figure 9. HLS tool work flow*
*Ren, 2014.*

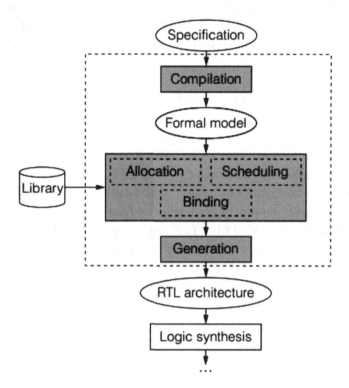

*Figure 10. Information about the HLS version used*

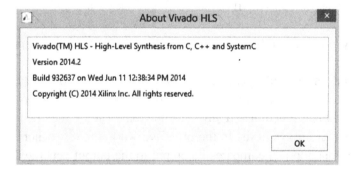

In a typical video stream using OpenCV functions, most of the algorithm will remain on the processor and remain using the OpenCV functions. Only the parts of the algorithm which need acceleration in the FPGA fabric will be synthesized and therefore updated to use the HLS video library.

HLS Video library includes commonly used OpenCV libraries as reference model, most video processing functions has the similar interface and equivalent behavior with corresponding OpenCV functions. The pre-built OpenCV libraries (with FFmed support) are also provided with Vivado HLS on different platforms, so users are able to use OpenCV directly without extra effort. The two header files that can help users start using HLS video library:

- **#include <hls_video.h>:** This must be included in the top design to access all specific video data structures and image/video processing functions. They are all synthesizable, when using the synthesizable part of HLS video library, it is required to use the HLS namespace.
- **#include <hls_opencv.h>:** This must be included in the test bench to access pre-built OpenCV libraries in Vivado HLS.

There are several limitations to the current OpenCV synthesizable library. The basic limitation is that OpenCV functions cannot be synthesized directly, and must be replaced by functions from the synthesized library. A second limitation is that hls::Mat<> datatype used to model images is internally defined as a stream of pixels, using the hls::stream<> datatype, rather than as an array of pixels in external memory.

Also streaming access implies that if an image is processed by more than one function, then it must first be duplicated into two streams, such as by using hls::Duplicate<> function. Another limitation is that OpenCV functions typically support either integer or floating-point datatypes. However, floating point is often more expensive and avoided when targeting programmable logic. A final limitation is that interface functions are only provided for AXI4 streaming video.

## Building Vivado HLS project

In order to build a Vivado HLS project, certain files must be added as input to the project being developed:

- **The Top C Function:** Written in C, C++, or System-C. The function can contain a hierarchy of sub-functions. In the presented work, the top C-function has been written in order to call the Sobel edge detector, and this is the function that needs to be synthesized.
- **Constraints:** The clock period, clock uncertainty, FPGA target. In the presented work, the default settings have been accepted, with 10 nanoseconds clock period and clock uncertainty 12.5% of the clock period.
- **Directives:** They are optional, they direct the synthesis process to implement a specific behavior or implementation.
- **C-Test Bench and Associated Files:** Vivado uses the test bench to simulate the C-function prior to synthesis and to automatically verify the RTL output using a C/RTL co-simulation. The C-test bench includes the main function and any sub-functions that are included in the hierarchy under the top-level function for synthesis. In the proposed work, the test bench was a simple program that calls the top function and compares its output to the output generated when using OpenCV on the computer's processor.

The first step in an HLS project is to confirm that the C code taken as an input is correct. This process is called C Validation or C simulation. In this project, the test bench compares the output data from the files that we added at the beginning of building the HLS project. The test bench file contains the top-level C main function, which in turn calls the function to be synthesized. The test bench performs the following:

- It saves the output image from the top function into an output file.
- The output file is compared with the input image file that was added at the beginning of the project.

- If both files' data match each other, a message is printed indicating the success of the process, and the main function returns 0.
- If both files' data didn't match each other, a message is printed indicating failure of verification, and the main function return 1.

Vivado HLS re-uses the test-bench during RTL verification and confirms the successful verification of the RTL if the test bench returns a value of 0. If any other value is retuned by the main function, including no return value, the RTL verification is considered to have failed.

The second step is synthesizing the C-design into an RTL design and review the synthesis report. When synthesis completes, the report file opens automatically. The third step is to perform verification, by choosing to do "co-simulation" in the toolbar. It reuses the C test bench to verify the RTL using simulation. In our project we used the RTL co-simulation default option to perform the simulation using the Vivado simulator and Verilog RTL. At the end of this step, the C test bench has generated input vectors for the RTL design, the RTL design is simulated and the output vectors from the RTL are applied back into the C test bench and the results-checking in the test bench verify whether or not the results are correct.

The final step is IP creation which means packaging the design as an IP block for use with other tools in the Xilinx Design Suite. By default every IP core generated by Vivado HLS is going to have the following signals:

- **AP_START:** Input, begin the computation.
- **AP_RST:** Input.
- **AP_CLK:** Input.
- **AP_IDLE:** Output, which states that the computation has not started yet.
- **AP_DONE:** Output, the computation has finished.
- **AP_READY:** Output, the core is ready to receive another input.

To summarize, the work flow used when working with Vivado HLS to build our Vivado HLS project is illustrated below:

- Define your function/Algorithm and create a program that uses this algorithm.
- Simulate the algorithm As compiled code.
- Synthesize (C/C++ →HDL).
- Co-simulate the HDL generated code.

## AXI4 Streaming Interface

AXI is a family of micro controller buses first introduced in 1996. AXI4 provides improvements and enhancements to the Xilinx product providing benefits to productivity, flexibility, and availability as it provides productivity by standardizing on the AXI interface, it provides flexibility by providing the right protocol for the application, and lastly, it provides availability by moving to an industry-standard, as we not only have access to the Xilinx IP catalog, but also to a worldwide community of ARM partners.

The AXI specifications describe interfaces between a single AXI master and a single AXI slave, representing IP cores that perform exchange of information between each other. Memory mapped masters and slaves can be connected together using an Interconnect block. Data can move in both directions between the masters and slave simultaneously, and data transfer sizes can vary according to the specifications. There are three main types of AXI buses:

- **AXI4:** High throughput for memory-mapped communication.
- **AXI4-Lite:** Low throughput for memory-mapped communication.
- **AXI4-Stream:** High throughput for streamed data.

## Integrating the Generated Intellectual Property (IP) Core in a Block Diagram

After generating the targeted IP core, we switch to Vivado software. First we have to add the Zynq processing system block, a (Direct Memory Access) DMA block and the generated IP that performs the FAST corner detection as well. After adding the DMA block we have to configure it to simple transfers and configure the required stream data width (in the proposed system it takes gray scaled images as input to the FAST corner detector), so we specify the stream data width to be 8 bits. Also the Zynq must be configures to use the slave HP port to connect with the DMA. Finally, an AXI timer block should be added, this will be how we will calculate time spent in running the FAST.

Vivado provides a facility that simplify the work on block diagrams which runs automatic connecting between IP cores.

## NEW FINDINGS AND LIMITATIONS

The main goal of this research is to achieve an optimal time performance for a real-time edge detection application. By using the OpenCV library which offers various accelerated computer functions such as: noise filtering, histogram equalization, object detection functions, etc. Acceleration is accomplished by implementing the edge detection operation on the Zedboard which yielded a 2.5x acceleration. Moreover, High-Level Synthesis has been used to easily optimize the design architecture and to describe the design at a higher level of abstraction. Also, HLS generates an optimized RTL hardware design regarding performance, area, and power requirements.

The hardware implementation is aimed to accelerate the edge detection operation by implementing it on the Zynq-7000 AP SoC XC7Z020 Zedboard. At first the abstraction level is raised from the RTL level to an algorithmic level to generate the IP core of the target algorithm to be accelerated. After that, the IP core generated with the complete hardware cores.

Xilinx Vivado Design Suite is the backbone for advanced generation-ahead hardware, software, and system development using All Programmable Abstractions. It enables the generation of comprehensive IP- and system-centric development environment that is commonly experienced during system-level integration and implementation.

Moreover, the Vivado Design Suite can reach high device utilization levels because it employs advanced fitting algorithms. In addition, the Vivado Design Suite employs advanced, efficient data models and structures to yield the smallest memory footprint.

Vivado HLS tool accelerates the development of real-time smart vision algorithms for systems based on Xilinx Zynq-7000 All Programmable SoC devices through pre-defined image and video functions integrated into an OpenCV environment, and these algorithms can run using software on the Zynq SoC's dual-core ARM processing system and hardware on the Zynq SoC's high-performance FPGA fabric.

In addition to the reduction of time latency, resource utilization percentage of the FPGA board has also been optimized by using the Zedboard which is well suited for real-time image and video processing through offering better suited processing elements, capacity, and connection ports.

## FUTURE RESEARCH DIRECTIONS

For the future work, this work can be continued to work on video streams of higher frames per second rate and with higher resolution.

Moreover, further improvements for the proposed model can be achieved by implying pre-processing techniques on the input frames and apply different noise filters to help in further improving of the image features which reflects on the system's accuracy in the next operations.

Also, Future work will focus on further improvements of the operator cells, such as decreasing power consumption and reducing resources consumption. More improvements could be done in order to enhance the performance of the operator cells when values consist of more than 8 bits.

## CONCLUSION

The main goal of this research is to achieve an optimal time performance for performing Sobel edged detection. Edge detection is performed by using the open source computer vision library OpenCV library which offers various accelerated computer vision functions such as: noise filtering, histogram equalization, object detection functions, etc. Moreover, High-Level Synthesis has been used to easily optimize the design architecture and to describe the design at a higher level of abstraction. Also, HLS generates an optimized RTL hardware design regarding performance, area, and power requirements.

In addition to the reduction of time latency, also resource utilization percentage of the FPGA board is optimized by using the Zedboard which is well suited for real-time image and video processing by offering better suited processing elements, capacity, and connection ports.

In this research a novel operator cell based on compressors is introduced. Delay enhancement is achieved when using 3:2 compressors that could be used to add nine 8-bit values together, it will yield the least delay compared to the other compressor cells and also the ripple carry adder cells. When using the ripple carry adder, each addition stage would cost 9.774 nanoseconds. As shown in Figure 2, four addition stages are needed, which produces a total of 39.096 nanoseconds delay, while using 3:2 compressor cells as shown in Figure 5, it only needs two addition stages with each stage producing a delay of 5.144 nanoseconds, and a total of 10.288 nanoseconds.

This improved behavior has been confirmed with experimental results that have shown a 26% increase in speed.

# REFERENCES

Abouelfarag, A., Elshenawy, M., & Khattab, E. (2016). High Speed Edge Detection Implementation Using Compressor Cells over RSDA. *Proceedings of the International Conferences Interfaces and Human Computer Interaction 2016, Game and Entertainment Technologies and Computer Graphics, Visualization, Computer Vision and Image Processing 2016*, 229-237.

Anusha, G., Prasad, T. J., & Narayana, D. S. (2012). Implementation of SOBEL Edge Detection on FPGA. *International Journal of Computer Trends and Technology, 3*(3).

Asanovic, K., Bodik, R., Catanzaro, B. C., Gebis, J. J., Husbands, P., Keutzer, K., & Yelick, K. (2006). The Landscape of Parallel Computing Research: A View from Berkeley. Retrieved from http://www2.eecs.berkeley.edu/Pubs/TechRpts/2006/EECS-2006-183.html

Bradski, G., & Kaehler, A. (2008). Learning OpenCV: Computer Vision with the OpenCV Library. O'Reilly Media.

Jain, R., Kasturi, R., & Schunck, B. (1995). *Machine Vision*. New York: McGraw-Hill, Inc.

Johnston, T. C., Bailey, D. G., & Gribbon, K. (2004). Implementing image processing algorithms on FPGAs. *Proc. Elev. Electron New Zealand ENZCon, 04*, 119–123.

Jones, D. H., Powell, A., Bouganis, C.-S., & Cheung, P. (2010). GPU versus FPGA for High Productivity Computing. *Proceedings of the International Conference on Field Programmable Logic and Applications*, 119-124. doi:10.1109/FPL.2010.32

Khidhir, A. M., & Abdullah, N. Y. (2013, June-July). FPGA Based Edge Detection Using Modified Sobel Filter. *International Journal for Research and Development in Engineering, 2*(1), 22–32.

Kumar, V., Sbirlea, A., Jayaraj, A., Budimlic, Z., Majeti, D., & Sarkar, V. (2015). Heterogeneous work-stealing across CPU and DSP cores. *Proceedings of the High Performance Extreme Computing Conference (HPEC)*. IEEE. doi:10.1109/HPEC.2015.7322452

Mccool, M. (2008). Signal Processing And General-Purpose Computing And GPUs. *IEEE Signal Processing Magazine, 24*(3), 109–114. doi:10.1109/MSP.2007.361608

Morris, T., Blenkhorn, P., & Zaidi, F. (2002). Blink Detection for Real-time Eye Tracking. *Journal of Network and Computer Applications, 25*(2), 129–143. doi:10.1016/S1084-8045(02)90130-X

Nayak, S., Pujari, S., & Dash, P. (2014). Implementation of Edge Detection Using FPGA and Model Based Approach. *Proceedings of the International Conference on Information Communication and Embedded Systems (ICICES)*. doi:10.1109/ICICES.2014.7033990

OpenCV. (2016). Retrieved from http://opencv.org/

Ren, H. (2014). A Brief Introduction on Contemporary High-Level Synthesis. *Proceedings of the IEEE International Conference on IC Design & Technology (ICICDT 2014)*. doi:10.1109/ICICDT.2014.6838614

Saponara, C., Casula, M., & Fanucci, L. (2008). ASIP-based reconfigurable architectures for power-efficient and real-time image/video processing. *Journal of Real-Time Image Processing, 3*(3), 201–216. doi:10.1007/s11554-008-0084-y

Schiel, J., & Bainbridge-Smith, A. (2015). *Efficient Edge Detection on Low Cost FPGAs*. Academic Press.

SlashGear. (2016). *Iris camera concept reinvents blink detection*. Retrieved from http://www.slashgear. com/iris-camera-concept-reinvents-blink-detection-01236626/

Sujatha, P., & Sudha, K. (2015). Performance Analysis of Different Edge Detection Techniques for Image Segmentation. *Indian Journal of Science and Technology*, *8*(14). doi:10.17485/ijst/2015/v8i14/72946

Xilinx.com. (2016). *Vivado High Level Synthesis*. Retrieved from https://www.xilinx.com/products/ design-tools/vivado/integration/esl-design.html

ZedBoard. (2016). Retrieved from http://zedboard.org/product/zedboard

Zhen-tao, L., Tao, L., & Jun-gang, H. (2013). A novel reconfigurable data-flow architecture for real time video processing. *Journal of shanghai Jiaotong University (Science), 18*(3), 348-359.

## ADDITIONAL READING

Coussy, P., & Morawiec, A. (2008). *High-level synthesis.* New York: Springer. doi:10.1007/978-1-4020-8588-8

Crockett, L., Elliot, R., Enderwitz, M., & Stewart, R. (2014). *The Zynq book.* Glasgow, UK: Strathclyde Academic Media.

Das, V. (2010). *Information processing and management.* Berlin: Springer. doi:10.1007/978-3-642-12214-9

Fingeroff, M. (2010). *High-level synthesis.* Xlibris Corporation.

Kehtarnavaz, N., & Gamadia, M. (2006). *Real-time image and video processing.* San Rafael, CA: Morgan & Claypool Publishers.

## KEY TERMS AND DEFINITIONS

**AXI Interfaces:** A family controller buses which enable standard and rapid stream data communication.

**Compressors:** Logic circuits that can add multiple bits simultaneously while eliminating the carry propagation delays.

**HLS:** High level synthesis is the process that enables hardware designers to easily optimize their design dealing with the algorithmic level instead of the RTL level.

**OpenCV:** An open-source computer vision library that offers accelerated pre-defined computer video and image processing functions.

**Real-Time Applications:** Applications that need to operate abiding by constrained time constraints in order to be operate in real-time interactive systems.

**Sobel Edge Detector:** An edge detection algorithm that makes use of convolutional kernels.

**Xilinx:** An American technology company which offers field-programmable gate array boards.

# Chapter 2
# Expansion of Uses and Applications of Virtual Reality

**Pablo Gobira**
*Universidade do Estado de Minas Gerais, Brazil*

**Antônio Mozelli**
*Universidade do Estado de Minas Gerais, Brazil*

## ABSTRACT

*The chapter shows the evolution of virtual reality interfaces and technologies to the current moment and verifies what led them to an alleged decline in early 1990. Due to the development of the industry of digital games, new forms of interaction have being researched and presented to the public. It will also be shown the application of virtual reality in different contexts of digital games, in addition to reporting a brief experience of the research group in art, science and technology, Lab\Front (Laboratório de Poéticas Fronteiriças - CNPq/UEMG).*

## 1. INTRODUCTION

This chapter presents a brief history of development and technological advances in virtual reality (VR) up to this moment which seems to be expanding. Due to advances in research and development of the game industry, virtual reality and its immersion technologies appear to be growing. In the 1990s, this technology promised to be a trend, but high production costs have limited their use and interest to only specific scientific communities.

Between 1990 and the middle of the first decade of this century, other forms of interaction and languages have been explored due to increasing Internet access and dissipation of data in virtual networks. The interests in VR have decreased more and more, as well as the attention of researchers and scientific centers to handle the subject. However, it is important to emphasize that innovation efforts as well as the varied interests, not ceased altogether. This is something that this chapter aims to demonstrate to the exposure of continuous events in a "story of the VR".

DOI: 10.4018/978-1-5225-2492-2.ch002

Current research in virtual reality area is realigning its focus to the development and growth of the area, mainly for the prospects of creating videogames with higher levels of realism, new technologies and immersion artifacts.

In this chapter, we present in the third section some of the experiences of the Laboratory of Front Poetics (Lab|Front) with virtual reality. The two experiments are a different use of virtual reality as expected primarily by industry: whether in the world of digital games (see Playstation VR or VR Samsung, for example); or in exploration of social experiences applications.

One is the development of an interactive art installation that aims to "imprison the look" of the interactor as an investigative attempt to immersion in virtual reality and the other is a curatorial experiment in virtual reality, where we simulate the art gallery of the Guignard School from the University of the State of Minas Gerias in order to propose an excercise of art work curatorship.

After the report of the two experiments it will be possible to envisage other uses of virtual reality that signal virtual reality uses in a continuous and expanding way at least since the 1990s.

## 2. THE DEVELOPMENT OF INTERFACES

### 2.1 Virtual Reality in Expansion

Since its beginning, virtual reality has been intended to something big: the possibility of experiencing other realities, of being transported to any other space without leaving their own place simulating their own world with its own rules and with lots of different ways of life. It is part of a system in which man interacts with the machine, but it is truly in the mind where everything happens. Even before the development of current virtual reality technologies and immersion, attempts in history have already shown the man's interest in mastering such artifacts.

In the seventeenth century, the church used the projections of Athanasius Kircher made with the optical principle called *camera obscura*, an early example in history. Athanasius created the "live" view of hell that caused great astonishment and served for many Christians as a powerful argument against sin. He made the mental picture of hell and demons possible through the smoke employment, inclusion of strange insects, which seemed magnified monsters. He used the simulation to make a fictional world real. The image hitherto unseen by the faithful could have caused a sense of immersion in another reality. The space of the church was intended to provide the observer with knowledge of the possible, that is, the virtual existence of the infernal world (Giannetti, 2006, p. 150).

When virtual reality is thought, many authors refer to the development of stereoscopy and the first images in three dimensions, as well as others point to interfaced experiences out of the body. The principle of stereoscopy presents each eye an image corresponding to their point of view. Thus, it is possible to simulate the sensation of depth and relief, since human eyes are distant from each other by a few centimeters, it does not have the same view of the world (Arantes, 2005, p. 114).

For most authors, it was between the years 1950 and 1960 that the pioneers started the development of stereoscopic instruments for immersion and graphic simulation. It should highlight the Sensorama of Morton Heilig in 1950 as a kind of synesthetic theater. In it, an immersive booth, a vibrating seat, handlebars, a binocular display device, a set of fans, stereo speakers and a nasal device simulated the experience of driving a motorcycle in specific places of the United States (Rejane, 2001, p. 29).

In 1962 at MIT, Ivan Sutherland developed the direct manipulation program called Sketchpad. Using a pen, one could draw directly on the cathode ray tube and displaying the image in almost real time. This was a major breakthrough in computer graphics research at the time. Later, between 1966 and 1970, Sutherland developed the Head-Mounted Display, a version of a more advanced stereoscopic viewing helmet, allowing interaction with located infographic images before the viewer's eyes (Giannetti, 2006, p. 121).

In 1968, Sutherland published an article in Harvard University, called "The Head-Mounted Three Dimensional Display," in which it was described the development of a stereoscopic helmet traceable. The helmet had two mini CRT displays that projected images directly into the user's eyes and you could track the head movements through a mechanical and ultrasonic interface. Sutherland developments made a landmark in the history of VR, thereby establishing the concept of immersion.

The Augmented Reality (AR), so common today, was based on the creation of interactive helmet video, developed by engineers from Philco, along with interactive helmet for computer graphics Sutherland. They both had tracking technologies. A few decades after this, the use of video, tracking and computer graphics integrated - and interacting in real time - enabled the development of augmented reality applications. (Kirner, 2008)

In the mid-1970s, a number of artifacts began to be developed for the evolution of virtual reality. In 1977 the glove Dataglove was designed to contribute to the multisensory aspects of the VR being marketed only in 1985, by the company VPL Research. In 1981, the US Air Force created one Cockpit simulator for pilots where it was possible to use an optical sight helmet with increased vision and aircraft information, visual indication of missiles available for shooting. The helmet had an acrylic display and allowed to mix view of the scene overlaid with images generated by projection of a CRT display inside the helmet. This was one of the first augmented reality projects, it cost was in the range of millions of dollars.

In 1989 the Power glove was released for the Nintendo video game, developed by Mattel company, but was not successful in the video game industry being adapted for virtual reality systems based on computers like the firsts Personal Computers (PC).

The appearance of CAVEs (Cave Automatic Virtual Environment), a virtual reality system for projection on walls as an alternative to the use of helmets, was shown in SIGGRAPH'92 event in 1992, developed at the University of Illinois at Chicago, by Carolina Cruz-Neira. Since 1992 computer graphics companies such as Silicon Graphics Inc. and Sense8 Co. has begun producing tools and software for the development of applications in virtual reality.

Softwares as WorldToolKit and Iris Inventor use their own library of functions in C and C ++ for modeling and 3D visualization, making it possible to increase productivity and quality of applications. They also have provided the structural foundation of what would become the VRML (Virtual Reality Modeling Language). In the academic community, conferences and workshops they appeared to discuss the research frontiers in virtual reality and in the year 1995 the IEEE VR event was created by combining the VRAIS'93 and Research Frontiers in Virtual Reality IEEE Workshop conferences.

In 1999 the ARToolKit, a free software written in C that allowed tracking video, aroused worldwide interest in augmented reality area and there were several other free tools led to virtual reality applications and augmented reality with the growth of the Internet and applications native Web.

In Brazil, the development in virtual reality area dates back to the early 1990s with masters and doctoral defenses, publications, events and creation of research groups. Guest researchers like Prof. Claudio Kirner (UFSCar) traveled to the United States allowing the approach and the deepenerin the area. The first major field event was the "1st Workshop on Virtual Reality - WRV'97" held at the Federal University of São Carlos and allowed to promote the integration of researchers, professionals and students interested.

Currently, the event is in its 17th meeting entitled "SVR 2015 - XVII Symposium Virtual Reality and Augmented Reality" and has evolved and incorporated other symposia on specific topics such as augmented reality. The SVR2015 has several topics of interest from systems of VR and AR tools, 3D interaction, virtual human and avatars, games for VR/AR, Social Impacts, economic and technical VR/ AR, among others.

New research groups have been formed, as well as virtual reality centers have been installed in large companies in Brazil. Large equipment have been purchased at universities and new graduate courses have begun to form masters and doctors in the area. Companies such as Petrobras and Embraer invested in technology centers applied to virtual reality and universities have invested and developed their own CAVE systems. Today, with the creation of several undergraduate courses in both technological level of Digital Games, Media Production, Computer Graphics, Digital Arts are beyond traditional degrees in Computer Science, Information Systems and engineering, virtual reality area is booming. Motion capture systems, capture and video editing, visual effects creation and development for mobile platforms have led to the industry investment trends. (Kirner, 2008)

This historical presented aims to highlight the evolution and development of virtual reality to the current scenario, where the VR is in fact expanding. Below we will discuss if there was really a fall of VR started in the 1990s in relation to this contemporary expansion.

## 2.2 Virtual Reality: From Fall to Growth?

During the past decades, developers and communities based their work on virtual reality trends suitable forthe features of the time. There are works in three-dimensional modeling with low quality rendering, primitive 3D graphics, initial studies on user interface and visual simulations with little interaction. Currently, the virtual reality field is expanding due to the access to the current game development tools and the film industry.

This section is intended to present the expansion of the area of a specific perspective. It points out the possible causes of the falling interest in VR in the last two decades. However, it does not mean that there was retrogression of interest in virtual reality or the augmented reality. As seen above, there has been continuity of research for development and innovation as well as conceptual and theoretical research of those same decades.

The revolution that virtual reality promised in the early 1990s with the emergence of the first Personal Computers was unsuccessful due to numerous factors. Basically the industry was not prepared for such ideals. The high development costs of the time did not allow further expansion in industrial terms. In the mid-1990s, due to increasing Internet access and dissipation of data in virtual networks, other forms of interaction and languages were explored (Rocha, 2010). Many researchers have abandoned virtual reality area and have migrated to the latest World Wide Web studies, as well as the entire industry attention has been redirected to the Internet and its possibilities.

According to the discussion held by Professor Mark Bolas (2011), from the Creative Technologies Institute of the University of Southern California (USC), there is a matter determined by the "hype". Hype is an English word which suggests the extreme promotion of an idea, person or product, as if coming into fashion. There was hype around virtual reality in the 1990s and it turned out impossible to carry out their promises.

This is a common phenomenon observed in the Gartner Hype Curve chart (Chart 1) developed by Jeremy Kemp at Gartner Inc., an American company Research in Information Technology. The graph shows that when a new technological potential is created, it also creates a media interest and publicity on this new potential, as well as the development of very new concepts about the potential. At this stage, usually there is no proven commercial feasibility to the potential yet and there are also no usable products. The second point of the graph shows a peak inflated of expectations about the potential developed, with the result of a number of success stories produced by advertising and also many stories of failure. At this point some companies pay attention while others can not provide it. The third point is called "Trough of Disillusionment", which is when many implementations and interests fail in their delivery. Investments remain only for those who can change the potential and thus meet the consumer trends, the so-called Early adopters. The fourth point of the graph refers to an inclination about how the technological potential can benefit the company and become more widely understood. New product generations begin to emerge from technology vendors and more enterprises begin to fund pilot projects. Also, at this point, more conservative companies remain wary. Finally, there is a productivity plateau, in which the mass of consumers begin to make use of technological potential. The criterias for access and viability are more clearly defined. The market can see the broad applicability for the technology.

This diagram describes the scenario of virtual reality in the 1990s and its current stability seen by the market and industry, especially the market of digital games. Many factors contributed to that stability in the recent decades. The evolution of computer's processors and telecommunications technologies have enabled the development of new computer technologies and a more mature perspective about the future.

Currently, specific hardware for graphics processing, such as 3D video cards, has achieved high performance when compared to the hardware of the 1990s. Cell phones have screens of ultra definition imagery, advanced technologies and wireless sensors for data network connection and high speed internet, global positioning sensors (GPS) and other sensors: gyroscopes; accelerometers; pedometers; barometers; and magnetic interfaces. The cameras on cellphones film in resolution compared to digital cinema with resolutions above the limit for the human eye. Inexpensive devices, such as cardboard boxes, are turning mobile phones into virtual reality goggles and helmets, in addition of besides the investment of large companies developing their own virtual reality interfaces.

*Figure 1. Hype cycle diagram, Jeremy Kemp*
*Source: Bolas, 2011.*

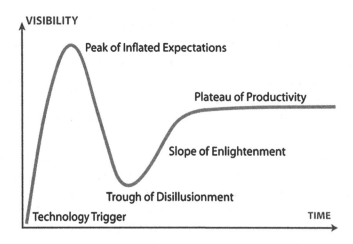

Game developers have persisted in creating experiences with higher level of engagement. The scenarios and virtual worlds have magnificent ability to simulate details. The growth areas such as scientific visualization, has made advances in distribution of computing and network games like World of Warcraft and other Massively Multiplayer Online (MMO) and they also have contributed to the stability of virtual reality.

Besides technological developments, societies around the world are more comfortable with the idea of virtuality than in the 1990s. Most people have cell phones and use the Internet to communicate across applications, instant messaging and e-mails, watch movies in digital format, play online games and have accounts on social networks. It can no longer fail to note the importance of digital artists who use the 3D modeling and virtual reality technologies. These are people who are directly linked to the film industry, production of digital games and follow careers in the construction of entire worlds and virtual environments, 3D objects, entertaining thousands of people. It seems that society has never been more receptive and engaged with the virtual reality.

We act like that actually there was no fall in the growth of the VR. There was a timid industrial development in the use and applications of VR that almost could generate a break. The development was in those years, for the reasons given above, did not have such a big advertising as we are seeing in the context of games that, on other occasions, tried to include virtual reality without much success. This lower investment in the VR is reversed now, as we shall see.

## 2.3 Virtual Reality, Games, and Industry

The gaming industry is investing largely in technologies and interfaces to better use of virtual reality. In the year 2016, the famous American event and the greatest influence on technological trends for the consumer - Consumer Technology Association (CES) - made history pointing to the year 2016 (and for years to come) the immersion technologies in virtual reality and output content to them. The focus of the event was the new interfaces for immersive virtual reality, that is, systems that are being developed by large companies in the area as Oculus, HTC and Sony, as well as new hardware for games, software and accessories designed for mobile devices, computers and video game consoles. The games and virtual reality market will expand by 77% on its forecast comparing 2015, according to the reports of Consumer Technology Association (CTA), a group that organizes CES (Baig, 2016).

When mobile devices such as cell phones, are used as binoculars interfaces for VR, they enable widespread access to such content. As example of these interfaces, companies like Google and Samsung have showed mid and low cost solutions for VR access. The model from Samsung, the Samsung Gear VR, presents a sophisticated plastic device with presence sensors and lenses to stereoscopy, which used along with a brand handset allows quality access in the execution of applications and content for VR. However, it must remember that only the most robust mobile phones of the brand are compatible with this solution. Google provides a low cost solution called Google Cardboard. It consists of a model made in cardboard plus two magnifying glasses and a magnetic system that serves as an interface to the user. The model is available at the company's website and it is possible to develop your own domestic solution with the use of a mobile device (Baig, 2016).

Other binocular interfaces were also presented to the public during the event. The most anticipated, especially by the public of the games, were the virtual reality systems Oculus Rift, HTC Vive and Sony's design, Project Morpheus, which works with the PlayStation 4 console. These are robust interfaces that require higher graphical processing of its hardware. With the main focus on immersion in digital games, these interfaces allow greater interaction with the game's elements as they are equipped with sensors and joysticks integrated into the body immersion system. One example is the HTC Vive that signals the user, through graphic signs on the screen, the approach of its user to possible obstacles outside the virtual environment, avoiding possible accidents. Another interface, in this case for augmented reality, is the product of Microsoft, HoloLens. A helmet with holographic projection system that combines virtual reality with the outside world, and allows viewing a mixed reality (Baig, 2016). Importantly, these more robust interfaces are also used for other virtual reality applications and experiments, expanding its use not only for the development of digital games.

The social network Facebook, which in 2014 bought the company that developed the Oculus Rift interface, affirmed that it wants to change the use of their social network by being able to share a more meaningful experience with its members. The company also said it is important to use virtual reality to develop a stronger presence rather than the current means of dissemination of media on its network. If it is now possible to share photos, videos and various digital information, with the adoption of virtual reality new forms of narrative and interactions should be tried as well (Schnipper, 2014).

A new market is also emerging, it is the mediating companies that work in the process of buying and selling digital products used in virtual reality universe. Three-dimensional modeling, algorithms and image rendering techniques, animation, games and characters to virtual worlds are being marketed through retail platforms using virtual reality. But, non virtual retail companies are also investing in virtual reality experiences to enhance product sales at its department stores (Baig, 2016).

Another trend that is also causing expansion in virtual reality is the companies producing content for VR. Today it's possible to follow the broadcast of basketball games as well as watching golf championships using virtual reality. The evolution of video cameras, that star to record 360° films and 3D, allows producers to reinvent ways to tell stories and generate new challenges for the cinematographic industry. (Baig, 2016)

With these examples we see not only that the use of virtual reality is expanding, but also that it is going beyond the field of the games industry, when using it to drive sales, as well as the development and knowledge of applied technologies. We have seen this strategy when was launched and popularizing the Kinect sensor technology, Microsoft (in 2010).

## 2.4 Applications of Virtual Reality

As Microsoft sensor, Kinect, is used for other applications, new virtual reality interfaces are also being used for other experiments. Companies, researchers and artists around the world, are enabling new uses for these interfaces.

Engineering and architectural companies are promoting the use of virtual reality to simulate virtual tours into new ventures. Model apartments and virtual show room are also being used as a potential conversion factor for sales. Customers can visit the apartment or condo without leaving their own home. The scientific visualization has also used the virtual reality capabilities to run simulations, enabling training in occupational safety and heavy operations with specific machinery.

The cultural industry also takes advantage of the new opportunities for media coverage of their products, from the promotion of blockbuster movies to full immersion in rock concerts. You can also pose as superheroes or participate in an earthquake in Asia.

The realistic and immersive nature of virtual reality has allowed the user to play the role of another person. Psychologists in the Virtual Human Interaction Lab, Stanford University (USA), are conducting several projects using virtual reality in order to generate empathy in users. Through the capabilities of technology, students can see their appearance and behavior reflected in a virtual mirror as someone who is different and may experience a scenario from the perspective of either party of a social interaction.

Studies have been applying virtual reality to teach empathy towards people with disabilities, with different skin color, with different economic goals, and different age groups. Another project called "Sustainable Behavior" from the same laboratory at Stanford University, grant users to experience a dive in a filled coral life which may be over, if our behavior on pollution do not change.

Not many people have the opportunity to dive like this, and the experience allows you to view various stages of ocean acidification. The laboratory also has a research project on a virtual learning environment, where the virtual environment allows greater focus and attention to the class goals. The engagement technology enables better interaction between content and students.

Something similar to what is developed at Stanford has been held since 2009 by professor and researcher Mel Slater, Department of Computer Science at University College London, where he studied "the exploration of virtual reality in the study of moral judgment."

Another work that also aims to teach empathy to people is the work of student Yifei Chai, from Imperial College London has developed a virtual reality system in order to give users the feeling of being in someone else's body and also to be able to control it. As a participant uses a binocular interface of VR, another uses a head support with an installed camera and also a cloth with electrical stimulation. Both bodies are tracked by a motion sensor. The camera feeds the binocular interface and it possible to them to look at their own body and see the body of another person, in addition to controlling the body movements of the other participant (Stuart, 2014).

Artists are proposing demonstrations and performances using virtual reality to show their work. An art installation, *The Machine to be Another*, allows the virtual exchange of genres among participants. It can use the body of another party through a system of cameras and glasses for VR. The concept of exchange and personification of virtual body, called digital embodiment (Munster, 2006), is widely used in virtual reality, especially in digital games. When taking on a character or avatar in a digital game the notion of itself is changed to a different notion of control.

Another artist, Thorston Wiedemann, tested his ability to stay on virtual reality for 48 hours in various virtual worlds in Games Science Center in Berlin (Germany). Among its activities, Thorston played tennis against himself, created snowmen through a virtual design tool, sometimes tickled a cat as solve puzzles, traveled to magical places with their virtual friends, posed with his pink suit as the US president at the White House and other activities (Pangburn, 2016).

## 3. AN EXPERIENCE OF ART AND VIRTUAL REALITY

This section describes an interdisciplinary experience of developing interactive interfaces of the research group in art, science and technology called Lab|Front - Laboratory of Front Poetics (CNPq/UEMG)[1]. Here we present two interactive experiments in immersive virtual reality performed in low cost with the use of digital games development technologies.

## 3.1 Art Installation Look at yourself

The developed installation aims to "imprison the look" of the interactor as an investigative attempt to immersion in virtual reality. Through 3D computer modeling, created forms simulate the head of the interactor and his/her look is produced by the camera located inside the head of the model in a way that the outside world is not seen concretely.

### 3.1.1 3D Artwork Development

The first stage of the development was the 3D modeling performed using the free software computer modeling Blender. We developed a model of a human skull that houses inside the camera that is the starting point of view of installation. The texturing process was performed using the mapping model with the UV Mapping technique. The developed texture, made from a drawing built in an image editing software, was meant to represent how the insight would be if we accommodate ourselves within a human head.

From the model created in Blender, the installation program was held in the graphics engine (game engine) to develop digital games Unity 5, using C# programming language. The camera was set to connect with the movements performed by the head of the interactor when merged in the installation. That was possible by mapping the gyro sensor, present in mobile devices like smartphone, to capture the angle required as data input to rotate and to tilt the virtual camera installation as data output. The Google Cardboard SDK was used to perform the image division for stereoscopy in conjunction with the LG Nexus 5 mobile with Android Kit Kat operating system. Tests were also conducted with Samsung Galaxy S4 and Samsung Note 4 devices with Android Jelly Bean operating system. The interaction with the interactor allows him to rotate around his own axis and also to tilt his head.

*Figure 2. Stereoscopic vision of the piece*
*Source: Setup Files.*

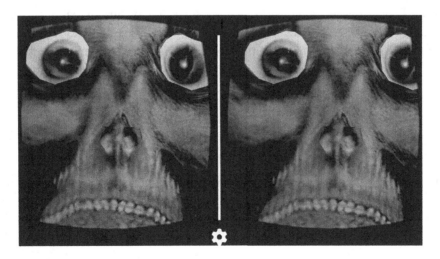

### 3.1.1 Sound Design and Anti-Immersion Concept

Besides the 3D model developed and visual features, the installation also includes the creation of sound effects that support and allow to emphasize the concept of "imprisonment look."

The immersion idea is linked to the need to be part of another environment, to enter it through the illusion of the senses. Since the first attempts to build interfaces for virtual reality, the means that perform the interaction between man and machine are designed to increase the communication capacity between system and user. Greater attention was given to the development of the installation in order to promote a possible denial of the dialogue between interactor and interface through sound resources that promote an alleged anti-immersion.

That anti-immersion sound would be a way to integrate the idea of imprisoning the interactor in his own head, filled with random thoughts with no way out. The anti-immersion concept is influenced by the thoughts and ideals of avant-garde movements of the twentieth century that still inspire today's contemporary artistic productions. In some avant-garde movements of the early twentieth century, random pictorial effects (also verbal and sound) were explored as a possibility to eliminate the pre-established conventions, and also to question paintings and poems elected as beautiful or significant. Deliberated offsets seen in the work of Marcel Duchamp, for example, in the exhibition of his ready mades, which intended to challenge the habits and prejudices that are behind the expectations of what art would be (Fer, Batchelor; Wood, 1998, p. 35). In the context of sound, concrete music and electronic music emerge and they are combined with the technological deviations in Pierre Schaeffer, in the dodecaphonism of Arnold Schöenberg and in the thoughts of John Cage. Music, as well as the sound development, breaks with the ideal tonals and harmony and opposes the pre-established musical conventions at that time.

When we think of sound effects in interactive installations and even in digital games, it is expected to hear sounds that allow a synchronization and contribute to a better user immersion in the simulated environment. The goal of disciplines such as sound design, for example, is to establish the need to create consistent soundscapes in relation to the interaction design. Opposing to that ground, the soundscape was designed to deny the communication among the sound effects of the installation and, thereby, create an immersion of disturbing experience.

Thus, the installation development team has striven to create a soundscape that would break with the expected tracks and sound effects that are commonly used to immersive support in virtual reality installations. There was the challenge of producing sounds that represent the various forms of existing thoughts within our own heads, and they shouldn't be an interator insert mode in a verbal or even dreamlike immersion

As the musical avant-garde of the twentieth century broke with tonal patterns, the sound elements were thought to deny the tonal and harmonic possibilities of sound production that are composed exclusively for humans. By applying sound algorithms that provide greater noise in the current sounds produced by the team. The sounds are triggered from the interactor head movements in the cyberspace of the installation. A poem made by one of the members is read through sound synthesis within the installation environment. Random rules defragment the reading of the poem while the interactor remains "trapped" in the installation.

## 3.2 Exhibition Leaving the Room

The development of this installation is the result of a research project on curating and exhibition spaces with the presence of digital technology. Through three-dimensional modeling of the art gallery in Guignard School (UEMG) it was possible to simulate how selected pieces of an extension project would be inserted in the space of the art gallery, and it was also possible to discuss the access to art and culture in the that institution. During the development of the installation, several questions have arisen about the virtual exhibition space, as well as the special features related to interactivity in immersive environments, it is necessary to rethink the development of these experiences and their relationship with the current design interaction methodologies, with the usability and the human-computer interaction.

The proposal of developing a virtual reality installation arises through the extension project "Living Room". The project aims to provide greater dialogue and also exchange of experiences between students, teachers, servers and people interested in the art world issues, as well as in experimentation and curatorial practices and exhibition space for debates at the university (Cesário, 2015). With the end of the semester and after an accumulation of curatorial experience resulting from the project, it was articulated by the organizers of the project "Living Room" the possibility to simulate a curatorial action through an immersive virtual reality, using the space of the art gallery in Guignard School (UEMG).

For the development of the installation, technologies for the creation of digital games, as the game engine Unity 3D 5 together with the SDK Cardboard, and a smartphone were used.

The installation was considered as low cost because we have chosen not to use robust solutions as current technologies and immersive industry interfaces such as Oculus Rift and HTC Vive. The possibility of using a cell phone as an operating platform allowing greater mobility for installation since it was not limited to the need of direct connection to power or to an external computer, and also it allows greater facility of public access and of testing on multiple mobile platforms.

### 3.2.1 The Development of the Installation

The development of the installation was divided into seven steps: three-dimensional modeling of the scenario; texturing the setting; importing models for the game engine Unity 3D; lighting application; programming of interactions; compilation tests; and tests with the user. The process has worked in a similar way to methodologies in cascade type of software engineering processes. It was often necessary to go through all the steps again to make changes.

For three-dimensional modeling of the art gallery of the school, the floor plans of the building and reference photos were used. It was used the free software Blender 3D. The original proportions of the space were respected and patterned ceiling details and support pilasters were made. The images of the process are below.

The texturing process of the three-dimensional modeling has aimed to provide greater realism to the virtual environment. Based on real space photographs, floor, walls, ceilings and doors have received the application of texture.The process of UV Mapping was used to enable greater fidelity to the application of 2D textures in 3D models with the lowest error possible.

*Figure 3. Basement floorplan drawing of Guignard School; the number 8 is the space of the gallery.*
Source: Bienales de Arquitectura, http://www.bienalesdearquitectura.es/archivo/imagenes/biau/01BI/01BI-15/01BI-15%20(5).jpg

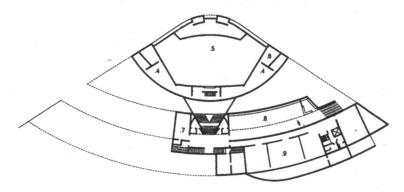

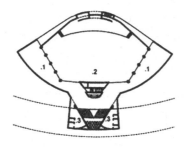

*Figure 4. Image of the 3D modeling*
*Source: Installation files.*

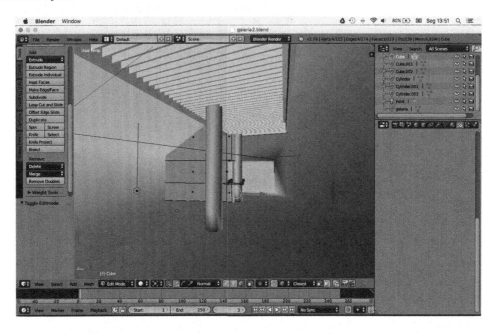

After the steps of modeling and creation of textures, the model was imported into the development environment and game engine Unity 3D. Proportion adjustments and the update of shaders were made. The curatorial action started being thought in relation to the disposal of the artwork in the virtual space of the art gallery. Data sheets and expographic elements were imported, as well as the displays for each work were put at the bottom left of each work, containing the title of the work, author, technique used and dimensions, as it is traditionally done in an art gallery.

The three-dimensional model tried to meet the real illumination conditions of the art gallery, taking into account processing conditions of the selected hardware to achieve a greater degree of realism. It was necessary to enable the processing of shadows, causing greater need for calculations by the system.

The goal of the installation was to allow the user to perform a virtual visit to the art gallery environment. For that reason some user needs were elected and some interactive solutions have been proposed. How to provide mobility in the virtual environment? What are the means of interaction with the environment?

The proposed virtual tour allowed the users to gain complete control of their location within the virtual space and involved a solution for movement of then within the virtual environment without the use of external interfaces (joysticks, motion sensors or cameras) as usual in digital games. Only the movements interfaced by the own mobile device sensors served as an interactive medium for the user to travel in the virtual environment. The input and output data relation through the user's head movements allowed the locomotion within the virtual gallery.

The operation of the interface occurs when the user moves lightly his head down or up, allowing him to move forward or stand still in the virtual environment. By turning his head to the left or right, his head (camera) turns in the gallery space. These movements are similar to the directional controls of video game joysticks.

*Figure 5. Image of the gallery in virtual reality after the curatorship of the selected works*
*Source: Setup Files.*

*Figure 6. Image of the gallery in virtual reality after the curatorship of the selected works*
Source: Setup Files.

*Figure 7. Stereoscopic image produced by the game engine Unity 5*
Source: Setup Files.

For developing this feature, a script in C# language has been used and adapted that is compatible with the SDK Cardboard, which automatically moves a player in the direction he is looking. You can activate the function by setting a limit angle and / or also through the trigger found in the Google Cardboard. You can set the limit of the look between 0° and 90°, and the player remains stopped from the time that he exceeds the threshold value, and he is moved forward when he negatively exceeds the stipulated limit (Borowski, 2015).

The first tests were conducted with the stereoscopy kit Google Cardboard in cellphone models LG Nexus 5 and Samsung Galaxy S4 Mini with Android OS, Jelly Bean and KitKat version.

After all the installation development stages, one last step regarding the user with tests was performed. The tests aimed to verify how the user's interaction was working in the virtual environment, specifically they checked adjustments in relation to virtual expography.

## 3.2.2 The Installation's Achievements

The relevant points of the application use can be quoted: the majority of users were surprised by the immersion capacity in a built environment with virtual reality; some users felt the need also to walk around the physical environment where the installation was; the works, selected and inserted into the immersive environment, had different repercussions in comparison to the works exhibited during the project "Living Room"; many users said they noticed the wealth of details in some works and were impressed with the dimensional character of the work in relation to the gallery space. In some works, the curatorial project changed the dimension of approximately 500% of the original size, for example, which provided astonishment in some users.

During the development stages of the installation, some questions have arisen regarding the curatorship and the interactive capabilities of the virtual exhibition elements. Questions like: is it possible to define a pre-set virtual path of visit for each application user? Is there a display order of the works? Do the works allow interaction with users? What kind and what information will be available to the visitor? Is it possible to mix other realities (augmented reality) to experience use of the application? How would this mixture occur with the external environment? How could the Interaction Design processes contribute to the solution of these issues involving virtual expography?

In order to propose a method for solving interaction problems, the user centered design comes up with its approach focused on the user and not on the technology. As a result, a well-designed system should withdraw the most of human trials and skills, and it should be also directly relevant to the work in question. It should support the user, and not limit their actions (Preece et al, 2005). The Interaction Design and all its features can help in breaking and/or constructing mental models, which are defined by Norman as models that people have of themselves, others, the environment and the things which they interact (Norman, 2002). Great part of the usability problems stems from the conflict among the different types of mental models that involve the development of relationship and use of a system, the mental model of the designer *versus* the mental model of the user. The goal of the interaction design is that it can, through processes and methodologies, understand users needs and then produce a system that meets those demands.

We realized, with this experience, that it is necessary to deep into the nature of human-computer interaction and contextualize the use of the interactive system. It's necessary to realize the human characteristics that influence the participation of people in the interaction. We must conduct the study of technologies and computational architectures, as well as their capabilities, limitations and development processes aimed to the use, as seen by Hewett et al. (*apud* Barbosa, 2010, p. 10.)

## 4. CONCLUSION

Many uses seem to be possible with virtual reality interfaces, and it seems that some stability has been achieved due to industry advancements and the mass adoption of the technology. It is even possible that the hype described by Bolas (2011) may be in manifestation and that some of these interfaces, especially for digital games, are only attracting the attention of consumers eager for news. But it is no longer possible to disregard the other manifestations in addition to those of the games industry.

The prospects for the development and use of these interfaces are challenging, however, many applications have already become references. In technological development perspective, it is necessary to readjust the current models of design and interaction design for virtual environments. New elements have been added for immersion development. The possibility of navigation in a virtual environment differs from a multi-touch environment in 2 dimensions, for example (Malaika, 2015).

The possibility of embody other body types, digital/virtual embodiment, allows the user new ways of expression and control over virtualized object. Research on brain-computer interface lead the innovations of what can be the future of these interactions. One is the recent development NESD notice (Neural Engineering System Design) of the DARPA (Defense Advanced Research Projects Agency), a neural interface that can stream audio and video communication in the brain with the machine.

Technological advances in virtual reality interfaces in the XXI century are in fact taking place and converging with other findings. We have seen in this chapter that the industry, mainly digital games, has keeping great interest in developing products for the general public. We finally confirm – including through the presented experiments – that applications of VR to overcome the game field borders to other areas guarantee the continuity of studies not only on virtual reality or augmented reality, but to study the potential of different realities.

## REFERENCES

Arantes, P. (2005). Arte e Mídia. São Paulo, Brazil: Senac.

Baig, E. C. (2016, January 2). CES 2016 will be virtual reality showcase. *USA Today*. Retrieved from http://www.usatoday.com/story/tech/columnist/baig/2015/12/31/ces-2016-virtual-reality-showcase/77564238/

Bolas, M. (2011). Keynote remixed: what happened to virtual reality. *Proceedings of ISMAR*. Retrieved from http://projects.ict.usc.edu/mxr/blog/keynote-remixed-what-happened-to-virtual-reality/

Borowski, D. (2015). Create a Virtual Reality Game For Google Cardboard. *Daniel Borowski*. Retrieved from http://danielborowski.com/posts/create-a-virtual-reality-game-for-google-cardboard/

Cesário, I. (2015). O Projeto Sala de Estar como Estímulo ao Acesso à Arte e à Cultura. *Proceedings of the 2ⁿᵈ Congresso de Extensão da Associação das Universidades do Grupo de Montevideo (AUGM)*.

Giannetti, C. (2006). *Estética Digital. Sintopia da Arte, a Ciência e a Tecnologia*. Belo Horizonte: C/Arte.

Heilig, M. (n.d.). *Morton Heilig Website*. Retrieved from http://www.mortonheilig.com/InventorVR.html

Kirner, C. (2008). Evolução da Realidade Virtual no Brasil. *Procedings of X Symposium on Virtual and Augmented Reality*, 1-11.

Malaika, Y. (2015). Interaction Design in VR: The Rules Have Changed (Again). *Proceedings of Game Developers Conference Europe*. Retrieved from http://www.gdcvault.com/play/1022810/Interaction-Design-in-VR-The

Munster, A. (2006). *Materializing New Media: Embodiment in Information Aesthetics*. Dartmouth College Press.

Norman, D. A. (2006). *O Design do dia-a-dia*. Rio de Janeiro: Rocco.

Pangburn, D. J. (2016). This Guy Just Spent 48hours in virtual reality. *In The Creators Project*. Retrieved from http://thecreatorsproject.vice.com/blog/48-hours-in-vr

Preece, J., & Rogers, Y. (2005). *Design de Interação: além da interacao homem-computador*. Porto Alegre: Bookman.

Cantoni, R.C.A. (2001). Realidade virtual: uma história de imersão interativa. Programa de Pós-graduação em Comunicação e Semiótica da PUC-SP.

Batchelor, D., Wood, P., & Fer, B. (1998). Realismo, Racionalismo, Surrealismo: a arte no entre-guerras. São Paulo: Cosac & Naify.

Rocha, C. (2010). *Três concepções de ciberespaço. Proceedings of the 9th Encontro Internacional de Arte e Tecnologia*. Brasília: PPG Arte/IdA/UnB.

Rocha, C. (2010). Três concepções de ciberespaço. Proceedings of 9° Encontro Internacional de Arte e Tecnologia.

Schnipper, M. (2014). The Rise and Fall and Rise of Virtual Reality: coming Monday - An Oculus Rift in every home? *The Verge*. Retrieved from http://www.theverge.com/a/virtual-reality/>

Stuart, K. (2014, November 20). What a virtual reality art show could say about the future of games. *The Guardian*. Retrieved from http://www.theguardian.com/technology/2014/nov/20/virtual-reality-art-future-games

## ENDNOTE

[1]   See: http://labfront.tk

# Chapter 3
# Multimodal Human Aerobotic Interaction

**Ayodeji Opeyemi Abioye**
*University of Southampton, UK*

**Glyn T Thomas**
*University of Southampton, UK*

**Stephen D Prior**
*University of Southampton, UK*

**Peter Saddington**
*Tekever Ltd., UK*

**Sarvapali D Ramchurn**
*University of Southampton, UK*

## ABSTRACT

*This chapter discusses HCI interfaces used in controlling aerial robotic systems (otherwise known as aerobots). The autonomy control level of aerobot is also discussed. However, due to the limitations of existing models, a novel classification model of autonomy, specifically designed for multirotor aerial robots, called the navigation control autonomy (nCA) model is also developed. Unlike the existing models such as the AFRL and ONR, this model is presented in tiers and has a two-dimensional pyramidal structure. This model is able to identify the control void existing beyond tier-one autonomy components modes and to map the upper and lower limits of control interfaces. Two solutions are suggested for dealing with the existing control void and the limitations of the RC joystick controller –the multimodal HHI-like interface and the unimodal BCI interface. In addition to these, some human factors based performance measurement is recommended, and the plans for further works presented.*

## INTRODUCTION

This chapter discusses the interfaces used in the control of small multirotor aerial robotic systems. In order to aid the discussion of these interfaces, a novel classification model for autonomy called the 'navigational control autonomy (nCA)' model, was presented and discussed intensively. This sets the background for discussing the RC joystick-controller control range and the control void existing beyond the tier-one nCA model. The limitations of the RC joystick controller were presented in the result section of this chapter. This chapter suggests two solutions that could address this control void revealed by the nCA model, as well overcome the limitation of the RC joystick controller. The first method suggests

DOI: 10.4018/978-1-5225-2492-2.ch003

the development of an interface that emulates multimodal human-to-human communication methods to address higher-level interaction problems. The second method extends the first solution into a beyond normal human interaction of mind control via brain-computer interfaces. The limitations of these suggestions are also presented under the discussion section. It then concludes by suggesting some further research works resulting from this chapter's investigation.

This section briefly discusses the background of the unmanned aerial vehicle and introduces the term 'aerobot', which is used to refer to aerial robotic systems in this chapter's discussion. Some aerial robot applications are also presented in this section.

## BACKGROUND

A particular class of unmanned aerial vehicles (UAVs) gaining wide popularity with applications cutting across diverse fields, is the small unmanned multirotor aircraft system. The most common application of this system is cost-effective image or data acquisition from remote locations, high altitudes, hazardous environments, or positions that are difficult or more expensive for a human to reach. Another rising application is drone delivery of goods, medical, or military supplies. However, in this research, a particular application of interest for these small multirotor aircraft systems is in aerial robotics. This research focuses on control for these aerial robots. Control for delivery applications or data/image acquisition can be achieved via a combination of manual or automatic control. However, for aerial robotic application, some higher-level control methods may be required. This chapter explores a few relevant control concepts.

### Aerobot

The term aerobot was derived from the following two words 'AERial rOBOT', as a way of referring to small unmanned multi-rotor aircraft robotic systems (Abioye, Prior, Thomas, & Saddington, 2016). The term, as adopted in this chapter, is used to give these multi-rotor aircraft systems (often seen as toys) an elevated status of a proper robotic system. Some researchers who seem to share this position are Kim et al. (2016), Muscio et al. (2016), and Verma (2016). Kim et al. (2016) demonstrated the concept of a vision-guided flying robotic arm (aerial robotic manipulator). Muscio et al. (2016) developed a control model for aerial robotic manipulators. The authors particularly identified the industrial applications of these multi-rotor aircraft as Unmanned Aerial Vehicle-Manipulator (UAVM), when equipped with grippers or multi-joint robotic arm manipulator. Verma (2016) also presented the idea of a flying robotic projector system that can be used to convert any plain surface as a display screen. Clearly, these are multi-rotor UAV systems acting as robots. Therefore, aerobots can be considered as unmanned multi-rotor aircraft systems with actuators, able to perform tasks analogous to fixed industrial robot manipulators. They are robot manipulators with an innate ability to hover or fly.

The applications of aerial robots are vast. Aerobots are being creatively adopted in many practical application scenarios such as working in human hazardous or radioactive environment, aiding search and rescue missions, performing military ISR (intelligence, surveillance, and reconnaissance) missions, undertaking logistics and transportation (DHL and Amazon examples), conducting space exploration missions (potential Mars rover attached aerobot missions), and videography/photography. Some civilian applications of aerial robots have been presented in Table 1, although some of these applications may be limited by current technological constraints.

*Table 1. Civilian applications of aerial robots*

| S/No. | Category | Applications |
|---|---|---|
| 1 | Aerial Inspection | • Rail Network Inspection<br>• Offshore oil drilling maintenance inspection |
| 2 | Disaster Relief | • Search and rescue operations<br>• Healthcare supply delivery |
| 3 | Emergency Services | • Law enforcement applications such as portable aerial surveillance<br>• Firefighting applications |
| 4 | Entertainment Applications | • Commercial Newsgathering<br>• Filmmaking<br>• Theatrical entertainment (Murphy et al., 2011)<br>• Drone racing |
| 5 | Environmental Application | • Wildlife conservation<br>• Habitat exploration<br>• Flood monitoring<br>• Open water monitoring |
| 6 | Field Application | • Aerial Survey & Mapping<br>• Agricultural applications |
| 7 | Industrial | • Aerial robotic manipulators - flying robotic arms in manufacturing<br>• Warehouse quick light-goods transportation<br>• Indoor inspection |
| 8 | Photography | • Selfies<br>• Sport Videography<br>• Mountaineering expedition |
| 9 | Transportation | • Drone delivery of goods e.g. Amazon & DHL delivery trials<br>• Drone rides transporting humans |

However, compared to their industrial robotic manipulator counterparts, the precision and accuracy currently achieved by aerobots is relatively poor, hence limiting their direct practical applications in industrial setups. This is probably due to their inherent aerodynamic complexity of flying in three-dimensional space, the continuously changing references, dynamic environmental conditions, dynamic environmental objects, its un-location to a fixed origin, and a slow sensor response. In order to address some of these navigational limitations and improve the aerial robot's overall performance, some advancement in navigational autonomy may be required.

## Autonomy Control Levels

*By Autonomous, it is meant the ability to be self-governing/operating within given constraints or rule sets. (Payne, 2007)*

The meaning of autonomy in robotics slightly differs from the political, philosophical, or biological meanings. This difference has been responsible for several contentions between experts on how this term is used. The argument as to whether robotic systems performing a task without external control commands are really doing so solely through their own ability to make decisions or through a decision-making method that has been pre-programmed into them. Especially when such systems, may be considered, to have been designed and developed to perform such specific functions and not a random system existing in nature. The designed artificial autonomous system process could be broken down into bits, understood, and hence predictable by the designer. Therefore, there seems to be a thin layer requiring further clarification as to whether:

- **Proponents:** A robotic system, performing a particular task without being told how to do such task, is simply autonomous or
- **Opponents:** Just executing a pre-defined program on how to make the right decisions that complete the task.

In order words, a clarification needs to be made as to whether executing a program, not of the task, but of how to decide on key elements that affects accomplishing the task, is autonomous or automatic. Clearly, executing a program of the task would be automatic as described by Clough (2002). In order to avoid being drawn into this debate, what is meant by autonomy in this chapter is defined in simple, clear, and unambiguous terms. Clough (2002) made a distinction between automatic and autonomous systems, "Automatic means that a system will do exactly as programmed, it has no choice. Autonomous means that a system has a choice to make free of outside influence…" According to Pfeifer and Scheier (1999), "autonomy means independence of control. This characterization implies that autonomy is a property of the relation between two agents, in the case of robotics, of the relations between the designer and the autonomous robot. Self-sufficiency, situated-ness, learning or development, and evolution increase an agent's degree of autonomy."

In this chapter, autonomy is conceptualised as being self-operating in a dynamic environment, within a given sets of rules or constraint, without relying on external control. This could be with the aid of a computer program working with sensors to guide decision-making, or some complicated artificial intelligence real-time learning and adapting algorithm. This could be a decision method that the operator may or may not understand, may or may not be able to predict, but is optimal enough to safely complete the assigned task to an acceptable standard. Autonomy, in this case, is void of continuous real-time control interaction during task execution but rather sparse real-time command, or just the initial command instruction may be given, in some cases.

Autonomy is an abstract concept difficult to measure empirically; hence, it is rather described qualitatively by analogically developed subjective hierarchical levels. The autonomy of an aerial robot can be considered in two context – navigation and payload. Usually, the payload autonomy level is expected to match the navigation autonomy as observed in Clough (2002) classification, which was adopted by the US Air Force Research Lab (AFRL) as the AFRL's ACL (Autonomous Control Levels). It was also used as a standard classification in other US military and government agencies, and by their contractors (Sholes, 2007). Clough (2002) identified eleven autonomy control levels:

1. Remotely Piloted Vehicle,
2. Execute Preplanned Mission,
3. Changeable Mission,
4. Robust Response to Real Time Faults/Events,
5. Fault/Event Adaptive Vehicle,
6. Real Time Multi-Vehicle Coordination,
7. Real Time Multi-Vehicle Cooperation,

8.    Battlespace Knowledge,
9.    Battlespace Cognizance,
10.   Battlespace Swarm Cognizance,
11.   Fully Autonomous.

The ACL incorporated a model of the human OODA (Observe, Orient, Decide, and Act) loop, a loop that seemed popular with the military (Clough, 2002). Sholes (2007) developed a simulation technique for evaluating multiple autonomy algorithms based on Clough AFRL (2002)'s ACL model. In a separate study by the Office of Naval Research (Horrigan & ONR's Committee, 2000) classified autonomy into the following six levels enumerated below:

1.    Human Operated,
2.    Human Assisted,
3.    Human Delegated,
4.    Human Supervised,
5.    Mixed Initiatives,
6.    Fully Autonomous.

Hill, Cayzer, and Wilkinson (2007) presented the modified PACT (Pilot Authority and Control of Task) autonomy level system, originally developed by the UK Defence Evaluation Research Agency (DERA), as a better classification of autonomy compared to the Clough's ACL. Firstly, they considered Clough's descriptive autonomy useful for vehicle level classification but inadequate for classification at functional levels. Secondly, Clough's ACL imposed an artificial ceiling on the autonomy level that can be achieved by an individual vehicle by introducing swarm behavioural requirements within it ACL. The PACT classification is as follows:

**Level 0:** Full pilot with no computer autonomy.
**Level 1:** Pilot assisted by computer only when requested.
**Level 2:** Pilot assisted by computer without pilot necessarily requesting it (computer advice continuously).
**Level 3:** Pilot backed up by computer.
**Level 4a:** Computer backed up by pilot – computer acts when authorized.
**Level 4b:** Computer backed up by pilot – computer acts unless pilot disapproves.
**Level 5a:** Computer monitored by pilot – computer informs human of actions.
**Level 5b:** Computer monitored by pilot – computer acts completely autonomously and need not inform the human of its decisions.

As may be observed, the PACT levels seemed similar to Horrigan and ONR Committee (2000) classification, which also closely aligns with the civilian aerial robot navigational control autonomy model presented in this chapter. In addition to the limitations already offered by Hill, Cayzer, and Wilkinson (2007), Clough's ACL was structured after military missions, therefore, its military-specifics context makes it difficult to adopt it in many emerging civilian applications. In addition, Clough's ACL was modelled as a generalised classification method for all types of military robotic systems – aerial, ground, and underwater.

Since autonomy, as a concept in robotics is a subjective non-quantitative (not measurable) analogical (but comparable) descriptor, perhaps its layers could be considered in fuzzy terms as overlapping strata expressed as a range of percentile rather than as discrete levels. Therefore, the autonomy levels presented in Figure 1, which is used as the basis of discussing the human aerobotic interfaces, is considered as a continuous, overlapping layer rather than quantized or discrete layers. For this reason, the presentation of the autonomy levels in Figure 1 is not presented in levels or vertical columns suggesting equal linear step size increments in autonomy. Sholes (2007) simulation plot and prediction of the growth of autonomy seems to supports this hypothesis of a non-linear step-size increase or change from one successive layer to another. Moreover, the concept of autonomy is a borrowed property from living organisms existing in nature and the ecological system, which is rarely linear.

Figure 1 presents a two-dimensional, expandable pyramidal model of Navigational Control Autonomy (nCA) levels for multi-rotor aerial robotic systems. In this model, autonomy is divided into three tiers: lower, intermediate, and upper tiers. Within each tier, autonomy level increases from left to right, and then across tiers from lower to intermediate to the uppermost tier. For this reason, it is termed the 'inverted lightning model of autonomy' as shown in Figure 2. This two-dimensional pyramidal model of autonomy is expandable rightwards and upwards to accommodate for new or missing autonomy level classes.

Unlike the ONR and Clough's Levels of Autonomy, the nCA model does not take into account the payload autonomy. However, payload autonomy is expected to match the aerial robot's navigation control level. The separation of navigational autonomy from payload autonomy simplifies the interaction relationship between an operator and an aerial robot (as considered in this chapter). Additionally, because autonomy classification may vary slightly across specific domains, the classification method used in this chapter have been developed specifically for multirotor aerial robotic systems' application in the civilian domain; as the AFRL's and ONR's classification were patterned towards military specific applications. Perhaps, with the rapidly evolving civilian applications of the aerobot, a less military objective-based classification may be worth considering.

*Figure 1. Multirotor aerial robot navigation control autonomy (nCA) levels*

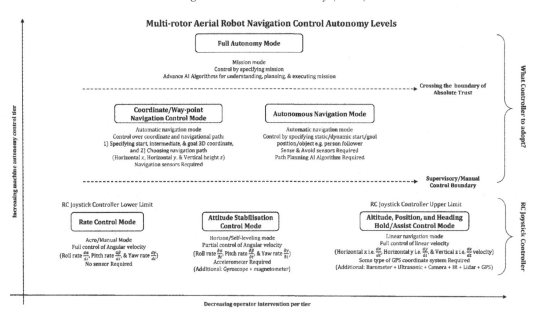

*Figure 2. The inverted lightning model of increasing autonomy*

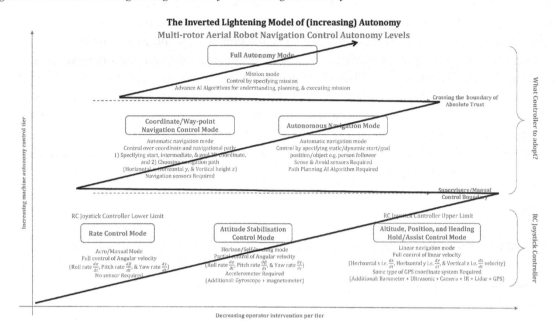

**The Inverted Lightening Model of (increasing) Autonomy**

Multi-rotor Aerial Robot Navigation Control Autonomy Levels

## Tier-One Control Levels

The nCA model described in Figure 1, has six components distributed in three tiers. The first tier consists of the following modes:

1.  Rate control,
2.  Attitude stabilisation control,
3.  Altitude, position, and heading hold/assist Control.

Rate control mode is the minimal level at which a human operator can control a small multirotor aircraft. In this mode, no sensor is needed. Full control of the three angular velocities (Roll rate $d\alpha/dt$, Pitch rate $d\beta/dt$, & Yaw rate $d\gamma/dt$) are given to the operator. This is usually performed with the aid of the RC joystick controller. A high level of skill is required to operate the multi-rotor aircraft at this level. This level is also called the Acro (short for Acrobatic) or Manual mode. RC hobbyist often prefer this mode when performing stunt manoeuvres for entertainment purposes. Flying at this level usually requires many training hours. It could take up to 600 or more hours of training to become an expert (from being a novice who has never flown before).

The Attitude stabilisation control mode is the next level after the rate control mode. In this mode, the operator is assisted with attitude stabilisation. The operator only has partial control over the three angular velocities (Roll rate $\partial\alpha/\partial t$, Pitch rate $\partial\beta/\partial t$, & Yaw rate $\partial\gamma/\partial t$). This is because the multi-rotor aircrafts flight controller, in this case, has a stabilization loop that continuously balances the aerobot horizontally, especially when the operator stops feeding new rate control data. The stabilization loop in this mode requires, at least, an accelerometer sensor. Additional or optional sensors may include the gyroscope and magnetometer. Data from a gyroscope could be collected and fused with the accelerometer data for a more accurate attitude stabilization control, because the accelerometer is prone to noise and the gyroscope to drift. A magnetometer could also be integrated to minimize yaw drift.

The next level after the attitude stabilisation, is the altitude, position, and heading hold/assist control mode. In addition to the attitude stabilisation from the previous mode, the operator is also assisted with the altitude, position, and heading direction. In this mode, the operator no longer has control over three angular velocity parameters. Control is performed by manipulating three linear velocities (Horizontal x i.e. $dx/dt$, Horizontal y i.e. $dy/dt$, & Vertical z i.e. $dz/dt$ velocity). In this mode, more sensors are required, such as GPS, Barometer, Ultrasonic, Camera, Infrared, Lidar, etc. for localization within the system specified coordinate system.

## Tier-Two Control Levels

The second tier of the nCA model consists of the following two modes:

1. Coordinate/waypoint navigation control mode,
2. Autonomous navigational mode.

The lowest level of the second tier is the coordinate/waypoint navigation control mode. This may also be called the automatic navigation mode. In this mode, low-level controls are completely abstracted from the operator. Navigation is specified by the user before execution. The start point, intermediate points, and goal point are pre-fed into the aerobot. Once execution starts, the multirotor flight controller is responsible for all low-level control required to achieve the goal point from the start point to the endpoint via the route specified by the operator. Execution would proceed as plan except the operator decides to abort the mission. In this mode, navigational sensors for location, continuously tracking flight route, are required. The system may or may not have a sense and avoid system and is, therefore, the responsibility of the operator to ensure that the specified route is safe enough for the aerobot to operate. The aerobot at this control level is expected to be able to perform some self-diagnostics check on itself, and relay issues requiring operator advice or intervention and may be robust enough to execute certain fundamental safety measures such as abort mission and return to launch.

The higher level of the second tier of the nCA model is the autonomous navigation mode. In this mode, the operator only needs to specify the goal position or object, which could be static or dynamic, as in the case of a person-following UAV. This mode requires: 1) sense and avoid (SAA) sensors and 2) a path planning AI algorithm.

## Tier-Three Control Level

The third tier consists of only one control mode – the full autonomy mode. At this point, the operator interaction with the aerobot is very sparse. The operator only needs to specify a mission and the aerobot takes care of the rest – planning and execution. In this mode, the aerobot must be well equipped with advanced AI algorithms, for understanding the prevailing scenarios or context within which mission has been given, planning the mission, and executing the mission.

Between tier one and tier two is the supervisory/manual control boundary. In order words, most of the operation performed in tier one is manual operator control, whereas tier two is mostly supervisory. The boundary separating tier-two from tier-three is the boundary of 'absolute trust.' For the aerobot autonomy to progress beyond this point, the operator must be willing to trust the aerobot's decisions absolutely.

## AFRL vs. nCA vs. ONR Autonomy Control Levels

This section relates how the nCA level model maps to the ONR's and Clough's AFRL ACL models. In 2000, a research committee for the Office of Naval Research (ONR), proposed six robotic autonomy level (Horrigan & ONR's Committee, 2000). In 2002, the Airforce Research Laboratory (AFRL) UAV program motivated Clough's research into developing a measurement metrics for autonomous vehicles (Clough, 2002). This was later adopted by the AFRL as a metric method of measuring their autonomous vehicles. Since then, software has been developed by various vendors and researchers based on this measurement metrics for used by government and military agencies (Sholes, 2007). These two widely recognised standard metrics for autonomy control levels were developed particularly for the military domain. The nCA model was developed to serve a similar purpose in the evolving civilian application domain of autonomous vehicles. These three ACL models are compared side-by-side, with similar levels mapped to each other, as shown in Figure 3.

The AFRL's eleven-level model maps to the nCA six-level model as shown in Figure 3. AFRL's level zero (Remotely piloted vehicle) maps to the three tier one component of the nCA model. AFRL's level 1-5 maps to the first component of the second tier of the nCA model. AFRL's level 6-9 maps to the second component of the second tier of the nCA model. A one to one mapping is observed in the highest column of both hierarchies, as AFRL's level 10 (fully autonomous) maps to the nCA third tiers only component, full autonomy mode.

The ONR's six-level model maps to the nCA six-level model as shown in Figure 3. Both the bottom and top most level of both model have a one to one mapping. The ONR's level 1 maps to the second and third components of the first tier of the nCA model. The ONR's level 2 maps to the first component

*Figure 3. Mapping relationship between AFRL, nCA, and ONR autonomy levels*

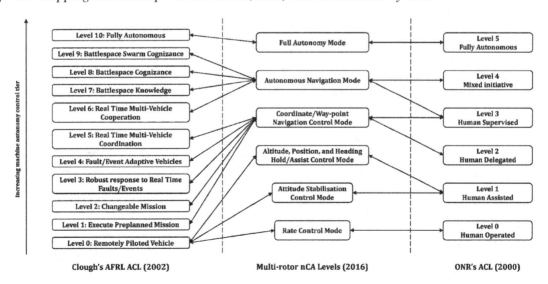

of the second tier of the nCA model. The ONR's level 3 maps to both components of the second tier of the nCA model. The ONR's level 4 maps to the second component of the second tier of the nCA model.

The mapping relationships of the nCA model with the AFRL and ONR models describes how robotic systems classified in any of these scales could be re-classified under the nCA scale. It also shows how robust and fully representative the nCA scale is, of previous models and domain application, despite being designed for the emerging multi-rotor aerial systems in the civilian domain.

## The Interface Problem

The Autonomy level of an aerial robot affects the range of selectable control communication interfaces that can be used for communicating control signals to it. Higher-level systems often require little or no operator intervention whereas low-level systems often require much operator control intervention. Different control interfaces offer varying level of intervention. For example, the RC controller enables the provision of much intervention and hence, it is suitable for low-level interaction; however, speech and gesture interfaces, though more convenient, offers less flexibility at such low-level. Figure 1 shows the application limits of the RC joystick controller. The RC joystick controller is a very suitable controller for the first tier of the nCA model. It has a dynamic range, with the rate control mode being its lower limit and the altitude-position-heading assist mode being the upper limit.

Although the RC joystick controller is widely accepted as a standard controller for the tier-one nCA model range, it is not without its limitations. These includes orientation un-intuitiveness (when the multirotor's front faces the operator), long training hours (estimated 600 hours to develop expert skill level), difficulty to learn for persons with neurological motor movement disorder (such as ataxia, dystonia, essential tremor, Parkinson's disease, and atypical Parkinsonism), and much cognitive effort requirement (depending on autonomy control level).

*Figure 4. Aerial robot control interfaces*

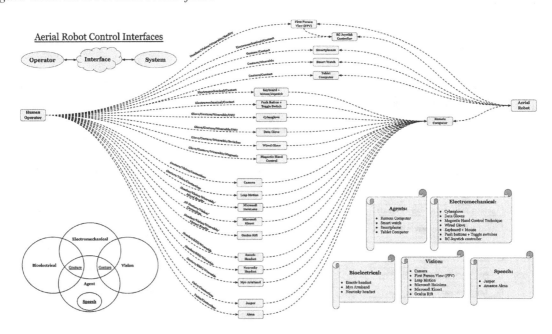

Therefore, if the RC joystick controller is a suitable interface for low-level (tier-one nCA levels) aerobotic interactions, but inadequate for higher-level interactions, then what controller should be adopted for higher-level (tier-two and tier-three nCA levels) interactions? This question forms the basis for investigating several human aerobotic interaction interfaces presented in the following sections.

## RESEARCH INVESTIGATION: HUMAN AEROBOTIC INTERACTION

Human aerobotic interaction can be considered as an association of three component: an operator, an interface, and a system, as shown in Figure 4. The operator, in this case, is the human and the system is the aerobot. Therefore, this research investigation is a problem of 1) how to get the human operator, to communicate their control intentions, to the aerobot; and 2) how to get the aerobot, to provide real-time feedback, to the human operator, so that the operator can make a more informed control decision. In this section, unimodal and multimodal human aerobotic interaction interfaces would be discussed.

### Unimodal Human Aerobotic Interfaces

As shown in Figure 4, the unimodal aerial robots interfaces discussed in this section would be grouped into five categories: agents, electromechanical, bioelectrical, vision, and speech.

### Agents

According to Nwana, (1996) an agent can be referred to as a software or hardware component that is capable of acting (in an exact manner) on behalf of its user, in order to accomplish a specific task. Agents, in the context of this chapter, refers to intermediate intelligent or smart systems capable of 1) being pre-instructed or programmed by the operator, 2) processing such high-level programmes into low-level control instructions that can be 3) relayed to an aerial robot, with the aim of providing continuous guidance in order to accomplish the operator's pre-defined task or objective. The most commonly used aerial robot control agent as described in this section is a remote computer system, which could be running a Windows, Linux, or Mac operating system. Other popular agents include the tablet computers (such as Apple's iPad Pro and Samsung's Galaxy Tab S), Smartphones (such as the iPhone 6s and Sony Xperia L), and Smart watches (such as the Apple Watch 2 and Samsung Gear S2). The control level of the agents, as described in this section, is limited to the first component of tier-two in the nCA model.

As shown in Figure 4, besides the remote computer being an independent agent, it also acts as an intermediate processing/relay terminal for many other control interfaces (as discussed in later sections). The remote computer can be pre-programmed for waypoint navigation (nCA tier-two, first component). It can accept electromechanical input and provide visual feedback of the aerial robot collected data and health status.

The tablet computer is often powerful enough to operate complex programs like the remote computer. It can also provide waypoint navigation, electromechanical contact/switch, touch screen, and accelerometer-based gesture interaction. In addition to this, it can also provide on-screen visual and haptic feedback of telemetry data, status, and other information.

The smartphone is a smaller version of the tablet computer. It can perform similar functions as the tablet computer although it has a smaller screen for visualising telemetry data, status, and other information.

The smart watch is a computing attempt to miniaturise the smartphone. Control using the smart watch could be relayed through the smartphone as demonstrated by Mark Ven (Reuters, 2015). Gesture control is achieved by collecting and processing the smart watch's IMU sensor data. Processing could be relayed through a smartphone, tablet computer, or a remote computer. Although, at the time of writing this chapter, the smartwatch is not capable of processing these data and hence directly controlling the aerial robot, this is a feat soon to be achieved by the collective efforts of the research communities at various research institutions and laboratories. However, unlike the other agents, the smart watch has the additional advantage of being a wearable technology.

## Electromechanical

Electromechanical interfaces describe a class of devices that utilises mechanically actuated switches in controlling the flow or current in an electrical circuit. This regulation of the flow of current is used to signal control intentions to a computer, machine, or robotic system. The most popular electromechanical control device for an aerial robotic system is the RC joystick controller. Other electromechanical devices includes the keyboard, mouse, push buttons, toggle switches, Cyber glove, data glove, wired glove, Shift thumb drone controller (Lavars, 2016), IMU HandMagic device (Calella, Ortega, Rishe, Bernal, & Barreto, 2016), and magnetic hand gesture device (Yinghong et al., 2011) among several others. Most electromechanical controller application varies from nCA tier-one levels to the first component of the nCA tier-two.

The RC (Radio Controlled) joystick controller consists of two joysticks, a few toggle switches, push buttons, and variable potentiometers as shown in Figure 5 (HobbyKing & Turnigy, 2015). A joystick can be conceptualised as a two-dimensional potentiometer (continuous variable resistor) that generates an analogue voltage divider circuit in each dimension. With each dimensional axis being mapped to a control (e.g. thrust) with a continuous range of intensity/values bounded by two extremes levels. The

*Figure 5. 10-channel Turnigy TGY-i10 (mode 2) telemetry RC joystick controller*

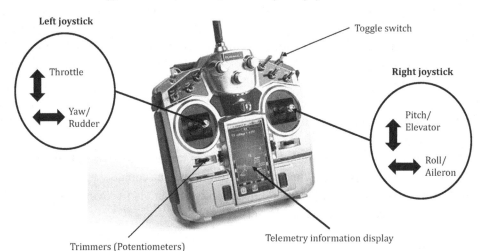

RC joystick controller, unlike most other electromechanical devices, does not require additional or intermediate processing by a remote computer. It is capable of interacting directly with the aerobot's flight controller. Additionally, it may be augmented with an FPV (First Person View) headset, a smartphone, or a tablet computer to provide visual image data from the aerobot's camera. Telemetry data could also be feedback to the controller via the smartphone, tablet, or a small screen, installed on the controller. It can also be augmented to provide haptic feedback of flight turbulence.

Cyber glove and Data glove are examples of IMU-based, glove-like, hand-wearable, computer input and control device. An accelerometer sensor is used to measure hand gesture orientation. A gyroscope sensor may be used to measure the rate at which a gesture is formed, hence increasing the vocabulary of possible gesture vocabulary. To further increase the gesture vocabulary, some gesture gloves may have switches that can be triggered by specific hand gestures. These gesture gloves require processing on a remote computer. They could be wirelessly connected to the computer using wireless technologies like Bluetooth or simple connected via wires. Unlike the IMU-based Cyber-glove and Data-glove, Wired-glove is based on finger/hand motions triggering switches embedded along the wearable glove structure (Renitto & Thomas, 2014). Another gesture glove of interest is the Magnetic-Hand gesture technique that is based on small magnets installed on the fingernails, generating a magnetic field that is tracked by a magnetic sensor bracelet installed on the wrist (Yinghong et al., 2011). HandMagic is an IMU based wristband for sensing human hand gesture (Calella et al., 2016). Although it is similar to the IMU based gesture gloves, it is being worn on the wrist, hence does not capture finger motions. Similar to some RC joystick controllers, some wearable gesture devices are also capable of providing haptic feedback.

Other electromechanical devices such as keyboard, mouse, pushbuttons, toggle switches, and joysticks are also used in combination with a remote station for communicating operator intentions to the aerial robots. They could be used as inputs for either direct or pre-programed computer control. Waypoint mapping is an example of pre-programmed control.

## Vision

Vision based control interfaces utilise the techniques of computer vision such as image capture/acquisition, filtering, segmentation, feature extraction, and classification, in identifying operator's control intentions. Image acquisition is usually performed with the aid of a regular camera, thermal camera, infrared camera, or some other specialised imaging system. Vision systems often require remote processing. Due to their low rate of feeding control signal which is in turn due to slow remote processing and communication medium lag, the vision control techniques are not suitable for high-rate low-level control function (first and second components of tier-one nCA model). Some devices in this category used for human aerobotic interaction includes regular standalone cameras, web cameras, stereo cameras, Leap Motion device, Microsoft Kinect. It may also include virtual, mixed, and augmented reality headsets such as the Oculus Rift and Microsoft HoloLens amongst others.

The following are examples of research were cameras and computer vision techniques are used. Soto-Gerrero and Ramrez-Torres (2013) demonstrated visual gesture interaction on a Parrot AR drone via an android-based mobile phone platform. Milanova and Sirakov (2008) and Qing et al. (2008) independently investigated systems to recognise expressions of joy, distress, surprise, interest, frustration, anger, disgust, fear, and a neutral expression among several human observable facial expressions. This could be potentially useful in emotional gesture interactions with aerobots.

## Bioelectrical

Bioelectrical control interfaces rely on electrical nerve impulses generated by muscular or neurological human activities. These electrical impulses are usually detected with the aid of some biomedical instruments and probes. The detected impulses may be recorded for immediate analyses on a remote computer, where it is then cross-referenced with a previously collected signal database already mapped to the user's control intention (vocabulary of the bioelectrical signal), for identification of the user's control intention. The identified control intention is then relayed by the remote computer to the aerobot for appropriate execution. Digital Signal Processors (DSPs) are often used to provide high-speed processing to reduce processing time lag and ensure near real-time response to users control input.

The Emotiv and Neurosky headsets are two examples of electroencephalography (EEG) measuring devices that are being used by researchers to investigate brain-computer interaction for robotic systems such as aerial robots (Emotiv, 2014; Hammacher Schlemmer, 2015). Lafleur et al. (2013) demonstrated BCI (telepathic mind) control of a quadcopter in three-dimensional space, using an EEG cap. The MYO armband is another example of a bioelectrical device that is used to capture electromyography (EMG) signal. The MYO device is worn on the arm and is able to capture, consistently, a few unique arm gestures, which are then used in robotic control applications such as the aerobot navigation (Cacace, Finzi, & Lippiello, 2016; Nagar & Xu, 2015; Thalmic Labs, 2015).

## Speech

Speech interfaces provide a method of communicating control intentions via voice commands. A microphone may be used to detect (and convert to an electrical signal) the sound wave generated by the operator's voice commands. The operator's speech command may be identified by querying a database of the aerobot's speech command vocabulary with the recorded speech signal. A successful match results in the matched control intention signal being sent by the speech processing system to the aerobot control system for control execution.

Harris and Barber (2014) investigated verbal speech interaction with a mobile robotic system. They converted the microphone-captured audio to text using the CMU Pocket Sphinx audio speech recognition (ASR) toolbox. With this method, a text command vocabulary can be defined instead of a speech command vocabulary; the transcript of the voice command can be compared with the predefined database of command, and the interpreted control intention is passed to the aerobot for execution. Recent advancement in speech technology is evident in a plethora of devices using the following voice assistant: Apple's Siri, Microsoft's Cortana, Google's Now, Amazon's Alexa, and the Jasper's ASR framework.

## Multimodal Human Aerobotic Interfaces

According to Oviatt (2002), "Multimodal system process two or more combined user input modes – such as speech, pen, gaze, manual gestures, and body movements – in a coordinated manner…" A multimodal interface could be a combination of any two or more compatible, complementary, unimodal interfaces. Multimodal interaction offers the flexibility of switching sequentially between communication modes without breaking the interaction or communicating via parallel modes simultaneously (Turk, 2014). There are a number of reasons, why multimodal interfaces are being investigated and developed. One may be an attempt to overcome the limitations of the constituting unimodal interfaces. However, there is also the complication associated with fusing multiple unimodal interfaces together. In this research's investigation, the multimodal combination of interests is one that emulates the human multimodal interaction method, as would be discussed subsequent sections.

## Interface Summary

Table 2 presents a summary of the merits and demerits of the unimodal and multimodal interfaces discussed in this section. It also highlights a few researchers and stakeholders involved in the development or investigation of such interfaces.

## RESULTS

## The Joystick-Type Controller Dilemma

Typically, the interaction between humans and aerobots fundamentally consists of a radio-controlled (RC) joystick transmitter controller, augmented with toggle switches, push buttons, and variable potentiometer, for improved control functionality as shown in Figure 5. The RC controller is plagued with a number of limitations. Firstly, learning to control an aerobot via the RC joystick controller requires an operator with a good neurological motor response. Although most UAV operators eventually adapt to the operation of this joystick-type controller and may become very skilful, getting used to it as a compound impulse response. Secondly, it is not a natural human interaction modality. Human interaction with one another occurs at a higher level of intelligence or autonomy. Thirdly, there may be side effects to briskly flicking both the left and right thumb, placed on the left and right joystick, in order to maintain horizontal level balance, within fractions of a second. Fourthly, there is the problem of too many controls. Besides operating the left and right joysticks, the operator might be required to operate switches to perform some other functions such as payload drop or snapshot from an onboard camera, at some specified time, altitude, distance, space, and location. Simultaneously executing this accurately may be difficult. Fifthly, there is the problem of un-intuitiveness of the controller, especially when the human operator and aerobot's forward orientation is out of alignment at 180 degrees. Sixthly, learning to fly the aerobot via the RC joystick controller often requires several training hours especially in the previously described un-intuitive orientation state. Seventhly, due to the control overload on a small unmanned multi-rotor aircraft's operator, the situational awareness of the operator is reduced; making it impossible to simultaneously control multiple aircraft (Cavett, Coker, Jimenez, & Yaacoubi, 2007). Finally, the level of control offered by the RC joystick controller is limited to tier-one of the nCA model. Interaction at a higher level of autonomy may require the adoption of some other interfaces.

## DISCUSSION: SOLUTIONS AND RECOMMENDATIONS

In order to address the joystick-type controller dilemma, described in the result section, two solutions are suggested. The first solution is the development of an interface that emulates typical human-human multimodal speech and visual interaction. The second solution is the development of unimodal mind

*Table 2. Aerobotic interface comparison*

| S/No | Interface Category | Interfaces | Merits | Demerits | Stakeholders/Researchers |
|------|-------------------|-----------|--------|----------|--------------------------|
| 1 | Electromechanical | • RC Joystick Controller • Keyboard + Mouse + Joysticks • Push buttons + Toggle switches • Wired Glove • Magnetic Hand Gesture Technique • Data Glove • Cyber Glove • Shift drone thumb controller • Google Project Soli | • Fast response • Very reliable • Easier to implement | • Long hours dedicated to training • Not natural - not a normal human interaction method • Not intuitive - especially when re-oriented towards operator • Demands high cognitive workload | • Futaba; Turnigy; DJI; Hobbyking; FrSky; Spektrum; • Raytheon • 3D Connection • VDCI • Ma et al. (2010) • Lavars (2016) • Google (2014) |
| 2 | Vision | • Camera • First Person View (FPV) • Leap Motion • Microsoft HoloLens • Microsoft Kinect • Oculus Rift | • Natural • Easy to learn | • Difficult to implement • Requires higher processing power • Occlusion | • Gupta and Ma (2001) • Huang and Chung (2004) • Nimble VR (2012) • Blanz (2007) • Leap Motion Inc. (2010) |
| 3 | Bioelectrical | • MYO armband • Emotiv headset • Neurosky headset | • Assistive technology • Gesture interaction • Stealth interaction | • Not natural due to wearable device requirement • High cognitive concentration workload • Security concerns - snooping EEG signals to potentially steal certain information like login pins, credit card number, etc. | • Thalmic Labs (2013) • NeuroSky (2011) • Emotiv (2014) • Martinovic et al. (2012) |
| 4 | Speech | • Jasper • CMU Sphinx • Julius • Amazon Alexa | • Natural • Easy to learn | • Difficult to implement • Not immune to prevailing environmental noise | • Bastianelli et al. (2015) • Lee et al. (2003) • Mu-Chun & Ming-Tsang (2001) • Amazon; Google; • Microsoft; Apple; |
| 5 | Agent | • Remote Computer • Tablet Computer • Smartphone • Smartwatch | • Easy to learn • Touch-screen gestures • Orientation-tilt feature • Waypoint programming | • Relative precision requirement over a small screen area • Severe fatigue on user's wrist | Huhn and Haewon (2014) |
| 6 | Multimodal | HHI-like interaction (Speech + gesture) | • Natural • Easy to learn • Robust - complementing interfaces overcomes unimodal limitations | Difficult to implement | • Harris and Barber (2014) • Oviatt (2003) • Shah and Breazeal (2010) • Lackey et al. (2011) • Reeves et al. (2004) • Bolt (1980) |

*Figure 6. Near interaction: human with aerobot and human with human*
Abioye et al., 2016.

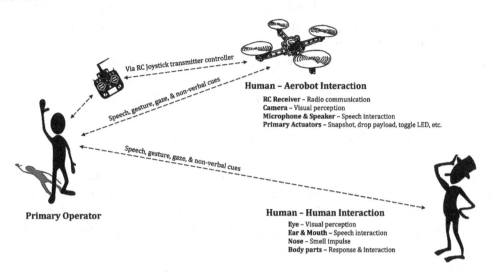

control (telepathic interaction) via brain-computer interfaces. In addition to discussing these two solutions, this section also discusses the need to measure the performance of such developed systems, from a human factors point of view. The limitation of each technique is discussed in each subsection.

## HHI-Like Aerobotic Control Interface

Human-human interaction (HHI) is a multimodal combination of speech and non-verbal expressions such as gestures and gazes (Green, Chen, Billinnghurst, & Chase, 2007; Sharma, Pavlovic, & Huang, 1998). The natural human-to-human interaction often occurs within the context of a very small geographical area, hence the term 'near-interaction' (as used in describing Figure 6). The idea of near-interaction is used to indicate the limit of up to a few hundred metres. If the human is too far away, it would be difficult to be heard; and difficult to be seen when much farther away. Therefore in HHI, it is difficult, if not impossible, to interact via speech, gaze, gesture, and other non-verbal methods, beyond a small geographical location radius. This range limitation could also affect HHI-like human aerobotic interaction, as it becomes difficult for the onboard camera to identify the human, or for the microphone to detect the human voice amid several other environmental noise sources. At such long distances, other long distance communication technologies may need to be adopted, as with HHI interaction. Figure 6 describes near human interaction between three actors. The first is an interaction between a human operator and an aerial robot. The second is an interaction between the human operator and another human. The human operator could potentially interact with the aerobot via RC joystick controller as shown or it could interact via normal human HHI-like methods. The second human in the figure, though not the primary operator, may also be able to initiate an interaction with the aerobot.

Generally, robots have been designed to reduce human workload, risk, cost, and human fatigue-driven errors. Fong and Nourbakhsh (2000) suggested that in order to achieve these objectives, it is crucial to make the human-robot interaction effective, efficient, and natural; which further suggests the use of multiple modalities of contact, dialogue, and gestures. According to Green et al. (2007), "It is clear that people use speech, gesture, gaze and non-verbal cues to communicate in the clearest possible fashion."

Therefore, it may be necessary to develop systems that could adopt some of these natural human-human interaction techniques. The essence of human-robot collaboration is probably the fact that robots can complement the human effort by optimising problem-solving techniques, performing tasks faster, and in many cases with greater dexterity.

In Figure 6, a hand gesture interaction was initiated which could suggest a human-human or hu-man- aerobot interaction. Some notable human-aerobot hand gesture interaction research includes the application of the data glove such as the AcceleGlove (Hernandez Jose, Kyriakopoulos, & Lindeman, 2002) and Magic glove (Chaomin, Yue, Krishnan, & Paulik, 2012), Magnetic hand tracking (Ma et al., 2010), Apple Watch (Reuters, 2015), and the MYO armband device (Nagar & Xu, 2015; Thalmic Labs, 2013). Gaze or eye tracking is a technique that seeks to determine the direction the eye is focused; per-haps, via the relative motion of the eye with respect to the head's position (Renitto & Thomas, 2014). Electrooculography (EOG) techniques could be used to approach this from a biomedical point of view.

Because the development of an HHI-like aerobotic interaction requires a multimodal approach (Sharma et al., 1998), there may be some technical complications associated with integrating the individual HCI interfaces – a control fusion problem. What happens when two unimodal interfaces receive contradictory commands? What happens when two contradictory actions result from individual unimodal interface interpretation of a particular human control interaction? What should be the conflict resolution model for such cases? Are the unimodal technologies sufficiently developed to meet the basic requirement of such multimodal interactions? These are just a few of many technical limitations that need to be addressed via further research investigation.

## Brain Control Interfaces: Telepathic Interaction

One unimodal solution that could address the limitations of the RC joystick controller, unlocking higher control levels in the nCA model is telepathic mind control via brain-computer interfaces (BCI). The advancement in the development of brain-computer interfaces can be attributed to the understanding of the human neurology and the advancement in biomedical signal processing. These interfaces now find applications in various robotic systems. Telepathy is not necessarily a human-human interaction modality. Unlike the regular human interaction methods of speech and visual gesture, which have a "feel it and it happens" or "feel it as it happens" sensation, telepathic interaction emphasises a "think it and it happens" interaction. In natural gesture interaction, machines are taught to interact via natural human methods. However, in mind control interaction, the machines are being equipped to interact with humans in a way that humans do not normally interact with each other, a way that is beyond the normal human-human interaction capability. Humans skillful in the art of manipulating other humans via induction, deception, and psychological means such as the psychic, medium, or paranormal extrasensory perception or the sixth sense, may argue otherwise.

A challenge that the BCI system faces, even though it is still under development, is security. The mere thoughts of the human vulnerability to telepathic credit card hack elicits a fearful response, and a natural reluctance to the adoption of such technology (as a defensive strategy), until the security of such systems can be guaranteed (Martinovic et al., 2012). This means security is put at the forefront of this development rather than taking a back seat, as is often the case with new technologies. While this may suggest the possibility of absolute transparency in interaction, the breach of privacy and human right could be called to question.

## Human Factors: Performance Measurement

A major consideration in the development of any system is how to measure the system's performance. According to (Lindquist, 1985), the effort-to-learn and the effort-to-use contribute to the usability of human-computer interaction (HCI) interfaces. The similarity of the developed interface to other known interfaces, the knowledge of similar interfaces, and the complexity of the developed interface, contributes to the effort-to-learn and usability of the developed system. Another performance metric of interest is probably a comparison of the interface's functionality with alternative existing interfaces. In this case, a comparison of the interface precision, accuracy, efficiency and effectiveness could be carried out. A performance benchmark could be drawn around the most generally accepted HCI interface such as the joystick-type controller for new aerobotic control interfaces.

Generally, a good interface design improves the overall user experience, makes interaction enjoyable, intuitive, easy to learn, and is functionally effective with an accepted level of precision and accuracy. As implied from (Chao, 2009), a good HCI is not about the human adapting to the limitation of the computer (as used to be the case), but about the computer adapting to the human's natural tendencies and expectations.

## CONCLUSION

The discussion in this chapter focused on human aerobotic interaction interfaces. These are interfaces used by humans to interact with aerial robotic systems, which were introduced as 'aerobots', a term used extensively in this chapter. A number of these interfaces were presented. Most of the interfaces presented were unimodal, and a few were multimodal. In order to develop the premises for the discussion of the control interaction interfaces, the concept of autonomy in robotic systems was intensively explored. Because of the limitations of the existing autonomy models (such as the AFRL and ONR), in aerobot navigational control autonomy classification, a new autonomy classification model called the navigational control autonomy (nCA) model, was proposed and developed. It was compared with the other existing models. The nCA model differs from the other models in eliminating step-size increment, supporting fuzzy classification between levels, presenting levels in a pyramidal order, and appropriately mapping the limits of aerobotic control interfaces (such as the RC joystick controller). The nCA model was used as the basis for discussing the unimodal human aerobotic control interfaces, in this chapter. The nCA model identified a control void beyond the tier-one components of the nCA model. An attempt was made to address this by suggesting two solutions, a multimodal HHI-like interface and a unimodal BCI interface. The limitations of each of these suggestions were also discussed. In addition to these, some human factors based performance measurement was recommended.

## FURTHER WORKS

The need for intuitive control interaction interfaces for aerobots beyond tier-one components of the nCA autonomy model opens up an opportunity to explore smart novel interaction techniques. The next phase of this work would be exploring the practical application/implication of a multimodal HHI-like interface that combines speech with visual gestures in human aerobotic interaction. A working practical prototype would be developed to demonstrate the feasibility of this approach and to investigate the practical implications of this method. This would enable further investigation into some of the technical limitations presented in the discussion subsection of the HHI-like interface. Another potential solution to that may be investigated further would be the telepathic interaction via BCI interfaces.

## REFERENCES

Abioye, A. O., Prior, S. D., Thomas, G. T., & Saddington, P. (2016). The Multimodal Edge of Human Aerobotic Interaction. In K. Blashki & Y. Xiao (Eds.), *International Conferences Interfaces and Human Computer Interaction* (pp. 243–248). Madeira, Portugal: IADIS Press.

Bastianelli, E., Nardi, D., Aiello, L. C., Giacomelli, F., & Manes, N. (2015). Speaky for robots: The development of vocal interfaces for robotic applications. *Applied Intelligence*. doi:10.1007/s10489-015-0695-5

Blanz, V. (2007). A learning-based high-level human computer interface for face modeling and animation. *Proceedings of the20th International Joint Conference on Artificial Intelligence, IJCAI 2007 - Workshop on Artificial Intelligence for Human Computing,LNAI* (*Vol. 4451*, pp. 296–315). Hyderabad, India: Springer Verlag. doi:10.1007/978-3-540-72348-6_15

Bolt, R.a. (1980). Put-that-there: Voice and Gesture at the Graphics Interface. *Proceedings of the 7th Annual Conference on Computer Graphics and Interactive Techniques - SIGGRAPH '80* (pp. 262–270). doi:10.1145/800250.807503

Cacace, J., Finzi, A., & Lippiello, V. (2016). Multimodal Interaction with Multiple Co-located Drones in Search and Rescue Missions. CoRR, abs/1605.0

Calella, J. C., Ortega, F. R., Rishe, N., Bernal, J. F., & Barreto, A. (2016). HandMagic: Towards User Interaction with Inertial Measuring Units. Proceedings of the IEEE Sensors 2016, Orlando, FL, USA. IEEE. doi:10.1109/ICSENS.2016.7808524

Cavett, D., Coker, M., Jimenez, R., & Yaacoubi, B. (2007). Human-computer interface for control of unmanned aerial vehicles. *Proceedings of the2007 IEEE Systems and Information Engineering Design Symposium, SIEDS,* Charlottesville, VA, USA. IEEE. doi:10.1109/SIEDS.2007.4374014

Chao, G. (2009, March 8-10). Human-computer interaction: Process and principles of human-computer interface design. In *2009 International Conference on Computer and Automation Engineering ICCAE '09*, Bangkok, Thailand (pp. 230–233). IEEE. doi:10.1109/ICCAE.2009.23

Chaomin, L., Yue, C., Krishnan, M., & Paulik, M. (2012). The magic glove: A gesture-based remote controller for intelligent mobile robots.*Proceedings of the SPIE - The International Society for Optical Engineering.* doi:<ALIGNMENT.qj></ALIGNMENT>10.1117/12.912186

Clough, B. T. (2002). Metrics, schmetrics! How the heck do you determine a UAV's autonomy anyway? *Proceedings of the 2002 Performance Metrics for Intelligent Systems Workshop,* Gaithersburg, MD, USA (pp. 313–319).

Emotiv. (2014). Wearables for your brain. Retrieved from https://emotiv.com/

Fong, T., & Nourbakhsh, I. (2000). Interaction challenges in human-robot space exploration. *Proceedings of the Fourth International Conference and Exposition on Robotics for Challenging Situations and Environments* (pp. 340–346). http://doi.org/doi:<ALIGNMENT.qj></ALIGNMENT>10.1145/1052438.1052462

Google. (2014). Google Project Soli: Your Hands Are the Only Interface You Will Need. Retrieved from https://atap.google.com/soli/

Green, S., Chen, X., Billinnghurst, M., & Chase, J. G. (2007). Human Robot Collaboration: An Augmented Reality Approach a Literature Review and Analysis. *Mechatronics*, *5*(1), 1–10. doi:10.1115/DETC2007-34227

Gupta, L., & Ma, S. (2001). Gesture-based interaction and communication: Automated classification of hand gesture contours. *IEEE Transactions on Systems, Man and Cybernetics. Part C, Applications and Reviews*, *31*(1), 114–120. doi:10.1109/5326.923274

Hammacher Schlemmer. (2015). The Mind Controlled UFO. Retrieved from http://www.hammacher.com/Product/Default.aspx?sku=84249&promo=Toys-Games-Remote-Control-Toys&catid=247

Harris, J., & Barber, D. (2014). Speech and Gesture Interfaces for Squad Level Human Robot Teaming. In R. E. Karlsen, D. W. Gage, C. M. Shoemaker, & G. R. Gerhart (Eds.), *Unmanned Systems Technology Xvi*, SPIE (Vol. 9084). doi:10.1117/12.2052961

Hernandez Jose, L., Kyriakopoulos, N., & Lindeman, R. (2002). The AcceleGlove a Hole-Hand Input Device for Virtual Reality. In *ACM SIGGRAPH Conference Abstracts and Applications*, 259.

Hill, A. F., Cayzer, F., & Wilkinson, P. R. (2007). Effective Operator Engagement with Variable Autonomy. *Proceedings of the 2nd SEAS DTC Technical Conference* (p. 7).

HobbyKing & Turnigy. (2015). Turnigy TGY-i10 10ch 2.4GHz Digital Proportional RC System with Telemetry (Mode 2). Retrieved from http://www.hobbyking.com/hobbyking/store/__58455__Turnigy_TGY_i10_10ch_2_4GHz_Digital_Proportional_RC_System_with_Telemetry_Mode_2_.html

Horrigan, F. A.ONR's Committee. (2000). *Review of ONR's Uninhabited Combat Air Vehicles Program*. Washington, D.C.: National Academy press.

Huang, C.-L., & Chung, C.-Y. (2004). A real-time model-based human motion tracking and analysis for human-computer interface systems. *EURASIP Journal on Applied Signal Processing*, *2004*(11), 1648–1662. doi:10.1155/S1110865704401206

Huhn, K., & Haewon, S. (2014). Evaluation of the safety and usability of touch gestures in operating in-vehicle information systems with visual occlusion. *Applied Ergonomics*, *45*(3), 789–798. doi:10.1016/j.apergo.2013.10.013 PMID:24231034

Kim, S., Seo, H., Choi, S., & Kim, H. J. (2016). Vision-guided aerial manipulation using a multirotor with a robotic arm. *IEEE/ASME Transactions on Mechatronics*, *4435*(c), 1–1. doi:10.1109/TMECH.2016.2523602

Lackey, S., Barber, D., Reinerman, L., Badler, N. I., & Hudson, I. (2011). Defining Next-Generation Multi-Modal Communication in Human Robot Interaction. *Proceedings of the Human Factors and Ergonomics Society Annual Meeting*, *55*(1), 461–464. http://doi.org/doi:10.1177/1071181311551095

Lafleur, K., Cassady, K., Doud, A., Shades, K., Rogin, E., & He, B. (2013). Quadcopter control in three-dimensional space using a noninvasive motor imagery-based brain-computer interface. *Journal of Neural Engineering*, *10*(4), 046003. doi:10.1088/1741-2560/10/4/046003 PMID:23735712

Lavars, N. (2016). Thumbsteered drone leaves you with a free hand. Retrieved from http://newatlas.com/shift-drone-thumb/46188/

Leap Motion Inc. (2010). Leap Motion Controller. Retrieved from https://www.leapmotion.com/

Lee, T., Meng, H., Lo, W. K., & Ching, P. C. (2003). The State of the Art in Human-computer Speech-based Interface Technologies. *HKIE Transactions Hong Kong Institution of Engineers*, *10*(4), 50–61.

Lindquist, T. E. (1985). Assessing the usability of human-computer interfaces. *IEEE Software*, *2*(1), 74–82. doi:10.1109/MS.1985.230052

Ma, Y., Mao, Z.-H., Jia, W., Li, C., Yang, J., & Sun, M. (2010, May 9-12). Magnetic hand tracking for human-computer interface. *Proceedings of the 14th Biennial IEEE Conference on Electromagnetic Field Computation CEFC '10*, Chicago, IL, USA. IEEE. Doi:<ALIGNMENT.qj></ALIGNMENT>10.1109/CEFC.2010.5481499

Martinovic, I., Davies, D., Frank, M., Perito, D., Ros, T., & Song, D. (2012). On the Feasibility of Side-Channel Attacks with Brain-Computer Interfaces. *Usenixorg*, 1–16.

Milanova, M., & Sirakov, N. (2008, December 16-19). Recognition of emotional states in natural human-computer interaction. *Proceedings of the 8th IEEE International Symposium on Signal Processing and Information Technology ISSPIT '08* (pp. 186–191). IEEE. doi:10.1109/ISSPIT.2008.4775663

Mu-Chun, S., & Ming-Tsang, C. (2001). Voice-controlled human-computer interface for the disabled. *Computing & Control Engineering Journal*, *12*(5), 225–230. doi:10.1049/cce:20010504

Murphy, R., Shell, D., Guerin, A., Duncan, B., Fine, B., Pratt, K., & Zourntos, T. (2011). A Midsummer Nights Dream (with flying robots). *Autonomous Robots*, *30*(2), 143–156. doi:10.1007/s10514-010-9210-3

Muscio, G., Pierri, F., Trujillo, M. A., Cataldi, E., Giglio, G., & Antonelli, G., ... Ollero, A. (2016). Experiments on coordinated motion of aerial robotic manipulators. *Proceedings of the IEEE International Conference on Robotics and Automation (ICRA)*, Stockholm, Sweden (pp. 1224–1229). doi:10.1109/ICRA.2016.7487252

Nagar, A., & Xu, Z. (2015). Gesture control by wrist surface electromyography. *Proceedings of the 2015 IEEE International Conference on Pervasive Computing and Communication Workshops* (pp. 556–561). doi:<ALIGNMENT.qj></ALIGNMENT>10.1109/percomw.2015.7134098

NeuroSky. (2011). Brainwaves. Not Thoughts. Retrieved from http://neurosky.com/biosensors/eeg-sensor/

Nimble VR. (2012). Nimble VR is joining Oculus. Retrieved from http://nimblevr.com/index.html

Nwana, H. S. (1996). Software Agents : An Overview. *The Knowledge Engineering Review*, *11*(3), 205–244. doi:10.1017/S026988890000789X

Oviatt, S. (2002). Breaking the robustness barrier: Recent progress on the design of robust multimodal systems. *Advances in Computers*, *56*(C), 305–341. doi:10.1016/S0065-2458(02)80009-2

Oviatt, S. (2003). Multimodal interfaces. In J. A. Jacko & A. Sears (Eds.), The Human-Computer Interaction Handbook: Fundamentals, Evolving Technologies, and Emerging Applications (pp. 286–304). London: Lawrence Erlbaum Associates, Incorporated.

Payne, K. (2007). *Autonomy - Proposal for a UK Route Map*. United Kingdom: BAE Systems.

Pfeifer, R., & Scheier, C. (1999). Embodied Cognitive Science: Basic Concepts. In R. Pfeifer & C. Scheier (Eds.), *Understanding Intelligence* (pp. 81–138). MIT Press.

Qing, C., Cordea, M. D., Petriu, E. M., Whalen, T. E., Rudas, I. J., & Varkonyi-Koczy, A. (2008). Hand-Gesture and Facial-Expression Human-Computer Interfaces for Intelligent Space Applications. *Proceedings of the IEEE International Workshop on Medical Measurements and Applications MeMeA '08* (pp. 1–6). doi:<ALIGNMENT.qj></ALIGNMENT>10.1109/MEMEA.2008.4542987

Reeves, L. M., Martin, J.-C., McTear, M., Raman, T., Stanney, K. M., Su, H., & Kraal, B. et al. (2004). Guidelines for multimodal user interface design. *Communications of the ACM, 47*(1), 57. doi:10.1145/962081.962106

Renitto, J. E., & Thomas, N. K. (2014). A Survey on Gesture Recognition Technology. *International Journal for Technological Research in Engineering, 1*(10), 1058–1060.

Reuters. (2015). Using The Force? No, it's an Apple Watch flying this drone. Retrieved from http://www.reuters.com/article/us-apple-watch-drone-idUSKBN0UE14Q20160101

Shah, J., & Breazeal, C. (2010). An Empirical Analysis of Team Coordination Behaviors and Action Planning With Application to Human-Robot Teaming. *Human Factors: The Journal of the Human Factors and Ergonomics Society, 52*(2), 234–245. doi:10.1177/0018720809350882 PMID:20942253

Sharma, R., Pavlovic, V. I., & Huang, T. S. (1998). Toward multimodal human-computer interface. *Proceedings of the IEEE, 86*(5 pt 1), 853–869. doi:10.1109/5.664275

Sholes, E. (2007). Evolution of a UAV autonomy classification taxonomy. *Proceedings of theIEEE Aerospace Conference Proceedings*. doi:10.1109/AERO.2007.352738

Soto-Gerrero, D., & Ramrez-Torres, J. G. (2013). A human-machine interface with unmanned aerial vehicles. *Proceedings of the 2013 10th International Conference Electrical Engineering, Computing Science and Automatic Control,* Mexico City, Mexico (Vol. 37, pp. 307–312). IEEE. http://doi.org/doi:10.1109/ICEEE.2013.6676045

Thalmic Labs. (2013). Homepage - Gesture Control Has Arrived. Retrieved from https://www.myo.com/

Thalmic Labs. (2015). Myo - Real Life Applications of the Myo Armband. Retrieved from https://www.youtube.com/watch?v=te1RBQQlHz4

Turk, M. (2014). Multimodal interaction: A review. *Pattern Recognition Letters, 36*(1), 189–195. doi:10.1016/j.patrec.2013.07.003

Verma, P. (2016). Flying User Interface. *Adjunct Proceedings of the 29th Annual Symposium on User Interface Software and Technology UIST '16,* Tokyo, Japan (pp. 203–204). ACM. doi:10.1145/2984751.2984770

Yinghong, M., Zhi-Hong, M., Wenyan, J., Chengliu, L., Jiawei, Y., & Mingui, S. (2011). Magnetic Hand Tracking for Human-Computer Interface. *IEEE Transactions on* Magnetics, *47*(5), 970–973. doi:10.1109/TMAG.2010.2076401

## KEY TERMS AND DEFINITIONS

**Aerobot:** A term derived from and referring to Aerial Robot.

**Control:** To operate a machine, a vehicle, or some other robotic systems such as an unmanned aerial vehicle, often with the aid of some device such as the RC joystick controller.

**Gesture:** Precise human body parts movement intended to communicate instructions to computers or robotic systems.

**HCI:** Abbreviation for Human-Computer Interaction.

**Interface:** A device used to operate a machine or robotic system e.g. joystick, keyboard, microphone.

**Multimodal:** A combination of two or more control interfaces, which could be, operated simultaneously or sequentially e.g. speech and gesture, keyboard and mouse.

**nCA:** Abbreviation for Navigational Control Autonomy, a concept introduced in this chapter.

**Unimodal:** A single control interfaces used to operate a machine, vehicle, or other robotic systems e.g. RC joystick controller.

# Chapter 4
# Methodology for Knowledge Management and Self-Directed, Science Program Engineering Computing

**Marcos Levano**
*Universidad Catolica de Temuco, Chile*

## ABSTRACT

*The following chapter shows the development of a learning methodology used to validate self-directed learning generic competences and knowledge management in a competence-based model in the engineering computer science program of the Universidad Católica Temuco (UCT). The design of the methodology shows the steps and activities of the learning-by-doing process, as shown gradually in the learning results of the competence. The designed methodological process allows creating working schemes for theory-based teaching and learning, and also for practicing and experimenting. The problematology as controlled scenarios is integrated in order to answer problems in engineering, allowing the process of validation in the self-learning and knowledge management competences. Thus, the achievements in the results have allowed helping the teachers to use their learning instruments.*

## INTRODUCTION

Nowadays, implementing the process of teaching practices in the classroom and workplace settings has led the students toward an educational training to review scripts and / or schemes (Yániz and Villardón, 2006) of how teaching and learning takes place in Chilean universities (Levano and Herrera, 2012). In this way, a set of trends in the world have allowed boosting major revisions in the way of delivering education. A common factor in many of these purposes is the orientation towards a competence-based training. Competences are those visible behaviours, skills, and attitudes that people provide in a specific scenery to perform effective and successfully (Tobón, 2007).

DOI: 10.4018/978-1-5225-2492-2.ch004

In its constant process of improvement about academic processes, ever since a few years ago, UCT is promoting a new educative model (Sánchez, 2008), which is composed of a significant learning focused on students, academic training based on competences, ICTs on the teaching and learning process, ongoing education, and humanistic and christian education.

The academic training based on competences has allowed for in-depth comprehension of the construct, going from a complex knowing and action to a competent performance in context (Sánchez, 2008), (Lévano and Herrera, 2012; Tobón, 2007) Thus, the competency-based educational model focuses on the student and his/her explanation of the concept in a given situation and context (Yániz and Villardón, 2006).

The new educational model has as pillar the competences training, responding to the needs of the environment and going hand in hand with international educational trends. The emphasis of the model are the generic competences, which give a hallmark to the students of the university.

One of the drawbacks that are exhibited in the validation of skills is the complexity of doing activities of teaching and learning in order to generate scaled schemes scenarios to replicate scenarios as they occur in the real context of a developer of a software product or a specialist in information technology management. Considering the above fact, here is proposed a design of a learning methodology for validation of the following generic competences; independent learning for level 1 and knowledge management for level 1 in a competence based-model in an engineering computer science program at the Universidad Católica Temuco, with the design of activities of learning by doing.

The design is supported by the previous works of Lévano and Oriel (2012), Lévano and Fernandez (2015) and Kolb (1984).

The research question to be resolved is how can you design a methodology to evaluate knowledge management competences and independent learning in undergraduate students for a professional training under a education approach competency-based?.

This paper is structured in the following sections: the UCT educational model, the design of the competences model for the engineering computer science program, the competences of knowledge management and independent learning, the model of experiential learning of Kolb, the model of integration of the metacognition in the curriculum of Lévano and Fernnadez, CDIO in the developement of generic and specific competences of Lévano and Albornoz, the design of the script for learning by doing, the design of the learning guide, learning methodology of learning by doing, results, discussion, limitations and future research, conclusions, acknowledgments and references.

## UCT EDUCATIONAL MODEL

The UCT (Universidad Católica de Temuco) defines competence as: "a knowledge act, by mobilizing own and external resources to effectively and ethically responsible solve real problems", (Sánchez, 2008). The educational model assumes the following types of competencies: generic competences are those shared with other professions; specifics competences are those related to the professional aspect.

In Figure 1, the five main pillars that support the whole educational competence-based model are observed. The UCT educational model is articulated on five main axes according to the study program formative itinerary, as it is explained below:

*Figure 1. Principal axes of the UCT educational model*

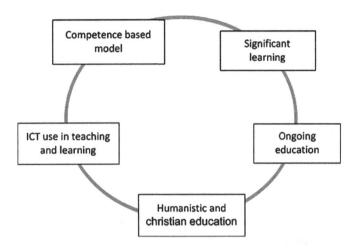

1.  Competence-based training: a commitment to the management of learning's quality – this implements 10 generic competencies.
2.  Significant learning centered on the student.
3.  Ongoing education: learning throughout life in a framework of equity – expects the continued education process in the graduate that develops an incremental complexity of the model.
4.  ICT in the process of teaching and learning – development that is immersed in the formative itinerary that is heading in the institutional strategy of incorporating intensive and critically the information and communications technology (ICT).
5.  A humanist and Christian formation - this incorporates an humanist and Christian formation, this is justified because the society of globalization requires clarity in ethical discernment of their professionals, solid disciplinary knowledge, ability to solve problems from different perspectives along its professional formation.

It is highlighted that since 2009 the UCT has been implementing the educational competences model and to date 100% of the study programs are developed in the context of competences.

The structure of the curriculum of the program consists of:

## Stage I

This stage consists on just one step, and it aims to create a professional graduate profile based on competences for each School inside the Faculties of the university. Due to the nature of some programs, some programs have specific competences in common.

**Step 1:** Creation of a professional graduate profile.

## Stage II

This stage has 4 steps and it aims to develop a curriculum that will be offered in the program in function of the new requirements.

**Step 2:** Learning outcomes.
**Step 3:** Definition of the curriculum.
**Step 4:** Development of programs.
**Step 5:** Development of learning guides.

## Stage III

This tow-stepped stage aims to implement the Educational Model of UCT. Also, it considers its assessment and tracing in order to make improvements.

**Step 6:** Implementation.
**Step 7:** Assessment and tracing.

## The Curriculum

The curriculum is built upon specific and generic competences, which are developed in different levels by doing activities during the courses.

- **Specific Competences:** They approach specific knowledge about each area (knowing), skills and abilities (doing) and attitude, commitment and values (being).
- **Generic Competences:** Those that account for the integral development of the future professional, both in their personal and interpersonal dimension. These competences are worked in all the programs and careers offered by the University as they constitute the institution's own training stamp.

## COMPETENCE BASED-MODEL FOR ENGINEERING COMPUTER SCIENCE PROGRAM

The Engineering Computer Science program joins the new educational model from 2010. The task of curriculum redesign and implementation took one year. Regarding the specific competencies to develop, four were defined (see Table 1), each in its three progressive levels of proficiency (Herrera et al, 2009; Lévano et al, 2016).

The strengths of the new formative itinerary or curriculum of engineering computer science program are justified on the following bases:

*Table 1. Specific competences of computer science curriculum*

| Specific Competences | Description |
|---|---|
| C1: Software development | Develops software solutions appropriate for one or more application domains using a software engineering approach that integrates technical, ethical, social, legal and economic aspects. |
| C2: IT Management | Manages systems that involve the use of hardware and software technologies in an organization to automate management systems and production processes. |
| C3: Modeling and applying methods in computer science | Models and implements software solutions, using methods of Computer Science, considering abstract-logical-scientific aspects, to provide solutions to the problems associated with real contexts, using algorithmic methods in automated information processes. |
| C4: Applying engineering sciences | Implements mathematical models in engineering and basic sciences using logical deductive reasoning skills to address problems of analysis and design of technological systems based on software linked to engineering specialties. |

## Educative Model

The new curriculum for the computer Engineering Science program of UCT is developed on a competence-based model of UCT (Sánchéz, 2008), on the curriculum of the ACM/IEEE-CS Joint Task Force on Computing Curricula (2013); ACM/IEEE Joint Task Force on Computing Curricula, Software Engineering (2014); ACM/IEEE Joint Task Force on Computing Curricula, Computer Engineering Curricula (2016); ACM/IEEE Association for Computing Machinery (ACM) IEEE Computer Society. Information Technology (2008); under the focus of the development of abilities CDIO (Crawley et al, 2007) and also it is developed based on the criteria given by the Chilean institution comisión nacional de acreditación (CNA, 2016).

## Competences in the Formative Itinerary

In the context (conceives, designs, implements and operates) CDIO in the formative itinerary four competences were developed such as the competence of software engineering (C1), information technology management competence (C2), competence called "models and applies procedures in computer science" (C3) and competence called "applies engineering sciences" (C4) (Herrera et al, 2009).

The competences meet professional profile (Herrera et al, 2009). The competences C1, C2, C3, and C4 are developed in three levels of complexity in engineering and engineering sciences of experiential learning. The formative itinerary levels of organization are built on reasoning and disciplinary knowledge, skills and personal and professional attributes and interpersonal skills (Figure 1), (Crawley et al, 2007), they together play the key in the application of knowledge and benefit of society under the Conceives, Designs, Implements and Operates model (CDIO) (Crawley et al, 2007); (ACM/IEEE Joint Task Force on Computing Curricula, Software Engineering, 2014); (ACM/IEEE Association for Computing Machinery (ACM) IEEE Computer Society, Information Technology, 2008).

## The Program in the Region

The university in the educational model (Sánchez, 2005) is part of a regional seal and is oriented to the sustainable development of economy of Chile to the world. Technical professionals, graduates in engineering sciences, engineers with mentions in software development and information technology, computer sciences engineers are exported, allowing a sustainable systemic balance between student and university, business and society and competence and professionals.

# COMPETENCES: KNOWLEDGE MANAGEMENT AND INDEPENDENT LEARNING

## 1. Knowledge Management in UCT Educative Model

The competence of Knowledge Management in the educational model of the UCT (Sánchez, 2008), is defined as: "The ability to identify and analyze information to a body integrating previous knowledge to generate new cognitive schemas. Skill of searching, evaluation, selection and efficient management of information, in terms of quality and relevance. Assess the various sources of information, in terms of quality and relevance, along with the willingness to analyze in depth the available knowledge". The UCT defines knowledge management as "the student processes information for the generation of knowledge which means to know, understand, apply, analyze, synthesize, evaluate and transform according to the needs of learning and work, and according to the requirements of the sociocultural environment".

This competence involves developing skills to manage knowledge in a progressive process from data and information to a higher level defined by the ability to understand the principles. The complexity in this regard will be defined by knowing how to contextualize the information to promote an act intelligently; also it will be achieved as far to create new, valid and reliable knowledge according to academic and disciplinary standards (UCT, 2008).

### Domain Levels

The domain levels set by the UCT educational model are explained in Table 2.

*Table 2. Domain levels for the knowledge management competence*

| Level 1 | Level 2 | Level 3 |
| --- | --- | --- |
| Recognizes the skills and / or cognitive processes with which he or she can identify, select, relate and interpret basic information regarding future information. | Applies the processes of analysis, synthesis, abstraction, inferences to new knowledge of the sociocultural and professional field. | Uses the information and knowledge to act responsibly to the demands of complex contexts that allow solving problems of sociocultural and professional reality. |

UCT, 2008.

## 2. Independent Learning in the UCT Educative Model

Independent learning competence in UCT educational model (Sanchez, 2008) is defined as: "the development of critical and reflective thinking that allows to become aware of their own learning processes (learning to learn). Ability to manage their own learning: efficient time management, learning strategies and constant evaluation of experience and the positive assessment of the building of own learning and willingness to learn in depth and for life".

The conception of learning that supports this competence, like others, is intended to promote the autonomous human and professional development. Learning that is essentially anticipatory, promotes forward-looking people, distinguished by the execution of complex tasks: they know what to do with knowledge. Similarly, the Christian vision of education puts at the center of the educational process the human being and the conquest of responsible autonomy (UCT, 2008).

### Domain Levels

The domain levels set by the UCT educational model are explained in Table 3.

## KOLB EXPERIENTIAL LEARNING MODEL

The model focuses on five learning components (Kolb, 1984)

- **Experiential Context:** This first component seeks to focus the student on the topic or issue that is being developed.
- **Reflective Observation:** The purpose of this phase is that the learner can question himself, since there can't exist meaningful learning if you do not question about it.
- **Conceptualization:** Conceptual learning is based on the acquisition of knowledge, scientific terminology, facts and data, methods and strategies, principles and theories that make up scientific knowledge of each subject.
- **Active Experimentation:** Means action, meaning it two key aspects: the internalized options, ie, experience, reflective observation and conceptualization that lead to action that favour. On the one hand, a gradual clarification of the priorities themselves and, secondly, action decisions based on their own beliefs / attitudes and values. The options that appear to the outside, the choice of personal and professional life performance in respect to one's own convictions and internalized values.

*Table 3. Domain levels of the independent learning competence*

| Level 1 | Level 2 | Level 3 |
|---|---|---|
| Knows and uses learning strategies and study and work habits, selecting those who are useful according to their learning needs. | Investigates into new knowledge areas from their own learning needs detected from metacognitive processes. | Solves problems of the professional area by the challenging and integration of theorists models from a personal and creative synthesis. |

UCT, 2008.

- **Evaluation:** In this model the term evaluation is defined as "the assessment of the merit and value of an object". The object of evaluation can be manifold: the learning, a method, a program, a student, a teacher, an institution, etc.

## MODEL OF INTEGRATION OF THE METACOGNITION IN THE CURRICULUM (MIMC)

The model of integration of monitoring in the metacognition curriculum (MIMC) is carried out by a thermal bath approach, for extreme feedback for the monitoring operations such as: learning guide, integration workshop, tracking of competency and teaching staff. Figure 1 shows the thermal bath model of MIMC for the student self-evaluation by means of the monitoring operations of the metacognition (Lévano and Fernandez, 2015).

## CDIO IN THE DEVELOPEMENT OF GENERIC AND SPEFICIC COMPETENCES

The modifications of the curriculum were made in two cycles of the students training. For the first cycle (first and second year) the modifications were focused on operate and then on implement and opearate; the second cycle (third and fourth year) is focused on implement and operate, then on design, implement and operate. The third cycle (fourth and fifth year) is focused on design, implement and operate and then on conceive, design, implement and operate (Lévano and Albornoz, 2016).

## DESIGN OF THE SCRIPT OF LEARNING BY DOING

The following use case design (see Figure 2) presents the design work schema that was developed by the teacher in front of students.

The design of the script responds to the active experiential process of learning by doing in the context of computer programming. This is based on the Kolb model (Lévano and Oriel, 2012); (Lévano and Fernandez, 2015); (Lévano and Herrera, 2012); (Kolb, 1984). The didactic process of the teacher is explained in the following use cases:

1. **To Plan:** This use case has the finality to allow the definition of teaching and learning activities in an instrument called the guide of student learning. This guide declares the systematization of the moments of Kolb, from the experiential context to active experimentation.
2. **To Schedule:** This use case has the finality to make the student programs instructions using a programming language at a high level in problems associated with engineering sciences, all done in situ with teachers and students.
3. **To Experience:** This use case has the finality to allow an experiential active process of the student in the problematology of engineering computer sciences. This allows the student to develop independent learning and knowledge management to achieve learning outcomes.
4. **To Provide Feedback:** This use case has the finality to allow feedback between teacher and student in order to sharpen the details of the experimentation process.

*Figure 2. Use case model of the script of learning by doing*

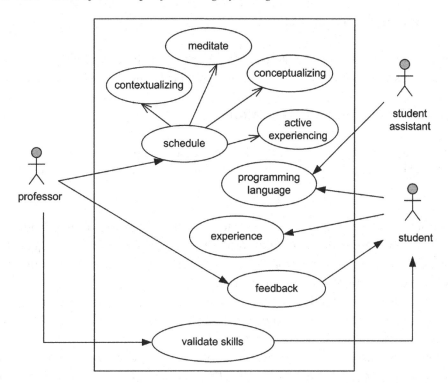

5.  **To Validate Skills:** This use case has the finality to allow the teacher to do the application of criteria for evaluating independent learning and knowledge management competences. The teacher designs a set of rubrics that allow him to pick the criteria as a learning strategy, time management, reflect on own learning strategies. Also it allows you to collect information management, knowledge building and knowledge transfer.

## Learning Guide Design

UCT defines the learning guide as an integrating element of the teachers of the course, where they should respond to the own competences of the subject. The focus is to work knowledge, skills, abilities and attitudes, respecting the time limits of this curricular activity.

The stages for the design and development of the learning guide are:

1.  Identify the general and specific competences to validate them in the learning guide.
2.  Definition of learning outcomes of what is expected the student be able to do at the end of the course.
3.  Instructional design of teaching and learning activities.
4.  Instructional design of activities of teaching and learning.
5.  Establishment holistically of protocols of competences evidences, which contributes to vertical integration of the curriculum.

6.  Coherence in the triple accordance that should exist in the learning guide. Relationship between methodology, learning outcome and assessment mechanism.

It is important to have explicit declarations of the learning outcomes that integrate specific and generic competences, as well as knowledge in the experiential cycle model and the structures in shown.

## Steps in the Learning Guide Elaboration

It is important to highlight the integration that has the subject with its own course program, which is stipulated in the formative itinerary of the study program. The steps in the design and elaboration of a guide are:

**1st Step:** Identification of competences and levels to validate them in the learning guide.
**2nd Step:** Comment and argue the description of the learning outcome for the subject. This involves defining the respective learning outcomes. It should be two or three learning outcomes, which must integrate generic and specific skills. The learning outcomes.
**3rd Step:** To design learning activities for the student. It is a sequence organized by weeks, where the set of activities during the semester is declared. The percentages of the contact hours, mixed hours and autonomous hours should be considered.
**4th Step:** Contemplates meetings (school executive committee) to integrate types of jobs that connect between two or more courses. This is done with the perspective to develop and demonstrate generic skills.
**5th Step:** The forms of evaluation, group or personal evaluation rubrics, references, test Schedule and the percentages of evaluations should be indicated, any evaluative and administrative element.

## Learning and Teaching Activities

The learning guide for the design of the activities is based on theory, practice, and experimentation. The method considers the following stages or learning processes. It aims to achieve a learning outcome.

- Experience.
- Analysis of the experience (What happened? How was the experience?).
- Learned lessons. Construction of knowledge.
- Future application, generalization, future projection.

## Learning Methods for Learning by Doing

In Figure 3, the methodology of student-centered learning by doing and under the Kolb approach is presented.

The teacher explains the theory in action and develops in-class practice activities while the students are learning in the process of doing. Additionally, students are learning how to operate with high-level

*Figure 3. Learning by doing methodology*

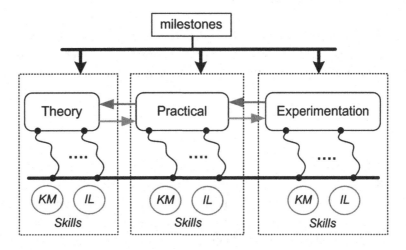

language tools. Then, the teacher proposes a case where engineering sciences are integrated. Many of the cases are activities that require the learner to develop independent learning and knowledge management skills. Figure 3 shows that the Theory articulates the two competences KM (knowledge management) and IL (independent learning). To do this, the teacher develops notes, problem activities and answer guides. Subsequently, it is used to validate the competences based on rubrics according to the criteria. In Practice, the operational work and programming skill in coordination with teachers and assistants is articulated. Similarly, it is used to validate the competences based on rubrics according to the criteria. Experimentation is the situation in context based on the problem situation in the engineering science area.

In a competence based- model the percentages of the subjects are in STC (system of transferable credits) (Ischinger and Alba, 2009), hours of the teacher job are distributed in contact hours, mixed hours and autonomous hours.

In the contact hours: teacher combines the learning by doing methodology, demonstrating a study case or problem. The problem situation leads them to iterate the learning cycle of Kolb where the transit by each phase occurs. In mixed hours: in the methodology, feedback in focus groups is done. This step is undertaken with support instructors like peer mentoring with senior students. The autonomous hours: in this period of time, the students can work in group or personally. The management of the resources which are part of learning is undertaken by a LMS platform, like Moodle.

## Strategies of Companies to Project a Profile

The companies the first thing they do is to determine a profile of the skills which the Engineers have and classifies them according to the professional's expertise. Afterwards a test and training process is carried out where the engineer must be involved in the field and / or project to which he is assigned, for this the engineer is integrated into groups and learns according to the planning and objectives of the company. In many cases computer engineers start as programmers, then process analysts, then system analysts, project managers, integration system managers.

## Program and Professional Practices

In order to integrate the engineers to the job market, the program inserts them into a period of supervised professional practice, so they can have a feedback from the company in which the practice is carried out. Connections are generated so the university is able to obtain information to enhance the curriculum.

## RESULTS

Among the results achieved with this proposed methodology of learning by doing under the competence based-model, the following progress are observed, and as key criteria establishment for validating the competences of knowledge management (see Table 4) and independent learning (see Table 5). It is achieved to assess the development of progress and the competences validation.

This investigation is made during the graduation period of the program and also during the third year. The program lasts five years.

*Table 4. Criteria for knowledge management*

| Criteria | Recognition of Skills and/or Cognitive Processes With Which Students can Identify, Select, Relate and Interpret Basic Information Related to Their Future Profession |
|---|---|
| Information management | • Uses search engines, Web sites easily accessible libraries or indicated by the teacher to find information.<br>• Expresses the information through charts and graphs proposed by the teacher.<br>• Expresses developed new skills or cognitive processes followed during the learning process. |
| Knowledge building | • Uses simple mental operations such as comparison and classification to build knowledge.<br>• Uses knowledge of a decoupled way to what the student tries to support.<br>• Quotes following the rules of the institution or accepted standards identified by the teacher. |
| Transference | • Presents the knowledge generated in pre-built or designated by the teacher formats.<br>• Participates in situations organized by the teacher in the classroom to disseminate the generated knowledge (oral presentations in class)<br>• Identifies the possible applications of the generated knowledge.<br>• Characterizes stages and processes developed in obtaining the learning. |

*Table 5. Criteria for independent learning*

| Criteria | Knows and uses Learning Strategies and Study Habits, Selecting Those That are Useful According to Their Learning Needs |
|---|---|
| Learning strategy | • Selects relevant terms of a matter for the management of technical language.<br>• Uses graphics organizers, such as conceptual, mental or semantic maps as learning strategy.<br>• Uses summaries as a learning strategy.<br>• Prepares comparative tables to understand the specific topics of the discipline.<br>• Questions, either individually or together, preparing assignments and tests. |
| Time management | • Has a schedule of assessments made during a semester.<br>• Is able to reflect on the effectiveness of times studies used for the preparation of a test.<br>• Following the reflections on the effectiveness / time with respect to an assessment, the student organizes consistently to time and the skills that possess. |
| Reflections on own learning strategies | • Reflects and recognizes their skills and difficulties regarding: organization of knowledge, written production, oral expression, reading comprehension, use of time and other skills that are necessary for the study of the subject.<br>• Uses the resources that the University offers to improve the learning process. |

The study consisted on two tips of cases, the first one was made during 2015 for a level of progress in the generic competences with a sample of 35 students of a section. The second case was made in 2014 with a population of 270 students.

The results advances were made for a population of 270 students, 20 teachers and 80 graduates of the engineering computer science program. According to the information in Table 6, we can see that both the 80% of students and 100% of teachers believe that the formative itinerary (curriculum) is suited to the requirements of the work world. Likewise they indicate that the formative itinerary properly integrates theoretical and practical activities; it is highlighted that 91% of students, 100% of teachers and 83% of graduates manifest "agree" on the surveys. Finally, 74% of students believe that the curriculum encourages students' creativity.

Survey results regarding entry and development of graduates to the work world (Table 7).

According to Table 7, the 90% of 2013 graduates in engineering computer science program took less than 3 months to get their first job. If we add those who took between 3 and 6 months (9%) gives an overall of 100% timely employability of graduates of the UCT engineering computer science program, ie, they found a job within the first 6 months after finishing university. This value is more than 17 points above the average of Engineering Faculty (83%) and the UCT average (82%). 85% claims to have appropriate employment, ie employment consistent with their professional training. Currently, 55% of respondents in the Engineering Computer science program are residing in the region of Araucania, while 36.4% are residing in the Metropolitan Region; the rest of the graduates are residing in the Region of Antofagasta.

Advances of results targeted for a sample of 35 students, of which 91.4% were male students and 8.6% were female students. 74.3% corresponds to the cohort of university entrance in 2010, 22.9% in 2011 and 2.9% in 2012, all of them were taught under the Educational Competence based- model, Now, results from according to each objective are presented.

**Specific Objective 1:** "To explore how students perceive generic competences implemented in the educational process" the following dimensions were measured:

*Table 6. Curriculum*

| Curriculum | Students | Teachers | Graduates |
|---|---|---|---|
| It is suited to the requirements of the labor market. | 80% | 100% | -- |
| Integrates properly theoretical and practical activities. | 91% | 100% | 83% |
| The subjects encourage students' creativity. | 74% | -- | -- |

*Table 7. Monitoring of graduates*

| General Results (2014) | |
|---|---|
| Timely employability | Less tan three months (90%); between 3 and 6 months (9%) |
| Appropriate employability | 85% appropriate employability |
| Region of residence | Araucanía (55%); Metropolitana (36%); Antofagasta (9%) |

## Level of Knowledge of the Competences

Faced with the question: Do you know the competences included in your training process? 77.1% of surveyed students declare to know the competences versus a 14.3% who do not know them and 8.6% do not know them or do not answer the question (Figure 4).

Facing the statement "are you able to clearly identify the meaning of each of the generic competences" As shown in Figure 4, most students, with 63% positioned in the line "agree and strongly agree", while 17% positioned in the line "disagree and Strongly disagree." Therefore, most of the surveyed students declare to know and identify the meaning of generic competences implemented in their training process.

In Table 8 dispersión of data can be observed. Students can identify the different competences that have been evaluated. However, the competences called "appreciation and respect for diversity", "Focus on quality" and "technological management" are those with the lowest percentage, hence there is a lower level of identification and knowledge. The competence called "focus on quality" has the lowest rate at

*Figure 4. Achieves clearly identify the meaning of each competition*

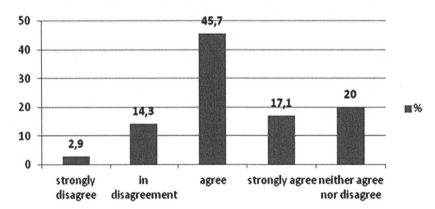

*Table 8. Level of identification and percentages of competences*

| The Following List of Generic Competences Includes Those That Have Been Evaluated From 1st to 4th Year | Answers | |
|---|---|---|
| | Number | % |
| Ethic act | 33 | 11,6 |
| appreciation and respect for diversity | 21 | 7,4 |
| Focus on quality | 20 | 7,0 |
| Creativity and innovation | 32 | 11,2 |
| **Independent learning** | **34** | **11,9** |
| English language | 30 | 10,5 |
| Teamwork | 34 | 11,9 |
| **Knowledge management** | **27** | **9,5** |
| Oral and written communication | 30 | 10,5 |
| Technology management | 24 | 8,4 |
| Total | 285 | 100,0 |

7%, while the "independent learning" and "teamwork" competences have a higher level of identification with 11.9%.

**Specific Objective 2:** "Describe the teaching and learning strategies that have been implemented to validate the competences from the perspective of students and teachers." The following dimensions were measured:

## Level of Competences Development (see Figure 5)

Just over half (51.4%) of the students considered that throughout their training process has succeeded in developing the evaluated competences. There is a greater inclination of the data for the "agree and strongly agree". However, it shows clearly that students have no clarity in the evaluation process. They only state that from their experiences have managed to develop competences.

## DISCUSSION

It can be understood that for validation of knowledge management and independent learning competences, these were validated together with other general competences, such that 97.1% admitted having passed the stage of validation of knowledge management competence (see Table 8). And 77.1% also admitted having gone through independent learning competence (see Table 8).

It is necessary to show that graduate students recognize that the curriculum gives them the possibility of joining a competitive work world. So, academics, students and graduates answer "yes," they are given tools to the workplace, they recognize that in the process they received practical and theoretical training, and also recognize that they were encouraged to develop their creativity in their discipline.

For academics is high demand to their job in doing a systematic and continuous process to validate the competences in context. Where the academics have created instruments that meet the needs depending on competences worked and developed by the students.

*Figure 5. Percentage of competences development in the curriculum design*

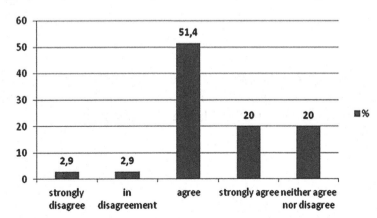

The instrument (learning guide) guides towards a clear performance and allows enunciate the various activities in situations that allow interaction to an active learning by doing in front of challenges where students achieve an objective in the transition process of Kolb phases.

Model metacognitive integration (Lévano and Fernandez, 2015) and the model of integration of generic and specific competences under CDIO approach (Lévano and Albornoz, 2016).

Chile has a growing demand for information technology companies, and the demand for employability of the 1st and 2nd. year of graduation of Computer Engineering is 88.8% and 93.2%.

## CHAPTER IMPORTANCE

The message left by this chapter is that it provides guidance to teachers to develop under a methodology of learning by doing, teaching and learning of the specialty in Informatics, in specialty subjects, like in software development and information technology management.

It allows to show the interventions activity by activity in the transition of Kolb cycle and according to the proposal of the theoretical practice and experimentation phase which integrates the model of metacognition in the curriculum (Lévano and Fernández, 2015). Also, implements the CDIO in the developement of generic and speficic competences (Lévano and Albornoz, 2016). It makes clear that the organization of biannual training project in the curriculum is aligned to the institutional model based on five keys axes towards the formative development.

## LIMITATIONS AND FUTURE RESEARCH

The limitations of this work described in this chapter, don't answer to the fact of having evaluated different learning styles of students under empirical studies (such as styles for those who observe, listen, read, do animations, and others), the study only focuses in answer a study of the application of the proposed methodology of learning by doing in the classroom due to the nature of the problems addressed in courses of specialty in engineering computer science program.

This work leaves the opportunity to measure and achieve results with different learning styles. It also exposes advances to develop training based on STEM context (science, technology, engineering and mathematics).

## CONCLUSION

This work provides a learning methodology for validation of the following generic competences: independent learning and knowledge management under a focus of learning by doing. Pedagogical teacher techniques focus on performing five activities: planning, programming, experience, feedback and the validation of competences.

The methodology allows generating schemes of work for teaching and learning based on the theory, practice and experimentation. As a result, the methodology establishes three validation criteria for knowledge management competence: information management, knowledge building and transfer. Similarly, the following criteria are set: learning strategy, time management and reflections on students own learning strategies.

The problematology, as controlled scenarios, integrates to solve engineering sciences problems, enabling the process of competences validation. However, this requires the teacher to use an adequate selection of problems to solve, in this way, the students must develop the selected competencies in an iterative and gradual process, which allows them to obtain the knowledge and skills required for the approval of a subject.

## ACKNOWLEDGMENT

In the process of making this paper, I would like to thank the support from UCT Engineering Computer Science Program.

## REFERENCES

ACM/IEEE Association for Computing Machinery (ACM) IEEE Computer Society. (2008). Information Technology 2008 Curriculum Guidelines for Undergraduate Degree Programs in Information Technology. Retrieved from http://www.acm.org//education/curricula/IT2008%20Curriculum.pdf

ACM/IEEE-CS Joint Task Force on Computing Curricula. (2013). ACM/IEEE Computing Curricula 2013 Final Report. Retrieved from https://www.acm.org/education/CS2013-final-report.pdf

ACM/IEEE Joint Task Force on Computing Curricula. (2015). Software Engineering 2014 Curriculum Guidelines for Undergraduate Degree Programs in Software Engineering. Retrieved fromhttp://www.acm.org/binaries/content/assets/education/se2014.pdf

ACM/IEEE Joint Task Force on Computing Curricula. (2016). Computer Engineering Curricula 2016 Curriculum Guidelines for Undergraduate Degree Programs in Computer Engineering. Retrieved from http://www.acm.org/binaries/content/assets/education/ce2016-final-report.pdf

CNA. (2016). Evaluation criteria for the accreditation of professional careers with bachelor's degree and bachelor's degree programs. National Accreditation Commission. Retrieved from https://www.cnachile.cl/Paginas/Acreditacion-Pregrado.aspx

Crawley, E., Malmqvist, J., Östlund, S., & Brodeur, D. (2014). *Rethinking engineering education: The CDIO Approach*. Cham, New York: Springer. doi:10.1007/978-3-319-05561-9

Herrera, O., Lévano, M., Mellado, A., Schindler, M., Donoso, G., & Contreras, G. (2009). *Profile of the Civil Engineering Degree in Computer Science. UCT*. Temuco: School of Computer Engineering.

Ischinger, B., & Alba, P. (Eds.). (2009). *Higher education in Chile. OCDE Chile*. París: Banco Mundial.

Kolb, D. A. (1984). *Experiential learning: Experience as the source of learning and development*. Englewood Cliffs, NJ: Prentice-Hall.

Lévano, M., & Albornoz, A. (2016). Findings in profesional training: computer engineering Science program. In J. Björkqvist, K. Edström, R.J. Hugo et al. (Eds.), *Proceedings of the 12th International CDIO Conference: CDIO Implementation* (pp. 528-537). Turku AMK: Turku University of Applied Sciences.

Lévano, M., & Fernández, C. (2015). A model for a Physical and Virtual Environment for Extreme Feedback in the Development of the Metacognition Supported by TICS: The Computer Engineer Career as Case of Study. *Lecture Notes in Electrical Engineering*, *330*, 1345–1352. doi:10.1007/978-3-662-45402-2_187

Lévano, M., & Herrera, O. (2012). Validation Strategies of Competences in a Computer Science Curriculum. *Proceedings of the31st International Conference of the Chilean Computer Science Society* (pp. 9-11). Valparaíso: Pontificia Universidad Católica de Valparaíso. doi:10.1109/SCCC.2012.8

Lévano, M., Herrera, O., Mellado, A., Rojas, J., Contreras, G., Peralta, B., & Caro, L. (2016). *Profile of the Civil Engineering Degree in Computer Science*. Chile, Temuco: School of Computer Engineering UCTemuco.

Sánchez, T. (2005). *Educational Model of the UC Temuco*. Temuco, Chile: Universidad Católica de Temuco.

Sánchez, T. (2008). *Educational Model of the UC Temuco*. Temuco, Chile: Universidad Católica de Temuco.

Tobón, S. (2007). *Metodología sistémica de diseño curricular por competencias*. Bogotá: Grupo cife.ws.

UCT (Ed.). (2008). *Generic competences for the integral formation of socially responsible citizens*. Temuco, Chile: Universidad Católica de Temuco.

Yániz, C. & Villardón, L. (2006). Planificar desde competencias para promover el aprendizaje. *Cuadernos Monográficos del ICE*, 12.

## KEY TERMS AND DEFINITIONS

**Competence-Based Model:** A model that leads to a mobilization of knowledge, and the integration of them in a holistic manner and linked with the context, assuming that people learn better if you have a global view of the problem that requires face. The competences should be considered part of cognitive behavioral adaptive capacity that is inherent in human beings, which are set up in order to meet the specific needs faced by people in specific socio-historical and cultural contexts, which implies a process of adaptation between the subject, the demand environment and his needs, in order to be able to provide answers and / or solutions to those demands.

**Educational Model Focused on the Student:** A set of rules and pedagogical teaching and learning schemes for cognitive development in higher education, centered on the student and focused on teaching, methodology, and evaluation.

**ICT:** Information and communication technologies supported by the Web 2.0 where the users can be advanced or not in the usage and exploitation technological resources.

**Knowledge Management:** The ability to identify and analyze information to a body integrating previous knowledge to generate new cognitive schemas. Skill of searching, evaluation, selection and efficient management of information, in terms of quality and relevance.

**Problemathology:** The way in which an observer defines the problems related to the images that he has about the real world he knows.

**Self-Directed Learning:** The process of the students' autonomous work, developed in a slow, reflexive, and critical way.

**Validation of Skills:** The learning and teaching process for the validation of skills in a context in which the students demonstrate the learning achievements required.

# Section 2
# Smart Technology and Health

# Chapter 5
# Adolescence Surveillance System for Obesity Prevention (ASSO) in Europe:
## A Pioneering Project to Prevent Obesity Using E-Technology

**Garden Tabacchi**
*University of Palermo, Italy*

**Joao L Viana**
*University Institute of Maia (ISMAI), Portugal*

**Monèm Jemni**
*Qatar University, Qatar*

**Antonino Bianco**
*University of Palermo, Italy*

## ABSTRACT

*Adolescents' obesity is a major concern in our modern life that could lead to significant increase in the rate of obese future generations and consequently in the health budget. The ASSO (Adolescence Surveillance System for Obesity prevention) project in Italy is tackling this new pandemic using the new e-technology through a multi facets monitoring system on life style including food consumptions, meal patterns and habits, alcohol, smoking, physical activity, fitness and sedentariness, and biological/genetic, and socio-cultural/environmental characteristics of adolescents. The project has been recently piloted in the South of the country. This chapter summarizes the design and structure of the ASSO system, its implementation and the results of an evaluation process for its possible extension to the whole Italian territory and to other European realities as a national surveillance system.*

## 1. INTRODUCTION

The world's population is facing an unprecedented obesity pandemic (Gortmaker, 2011; Swinburn, 2011; WHO, 2006; WHO 2014). Not only are the rich and occidental countries struggling with alarming numbers of obese people but also poorer countries are also reporting an increasing number of deaths directly or indirectly related to obesity (Bhurosy & Jeewon, 2014; Popkin, 2012). The World Health

DOI: 10.4018/978-1-5225-2492-2.ch005

Organization (WHO) showed that the main cause for mortality is cardiovascular disease (WHO 2014), with obesity one of the major determinants.

Longitudinal studies in all countries since the early 2000s have found increasing rates of overweight specifically in children and adolescents (UNICEF-WHO-World Bank, 2015). Recent data show that in Europe 8-29% of adolescents are overweight/obese, with a growing gradient from Northern to Southern countries (HBSC, 2016a). The HBSC study in Italy (HBSC, 2016b) shows that the prevalence of overweight/obesity in adolescents is on average around 19%.

It is well known that obesity and its associated non communicable diseases are common illnesses of childhood and adolescence representing an emergent public health issue (Ng, 2014; WHO, 2014). There is at least a moderate correlation between weight in childhood and adulthood, as well as obesity in childhood and later health problems (Freedman, 2005; Hills, 2007).

Collecting data on adolescents' health and behaviours through a standardized surveillance system is essential to understand diet- and physical activity-related health problems, in order to implement appropriate, effective and sustainable action plans. Data collected through a public health surveillance system represents a source that can be used for action, planning, evaluation, and formulating research hypotheses (German, 2001).

Few national surveillance systems have been established worldwide in the field of adolescents' obesity and lifestyles, such as the Youth Risk Behavior Surveillance System (YRBSS) in the USA (Brener, 2013) and the Health Behavior in School-aged Children Study in Europe (Currie, 2009). In Italy, the paper-based HBSC system is currently being up-taken every two years to collect health behavior information in adolescents, but the need for a web-based, user-friendly, low cost, valid and obesity/fitness-focused instrument has been highlighted recently (Tabacchi, 2014).

The Project "An innovative surveillance system for obesity and lifestyles in adolescents applied to the public health service", acronym "ASSO" (Adolescence Surveillance System for the Obesity prevention), was funded by the Italian Ministry of Health, involved different national and international partners, and was recently piloted in a Southern area of the Italian territory. It was launched with the aim of developing an innovative web-based system for a standardized and continuous collection of data on obesity and lifestyles among adolescents. To this purpose, different instruments included in an ASSO-toolkit were developed within the Project, and a software called ASSO-NutFit (Nutrition and Fitness assessment) was developed to allow for a web-based data collection.

The objective of the present chapter is to provide an overview of the ASSO Project architecture, with detailed descriptions of the design and structure, the actors involved, the tools developed, as well as the procedures used for sampling, recruiting, training, collecting and analysing data. Moreover, the project implementation is shown, together with a technical and procedural feasibility assessment. An assessment of the different steps of the Project is also performed to weigh how well it operates to achieve its objectives (Buehler, 1998; Teutsch & Thacker, 1995). The evaluation of the surveillance system as a whole is shown finally, with the purpose of assessing its suitability to be adopted as an effective, sustainable and continuous national surveillance system, and to be possibly adapted to other countries thanks to its web-based nature.

## 2. BACKGROUND

### 2.1 Obesity Drivers Among Adolescents

Different obesity drivers have been debated in children and adolescents, including factors related to nutrition in pregnancy, infant and child feeding practices, the quality and frequency of family foods and lifestyle, and aspects related to declining physical activity and low fitness levels (Bleich, 2011). Excess body weight is due mainly to excessive consumption of energy, saturated fats, trans fats, sugar and salt, as well as low consumption of vegetables, fruits and whole grains (EU, 2014). Important risk factors have to be recognized in socio-economic factors; socioeconomic disparities in child overweight are increasing and association between socioeconomic inequality and prevalence of child overweight in European countries have been documented. A recent study revealed heterogeneity in the association between parental socioeconomic indicators and childhood overweight or obesity in five countries located in different parts of the WHO European Region; both positive and negative associations were found out. This underscores the need to continue documenting socioeconomic inequalities in obesity in all countries through international surveillance efforts in countries with diverse geographic, social and economic environments (Lissner, 2016).

Also physical activity in youth is critical in Europe, with low children's and adolescents' engagement with sport and/or exercise (EU Special Eurobarometer 412, 2014). Physical fitness, in particular, has not been deeply investigated in Europe, although it is a powerful health marker and influences many life aspects (Bailey, 2013). Many countries have actually recognized the importance of assessing physical fitness in schools, and have included assessment strategies in their education syllabus (Cvejić & Ostojić, 2013).

### 2.2 Current Systems for Adolescent Dietary Evaluations

The assessment and the monitoring of all these factors as possible obesity risk behaviors represent important strategies to intervene appropriately and contribute in the avoidance of new young obese generations. The European Commission is taking the prevalence of adolescence's obesity very seriously and has put together a long-term strategy to tackle the pandemic from different perspectives. The EU has set out actions based on priority themes by mid 2013, such as putting together a monitoring process for children and adolescents obesity (EU, 2014). The way the monitoring processes are carried out is crucial for an effective surveillance system. To maximize benefits while minimizing risks, surveillance systems should aim to become wholly automated end-to end, e.g., becoming all electronic reporting systems. These last are computerized systems hosting medical records on diseases/health events (ECDC, 2014). Currently, there are not European national surveillance systems specific to obesity and its risk factors and based on e-technology as a whole. Nonetheless, innovative technology has been used in different dietary assessment instruments, with Personal Digital Assistant-, Mobile-phone-, Interactive computer-, Web-, Camera- and tape-recorder- and Scan- and sensor-based technologies (Illner, 2012). In particular, web-based Food Frequency Questionnaires have been shown to be more valid in estimating individual dietary intake, since compared with paper-based tools the underlying methodology is unchanged by the technology (Illner, 2012).

The use of technology in dietary assessment in particular for adolescents has been demonstrated to be attractive for that age range, thus improving participation rates; it provides an efficient, cost-effective and practical solution to assess dietary intake, and it is less burdensome to respondents and reduces errors and bias (Storey, 2015; Illner, 2012); the quality of the data collected is higher because the lower burden of the method is less likely to impact on habitual intake (Svensson, 2014).

The use of technology in dietary assessment with children has the potential to reduce respondent burden and to make participating in dietary studies more attractive and engaging. This could improve not only participation rates, but also the quality of the data collected because the lower burden of the method is less likely to impact on habitual intake (Howat, 1994). Computerised 24-h dietary recalls have been developed and used successfully with adults and children in the US (Baranowski, 2002; Subar, 2007) and adolescents in Europe (Vereecken, 2005). Nowadays, some questionnaires in Europe have used web-based methods, such as the FFQ from Matthys (2007), the 24-HR "Synchronised Nutrition and Activity Program™" (SNAP™) (Moore, 2008), the 24-HR YANA-C (Vereecken, 2005; Vereecken 2008), the HBSC FFQ (Vereecken, 2006) and the HELENA FFQ (Vereecken, 2010). However, as already mentioned, there is an ongoing need for the refinement of existing approaches, especially ones that can be used in large epidemiological studies (Tabacchi, 2014). In fact, all dietary methods validated and used for adolescents are different worldwide, this making comparison of data often difficult or unfeasible; standardized surveillance systems are needed, in order to collect valid and accurate estimates of food and nutrient intakes. A standardized and sustainable collection of data on adolescents' food consumption and lifestyles is useful to understand the diet-related public health problems and implement appropriate actions for the prevention of the related diseases.

It also has to be considered that physical activity and eating behaviors that affect weight are influenced by many sectors of society, including families, community organizations, health care providers, faith-based institutions, businesses, government agencies, the media, and schools (MMWR, 2011). Schools and colleges represent a perfect environment to collect data related to the current generation's health and they are ideal sites to undertake pioneering interventions on a wider scale that may impact the future of a country (Simovska, 2012). Published literature has shown that school programs can effectively promote healthy eating, physical activity and reductions in television viewing time (De Bourdeaudhuij, 2010; Buijs, 2009; CDC, 1997; Gortmaker, 1999; Robinson, 1999). Therefore the ASSO system has been piloted within a school environment, at a local level in Southern Italy, with the aim of collecting information on obesity and its determinants. The issue is whether it can be applied as a surveillance system that uses e-technology in the whole Italian territory and in other European countries. This chapter will clarify the potential use of ASSO as a national surveillance system to prevent obesity in adolescents, highlighting the attributes that such a system should have in order to be effective.

# 3. THE ASSO WEB-BASED SYSTEM

## 3.1 The ASSO Actors

The multidisciplinary ASSO team included professionals from the fields of nutrition, physical activity, epidemiology, medicine, psychology, informatics, biology, graphics and communication, recruited both from the academic and non academic sector. The ethical approval was given by the ethical committee of the "Azienda Ospedaliera Universitaria Policlinico Paolo Giaccone" (approval code n.9/2011).

Contacts were established with the Regional Education Office, which provided the list of all the schools in the territory, allowing the selection and recruitment of the required sample. After the school selection, an agreement was signed by their dean and the Ministry of Health in order to perform the activities. Schools provided the structures and equipment for the Project activities, guaranteeing their commitment in recruiting the pupils and their parents' consent. Two reference teachers were selected by the dean within each school, one in the scientific area and the other in the physical activity area; they covered a very important role in supporting students during the questionnaire compilation and in collecting the anthropometric and fitness data, respectively.

## 3.2 The ASSO Design

The ASSO Project is inspired by the EU policies and guidelines. It addresses key issues related to monitoring scholarly adolescent's health variables by applying the latest e-technology for effectiveness. The overall outcome of the ASSO Project is to create an online sharable database that provides information on different obesity- and health-related aspects: dietary, drinking and smoking habits, body composition, physical activity and physical fitness, beyond demographic and socio-cultural characteristics. Although the system is built up to be accessible within the school environment, all the described variables are monitored via a guided system during different locations and periods: at school, at home with the parents/guardians, with relatives, during holiday, week days and weekends, as they could vary according to the context, hence providing a holistic picture of the adolescents life style behaviour change in different environments.

The Project was structured in six Work Packages (WPs), which interrelated to each other as showed in Figure 1.

### 3.2.1 The Asso Toolkit

#### 3.2.1.1 Systematic Literature Reviews and Meta-Analyses

In order to come up with a relevant and a scientifically based assessment tool, an analytic review of the current state of the art literature and/or a meta-analysis has been undertaken by a team of experts. Two Systematic Literature Reviews (SLRs) on the most valid dietary and fitness assessment methods used in the target population (Bianco, 2015; Tabacchi, 2014) and a meta-analysis of the validity of food frequency questionnaires targeted to adolescents (Tabacchi, 2015) were performed. The obtained results, i.e. the suggestion on the need of a new FFQ and the selection and incorporation of five fitness tests in a new battery, together with the consultation of the different involved experts, were useful for the development of the ASSO-toolkit.

#### 3.2.1.2 Tools

As shown in Figure 2, the ASSO-toolkit consists of four questionnaires (ASSO-PIQ, Personal Information Questionnaire; ASSO-PASAQ, Physical Activity, Smoke and Alcohol Questionnaire; ASSO-FHQ, Food Habits Questionnaire; ASSO-FFQ, Food Frequency Questionnaire); one ASSO-BFMT (Body and Fitness Measures Tool) including a form (ASSO-BFMF, Body and Fitness Measures Form) and a Fitness Tests Battery (ASSO-FTB); and Standard Operating Procedures (SOPs).

*Figure 1. Overall structure of the Adolescence Surveillance System for the Obesity Prevention Project (ASSO)*

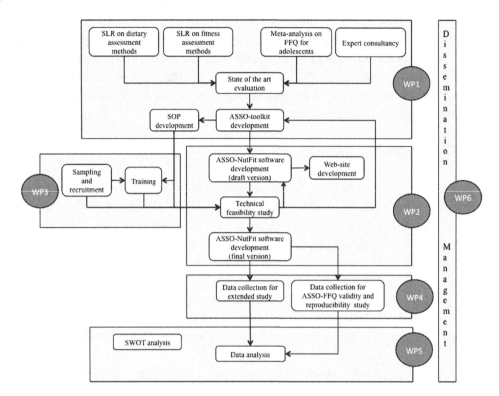

The ASSO-PIQ includes questions regarding participant and family information, neonatal and clinical assessment. The ASSO-PASAQ consists of three sections: physical activity, smoking, alcoholic drinks and other beverages. The ASSO-FHQ consists of six items regarding: breakfast, school break, lunch, afternoon break, dinner, and various habits.

The need of refining dietary consumption approaches advocated the FFQ method for the ASSO system, and suggested the development of a new quantitative FFQ that could fit the purposes of the ASSO project. The ASSO-FFQ is structured in three sections (foods, beverages and supplements) including 20 major groups: 12 food groups (fruit/vegetables/legumes, cereals/bread/substitutes, pasta/rice/couscous, potatoes, sweets, cheeses/yogurt, fishery products, meat, eggs, fats/oils, savory foods, regional dishes); 7 beverages groups (water, soft drinks, juice/milkshakes, milk, tea, coffee, alcoholic drinks), and 1 supplements group. Each main group was stratified into subgroups, for a total of 106 items. This classification was put together according to the European Food Safety Agency (EFSA, 2011), on the basis of the common nutritional properties. The adopted classification considered the different methods of cooking foods, distinguishing between raw and cooked vegetables, and the different cooking techniques e.g. for potatoes. For every food subgroup, a legend was added that explained what foods/beverages/supplements were included in that group. The consumption frequency was set on eight different frequencies, and the portion size was assessed through the use of pictures taken by the ASSO team and where necessary household units were used. The use of pictures with different sizes made the portion size estimation much easier and more accurate, and therefore helped the subjects to better evaluate and choose the size closer to their real consumption (the errors reported when these kind of portion size estimation methods

*Figure 2. Tools included in the ASSO-toolkit*

| ASSO-toolkit | | Duration, min | Outcome/Measure/Objective |
|---|---|---|---|
| **Tool** | **Sections** | | |
| ASSO-PIQ (Personal Information Questionnaire) | Section A. General information<br>Section B. Family information<br>Section C. Neonatal information<br>Section D. Clinical information | 10 | General, family, neonatal and clinical information |
| ASSO-PASAQ (Physical activity, Smoke and Alcohol Questionnaire) | Section A. Physical activity<br>Section B. Smoke<br>Section C. Alcohol | 10 | Physical activity, smoke and alcohol consumption |
| ASSO-FHQ (Food Habits Questionnaire) | Section A. Breakfast<br>Section B. School recess<br>Section C. Lunch<br>Section D. Afternoon snack<br>Section E. Dinner<br>Section F. Various food habits | 5 | Meals practices and food habits such as organic products consumption, precooked foods |
| ASSO-FFQ (Food Frequency Questionnaire) | Section A. Foods<br>Section B. Beverages<br>Section C. Supplements | 20 | Foods, beverages and supplements consumptions |
| ASSO-BFMT (Body and Fitness Measures Tool) | | 45 | |
| Anthropometrics | Weight<br>Height<br>Waist circumference | 5 | BMI, metabolic risk |
| ASSO-FTB (Fitness Tests Battery) | Hand grip test | 3 | Maximum isometric strength of hand and forearm muscles |
| | Standing broad jump test | 3 | Lower body power |
| | Sit up test | 3 | Abdominal muscular endurance |
| | 4x10 m shuttle run test | 5 | Speed and agility |
| | 20 m shuttle run test | 15 | Maximal aerobic fitness |
| ASSO-BFMF (Body and Fitness Measures Form) | | | Sheet where reporting anthropometric and fitness measures |
| SOP (Standard Operating Procedures) | 1. General procedure<br>2. Procedures for the collection of data from questionnaires<br>3. Procedures for the collection of body measures and fitness test measurements | | Standardize methods and procedures |

are used are sufficiently small, within 5-10%) (Willett, 2012). A subsection related to the reporting of regional/local products was introduced.

The validity and reproducibility of the ASSO-FFQ were performed. Validity of the ASSO-FFQ was carried out in a small subsample of 92 boys and girls aged 14-17 from three of the selected schools, after completing both the ASSO-FFQ and a seven-day weighted food record (WFR). A hardcopy of the WFR was distributed to participants on the same day of the ASSO-FFQ administration, in order to be filled in the week following the ASSO-FFQ compilation. This study suggested that the ASSO-FFQ could be considered as a valid instrument for ranking subjects on a range of food and nutrient intakes (Tabacchi, 2015). In fact, high cc (>0.40) were found for soft drinks, milk, tea/coffee, vegetables, and lactose; fair energy adjusted cc (0.25-0.40) for water, alcoholic drinks, breakfast cereals, fishery products, savory food, fruit juice, eggs, and 19 nutrients; the subjects classified in the same or adjacent quintile for food groups ranged from 40% (alcoholic drinks) to 100% (dried fruit); for energy and nutrients from 43% (phosphorus, thiamin, niacin) to 77% (lactose); mean differences were not significant for water, soft drinks, meat, sweets, animal fats, milk and white bread, and vitamin B12 and folate.

The ASSO-FFQ was compiled twice by a sample of 185 students for the reproducibility study that were selected by stratifying per age and type of school. The analysis revealed that the ASSO-FFQ was a reliable instrument for estimating food groups, energy and nutrients intake in adolescents, with mean values of weighted kappa 0.47 and 0.48, respectively for food groups and nutrients; fair to good ICC values (>0.40) were assessed for thirteen food groups, energy and forty-three nutrients; Limits of Agreement were narrow for almost all food groups and all nutrients (Filippi, 2014). The ASSO-FFQ, therefore, can be used in epidemiological studies on large scale to obtain valid and reliable estimations over time.

For the compilation of all questionnaires a total time of 45 min were needed, with the only FFQ taking 20 min to be filled in; other developed questionnaires reported a similar or even longer time for compilation (Bertoli, 2005; Hoelscher, 2003; Hong, 2010; Matthys, 2007; Shatenstein, 2010; Watanabe, 2011). All the questionnaires were compiled in the classroom setting, with teachers available to answer possible questions; if the student was not present the day of the data collection, the teacher assigned it to him as a homework, so that a bunch of students filled their questionnaires in from home.

The ASSO-BFMT included the description of methods to collect anthropometric measurements, including body weight, height, waist circumference, and to perform the FTB administration. Anthropometric measurements were collected through the use of a weight scale, a stadiometer and a non elastic meter, all instruments commonly available within the schools and used by the teachers themselves to collect these data during their school curriculum.

The ASSO-FTB was accurately selected by the ASSO team experts and the final version included five tests: Handgrip test; Standing broad jump test; Sit up test to exhaustion; 4x10 m shuttle run test; 20m shuttle run test (Figure 2). They allowed the estimation of upper body maximal strength, lower body maximal strength, abdominal endurance, speed/agility/coordination and cardiorespiratory endurance respectively. All these tests were easily performed within the school since they require few tools and easy equipment generally available in the school; only the handgrip was provided by the University, as it was not a common tool used within the school environment. A total time of 30 min per student was needed for the collection of anthropometric measurements and the performance of all fitness tests; some of them could be administered to more students at a time, hence reducing the total time needed for the whole class.

An ASSO fitness index was developed starting from the data collected through the ASSO-FTB (Bianco, 2015b). The health-related fitness components were detected in a convenient sample of adolescents and a fitness index model was provided incorporating all these components for an intuitive classification of fitness levels. The monitoring of these variables will allow early detection of health related issues in a mass population and hence will give the opportunity to plan appropriate interventions.

The ASSO-BFMF included in the tool was useful for teachers to report on all these measurements, before transferring them to the software.

A total time of 75 min was required per student to perform the entire ASSO-toolkit, this being considered a reasonable time to promote the introduction of the ASSO in schools as a continuous surveillance system strategy.

### 3.2.1.3 Standard Operating Procedures

The SOPs included: a general procedure, for the activities preceding the data collection (namely selecting schools, classes, students and teachers and configuring them in the ASSO-NutFit software), training teachers, preparing all the materials and tools necessary for the data collection; procedures for the collection of data from questionnaires; procedures for the collection of anthropometric and fitness test measurements. These procedures were addressed to all ASSO operators and teachers involved in the collection of lifestyle data of adolescents within the schools and provided information on the modalities to: standardizing methods and procedures in order to prevent systematic errors in the data collection and reporting; providing reminders of the correct way to perform a procedure; dealing with the information material and tools related to the study; supporting students in the self-administration of the questionnaires; collecting anthropometric and fitness data; storing the collected information.

## 3.2.2 The ASSO-NutFit Software and Website

### 3.2.2.1 The ASSO-NutFit Draft Software

The ASSO team and IT engineers have worked closely to create a relatively straightforward and user-friendly Software called the ASSO-NutFit, which was developed with the aim of obtaining an instrument for a web-based collection of data. Software implementation was done using J2EE (Java 2 Enterprise Edition), using MySQL as database engine with InnoDB configuration type. The software's architecture is shown in Figure 3.

Data are input by the administrators, teachers and students, and are recorded on the relational database MySQL, in a database named *master*, which is accessible uniquely by the developed application and for security reasons it can be modified only with an extraordinary maintenance intervention. Data from *master* are synchronized daily with those on a database called *slave* that contains a simplified and normalized image of the *master* database, and that is directly accessible by a series of users and internet

*Figure 3. The ASSO-NutFit software architecture*

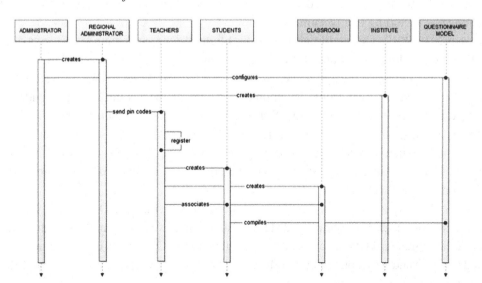

enabled accesses. Through the commercial software Access MySql Converter it is possible to acquire data from the *slave* database and recording them on a Microsoft Access database of identical structure, for the subsequent statistical elaborations.

Some of the tools developed for the ASSO-toolkit were included within the software, i.e. the four questionnaires and the BFMF. Data gathered in the database are crossed and checked throughout the duration of the data collection.

During data acquisition, two types of validation are applied: single data field validation and business function cross-field validation. In the field validation, the platform performs a syntactic validation to check whether the data is valid for the specific field. Once the toolkit has validated the data syntactically, it could then validate the data semantically. Semantic validation checks whether the data conforms to specified business rules. After that, the platform performs a cross-field validation of the relationship between the current field's value and the value of the other fields.

Different snapshots of the ASSO-NutFit interfaces are showed in Figures 4 and 5.

Figure 4A shows a snapshot of the ASSO-NutFit interface with Administrators registering Institutes and teachers from each school. Once teachers are registered, a username and password is automatically sent to them, so they can have access to the software. Teachers from the science area have the role of registering students (Figure 4B), who are automatically provided in their turn with username and password to their e-mail addresses. Students can then have access to the application and complete the questionnaires.

In Figure 5 a snapshot of the interface of the ASSO-FFQ compiled by the students is provided.

Physical Education teachers have the role of reporting all the anthropometric and fitness data into the paper ASSO form and then transfer them to the ASSO-BFMF on the software.

### 3.2.2.2 Technical Feasibility Study

At the first stage data was collected on a subsample of population for a technical feasibility assessment of the data collection through the ASSO-NutFit software and of the developed procedures. This study allowed testing the applicability of the system before extending it to the total sample of adolescents, and provided the ASSO team with the information needed to guide the project's strategy towards achieving objectives, identifying activities and processes that needed amendments.

A sample of 100 boys and girls aged 14 to 17 years was recruited from three of the selected high schools in Palermo, including one lyceum, one technical and one professional institute, to conduct this study in the year 2011-2012. This preliminary study highlighted different technical and procedural issues, related both to the developed tools and the software structure, which subsequently led to modification and adaptation of the tools and the application software for a more accurate data collection.

Different issues arose during the tools development. In general, the few initially open-ended questions were converted into closed-ended questions. Sometime the questions' structure was changed in order to obtain a more accurate answer. When numerical answers had to be given, some student provided implausible responses; hence limited ranges were imposed for the reply in the software's structure. Some terms were not understandable by all students, therefore they were exchanged with more suitable ones; alternatively some legend was introduced.

With regards to the question related to parent's occupation in the ASSO-PIQ, the 9 categories of the ISTAT classification CP2011 (http://cp2011.istat.it/), which were obtained through an adaptation of the International Standard Classification of Occupations - ISCO08, were initially considered. Since they resulted too long and time consuming for the students, a shorter classification was carefully created including only four main occupation categories.

*Figure 4. Snapshot of the ASSO-NutFit interface with Administrators registering Institutes and teachers from each school*

The ASSO-FFQ was the most challenging questionnaire. Its first version was too long and time consuming. A shorter version was then suggested, by slightly modifying the EFSA classification and deleting or incorporating some groups such as the whole pasta/rice/couscous with different types of condiments, which was integrated into a unique group of pasta/rice/couscous.

The quantification of the portion size was identified using units such as "number" (e.g. number of dried fruits, nuts, biscuits, candies/chewing gums), that were initially grouped into classes and subsequently substituted by a slider that quantified the exactly amount. The same thing was suggested for the number of bottles of water, soft drinks and energy drinks.

Cocoa powder intake was not included as a subgroup for the sweets group, but the feasibility study evidenced that many adolescents consume this product; therefore it was added in the main questionnaire. Different students also eat "crepes" (pancakes) as a sweet, thus they were introduced as a subgroup in the sweets group. Salted crepes, anyway, together with precooked food and quiches were also a commonly eaten food in the territory, and therefore included as a subgroup under "other foods". In the first version, cream and béchamel were not included in the fat group, and since many students often consumed these products as condiment for the pasta, this was added to the fat group. The box relative to the extra virgin olive oil was initially divided from the olive oil in this main group, but then the two boxes were collapsed.

*Figure 5. Snapshot of the ASSO-NutFit interface with the ASSO-FFQ compiled by the students*

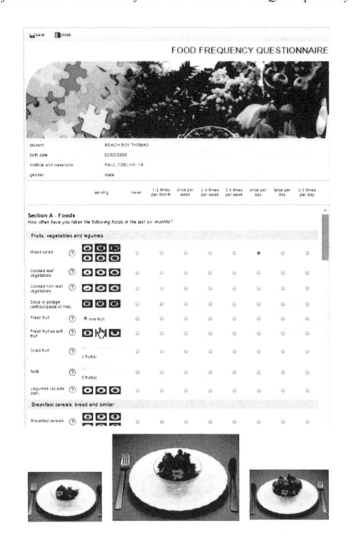

In the first ASSO-FFQ there was no question for the assessment of episodes of binge drinking (five or more drinks in a row), a phenomenon that is quite frequent in adolescence. Thus, a question was introduced to assess eventual episodes of binge drinking.

The classification of supplements was difficult in the first stage, as a wide range of types exist on the market; moreover, a database with all the nutrient components does not exist. It was, therefore, necessary to create such a database and include it within the ASSO-FFQ.

Some issues were highlighted in the structure of the ASSO-NutFit software. The software architecture was based on J2EE paradigm, using ZK Framework library to enhance user experience and following the same interface interaction as the common desktop applications. The application was based on a pluggable component and event-driven programming model; therefore, the platform was open to other developers to add functions to respond to events of components that were triggered by user interaction, such as adding supplementary validation procedure, or different input controls.

The use of Hibernate component in the platform architecture was made to maintain isolation from having to know the underlying database; so, it's possible to enhance the platform using a more powerful commercial database engine, to reach desired scalability. Hibernate, in fact, makes use of the database and configuration data to provide persistence services (and persistent objects) to the application.

### 3.2.2.3 The ASSO-NutFit Final Software

The final versions of the tools, software and procedures were then realized, and the study was extended to the whole sample population, consisting in more than 1,000 students. A huge quantity of data was retrieved, and while most of them have been elaborated, a part is still being analyzed. The results of statistical analyses do not fall within the aims of the present chapter. They will be found in future publications.

The created database shows that collected data are quite complete, valid, plausible and clear, and the partial elaboration guaranteed by the NutFit software made them suitable for a fast statistical analysis. No issues arose from the high number of data collected (e.g. server capacity). The time used for the data collection was acceptable (75 min for each student) and satisfaction of students and teachers was accomplished through an interview administered after the intervention.

### 3.2.2.4 Website Development

A website of the project (http://www.assoproject.info) was built up in order to disseminate the project's contents and allow collaboration between the researchers involved. User data synchronization was maintained between the website and the ASSO-toolkit to send communications to different actors involved (students, teachers).

## 3.2.3 Sampling, Recruiting and Training

### 3.2.3.1. Sampling and Recruiting

Public and private high schools of every type (lyceum, technical institute and professional institute) were all represented in the study with the aim of including all the socio-economic levels of Palermo city. A multistage sampling was applied for the schools and subjects' selection. The total sample size was calculated for an estimate precision of ±3% and CI 95%, evaluated in accordance to the frequency of overweight/obese subjects of 25% in Southern Italy (HBSC Study 2011). A required sample size of 800 subjects was calculated. However, relevant literature shows that the attrition rate in such studies is around 37% (Moreno, 2003), therefore, an over-sampling proportional to the questionnaire completion was required to make the total sample size of 1,096 (800+296). Hence, as seven schools were selected, it was necessary to collect around 160 students per school, which corresponded to around six classes per school, for a total of 1,021 students.

Seven secondary schools were recruited, including one private and six public institutes; the first four classes were considered, since in the fifth classes many students aged 18 or more were present. A class was considered eligible if the participation rate was at least 85%, and when this rate was not reached, that class was excluded and another class in the same year was chosen in the same school.

All students were provided with an information sheet about the Project and an informed consent form to be signed by their parents/guardians. Obtaining signed consent was the first criteria to consider the subject eligible. The number of obtained signed consent forms was 919, with a total non-respondents percentage of 22.8%. The reasons of non-participation were investigated, and almost 92% declared that the reason for non-adhering the survey laid on privacy issues and was connected to the sensitive data that should have been provided. A small percentage (6%) was not aware of the reasons why their parents did not sign the consent form, while the rest refused to respond.

Disabled students and all those students for whom a proper collection of data was not possible, were initially included in the study but not included in the database for data elaboration and analysis.

All sensitive data were protected according to the Italian privacy law n.196/2003. For the registration of participants, an identification code (i.e. the fiscal code) was used instead of name and surname.

### 3.2.3.2. Training

All teachers involved in the schools were subjected to a four hour training session in the afternoon, with the aim of standardizing the methodologies for data collection and well manage materials and tools. Different PowerPoint presentations and a specially designed web-based tutorial for the compilation of food records were created and shown. The ASSO team showed a live demo of the application, and explained in detail how to access the software, complete the online questionnaires and include fitness data. The Standard Operating Procedures (SOP) developed by the team and described further on in this paper, and all needed materials, were distributed to the teachers during the training session.

In a second four-hour afternoon session, each physical activity teacher participating the previous session completed reliable measures on approximately 10 volunteer participants and was certified for body composition and fitness measurements. Intraobserver reliability was higher than 95%; interobserver reliability was higher than 90% (Moreno, 2003).

## 4. THE ASSO EVALUATION FOR APPLICABILITY AS A SURVEILLANCE SYSTEM

An ASSO Project evaluation was completed according to a SWOT analysis to identify strengths, weaknesses, opportunities and threats (Humphrey, 2005), and according to the guidelines provided by the CDC (German, 2001). This evaluation was performed by the ASSO staff members involved in the design and management of the Project and other staff members, such as teachers selected within the schools.

The results of the SWOT analysis are listed in Figure 6, and system attributes are showed in Figure 7.

Firstly, the ASSO system is focused on a disease that is considered an emergent public health issue, of public interest and highly preventable; as the public health importance of health-related events are influenced by their level of preventability (German, 2001), the system should be considered a priority for the National Health System (NHS). Moreover, the possibility of easily adapting this system to younger populations of schoolchildren can shift the prevention to that age as well, thus making the system even more efficient. The health costs related to obesity would be reduced, as well as eventual inequities related to the access to public health cares.

The usefulness of the ASSO surveillance system lies in the possible effective dissemination of health data so that decision makers at all levels can readily understand the implications of the information (Teutsch & Thacker, 1995). Options for disseminating the collected data include electronic data interchange, public-use data files, the Internet, press releases, reports, newsletters, publication in scientific journals, and poster and oral presentations. The audiences for disseminated information include public

*Figure 6. Results emerged from the Strengths, Weaknesses, Opportunities, and Threats (SWOT) analysis of the Adolescence Surveillance System for the Obesity Prevention Project (ASSO)*

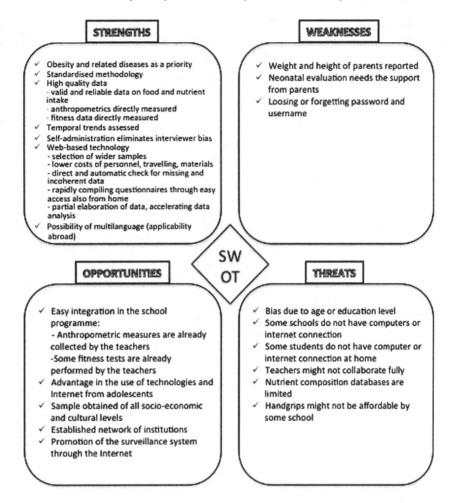

health practitioners, health-care providers, members of affected communities, professional and voluntary organizations, policymakers, the press, and the general public. These data are useful to detect obesity and all associated diseases in adolescents; monitor trends in obesity; identify obesity risk factors; allow assessment of the effect of prevention and control programs; stimulate research intended to lead to prevention or control of obesity.

The web-based technology allows the selection of wider samples; the lower costs of personnel, travelling, materials; the direct and automatic check for missing and incoherent data; the possibility of rapidly compiling questionnaires through easy access also from home; the partial elaboration of data (means and percentages are automatically estimated; BMI and weight status are automatically calculated, as well as other variables such as family affluence scale, etc.), thus accelerating data analysis; and the possibility of multilanguage, that provides the potential to be extended abroad, to deliver a complete framework with the possibility of regional comparisons for information on adolescent lifestyles. A characteristic of the ASSO, in fact, is its flexibility, that allows modifying fewer components in order to adapting the system to other realities. Moreover, it is based on electronic data that could easily be integrated with

*Figure 7. The ASSO system attributes many strengths and opportunities were underlined together with important attributes of the system.*

| ASSO system attributes | Description |
|---|---|
| High public health importance | Focused on an emergent public health issue: obesity in adolescents |
| Useful | Data collected and disseminated by the ASSO system can be used by different stakeholders, the press, and the general public. These data are useful to detect obesity and all associated diseases and their trends in adolescents; identify obesity risk factors; suggest prevention and control programs against obesity. |
| Flexible | There is the possibility of easily modifying the tools included in the ASSO-NutFit software and adapting to other realities |
| Providing high quality and sensitive data | Collected data are complete and valid, due to the highly standardized procedures, and to the validity and reproducibility of the tools developed |
| Acceptable | The students refusal rate was 22.8%. Satisfaction by all the involved actors (personnel and students) was assessed. The system has the ability to protect privacy and confidentiality |
| Timeliness | Data are made available after only 3 months after survey completion. |
| Stable | Able to collect and manage data properly without failure for most of the time needed |
| Simple | Moderate simplicity, since data collection is labor intensive and requires expertise and complex survey design; however, staff training and method of managing data and analyse them are simple; time spent on maintaining the system is short; integration with related system is easy. |
| Representative | The system is representative of the adolescent population, of different socio-economic and cultural level, from urban and non urban areas. After a scale-up at national level, it can be representative of all geographical population of adolescents |

other existing systems. Another advantage of the system is the possibility of online staff training; in fact, beyond the on-site sessions, the staff training could be performed also on-line through a web-based procedure that uses the developed SOP and interactive tutorials.

The establishment of a highly standardized methodology with SOPs in ASSO allows all the involved operators to perform their activities following precise indications that guarantee a high quality, validity and reproducibility of collected data. ASSO helps identifying risk indicators and correctly addressing overweight/obesity in adolescents; e.g data collected on health and obesity determinants have been used to determine a combined effect of the socio-demographic variables, early factors and lifestyles and identify different patterns and groups of young people more at risk that should be prioritized in interventions (submitted for publication). The system provides accurate data on food consumptions, by using a validated and reproducible FFQ; it correctly estimates food habits and lifestyles, as all the questionnaires used for their assessment have been developed following high standards and expert consultations. It helps identifying disease symptoms that could be predictor of future diseases in adolescents, through a properly performed and validated malaise index estimated in a subsection of the PIQ; these data have been used to develop an index of malaise a score for classifying adolescents in different malaise level categories (submitted for publication). It collects anthropometric measure directly, thus providing accurate estimates of the obesity status in the adolescent population, as well as their overall health and nutritional status, thus the system can be considered very sensitive. It correctly and completely estimates fitness levels of adolescent, by the application of a test battery accurately selected and validated through the support of national and international expertise; these data were useful to develop a fitness score to categorize adolescents in fitness levels (Bianco, 2015). The system also would allow the identification of trends over time, leading to improved behavioural practices and stimulating research on the prevention and control of obesity.

ASSO could be considered in general as an acceptable system according to: the satisfactory subjects participation rate with low refusal rates; the completeness of the obtained questionnaires; the satisfaction degree by all the involved actors (personnel and students); the ability of the system to protect privacy and confidentiality. It has been observed that students acquired more awareness on the quality and quantity of their consumed food and on their fitness abilities.

Timeliness is another important attribute of the system, since data can be made available after only 3 months after survey completion.

The system could be considered stable since it is able to collect, manage, and provide data properly without failure for most of the time needed.

A moderate simplicity has been evidenced within the system, since data collection is labor intensive and requires expertise and complex survey design. However, staff training is simple, method of managing data (including time spent on transferring, entering, editing, storing, and backing up data) and their analysis is simple; time spent on maintaining the system is short; integration with related systems could be easy.

Regarding representativeness, the system is representative of the adolescent population, belonging to different socio-economic and cultural level, from urban and non urban areas. After a scale-up at the national level, it can be representative of all geographical population of adolescents.

Few weaknesses and threats were detected (Figure 6). Some of them are linked with the availability and access to the Internet connection and on the stability of the server; in fact, this could delay the time for collecting data: e.g. in the day established for questionnaire compilation in the school (or at home) an outage of the server may occur; computers in the school could break down and need time for repairing; when exporting data for the analysis the server could be unavailable.

Another weakness of the system consists in the need of parents' advice when compiling the questionnaire's part related to the neonatal evaluation and in the weight and height of parents that are reported. Furthermore, students often lose or forget their password and username to access their own email address, or they forget to write the password that is automatically sent by the system to access the application.

Specific threats identified were the possibility that some schools do not have computers or internet connection, or some students do not have a computer or internet connection at home. Moreover, issues related to the school staff collaboration were identified, as well as the handgrips instruments that are not sometime affordable by the schools.

One issue was also found on the nutrient composition databases that are often limited and different from one country to another.

Another limitation concerns the representativeness of the system. Data collected within ASSO are also used to identify groups at high risk and to target and evaluate interventions; sometime these data collection could lead to different results when gender is considered; e.g. females estimate their food intake better than males, thus the ASSO-FFQ is more valid for assessing food and nutrient intake in females rather than in males, and this could lead to misleading conclusions about the risk factors associated to obesity.

Moreover, for the nature of this "pioneering" project, the sample collected so far is not representative of the entire Italian population, and an important issue will have to be solved with regard to the financial resources that will be potentially used for sustaining the implementation and maintenance of the proposed system at national level.

## 5. SOLUTIONS AND RECOMMENDATIONS

As mentioned above, ASSO is a web-based system, thus it relies on the availability and access to an Internet connection and on the stability of the server. Since this is an issue not depending on the ASSO system itself, the only solution in the case of a connection failing on the fixed day of the questionnaire filling is to postpone the day of the administration.

Moreover, among the identified *threats*, the possibility that some schools do not have computers or internet connection still exists, as well as some students that do not have computer or internet connection at home. This limits the accessibility to the system and those schools presumably could not participate in the data collection. It is thus recommended that those who are responsible of the school recruiting get information about the existence of computer halls within the schools and their connection capacity.

Other issues concern the need of parents' advices when compiling the questionnaire's part related to the neonatal evaluation, and the fact that weight and height of parents are reported. It is recommended that teachers show and explain the question to the students the day before the questionnaire administration, and they advice students to ask help their parents so they can be ready when filling the questionnaire.

In the phase of enabling students to have access to the software, it has been noted that students often lose or forget their password (pw) and username to access their own email address, or they forget to record the pw that is automatically sent by the system to access the application. In these cases the recommendation is that teacher record the pw on a sheet and keep it in case the student forgets it, always respecting privacy issues; moreover, teachers should make students to feel responsible for their pw and username memorization.

Some concerns related to the school staff collaboration were identified, with some of teachers complaining about the time spent collecting data through the system, even though, as previously mentioned, the time requested is really affordable and short. A possible recommendation is that the school dean organizes brief meetings aimed to train teachers on the importance of collecting such data.

It has been noted also that the handgrip instruments are sometimes not affordable for the schools. In this case the recommendation is to collect the other data, in order to have as much information as possible.

One issue was also found on the nutrient composition databases that are often limited and different from one country to another. So, if the system has to be adopted in other countries, it is necessary to make some modifications on the databases used for the conversion from food consumption to nutrient intakes. The same problem regards the typical local foods, which should be modified within the ASSO-FFQ according to the country where the questionnaire has to be administrated.

Since the system is only moderately simple, with data collection being labor intensive and requiring expertise and complex survey design, although a short collection training, the recommendation is that some improvements in funding methods that facilitate the administration should be searched.

With regard to the representativeness of the system, the fact that it is more valid for assessing food and nutrient intake in females rather than in males can be solved by introducing correction factors when analyzing the data.

Moreover, since the sample collected so far is not representative of the entire Italian population, a study extended to the territory is needed to evaluate the system as a whole.

As mentioned in the previous session, an important issue to be solved is the financial resources used for sustaining the implementation and maintenance of the proposed system at national level. An accurate estimation of the national health expenses in this field should be conducted. Unfortunately, this estimation is very complex, but some data exist related to Europe. Studies in the WHO European Region indicate that the direct health care costs of obesity account for 2–4% of national health expenditure (Fry & Finley, 2005), these including the direct costs of health services, the indirect costs associated with lost economic production and individual costs, such as the purchase of slimming products. Among the direct costs, a great part of them is due to the treatment of cardiovascular diseases, hypertension and type II diabetes. These high costs associated with obesity and unhealthy lifestyles demonstrate that savings may result from health promotion and prevention, at least in the short term; even though the long-term health savings are not known, obesity prevention programs will almost certainly lead to both short- and long-term gains in economic productivity (Branca, 2007). Hence, it is hypothetical that the costs of maintaining a surveillance system on obesity and lifestyles could be sustainable. These costs would be referred to the costs within the Institutions involved (Ministry of Health, Regional Health Commissions, Regional Education Offices and the University), related to: personnel, that includes the time to operate the system, such as contacting Institutions, editing and analyzing data, and disseminating data; computer and other equipment (software for statistical analysis), telephone, mailing and media; server where store data; printed material for dissemination. Since the system is web-based, there are no costs of travelling and collecting data. Nevertheless, a quantitative analysis of the costs should be done after applying the system at a national level.

A proposed flow chart of the national and local Institutions that should interact in the ASSO system implementation and maintenance is shown here (Figure 8). The web-based system was designed to be available for all schools and super-administered by a leading institution, which provide directions to the other administrators in the regional focal points. As it can be evinced, a network between Ministry of Health/Regional Health Commissions, Universities and Regional Education Offices was established, that could contribute in a synergic way to achieving the objectives. The Ministry of Health would have the role of contacting the Regional Health Commissions, which in their turn would interact with the Regional Education Offices to recruit schools and provide them access to the web platform and training sessions. The data collected within the schools could be analyzed by researchers from University and results can be later diffused to the Regional Health Commissions, the Ministry of Health, and to the public.

## 6. FUTURE RESEARCH DIRECTIONS

The results from this chapter provide evidence that a surveillance system based on e-technology could be appealing for adolescents and effective in the health data collection particularly related to obesity, lifestyle, food consumptions and fitness. As previously mentioned, the other national surveillance system on adolescent lifestyles in the Italian territory is the paper-based HBSC system carried out by the Regional Health Commissions as well. What it is suggested and proposed in this chapter for the future is

*Figure 8. Flow chart of the possible interrelations between the Institutions involved in the surveillance system proposed by the Adolescence Surveillance System for the Obesity Prevention Project (ASSO)*

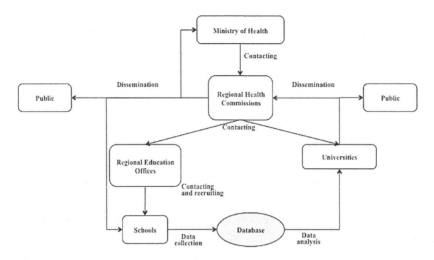

that an effort should be made to integrate these two systems, through a dialogue and an evaluation of all the different and common characteristics between the two systems and related critical issues. This could prevent duplication of efforts and lack of standardization that can arise from parallel analogous systems (Morris, 1996). E.g. the ASSO system first of all could provide web-based data, that, compared to HBSC paper-based data, are easier to be managed and analysed and allow saving of human and economical resources; it can integrate the HBSC lack of validated and reproducible data on food consumptions; it can provide measured anthropometric parameters on adolescents, which are missing at the moment; finally, it is the first system providing fitness data of adolescents, that are commonly good markers of health.

It is to be noted that the HBSC is running in all Europe, this suggesting that the ASSO system could be adopted as such in all European territory, after the appropriate amendments. Thus, a first proposed step should be moved to the scaling-up of the system at Italian level, in order to assess the sustainability of a huge database on scholars' information, together with agreements signed by the Institutions involved. Subsequently, the system could be adapted to the different countries and used as national surveillance organism.

Different stakeholders could benefit from such a lifestyle surveillance system. Although the system was designed to be allocated by the Ministry of Health in the schools free of charge, it can be relevant also within some business environments. Amongst them, private sport and athletic centers, or sport societies, which are interested in the assessment of nutritional and fitness status of adolescents, could purchase the ASSO e-toolkit in order to quickly and reliably obtain data and improve nutritional and training plans. Similarly, weight loss clinics, wellness centers or centers to treat eating disorders could use the ASSO e-questionnaires to perform a detailed dietary and lifestyle history of the adolescent patient. These centers can have access to the e-platform, and to the database, thus managing collected data and comparing them throughout time. food supply, e.g. food availability and composition of foods food reformulation and food labelling food fortification nutritional supplements.

## 7. CONCLUSION

The present chapter provides a detailed overview of the ASSO Project's design and implementation and describes the results of its evaluation process as a national surveillance system in all Europe.

The ASSO web-based system design was based on the state of the art research in the lifestyle assessments specifically for teenagers, and it is consistent with the country needs and priorities. Through the developed toolkits, it allows the collection of valid and reliable data on adolescents' obesity, food consumptions, meal patterns and habits, alcohol, smoking, physical activity, fitness and sedentariness, and biological/genetic, and socio-cultural/environmental characteristics of adolescents, not only at school but also at home and in different times of the year. The system is quite easy and fast to use and well-accepted by the users, and its standardized methodology makes it reproducible in different arenas.

The ASSO e-toolkit was designed to be administered by a leading institution that could give directions to the local government. It could provide live and current evidence-based conclusions and facilitate a network between the Ministry of Health and schools.

Even though few weak points and threats were identified, they are not likely to undermine the basic objectives and feasibility of the system. The emerged strengths and opportunities suggested that the ASSO system was valid and effective at the local level. A scale-up of the system is needed in order to test the feasibility on the whole territory. Results obtained confirm that it could be adopted within the National Health Service representing a permanent source of high quality and standardized data to help identify risk factors and implement appropriate preventive actions.

The application of such a surveillance system on a large scale could have a significant impact on national public health services. The result would be an improvement in the efficacy and the quality of the surveillance and prevention in the field of nutrition and physical activity at a national level. Accurate reports could be drawn and relevant measures could be applied when necessary, all within a synergic way to achieving the government, the EU objectives and possible saving future lives. Obesity and chronic diseases policies and interventions can be translated into a decrease in the burden of disease, thus improving population health and reducing economical public expenses.

## REFERENCES

Bailey, R., Hillman, C., Arent, S., & Petitpas, A. (2013). Physical Activity: An Underestimated Investment in Human Capital? Richard Bailey, Charles Hillman, Shawn Arent, and Albert Petitpas. *Journal of Physical Activity & Health*, 10(3), 289–308. doi:10.1123/jpah.10.3.289 PMID:23620387

Bertoli, S., Petroni, M. L., Pagliato, E., Mora, S., Weber, G., Chiumello, G., & Testolin, G. (2005). Validation of food frequency questionnaire for assessing dietary macronutrients and calcium intake in Italian children and adolescents. *Journal of Pediatric Gastroenterology and Nutrition*, 40(5), 555–560. doi:10.1097/01.MPG.0000153004.53610.0E PMID:15861015

Bhurosy, T., & Jeewon, R. (2014). Overweight and Obesity Epidemic in Developing Countries: A Problem with Diet, Physical Activity, or Socioeconomic Status? *TheScientificWorldJournal*. doi:10.1155/2014/964236 PMID:25379554

Bianco, A., Jemni, M., Ramos, J., Thomas, E., & Tabacchi, G. (2015a). A systematic review to determine reliability and usefulness of the field-based test battery for the assessment of physical fitness in adolescents. The ASSO project. *International Journal of Occupational Medicine and Environmental Health*, *28*(3), 445–478. doi:10.13075/ijomeh.1896.00393 PMID:26190724

Bianco, A., Palma, A., Jemni, M., Filippi, A. R., Patti, A., Thomas, E., & Tabacchi, G. et al. (2015b). A fitness index model for Italian adolescents living in Southern Italy. The ASSO project. *The Journal of Sports Medicine and Physical Fitness*, (Oct), 16. PMID:26472604

Bleich, S.N., Ku, R., & Wang, Y.C. (2011). Relative contribution of energy intake and energy expenditure to childhood obesity: a review of the literature and directions for future research. *International Journal of Obesity*, *35*(1), 1–15. doi: pmid:2111966910.1038/ijo.2010.252

Branca, F., Nikogosian, H., & Lobstein, T. (Eds.). (2007). *The Challenge of Obesity in the WHO European Region and the Strategies for Response*. Copenhagen, Denmark: World Health Organization Regional Office for Europe.

Brener, N., Kann, L., Shanklin, S., Kinchen, S., Eaton, D. K., Hawkins, J., & Flint, K. H. (2013). Methodology of the Youth Risk Behavior Surveillance System -. *MMWR. Recommendations and Reports*, *62*(1). Retrieved from http://www.cdc.gov/mmwr/pdf/rr/rr6201.pdf PMID:23446553

Buehler, J. W. (1998). Surveillance. In K. J. Rothman & S. Greenland (Eds.), *Modern epidemiology* (2nd ed.). Philadelphia, PA: Lippencott-Raven.

Buijs, G. (2009). Better schools through health: Networking for health promoting schools in Europe. *European Journal of Education*, *44*(4), 507–520. doi:10.1111/j.1465-3435.2009.01410.x

Centers for Disease Control and Prevention. (1997). Guidelines for School and Community Programs to Promote Lifelong Physical Activity Among Young People. *Morbidity and Mortality Weekly Report*, *46*(RR-6), 1–36. PMID:9072670

Centers for Disease Control and Prevention. (2011). School Health Guidelines to Promote Healthy Eating and Physical Activity. *MMWR*, *60*(5), 1–80. PMID:21918496

Currie, C., Nic Gabhainn, S., & Godeau, E.International HBSC Network Coordinating Committee. (2009). The Health Behaviour in School-aged Children: WHO Collaborative Cross-National (HBSC) Study: origins, concept, history and development 1982–2008. *International Journal of Public Health*, *54*(2), 131–139. doi:10.1007/s00038-009-5404-x PMID:19639260

Cvejić, D. P. T., & Ostojić, S. (2013). Assessment of physical fitness in children and adolescents. *Physical Education and Sport*, *11*(2), 135–145.

De Bourdeaudhuij, I., van Cauwenberghe, E., Spittaels, H., Oppert, J. M., Rostami, C., Brug, J., & Maes, L. et al. (2010). School-based interventions promoting both physical activity and healthy eating in Europe: A systematic review within the HOPE project. *Obesity Reviews*, *12*(3), 205–216. doi:10.1111/j.1467-789X.2009.00711.x PMID:20122137

European Centre for Disease Prevention and Control. (2008). *Surveillance of communicable diseases in the European Union. A long-term strategy: 2008–2013*. Stockholm: ECDC.

European Centre for Disease Prevention and Control. (2014). *Data quality monitoring and surveillance system evaluation – A handbook of methods and applications.* Stockholm: ECDC.

European Food Safety Authority. (2011). Evaluation of the FoodEx, the food classification system applied to the development of the EFSA Comprehensive European Food Consumption Database. *EFSA Journal, 9*(3), 1970. doi:10.2903/j.efsa.2011.1970

European Union. (2014). Special Eurobarometer 412. Sport and physical activity (Report). Retrieved from http://ec.europa.eu/health/nutrition_physical_activity/docs/ebs_412_en.pdf

European Union (EU). (2014). *EU Action Plan on Childhood Obesity 2014–2020.* Online.

Filippi, A., Amodio, E., Napoli, G., Breda, J., Bianco, A., Jemni, M., & Tabacchi, G. et al. (2014). The web-based ASSO-food frequency questionnaire for adolescents: Relative and absolute reproducibility assessment.[Internet].*Nutrition Journal, 13*(1), 119. Retrieved from http://nutritionj.biomedcentral.com/articles/10.1186/1475-2891-13-119 doi:10.1186/1475-2891-13-119 PMID:25518876

Frank, L. D., Andresen, M. A., & Schmid, T. L. (2004). Obesity relationships with community design, physical activity, and time spent in cars. *American Journal of Preventive Medicine, 27*(2), 87–96. Retrieved from http://www.ajpmonline.org/article/S0749-3797(04)00087-X/pdf doi:10.1016/j.amepre.2004.04.011 PMID:15261894

Freedman, D. S., Khan, L. K., Serdula, M. K., Dietz, W. H., Srinivasan, S. R., & Berenson, G. S. (2005). The relation of childhood BMI to adult adiposity: The Bogalusa Heart Study. *Pediatrics, 115*(1), 22–27. doi:10.1542/peds.2004-0220 PMID:15629977

Fry, J., & Finley, W. (2005). The prevalence and costs of obesity in the EU. *The Proceedings of the Nutrition Society, 64*(3), 359–362. doi:10.1079/PNS2005443 PMID:16048669

German, R.R., Lee, L.M., Horan, J.M., Milstein, R.L., Pertowski, C.A., & Waller, M.N. (2001). Guidelines Working Group Centers for Disease Control and Prevention (CDC). Updated guidelines for evaluating public health surveillance systems: recommendations from the Guidelines Working Group.

Gortmaker, S. L., Peterson, K., Wiecha, J., Sobol, A. M., Dixit, S., Fox, M. K., & Laird, N. (1999). Reducing Obesity via a School-Based Interdisciplinary Intervention Among Youth: Planet Health. *Archives of Pediatrics & Adolescent Medicine, 153*(4), 409–418. doi:10.1001/archpedi.153.4.409 PMID:10201726

Gortmaker, S. L., Swinburn, B. A., Levy, D., Carter, R., Mabry, P. L., Finegood, D. T., & Moodie, M. L. et al. (2011). Changing the future of obesity: Science, policy, and action. *Lancet, 378*(9793), 838–847. doi:10.1016/S0140-6736(11)60815-5 PMID:21872752

HBSC. (2016a). *4th Italian report from the international study HBSC* (F. Cavallo, P. Lemma, P. Dalmasso, A. Vieno, G. Lazzeri, & D. Galeone, Eds.).

HBSC (2016b). Growing up unequal: gender and socioeconomic differences in young people's health and well-being (International Report from the 2013/2014 Survey). Health Policy for children and adolescents.

Hills, A. P., King, N. A., & Armstrong, T. P. (2007). The contribution of physical activity and sedentary behaviours to the growth and development of children and adolescents: Implications for overweight and obesity. *Sports Medicine, 37*(6), 533–545. doi:10.2165/00007256-200737060-00006 PMID:17503878

Hoelscher, D. M., Day, R. S., Kelder, S. H., & Ward, J. L. (2003). Reproducibility and validity of the secondary level School-Based Nutrition Monitoring student questionnaire. *Journal of the American Dietetic Association, 103*(2), 186–194. doi:10.1053/jada.2003.50031 PMID:12589324

Hong, T. K., Dibley, M. J., & Sibbritt, D. (2010). Validity and reliability of an FFQ for use with adolescents in Ho Chi Minh City, Vietnam. *Public Health Nutrition, 13*(3), 368–375. Retrieved from http://www.ncbi.nlm.nih.gov/pubmed/19706213 doi:10.1017/S136898000999125X PMID:19706213

Humphrey, A. S. (2005). SWOT Analysis for Management Consulting. *SRI Alumni Assoc Newsletters, 7*, 8. Retrieved from http://www.sri.com/sites/default/files/brochures/dec-05.pdf

Illner, A. K., Freisling, H., Boeing, H., Huybrechts, I., Crispim, S. P., & Slimani, N. (2012). Review and evaluation of innovative technologies for measuring diet in nutritional epidemiology. *International Journal of Epidemiology, 41*(4), 1187–1203. doi:10.1093/ije/dys105 PMID:22933652

Italia, H. B. S. C. (2011). Stili di vita e salute dei giovani in età scolare - Rapporto sui dati regionali HBSC 2009 -2010. Istituto Superiore di Sanità. Retrieved from http://www.hbsc.unito.it/it/images/pdf/hbsc/sicilia_report_hbsc_2010.pdf

Lissner, L., Wijnhoven, T. M. A., Mehlig, K., Sjöberg, A., Kunesova, M., Yngve, A., & Breda, J. et al. (2016). Socioeconomic inequalities in childhood overweight: Heterogeneity across five countries in the WHO European Childhood Obesity Surveillance Initiative (COSI–2008). *International Journal of Obesity, 40*(5), 796–802. doi:10.1038/ijo.2016.12 PMID:27136760

Matthys, C., Pynaert, I., De Keyzer, W., & De Henauw, S. (2007). Validity and reproducibility of an adolescent web-based food frequency questionnaire. *Journal of the American Dietetic Association, 107*(4), 605–610. Retrieved from http://www.sciencedirect.com/science/article/pii/S0002822307000247 doi:10.1016/j.jada.2007.01.005 PMID:17383266

Moore, H. J., Ells, L. J., McLure, S. A., Crooks, S., Cumbor, D., Summerbell, C. D., & Batterham, A. M. (2008). The development and evaluation of a novel computer program to assess previous-day dietary and physical activity behaviours in school children: The Synchronised Nutrition and Activity ProgramTM (SNAPTM). *The British Journal of Nutrition, 99*(06), 1266–1274. doi:10.1017/S0007114507862428 PMID:18042307

Morbidity and Mortality Weekly Report (MMWR). (2011). School Health Guidelines to Promote Healthy Eating and Physical Activity. *Recommendations and Reports, 60*(RR05), 1-71.

Moreno, L. A., Joyanes, M., Mesana, M. I., González-Gross, M., Gil, C. M., Sarría, A., & Marcos, A. et al.AVENA Study Group. (2003). Harmonization of anthropometric measurements for a multicenter nutrition survey in Spanish adolescents. *Nutrition (Burbank, Los Angeles County, Calif.), 19*(6), 481–486. doi:10.1016/S0899-9007(03)00040-6 PMID:12781845

Morris, G., Snider, D., & Katz, M. (1996). Integrating public health information and surveillance systems. *Journal of Public Health Management and Practice, 2*(4), 24–27. doi:10.1097/00124784-199623000-00007 PMID:10186689

Ng, M., Fleming, T., Robinson, M., Thomson, B., Graetz, N., & Margono, C. et al.. (2014). Global, regional and national prevalence of overweight and obesity in children and adults 19802013: A systematic analysis. *Lancet, 384*(9945), 766–781. Retrieved from https://www.ncbi.nlm.nih.gov/pmc/articles/ PMC4624264/ doi:10.1016/S0140-6736(14)60460-8 PMID:24880830

Popkin, B. M., Adair, L. S., & Ng, S. W. (2012). Now and then: The Global Nutrition Transition: The Pandemic of Obesity in Developing Countries. *Nutrition Reviews, 70*(1), 3–21. doi:10.1111/j.1753-4887.2011.00456.x PMID:22221213

Robinson, T. N. (1999). Reducing Children's Television Viewing to Prevent Obesity: A Randomized Controlled Trial. *Journal of the American Medical Association, 282*(16), 1561–1567. doi:10.1001/ jama.282.16.1561 PMID:10546696

Shatenstein, B., Amre, D., Jabbour, M., & Feguery, H. (2010). Examining the relative validity of an adult food frequency questionnaire in children and adolescents. *Journal of Pediatric Gastroenterology and Nutrition, 51*(5), 645–652. doi:10.1097/MPG.0b013e3181eb6881 PMID:20871415

Simovska, V., Dadaczynski, K., & Woynarowska, B. (2012). Healthy eating and physical activity in schools in Europe: A toolkit for policy development and its implementation. *Health Education, 112*(6), 513–524. doi:10.1108/09654281211275863

Storey, K. E. (2015). A changing landscape: Web-based methods for dietary assessment in adolescents. *Current Opinion in Clinical Nutrition and Metabolic Care, 18*(5), 437–445. doi:10.1097/ MCO.0000000000000198 PMID:26125112

Svensson, A. (2014). *Assessment of dietary intake in young populations using new approaches and technologies*. Umeå, Sweden: Print & Media. Retrieved from http://umu.diva-portal.org/

Swinburn, B. A., Sacks, G., Hall, K. D., McPherson, K., Finegood, D. T., Moodie, M. L., & Gortmaker, S. L. (2011). The global obesity pandemic: Shaped by global drivers and local environments. *Lancet, 378*(9793), 804–814. doi:10.1016/S0140-6736(11)60813-1 PMID:21872749

Tabacchi, G., Amodio, E., Di Pasquale, M., Bianco, A., Jemni, M., & Mammina, C. (2014). Validation and reproducibility of dietary assessment methods in adolescents: A systematic literature review. *Public Health Nutrition, 17*(12), 2700–2714. doi:10.1017/S1368980013003157 PMID:24476625

Tabacchi, G., Filippi, A., Amodio, E., Jemni, M., Bianco, A., Firenze, A., & Mammina, C. (2015). A meta-analysis of the validity of food frequency questionnaires targeted to adolescents. *Public Health Nutrition, 19*(7), 1168–1183. doi:10.1017/S1368980015002505 PMID:26354204

Tabacchi, G., Filippi, A. R., Breda, J., Censi, L., Amodio, E., Napoli, G., & Mammina, C. et al. (2015). Comparative validity of the ASSO Food Frequency Questionnaire for the web-based assessment of food and nutrients intake in adolescents. *Food Nutrition Research, 59*(1), 26216. doi:10.3402/fnr.v59.26216 PMID:25882537

Teutsch, S. M., & Thacker, S. B. (1995). Planning a public health surveillance system. *Epidemiological Bulletin: Pan American Health Organization, 16*, 1–6. PMID:7794696

UNICEF, WHO, World Bank. (2015). *Levels and trends in child malnutrition: UNICEF-WHO-World Bank joint child malnutrition estimates.* Washington, DC: World Bank.

Vereecken, C. A., Covents, M., Matthys, C., & Maes, L. (2005). Young adolescents' nutrition assessment on computer (YANA-C). *European Journal of Clinical Nutrition, 59*(5), 658–667. doi:10.1038/sj.ejcn.1602124 PMID:15741983

Vereecken, C. A., Covents, M., Sichert-Hellert, W., Alvira, J. M., Le Donne, C., De Henauw, S., & Moreno, L. A. et al.HELENA Study Group. (2008). Development and evaluation of a self-administered computerized 24-h dietary recall method for adolescents in Europe. *International Journal of Obesity, 32*(5), S26–S34. doi:10.1038/ijo.2008.180 PMID:19011650

Vereecken, C. A., De Bourdeaudhuij, I., & Maes, L. (2010). The HELENA online food frequency questionnaire: Reproducibility and comparison with four 24-hour recalls in Belgian-Flemish adolescents. *European Journal of Clinical Nutrition, 64*(5), 541–548. doi:10.1038/ejcn.2010.24 PMID:20216566

Vereecken, C. A., & Maes, L. (2006). Comparison of a computer administered and paper-and-pencil administered questionnaire on health and lifestyle behaviors. *The Journal of Adolescent Health, 38*(4), 426–432. doi:10.1016/j.jadohealth.2004.10.010 PMID:16549304

Watanabe, M., Yamaoka, K., Yokotsuka, M., Adachi, M., & Tango, T. (2011). Validity and reproducibility of the FFQ (FFQW82) for dietary assessment in female adolescents. *Public Health Nutrition, 14*(2), 297–305. doi:10.1017/S1368980010001618 PMID:20537215

WHO Regional Office for Europe. (2006, November 15–17). European charter on counteracting obesity (document EUR/06/5062700/8).

Willett, W. C. (2012). Overview of Nutritional Epidemiology. In W. C. Willett (Ed.), *Nutritional Epidemiology.* Oxford Scholar Online. doi:10.1093/acprof:oso/9780199754038.003.0001

World Health Organization. (2014). Global status report on noncommunicable diseases.

World Health Organization. (2016). WHO Library Cataloguing-in-Publication Data Report of the commission on ending childhood obesity.

# Chapter 6

# An Intelligent Ecosystem to Support the Development of Communication Skills in Children with Autism:
## An Experience Based on Ontologies, Multi-Sensory Stimulation Rooms, and Robotic Assistants

**Vladimir Robles-Bykbaev**
*Universidad Politécnica Salesiana, Ecuador*

**Martín López-Nores**
*University of Vigo, Spain*

**Jorge Andrés Galán-Mena**
*Universidad Politécnica Salesiana, Ecuador*

**Verónica Cevallos León Wong**
*Universidad Politécnica Salesiana, Ecuador*

**Diego Quisi-Peralta**
*Universidad Politécnica Salesiana, Ecuador*

**Diego Lima-Juma**
*Universidad Politécnica Salesiana, Ecuador*

**Carlos Andrés Arévalo Fernández**
*Universidad Politécnica Salesiana, Ecuador*

**José Pazos-Arias**
*University of Vigo, Spain*

## ABSTRACT

*The term Autism Spectrum Disorders (ASDs) covers conditions such as autism, childhood disintegrative disorder and Asperger syndrome. In this line, the World Health Organization (WHO) points that core symptoms of ASD are: a mixture of impaired capacity for reciprocal socio-communicative interaction and a restricted, stereotyped repetitive repertoire of interests and activities. Therefore, it is fundamental for a person with ASD to develop skills to communicate with his/her peers, share ideas, and express feelings. On those grounds, this chapter presents an intelligent ecosystem to support the development*

DOI: 10.4018/978-1-5225-2492-2.ch006

*of social communication skills in children with ASD. The ecosystem uses a knowledge model that relies on ontologies, and defines the main elements that will be used for psychological intervention process. The different activities that will be carried out during the therapeutic intervention can be done using a robotic assistant or a Multi-Sensory Stimulation Room. This proposal has been tested with 47 children of regular schools, 9 specialists on ASD, and 36 children with ASD.*

## INTRODUCTION

World Health Organization (2016) data show that 1 in 160 children present an Autism Spectrum Disorder, and some other resources (CDC, 2016) point about 1 in 68. Far from being a disease, this condition obeys to a developmental disorder, which implicates impairments in social interaction, social communication disabilities, repetitive behavior and restricted interests (American Psychiatric Association, 2014). New conceptualizations of autism are presented within the latest version of the Diagnostic Statistic Manual (American Psychiatric Association, 2014) to adjust the diagnosis to the particular characteristics of individuals. In this line, a person with Autism is diagnosticated considering the main traits of the spectrum, but also describing his/her performance in different areas such as cognition, language and the seriousness level of the main symptoms.

Children with ASD present difficulties to adjust their behavior to social situations, which frequently leads them to remain excluded from their peer group. In serious cases of autism, children may show impairments to even recognize simple conventional behavior such as associating objects with specific places or different types of behavior needed to execute simple tasks, such as using silverware correctly. Visual tools have shown to effectively enhance the development of communication and social skills, by helping the child with ASD to understand and integrate conventional information and develop social skills that may allow them to be more tolerated and accepted within the peer group.

Deficits in conventional language and communication are associated with poor social skills in this population; this demands a progressive intervention in which the child can be introduced to basic social patterns and eventually enhance his/her relationship with other significant human being. These interventions are aimed to get the child to be better tolerated and accepted by his/her peer group, by helping him/her to integrate social skills through stories presented in a visual manner.

In addition, children with ASD usually present a preference to interact with objects rather than with humans, which may cause withdraws during the therapeutic work. In this scenario, it is needed the assistance of mediators, which nowadays can be represented by robotic devices. The implementation of artifacts of this kind would reduce the anxiety that children with ASD commonly present towards the interaction with adults or peers, allowing the interventions to be more progressive and respectful with the child's particular characteristics and needs.

Neurobehavioral models of autism consider it as a "disorder of complex information processing system" in which skilled motor, complex memory and language, and reasoning domains present impairments, while, in contrast, attention, simple memory and language, and visual–spatial domains show a high level of performance (Minshew and Goldstein, 1998). Considering the fact that visual-spatial domains are a strength in these individuals, most of interventions proposed to enhance their life quality are based on visual supports, addressed to attract the child's attention, anticipate facts and reduce the associated anxiety, understand abstract messages by making them more concrete, as well as helping them to express ideas and feelings (Rao and Cagie, 2006).

These visual supports consist in words, images or perceptible objects which the child can easily recognize and interpret, especially when he/she has to handle abstract or unfamiliar information (Hayes et. al, 2010). Visual tools allow a child with autism to organize better his/her surrounding world, which is perceived as uncertain and consequently generates anxiety and uncomfort. Research has shown that picture based systems reduce the symptoms associated with Autism Spectrum Disorders (Williams et. al., 2006 in Hayes et. al., 2010).

Since in the past, Autism Spectrum Disorders were considered as a disability, social interventions were addressed in this line, focusing on pathology, more than in the patient him/herself. Current models advocate an attendance centered on the person, considering his/her particular characteristics and, most importantly, his/her personal aspirations. (Tamarit, J., 2005). Various social and professional politics have been implemented worldwide, to enhance life quality of persons with ASD, ensuring their wellbeing and rights compliance.

An opportune diagnosis will conduct to an intervention over the child with ASD, his/her family and environment to attend permanent or transitory necessities that children with ASD may present. (Mulas, et al., 2010) This intervention are applied in different environment in which the person develops, such as school or occupational spaces, where, it is pretended, that the person counts on structured spaces, adapted to their particular way of understanding and processing the surrounding information. (Tamarit, J., 2005).

There is a variety of clinical and educational intervention models, addressed to develop skills that may present deficits, such as social interaction and communicational abilities; promote personal autonomy, and supporting the person with ASD's family. Interventions on Autism Spectrum Disorder focus on three main models: pharmacological, developmental, and behavioral interventions.

Medication is not prescribed to the ASD symptoms themselves, but to the comorbid syndromes or disabilities that ASD may present, such as Epilepsy or behavioral disorders. (Mulas et al., 2010). Developmental intervention focus on developmental processes that are behind the symptoms, and allow future cognitive, affective and social development. Floortime and RDI are two approaches that highlight among this model. Floor Time is a child-oriented model, carried out by parents, which focuses on the development of the child's own social, communicational and affective skills. Meanwhile, RDI, also executed by parents, consists in semi-structured activities addressed to enhance language skills, cognitive flexibility, social coordination, and affective retrospect development (Alessandri, Thorp, Mundy and Tuchman, 2005).

Behavioral models center on behavioral analysis and skills development through structured environments (Montalva, Quintanilla y Del Solar, 2012). These kinds of interventions are frequently used in institutions that attend Autism Spectrum Disorders, particularly in the Center for Multidisciplinary Intervention for Autism ("Centro Intervención Multidisciplinario para el Autismo, CIMA"), in which the developed ICT devices have been implemented and tested.

ABA (Applied Behavior Analysis) is founded on learning theory, to modify (increase, decrease, maintain or generalize) behaviors in a structured and measurable manner (Mulas et al., 2010). It considers the relationships between behavior and environment, identifying problematic behaviors and using reinforcement to improve adaptive responses on the person with ASD. (Alessandri et al, 2005).

The TEACCH method, (Treatment and Education of Autistic and Related Communication Handicapped Children) is based on two main principles: increasing comprehension and skills development in persons with ASD, and making environments more comprehensible for them. (Montalva Quintanilla y

Del Solar, 2012). This model contains five guidelines which are centering on structured learning, using visual strategies to guide the children, learning of pre-academic abilities, and parental training as co-therapists. It pretends to enhance adaptive behavior in children with ASD, increasing life quality and reducing family stress (Mulas et al., 2010).

The rest of this chapter is organized as follows. Section 2 presents a general overview of some relevant works related with the use of ontologies in mental health care as well as robotic assistants for the intervention in of patients with ASD. The proposed ecosystem and the psychological basis of this work are described in Section 3. Section 4 presents an experiment carried out with 47 children of regular schools and 9 experts that work with children with ASD. Finally, in Section 5 are described the conclusions and some ideas of future work.

## Background

In the last 10 years several researches have been developed in the area of health-care with the aim of supporting decision making. Some of these proposals rely on knowledge modeling strategies such as ontologies, Electronic Health Records (EHR), archetypes, etc.; however, in the SLT area only few proposals exist nowadays, that use knowledge modeling to contribute in the improvement of tasks such as diagnostic, therapy planning and therapeutic intervention.

In the line of the patient's health-care, Iroju, Soriyan and Gambo have proposed the use of ontology matching for supporting the semantic interoperability between systems. This research has the aim of identifying and interpreting similar medical terms that are represented heterogeneously in different systems. With this, it will be possible to detect correlation between elements of one or more overlapped/disjoint ontologies and provide a better service for patients (Iroju, Soriyan, and Gambo; 2012)

Riaño et al. (2012) have developed a system to support decision making for patients with chronic diseases using a knowledge database based on ontology (Case Profile Ontology, CPO) and formal intervention plans. The CPO represents all concepts related with the patient's care. Each disease, syndrome or social issue has an intervention formal plan that is represented by state-decision-action diagrams. With this aim, this proposal introduces two personalization processes and a decision support tool. In the first process, the ontology is adapted to the particularities observed in the health-care record of a given concrete patient, automatically providing a personalized ontology containing only the clinical information that is relevant for health-care professionals to manage that patient. In the other hand, the second personalization process uses the personalized ontology of a patient to automatically transform intervention plans describing health-care general treatments into individual intervention plans. In order to analyze the real feasibility of this proposal, the authors have conducted an evaluation process with several professionals of 7 health-care centers. The achieved results shown that the professionals agree with the quality (84\%) and utility of the tool (90%).

In the other hand, recent studies have shown that children with disabilities can be more receptive towards robotic assistants in comparison to their peers. In this line, Lee and Hyun (2015) present a research where the robot iRobiQ was programmed with several activities and exercises to promote the language development in children with communication disorders. This approach was tested with four children with an Autism Spectrum Disorder and intellectual disability, and as result of therapies, children learnt to initiate conversations with the robot through the emotional exchange of expressions (Lee and Hyun, 2015).

Likewise, Wainer et. al (2014) present a novel proposal of a triadic collaborative game which involves the participation of two children with an Autism Spectrum Disorder (ASD) and KASPAR, a robotic assistant. One of the main goals of this research is to prove the possibility to use a robotic assistant to improve social communication and social skills in these children in a collaborative environment. The pilot experiment was carried out with 6 children during 78 playing sessions, and all participants have shown an important improvement in their social behavior.

Bugnariu et. al (2013) have developed a robotic assistant that analyzes kinematic data and uses a Dynamic Time Warping algorithm with the aim of evaluating and quantifying the imitation behavior of children with ASD. This robot named Zeno has a human form and has been developed by Hanson Robotics. During the data collection, each child and Zeno are put one in front of the other, and the robot interacts with child through this behaviors: verbal dialog ("look at me", "and follow me"), imitate my facial gestures, imitate my head-eye motion, imitate my arm and hand movement. The results of this experiment show that children with ASD consistently perform worse the imitation behavior than their age-match control pairs (children without ASD). All children have reacted in a positive way to the robot, possibly because they perceive that it is a toy (Bugnariu et. al, 2013).

Additionally, in the area of e-learning systems, Judy, Krishnakumar and Narayanan (2012) have proposed a personalized system for students with autism. This proposal relies on soft semantic web technologies and implements a Genetic Algorithm (GA) to personalize education plans for each student. To this aim, the authors propose establishing and generating educational guidelines through Individual Education Plans (long-term and short-term goals, personal and educational data, student's strengths and needs, etc.). In the same line, Venkatesan et al. (2013) have developed a hybrid approach based on ontologies and e-learning expert systems. In this proposal are modeled two main blocks: (i) learning contents and learning strategies for students with ASD, and (ii) the profile of children with autism and language disorders. With this information, the authors use a rule based ontology mapping system, with the objective of expressing the educational curriculum in form of rules. Alcorn, Good and Pain (2013) present an exploratory study of system-side errors as potential strategy for virtual learning environments. This proposal analyzes the reaction of children with ASD to interaction that take place in a virtual "Magic Garden". Each child has a Virtual Character (VC) that can be controlled inside the virtual environment. The system includes errors in some communication and activities that are carried out by the VC. Therefore, in this study was possible to determine that 8 participants (children with ASD) were able to note these errors or discrepancies between the "correct behavior" and the "behavior carried out".

As it can be seen, the most of the developed approaches are focused in the treatment of some specific disorders and areas of psychological intervention. In the same way, the proposed approaches do not consider some important aspects like the following:

- The informatics systems, robotic assistants, and in general, the intelligent ICT tools must be able to adapt itself to the specific requirements of each patient and his/her environment (family, scholar, etc.).
- Even two patients with ASD have the same diagnosis, and they could require different kind of therapeutic exercises or activities.
- The tools used to provide support in diagnosis and intervention of children with communication disorders and ASD, must contain information about the progress of each patient as well as the response to tools and to therapy.

In light of above, in this chapter is presented a complete ecosystem able to provide a comprehensive support for diagnosis and intervention of children with ASD and communication disorders. In the same line, in this document are described some of the most relevant features of the proposed approach as well as the preliminary results achieved during a pilot experiment conducted with children of regular schools (as the first stage the incorporation of the ecosystem to specialized centers that work with children with ASD in Cuenca, Ecuador).

## METHODOLOGY

In order to provide a complete support for the diagnosis and rehabilitation processes of children with ASD, we have developed an ecosystem that relies on ontologies, Multi-Sensory Stimulation Rooms (MSSR), and robotic assistants. The main objective of this ecosystem is providing an adaptable environment for both patients, and their families/caregivers. Likewise, given that the ecosystem uses an architecture based on layers and modules, it is easy to include more elements or components to cover new areas, such as interfaces to provide environmental intelligence services, sporadic learning/health monitoring networks, virtual intermediaries for supporting teaching, etc.

### Main Components of the Ecosystem

Our intelligent system relies on two layers (services and intelligent system) and several modules. This aspect allows us to easily incorporate new functionalities in a given module, without affecting the functionalities that are provided by others modules and layers. Below we describe some of the most important aspects of each layer that is part our system (Figure 1):

- During the therapy sessions the therapist, and the patient and their parents/caregivers interact with the Multi-Sensory Stimulation Room (MSSR) and robotic assistant. In order to determine the interaction guidelines, the psychologist selects the patient's profile from a remote database, and the system automatically loads the ontology that relates the therapy guidelines, activities, and patient's profile. To do this, the ecosystem provides a set of web services that can be accessed from desktop, mobile or web-based environments. In the same way, it is important to mention that MSSR and robotic assistant can be controlled by any kind of mobile device based on Android (tablet or smartphone).
- The robotic assistant has several costumes that can be easily changed to improve the engagement with each patient (according to his/her preferences and needs). In the same way, some of the most relevant features of the robot are the following:
  - Has two different systems to provide energy (one for Raspberry and other for servo motors).
  - Has four degrees of freedom (head, arms, and can move in a table/ground through the two wheels of his base).
  - Has a low consumption of energy, given that uses a resistive display, can take pictures and make videos through a RaspiCam that is under his jaw.
  - Has six hours of autonomy in the complete functioning mode (using the Raspberry and moving the arms, head, and wheels)

*Figure 1. General overview of services, layers, and components that make up the proposed ecosystem*

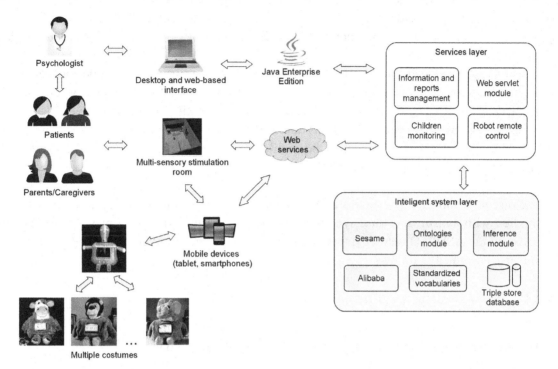

- ○ Can play videos, songs, and incorporates a Text To Speech System (TTS) and an Automatic Speech Recognition System (ASR).
- In the services layer the system provides several functionalities that allow monitoring the patient's progress, registering therapy sessions, generating reports, and control remotely the robot. Likewise, this layer contains the published ontology, as well as the Resource Description Framework (RDF) instances (web servlet module).
- The intelligent system layer allows managing all the information of our system as graph structures for semantic queries with nodes. For this purpose we use two elements:
  - ○ An interface (Sesame) to access and manage all the information stored in the triplestore (Broekstra, Kampman and Van Harmelen, 2002).
  - ○ A mapping interface (Alibaba) to convert each tripleta to Java objects and create the links with the Resource Definition Framework Annotation, RDFa (Adida, 2008).
- With the aim of extending and sharing our proposal through the semantic web, we use standardized vocabularies like DSM-5 and ICD-10. In the same way, this layer contains an ontology-based reasoner (inference module), and a triple database store.

## Knowledge Model: Ontology Design

Designing a therapy plan is considered one of the most complicated tasks of the psychological intervention in patients with ASD. This task requires an important effort on the part of the team in charge of patient's rehabilitation (psychologists, special educators, therapists, etc.), because it is not possible to generalize intervention guidelines. For these reasons, the proposed ecosystem implements an ontology that extends strategies provided in the Autism Spectrum Disorder Phenotype Ontology (ASDPTO) (Mc-Cray, Trevvett, and Frost; 2014), incorporating new elements and relations that allow to automatically generate an intervention plan.

To illustrate the developed ontology (Figure 2), we present the way in which we model the relationship between therapists and patients at CIMA, a specialized institution for ASD assistance, where different support elements are used by the therapists, to develop certain abilities in children.

Among these elements, they count on tools developed in the present research, based on the various necessities present in the institution, such as the mobile application for the development of social codes, which is an extension of the ontology modeling.

- The discourse universe D contains all the elements within playful activities in the treatment of children with autistic spectrum syndrome, elements used in autism therapies, and phenotypes based on the ASDPTO ontology, that are a frame of reference in affected skills evaluation. The universe is defined as follows:

$$D = \left\{ Autism\_Phenotype1, ..., Therapy1, ..., User1, ... \right\}$$

- The main unary relationships defined in our ontology are the following:

*Figure 2. General structure of proposed ontology*

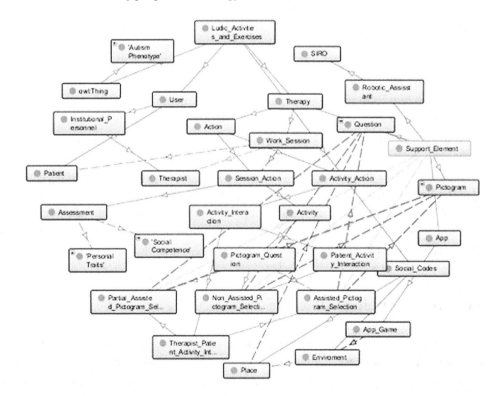

- ○ **Autism_Phenotype:** Set of affections present in children with autistic spectrum syndrome that are visible, taking as reference the ASDPTO ontology.
- ○ **Therapy:** All the means that allow treating the affected abilities of patients; among these are the work sessions between the therapists and the patients, the types of interaction in the sessions, and the different support elements that are used in a session.
- ○ **Action:** These are the types of interaction that therapists and patients have in the different activities they perform in the work sessions, which are usually three: therapist-assisted activities, partially assisted activities, and non-assisted activities.
- ○ **Activity:** Are all the actions performed in the work sessions, including activities that are specialized for the treatment of autism, as well as the evaluations that are performed to the patients.
- ○ **Item_Activity:** Consensus of the name given to an activity developed in a work session.
- ○ **Support_Element:** Tools used within the therapies with the patients, which help to obtain better results.
- ○ **Question:** Type of support element that has a question linked to different responses in the form of a pictogram, which develops a skill present in the phenotypes of autism.
- ○ **Pictogram:** Type of support element consisting in a picture which represents an object, action, idea or command.
- ○ **Work_Session:** Space of time in which different actions are carried out such as activities and evaluations between the therapist and the patient.
- ○ **Therapist:** Person who applies the different activities in the work sessions with patients.
- ○ **Patient:** Person who has affectations in different abilities, diagnosed with autistic spectrum syndrome.
- The binary relations that were modeled in the ontology are the following:
  - ○ **hasTheraphist:** Indicates the therapist who develops the work session.
  - ○ **hasPatient:** Indicates the patient to whom the work session is addressed.
  - ○ **work:** Specifies the activity items that are developed in a work session.
  - ○ **hasWorkSession:** Used to signal the work session to which an activity belongs.
  - ○ **hasItemActivity:** Indicates the activity item to which an activity belongs in a work session.
  - ○ **hasAction:** Allows to specify the actions that are performed in an activity.
  - ○ **developsASkill:** Indicates the ability within the autism phenotypes that develops a question.
  - ○ **hasAnswer:** Used to point out the different answers in the form of pictograms that a question has.
  - ○ **hasCorrectAnswer:** Used to indicate the correct answer in the form of a pictogram that a question has.
- The set of relations R is defined as follows:

$$R = \left\{ \begin{array}{l} Theraphy, Action, Activity, Item\_Activity, Support\_Element, \\ Patient, Therapist, Work\_Session, Autism\_Phenotype, Question, \\ Pictograma, work, hasWorkSessionhasItemActivity, hasAction, \\ hasPatient, hasTherapist, developsASkill, hasAnswer, hasCorrectAnswer \end{array} \right\}$$

- We specify the subcontracts of unary relationships:

$$O_1 = \left\{ \begin{array}{l} Action(x) \rightarrow Therapy(x), Activity(x) \rightarrow Therapy(x), Item\_Activity(x) \\ \rightarrow Therapy, Support\_Element(x) \rightarrow Therapy(x), Work\_Session(x) \\ \rightarrow Therapy(x), Patient(x) \rightarrow User(x), Therapist(x) \\ \rightarrow User, Question(x) \rightarrow Support\_Element(x), Pictogram(x) \\ \rightarrow Support\_Element(x) \end{array} \right\}$$

- Specifying the domains and ranges of binary relations:

$$O_2 = O_1 \cup \left\{ \begin{array}{l} hasPatient(x,y) \rightarrow Work\_Session(x) \wedge Patient(y), \\ hasTherapist(x,y) \rightarrow Work\_Session(x) \wedge Therapist(y), \\ work(x,y) \rightarrow Work_{Session(x)} \wedge Item\_Activity(y), \\ hasWorkSession(x,y) \rightarrow Activity(x) \wedge WorkSession(y), \\ hasItemActivity(x,y) \rightarrow Activity(x) \wedge ItemActivity(y), \\ hasAction(x,y) \rightarrow Activity(x) \wedge Action(y), \\ hasAnswer(x,y) \rightarrow Question(x) \wedge Pictogram(y), \\ hasCorrectAnswer(x,y) \rightarrow Question(x) \wedge Pictogram(y), \\ developsASkill(x,y) \rightarrow Question(x) \wedge Autism\_Phenotype(y) \end{array} \right\}$$

With the complete definition of the ontology, we can execute multiple queries such as the following:

- To determine which skills are affected by the autism phenotypes in the patients through the assessments.
- To know the response of the patients to the activities, according to the type of assistance they obtain from the therapists, in their interactions.
- To get the best questions from the "pictogram question" activity, basing on the affected skills of the patients, detected in the assessments.
- To know the response of patients to different support elements in the activities of the work sessions.

Based on the above, we present in Figures 3 and 4, the structure of the created instances that show us how a patient and a therapist relate to a work session and the activities they develop in the it. The illustrations show the performance of an evaluation and a "Pictogram Question" activity (Figure 3) and interactions between activities (Figure 4).

## Information Management System

The system was built for the administration of information and as a recommender of activities, exercises and games that need the therapists to attend patients with ASD. Within administration of information,

*Figure 3. Ontology of the interaction of patients and therapists in the work sessions, generated in Protégé*

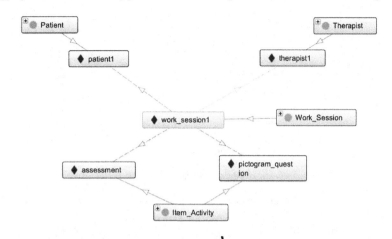

*Figure 4. Ontology generated in Protégé, representing interactions of activities*

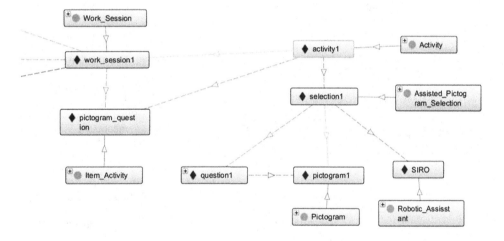

we can manage the medical history of each of the children; we can generate reports and visualize the progress of each child, and store the process therapy through the used applications (Figure 5).

The expert system uses the ontology to describe and model the various relationships that exist in the process of therapy. This information and the rules set are the inputs necessary for the inference motor to generate a set of activities suggested for the child, based on his or her profile.

It is important to note that the information will be stored on two different databases, the first one oriented to transactional data and the second one to the explicit representation of tacit knowledge. Each component of the system is described below:

- **Applications:** This module is composed of a set of mobile, desktop and web applications. It provides access to the various features offered by the system. Some of its features are detailed below:

Within the mobile applications, some activities can be done to enhance the child's abilities, such as games, exercises and ludic activities that the therapists can execute with their patients with ASD.

*Figure 5. General architecture of informatics system*

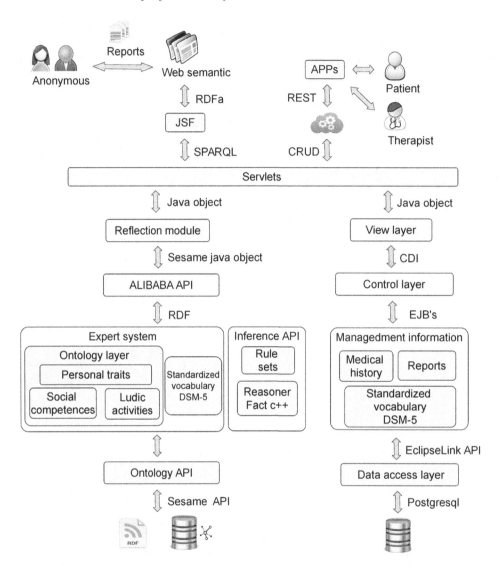

All the activities that the child carries out are stored in a centralized database using REST (Representational State Transfer) like web services. Some of the features stored are: number of errors and successes, application usage time, child's time of response, etc.

Moreover in desktop applications allow to create, update, read and delete (CRUD) the therapist's information and the children's therapy records. This information is stored in the centralized database.

The web application allows the user to publish information semantically on the web and to be a recommender that, through a search engine allows the display of exercises and activities that can be performed based on the child's profile. Finally, all this is done through the use of JSF (JavaServer Faces) and Primefaces to generate views and RDFa tags for web semantics.

- **Servlets:** This allows us to generate dynamic content using java. Therefore they are responsible for attending the requests from different customers. Within this module we count on application and control servlets. The application is responsible for managing the connection to the database triplets and the transactional database, while the control servlets manage information handling tuples.

As mentioned before, the system supports data and transactional data based on triplets; for this reason, it is divided into two architectures according to handled data.

For managing transactional data of children, therapists and therapies, 7 stack of JEE (Java Enterprise Edition) was used, following a MVC architecture (Model, View and Controller). The components of the system are briefly described below.

- **View Layer:** Using CDI (Contexts Dependency injection) interaction between EJB (Enterprise JavaBeans) and JSF can be done. Is it possible to obtain data from the user interface and work with them as objects in Java for transactional data.
- **Control Layer:** Using EJBs, the following features can be implemented: the publication of web services for managing data that is accessed by different applications, application security and user permissions management, ACID (Atomicity, Consistency, Isolation and Durability) management in the boards and the data access object records
- **Data Access Layer:** It is responsible for communicating with the DBMS (DataBase Management System) and performing DML (Data Manipulation Language) processes on the database. In this system, Postgresql is used as DBMS. Finally, standard JPA (Java Persistence API) and specifically the implementation of EclipseLink is used for mapping the OOP (Object Oriented Programming).
- **Management Information:** The information managed by this architecture is divided into three main modules: The medical history, which is responsible for having all medical records and treatment of each patient. The reports can synthesize or summarize the information and see the progress that the patient has had. In this line, all this information is stored under standardized vocabularies (DSM-5) to be able to be contextualized worldwide.

On the other hand, for the management of triplets a hybrid architecture (Transactional - RDF) was performed. Mainly because development language is object-oriented (JAVA) and this does not directly support data management in RDF format. The expert system uses the ontological model and the inference engine to infer new knowledge based on logic first level. In this context, it allows us to build an activities, exercises and games recommender system that the child can use to improve skills.

- **Reflection Module:** The purpose of this module is to solve the incompatibility between Poos and Sesame Object. For example, when making a query to the database triplets these results must be mapped to object instances. And this way, be able to present and manipulate within the JVM. For this, the reflection of java was implemented to build objects at runtime and populate them with data obtained from the consultation, for this to be a generic process and useful to any kind of development through generic programming. In this context, this process is bidirectional, because the change in the objects must also translate into triplets database.

- **ALIBABA API:** This library allows extracting and manipulating data in RDF graphs or from a database of triplets, the same that are based on an ontological model. These data are mapped and managed to level objects in JAVA.

- **Ontology API:** This module is responsible for storing, querying and DML processes performing on RDF data type, for which it uses the SPARQL language for data management. Among some features, we count on that data can be stored in three different ways: first as a database, the second within a file or, the third one, just within the virtual memory of the computer. Data access can be done by using Web services, repositories can be created and triplets, exported to a file in RDF format; it counts on a stack of libraries that can have access to this information by using JAVA.

- **Expert System:** The expert system allows working with an ontological model. Within this model, personal trait, social competences and ludic activities are modeled, describing how they relate, and entering a set of rules that best describe these objects. With this information the inference engine can generate new knowledge by applying first level logic. In light of the above, it can recommend different activities based on the child's profile. To do this the reasoner FaCT ++ was used. Finally, all this information used standardized vocabularies.

In conclusion, the information management system is designed to support the different requirements of stakeholders (patients, therapists and users), which need to take control and management of patient, therapists and therapies data. Likewise, it allows any user to query the system, and the system itself to recommend activities to improve the skills in children with ASD. All this information is semantically presented on the web allowing defining better the data and having interoperability between systems, thus obtaining better results when searching for information..

## The Architecture of the Multi-Sensory Stimulation Room

The MSSR relies on several modules that are aimed to support the psychological and therapeutic intervention activities for children with autism spectrum disorders. Likewise, its general architecture was designed according to the requirements established by CIMA.

In order to configure the MSSR according to the requirements of each patient, we have developed a mobile application that allow configuring several elements of the room such as the colors of the lights, the volume of the sounds used to provide feedback for patients, the number and types of therapeutic activities, etc.

The configuration of the room is provided by the ontology and is executed by a central processor (a Raspberry PI module) that is connected to several educational and therapeutic modules through radio frequency communication modules (Xbee, O. E. M., 2012). With this model is possible to easily incorporate new modules without making connections with cables.

The main stimuli that are currently provided by the MSSR are visual (RGB color leds), auditory, and kinesthetic (through the robotic assistant). At this time, our MSSR contains the following modules:

- **Piano With Stimulation Lights:** This module is aimed to support memory, attention and concentration development in children. During the therapy session, this module presents a lights activation sequence that must be reproduced by the patient. To do this, the patient must push the buttons in the same order in which they were presented by the system. As the patient progresses in the exercises, the system will present more complex sequences (increasing the number of lights on, increasing the speed of activation, etc.). Likewise, the system is able to register the level of force applied by the patient during the use of the piano (high, medium or low). This variable is useful to determine the anxiety level that the patient presents during therapy.

- **Pictograms Panel:** It is focused in the development of patient's visual, auditory and tactile skills. This module incorporates several pairs of buttons and pictograms that represent concepts, ideas, actions, etc. The patient must select the pictogram (pressing the button) that represents the concept or element presented aurally by the system. The responses provided by the patient are used to determine which are the concepts, categories, etc. that must be improved through therapy.
- **Stair of Lights:** It is used to work in vocalization and visual stimulation areas. The exercise consists on requesting patient to produce vocalizations with different levels of voice volume. According to each vocalization and voice volume, the system will activate the lights.
- **Bubbles Panel:** This module is used to develop simultaneously motor and visual skills. This panel consists on a transparent box that contains water inside. When a patient stands on the box, the system produces bubbles (using a motor) of a specific color (that can be defined using a mobile application). This activity is helpful to relax patients too.
- **Dice of Colors:** Consists on a big dice that has a different color in each face. This module is used to change the color and intensity of the room's lights when the patient throws the dice.
- **Module for Augmented Reality:** It has the objective of supporting the development of motor skills in children. This module presents different kinds of concepts that must be learnt by the patient. Some examples of these concepts are: geometric figures (spatial skills), cardinal points (how to position themselves on the physical plane), images and virtual stimuli, etc.

## A Mobile Application to Develop Social Communication Skills

Considering the visual style to process information in individuals with ASD, a series of interfaces containing multiple exercises based on images related to the child's common situations have been developed. In Figure 6 it is possible to see a screen capture of the menu that contains some options to work with social codes at home (other categories are school and external places).

These exercises are aimed to better visualize the situations in which the child may present drawbacks, so he/she can be able to anticipate other's behavior and different situations, to rehearse some conventional responses he/she needs to give in return.

The intervention program has a progressive approach, so the child initially works with some conventional information related to daily life behaviors such as using silverware or depositing the garbage in the correct place, and eventually rehearse more complex interactive behavior that usually appear at home or school.

The exercises present a situation in interrogative format, and three different options of answer, to which the child needs to choose the correct response, integrating new alternatives to his/her behavioral spectrum.

Interventions of this kind may offer the child with ASD the structured behavioral and communicational patterns he/she needs to develop satisfactorily within his/her own environment.

*Figure 6. A screen capture of the menu that contains exercises to develop communication skills that are needed at some home's places*

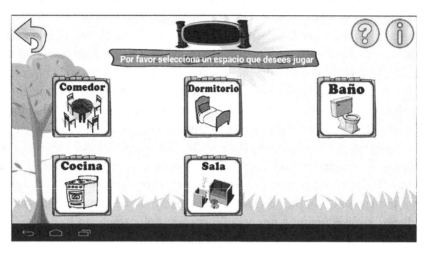

## Pilot Experiment and Preliminary Results

In order to analyze the real feasibility of our system, we have conducted a pilot experiment with the aim of analyzing the following aspects: (i) the reaction of children of regular schools to the robotic assistant, (ii) the feasibility of using the therapeutic activities selected by the ontology, (iii) the valuation of professionals about the MSSR and its integration with the robotic assistant, and (iv) the reaction of children with ASD to the robotic assistant in real therapy scenarios.

To accomplish this objective, we have worked with 47 children of regular schools, and 9 experts of CIMA foundation. The children attend to different schools of Cuenca city and are aged between 5 and 14 years. This CIMA Foundation works with 90 children with autism spectrum disorders, and has 10 professionals of different areas (psychologists, special educators, educational psychologists, and speech-language therapists). On the other hand, the children with ASD assist to CIMA Foundation and present the characteristics described in Table 1. As it can be seen, all 36 children present ASD (International Classification Diseases Code: F84.0), and two of them have associated disorders (intellectual disability, and epilepsy).

In the following subsections we describe the results achieved with each experimentation process that was applied to put to test the developed ecosystem.

## Preliminary Validation of Robotic Assistant with Children of Regular Schools

The aim of this experiment was to analyze the response of children to the robot as intermediary, and at the same time, determine if it appearance and functionalities of the robot arouse interest in children. With this objective, we have carried out several ludic and interactive activities between children and the robot, such as playing some basic games, conducting short dialogs, etc. Following that, we have applied a survey to know what children think about the functionalities of the robot, according to a Likert scale (very good, good, average, bad, and very bad). The results show that 41 children think that the robot is "very good", while 6 of them think that it is "good".

*Table 1. Characteristics of children with ASD with which was tested the robotic assistant in real therapy sessions*

| Chronological Age Range | Cognitive Age Range | Developmental Language's Age Range | Patients' Diagnostic and Related Disorder |
| --- | --- | --- | --- |
| 1 year 5 months - 11 year 7 months | 1 year 6 months - 11 years | 1 year 1 month – 10 years 3 months | Autism Spectrum Disorder (ICD-10 Code: F84.0) for all 36 cases) |
| Average: 6 years 7 months | Average: 5 years 9 months | Average: 4 years 6 months | Intellectual disability (1 case), Epilepsy (1 case) |

Finally, we have considered fundamental to determine the following aspects related to the robot:

- *What kinds of activities are preferred by children when they come into contact with the robot?* In order to obtain this information, we asked children what activities are most interesting to perform with the robot, and the first four choices proposed by children were: playing games, dancing, talking and walking/running (Figure 7, top).
- *The children's preferences about the robot's appearance (costumes).* In order to determine the level of preference for each costume, we have carried out several ludic activities with children and the robot. During the ludic and familiarization activities, the robot was presented with four different costumes (dog, cow, dinosaur, and elephant), and after that, we have asked children about their preferences about presented costumes and any Other option that they want (through a survey). As it can be seen, the most of the children prefer costumes of a dog, cat, and dinosaur (Figure 7, bottom).

## Ontology Validation

On the base of the different activities that are carried out by the experts of CIMA foundation, we have able to define several relations between the ASDPTO ontology and the different social and communication skills that are possible to develop through the mobile application. Thereby, it is possible to have an ontology adapted to the requirements of patients involved in the program that uses the mobile applications as well as MSSRs. These relations between therapeutic activities and ASDPTO ontology allows the ecosystem inferring which exercises are the most appropriate to address the different patients' disorders raised in ASDPTO's areas. For example, with the query described below, we can determine which are the most adequate exercises for the activity of "*selecting a pictogram*" for a patient that presents problems related with "*Adherence to Rules in the Community*". The results provided by ontology show that objects labeled as "*r10*" and "*r11*" (*nodeQuestion* variable) are the best to carry out the therapeutic activities required by patient:

- **Query:**

```
        SELECT (STR(?skill) AS ?labelSkill)  ?nodeQuestion
(STR(?question) AS ?labelQuestion)
WHERE { ?nodeQuestion cima:developsASkill ?nodeSkill.
             ?nodeSkill rdf:type ?skillClass.
```

*Figure 7. Children's preference about robot appearance and the interactive activities to carry out with the robot*

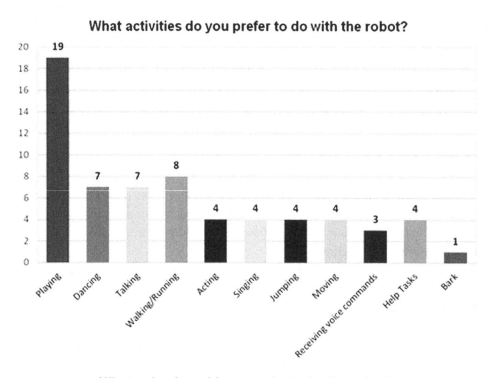

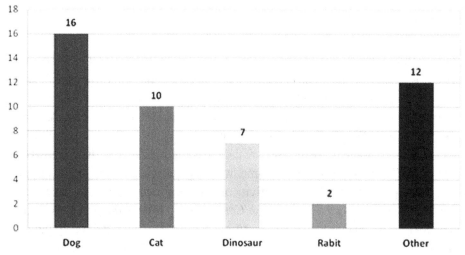

```
?skillClass rdfs:label ?skill.
?skillClass rdfs:label "Adherence to Rules in the
Community"^^<http://www.w3.org/2001/XMLSchema#string>.
?nodeQuestion cima:text ?question}
```

- **Result 1:**
  ○ **Skill:** Adherence to Rules in the Community.
  ○ **Node Question:** r10.
  ○ **Question:** What should do in the movie theater?
- **Result 2:**
  ○ **Skill:** Adherence to Rules in the Community.
  ○ **Node Question:** r13.
  ○ **Question:** What should do if I'm in the movie theater and I have wanted to go to the bathroom?

Likewise, is noteworthy that our ontology allows analyzing two key aspects: (i) the patient's development, and (ii) the disturbances in different communication and social skills that can appear during the patient's development. As it can be seen in Figure 8, the patient "*User 1*" starts developing himself at the moment that interacts with an application of the ecosystem that relies on activities related with questions and pictograms selection in three modes: assisted, partially-assisted and non-assisted. The procedure is the following: the patient should answer the question about what to do in a specific place and then, select a pictogram. As we can see, the platform registers the time needed by patient to complete the exercise as well as the selected answer, and the correct answer.

## MSSR Valuation and Analysis

This pilot experiment was aimed to analyze the following aspects of the MSSR:

- Determining the level of integration between the MSSR and robotic assistant. Currently, the robotic assistant is able to perform several joint activities with the MSSR. Therefore, we have asked experts about the importance of including robot inside the room and developing joint activities with the modules of MSSR. The results show that 7 experts considers that is important to have high (3) or medium (4) level of integration, whereas the other 2 experts consider that is very high (1) and low (1).
- Analyze which elements of the MSSR are the most relevant to control: (a) color of the lights, (b) lights intensity, (c) sounds volume or (d) temperature. We have asked professionals which of the previous variables is more important to control (considering that is possible to choose more than one option), and the results show 7 votes for option (a), 3 for (b), 7 for (c) and 1 for (d).
- Button's pressure level: it is important to determine the force used to press the different buttons of the MSSR, given that it can be an indicator of anxiety or similar conditions. In a scale of three possible values of importance (high, medium and low), 8 experts are agree that is very important (high) measuring the press ion, whereas 1 considers that is important (medium).

*Figure 8. An example of a SPARQL query that is automatically assembled by the system to provide therapeutic exercises for the patients*

```
 8  SELECT (STR(?patient) AS ?labelPatient) ?typeSelectPictogram
 9  (STR(?question) AS ?labelQuestion)  (STR(?selectAnswer) AS ?labelSelectAnswer)
10  (STR(?correctAnswer) AS ?labelCorrectAnswer) (STR(?time) AS ?timeLabel)
11  WHERE {
12  ?nodeWorkSession cima:hasPatient ?nodePatient.
13          ?nodePatient cima:nameId ?patient.
14          ?nodeWorkSession cima:hasSessionAction ?nodeSessionAction.
15          ?nodeSessionAction rdf:type cima:Pictogram_Question.
16          ?nodeSessionAction cima:hasSelectPictogram ?nodeTypeSelectPictogram.
17          ?nodeTypeSelectPictogram rdf:type ?typeSelectPictogram.
18          cima:hasSelectAnswer rdfs:domain ?typeSelectPictogram.
19          ?nodeTypeSelectPictogram cima:hasSelectAnswer ?nodeSelectAnswer.
20          ?nodeSelectAnswer cima:text ?selectAnswer.
21          ?nodeTypeSelectPictogram cima:time ?time.
22          ?nodeTypeSelectPictogram cima:hasSelectQuestion ?nodeQuestion.
23          ?nodeQuestion cima:text ?question.
24          ?nodeQuestion cima:hasCorrectAnswer ?nodeCorrectAnswer.
25          ?nodeCorrectAnswer cima:text ?correctAnswer
26  }
```

| QUERY RESULTS | | | | | |
|---|---|---|---|---|---|
| Patient | Assistence Type | Question | Select Answer | Correct Answer | Time |
| "User 1" | Non_Assisted_Pictogram_Selection | What should do in the movie theater? ("En la sala de cine ¿debemos?") | Sleep ("Dormir") | Be quiet ("Hacer Silencio") | 45 |
| "User 1" | Non_Assisted_Pictogram_Selection | What should do in the movie theater? ("En la sala de cine ¿debemos?") | Be quiet ("Hacer Silencio") | Be quiet ("Hacer Silencio") | 4 |
| "User 1" | Assisted_Pictogram_Selection | What should do if I'm in the movie theater and I have wanted to go to the bathroom? ("Si estoy en el cine y tengo ganas de ir al baño ¿Qué hago?") | I get out of room and go to the bathroom ("Salgo de la sala y voy al baño") | I get out of room and go to the bathroom ("Salgo de la sala y voy al baño") | 18 |

- Finally, we have asked experts making a judgment about what are the most relevant benefits that can be provided by the MSSR. The results obtained with survey show the following benefits and punctuations:
  - Senses stimulation: 3
  - Improving the communication: 2
  - Cognitive development: 1
  - Therapeutic activities reinforcement: 1
  - Increasing motivation: 3
  - Sensorial integration: 3
  - New working methods: 3
  - Improving the concentration: 2
  - Acquiring new skills: 3
  - Improving the perception as well as notions: 1

## Validation of Robotic Assistant with Children with ASD

Once we have determined that robot is adequate to work with children and the ontology is able to automatically generate therapy guidelines, we have introduced the robot in real therapy sessions with children with ASD. To achieve this objective, we have worked with the 36 children mentioned previously during they therapy sessions. The procedure that was carried out is described below:

1. Each therapy session was conducted by a therapist of CIMA Foundation in a special classroom where children commonly receive therapy. As the activities are carried out by therapist and child, a team of engineers monitors and registers the robot's response to stimuli and orders provided.
2. During the therapy session, the therapist has applied the guidelines selected by our expert system (through ontology). For example, for the patient No. **12** that has the following profile:

Chronological age = 7 years 7 months

Cognitive age = 7 years 3 months

Language development age = 5 years

The ecosystem was able to determine that must be conducted the following activities:

- It is necessary to develop social competencies through interactive/communication activities and games developed with robotic assistant ("Simon says game", imitating gestures, follow the steps to wash the hands or use the toilet, etc.).
- The virtual scenarios where must be developed the therapy activities are: bathroom, and dining room.
- The child's vocabulary must be improved through pictogram-based exercises (describe activities, follow simple orders, etc.).
- Develop relaxation activities in the MSSR with the aim of reducing the anxiety of child and their parents/caregivers: use the dice of color (change the ambient perception), work with stair of lights (vocalization), etc.

The robot as well as the MSSR automatically stores (through the ontology and information management system) all interaction process with the children and parents/caregivers.

Once the therapy session is over, the therapists have applied polls to each child with the aim of determining whether the robot had a positive impact on children. In Figure 9 are depicted the achieved results for the following areas: (i) interaction between children and the robot (30 were able to use the robot without assistance of the therapist), (ii) level of interest showed by children (32 were interested in the robot), (iii) visual and physical appearance (27 liked robot very much, 4 did not like and 5 did not provide a response), and (iv) motivation to handle the robot (28 children were motivated to use the robot).

*Figure 9. Children's response to robotic assistant in the following areas: interaction, level of interest, appearance, and motivation to handle*

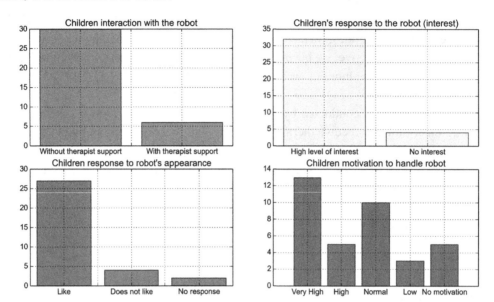

## FUTURE RESEARCH DIRECTIONS

It is important to take into account that each year the prevalence of autism in children increases. Therefore, it is fundamental to have adequate tools to support the educational process of these children. An early intervention process can reduce the impact of the disorder, and can increment the opportunities to have a better life quality in the future. For these reasons, it is fundamental to create tools and mechanisms that can provide services to adapt the environment or the form in which a person with ASD perceives the world. The virtual reality or augmented reality tools can constitute an important input to achieve this goal. In the same way, nowadays some emerging technologies such as sporadic networks constitutes a non-explored area that can be used to provide effective support for people with ASD:

- To have a communication structure able to monitor children behavior (despite their age, some patients with ASD are not aware of how dangerous are some actions, for example, crossing the streets without paying attention, talking with strange people, etc.).
- To automatically adapt educational contents to each patient using virtual or robotic intermediaries for improving the interaction flow in teaching-learning process.
- To adapt the environment (lights, sounds, and in general stimuli) to patient needs using the information collected from wearables or other kinds of sensors.

## CONCLUSION

The robotic assistant showed to have a very high level of acceptance among the sample. These aspects allow us establishing master lines with the objective to carrying out the same experiment with children with ASD, and determine the most relevant characteristics of the robot according to age, medical diagnosis, and related disorders.

The sample also exhibited a preference for customs associated with familiar animals like dogs, which can help them feel more comfortable and accompanied in unknown places or situations that commonly causes them to suffer from anxiety.

In the same way, it is fundamental to mention that ecosystem and robotic assistant have mechanisms to adapt the activities, intervention strategies, and they behavior according to each child's profile, and their needs.

In the other hand, it is important to incorporate inference mechanisms that allow automatically determining the best activities for each patient, under that the ASD cover a broad spectrum of disorders where a minimum variation in some variable of patient's profile can require totally different intervention plans.

One of the most important contributions of this work is the perspective of using an integrative environment that uses effectively ICT tools such as robotic assistants, mobile devices, MSSR, etc. and methodologies for modeling knowledge and making inferences (ontologies). Our proposal can easily incorporate more modules or components with the aim of covering new areas, such as: remote therapy support (to conduct reinforcing activities with patients at home), adaptable learning objects (using the ontology is possible to adapt the educational contents according to patient profile), stress or anxiety detectors (is possible to incorporate sensing modules to determine the patient's state of mind), among many others.

As lines of future work we propose the following ones:

- To develop sensing application for wearables devices, with the aim of determining the physical response of children to therapy and some intervention activities.
- To develop a remote support application for patient relatives, with the aim of gathering information that can provide data about the behavior pattern of children at home.
- To design and develop a sporadic network to automatically adapt educational contents for patients as well as to provide monitoring support in the daily life activities execution.

## LIMITATIONS

Currently our proposed approach presents some limitations that are mainly related with 3 areas: (i) knowledge modeling, (ii) patient and therapist feedback, and (iii) the level of granularity of the therapy plan generated.

The knowledge modeling related with autism constitutes a complex challenge, given due is a broad area in which it is relevant consider several concepts such as:

- **Speech and Language Disorders:** A person that presents ASD commonly has disorders related with communication. In this line, it is necessary to extend the ontology to provide a complete coverage of rehabilitation process.
- **Concomitant Disorders:** The ASD can be present with other disorders/disabilities such as epilepsy, intellectual disability, etc. These cases are very complicated to treat and require a very specialized knowledge model as well as support tools and methodologies.

- **Relevance Feedback:** Currently our ecosystem does not implement mechanisms to collect the feedback provided by the different actors (patients, therapists, and parents/caregivers). In the same way, it is fundamental to value the different sources that provide the feedback (relevance).

## ACKNOWLEDGMENT

The authors from the Universidad Politecnica Salesiana have been supported by the "Sistemas Inteligentes de Soporte a la Educación (SINSAE v4)" research project and the "Cátedra UNESCO – Tecnologías de apoyo para la Inclusión Educativa" initiative. The authors from the University of Vigo have been supported by the Ministerio de Educación y Ciencia (Gobierno de España) research project TIN2013-42774-R (partly financed with FEDER funds).

## REFERENCES

Adida, B., Birbeck, M., McCarron, S., & Pemberton, S. (2008). RDFa in XHTML: Syntax and processing. Recommendation. *W3C*.

Alcorn, A. M., Good, J., & Pain, H. (2013). Deliberate system-side errors as a potential pedagogic strategy for exploratory virtual learning environments. *Proceedings of theInternational Conference on Artificial Intelligence in Education*. doi:10.1007/978-3-642-39112-5_49

Alessandri, M., Thorp, D., Mundy, P., & Tuchman, R. F. (2005). ¿ Podemos curar el autismo? Del desenlace clínico a la intervención. *Revista de Neurologia*, *40*(1), 131–136.

American Psychiatric Association. (2014). Guía de consulta de los criterios diagnósticos del DSM-5 [Desk Reference to the Diagnostic Criteria From DSM-5]. American Psychiatric Pub.

Brickley, D., & Miller, L. (2012). FOAF vocabulary specification 0.98. Namespace document, 9.

Broekstra, J., Kampman, A., & Van Harmelen, F. (2002, June). Sesame: A generic architecture for storing and querying rdf and rdf schema. *Proceedings of theInternational semantic web conference* (pp. 54-68). Springer.

Bugnariu, N., Young, C., Rockenbach, K., Patterson, R. M., Garver, C., Ranatunga, I.,... Popa, D. (2013). Human-robot interaction as a tool to evaluate and quantify motor imitation behavior in children with Autism Spectrum Disorders. *Proceedings of the2013 International Conference on Virtual Rehabilitation (ICVR)* (pp. 57-62). doi:10.1109/ICVR.2013.6662088

CDC. (2016). Facts about Autism Spectrum Disorders. Retrieved from http://www.cdc.gov/ncbddd/autism/data.html

Hayes, G. R., Hirano, S., Marcu, G., Monibi, M., Nguyen, D. H., & Yeganyan, M. (2010). Interactive visual supports for children with autism. *Personal and Ubiquitous Computing*, *14*(7), 663–680. doi:10.1007/s00779-010-0294-8

Iroju, O., Soriyan, A., & Gambo, I. (2012). Ontology matching: An ultimate solution for semantic interoperability in healthcare. *International Journal of Computers and Applications*, *51*(21).

Judy, M. V., Krishnakumar, U., & Narayanan, A. H. (2012). Constructing a personalized e-learning system for students with autism based on soft semantic web technologies. *Proceedings of the 2012 IEEE International Conference on Technology Enhanced Education (ICTEE)*. doi:10.1109/ICTEE.2012.6208625

Lee, H., & Hyun, E. (2015). The intelligent robot contents for children with speech-language disorder. *Journal of Educational Technology & Society*, *18*(3), 100–113.

McCray, A. T., Trevvett, P., & Frost, H. R. (2014). Modeling the autism spectrum disorder phenotype. *Neuroinformatics*, *12*(2), 291–305. doi:10.1007/s12021-013-9211-4 PMID:24163114

Minshew, N. J., & Goldstein, G. (1998). Autism as a disorder of complex information processing. *Mental Retardation and Developmental Disabilities Research Reviews*, *4*(2), 129–136. doi:10.1002/(SICI)1098-2779(1998)4:2<129::AID-MRDD10>3.0.CO;2-X

Mulas, F., Ros-Cervera, G., Millá, M. G., Etchepareborda, M. C., Abad, L., & Téllez de Meneses, M. (2010). Modelos de intervención en niños con autismo. *Revista de Neurologia*, *50*(3), 77–84. PMID:20112215

Rao, S. M., & Gagie, B. (2006). Learning through seeing and doing: Visual supports for children with autism. *Teaching Exceptional Children*, *38*(6), 26–33. doi:10.1177/004005990603800604

Riaño, D., Real, F., López-Vallverdú, J. A., Campana, F., Ercolani, S., Mecocci, P., & Caltagirone, C. et al. (2012). An ontology-based personalization of health-care knowledge to support clinical decisions for chronically ill patients. *Journal of Biomedical Informatics*, *45*(3), 429–446. doi:10.1016/j.jbi.2011.12.008 PMID:22269224

Tamarit, J. (2005). Autismo: Modelos educativos para una vida de calidad. *Revista de Neurologia*, *40*(1), 181–186.

TEACCH, Y. (2012). Modelos de intervención terapéutica educativa en autismo: ABA y TEACCH. *Revista Chilena de Psiquiatría y Neurología de la Infancia y Adolescencia*, *23*(1), 50.

Venkatesan, K., Nelaturu, S., Vullamparthi, A. J., & Rao, S. 2013. Hybrid ontology based e-Learning expert system for children with Autism. *Proceedings of the 2013 International Conference of Information and Communication Technology (ICoICT)*. doi:10.1109/ICoICT.2013.6574555

Wainer, J., Robins, B., Amirabdollahian, F., & Dautenhahn, K. 2014. Using the Humanoid Robot KASPAR to Autonomously Play Triadic Games and Facilitate Collaborative Play Among Children With Autism. IEEE Transactions on Autonomous Mental Development, 6(3), 183-199. doi:10.1109/TAMD.2014.2303116

World Health Organization. 2016. Autism spectrum disorders. Retrieved from http://www.who.int/mediacentre/factsheets/autism-spectrum-disorders/en/

Xbee, OEM. (2012). OEM RF Modules by MaxStream. Inc. Specifications. *ZigBee*, *802*(15), 4.

# Chapter 7
# Auditory Feedback in a Computer Game for Blind People

**Ana Teixeira**
*Polytechnic of Coimbra, Portugal*

**Anabela Gomes**
*Polytechnic Institute of Coimbra, Portugal*

**Joao Gilberto Orvalho**
*Polytechnic of Coimbra, Portugal*

## ABSTRACT

*The study presents an adaptation of the Mastermind game for blind users called MasterBlind. The game mechanics were simplified and auditory feedback introduced. The research object was to understand what kind of sounds would work better to help blind people play the game. Three versions were presented to the subjects - pentatonic notes, animal sounds and vowels - to help users recall previous steps in the game. The main hypothesis predicted that blind users would consciously benefit from the auditory feedback provided. The second hypothesis predicted that users would benefit less from the feedback that doesn't provide semantic information- auditory icons versus earcons. The results were congruent with the hypothesis. MasterBlind can be a usable, enjoyable and a challenging experience for blind users as long as it provides semantically significant feedback. However, new developments are in progress to prove our ideas having in mind the inclusion of blind people.*

## INTRODUCTION

This work aims to discuss the most important aspects related to the development and integration of audio-based educational games as a novel and efficient learning strategy for visually impaired people. Audio games have the potential to promote learning, enhance memory and develop cognitive skills and thus can significantly improve the quality of life of visually impaired people. A review of the literature on the integration of non-speech sounds to visual interfaces and applications from an usability perspective is done.

DOI: 10.4018/978-1-5225-2492-2.ch007

## Background

Over the past decades video games have become a worldwide phenomenon and one of the preferred leisure options for many people. However, game accessibility remains an unresolved matter, due to its strong visual and interactive nature. Even though the majority of these games also use audio, most (relevant) information is provided through images. This way, it is very difficult for low vision users, and impossible for blind users, to play the games independently. Therefore it is urgent to include new computer interaction techniques for visually impaired people and those with physical disabilities. Most of them rely in controlling the environment with movements and getting feedback via compensatory sensorial channels (for instance, hearing). The majority of the solutions uses sound, touch screens, haptic equipment, and specially designed hardware.

A common approach to help them develop spatial orientation and mobility skills is the employment of audio-based computer games as a practical, interactive and user-centred learning approach. The purpose of audio-based games is to improve knowledge, spatial representation and localization, orientation and mobility, contextual and associative memory and to enhance the ability to perform problem-solving tasks. Miller, Parecki and Douglas (2007) show an approach to develop video games for people with visual impairment using sensory substitution.

A number of virtual environments have been developed for blind people based on different type of audio, from simple sounds to 3-D audio. We can highlight, for instance, AudioMUD (Sanchez & Hassler, 2007) using spoken text to describe the environment, navigation, and interaction. It also includes some collaborative features into the interaction between blind users and includes a simulated virtual environment inside the human body. During the last years different techniques of the use of sounds to represent visual scenes, especially for blind people were proposed. The sonification processes varied from the parameters used to acoustically describe an image, as well as the number of channels and the dimensional complexity of the sonification produced.

The purpose of audio-based games is to improve knowledge, spatial representation and localization, orientation and mobility, contextual and associative memory and to enhance the ability to perform problem-solving tasks.

However, new approaches start to appear, for example, the Sonic-Badminton game. It is an audio-augmented badminton game that uses a virtual shuttlecock implied by audio feedback. It uses a real badminton racket and simple stereo sound to guide virtual shuttlecock (Kim, Lee, & Nam, 2016).

The highly immersive and attractive nature of audio games enables blind people to create a spatial representation of their environment that can be assigned to aid performing real-life navigation tasks.

Balan, Moldoveanu, Moldoveanu and Dascalu (2014) make a review and outline the most notable audio-based games in what concerns their usability as an educational tool for the visually impaired students is also presented. These games follow a user-centred design approach; taking into account the cognitive mental model of sensory perception and information processing that is specific to blind individuals. Balan, Moldoveanu and Moldoveanu (2014) proposed a new method of training blind people, consisting in a navigational 3D audio-based game. In this exploratory game the player has to perform route-navigational tasks under different conditions with the goal to exercise and test their orientation and mobility skills, relying exclusively on the perception of 3D audio cues.

These games follow a user-centred design approach; taking into account the cognitive mental model of sensory perception and information processing that is specific to blind individuals.

Ibrahim and Embug (2014) presented a new solution, consisting in the replacement of voice and touch forms of instructions of trainers or therapist into non-speech sound instructions. The method involves transforming 3-dimensional data of body movements (kinematics) into sounds. The idea is that by only listening to the sounds, a person should be able to follow the exact movements of the body of another person or instructor without any voice commands or instructions. This research uses Kinect as the live 3D movement input data stream.

Tayebi and Sedano (2014) reported a literature review of non-speech audio between the period of January 2000 and March 2014. The patterns, which emerged from the selected publications, delivered five categories with a clear focus on the research of non-speech audio.

Other projects can be cited, for example Finger Dance is an original audio-based rhythm-action game developed specifically for visually impaired people.

Another tendency in sonification consists in mapping arbitrary information such as the distance to an obstacle or changes in temperature into sound. It consists in the systematic representation of data using sounds, such as text-to-speech, colour readers, Geiger counters, acoustic radars, and MIDI synthesizers. Sanz, Mezcua, Pena and Walker (2014) survey existing sonification systems and suggest a taxonomy of algorithms and devices. Another issue is the representation of Non-verbal sound cues that can be used to convey different kinds of information and are often used for both simple and more complex types of feedback in computer games. Non-verbal sound cues can be divided into two different categories; auditory icons, that are sounds that represent real world events and earcons and morphocons, that are abstract synthetic or musical sounds. In contrast to earcons (the audio analog of icons), which map a unique sound to a particular meaning, morphocons are short audio units that are used to construct a sonic grammar based on temporal-frequency patterns, rather than fixed sound samples.

Another type of solution consists in having elements of the visual display replaced by auditory and/ or haptic displays. The access to the three-dimensional graphic computer world is done through the sense of touch (using a new dual-finger haptic interface) and augmented by audio output and voice commands. As an example of this system we can cite the one presented in the work of Iglesias and colleagues (Iglesias et al., n.d.). It consists in three applications for visual impaired people: an adventure game, a city map explorer and a chart explorer. There are other projects using different types of haptic feedback to substitute visual stimuli. For instance, Yuan and Folmer (2008) uses a glove that transforms visual information into haptic feedback using small pager motors attached to the tip of each finger. This allows a blind player to play Guitar Hero. Some systems include both sonic and haptic interaction. For instance, the auditory platform "From Dots to Shapes" (FDTS) is composed by three classic games (Simon, Point Connecting and concentration game). Each game was adapted to work on a concept of the Euclidean geometry.

Over the last years, the interest in the field of virtual reality based learning tools for the visually impaired people has considerably increased. Grabski and colleaugues (Grabski, Toni, Zigrand, Weller, & Zachmann, 2016) describe an accessible game allowing a competition between sighted and blind people in a shared virtual 3D environment. They use an asymmetric setup that allows touch less interaction via Kinect, for the sighted player, and haptic, wind, and surround audio feedback, for the blind player. Another approach can be seen in (Lee et al., 2013), a prototype game designed for both the visually healthy people and the blind people. They can play together in the game in order to construct interaction between their social lives. The hardware of the proposed game employs passive RFID technology, the Arduino microcontroller, a sound module, and a NAND Flash device.

Gesture-based interaction is a new trend that adds a new level of immersion to video games. However, players who are blind are unable to play them as these games use visual cues to indicate what gesture to provide and when. Therefore, a solution could be the use of vibrotactile stimulation of skin receptors to guide visually impaired people. Adame, Jing Yu, Moller and Seemann (2013) presented different wearable low-budget prototypes that integrated vibration motors as the ones used in mobile phones. Morelli and Folmer (2014) discussed a solution that uses real-time video analysis to detect the presence of a particular visual cue, which is substituted by a vibrotactile cue that is provided with an external controller.

There are also other projects based on braille. For instance, BraillePlay is a suite of accessible games for smartphones that teach Braille character encodings. The BraillePlay games are based on VBraille, a method for displaying Braille characters on a smartphone (Milne, Bennett, Ladner, & Azenkot, 2014). Another approach of this type is VBGhost (Milne, Bennett, & Ladner, 2013) an accessible educational smartphone game using audio and haptic feedback to reinforce Braille concepts. Players enter letters in the game by using Braille dot patterns on a touchscreen interface. Tang (2015) presented the Blind Mahjong Game (BMG). It also uses low-cost RFID as the mediation between the blind player and computer.

The TIM project used a specially designed keyboard and a scripting language to adapt existing educational games for visually impaired children (Archambault & Burger, 2000). Another approach could be the use of multimodal interfaces. Sánchez, Darin, and Andrade (2015) presented a summary of approaches and technologies currently in use for the development of mental maps, cognitive spatial structures, and navigation skills in learners who are blind by using multimodal videogames. This work shows some trends in interface characterization and interaction style that worth to be mentioned. One aspect is that all of the 21 applications used at least one aural interface element, although most of the cases combined two or more aural elements. The prevailing combination was between iconic and spatialized sound in 3D environments. Iconic sounds were the most common type of sonorous feedback (16 applications), followed by spatialized sounds (11 applications). The spoken audio (11 applications) was more prevalent than speech synthesis (7 applications), even though 5 applications combine the two types. Stereo sound was also used in 5 applications. Only one application used music/tones to represent different objects. Another aspect worth to be mentioned was the fact that 20 applications presented a graphic interface in addition to the aural elements and there were not applications with sound-only interfaces. It is also important to stress that the most common interaction pattern was the keyboard, used by 15 applications. The second more used interaction form was the joystick (7 applications). Two applications allowed the use of the mouse together with the keyboard and one application had the mouse as the primary interaction mode. Only 2 applications allowed the user to give natural language commands.

Darin, Sánchez and Andrade (2015) presented and discussed a 4-dimension classification: Interface, Interaction, Cognition, and Evaluation, to analyse the design of multimodal videogames for the cognition of blind people is presented and discussed. Another research line in which we are interested in is the use of games in mobile devices. Csapó, Wersényi, Nagy and Stockman (2015) presented an overview of developments concerning mobile and handheld devices is presented. It is of the utmost importance to start thinking in making accessible products and games, for all. Mangiron and Zhang (2016) analyse the current state of game accessibility, particularly for the blind and visually impaired. They discuss the barriers and gaming options for this target group, they also propose the application of audio description to video games, which would potentially enhance game accessibility for blind and visually impaired players.

## Masterblind Application

One of the most significant cognitive issues for people who are blind is the development of orientation and mobility skills so that the individual can become autonomous and independent. For an efficient navigation and the development of orientation skills, a person needs to construct a mental representation or mental map of the surrounding environment. However, the absence of vision adds more complexity to easy tasks that require spatial representation (Lahav & Mioduser, 2008). Therefore, a person who is blind needs to use complementary non-visual stimuli to perceive the environment and construct mental maps. Sound has a fundamental role to perceive and interact with the environment. In this work a study was performed to understand which kind of sounds work better to help blind people to play games.

A computer game adaptation of the board game Mastermind ("MASTERMIND | Toys for Kids | Hasbro Games," n.d.) was designed and prototyped to address the difficulties in visual interfaces blind users may have - *MasterBlind*. The main design problem was to understand how the original concept of Mastermind, that relies so much on visual information, could be adapted to a computer game for blind users without any visual output. Three main aspects of the role of visual information were identified and hypothesized to have a significant role on the mechanics of the original game:

1. Distinctive capacity of the user to clearly identify each element of the secret key;
2. Accurate, but at the same time, vague feedback that provides just enough information for the player to derive the correct solution without losing the puzzling element that is essential for these kind of games;
3. Accessibility of information about the previous plays to minimize repeated answers in the following attempts.

To address these aspects, several design choices were made. Following the direction of Targett and Fernstrom (2003) using audio feedback and simplifying the game mechanics has driven those choices. To keep the balance between enjoyability and the challenge that one derives from a puzzle game such as this one, the number of possible elements for the secret keys was reduced from eight to only four elements and repetitions were excluded. Verbal feedbacks about the number of right positions in each round provided enough information to try new combinations and derive the secret key, without reducing the challenge of the task. Research has shown that blind people seem to be more efficient in remembering routines and patterns (Raz, Striem, Pundak, Orlov, & Zohary, 2007) and have more efficient auditory short-term and long-term memory (Hötting & Röder, 2009) - although there are differences between congenital and non-congenital blindness in the accuracy and fidelity in memory tests (Pasqualotto, Lam, & Proulx, 2013). But, what kind of sounds would work better to help users recall the last sequence? In designing auditory cues in a user interface a distinction is made between auditory icons and earcons (Absar & Guastavino, 2008). An auditory icon is a brief sound that is used to represent a specific event, object, function, or action. They are essentially emulations or caricatures of naturally occurring sounds in everyday life taking advantage of the user's prior knowledge and natural auditory associations between sounds and their results (Absar & Guastavino, 2008). Auditory icons can represent directly or indirectly an object, either by using the sound made by the target event, or by substituting a surrogate for the target - requiring additional learning to develop the relationship between the sound and a specific event (Absar & Guastavino, 2008). Earcons are brief, nonverbal, distinctive audio sounds used to represent a specific event, usually abstract, synthetic, and mostly musical tones or sound patterns that can be used in structured combinations. Since they don't deliver any natural representational value they require more learning than direct auditory icons (Absar & Guastavino, 2008). The prototypes were developed with the Scratch tool ("Scratch - Imagine, Program, Share," n.d.), a programming platform, that allows simple and easy programming through direct manipulation of blocks and visual elements. The users interact with the game using the Makey Makey ("Makey Makey | Buy Direct (Official Site)," 2016) - a circuit board that connects any conductive physical object to a computer by replacing the keyboard and mouse click signals with touch on real objects. The Makey Makey player can choose any four everyday objects of his/her choice (as long as they are conductive) but in this case it was not possible to refer the objects by their names (speech) or a direct auditory representation (auditory icon). The research of Mynatt (1994) suggests that although more realistic sounds, such as auditory icons reveal greater functional utility, there may be a preference for abstract musical sounds. Therefore we sought to find a compromise between the realism and the abstraction of the designed sounds, in order to provide further meaning to the user, exploring different levels of meaning either in the relationship between the sounds, or in the semantic and naturalistic relation that the sounds have in relation to the learning process of the users. Three alternatives for auditory feedback were designed and three different prototypes corresponding to those alternatives were used to test their efficiency. One alternative associates each object to a note of the pentatonic scale. The ease in creating recognizable melodies with different combinations of the notes of this scale provides additional melodic information over tonic sounds, introducing a second level of meaning that might strengthen memorization - earcons. Other alternative links voices of animals (cow, rooster, cat, sheep) reinforcing the recalling power through association with realistic sounds that are clearly identifiable to users and through conceptual immersion on the animal topic - auditory icons. The last one uses the sounds of vowels ("a", "e", "i", "o"), using basic speech sounds with a long history of learning and semantic and sequential value - providing an order familiar to most users – auditory icons that may benefit memorizing strategies. The main hypothesis of the present study predicts that blind users will consciously benefit from the auditory feedback provided and use it to better recall previous sequences. The second hypothesis predicts that, although users may find it more enjoyable, they will benefit less from the feedback that does not provide semantic or conceptual information.

## Chapter Organization

This chapter is organized as follows: Section 2 presents the Sample description and the Game description. Section 3 describes the methodology used in this research: initial interview; usability tests; retrospective think aloud and questionnaires. The results and their discussion are presented in Section 4, and in Section 5 some conclusions are provided. Two topics of further work are discussed in Section 6. The bibliography is in the last section.

## EXPERIMENTAL PROCEDURE

The following subsections describe the sample used and the principal features that might be important to the game prototype. The game is also described in detail in section 2.2.

## Participants

The study took place over a period of two months at the headquarters of ACAPO (a Portuguese acronym for Association of the Blind and Partially Sighted of Portugal) Coimbra ("ACAPO - Associação dos Cegos e Amblíopes de Portugal," 2016) carried out by students of Master Human Computer Interaction (HCI) of Coimbra Polytechnic Institute ("Human Computer Interaction - ESEC," 2016). We performed a set of nine individual sessions with blind volunteers, divided between 5 males and 4 females with ages ranging from 21 to 66 years old, education levels between the 4th grade and post-graduation, and a diverse background of job occupations. Although only four of the volunteers had smartphones, we found that almost all of them were already familiarized with a computer, whether it be in work related tasks or leisure. It's also noteworthy mentioning that most of them were not used to play video games, playing more palpable and physical games instead, like cards, dominoes and various board games. Thus, all characterization information of the participants is resumed in Table 1.

## The Game

*MasterBlind* is a computer game adaptation of the board game Mastermind designed and prototyped to address the difficulties in visual interfaces blind users may have. There are several variations of the game, but the original concept is based on having a player generating/choosing a secret key of four coloured pieces out of a set of eight different colours - with or without repetitions of the same colour - while the other player, in several rounds, tries to guess the correct secret key previously generated. At each round the second player tests a combination of coloured pieces and according to the feedback given by the first player, he tries to deduce the key by presenting new combinations. The feedback provided by the first player consists in informing the second player of how many pieces are the correct colours in the correct position, and how many pieces are the correct colours but in the wrong position. The game ends when the key is discovered or the number of maximum attempts is reached. Concerning the duration of the exploration, it should be noted that the participants were not limited in time to accomplish the task. To address the fact that the original game relies largely on visual information, several design choices were made such as simplifying the game mechanics and implementing audio feedback. The number of

*Table 1. Information of all users considering: age, gender, scholarship, smartphone, videogames and computational literacy*

|  | Age | Gender | Scholarship | Smartphone | Videogames | Computational Literacy |
|---|---|---|---|---|---|---|
| Ind1 | 52 | M | 6th grade | No | Yes | Poor |
| Ind2 | 53 | F | 9th grade | No | No | Median |
| Ind3 | 66 | M | 4th grade | No | No | Poor |
| Ind4 | 49 | M | 4th grade | No | No | Median |
| Ind5 | 34 | F | 12th grade | Yes | No | Median |
| Ind6 | ND | F | post-graduation | No | No | High |
| Ind7 | 447 | M | graduation | Yes | No | High |
| Ind8 | 21 | F | 12th grade | Yes | No | Median |
| Ind9 | 24 | M | 12th grade | Yes | No | High |

possible elements for the secret keys was reduced from eight to only four elements and repetitions were excluded. This way, due to the secret key also having only four elements in total and the repetitions no longer being allowed, one could eliminate the need for excessive feedback and consequent confusion. The possible elements to choose for the secret key and that same secret key are both limited to four elements, so it is already implied that the player is using the correct elements, thus reducing the feedback just by informing the player about how many elements are in the correct position. Then, the role of colour in the original game was replaced by using real physical objects - through Makey Makey and a distinctive sound, elicited when the player touched the object (and repeated in a sequential order at the end of each round) was associated to each one of the objects. Through this step, the distinctive aspect of the elements was improved and the availability of information about the last play was reinforced by repetition and auditory memory. Furthermore, the availability of information about previous plays might need further addressing. Possible trajectories could be adding more features to the prototype (decreasing its simplicity) or improving the ability of the content to be remembered.

In short, to play *MasterBlind*, a secret key is generated in the beginning of the game, and a user has ten attempts to guess it. In each try, a user must touch two times in each of the four objects, the first time to identify the object, and if that object is the one intended a second touch is needed to confirm the choice. Note that for all versions, the objects selected were four fruits - banana, kiwi, apple and orange. When all of the four objects are chosen/confirmed, the user will hear the sounds associated to each one of the objects by the order they have chosen and a verbal feedback informing the number of correct positions in that guess/attempt. As in the original game, the game ends when the key is discovered or the number of maximum attempts (10) is reached. Three versions of the *MasterBlind* game, Figure 1, were developed and differed on the feedback that was transmitted to the player about the outcome of each round of the game, one had a pentatonic scale, the other had animal sounds (a rooster, a cat, a sheep and a cow) and the last one had spoken vowels ("a", "e", "i","o"). The versions are available in the following online links:

- Pentatonic Scale available in https://scratch.mit.edu/projects/81471814/;
- Vowels available in https://scratch.mit.edu/projects/81471958/,
- Animals Sounds in https://scratch.mit.edu/projects/81471880/.

*Figure 1. MasterBlind game*

## METHODOLOGY

The methodology used to understand what kind of sounds would work better to help blind people play the *MasterBlind* game was divided into four sets. Each session took around 30 minutes and different qualitative research methods were employed:

1.    A semi structured survey - Initial interview;
2.    A set of three usability tests;
3.    Three retrospective think aloud (one after each test);
4.    A questionnaire which was rated through a Likert scale (Likert & R., 1932) (a tool used in which participants are asked to respond to statements on a scale ranging from "strongly agree" to "strongly disagree").

## Initial Interview

Semi structured interviewing starts with more general questions or topics. Relevant topics are initially identified and the possible relationship between these topics and the issues such as availability, expense, effectiveness become the basis for more specific questions which do not need to be prepared in advance (Holtzblatt, Wendell, & Wood, 2005).

We started with individual semi-structured interviews where we collected data on the following topics:

1.    Demographic data;
2.    Education;
3.    Occupation;
4.    Computer usage frequency/proficiency;
5.    Smartphone usage frequency/proficiency;
6.    Games and computer games habits.

The results of contextual inquiry were used to define requirements, improve a process, learn what is important to users and customers, and just learn more about a new domain to inform future projects.

## Usability Tests

The primary goal of a usability test is to improve the usability of the product being tested. While there can be wide variations in where and how to conduct a usability test, we made an effort to have the following characteristics based from the book of Dumas and Redish (1999):

1.    The participants represent real users. We used blind people from ACAPO.
2.    The participants did real tasks.
3.    We observed and recorded what participants did and said.
4.    We analysed the data, diagnosed the problems and have in mind changes to fix those problems.

We also considered it was not required to have a usability laboratory or a formal test report. However, several aspects were taken in consideration:

1.  **The Duration of Tests:** Even though, in the majority of situations the time for testing is reduced as it has implications for budgets and schedules, in this situation we were not preoccupied with it and gave to participants the time they wanted. However, the total duration never exceeded 1 session of 1h for each participant.
2.  **The Type of Tasks:** Even though, in the majority of situations each test covers only a few features or relevant tasks of a product, in this situation and given the characteristic of the game we chose to test the complete game.
3.  **The Planning of Tests:** it involved defining the goals, deciding who should be the participants, recruiting participants, organizing the tasks to test, creating task scenarios, deciding how to measure usability, preparing other materials for the test and preparing the test environment.

As we tested a product that people were so interested in, there were no payments or incentives. However, it should be noticed that it is the exception rather than the rule. But we had an enthusiastic cooperation of these type of users. Nevertheless, lots of careful was put in all the process. We thanked the participants for agreeing to participate, we explained those thinks such as: the date and time we expect them to be there, how long to expect to be with them, the purpose of the test, that they need not to bring anything, that there were no payment (it is an academic work). We also remembered they were being observed and that they have three retrospective think aloud questioning (one after each test) and a final questionnaire. In order to minimize the inconveniences of the participants we also moved to the place indicated by them. We also gave our name and phone number to call if they have questions or need to reschedule.

After deciding the list of tasks for the test, we presented those tasks to participants telling them what we wanted them to do during the test. At the beginning of the test, the person (briefer) who interacts with the participant, also reminded the participant: to wait for the briefer to say when to begin the first task, to say out loud when the task is done, to wait again between each task until the briefer says to go ahead.

Before the real usability tests we also conduct a pilot test in order to rehearsal for the usability test to follow. The idea was to "debug" the equipment, software, materials and procedures to be used for the test and to practice the activities to be used.

Before starting the usability tests, we introduced the game prototype to each participant so they could have a first contact with it and clearly understand the rules of the game. There was an initial training period of around 10 minutes, so that the subjects could get familiar with the task and the sounds. During the training period the subjects could hear the sounds in the order they wished and repeat them as often as necessary. During training the subjects received feedback, but once the actual test started no more feedback was given.

We tested three different versions of the game in which the order of the tests was randomized for every participant. Each version consisted in ten rounds in which the user could try to guess the correct key.

## Retrospective Think Aloud

At the end of each test the participants were asked to explain their reasoning in the game in order to guess the correct key. Think aloud methods are often used when trying to detect usability problems. The most successful form of think aloud to use together with a system is a retrospective think aloud methodology (RTA), which means that participants verbalize their thoughts after completing a task or a set of tasks. RTA allows the participant to complete a task on his/her own and in silence. This method is also called post-task testing, retrospective protocol, retrospective report or think after (Guan, Lee,

Cuddihy, & Ramey, n.d.). RTA has been widely used, and people do believe that it provides valuable data. The method has a host of advantages. Most important, it serves as a window to the soul, allowing the discovery of what users really think about the design. In particular, we hear their misconceptions, which usually turn into actionable redesign recommendations: when users misinterpret design elements, we need to change them. Even better, we usually learn *why* users guess wrong about some parts of the interface and why they find others easy to use.

## Questionnaire

The questionnaire step is an essential input to requirements and the planning of other usability methods. It may be collected at an early stage during planning and feasibility, or in more detail as part of the usability requirements (Chin, Diehl, & Norman, 1988).

At the end of the series of tests, participants were asked to answer a questionnaire based on a Likert scale, in order to gather feedback about the comparative efficiency of the different approaches. The scale has five-level Likert item that means: 1) Strongly disagree; 2) Disagree; 3) Neither agree nor disagree; 4) Agree; 5) Strongly agree. In the questionnaire, eight questions (statements) for evaluation by the users were considered:

**Q1:** It was easy to remember the previous combinations when I heard the pentatonic scale.
**Q2:** Listening to the spoken vowels helped me more than listening to the pentatonic scale.
**Q3:** It was easy to remember the previous combinations when I heard the animal sounds.
**Q4:** It could not guide myself by the sounds.
**Q5:** Listening to the pentatonic scale helped me more than listening to animal sounds.
**Q6:** It was easy to remember the previous combinations when I heard the spoken vowels.
**Q7:** Listening to the animal sounds helped me more than listening to the spoken vowels.
**Q8:** The sounds only hindered me.

## RESULTS AND DISCUSSION

In order to validate the system we made a pilot study with visually impaired subjects. The goal of this study was to understand which prototype could efficiently work better. Results show that the users were overall more successful with the prototype using animal sounds and sounds of vowels than the prototype with pentatonic notes as feedback.

Figure 1 presents the results by user, which successfully identified the correct key for each version of the prototype, as well as, the users that failed.

By the results it can be concluded that three users (Ind3, and Ind5 Ind8) do not hit the key, regardless of the considered prototype. Furthermore, only one user hits the key for all prototypes (Ind. 7). Making a global analysis, it is verified that the prototype with higher success rate is the prototype of animals' sounds – auditory icons. Note that the spoken vowels as well as pentatonic scale versions of the prototype present a small accuracy (less than 50%).

The number of unsuccessful tries (in 10) for each version of the prototype, by each user, must be in account, Figure 3. Considering only the tries related for each version by users associated to the success,

*Figure 2. Results to identify the correct key in each version of the prototype (pentatonic, animals and vowels) by user (Ind1 – Ind9) where 1 represents the success and -1 represents the unsuccessful*

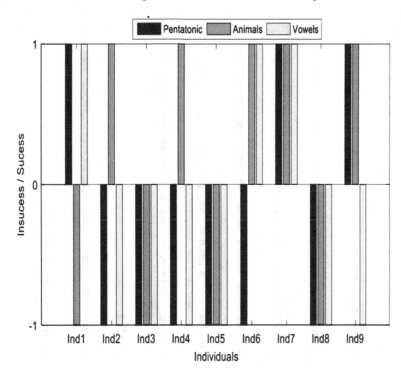

it is possible to conclude that in average pentatonic version presents the best result. In average, 3.8 tries are necessary for the users to be successful with pentatonic scale, 4 tries are necessary for the users to be successful with spoken vowels and with the version where users were more successful (Figure 2) – animal sounds – requires in average a greater amount of tries (4.6).

Crossing the data of Figure 2 and Figure 3 it is possible to infer that the prototype of animal sounds is the most successful, however the number of attempts to hit the key is higher compared to other prototypes. The pentatonic prototype has a small number of attempts to hit the key.

The computational literacy is also an important factor that should be account in this discussion. Ind. 7 presents the better results and is the only the user with high scholarship. On the other hand, Ind. 1 is the second user with best performance but his scholarship and computational literacy are poor. Thus, it is possible to conclude that this application can be accessible by users, independently of their computational literacy as well as their scholarship.

After finishing the experiments for each of the versions of the prototypes, users expressed their opinion regarding the game, their interaction with the game-retrospective think-aloud. The think-aloud was fruitful to understand the importance of auditory stimuli or other strategic references for memorizing sequences. The opinions of the users were divided considering three important variables: auditory feedback, spatial awareness and multimodal interaction (auditory feedback + spatial awareness).

Figure 4 shows that users pay more attention to auditory feedback only in the versions with animal voices; in the pentatonic notes version the users describe consciously to ignore the sounds and pay attention to spatial awareness and in vowels version the users describe paying more attention to spatial awareness. Users reported multimodal interaction as the less important interaction in all prototype versions.

*Figure 3. Number of unsuccessful tries for each version of the prototype (pentatonic, animals and vowels) by user (Ind 1 – Ind 9)*

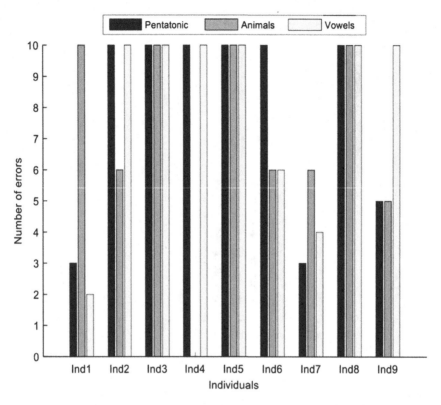

*Figure 4. Restropective Think-Aloud results considering three categarization: audio, spatial and mul-timodal interation*

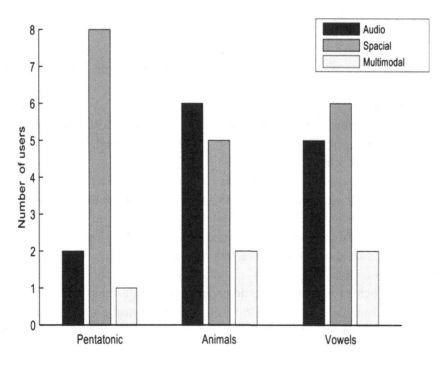

In the end of the tests, as explained in the last section, a questionnaire was done to better understand the users and their interaction with the system. Statistic information about the classification by all participants is presented for each question (Q1 – Q8) in Table 2 and Figure 5. The results are consistent with the results obtained by the usability tests and by the retrospective think-aloud methodology. Animal sounds are presented as the better alternative compared with both the vowel sounds version and the pentatonic notes version - which, comparatively, is the worst alternative. Both think-aloud and questionnaires results indicate that auditory feedback was not the only variable, and often not the most important, for recalling previous sequences. Spatial awareness of the objects seems to play an important role in this process.

*Table 2. Classification results by the Likert Scale for all questions (Q1 to Q8) considering the mean, the standard deviation and the mode, as parameters*

|        | Mean (μ) | Standard Deviation (σ) | Mode |
|--------|----------|------------------------|------|
| **Q1** | 3,11     | 0,99                   | 4    |
| **Q2** | 3,78     | 1,14                   | 5    |
| **Q3** | 3,67     | 1,33                   | 5    |
| **Q4** | 2,56     | 1,16                   | 1    |
| **Q5** | 2,67     | 1,11                   | 2    |
| **Q6** | 3,56     | 0,94                   | 3    |
| **Q7** | 3,67     | 0,89                   | 4    |
| **Q8** | 1,78     | 0,86                   | 1    |

*Figure 5. Boxplots of the classification of all questions, considering all users and the Likert scale*

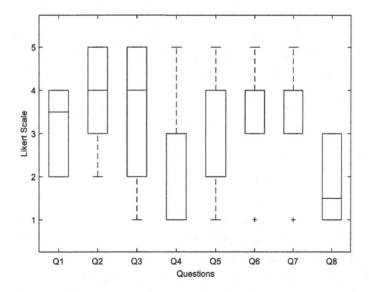

## FUTURE RESEARCH DIRECTIONS

Several tests and developments are underway. However, we are mainly interested in following two types of approaches: a development of a mobile version of *MasterBlind* and the use of a Brain Computer Interface (BCI) to extract and analyse information of interest while users play *MasterBlind*. Nevertheless, further developments about the understanding of what people think they hear are planned. Consequently, the first step to follow in a near future is to conduct listening tests. The following subsections describe our ideas underlying these two approaches. After these developments an extended sample will be used.

### Mobile MasterBlind Version

Smartphones are nowadays-essential accessories for people. More and more people interaction occurs on mobile devices. The use of Smartphones has improved the life of everyone and also those with disabilities. However, the majority of mobile applications remain inaccessible to people with visual impairment.

In this study, we want firstly to know how people with visual impairment use mobile phones. We want to have participants with visual impairment performing specified technologic tasks. For that, we will follow several usability/accessibility techniques: the observation, think aloud and interviews. We believe that the conjugation of all these methods could determine the use patterns that give us the best orientation.

As Braille is a method widely used by blind people to read and write, we also intend to experiment several interactions with "Focus Braille". This equipment combines the latest Braille technology with a user-friendly keyboard and control layout, plus USB and Bluetooth connectivity. It easily connects to mobile devices. We already used Heuristic walkthrough method with experts with normal vision trying this equipment; however only after their utilization with impaired users we can confirm their utility.

Then, we want to implement a new version of *MasterBlind* using the "MIT App Inventor". It is a tool developed in MIT, and like Scratch it enables an innovative beginner's introduction to programming. It enables the creation of applications through drag-and-drop visual building blocks instead the use of complex language of text-based coding. This new game will be developed according to the previous results and also systematic guidelines and standards of designing accessible mobile applications. Regarding the latter aspect, a compilation of literature about how to design mobile environments for people with disabilities will be done. Works such as the one made by Plos and Buisine (2006), Krajnc, Feiner, and Schmidt (2010), De Souza, Sánchez and Gomes (2011), Kane, Wobbrock and Ladner (2011), Chiti and Leporini (2012), Liimatainen, Häkkinen, Nousiainen, Kankaanranta and Neittaanmäki (2012) and will serve as the base for this research.

### Assessment of Audio Sounds

It is unquestionable that using sound for representing interaction is very convenient for non-visual communication in general. However, designing interactive sonifications requires a number of issues to be considered, especially where, how and what sonification is appropriate for.

We consider that when projecting systems for the visually impaired the sound is a crucial way to enhance interaction, however ways of creating and testing auditory metaphors need to be deeply explored in order to determine where sound contributes to the users' performance. To design with sound, we need a high-level understanding of what and how we hear (Gaver, 1986).

A crucial aspect to consider is how to select sounds to be suitable for a particular interaction and task. In general, depending on users, tasks and context, the chosen sounds should be more concrete (auditory icons) or abstract (earcons). Our main concern is to have audio messages with good mappings and metaphors for very effective feedback.

Auditory icons, if adequately chosen, have the advantage of being easily learnt and remembered, as they are natural and relatable to everyday things. However, there are functions and objects without real-world equivalents making it hard to find a good metaphor to represent them.

Earcons have the opposite disadvantage as they have no natural intuitive link to some functions or objects they have to be learned and remembered, however they have the advantage of being highly structured.

To further develop our understanding of what people think they hear we are planning to conduct listening tests in a near future, an approach also used by many other researchers (Brewster, 1997; Talsma, Doty, & Woldorff, 2006).

Our main concern is to test where (different environments, task situations and users) auditory icons and earcons are more effective. For this we will have different types of sounds that will be tested in a number of ways. For instance, we will have tasks consisting of listening to the recorded sounds in random order using headphones, and the user will have to identify what each sound is. We are interested in having quite different sounds that will follow well-defined criteria in order to avoid issues of ambiguity and loss of context. As designers we also must take into account the users' capabilities, while carrying out tasks in real environments, and also consider that surrounding noise levels might mask the system's sounds. The context is an important factor to consider. While it is assumed that everyday sounds have inherent meaning, learnt from our everyday activities, hearing such sounds in isolation without context can be quite confusing.

Another question to analyse is the number of sensorial channels to be used and exploited. The cognitive ability to focus attention on information in one sensory modality while ignoring information in another remains poorly understood. Should we present sounds in unimodal or bimodal way? Individual sounds or simultaneously with haptic technology (touch based interfaces).

Even though our research shows that non speech audio is an effective means of communicating information to the user in the computer interface, be it via auditory icons or earcons, there has been no fully conclusive evidence to be able to say that one method of feedback is most certainly better than the other in a certain environment. We think that more studies are needed on what people hear with different types of sounds in order to increase our understanding of the perceptual and cognitive processes involved. First of all we want to test the same sounds in a multitude of applications in order to say if the same results are maintained. Hence, for future research, it would be worth investigating these functional mappings more closely, design more general tasks and environments, and evaluate if they are truly optimal for those respective contexts.

Hence, designing formal evaluations of more functions and utilities of auditory icons in different task environments, in the context of human-computer interfaces, also merits further research. Further research is also required to combine the two types of auditory feedback in a single system, by using both types of sounds to their full potential and capabilities.

With the findings of the listening tests, we can suggest possible auditory representations and metaphors more suitable for interaction design.

## Brain Computer Interaction Analysis

We are preparing initiatives to use new forms of interaction as Brain Computer Interfaces (BCI) using body signals to extract information of interest.

The first phase of this work intends to acquire measurements on aspects of interest (emotions, concentration, frustration, load/stress, cognitive level) in different scenarios where "normal" and "impaired" visual people playing *MasterBlind* will be compared. BCI research seeks to develop an alternative communication channel between humans and machines. These devices determine the intent of the user from scalprecorded electrical brain signals (EEG Electroencephalogram) or from electrodes surgically implanted on the cortical surface (ECoG ElectroCorticoGraphy) or within the brain (neuronal action potentials or local field potentials) (Chiti & Leporini, 2012). These signals are translated into commands that operate a computerized application. Despite advances in this research field the BCI systems are still presenting several challenges that can be resumed in: Usability, Accuracy and Speed. Many factors determine the performance of a BCI system, among them is the quality of the brain signals, the methods used to extract signal information and the output applications. A BCI device must take into account all of these factors to provide a reliable performance (Kane et al., 2011). The traditional BCI system has two distinct stages. The first one is the training stage, where mutual adaptation of the BCI system and the user is performed. During this stage, the BCI parameters are tuned based on specific training scenarios. The second stage corresponds to the normal functioning of the BCI, termed as the online stage, where the BCI parameters are fixed. However the EEG signals are nonstationary, their statistics can suffer significant changes over time, and periodic calibration of the system may improve its reliability. In order to address these issues, the key characteristic of the BCI is its adaptability. The BCI system must be able to identify malfunctioning events (for example accumulation of errors in interpreting the user intentions) and provide a way to correct them (Kane et al., 2011). A new adaptive BCI architecture is used which can switch back to the training stage in order to adapt the BCI parameters in malfunctioning situations. Such situations are detected by extracting EEG Error Potentials.

We are preparing the use of this kind of BCI systems to make new usability/accessibility tests with blind people. In the context of substituting the visual channel for the auditory channel, this study aims to verify if it is possible to substitute visual feedback for its auditory equivalent and assess the impact that different type of auditory (mono, stereo, 3D,...) feedback has on BCI performance. A BCI not reliant upon the visual modality not only releases the visual channel for other uses but also offers an attractive means of communication for the physically impaired who are also blind or vision impaired. Tests will measure which group (The visual group or the impaired visual group) perform best and which type of auditory feedback methods and sounds are more intuitive. The results will also be used to select the most appropriate sounds for auditory feedback. We are also interested in analyse if there are differences in brain organization and performance capabilities between individuals who are "early blind" and "late blind".

## CONCLUSION

This chapter presents a study consisting in an adaptation of the Mastermind board game for blind users called *MasterBlind*. In this game the usual visual clues were substituted by audio. However, in order to understand what kind of sounds would work better to help users recall the last sequence, three types of auditory feedback were designed. The main hypothesis predicted that blind users would consciously benefit from the auditory feedback provided and use it to better recall previous sequences. Although users described having used more often spatial awareness as a strategy to recall previous sequences, they were actually more successful when they paid attention to sounds, alone or in combination with spatial awareness. The less they used auditory feedback the less successful they were. The second hypothesis may provide an explanation for the differences in users behaviour regarding attention to auditory feedback. Predicting that users would benefit less from the feedback that does not provide semantic information (earcons), was an assumption made on familiarity with the sounds (animal sounds, vowels) and the very structure of semantic memory (auditory icons). A sound like pentatonic notes that are less distinct, less familiar and is semantically irrelevant to the user, provide less power to the recalling process of previous sequences. Therefore, *MasterBlind* can be a usable experience for blind people, as long as it uses semantically significant auditory feedback. Overall, the study offers evidence that an adaptation of a board game, such as Mastermind, that relies mostly in visual information can be successfully adapted to blind users and still provide a challenging and enjoyable experience - even with users that have little to no experience in computer games.

Despite the fact that only with a more extensive and accurate analysis be possible to obtain final conclusions, the results and analysis already done present some slight evidences that allow to weave the above considerations, namely proposed developments in the next stage of the whole project.

## ACKNOWLEDGMENT

We would like to thank Dr. José Mário Albino of the Blind and Partially Sighted Association of Portugal (ACAPO - Coimbra).

## REFERENCES

Absar, R., & Guastavino, C. (2008). Usability of non-speech sounds in user interfaces.*Proceedings of the 14th International Conference on Auditory Display*. Paris France.

ACAPO - Associação dos Cegos e Amblíopes de Portugal. (2016). Retrieved October 23, 2016, from http://www.acapo.pt/

Adame, M. R., Jing, Yu., Moller, K., & Seemann, E. (2013). A wearable navigation aid for blind people using a vibrotactile information transfer system. *Proceedings of the2013 ICME International Conference on Complex Medical Engineering* (pp. 13–18). IEEE. http://doi.org/ doi:10.1109/ICCME.2013.6548203

Balan, O., Moldoveanu, A., & Moldoveanu, F. (2014). Navigational 3D audio-based game-training towards rich auditory spatial representation of the environment. *Proceedings of the 18th International Conference on System Theory, Control and Computing (ICSTCC)* (pp. 682–687). http://doi.org/ doi:10.1109/ICSTCC.2014.6982496

Balan, O., Moldoveanu, A., Moldoveanu, F., & Dascalu, M. I. (2014). Audio Games – A novel approach towards effective learning in the case of visually-impaired people. *Proceedings of the7th International Conference of Education, Research and InnovationICERI '14* (pp. 6542–6548). IATED.

Brewster, S. A. (1997). Using Non-Speech Sound to Overcome Information Overload. *Displays*, *17*(3), 179–189. Retrieved from http://eprints.gla.ac.uk/3249/ doi:10.1016/S0141-9382(96)01034-7

Chin, J. P., Diehl, V. A., & Norman, L. K. (1988). Development of an instrument measuring user satisfaction of the human-computer interface.*Proceedings of the SIGCHI conference on Human factors in computing systems CHI '88* (pp. 213–218). New York, USA: ACM Press. doi:10.1145/57167.57203

Chiti, S., & Leporini, B. (2012). *Accessibility of Android-Based Mobile Devices: A Prototype to Investigate Interaction with Blind Users* (pp. 607–614). Springer. doi:10.1007/978-3-642-31534-3_89

Csapó, Á., Wersényi, G., Nagy, H., & Stockman, T. (2015). A survey of assistive technologies and applications for blind users on mobile platforms: A review and foundation for research. *Journal on Multimodal User Interfaces*, *9*(4), 275–286. doi:10.1007/s12193-015-0182-7

Darin, T., Sánchez, J., & Andrade, R. M. C. (2015). Dimensions to Analyze the Design of Multimodal Videogames for the Cognition of People Who Are Blind. Proceedings of the XIV Simpósio Brasileiro sobre Fatores Humanos em Sistemas Computacionais Conference (IHC '15), Salvador Baia, Brasil. Doi:10.13140/RG.2.1.1749.9287

Dumas, J., & Redish, J. (1999). *A Practical Guide to Usability Testing*. Portland.

Galinhas, B. (2011). Developing an accessible interaction model for touch screen mobile devices: preliminary results. *Proceedings of the 10th Brazilian Symposium on Human Factors in Computing Systems and the 5th Latin American Conference on Human-Computer Interaction* (pp. 222–226). Brazilian Computer Society.

Gaver, W. (1986). Auditory Icons: Using Sound in Computer Interfaces. *Human-Computer Interaction*, *2*(2), 167–177. doi:10.1207/s15327051hci0202_3

Grabski, A., Toni, T., Zigrand, T., Weller, R., & Zachmann, G. (2016). Kinaptic - Techniques and insights for creating competitive accessible 3D games for sighted and visually impaired users. *Proceedings of the2016 IEEE Haptics Symposium (HAPTICS)* (pp. 325–331). IEEE. http://doi.org/ doi:10.1109/HAPTICS.2016.7463198

Guan, Z., Lee, S., Cuddihy, E., & Ramey, J. (n. d.). *The Validity of the Stimulated Retrospective Think-Aloud Method as Measured by Eye Tracking*.

Holtzblatt, K., Wendell, J. B., & Wood, S. (2005). *Rapid contextual design : a how-to guide to key techniques for user-centered design*. Elsevier/Morgan Kaufmann.

Hötting, K., & Röder, B. (2009). Auditory and auditory-tactile processing in congenitally blind humans. *Hearing Research*, *258*(1–2), 165–174. doi:10.1016/j.heares.2009.07.012 PMID:19651199

Human Computer Interaction - ESEC. (2016). Retrieved from https://www.esec.pt/pagina.php?id=429

Ibrahim, A. A. A., & Embug, A. J. (2014). Sonification of 3D body movement using parameter mapping technique. *Proceedings of the 6th International Conference on Information Technology and Multimedia* (pp. 385–389). IEEE. http://doi.org/ doi:10.1109/ICIMU.2014.7066664

Iglesias, R., Casado, S., Gutierrez, T., Barbero, J. I., Avizzano, C. A., Marcheschi, S., & Bergamasco, M. (n.d.). Computer graphics access for blind people through a haptic and audio virtual environment. *Proceedings. Second International Conference on Creating, Connecting and Collaborating through Computing* (pp. 13–18). IEEE. http://doi.org/ doi:<ALIGNMENT.qj></ALIGNMENT>10.1109/ HAVE.2004.1391874

Kane, S. K., Wobbrock, J. O., & Ladner, R. E. (2011). Usable gestures for blind people.*Proceedings of the 2011 annual conference on Human factors in computing systems - CHI'11* (p. 413). New York, New York, USA: ACM Press. doi:10.1145/1978942.1979001

Kim, S., Lee, K., & Nam, T.-J. (2016). Sonic-Badminton. *Proceedings of the 2016 CHI Conference Extended Abstracts on Human Factors in Computing Systems - CHI EA '16* (pp. 1922–1929). New York, USA: ACM Press. http://doi.org/ doi:10.1145/2851581.2892510

Krajnc, E., Feiner, J., & Schmidt, S. (2010). *User Centered Interaction Design for Mobile Applications Focused on Visually Impaired and Blind People* (pp. 195–202). Springer Berlin Heidelberg; doi:10.1007/978-3-642-16607-5_12

Lee, Y.-C., Yao, C.-Y., Hsieh, C.-Y., Wu, J.-Y., Hsieh, Y.-H., & Chen, C.-H., … Chen, Y.-S. (2013). Egg Pair — A hearing game for the visually impaired people using RFID. *Proceedings of the2013 IEEE International Symposium on Consumer Electronics (ISCE)* (pp. 3–4). IEEE. http://doi.org/ doi:10.1109/ ISCE.2013.6570237

Liimatainen, J., Häkkinen, M., Nousiainen, T., Kankaanranta, M., & Neittaanmäki, P. (2012). *A Mobile Application Concept to Encourage Independent Mobility for Blind and Visually Impaired Students* (pp. 552–559). Springer. doi:10.1007/978-3-642-31534-3_81

Likert, R. (1932). A technique for the measurement of attitudes. *Archives of Psychology*.

Makey Makey | Buy Direct (Official Site). (2016). Retrieved from http://www.makeymakey.com/

Mangiron, C., & Zhang, X. (2016). Game Accessibility for the Blind: Current Overview and the Potential Application of Audio Description as the Way Forward. In Researching Audio Description (pp. 75–95). London: Palgrave Macmillan UK. doi:10.1057/978-1-137-56917-2_5

MASTERMIND | Toys for Kids | Hasbro Games. (n. d.). Retrieved from http://www.hasbro.com/en-ca/ product/mastermind:93765D16-6D40-1014-8BF0-9EFBF894F9D4

Miller, D., Parecki, A., & Douglas, S. A. (2007). Finger dance. *Proceedings of the 9th international ACM SIGACCESS conference on Computers and accessibility - Assets '07* (p. 253). New York, USA: ACM Press. http://doi.org/ doi:10.1145/1296843.1296898

Milne, L. R., Bennett, C. L., & Ladner, R. E. (2013). VBGhost. *Proceedings of the 15th International ACM SIGACCESS Conference on Computers and Accessibility - ASSETS '13* (pp. 1–2). New York, USA: ACM Press. http://doi.org/ doi:10.1145/2513383.2513396

Milne, L. R., Bennett, C. L., Ladner, R. E., & Azenkot, S. (2014). BraillePlay. *Proceedings of the 16th international ACM SIGACCESS conference on Computers & accessibility - ASSETS '14* (pp. 137–144). New York, USA: ACM Press. http://doi.org/ doi:10.1145/2661334.2661377

Morelli, T., & Folmer, E. (2014). Real-time sensory substitution to enable players who are blind to play video games using whole body gestures. *Entertainment Computing*, *5*(1), 83–90. doi:10.1016/j.entcom.2013.08.003

Mynatt, E. D. (1994). Designing with auditory icons - how well do we identify auditory cues? Proceedings of the Conference companion on Human factors in computing systems CHI '94 (pp. 269–270). New York, USA: ACM Press; doi:10.1145/259963.260483

Pasqualotto, A., Lam, J. S. Y., & Proulx, M. J. (2013). Congenital blindness improves semantic and episodic memory. *Behavioural Brain Research*, *244*, 162–165. doi:10.1016/j.bbr.2013.02.005 PMID:23416237

Plos, O., & Buisine, S. (2006). Universal design for mobile phones. In *CHI '06 extended abstracts on Human factors in computing systems - CHI EA '06* (p. 1229). New York, New York, USA: ACM Press; doi:10.1145/1125451.1125681

Raz, N., Striem, E., Pundak, G., Orlov, T., & Zohary, E. (2007). Superior serial memory in the blind: A case of cognitive compensatory adjustment. *Current Biology*, *17*(13), 1129–1133. doi:10.1016/j.cub.2007.05.060 PMID:17583507

Sánchez, J., Darin, T., & Andrade, R. (2015). *Multimodal Videogames for the Cognition of People Who Are Blind: Trends and Issues*. Springer International Publishing. doi:10.1007/978-3-319-20684-4_52

Sanchez, J., & Hassler, T. (2007). AudioMUD: A Multiuser Virtual Environment for Blind People. *IEEE Transactions on Neural Systems and Rehabilitation Engineering*, *15*(1), 16–22. doi:10.1109/TNSRE.2007.891404 PMID:17436871

Sanz, P., Mezcua, B., Pena, J., & Walker, B. (2014). Scenes and Images into Sounds: A Taxonomy of Image Sonification Methods for Mobility Applications. *Journal of the Audio Engineering Society*, *62*(3), 161–171. doi:10.17743/jaes.2014.0009

Scratch - Imagine. Program, Share. (n. d.). Retrieved from https://scratch.mit.edu/

Talsma, D., Doty, T. J., & Woldorff, M. G. (2006). Selective Attention and Audiovisual Integration: Is Attending to Both Modalities a Prerequisite for Early Integration? *Cerebral Cortex*, *17*(3), 679–690. doi:10.1093/cercor/bhk016 PMID:16707740

Tang, J. (2015). A new RFID-based and ontological recreation system for blind people. *International Journal of Radio Frequency Identification Technology and Applications*, *4*(4), 291. doi:10.1504/IJR-FITA.2015.070548

Targett, S., & Fernstrom, M. (2003). Audio games: Fun for all? All for fun! Tayebi, A., Islas Sedano, C., Tayebi, A., & Islas Sedano, C. (2014). What can your ears do? A systematic literature review regarding the role of non-speech audio. *Proceedings of EdMedia: World Conference on Educational Media and Technology*, *2014*, 2653–2663.

Yuan, B., & Folmer, E. (2008). Blind hero. *Proceedings of the 10th international ACM SIGACCESS conference on Computers and accessibility - Assets '08* (p. 169). New York, USA: ACM Press. http://doi.org/ doi:10.1145/1414471.1414503

## ADDITIONAL READING

Absar, R., & Gustavino, C. (2008). Usability of non-speech sounds in user interfaces.*Proceedings of the 14th International Conference on Auditory Display,*Paris, France (pp. ICAD08-1-ICAD08-8).

Balata, J., Franc, J., Mikovec, Z., & Slavik, P. (2014). Collaborative navigation of visually impaired. *Journal of Multimodal User Interfaces*, *8*(2), 175–185. doi:10.1007/s12193-013-0137-9

Cancar, L., Diaz, A., Barrientos, A., Travieso, D., & Jacobs, D. M. (2013). Tactile-Sight: A sensory substitution device based on distance-related vibrotactile flow regular paper. *International Journal of Advanced Robotic Systems*, *10*. doi:10.5772/56235

Chan, C., Wong, A., Ting, K., Whitfield-Gabrieli, S., He, J., & Lee, T. M. C. (2012). Cross Auditory-Spatial Learning in Early-Blind Individuals. *Human Brain Mapping*, *33*(11), 2714–2727. doi:10.1002/hbm.21395 PMID:21932260

Chekhchoukh, A., Vuillerme, N., & Glade, N. (2011). Vision substitution and moving objects tracking in 2 and 3 dimensions via vectorial electro-stimulation of the tongue. Proceedings of the Conférence Internationale Sur L'accessibilité et Les Systèmes de Suppléance Aux Personnes En Situations de Handicaps.

Fakrudeen, M., Yousef, S., & Hussein, A. (2014). Analyzing App Inventor for Building Usable Touch Screen Courseware for Blind Users. Retrieved from http://edlib.net/2014/ic5e/ic5e2014001.pdf

Hakobyan, L., Lumsden, J., OSullivan, D., & Bartlett, H. (2013). Mobile assistive technologies for the visually impaired. *Survey of Ophthalmology*, *58*(6), 513–528. doi:10.1016/j.survophthal.2012.10.004 PMID:24054999

Joy, A., Kenny, A. T., Nishal, G. & Namitha, T. (2015). Android Based Color Routing Wizard. *International Journal Computer Science Trends and Technology, 3*(2).

Kumar, M. A., Jilani, S. A. K., Sreenivasulu, U., & Hussain, S. J. (2015). Automated Color Recognition System for Visually Challenged and Achromatopsia People using Arduino and Mobile App. *International Journal of Advanced Research in Electronics and Communication Engineering*, *4*(8), 2106–2110.

Lee, H. P., Huang, J.-T., Chen, C.-H., & Sheu, T.-Z. (2011). Building a Color Recognizer System on the Smart Mobile Device for the Visually Challenged People. *Proceedings of the Sixth International Multi-Conference on Computing in the Global Information Technology(ICCGI '11)*, Luxembourg City, Luxembourg (pp. 95—98).

Maidenbaum, S., Abboud, S., & Amedi, A. (2014). Sensory substitution: Closing the gap between basic research and widespread practical visual rehabilitation. *Neuroscience and Biobehavioral Reviews*, *41*, 3–15. doi:10.1016/j.neubiorev.2013.11.007 PMID:24275274

Michalevsky, Y., Boneh, D., & Nakibly, G. (2014) Gyrophone: recognizing speech from gyroscope signals.*Proceedings of 23rd USENIX security symposium*, San Diego, CA, USA.

Moldoveanu, A., Balan, O., & Moldoveanu, F. (2014). Training System for Improving Spatial Sound Localization. *Proceedings of the eLearning and Software for Education Conference (eLSE'14)*, Bucharest, Romania (pp. 79-85).

Park, K., Goh, T., & So, H.-J. (2015). Toward accessible mobile application design: developing mobile application accessibility guidelines for people with visual impairment. *Proceedings of HCI Korea (HCIK'15)*, Seoul, Republic of Korea (pp. 31–38). Retrieved from http://dl.acm.org/citation.cfm?id=2729485.2729491

Picinali, L., Feakes, C., Mauro, D. A., & Katz, B. F. (2012) Spectral discrimination thresholds comparing audio and haptics for complex stimuli. *Proceedings of international workshop on haptic and audio interaction design (HAID 2012)*, Lund, Sweden (pp. 131–140). doi:10.1007/978-3-642-32796-4_14

Ra, M.-R., Liu, B., La Porta, T. F., & Govindan, R. (2012) Medusa: a programming framework for crowd-sensing applications. *Proceedings of the 10th international conference on mobile systems, applications, and services*, Ambleside, United Kingdom (pp. 337–350). doi:10.1145/2307636.2307668

Sanchez, J. Borba Campos, M. Espinoza, M. & Merabet, L. (2014). Audio Haptic Videogaming for Developing Wayfinding Skills in Learners Who are Blind. *Proceedings of the 19th International Conference on Intelligent User Interfaces*, Haifa, Israel (pp. 199-208). doi:10.1145/2557500.2557519

Sjöström, C. (2001). Using haptics in computer interfaces for blind people. *Proceedings of CHI '01* (Vol.1, pp. 245–246). doi:10.1145/634211.634213

Strothotte, T., Fritz, S., Michel, R., & Raab, a. (1996). Development of dialogue systems for a mobility aid for blind people: initial design and usability testing. *Proceedings of the second annual ACM conference on Assistive technologies Assets '96* (pp. 139–144). doi:10.1145/228347.228369

Szücs, V., Lanyi, C. S., Szabo, F., & Csuti, P. (2014). Color-check in stroke rehabilitation games. *Proceedings of 10th International Conference on Disability, Virtual Reality and Association Technologies*, Gothenburg, Sweden (pp. 393-396).

Tian, Y., Yuan, S. & Yang, X. (2014, April). Assistive Clothing Pattern Recognition for Visually Challenged People. *IEEE Transactions on Human-Machine Systems*.

Ye, H., Malu, M., Oh, U., & Findlater, L. (2014). Current and Future Mobile and Wearable Device Use by People With Visual Impairments. *Proceedings of CHI'14* (pp. 3123–3132). http://doi.org/doi:10.1145/2556288.2557085

## KEY TERMS AND DEFINITIONS

**Accessibility:** The design of products, devices, services, or environments for people who experience disabilities. The concept of accessible design and practice of accessible development ensures both "direct access" (i.e. unassisted) and "indirect access" meaning compatibility with a person's assistive technology.

**Assistive Technology:** A general term that includes assistive, adaptive, and rehabilitative devices for people with disabilities and also includes the process used in selecting, locating, and using them. Assistive technology promotes greater independence by enabling people to perform tasks that they were formerly unable to accomplish, or had great difficulty accomplishing, by providing enhancements to, or changing methods of interacting with, the technology needed to accomplish such tasks.

**Auditory Icon:** The auditory equivalent of visual icons used in the desktop user interface metaphor. It makes use of natural everyday sounds in order to represent objects and actions on the interface. Auditory icons use an intuitive linkage between the model world of sonically represented objects and events, using sounds familiar to listeners from the everyday world.

**Brain Computer Interface (BCI):** A direct communication pathway between an enhanced or wired brain and an external device. BCIs are often directed at researching, mapping, assisting, augmenting, or repairing human cognitive or sensory-motor functions. BCIs acquire brain signals, analyse them, and translate them into commands that are relayed to output devices that carry out desired actions. BCIs do not use normal neuromuscular output pathways. The main goal of BCI is to replace or restore useful function to people disabled by neuromuscular disorders.

**Cognitive Modeling:** An area of computer science that deals with simulating human problem solving and mental task processes in a computerized model. Such a model can be used to simulate or predict human behavior or performance on tasks similar to the ones modeled.

**Cognitive Walkthrough:** A usability inspection method used to identify usability issues in interactive systems, focusing on how easy it is for new users to accomplish tasks with the system. It starts with a task analysis that specifies the sequence of steps or actions required by a user to accomplish a task, and the system responses to those actions. The designers and developers of the software then walk through the steps as a group, asking themselves a set of questions at each step. Data is gathered during the walkthrough, and afterwards a report of potential issues is compiled. Finally the software is redesigned to address the issues identified.

**Earcon:** A pun on the term icon. As icon sounds like "eye-con" and is visual, D.A. sumikawa coined the term earcon its auditory equivalent, in a 1985 article, "Guidelines for the integration of audio cues into computer user interfaces". It is a brief, distinctive sound used to represent a specific event or convey other information. An Earcon is a structured audio message based on musical sounds, which conveys information about the tasks being carried out.

**Haptic Interfaces:** Ways to recreate the sense of touch by applying forces, vibrations, or motions to the user. This mechanical stimulation can be used to assist in the creation of virtual objects in a computer simulation, to control such virtual objects, and to enhance the remote control of machines and devices. Haptic devices may incorporate tactile sensors that measure forces exerted by the user on the interface.

**Morphocons:** Short audio units that are used to construct a sonic grammar based on temporal-frequency patterns, rather than fixed sound samples. In contrast to earcons, which map a unique sound to a particular meaning. As morphocons are described using simple morphological shape, they can be applied to any type of sound.

**Multimodal Interaction:** Provides the user with multiple modes of interacting with a system. A multimodal interface provides several distinct tools for input and output of data. It responds to inputs in more than one modality or communication channel. Multimodal interfaces process two or more combined user input modes (such as speech, touch, manual gesture, gaze, head and body movements) in a coordinated manner with multimedia system output.

**Pentatonic Scale:** A musical scale or mode with five notes per octave that's why it is also sometimes referred to as a five-tone scale or five-note scale. The word "pentatonic" comes from the Greek word pente meaning five and tonic meaning tone. Pentatonic scales are divided into those with semitones (hemitonic) and those without (anhemitonic).

**Retrospective Think Aloud Protocol:** A technique used in usability tests to gather qualitative information on the user intents and reasoning during a usability test. It's a form of think aloud protocol performed after the user testing session activities, instead of during them. Think-aloud protocols involve participants thinking aloud (what they are looking at, thinking, doing, and feeling) as they are performing a set of specified tasks.

**Sonification:** The use of non-speech audio to convey information or perceptualize data. It is the transformation of data relations into perceived relations in an acoustic signal for the purposes of facilitating communication or interpretation. Auditory perception has advantages in temporal, spatial, amplitude, and frequency resolution that open possibilities as an alternative or complement to visualization techniques.

**Think-Aloud Protocol:** A protocol used to gather data in usability testing in product design and development still collecting valid data. Think-aloud protocols involve participants thinking aloud as they are performing a set of specified tasks. Participants are asked to say whatever comes into their mind as they complete the task. This might include what they are looking at, thinking, doing, and feeling. This gives observers insight into the participant's cognitive processes, to make thought processes as explicit as possible during task performance.

**Usability:** The ease of use and learnability of a human-made object such as a tool or device. In software engineering, usability is the degree to which a software can be used by specified consumers to achieve quantified objectives with effectiveness, efficiency, and satisfaction in a quantified context of use.

**User Experience Design:** The process of improving user satisfaction with a product by enhancing the usability, accessibility and satisfaction provided in the interaction with the product. User experience design encompasses traditional Human–Computer Interaction design, and extends it by addressing all aspects of a product or service as perceived by users.

# Chapter 8
# Experiences with a Research Product:
## A Robot Avatar for Chronically Ill Adolescents

**Jorun Børsting**
*University of Oslo, Norway*

**Alma Leora Culén**
*University of Oslo, Norway*

## ABSTRACT

*This chapter discusses challenges related to studying the use and usefulness of research products (robust, high fidelity prototypes placed in real use contexts for research purposes). Methods and methodologies for studying use and usefulness of such research products embedded in users' everyday lives are still lacking and need to be better established. By presenting a case of such research product in use, a robot avatar, we wish to illustrate how new knowledge of relevance for both designers and users can be gained. The robot avatar was designed to represent chronically ill adolescents at school, improving his/hers learning opportunities, as well as helping maintain social connections with peers. The chapter shows how methods were adapted and tools designed to work with this user group and learn about the role of avatars in education and reduction of social isolation. The value of using the avatar, and similar research products, is considered.*

## INTRODUCTION

In this chapter, we revisit the design of new digital artifacts, one of the core activities within Human–Computer Interaction (HCI). Specifically, we focus on the stage of the design process that is beyond the usability testing of high-fidelity prototypes and wish to highlight opportunities and challenges related to studying the actual use and usefulness of new digital artifacts in real-life use contexts and over time. This extension of the design process into actual, situated use is of increasing interest within the HCI

DOI: 10.4018/978-1-5225-2492-2.ch008

community. Moving away from exploring high-fidelity prototypes in the labs or short-term tests in the wild, researchers embrace research into the intricacies of everyday use and the complexities of human–technology relationships.

In their paper (Odom et al., 2016), authors address this problem, suggesting that the notion of a *prototype* may not be entirely sufficient to support the inquiries into actual everyday use. They propose to distinguish digital artifacts that are ready to be placed in the lives of real users from prototypes and call such artifacts *research products*. Research products are further distinguished from *research prototypes* by arguing that research prototypes may be a manifestation of a theoretical concept and are not to be judged for their actuality but rather for their potential. In contrast, research products are what they are and are not judged for their potential (like research prototypes), or seen as placeholders for something else (like prototypes) (Lim, Stolterman, & Tenenberg, 2008). Rather than focusing on prototypes as ways of furthering design practice agendas by helping generate and test new forms, functions, systems, etc., we wish to present a case that illustrates how research products open up new research opportunities in design-oriented HCI research.

In this chapter, we thus discuss a specific research inquiry related to use of a newly designed digital artifact/ research product. The research product described in the chapter is a robot avatar (see Figure 1). The avatar was designed to represent chronically ill children and adolescents at school. Behind the design and development of the avatar is a new startup company ("No Isolation," 2015). We started a research cooperation with the startup at the phase when the robot avatar was still a concept, and we have made an agreement to work with 10 exemplars as research products, studying their use in real life. The avatar was designed with the intention to improve learning opportunities, as well as to help maintain social connections with peers. For our research participants, we have chosen adolescents who suffer from Myalgic Encephalomyelitis/ Chronic Fatigue Syndrome (ME/CFS) and who, due to their illness, cannot attend school. As a consequence, they often suffer from social isolation. The research question

*Figure 1. The robot avatar in the classroom*
*Photo: Marius Vabo.*

that we were interested in was: do robot avatars help adolescents with ME/CFS to attend lectures more frequently and re-establish social connections with classmates as a consequence?

We believe that the case is illustrative of the advantages of using research products in everyday life and using research through design (RtD) as a methodology to tackle the complexities of actual use and the forging of human–technology relations. Our findings reveal how human values, points of view, the design of the product, and interactions with other people and other technologies around the product can change users' perceptions of the use and usefulness of the product. Further, the chapter addresses how methods were adapted, and tools made to work with chronically ill adolescents, their teachers, and peers concerning the role of avatars in education and the reduction of social isolation. Our findings also reveal some methodological challenges. Careful consideration of how methods are chosen and implemented needs to be made for each case of situated use. Theoretical frameworks for studying the use of research products embedded in users' everyday lives are currently lacking and need to be established. However, we do show how we adapted methods and tools to work with chronically ill adolescents and their schools in order to learn about the role of avatars in education and explore their impact on social isolation.

The chapter is organized as follows: the next section provides some background on previous work with chronically ill adolescents and the design of new technologies with and for them, as well as methodological approaches that are relevant both for working with the user group, as well as for other research on the situated use of research products. The subsequent section describes the case and research findings in detail. Discussion, future research, and, finally, our conclusions follow.

## BACKGROUND

The literature review presented in this section is separated into three parts. The first part briefly addresses research through design as a methodology and research products as a way to gain new knowledge about experiences with the product in real-life use. The second part of the review is dedicated to a brief review of design for and with adolescents who are chronically ill. Finally, we touch upon value-sensitive design as it applies to this research.

### Research through Design

Research through Design (RtD), a methodology originating from design research, has emerged as a valid and increasingly accepted research approach in design-oriented HCI. However, there is still an ongoing debate regarding its relevance for HCI, and types of novel knowledge contributions that it can offer (Gaver, 2012; Höök et al., 2015; Koskinen, Zimmerman, Binder, Redstrom, & Wensveen, 2011; Krogh, Markussen, & Bang, 2015; Zimmerman & Forlizzi, 2014). The debate also addresses the diverging nature of scientific research and design research (Dalsgaard, 2016; Owen, 2007).

Research through Design has also been proposed as an approach to tackle *wicked problems* (Buchanan, 1992; Rittel & Webber, 1973), problems that are complex, inter-dependent and messy. It is this aspect of RtD that makes it suitable for studying everyday use and lived experiences with new technologies. It allows designers and researchers to take a closer look at what it means to design not only a digital artifact, but also relationships with it that get formed over time (Mazé & Redström, 2005). The knowledge gained by focusing on the design of the artifact and lived experiences with it contributes to HCI design research, but may also contribute to other fields of research. For example, reflecting on the meaning of new technology and relations it mediates may contribute to the philosophy of technology. If the artifact embeds political, or policy related views, it may contribute to discussions in those fields. The robot avatar described in this chapter actually does this: it can be seen as an educational tool that policymakers in education should take a stance on, or as an assistive technology, passing the ball to policymakers in the health sector. However, this discussion is outside the scope of the chapter.

In (Odom et al., 2016), authors suggest that research products have distinct qualities, and look into their own RtD projects and research products through the lens of these four qualities: *Inquiry-driven*, *Finish*, *Fit* and *Independent* (IFFI). These are explained here very briefly. Inquiry-driven quality implies a research inquiry that unfolds through the making and experience of a design artifact. Finish quality implies that the artifact is what it is rather than what it could be. Fit relates to lived experience of the product, a fit between the product and the context of use. Independent quality mans that a research product is usable in real life and does not require researcher's intervention. We have found these helpful for differentiating research products from prototypes, but also for reflection over research intentions. The latter was helpful to broaden the scope of the research, and at the same time remove the focus from the idea that improvement, or redesign opportunities guide the inquiry alone. This was important for our case, as the research product, the avatar, was to become, and has been recently launched as a commercial product. However, for about a year, it was used as a research product for the study described here. The route from a research product to a commercial product is not a simple one, in likeness with other HCI prototypes, (Chilana, Ko, & Wobbrock, 2015). We believe that the knowledge gained through working with the robot avatar as a research product has contributed to making a better commercial product. However, the main gain from the research is a very rich set of data and insights, beyond design improvement implications. We have learned about practices created around robot avatars at school, views on robots and privacy, impact on social relations with peers, among many other valuable lessons. The robot avatar has also generated a rich set of future research opportunities.

## Designing for and with Chronically Ill Adolescents

Adolescents represent nearly a fifth of the population, yet the interaction design literature offers little guidance on the unique needs, opportunities, and challenges of designing technology with and for this age group (Little, Fitton, Bell, & Toth, 2016; Poole & Peyton, 2013). The literature on designing with adolescent patients is even scarcer, due to extra challenges related to their vulnerability with respect to health, and the ethical implication that these risks bring with them (Lang, Martin, Sharples, Crowe, & Murphy, 2012; Velden, Sommervold, Culén, & Nakstad, 2016).

Currently, a significant increase in chronic diseases is observed in general, and particularly so among adolescents (Perrin, Anderson, & Van Cleave, 2014). Among these chronic illnesses, Myalgic Encephalomyelitis/Chronic Fatigue Syndrome (ME/CFS) has become a growing concern (Farmer, Fowler, Scourfield, & Thapar, 2004). For these adolescents, the health issues make for a unique combination of the usual challenges of adolescence (cognitive, emotional, social, and physical changes), and increased number of stakeholders (for example, parents, doctors, teachers) with varying degree of power, authority and say. In particular, adolescents with ME/CFS are known as a user group that has serious issues with school attendance (Crawley & Sterne, 2009). Thus, these adolescents became a group of choice for the use of the robot avatar.

Adolescents with ME/CFS have several challenges that are specific to the illness. Exhaustion at the cognitive and physical level, joined with reduced tolerance to noise and light, as well as nausea and muscle pains are frequent. These problems, naturally, impact their experiences concerning technologies. Particular attention is also needed when new technologies are introduced into their lives. Most importantly, one needs to ensure that the research product causes no further harm to their health. Medical research indicates that energy modulation has an impact on the condition (Jason, Benton, Torres-Harding, & Muldowney, 2009). Overuse of energy for some task results in extra exhaustion lasting between several hours to several days, leading to increased pain, sensitivity and overall worsened cognitive and physical health. The person with ME/CFS often cannot estimate in advance negative health outcomes of activities, such as meeting a friend, and this makes the energy modulation challenging.

The two main challenges for chronically ill adolescents, besides health, are found to be educational and social (Wadley, Vetere, Hopkins, Green, & Kulik, 2014). We found relatively little previous research related to technologies that aim to support adolescents in these areas, especially isolation. In (Grajales III, Sheps, Ho, Novak-Lauscher, & Eysenbach, 2014), the authors report on the social media usage by this user group. Their findings were based on a literature review that included 76 articles, 44 websites, and 11 reports/policies. Results were presented based on ten diverse categories of social media use, where the most relevant were blogs (e.g., WordPress), micro-blogs (e.g., Twitter) and social networks (Facebook). The SecondLife, a virtual world, was also mentioned in relation to adolescents with ME/CFS in the work of Best and Butler (Best & Butler, 2013). Education, through remote learning, was discussed in several articles, for example, (Sheridan et al., 2013), and robot based telepresence for social interactions in (Tsui & Yanco, 2013).

## Value Sensitive Design

Value Sensitive Design (VSD) is a methodology used in the design of technology that accounts for human values in design processes (Le Dantec, Poole, & Wyche, 2009; Sellen, Rogers, Harper, & Rodden, 2009). Values have always been important in HCI, and were often embedded in the choice of methodological approach to design, such as user-centered design or participatory design. However, there is a growing concern within the field that the view on values has been too narrow and the questions asked about new technologies not reaching far enough. The problem is that it is difficult, during the design itself, to grasp the consequences, see the impacts and so on. As pointed out in (Sellen et al., 2009), this too is a complex task. "Making judgments about new computer technologies, and how they will affect us and the social fabric of which we are a part, is not straightforward. Research methods must capture how the use of technologies may unfold over time and in different situations" (ibid.). Using research products as artifacts in everyday life makes this task somewhat more transparent, and easier to grasp when the technology is part of the lived experience (Le Dantec et al., 2009).

This background section on designing for and with chronically ill adolescents, and on the importance of being sensitive to meaning and values of designed artifact is certainly not complete. However, rather than aiming for completeness, it aims to illustrate the complexity and intricacy of the research domain that is laden with ethical challenges, diversity of values, health challenges, school policies, privacy issues, as well as, lack of theoretical frameworks and similar previous empirical research.

## SITUATING ROBOT AVATARS IN THE LIVES OF ADOLESCENTS WITH ME/CFS

The research questions that led the inquiry explored the potential of the robot avatars to support adolescents with ME/CFS in attending school courses more frequently and easily and thus enabling better continuity in education and keeping in touch with peers. Is there a future in which these avatars enable chronically ill youth to get better continuity in their studies? Can avatars, such as they are, be perceived as actual representatives of sick adolescents, and could they help to reduce the sense of distance from peers?

The research product is shaped like a small robot (see Figure 2) that stands approximately 27 cm tall. The form essentially houses a camera, speakers, a microphone, a battery and a motor that enables 360-degree rotation at the base, as well as a 40-degree up and down head movement. It weighs ca. 1 kg. It is made so that classmates can easily pick the avatar up and carry it to places such as the schoolyard during breaks or on class excursions. Integrated 4G intend to enable the avatar's use everywhere, even when Wi-Fi is not available.

Adolescents control the avatar remotely, in real time, via an app installed on a personal mobile device, such as a smartphone or a tablet. The app is easy to use. The main functionality of the app is turning the robot on, rotating the body of the robot, and giving the light signal when a user wishes to initiate communication. It is important to note that the avatar can only stream video. It has no recording or data-storing abilities.

Robot avatars were placed in the classrooms of recruited participants with the intent to inquire into possibilities to improve classroom presence and decrease loneliness. The length of use of the avatars varied between participants—from one month to nine months. Researchers' involvement related to the functioning of the avatar was not needed at all. The participants could use the avatar in any way they wished. The researchers had no guidelines or requirements for the use of avatars; it was just like any product they would purchase, except that they agreed to participate in this research by providing information on their experiences with the avatar. Similar arrangements were also made with the schools and families of the participants.

From the above paragraph, we can conclude that the avatars had qualities of research products IFFI, discussed in the RtD subsection above.

### The Recruitment of Participants

The recruitment of participants for our study was conducted through a collaboration with the Norwegian ME/CFS Association ("Norwegian ME Association," 2016). The recruited participants were adolescents between 12 and 16 years of age with ME/CFS. Four girls and five boys were recruited.

We learned that the recruitment of participants was a much easier task than getting their schools on board. Therefore, only four participants are mentioned in the text of this chapter. Those are the participants whose schools were quickest in deploying the avatars in the classroom. All nine schools brought up issues related to the use of the robot avatar, and these had to be addressed before the school administration, teachers, and parents allowed the use of the robot at school. Even though the school principals, teachers, and parents of classmates were provided with thorough information about the study and were, therefore, aware that the robot avatars do not store any data and that the streamed data are always encrypted, some parents still felt uneasy about the possibility that their child could be observed from a remote location, where they had no control over who watches the video. The argument was that even though the sick adolescent says that he or she will be the only one watching, there is no guarantee that this will be so. A parent or a friend could easily accidentally oversee something that he or she should not. For the participants and their families, this was difficult to handle, as it implied a lack of trust and potential misuse of the robot on their end.

## Participants

As established through previous research with vulnerable adolescents (Culén & Karpova, 2014; Culén & Velden, 2013; Velden et al., 2016), vulnerability is viewed as a set of risks that are to be reduced by new technologies, such as the robot avatar. Hence, the health of the adolescents was not to decline due to extended school attendance and poor energy modulation strategies or social activities supported by the robot avatar. Our research inquiries also had to be done in a way that does not cause additional stress or fatigue for participants. This required ethical sensitivities that were higher than usual, as the research was done in participants' homes, and it could cause discomfort or pain much faster than with healthy adolescents.

The work with the startup company on planning the deployment of avatars as research products started in September 2015. The work with participants, their families, and their schools started in early January of 2016. As mentioned, we address the deployment of avatars in this chapter with Peter, Hannah, Ethan, Jon (fictive names), and their schools. Working with the four participants helped shape our methods, discover problems related to use, and uncover some interesting leads for our current and future research.

The first research avatar ever made was given to Jon in February of 2016. Peter's avatar was subsequently made and handed to Peter two weeks later. Hannah's and Ethan's avatars were ready for use two months later. Everyone got a week to get familiar with his or her robot and to use/play with it as he or she wished. After that week, the robot was taken to the participant's school. At the time of this writing, Jon and Peter have had their robots in the classroom for nine months, while Hannah and Ethan have had theirs for about six months.

Table 1 provides some basic information on these participants: how long they were ill, how far they live from school, and how often they are capable of attending school. The table shows that Peter can attend school less than one hour per week on average. One hour was actually his personal goal, but he could not reach it.

*Figure 2. a) Jon's old and new avatars, research products: the old, black one, has a red sticker encircled, a mark from the class trip to the museum; b) Peter's classmates made a smile for his robot avatar; c) the app showing how Jon sees a remote location; d) the avatar as a commercial product*

*Table 1. Data about our four participants at the time of recruitment to our study*

| Participant | Gender | Age | Time Since Receiving ME/CFS Diagnosis | Remoteness to School | School Attendance/Home Tuition per Week |
|---|---|---|---|---|---|
| Peter | M | 12 | 1 year | 2 km | <1 hour |
| Jon | M | 13 | 4 years | 24 km | 3 hours |
| Hannah | F | 13 | 5 years | < 1km | 3 hours |
| Ethan | M | 15 | 3 years | < 1km | 1 hour |

After opening the app, a participant can see his or her classroom through a video feed on a smartphone or a tablet. The video is one-way. Teachers and classmates see only the avatar as the representative of the participant and not the participant. This is important with respect to the participants' condition. They are often unable to sit or follow conversations in the classroom, or they have other symptoms that prevent them from going to school in the first place. However, if the participant is ready to take part in a conversation, he or she can turn on the light signal on top of the avatar's head, indicating that he or she wishes to participate.

## RESEARCH METHODS

As mentioned, the initial research inquiry focused on how social connectedness and learning are supported by the robot avatar. In order to discuss these issues, we felt that we needed to find out what our participants value in relation to social contacts, what their actual social situation was before the use of the robot, who the important actors in their lives are, how much education they were getting, and how their condition changes with diverse activities, particularly those activities that involve digital artifacts. Second, after a period of use, we needed to compare findings with design intentions and see whether and how they align. Consequently, we needed to select tools and methods that will allow us to collect data before and after use of the robot to see how findings aligned with design intentions and with the described research goals. We were also interested in other data that could help us to understand the trade-offs between human values, design, the physical condition of participants, and social factors that emerge through the use of the avatar. At the end of the research period, however, we have had a lot more open questions than concrete answers. This is in line with the generative nature of RtD.

The main methods used were interviews and observations. However, we adapted and made several map-based tools to use in interview sessions with participants. These were to help us ask specific questions that were relevant to the inquiry and their illness. In order to make good interview tools, we needed to gain some basic knowledge on ME/CFS. To this end, we used a literature search on ME/CFS from diverse perspectives (diagnosis, treatment, therapies, and behaviors) and then organized an expert sense-making session concerning adolescents with ME/CFS. The session participants had in-depth knowledge of ME/CFS acquired through daily contact with adolescents with ME/CFS and their families (representatives from the Norwegian ME Association, the ME/CFS youth organization, and a medical physician participated). The insights gained from this expert session were reported in another article (Børsting and Culén, 2016). Among numerous concerns that we understood were important, we chose to make tools focusing on social interactions, existing technology use patterns, technology preferences, and a tool that addresses envisioned and desired opportunities that may arise when using the robot avatar. This was done to make the comparison between different participants visual and simple. Using the same tools after the use of avatars, we were also able to compare the maps at the start and the end of the study (for each participant). Other concerns were addressed through a semi-structured interview format. We traveled to participants' homes to deliver robots and conduct the initial interviews at the same time. We started by interviewing the participant and then assisted him or her in installing the app and bringing the robot to life, ensuring that he or she would know how to use it. When the robot was given to Jon, our first participant, this initial visit lasted for roughly three hours due to several technical problems (unstable coverage at the location and our own lack of experience). All other interviews took between 30 and 60 minutes, duration mostly depending on the adolescent's health status at the time of the interview.

## The Interview Tools

During the interviews, we used four tools that we call the *Social Communication Map*, *Technology Usage Map*, *Avatar Expectations Map*, and *Cool Wall* (see Figure 3). As per consent, photos could be taken during interviews. Interviews were audio recorded and subsequently transcribed.

## The Cool Wall

The Cool Wall was presented by Fitton and others in (Fitton, Horton, Read, Little, & Toth, 2012). Technologies that are developed to be used by adolescents should have an element of 'coolness'; this increases the chances for the technology to be used and accepted by the teenage users (see also Culén & Gasparini, 2012; Read et al., 2011). This is especially important for adolescents who have a chronic illness, because technologies that are perceived as cool may result in better experiences with the technology. The Cool Wall was used as a way to collect data on what these adolescents perceived as cool (see Figure 3 and 7 a). It was also employed as an icebreaker technique that enabled us to discuss apps and games they perceive as cool and why. Magnets and the board allowed for easy placement of items and

*Figure 3. The Cool Wall and some of the icons used on the magnets*

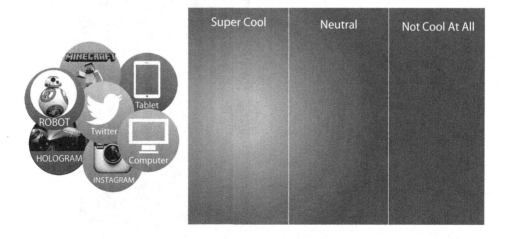

easy re-sorting when needed. Some icons that we deemed likely to be used by our participants were made a priori. Others were left blank so that the participants could add their own icons or words. Importantly, we also asked if any of the things considered neutral or cool tired them and why (e.g., loud sounds or too intense cognitive effort).

## The Social Communication Map

Figure 4 and Figure 7 b) show Social Communication Map where the participant is placed in the middle of the map (the square at the bottom labeled as Me), surrounded by a sphere containing close social relations that were nurtured by daily interactions, and then a space comprising of people with whom the communication with the participant was occasional. Cutouts of people, in different colors, were used to classify people into categories such as family, friends, doctors, teachers, best friends, etc. Each participant could define their own categories and chose colors to represent them.

## The Technology Usage Map

The Technology Usage Map shown in Figure 5, was a way to collect data on technology usage (frequency and length) and other habits around technology (Culén, 2015). We also tried to find out if there were technology platforms that had an adverse impact on their well-being, for example, that increased illness symptoms. We used the same icons as used for the Cool Wall, self-made ones were also included, to talk about their technology habits such as use of computers, TV, Skype, smartphones, etc.

## The Avatar Expectations Map

The Avatar Expectations Map explores the envisioned future use of the robot avatar, see Figure 6 and 7 c). Participants could write down on the map itself their thoughts on how they would use the robot

*Figure 4. The Social Communication Map*

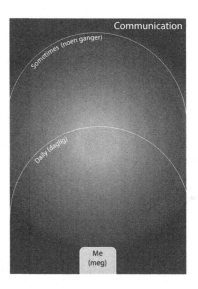

*Figure 5. The Technology Usage Map*

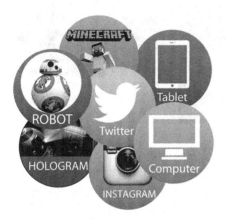 

avatar (have used, for the final interview). The same procedure was carried out with all participants. This also served as an opportunity to ask the participants if they would be (were, for the final interview) comfortable with the robot representing them socially, and how relevant this was.

## Other Inquiry Methods

Post-interview data on Ethan's, Hannah's, Jon's, and Peter's experiences with the avatar were collected through various emails with parents. In total, 195 messages were exchanged for these four participants: 106 emails concerned organizational issues with schools and teachers, and 89 were feedback on use. After six weeks of use, a structured online interview consisting of 17 questions was given to Hannah, Ethan, Jon, and Peter. This allowed participants to answer when they were well enough, at the time of their choosing. After 10 weeks of use, a questionnaire consisting of 14 questions was given to six schoolteachers, two from Jon's and Hanna's schools and one from Ethan's and Peter's schools. Subse-

*Figure 6. The Avatar Expectations Map*

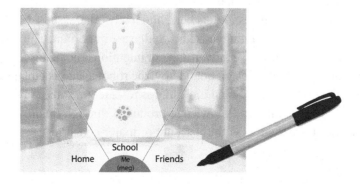

*Figure 7. Tools in use: a) Cool Wall; b) Social Communication Map; c) Avatar Expectations Map*

quently, observations were conducted at Peter's and Jon's schools, while Peter and Jon attended their lectures remotely through the robot avatar. After the class observations, nine-question questionnaires were distributed to their classmates. Lastly, a closing interview with participants, using the same tools as in the first interview, was conducted. In addition, field notes on other meetings, in particular those with teachers and school principals, were kept.

## FINDINGS

Prior to discussing findings, it is appropriate to mention that there were some issues with the two first avatars that were given to Jon and Peter. For example, one had to take the battery out of the robot manually and charge it daily. One also needed to charge the modem independently. Furthermore, 4G coverage was supposed to work everywhere, so the robots were developed based on the existence of good 4G coverage, but this was not the case. These two problems have, naturally, affected the experiences with the avatars, especially those of teachers and classmates who had to make sure the robot avatars were ready for use. Coping strategies that emerged to address these issues were interesting for this research. At Jon's school, the robot was marginalized (also not used when it was needed), while at Peter's, the students decided to rotate in taking the responsibility and making sure that Peter could attend classes. Peter's and Jon's avatars were replaced with better versions after some months. The charging activities were then no longer an issue.

The problems with 4G coverage were not expected, but they became an issue that shaped the experience for Jon, as the 4G coverage in his area was not good enough. Usability issues were not the main line of research inquiry, but they certainly affected experiences with the robot, more so for Jon.

The amount of data collected through this study is large and themes that emerged rather diverse, that is, we could discuss design, privacy, personalization, the meaning of the robot as a representation of a person, what benefits it brings, challenges for teachers, and many other issues. For such open inquiry as ours was, we feel that methods for generating new knowledge are important. The methods in themselves are rather traditional HCI methods. However, given that our intention is not focused solely on the usability of the product or implication for future design but on how the robot avatar is embedded in everyday life, we needed to reflect on the use of methods and tools in this research in some way. As pointed out in the introduction, methods, as well as kinds of knowledge produced through this research that rests on the use of research products and experiences with those, are of major concern.

## Reflection on Interview Tools

We begin by reflecting upon the methods and tools for making our inquiry. The Cool Wall served well as an icebreaker and conversation starter. It was an easy exercise to do and allowed us to address a wide range of topics on technology use and, more importantly, adolescents personal likes and dislikes. It was also useful when addressing topics that could be perceived as difficult to talk about, such as how long they can play before they get tired or how many close or distant friends they have. We found out that the use of these tangible magnets, pens, and maps enabled us to collect more and richer data than we would have gotten if we had just asked questions, addressing these same topics directly. Ethan, Jon, and Peter found these exercises fun; this was reported in online questionnaires and was easily observed during the interviews. Since Hannah's, Ethan's, and Jon's mothers (and both parents in Peter's case) were present during the interview, these tools enabled us to have a more direct dialogue with the interviewee only. They also enabled an easy overview of changes between the initial and final interviews, in addition to ensuring that important data were collected and could be compared across individuals.

As shown in Table 2, all four participants reported that they found the use of tools to be a positive experience. When asked about their experiences with maps and the experiences regarding the first interview, Hannah said that the tools were fun. When asked if she got worse from the interview and if she had any advice for improving the initial face-to-face interview, she said: "I get tired from long conversations regardless of whom I talk to, ☺ but it was worth it since I got to be part of this project." Ethan commented, "I thought it was okay, I did not get any more tired than I usually do, but there is nothing one can do about that, it was okay. But being part of the robot project has been really fun."

## Results from the Cool Wall in Initial Interviews with all Nine Participants

Graph 1 shows the results from the Cool Wall use in our initial interviews (with all nine participants).

One of the purposes of deploying the tools, such as the Cool Wall, during the initial interview was to collect data to understand our participants—in particular, what they like and think is cool. Graph 1 shows what this youth considered cool at the start of the study. Changes in this graph were important to

*Graph 1. The technologies categorized as cool by participants at the start of the study*

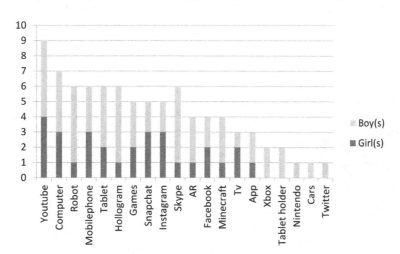

*Graph 2. The technologies categorized as cool in initial interview recalculated into percentages, to balance out an uneven number of girls (4) and boys (5)*

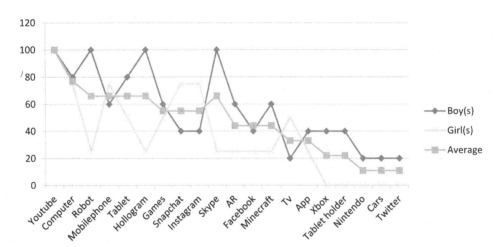

us, as we wanted to see if, how, and what the avatars would affect. The next graph, Graph 2, illustrates how even such small findings from a cool wall can be generative of new sets of research questions—for example, related to gender differences in what is considered cool. For example, only one girl thought that the robot was cool at the start; others did not place it in the cool category, justifying this by saying that they did not know yet. All the boys thought that the robot was cool.

Another example of research questions that became apparent by looking at the Cool Wall data was the difference in age with respect to what they considered cool (see Graph 3).

Upon careful analysis of what participants stated as a reason for them to call something cool, we found that the things that were categorized as cool were most often the ones that connected them to others. For some, this was Snapchat, Facebook, Instagram, or their mobile phones. For four of our users, Minecraft was used to meet friends and perform tasks in the game together. The age had an impact on

*Graph 3. a) To the left are the technologies categorized as not cool in the initial interview by some and cool by others. b) To the right, the ones that found these technologies to be cool*

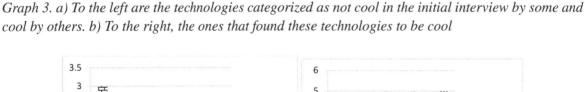

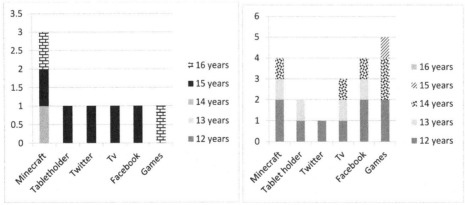

*Graph 4. The technologies that the participants use every day*

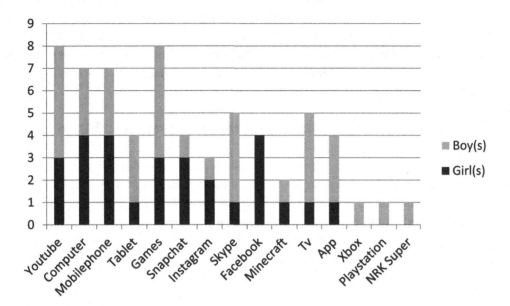

the games of choice. Older participants mentioned other kinds of games, such as FIFA, Counter-Strike, and Battlefield, often on Steam. When playing either Minecraft or other games such as FIFA, they usually used headphones and Skype to talk during the gameplay. The headphones were used as a strategy to control the exposure to sound and to avoid high sound levels during gameplay.

## Technology Use and Concerns

In Graph 4, the technologies our participants use every day are displayed. One participant explained that he did use YouTube both for game walk-throughs and for figuring out difficult math homework. Even though the computer is used daily by seven of our nine participants, some concerns regarding computers were raised during the initial interview. Jon stated that using a stationary computer can worsen his symptoms. Other participants said that they had to take regular breaks in order to not get worse. Peter's parents reported that it was their impression that Peter gets worse with prolonged use of the stationary computer. In particular, they stated that he gets worse if the sound levels in the games he plays are high. The adverse reaction to noise was also an important issue at school. The parents pointed out that lots of noise in the classroom could also be a problem when using the robot avatar. Peter did not comment on the use of the stationary computer and health consequences. He said that he favored the computer for playing the game of Minecraft. That game connects him to the three friends he has. Minecraft and Skype on the computer were the primary routes to social contact for Peter. Jon was also using his phone, SMS, Skype, and diverse games to connect daily with his friends and actively keep close contact.

## Social Mapping Results

The fact that we worked with adolescents who are not healthy was apparent from their social maps. Most of them immediately placed the closest family members on the map. For two of our participants, their pets (dogs) were the ones first placed in the area for important daily relations. When it came to friends and how often they had contact, it varied greatly from person to person. Three of our participants had daily contact with a best friend, whom they met online, and their parents did not even know about these friends. Doctors and teachers were placed on the map only after we explicitly asked about them. For all, the communications were very limited, and we could see firsthand how social isolation was an important issue.

## Results from Online Interviews with Hannah, Jon, Peter, and Ethan

Table 2 shows the findings related to social and educational issues reported in the online interviews. Both Peter and Jon reported that they have been able to tend to their education much more frequently than before. Peter reported that he was able to attend remotely in one week as much as he had been able to attend during the three-month period prior to the use of the avatar. He also stated that in periods of increased illness symptoms, he was still able to attend school—something that would not be possible without the robot avatar. This example highlights another line of inquiry related to the worsened health condition and the use of the avatar.

## Findings Related to Robot-Facilitated Learning for Adolescent ME/CFS Sufferers

We found that when developing or introducing technology in the lives of young ME/CFS sufferers, it is especially important to be aware of, and sensitive towards, challenges related to energy modulation in order not to cause post-exertion malaise. This malaise can be a result of any heightened sensory inputs or physical and cognitive activities related to the use of the robot that exceeds participants' limits. The worsened symptoms can last for days. Therefore, it is imperative to know that adolescents could easily exceed their boundaries by either adhering to demands from others (parents or teachers) or simply by experiencing joy from being with friends or going on a class tour. When Hannah was asked if she ever felt pressured into using the robot beyond her limits, she answered *"Sometimes."* Ethan said, *"Yes, Mom can push a bit about using it, but I decide."* This should be taken seriously in each individual case and strategies around the issue developed according to the needs of each participant. If not addressed, the opportunity to attend school more often may turn into worsened health symptoms.

*Table 2. Some research findings related to four of our participants*

| Participant | Participation in User Research | Tools | 4G Coverage | Social Benefit of Robot Use | Educational Benefit of Robot Use | Perception of Robot |
|---|---|---|---|---|---|---|
| Peter | Positive | Positive | Good | Yes/Some | Yes | Cool |
| Jon | Positive | Positive | Bad | Yes | Yes/Some | Neutral |
| Hannah | Positive | Positive | Good/poor | No | Yes | Cool |
| Ethan | Positive | Positive | Good | Yes | Yes/Some | Cool |

From our data analysis, we see the importance of technologies that mediate autonomy and control by the user to accommodate the fine-tuned energy modulation when designing technologies to support adolescent ME/CFS sufferers. More specifically, the important factors that the user should be able to control are the following:

1.  **Noise:** The ability to regulate the level of sound, both ways between the classroom and the participant (the class could clearly hear sounds from participants' homes, and participants often resented the loudness coming from the classroom).
2.  **Light:** What the users see and their ability to easily regulate the brightness of the screen without stopping the streaming.
3.  **The Level of Activity:** The level of autonomy the users have to define the level of participation in classroom teachings.
4.  **Movement:** What the users see and their ability to control the movement of the video view.
5.  **Flexibility:** The level of autonomy the users have to initiate, regulate, or terminate current usage of the avatar.

The users control the noise of the robot by using headphones when using the tablet and adjusting the volume on the iPad. They also wanted to turn off the sound going to the classroom if needed and lower the voice of the robot if they only wanted to talk to the classmates sitting closest to them. The light is also lowered to a preferred state both on screen and in the room that the participant is in when using the robot.

The level of activity is addressed in a design solution by users, where the light on top of the robot signals if the users only want to watch that day and not actively participate in classroom activities such as group work. Regarding the movement of the robot, we have observed that one participant preferred that the robot had a fixed position facing the blackboard and did not move the robot at all. We asked participants if they would like the movement of the robot to be automatic toward the person who talked. They did not want this. One said that she thought she would get dizzy and that she much preferred to be in control of the movements. Another user said that the control of the movement is important. She exemplified by saying that if she watched her brother play games on TV while moving around, she got a headache, but if she played and controlled the movement herself, she did not have this problem. In the initial interview, a parent stated that the movements in the classroom could have a negative impact on the health of his daughter because he knew that she used to respond badly toward environments in which many people are moving around her.

The need for flexibility in use is both stated by our users and seen in the reports on how they use the robot. Some periods in which they can use the robot more and for longer than other times and when and if they are able to use the robot are very different from day to day. The participants want to be able to control the level of activity by having the possibility to log in during the whole school day, but they do not want the time to be planned in advance or regulated.

Flexibility is especially important because the user's health varies greatly on a day-to-day basis and, for some, even from minute to minute. Therefore, the user has to be able to initiate use when he or she feels like it and end it when needed. This is something that is impossible to plan for. Transportation to schools takes time, and home tuition has to be planned and, therefore, often cannot provide this kind of flexibility. For our participants, this resulted in the planned teachings often being canceled, but after receiving the robot, they have all increased their time spent in the classroom. This cannot, however, substitute the individual tailoring of teachings provided by home tuition. ME/CFS sufferers often get behind on their schoolwork and teachings because of absence in times when they are bed-bound and have heightened illness symptoms. This way, home tuition is a way to catch up and ensure that they receive optimal educational teachings.

## Findings Related to Social Interactions with the Robot

Regarding social interaction with peers at school, the reactions of our participants differed. While Jon felt that the use of the robot during school breaks was very beneficial, Ethan found that he did not like it. For Ethan, the robot served as a painful reminder that he could not be there in person—something that he wants most of all. Jon wrote in the online interview, "I have had great pleasure from using the robot. I've learned something new and feel that I am more included." Jon has used the robot avatar actively to talk to some of his classmates during breaks at school when the teacher was not present. In addition, he could use it during group work in the class. After some months of free use, Jon's school decided that the robot could no longer be used during breaks because the robot is expensive and the school could not be accountable if the robot were stolen or broken. Since Jon could not use the robot in breaks anymore and the video streaming was unstable in his location, the robot went from being perceived as cool to being perceived as neutral. After the commercial sale of robots started, they could be fully insured by the startup. So, the commercial products can be used during breaks now.

Regarding the use of games for social purposes, we have found out that our participants easily related to the factors mentioned above. Games were often played with headphones; sound could be regulated; and Skype and other apps, such as Messenger, were easy to use for social contact. Comparing the avatar to games and communication apps, in the users' experience, the avatar provided the same level of autonomy and social connectedness with peers. The majority of feedback remarks related to the design and functionality of the avatar were directed toward making improvements that could mediate more autonomy and control from the users related to the five factors mentioned above.

## DISCUSSION

The findings described in the previous sections are not the entire collection of findings related to education and social isolation but are representative of the kind of knowledge that could be gained from the use of research products. Many of these points are not likely to be found through the usual prototype testing. The length of use is certainly an important factor in understanding the relationship between the participant, the artifact, and the context of use.

The biggest challenges for us in this research were methodological. In the end, to get to some findings and results, we have fallen back to rather traditional ways of doing research in HCI. We are still looking for ways to help us organize and understand the magnitude of data and reflect upon the large number of research possibilities that emerged during the course of the research. Also, how do we report on the diverging nature of some of the findings (that we did not present here because we still do not know how to articulate findings that are widely diverse)? Is it OK to present just raw data? We argue that methods and methodologies for studying the use and usefulness of such research products embedded in users' everyday lives are still lacking and need to be better established within the field. In our research study, RtD using the field approach (see Zimmerman & Forlizzi, 2014) to study experiences with a research product was found to be a promising way to provide insights into the nature of future use and usefulness in the chosen context. Each context will require an independent and careful reflection over tools and methods for research.

In addition, since our users were adolescents suffering from an illness, it was also important to consider what RtD can offer to vulnerable users. We believe that by focusing on experiences with the avatar and the particular set of risks to which ME/CFS adolescents are exposed, we managed to gain some knowledge about how the use of avatars was experienced by these particular users. Some of the insights are generalizable to many adolescents with ME/CFS, and others are not. In some cases, the conclusion might be that the technology should not be made or made available on the marked based on the harmfulness of the unintended effects. In other cases, the knowledge of such effects could empower the designer to redesign and take measures to ensure that such an effect does not occur. For example, the avatar simply streamed video from the classroom to the user one way. Because the teacher could not see the avatar user, it was impossible to evaluate his or her form and thus decide how the student should be integrated into the teaching that day. If the student is in bad shape that day, the teacher should not involve the student in activities such as group work or have him or her answer questions. Conversely, if the student is in good shape that day, it could be wrong for the teacher not to try to include the student in such activities. Because the robot's design did not allow for different levels of participation or a way to communicate to the teacher the student's health condition at the time of the lecture, it makes the teacher's role in taking care of his or her student even more difficult. If this problem is not addressed at the design level, one might expect that it would result in either poorer health for the user or that the findings from the use of the robot avatar do not match its design intentions, likely resulting in the robot being abandoned altogether.

When working with vulnerable users, it is important to prioritize human values in the design process. During the use of our research products, we experienced that they provoked many non-users (such as parents of classmates) to express their values in relation to the use of the avatar at school. Some of them had little knowledge about ME/CFS, and thought that robots are a step in the wrong direction and that the real, physical presence and shared social experiences need to be sought. One could easily imagine that this attitude is related to the stigmatization that is attached to ME/CFS; because all the adolescents in our study were too ill to attend school like their peers, for them, their absence was not a choice. In fact, all participants expressed a strong desire to attend school as much as possible. On the other hand, teachers and physicians who had high levels of knowledge about the illness valued the possibility to attend remotely on the days that physical presence was not an option either due to their form that day or if it was the flu season and they had to stay home to avoid being infected because of the impact of ME/CFS on their immune system.

We argue that the orientation in HCI toward values emerging in lived contexts is well supported by RtD and the research product, enabling both empirical research and reflections on design and use. Together, RtD and VSD provided researchers with new opportunities regarding directions the research can take. Is this technology needed? What do robot avatars do in terms of long-term learning opportunities? Does increased attendance at school translates to better learning opportunities? How do robots make adolescents act differently? In the case of the robot avatar, many ethical issues easily surface, given that they are used by a vulnerable group of users. In addition, other questions specific to isolation and education also become relevant. For example, does the robot indeed enable social connections? Does it do it in the appropriate ways? Does the use of the robot make me more autonomous in deciding when to attend courses at school? How do peers perceive my robot avatar? How is it for teachers to address robots instead of humans? What do they need to do to keep students connected? Are other parents concerned with the privacy of their child even after a period of use of the robot?

Another challenge when working with new technologies is to find out if the technologies that are initially well perceived and adopted by the intended user group will eventually lose their novelty and in time be rejected by the same users? In (Read et al., 2011), authors discuss one of the essential features that make teens perceive technologies as cool, i.e. their newness, innovativeness. Based on this, one could predict that if it is only the "newness" that makes the robot well perceived by adolescents, the chance of the technology losing its novelty is higher than if the technology also pertains to other desired characteristics. This makes it necessary to investigate in detail how the robot is perceived by the user and his or her peers. In addition to exploring the users, the technology uses habits and technology preferences. What technologies do they currently use that they perceive to be cool and why? As mentioned, we used surveys, observations, and interviews to collect opinions about the robot and their situation before starting to use the robot. Tools also become necessary to lower the strain of participating in the interview but also to collect data to investigate predefined questions of interest in detail. Methods and tools described in the literature were designed and tailored to work with this user group and learn about the role of avatars in education and their possibility to reduce exposure to social isolation. We found that if robot avatars are to provide access to schools successfully, they need to be in perfect functioning order, easy to use, and useful. The level of "being finished" that our avatars had could not work for a commercial product. But they were absolutely amazing as research products (Odom et al., 2009). We got a lot of great data, in particular, related to design and personalization, because avatars were indeed seen as something that can be improved, and thinking about suggestions was worthwhile. However, when it came to access and socialization, they were somewhat impeded by this "prototype" status.

As mentioned in the literature survey, there were attempts to use tablets and similar devices to ensure access to school (Sheridan et al., 2013). However, considering tablets as representatives of a child were not the issue that was brought up. It was important to explore the emotional aspect that physical representation of a child by an avatar opens up. The stronger the emotional connection with the avatar as a representative of the child, the better outcomes can be expected from its use regarding social connections. A good example of this is the fact that Jon's teachers, and in particular, the substitute teacher mentioned earlier, do not see the robot as Jon. If they did, they most certainly would not lock him in the closet whenever Jon did not attend a lesson. Jon's mother did make an emotional connection with the avatar and voiced her opinion as "it is like locking him (Jon) in a closet," identifying Jon's ability to access friends and teaching with that of the avatar. Jon has increased the number of closest friends by one and added a few more to the group of occasional contacts, and he thinks that this is due to the use of the robot, despite the fact that lately, it has been living in the closet. This increase he attributes to the ability to talk to them more often and to participate in social interactions with peers during breaks. Jon was much more positive toward the robot when he could use it to talk to friends during the breaks than after this possibility was eliminated. When Jon was able to participate during breaks with the robot, he described that he felt more included socially in his class (as was reported through the online interview). His parents also noted that, in general, he seemed more emotionally satisfied and happy. For teachers, it was naturally easier to see the robot as a prototype, because they were the ones having to do extra work, of which charging the robot or placing the modem where there is reception are only one aspect. They also had to think how not to forget the child, as Peter's teacher pointed out. They had to find natural ways to include the child properly in a conversation, as well as when what they are doing in the classroom is not easy to attend remotely. How willing they are to address these issues determines how well the robot can be used. In our cases, at one school, the teachers used a workaround, where students performed the charging activities, while at the other school, the robot avatar was used less and less.

Do robot avatars enable easier access to education and reduce isolation? We found that they need to be completely functional, but all of our participants believe in the potential they promise. In our research, the avatar seen as a research product provided us with valuable new knowledge of relevance about the context, use, and usefulness of the robot avatar and insights that are imperative for the robot to be designed in a way that it supports chronically ill adolescents and improves their learning opportunities, as well as helping maintain social connections with peers.

## FUTURE RESEARCH DIRECTIONS

Reflections after carrying out the research presented here point in the direction that methods and methodologies for studying the use of research products embedded in users' everyday lives are still lacking and need to be better established. We have illustrated how RtD, in combination with research products, produces a rich set of data and is generative in the sense that it opens a range of possible new research directions. The main challenge that we experienced in relation to the use of research products and RtD, is how to handle the richness of the data that this approach yielded. How should findings be categorized and prioritized in order to produce rigorous and relevant research results through the RtD approach? For the presentation in this chapter, we have selected only a small subset of data, and tried to show the openings and leads for future research, but we have not done a complete analysis of results from the study. In a way, the whole chapter itself is a demonstration of generativeness, rather than rigor and relevance.

In addition, there are many ethical concerns related to the research case presented that can be further explored. An important concern is how RtD should be carried out with vulnerable adolescents, as in the case described. In this regard, we have shown how methods and tools can be tailored and used with youth suffering from a chronic illness in a specific research context, but much more can be done in this direction.

The methodological approach followed in this paper could also inspire or be useful for designers or researchers developing technologies aiming to support adolescents suffering from a range of other chronic illnesses.

## CONCLUSION

In this chapter, we have explored issues related to studying the use and usefulness of research products placed in real-use contexts for research purposes. We have shown how research products and RtD guided the inquiry around the experiences with the robot avatar as a representative of chronically ill adolescents at school. Our inquiry was twofold. First, we wanted to illustrate how research products are generative of new research directions in ways that are different from prototypes. Second, we wanted to discuss methods and tools that would enable researchers to capture data in real-life use. We have also argued that research products facilitate the emergence and understanding of values through the real-life use of a designed artifact. We experienced how the context determines and guides the research. For example, sensitivity to and awareness of issues related to ME/CFS were profoundly important for the research with this particular group of participants.

The use of a research product, the avatar, offered a way to gain knowledge about the avatar's potential as a technology for education and the reduction of social isolation. Our findings show the tremendous potential of the technology. The participants, their parents, and the schools reported many positive experiences with the product. For us as researchers, the knowledge gained from lived experiences with this new technology was invaluable. The emergence of values, understanding where challenges in use can occur, and the ways in which interactions between schools and participants can get difficult became easier, or possible, by using the avatar as a research product.

## REFERENCES

Best, K., & Butler, S. (2013). Second life avatars as extensions of social and physical bodies in people with Myalgic Encephalomyelitis/Chronic Fatigue Syndrome. *Continuum, 27*(6), 837–849. doi:10.108 0/10304312.2013.794190

Buchanan, R. (1992). Wicked Problems in Design Thinking. *Design Issues, 8*(2), 5–21. doi:10.2307/1511637

Chilana, P. K., Ko, A. J., & Wobbrock, J. (2015). From User-Centered to Adoption-Centered Design: A Case Study of an HCI Research Innovation Becoming a Product. In *Proceedings of the 33rd Annual ACM Conference on Human Factors in Computing Systems* (pp. 1749–1758). New York: ACM. doi:10.1145/2702123.2702412

Crawley, E., & Sterne, J. C. (2009). Association between school absence and physical function in paediatric chronic fatigue syndrome/myalgic encephalopathy. *Archives of Disease in Childhood, 94*(10), 752–756. doi:10.1136/adc.2008.143537 PMID:19001477

Culén, A. L. (2015). Later Life: Living Alone, Social Connectedness and ICT. *International Conference on Digital Human Modeling and Applications in Health, Safety, Ergonomics and Risk Management.* (pp. 401–412). Springer International Publishing. doi:10.1007/978-3-319-21070-4_40

Culén, A. L., & Gasparini, A. (2012). Situated Techno-Cools: Factors that contribute to making technology cool and the study case of iPad in education. *PsychNology Journal, 10*(2), 117–139.

Culén, A. L., & Karpova, A. (2014). A Researcher's Perspective: Design for and with Children with Impairments. In Human-Computer Interfaces and Interactivity: Emergent Research and Applications Book (pp. 118–136). IGI Global.

Culén, A. L., & van der Velden, M. (2013). The Digital Life of Vulnerable Users: Designing with Children, Patients, and Elderly. In M. Aanestad & T. Bratteteig (Eds.), *Nordic Contributions in IS Research* (pp. 53–71). Springer Berlin Heidelberg. doi:10.1007/978-3-642-39832-2_4

Dalsgaard, P. (2016). Experimental Systems in Research Through Design. In *Proceedings of the 2016 CHI Conference on Human Factors in Computing Systems* (pp. 4991–4996). New York, NY: ACM. doi:10.1145/2858036.2858310

Farmer, A., Fowler, T., Scourfield, J., & Thapar, A. (2004). Prevalence of chronic disabling fatigue in children and adolescents. *The British Journal of Psychiatry, 184*(6), 477–481. doi:10.1192/bjp.184.6.477 PMID:15172940

Fitton, D., Horton, M., Read, J. C., Little, L., & Toth, N. (2012). *Climbing the cool wall: exploring teenage preferences of cool*. ACM Press. doi:10.1145/2212776.2223758

Gaver, W. (2012). What Should We Expect from Research Through Design? In *Proceedings of the SIGCHI Conference on Human Factors in Computing Systems* (pp. 937–946). New York, NY: ACM. doi:10.1145/2207676.2208538

Grajales, F. J. III, Sheps, S., Ho, K., Novak-Lauscher, H., & Eysenbach, G. (2014). Social Media: A Review and Tutorial of Applications in Medicine and Health Care. *Journal of Medical Internet Research, 16*(2), e13. doi:10.2196/jmir.2912 PMID:24518354

Höök, K., Dalsgaard, P., Reeves, S., Bardzell, J., Löwgren, J., Stolterman, E., & Rogers, Y. (2015). Knowledge Production in Interaction Design. In *Proceedings of the 33rd Annual ACM Conference Extended Abstracts on Human Factors in Computing Systems* (pp. 2429–2432). New York, NY: ACM.

Jason, L., Benton, M., Torres-Harding, S., & Muldowney, K. (2009). The impact of energy modulation on physical functioning and fatigue severity among patients with ME/CFS. *Patient Education and Counseling, 77*(2), 237–241. doi:10.1016/j.pec.2009.02.015 PMID:19356884

Koskinen, I., Zimmerman, J., Binder, T., Redstrom, J., & Wensveen, S. (2011). *Design Research Through Practice: From the Lab, Field, and Showroom* (1st ed.). Waltham, MA: Morgan Kaufmann.

Krogh, P. G., Markussen, T., & Bang, A. L. (2015). Ways of Drifting—Five Methods of Experimentation in Research Through Design. In *ICoRD'15 – Research into Design Across Boundaries* (Vol. 1, pp. 39–50). New Delhi: Springer. doi:10.1007/978-81-322-2232-3_4

Lang, A. R., Martin, J. L., Sharples, S., Crowe, J. A., & Murphy, E. (2012). Not a minor problem: Involving adolescents in medical device design research. *Theoretical Issues in Ergonomics Science*, 1–12.

Le Dantec, C. A., Poole, E. S., & Wyche, S. P. (2009). Values As Lived Experience: Evolving Value Sensitive Design in Support of Value Discovery. In *Proceedings of the SIGCHI Conference on Human Factors in Computing Systems* (pp. 1141–1150). New York, NY: ACM. doi:10.1145/1518701.1518875

Lim, Y.-K., Stolterman, E., & Tenenberg, J. (2008). The Anatomy of Prototypes: Prototypes As Filters, Prototypes As Manifestations of Design Ideas. *ACM Trans. Comput.-Hum. Interact., 15*(2), 7:1–7:27.

Little, L., Fitton, D., Bell, B. T., & Toth, N. (Eds.). (2016). *Perspectives on HCI Research with Teenagers*. Cham: Springer International Publishing. doi:10.1007/978-3-319-33450-9

Mazé, R., & Redström, J. (2005). Form and the computational object. *Digital Creativity, 16*(1), 7–18. doi:10.1080/14626260500147736

No Isolation. (2015). Retrieved March 2, 2016, from http://www.noisolation.com/en/

Norwegian M. E. Association. (2016). Retrieved from http://me-foreningen.com/

Odom, W., Wakkary, R., Lim, Y., Desjardins, A., Hengeveld, B., & Banks, R. (2016). From Research Prototype to Research Product. In *Proceedings of the 2016 CHI Conference on Human Factors in Computing Systems* (pp. 2549–2561). New York, NY: ACM. doi:10.1145/2858036.2858447

Owen, C. (2007). Design thinking: Notes on its nature and use. *Design Research Quarterly, 2*(1), 16–27.

Perrin, J. M., Anderson, L. E., & Van Cleave, J. (2014). The Rise In Chronic Conditions Among Infants, Children, And Youth Can Be Met With Continued Health System Innovations. *Health Affairs*, *33*(12), 2099–2105. doi:10.1377/hlthaff.2014.0832 PMID:25489027

Poole, E. S., & Peyton, T. (2013). Interaction Design Research with Adolescents: Methodological Challenges and Best Practices. In *Proceedings of the 12th International Conference on Interaction Design and Children* (pp. 211–217). New York, NY: ACM. doi:10.1145/2485760.2485766

Read, J., Fitton, D., Cowan, B., Beale, R., Guo, Y., & Horton, M. (2011). Understanding and designing cool technologies for teenagers. In *Proceedings of the 2011 annual conference extended abstracts on Human factors in computing systems* (pp. 1567–1572). New York, NY: ACM. doi:10.1145/1979742.1979809

Rittel, H. W. J., & Webber, M. M. (1973). Dilemmas in a general theory of planning. *Policy Sciences*, *4*(2), 155–169. doi:10.1007/BF01405730

Sellen, A., Rogers, Y., Harper, R., & Rodden, T. (2009). Reflecting Human Values in the Digital Age. *Communications of the ACM*, *52*(3), 58–66. doi:10.1145/1467247.1467265

Sheridan, A. K., Scott, L., MacDonald, N., Murray, L., Holt, S., & Allen, K.Scottish Cross Party Working Group: Education of Children & Young People with M.E. (2013). Exploring E-learning provision for Children with ME in Scotland. *Other Education: The Journal of Educational Alternatives*, *2*(1), 78–80.

Tsui, K. M., & Yanco, H. A. (2013). Design Challenges and Guidelines for Social Interaction Using Mobile Telepresence Robots. *Reviews of Human Factors and Ergonomics*, *9*(1), 227–301. doi:10.1177/1557234X13502462

van der Velden, M., Sommervold, M. M., Culén, A., & Nakstad, B. (2016). Designing Interactive Technologies with Teenagers in a Hospital Setting. In L. Little, D. Fitton, B. T. Bell, & N. Toth (Eds.), *Perspectives on HCI Research with Teenagers* (pp. 103–131). Springer International Publishing. doi:10.1007/978-3-319-33450-9_5

Wadley, G., Vetere, F., Hopkins, L., Green, J., & Kulik, L. (2014). Exploring ambient technology for connecting hospitalised children with school and home. *International Journal of Human-Computer Studies*, *72*(8–9), 640–653. doi:10.1016/j.ijhcs.2014.04.003

Zimmerman, J., & Forlizzi, J. (2014). Research Through Design in HCI. In J. S. Olson & W. A. Kellogg (Eds.), *Ways of Knowing in HCI* (pp. 167–189). Springer New York. doi:10.1007/978-1-4939-0378-8_8

## ADDITIONAL READING

Afari, N., & Buchwald, D. (2003). Chronic Fatigue Syndrome: A Review. *The American Journal of Psychiatry*, *160*(2), 221–236. doi:10.1176/appi.ajp.160.2.221 PMID:12562565

Asaro, P. M. (2000). Transforming society by transforming technology: The science and politics of participatory design. *Accounting. Management and Information Technologies*, *10*(4), 257–290. doi:10.1016/S0959-8022(00)00004-7

Beckman, S. L., & Barry, M. (2007). Innovation as a learning process: Embedding design thinking. *California Management Review*, *50*(1), 25–56. doi:10.2307/41166415

Bjögvinsson, E., Ehn, P., & Hillgren, P.-A. (2012). Design Things and Design Thinking: Contemporary Participatory Design Challenges. *Design Issues*, *28*(3), 101–116. doi:10.1162/DESI_a_00165

Bowers, J. (2012). The Logic of Annotated Portfolios: Communicating the Value of "Research Through Design." In *Proceedings of the Designing Interactive Systems Conference* (pp. 68–77). New York, NY, USA: ACM. doi:10.1145/2317956.2317968

Desmet, P., Overbeeke, K., & Tax, S. (2001). Designing Products with Added Emotional Value: Development and Appllcation of an Approach for Research through Design. *The Design Journal*, *4*(1), 32–47. doi:10.2752/146069201789378496

Friedman, B., Jr. P. H. K., Borning, A., & Huldtgren, A. (2013). Value Sensitive Design and Information Systems. In N. Doorn, D. Schuurbiers, I. van de Poel, & M. E. Gorman (Eds.), Early engagement and new technologies: Opening up the laboratory (pp. 55–95). Springer Netherlands.

Hammersley, M., & Traianou, A. (2012). *Ethics in qualitative research: controversies and contexts. Los Angeles* [i.e. Thousand Oaks, Calif.]. London: SAGE Publications. doi:10.4135/9781473957619

Hare, C., Law, J., & Brennan, C. (2012). The vulnerable healthcare consumer: An interpretive synthesis of the patient experience literature. *International Journal of Consumer Studies*, 299–311.

Höök, K., Dalsgaard, P., Reeves, S., Bardzell, J., Löwgren, J., Stolterman, E., & Rogers, Y. (2015). Knowledge Production in Interaction Design. In *Proceedings of the 33rd Annual ACM Conference Extended Abstracts on Human Factors in Computing Systems* (pp. 2429–2432). New York, NY, USA: ACM.

Höök, K., & Löwgren, J. (2012). Strong Concepts: Intermediate-level Knowledge in Interaction Design Research. *ACM Trans. Comput.-Hum. Interact.*, *19*(3), 23:1–23:18.

Krogh, K., & Lindsay, P. (1999). Including people with disabilities in research: Implications for the field of augmentative and alternative communication. *Augmentative and Alternative Communication*, *15*(4), 222–233. doi:10.1080/07434619912331278765

Krogh, P. G., Markussen, T., & Bang, A. L. (2015). Ways of Drifting—Five Methods of Experimentation in Research Through Design. In *ICoRD'15 – Research into Design Across Boundaries* (Vol. 1, pp. 39–50). New Delhi: Springer. doi:10.1007/978-81-322-2232-3_4

Schön, D. A. (1983). *The reflective practitioner: How professionals think in action* (Vol. 5126). Basic books.

Vines, J. (2013). Designing For- and With- Vulnerable People. Retrieved October 4, 2013, from http://www.academia.edu/2989640/Designing_For-_and_With-_Vulnerable_People

# Chapter 9
# Human–Data Interaction in Healthcare

**Federico Cabitza**
*Università degli Studi di Milano-Bicocca, Italy*

**Angela Locoro**
*Università degli Studi di Milano-Bicocca, Italy*

## ABSTRACT

*In this chapter, we focus on an emerging strand of IT-oriented research, namely Human-Data Interaction (HDI) and on how this can be applied to healthcare. HDI regards both how humans create and use data by means of interactive systems, which can both assist and constrain them and the operational level of data work, which is both work on data and by data. Healthcare is a challenging arena where to test the potential of HDI towards a new, user-centered perspective on how to support and assess "data work". This is especially true in current times where data are becoming increasingly big and many tools are available for the lay people, including doctors and nurses, to interact with health-related data. This chapter is a contribution in the direction of considering health-related data through the lens of HDI, and of framing data visualization tools in this strand of research. The intended aim is to let the subtler peculiarities among different kind of data and of their use emerge and be addressed adequately. Our point is that doing so can promote the design of more usable tools that can support data work from a user-centered and data quality perspective and the evidence-based validation of these tools.*

## INTRODUCTION

Twenty-five years ago, medical informatics was defined as "dealing with the storage, retrieval and optimal use of biomedical data" (Shortliffe et al. 1990). At that time, little emphasis was put on the practices of data production, that is on how medical practice, and single stories of illness, care and recovery are represented, accounted and "datafied" in some valid and reliable manner. However, these practices, which include policies, rules, habits, conventions, tools and techniques, have always been intertwined with and affected by the available ITs, as well as by the expectations of the stakeholders on how to make sense and use of health-related data. Different perspectives on these expectations, and on what valuable health

DOI: 10.4018/978-1-5225-2492-2.ch009

data are, lead to manifest chasms between primary use and other uses of health information, as often discussed in the specialist literature (Fitzpatrick and Ellingsen, 2013). To try to cross these chasms, we need to create the suitable language to describe the differences and give some operational definitions.

We distinguish between three different macro-types of data and the related processes in which these data are either produced, processed or consumed: namely, primary data, which come from a broad range of sources and are produced within a caring process to make its unfolding seamless and smooth (Berg, 1999); secondary data that are derived from the primary data for purposes different than care, like accounting and medical billing (Abdelhak, Grostick, & Hanken, 2012); and tertiary data, that are produced from the secondary data for any unanticipated need of the potential consumers of health services (see Figure 1).

To illustrate this tripartition, an analogy from the agriculture domain can be drawn (Locoro, 2016): primary data are like the produce of the land, which farmers grow for themselves as well as the external market. Secondary data are the product of a transformation of these primary data, like the one performed in food industry where vegetables are cleansed and chopped. Tertiary data are further transformed from secondary data to make them more easily consumable, that is suitable for and conveyed to a broader population of consumers in terms of information services, like fresh-cut vegetable products can be seen as the service to have vegetables already ready-to-eat.

The definitions mentioned above shed light on the relationship between data and their uses, which cannot be overstated. The tripartition that we propose reflects the different uses and practices in which data are produced and consumed and it calls for a specific area of research focusing on how to support people in interacting with their data of concern and in gaining insight from them: Human-Data Interaction (HDI).

## BACKGROUND

As rightly noted by Hornung et al. (2015), the expression HDI is neither specific nor new. On the one hand, humans have always interacted with data, that is they have inscribed, read and communicated data in terms of simple marks, more complex symbols and any kind of meaningful signs[1]. On the other hand, this interaction has predominantly been mono-directional until interactive systems have allowed users to

*Figure 1. The three kinds of data and ambits proposed for HDI in healthcare*

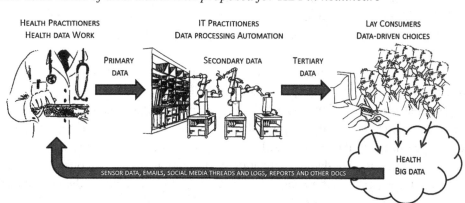

get access to data according to their peculiar and situated needs. In the computing literature, the expression has been used since the 1990s, e.g., by Kennedy et al. (1996), to address the needs of the users in the context of data intensive settings and hence "the problem of delivering personalized, context-aware, and understandable data from big datasets" (Cafaro, 2012). More recently a number of authors have tried to define Human-Data Interaction, by focusing on different aspects: Elmqvist (2011) and Cafaro (2012) focused on the material and embodied aspects of interaction; Crabtree and Mortier (2015) prefer to assimilate HDI to "the management and use of personal data in society at large" where *personal* here means that data are either "about individuals" or are delivered in terms of "personalized experiences". In particular, Elmqvist (2011) defines HDI as "the human manipulation, analysis, and sense making of large, unstructured, and complex datasets" and Cafaro sees HDI systems "as technologies that use embodied interaction to facilitate the users' exploration of rich datasets". We agree with Hornung et al. (2015) and Crabtree and Mortier (2014) in regard to the fact that "HDI does not only refer to embodied interaction, but to all kinds of interaction" and that "HDI should investigate 'data that affects people' ".

These reflections highlight the twofold meaning of HDI that we clarify in what follows. HDI is both a phenomenon and a research field that focuses on this phenomenon. As a phenomenon that is an object of research, we propose to see HDI as the class of actions where, on the one hand data are produced, processed and exploited by humans; this encompasses, at the two extremes of the action spectrum, both the "datafication" of facts, that is the process by which portions of the reality of interest are translated into the domain of words, symbols and numbers (through coding, classification, and measure[2]); and what we call data telling, that is the creation of accounts and stories that human can tell according to the data they make (a) sense of. On the other hand, HDI also regards actions in which humans are affected by data, that is in which their interpretations, opinions, beliefs and decisions are made by, or better yet according to, data.

Moreover, as a research area focusing on this kind of interaction it lies at the intersection of data science, data visualization and human-computer interaction. Researchers involved in HDI study how humans record and use data by means of Information Technologies; and design interactive systems that allow humans to retrieve and explore complex data sets in order to gain value in their learning, insight in their decisions, and feedback in their action. Considering HDI a distinct research field, although deeply grounded in the intersection between data visualization and human-computer interaction means to highlight the typical tenets of HCI about the centeredness of users in successful design and the importance to consider "complex contextual factors including the systems of beliefs, values and norms of the involved people" (Hornung et al. 2015) when designing systems by which humans can explore and interpret data according to their skills, competences, desires and needs. Moreover, it also means to borrow from HCI the attitude to evaluate the impact of these systems on the people life and investigate systematically "data production, collection, processing and use [by] focusing on the social impact they provoke" (Hornung et al. 2015).

In this chapter, we mainly focus on HDI as an evidence-based approach to the design of ICT systems. Our main contribution is a tripartite conceptual framework to help practitioners separate the concerns and address design related aspects peculiar to primary and tertiary data type, data work and data users. Three studies are also presented to exemplify the typical approaches within HDI and the related framework to the design, development and evaluation of healthcare supporting technologies. In particular, the first case refers to the heuristic evaluation of data visualization prioritization, the second one to a user test on data customization for citizens, and the third case to a research through design of a data visualization tool.

## INTERACTION AS KEY TO UNDERSTAND HEALTH DATA

In this section we discuss how to consider interaction central to characterize and distinguish among the roles of health data, as an alternative to top-down, and abstract ways to classify them: in short we propose an analytical framework where considering who is going to use health data, and why (that is for what objective in what task) is more important than investigating the intrinsic attributes of data to understand how to better manage them (Strong, et al. 1997).

In virtue of these primary concerns, we distinguish between primary, secondary and tertiary (health) data. For a straight metonymy, we intend primary data as entangled with the primary use of data, by definition; secondary data with secondary use(s); tertiary data with tertiary uses. The "primary use" of health information is "to use it to directly support patient care", both by aiding medical decision-making and by ensuring continuity of care by all providers, that is both interpretation of medical signs (represented by data) for decision making, and coordination among the actors involved "around" the patient (Berg, 1999). Secondary use regards both other uses of the same data collected for the primary use within the administrative domain, and the generation of derivative data for other aims than care, like billing and reimbursement, performance and care quality evaluation, resource planning and management, service design and public policy making. Tertiary use regards the heterogeneous uses through which tertiary data are put to the test of users' life: this can encompass the publication and dissemination of valuable indications for the citizens and the taxpayers about the available healthcare services, so as to orient them in the choice of the best healthcare provider (or just the closest one to their shelters – cf. Cabitza et al. 2015b); the policy makers and facility or agency manager, to facilitate the monitoring of suitable outcome and performance indicators and to enable the benchmarking and comparison of care facilities; as well as the researchers and epidemiologists to make sense of the great numbers of "similar" patients that are treated and detect trends and patterns of treatment appropriateness and efficacy.

On a more general level, three concepts characterize uses and data in each of these three ambits: primary use is related to what has been often called "data work" (Bossen et al. 2016). Secondary uses with data storing and processing. Tertiary uses with data value. Data storing and processing are self-explanatory concepts in computer science and regard the set-up of efficient data bases and the automation of accurate procedures by which to structure data, run searches and extract complex reports for disparate purposes. As secondary data and secondary processes usually entail little interaction by humans and these are always IT specialists and consultants who have always considered usability a relative concern, we will focus on the primary and secondary domains, and hence on data work and data value.

Data work is quite never defined in the specialist literature; although it is often mentioned, it is a slippery notion. We see it as a modern (but not at all recent) coinage after the word paperwork, of which it represents an abstraction, with respect to the medium of data representation; but also an extension, with respect to what people manage as data of their interest (besides accounting and resource management). As such data work is not only "working on data", typically producing new data in accounting for and recording a faithful representation of the work done; but also that portion of work that can be accomplished only by relying on some accurate data, i.e., "working by data". These two kinds of work are usually so deeply intertwined that distinguishing between them is useless and probably wrong: in the healthcare domain, the studies by Berg (Berg, 1999), for instance, clearly show that clinicians record data on the patient record not only to accumulate data for archival reasons (and for many other secondary uses), but also to coordinate with each other, articulate the resources around a medical case, and take informed decision in a written, distributed communication with themselves and the other colleagues taking care of the same patient. In healthcare, data work regards the additional effort paid by caregivers in making the record a "working record" (Fitzpatrick 2004), that is a resource capable of keeping disparate competencies and roles bound together and connected around the same cases over time and space.

On the other hand, tertiary use of tertiary data regards the concept of data value, that is how to exploit data to achieve some relevant goal for the user (even just to be informed about something), so that we can say that the user finds value in the data (also: she finds data valuable), or she gains value to some aim. Whether value is already in the data or rather it is created by an active stance of its consumers looks like an idle question: in a HDI perspective, value is the result of interacting with data and being capable to exploit them by tertiary users, that is lay people moved by unpredictable motives and toward unanticipated aims. In other words, on one hand data have got value if they are true and have been made accessible and comprehensible; on the other hand, their value lies in the comprehension itself, in the acquisition of true information, in learning notions, techniques, practices, and in the resulting knowledgeable behaviors, in their turn producing some positive effect, on either the single person or her community[3]. Thus, data value can be defined as the potential of data (for its intrinsic qualities) to enable processes of value creation by someone for anyone (either herself, or the others) in some given context.

## HDI CONTRIBUTIONS FOR THE QUALITY OF INFORMATION

While this tripartition is general enough to be applied in any domain where many different roles partake to the generation and transformation of data in the same supply chain, so to say, from the practitioner working in the field, to the final consumer of information services, its application to healthcare can be justified for its role in addressing the problem of the still relatively low quality of the data of patient records (Liaw et al. 2013), both in regard to completeness, accuracy and timeliness (Cabitza & Batini, 2016). Indeed it allows, on one hand, to highlight differences, separate concerns, and identifying ambits of use that are irreducible to one another; on the other hand, it allows to see the (existing) "seams" between these ambits (Berg and Goorman 1999) and therefore to address cooperation and interoperability without reckless neglect.

In regard to this latter point, it is time to acknowledge that chasms between primary and other uses exist and they go beyond the usual tension between clinical vs. administrative purposes because it is the concept of "adequate quality" that should be adopted to assess care-oriented data; likewise, crossing the chasm between the secondary and tertiary domains requires more than merely making secondary data more open and accessible, because also the end consumers' readiness to access, comprehend and exploit them, as well as their unpredictable purposes, are to be considered. Thus, the challenge to bridge the chasms mentioned above can be seen in terms of the problem of reusing primary data, which is "always entangled with the context of its production" (Berg and Goorman, 1999), in different contexts (either secondary or tertiary ones).

As Berg and Goorman note, reuse is possible only if data are made "transportable", that is sufficiently disentangled from their context of production; and this can occur only if specialized additional work is performed on data. So it is not a matter of improving, automating or changing current data work, but rather to invest on new and different data work, and corresponding new organizational roles (e.g., data nurses).

In regard to the separation of concerns, our distinction between primary, secondary and tertiary data is quite different from other frameworks discussed in the Data Quality literature: for example, the one inspired by the manufacturing domain (Shankaranarayan et al., 2003) which distinguishes between raw data, component data items, that is semi-processed information and information products, which are composed out of these items. Primary data are not necessarily raw (Gitelman, 2013), because they are meaningful to and usable by the primary consumers that generated them. On the other hand, secondary and tertiary data are unfinished information products: the former ones are resources for specialist work (both clerical and managerial) within specific organizational boundaries and processes, while tertiary data result from the enactment of information services conceived for the non specialist and the external consumers, that is for the public. The distinction introduced by Shankaranarayan and his colleagues focuses on an incremental definition of the information product, and is often mentioned in regard to how Data Quality (DQ) can be assessed, monitored and continuously improved (e.g., Wang, 1998)

Differently from the Information Product perspective, our tripartite perspective focuses on the different roles that produce and consume different information products that can be considered "definitive" only in relation to their context of use. Consequently, a HDI approach to DQ issues grounds on the interpretation of quality of data as their "fitness for use" (Wang & Strong, 1996). Our proposal is aimed at detecting and taking the differences from the various uses in healthcare seriously (Bossen et al. 2016).

According to our metaphor, secondary data and secondary data-centered processes are like industrial processes, that need standardization to achieve regularity and efficiency and that involve relatively few people with specific skills and motives, like the competent and trained operators of assembly lines at the shop floor of plants. This is why HDI regards secondary data and processes only marginally, and to a much greater extent the primary and tertiary contexts. In primary settings, HDI addresses the challenges of fitting "data work" to work, that is of reconciling the articulation of cooperative activities performed by knowledgeable experts with their effort in continuous recording relevant events and information about what has been carried out, and often also of why and how. On the other hand, in the broader ambits of tertiary use, HDI deals with the manifold challenge to design data structures, visualization controls and interaction affordances, for both unintended uses and unanticipated needs, for both the practitioners without particular e-literacy and numeracy, and lay people from the general public.

We would argue that quality of information should not be assessed irrespective of the distinction between primary / secondary / tertiary uses, that is, by adopting the same metrics and methods in a context-independent manner: on the contrary, data used in care processes should be evaluated on the basis of the efficacy they enable appropriate and timely action (fit to use), also on the basis of work conventions and tacit knowledge that are difficult to bring back to the usual dimensions of accuracy, completeness and consistency (Gregory et al., 1995). This is in line with the idea to measure the quality of primary (health) data in terms of appropriateness and as a function of the health outcome they help to achieve. Bad quality should not be related to completeness, timeliness or, even, accuracy, since health practitioners can perfectly make sense of "bad" data and to some extent they even expect them (Bossen et al. 2016); but rather to "information failure" and its impact, that is the number of times data work is either direct or indirect cause of adverse event or near misses (Pipino & Lee, 2011). Despite the authorities that advocated for more research on this concept (Pipino & Lee, 201; Cabitza & Batini 2016), information failure (or error) is still under-researched and a taxonomy of cases to guide analysis and comparison still missing, for instance one that could distinguish between cases in which wrong or late decisions were carried out with accurate and timely data, respectively, and the other way round, a right and timely interpretation has been based on wrong and obsolete data, and so on[4].

Similarly, further research is needed for the evaluation of the quality of tertiary data: this is highly correlated with the quality of the information services conceived for the general public, which should be evaluated in terms of the extent to which data are "informative" and can be appropriated by consumers and appreciated in their lives (i.e., according to its social value), that is if they affect decisions for the better.

This is where HDI can fit in and be a novel way to address long-standing problems of low quality that neither incentivizing structures nor sanctions seem to solve completely. Indeed, HDI covers three phases: design, development and evaluation of the systems by which to extract information and support knowledge in data-intensive application domains. As HDI approaches operate at the upper layer of the well known ISO-OSI standard, i.e., the application layer, or, better yet, the data visualization layer, the scope of HDI is not to tackle which data are to be shown in terms of ethical or security issues (which are tasks usually delegated to the lower layers of the ISO-OSI pillar, such as model and control layers, e.g., a database, a middleware, and so on), but how data are to be shown instead, e.g., in terms of ergonomic and usability issues. The scope of an HDI approach is mainly that of the design, development and evaluation of data visualization interfaces. In particular, HDI regards the user-centered elicitation of better requirements of configuration, adaptation and appropriation of big data analytics cockpits and dashboards to optimize usability and the user experience, i.e., efficiency, effectiveness and satisfaction; the application of End-User Development techniques and tools to allow end-users tweak the tools by which data are extracted and visualized; and user-centered methodology for the assessment and continuous improvement of the quality of the interaction of the humans with their data of interest, so as to reduce both information overloading and information funneling/complacency (Parasuraman and Manzey, 2010), and improve awareness. This also includes the exploration of new techniques toward better interactive visualization environments and above all better data-telling, that is the capability to build and share stories that can explain data and facilitate correct interpretations (e.g., in medical domain by adopting a natural frequency approach - Hoffrage et al., 2002) and to allow, instead of curbing, the social exchange within a community of data-users of multi-perspective, sound and viable interpretations around the data that are supplied by the computational systems to inform decision making and knowledgeable action.

Summarizing, HDI can contribute in addressing the reconciliation of needs in health data production and use by providing methods and techniques that investigate the following two research strands:

1.  The design of interfaces that could promote mutual awareness between data producers and consumers: on the one hand, by increasing commitment and awareness of consequences in the producers of the primary data; and, at the same time, by raising awareness in the secondary consumers of the contextual and social nature of primary data and hence of their limitations. This can be achieved, for example, by endowing the interfaces by which data are collected and presented with specific affordances that adapt to the context according to specific business rules in order to convey the so called "awareness promoting information" (Cabitza and Simone, 2012); this can be done also by means of simple visual clues like text highlighting or side messages, which do not impose any behavior to the data producers but help their interpretation.

2.  The design of interactive visual interfaces that could support the understandability of data analytics. The transformation of data into information services does not necessarily require a massive processing of data but rather the application of state-of-the-art human interaction techniques to develop interactive infographics and highly tailorable dashboards that enable user-friendly online analytical processing and hence the transformation, even by end users (Lieberman, Paternò, Klann, & Wulf, 2006), of secondary data into socially valuable information.

## AN HDI APPROACH TO FOSTER EVIDENCE-BASED DESIGN

The phrase evidence-based design is not totally new but still not really common, especially in the computer science literature and there is little wonder that also recently (Ammenwerth & Rigby, 2016) it has been applied to the fields of informatics that are closer to medicine and healthcare. In fact, the parallel with the approach to medical practice known as "Evidence-Based Medicine" (EBM)(VV.AA., 1992) is not coincidental, and indeed, it constitutes a sort of natural extension of that methodological empirical attitude to the design of computerized tools that can have an impact on medical decision and care quality. Shortly speaking, an evidence-based approach to IT design requires to back up any claim of utility or usability of a particular solution or tool with empirical studies that collect data from real users (including the perceptions of domain experts) and undertake standard statistical tests and group comparisons (Longhurst et al. 2013). Even more than this, an evidence-based approach must consider findings from the field of work in combination with the expertise of IT practitioners and the needs and wishes of the intended prospective users (e.g., patients and shopfloor doctors and nurses). Especially this latter aspect is typical in the Human-Computer Interaction field, and we also proposed it for studies accomplished within the HDI field (Cabitza et al., 2016).

To give more concreteness to the notion of HDI and evidence-based design, in the rest of this chapter we will report about three small-scale user studies in the domain of health information. The common element of these studies is the collection of empirical "proofs" (that is evidence) about solutions that were designed to increase the perceived value of interfaces and data visualization tools in the healthcare sector. To our knowledge the most relevant of the similar initiatives is the "Visualizing Health" project (http://www.vizhealth.org/), developed by the University of Michigan and the Robert Wood Johnson Foundation. In this project, which is subtitled "a scientifically vetted style guide for communicating health data", the involved researchers compared tens of different styles by which to communicate risk-related information in order to select the best ones for the general public according to a series of empirical tests involving real users. The main finding, which we also back up, is that when it comes to presenting health information, there is no single "best" graphic, as this depends on the intended goal and, in a subtler way, on what matters most to the intended users of the diagrams and infographics (Cabitza et al. 2015b). This calls for an evidence-based approach to this kind of evaluations, which must be tailored to specific groups of people (e.g., practitioners, patients) and contexts of use (Solomon et al. 2016).

*Figure 2. The ranking of data item in radiology; items are enumerated according to their fine-grained ranking within the macro-category of priority level. Levels are established according to statistical testing.*

| Data Item in the Main Page of the Radiographer | Level of Priority |
| --- | --- |
| Patient ID, Exam Date, Birth Date, Radiographist Name. | Higher |
| Level of urgency, Name of the patien, Time of execution, Patient Gender, Responsible Radiologist, Access number, Alert, Body section, DICOM ID, Patient fiscal code, Modality Type, Referring facility. | Probably Higher |
| Ordering Radiologist, Exam description, Phone number, Room ID, patient's current address, patient's municipality, how the patient arrived, cost center. | Probably Lower |
| Patient nationality, Patient height. | Lower |

# EXAMPLES OF USER STUDIES IN HEALTHCARE HDI

In this section we will report about three small user studies we accomplished under the tenets of HDI for an evidence-based design of data visualization tools for the healthcare sector. This is also aimed at showing that an evidence-based approach can be adopted also for small software development projects and without the need of relevant budgets. In particular, the first study regards primary data in radiology work, in terms of the identification of what data the practitioners should be required to record for their primary aim, and what data they deem less useful to this aim. The second study regards the value of tertiary data about hospital quality and availability, as this is evaluated by citizens that would need to gain information about the hospitals of their catchment area to choose where to go according to their needs and preferences. We will just outline the first two studies and give some more details of the third one, which regards the acceptance of an innovative system of data visualization for aggregate patient data by a sample of general practitioners (family doctors).

## The Radiology User Study

In this study, we asked 15 expert technicians from different radiology facilities of Northern Italy to indicate the usefulness for their work of 31 information items on an ordinal scale, from 1 (negligible) to 6 (essential). The items regarded either the assessment of patients, their management for the execution of digital imaging examinations, or the preliminary evaluation of radiographic media, and they were collected by considering the Italian guidelines for quality assurance in teleradiology (Working Group for Quality Assurance in Diagnostic and Interventional Radiology, 2010).

The aim of the study was to rank those items from the most useful to the least, so that the interface of their information system could be optimized. Here, the concept of optimization should be interpreted as follows: either in terms of having the radiological information system display and require only those data that the radiographers considered certainly useful for their job; or, at least, in terms of a system that would not urge the users to fill in the low priority fields as mandatory data that block the application unless radiographers insert them. The online questionnaire platform displayed the 31 items in different order to minimize order bias and the task was carried out as part of an assignment of a first Level Master degree class on IT management for radiographers.

We then applied an original ranking method, discussed in (Cabitza et al. 2015a) by which we classified each item in one of four levels of priorities (see Figure 2). An informal interpretation of the result could consider the first group (see the green block in Figure 2), i.e., Patient ID, patient birth date, exam date, operator name, radiographer name (if these latter are not the same) as those items that cannot be missing in the radiographer screen, and that indeed need to be emphasized at the interface level (e.g. by being rendered at a proper font size) and double checked by the operators involved to avoid potential mistakes and adverse events. The second group of items (including the name of the patient, the ordering radiologist, the access number) are data of lower priority but still very important, that radiographers should consider mandatory to fill in. Conversely, low priority items like patient nationality and patient height (see the red block in Figure 2) could be considered those that should not be imposed to the data work of radiographers, nor displayed irrespective of the specific examination, as these unnecessary items could contribute to clutter the user interface and hide more relevant information.

In our future work, we will perform the same user study in different groups of users of the radiological information system, like the medical radiologists and the administrative clerks, so as to make the interfaces adaptive according to the role logged in, and have the systems display awareness promoting information (Cabitza & Simone, 2012) about the different perception of utility (if any) by different worker categories. For instance, let us assume that the administrative clerks in a given hospital would consider the indication of the cost center and the billing address of the patient essential data items for their paperwork; in this case, radiographers, who conversely attach a low priority to these items (see Figure 2), could be notified that these data are important for someone else in the same facility (e.g., by means of some iconic indication or by a warning message at the end of the work shift) and be made aware (see above) of the data-related needs of other professionals that are connected by the same patient case.

## The Open Data Study

In this second study, we collected 330 complete questionnaires from a population of citizens living in an urban area and aged 18 or older. To this aim, we invited personal friends and acquaintances, all of the colleagues of our university department, and the students of two master classes from the same university. Sample representativeness was achieved by weighting the response set by both age and gender according to the latest national census. The respondents had to evaluate the utility of 11 information items in different scenarios of urgency and serious health conditions. The information items had been selected from those that can be conveniently extracted from some of the most important big open healthcare data sets available in the USA, in Canada and in Italy (taken, respectively, from healthdata.gov, www.cihi. ca and dovesalute.gov.it).

The sample exhibited (statistically) significant appreciation for three information items above all the others: the hospital ranking by number of admissions for the pathology of interest; the ranking by average wait time for the pathology of interest; and the ranking of facilities by their reaching time from one's place. The rankings evaluated the least useful were the rankings produced according to either the perceived level of care quality by all the hospitalized patients, or by the percentage of patients that had to be hospitalized again within six months since the first discharge. While the latter information is quite technical, perhaps too much to be appreciated by a sample of lay people, the former indication came unexpected and quite puzzling.

All of the collected indications are useful to design healthcare portals that show their users a minimal set of items with the highest potential to satisfy the users' needs, on default of other information, leaving the other items accessible on demand. Interestingly, we detected significant differences in the perception of information usefulness between different user profiles. For instance, male respondents attached more importance than women to the ranking based on georeferenced information. Not surprisingly, expert users considered the ranking by number of admissions for the pathology of interest more important than people self-declaring non-expert. We also probed the sample preferences for different ways to display the same information, either by simple and essential tables or by richer and more appealing infographics. Also in this case we detected a statistically significant difference between females and males, as the former ones found infographics to be clearer and more intuitive than men; and between young respondents and the elderly as the former ones, quit unexpectedly, found the tabular form more clear than the latter ones. These differences suggest that the usability of a healthcare portal can be maximized even considering basic profiling information and user satisfaction can be improved by asking the user only a few data, like gender and age.

## The General Practice Study

We will focus now on the third user study that in some way integrates the research question of the former two studies regarding perceived utility with one of the central issues for the HDI field of whether interactivity improves the perceived value of data. Thus, the first research question is: What health open data are perceived as *more useful* in general practice (if any)? The second one is: Would visualizing these open data by means of *interactive* (that is browsable, zoomable, etc.) maps make these data to be perceived as *more useful and usable*? To further investigate this latter question we addressed it also in case of innovative visualizations, like in the case of diagrams displaying *parallel coordinates* (Inselberg, 2009) (see Figure 3). Thus, in particular, we wondered whether this kind of tools are effective means to represent patient data at various levels of description and to help GPs understand population trends, discover (frequency-based) normal and abnormal conditions, and detect correlations between multiple conditions.

To these above aims, we conceived a short questionnaire to be administered as a Computer-Aided Web Self-Interview (CAWI). This questionnaire consisted of four sections, which were to be rendered each in a different Web page: in the first page, the platform presented a list of 13 datasets that the authors had previously selected among the health open datasets made available on the DatiOpen.it platform (http://www.datiopen.it/en), which is one of the biggest Italian open data portals collecting more than 2,000 thousand datasets. In particular the respondents were asked to choose at least one dataset (and at most three) that they could want to consult in an online and customized "visual dashboard" supporting their own professional practice. In the second page we further selected 6 datasets for their suitability to be mapped into a georeferenced map like the one depicted in Figure 4.a, and asked the doctors to evaluate the degree of *utility for their profession* of each dataset on a six-value ordinal scale, from 1 (not useful at all) to 6 (very useful).

*Figure 3. The parallel coordinate diagram shown to the user panel; the thick red and orange lines indicate the average values and standard deviations respectively. Blue lines represent single male patients. Pink lines female patients.*

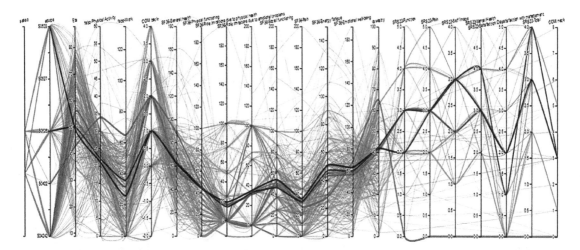

Then, we asked the doctors to imagine to be able to interact with the map, so that they could browse the map by dragging, and zooming in and out at the desired level of visualization (e.g., province, city, neighborhood if possible) and get a *heat map* like the one depicted in Figure 4.b. We then asked whether visualizing the above datasets on such a browsable map would make the data more useful or not (on a 5-value scale ranging from 1 "the data would be much *less* useful" to 5 "the data would be much *more* useful", passing through a middle value 3 "it wouldn't make almost any difference"). Finally in the third section, the questionnaire displayed a parallel coordinates diagram like the one depicted in Figure 3. We asked to indicate on a six-value ordinal scale the degree of informativity of such a way to represent patient data (from 1 not informative at all, to 6, very informative).

The questionnaire was left open for two weeks after the invitation had been sent to potential respondents. In this time lapse no reminder was sent. When we closed the survey, 29 GPs had accessed the questionnaire; 23 of them had completely filled in every item of the questionnaire in an average time of 5.9 minutes (SD=2.6 minutes). In this respondent sample, 5 out of 10 have been family doctors for more than 30 years, 9 out of 10 for more than 20 years; no respondent had less than 10 years of work experience so that we can consider the sample composed of experts in the Family Medicine domain.

The majority of the respondents (65%) claimed to be competent in Information Technology (IT) but neither experts nor enthusiasts. These latter ones were, respectively, approximately one third and one fifth of the sample. We detected a statistically significant and moderately negative correlation between age and IT expertise (-.49, p=.018), as it could be expected.

The respondents were asked to choose the three most useful datasets to be visualized on a personal dashboard for their daily practice by selecting them out of a list of 13 data sets. These had been selected for their popularity in terms of number of downloads from a comprehensive collection of Italian health open datasets. The sets chosen more frequently by the respondents were:

1. Regional distribution of the percentage of elderly people involved in the program of Integrated Home Care (in Italian: Assistenza Domiciliare Integrata).
2. Number (and details) of the Rehabilitation facilities for the elderly (in Italian: Istituti di Riabilitazione Extraospedaliera per Anziani).
3. Inpatient care average length of stay.

*Figure 4. The static map (on the left, a) shown to the general practitioners; the heat map (on the right, b) resulting from interacting with the map depicted on the left*

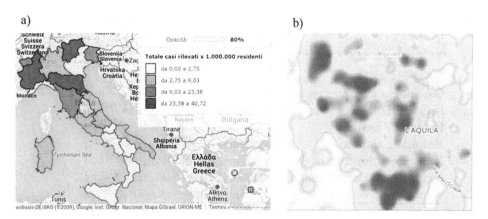

These datasets were selected by approximately one third of the sample (38%, 33% and 30% respectively). The other datasets collected much fewer preferences, with the "number of cases affected by pneumococcal disease by year" that was not chosen by any respondent.

In regard to the utility of data sets to be displayed on a georeferenced map, we got statistical significance for two sets only, which were considered useful for general practice, namely:

1.    Number of registers on exposure to carcinogens (.5 vs..95, p=.000).
2.    Hospitalization rates, by regime, patient genre and region (.26 vs..74, p=.035).

For the other data sets we did not get statistical significance: however, the "number of medical prescriptions delivered" can be considered the least appreciated information set (.64 vs..36).

We also asked whether putting all of the above datasets into an interactive map, instead of a static one, would change the perceived utility of the datasets themselves. The majority claimed mapping data would make a difference, and that in so doing the datasets would be more useful (.83 vs..17, p=.003, one third of the GPs even claiming that the data "would be much more useful"). The ranking of relative utility of mapping open data sets is reported in Table 1.

As a visualization aid to the comprehension of patient data and their correlation on multiple dimensions, parallel coordinates, like those depicted in Figure 3 and 5 were found to be highly informative: the responses were positive for the majority (.64 vs..46, p=.286). Furthermore, almost every GP involved in the user study claimed that the interactive version (see Figure 5) of the diagram was much more informative than the static view (.96 vs..04, p=.000, 60% "much more informative").

The characteristics of the respondent sample, in terms of work experience and attitude towards Health IT suggest that the respondents can be considered representatives of a population of real domain experts and that the potential (positive) bias introduced by the IT enthusiasts should be low. Besides the results reported above, the questionnaire also allowed the respondents leave free text comments in order to suggest datasets and applications to be considered in further studies, give advice on potential improvements to the visual tools presented, and more generally share remarks with the research team.

In particular, we report two comments that suggested relevant improvements to the Parallel Coordinate (PC) dashboard. One GP suggested to implement PCs indicating explicitly central tendency parameters on their axes (wherever applicable), like means and medians, standard deviations and interquartile ranges,

*Table 1. Open datasets to be visualized in maps ranked by perceived utility*

| Dataset | Priority level[(sig.)] | Perceived utility[(sig.)] | Median |
|---|---|---|---|
| Carcinogen exposure registers | Higher[(*)] | Positive[(***)] | 5 |
| National Drug Consumption | Uncertain[(NS)] | Positive[(NS)] | 4 |
| Home care patients | Uncertain[(NS)] | Positive[(NS)] | 4 |
| Hospitalization rate | Uncertain[(NS)] | Positive[(*)] | 4 |
| Incidence of invasive diseases | Uncertain[(NS)] | Positive[(NS)] | 4 |
| Incidence of occupational diseases | Uncertain[(NS)] | Positive[(NS)] | 4 |
| Number of prescriptions | Uncertain[(NS)] | Negative[(NS)] | 3 |

*Figure 5. The parallel coordinate diagram shown in Figure 3 after having interacted with it; in particular three specific ranges of data have been specified to filter the patient data to be highlighted: more precisely, female patients treated by two specific medical teams (equipe) and between 70 and 50 years of age*

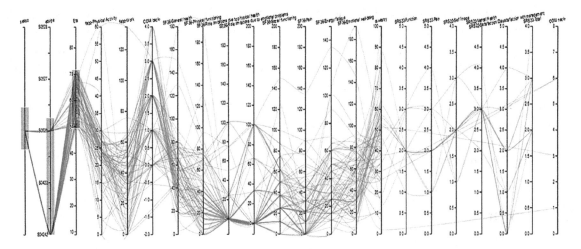

both at the level of the single GP patient set, and (if available) at the regional and national level. This doctor noticed how the bundle of lines, in virtue of their variable thickness at the intersection with the different coordinates, would nicely and visually represent the frequency distribution of the values within the subject population. Another GP suggested to allow the user to switch from a cross-sectional view (i.e., the default one) where each line represents the current conditions of a single patient, to a longitudinal view. In such a view, the current conditions would be represented as a highlighted line, while the bundle of the other lines would represent the different conditions that the same patient exhibited in the past, as these are recorded on the medical record of the GP or in the patient's health record.

We are aware of the limitations of this study. For instance, the fact that the involved doctors had to imagine the novel interaction, by looking at static pictures of how the visualization tools would change according to their actions. However, giving doctors real dashboards with which to interact and ask about their perceptions would have been problematic for the impossibility to give them a uniform training and to check remotely their interaction with the tool to evaluate. Using an interactive prototype would have implied a training phase of all the doctors involved in the experiments, and a physical presence during the usage of the interactive prototype to observe and record the experiment for further examination. A uniform training phase could have being achieved by preparing a video animation to show how to use the interactive prototype, but we could not do it due to two main reasons: (i) the lack of human resources that should also be present during the experimental sessions, and hence the impossibility to control the experiment adequately; (ii) the dread that the respondents, acting remotely without our presence, could assess the video animation and not the interactive prototype. However, we believe that studies like the present one, where interactivity is simulated in terms of its effects, could be useful anyway in a preliminary phase of development, where to understand if endowing visual tools with some kind of interactivity would be worth the effort.

## FUTURE RESEARCH DIRECTIONS

In light of the evidence collected in this study, we can conclude that designing for a better interactivity of open data platforms for general practice is worth further efforts. From the HDI perspective, this conclusion was desirable; although it might also seem easily predictable, nevertheless that conclusion could not be taken for granted in a committed *evidence-based approach* to Health IT design (Rigby et al. 2013, Longhurst et al. 2013, Cabitza et al. 2016). For this reason, our studies are just a small but necessary contribution in the research agenda outlined in the Introduction and that we advocate as future research directions of an increasing number of researchers in the health informatics, data science and human computer interaction fields. These future researches should be aimed at gaining feedback and design-oriented indications from both caregivers and patients to improve their experience in interacting with the next data visualization tools to come.

## CONCLUSION

In this chapter we have proposed a tripartite perspective to health data by which to distinguish between primary data, i.e., the content of health records that clinicians and nurse produce and consume in their decisions and treatments; secondary data, i.e., the content of structured data bases, data warehouses and the reports that automated procedures produce and display on interactive data visualization tools (or dashboards) to support the tasks of clerical and managerial roles (including policy makers); and tertiary data, i.e., particular content that has been selected and optimized in terms of clarity, understandability and appeal, in one word usability, to be offered online for the general public and hence for unanticipated needs and aims. The distinction has been proposed to separate concerns and differentiate agendas. The one-size-fits-all approach to data quality improvement simply does not work (Pipino et al. 2002), nor solve the still present problems of low use of and low satisfaction for the Electronic Health Record (Cabitza et al. 2015a). Moreover, such a simple separation of concerns also allows to emphasize the concept of "use and reuse" of health data (Berg and Goorman, 1999), which is important to keep in mind when setting quality requirements and imposing ideal data model to health practitioners and their patients.

Human Data Interaction (HDI), as a research approach, can provide alternative methods to address these challenges, which are becoming more and more urgent especially in our current age of increasing opportunities and threats regarding the "datafication" of medicine and the consequent production of health big data (Murdoch & Detsky 2013). In particular, HDI approaches would focus on evaluating how ICT supports data (producing) work by relieving doctors and nurses from form-filling, coding and other administrative tasks; and on evaluating the usability and the user experience related to interacting with tertiary (health) data, to understand the actual value these convey in decision making and information-intensive tasks. Put it in another way, through HDI a design approach more sensible to relieving doctors from administrative tasks should become the primary concern behind ICT systems for supporting healthcare practices. It goes without saying that there is not an ultimate solution to achieve this goal, and HDI is no exception. Nevertheless, HDI may promote an attitude and awareness to cognitive ergonomics aspects, to usability studies applied to healthcare information systems, and so on. The HDI perspective is aimed to let emerge that doctors should not work with data as information *per se* (e.g., by forcing them to fill a form of a database table full of tedious completeness constraints aimed to achieve an intrinsic data quality), rather they should use their time to work and reflect *upon* data, in order to enhance their daily work, practices and decisions. As a final consideration, HDI may be considered as an approach through which nothing is advisable *a priori*, unless it is packed-up with an evidence-based design and empirical evaluation. HDI cannot be directly connected to better outcomes, but to trace back all of the ICT recommendations and solutions to the evaluation of their impact in daily practices in terms of outcome efficiency and effectiveness, rather than in terms of intrinsic characteristics of a data system *per se*.

## REFERENCES

Abdelhak, M., Grostick, S., & Hanken, M. A. (Eds.). (2012). *Health information* (4th ed.). Elsevier.

Abiteboul, S. et al.. (2000). *Data on the Web: From Relations to Semistructured Data and XML*. San Francisco, CA: Morgan Kaufmann Publishers.

Ammenwerth, E., & Rigby, M. (Eds.). (2016). *Evidence-Based Health Informatics: Promoting Safety and Efficiency Through Scientific Methods and Ethical Policy* (Vol. 222). IOS Press.

Authors, V. (1992). Evidence-based medicine. A new approach to teaching the practice of medicine. *Journal of the American Medical Association, 268*(17), 2420. doi:10.1001/jama.1992.03490170092032 PMID:1404801

Berg, M. (1999). Accumulating and coordinating: Occasions for information technologies in medical work. *Computer Supported Cooperative Work, 8*(4), 373–401. doi:10.1023/A:1008757115404

Berg, M., & Goorman, E. (1999). The Contextual Nature of Medical Information. *IJMI, 56*, 51–60. PMID:10659934

Berg, M., & Toussaint, P. (2002). The mantra of modeling and the forgotten powers of paper: A sociotechnical view on the development of process-oriented ICT in health care. *JMI, 69*(2-3), 223–234. PMID:12810126

Bossen, C. (2016). Data-work in Healthcare: The New Work Ecologies of Healthcare Infrastructures. *ACM International Conference on Computer-Supported Cooperative Work and Social Computing, CSCW 2016*. doi:10.1145/2818052.2855505

Cabitza, F., & Batini, C. (2016). Information Quality in Healthcare. In Data and Information Quality, (pp. 421–438). Springer. doi:10.1007/978-3-319-24106-7_13

Cabitza, F., Del Zotti, F., & Misericordia, P. (2014). Electronic Records for General Practice – Where we Are, Where we should Head to Improve Them. In *Healthinf'14:Proceedings of the International Conference on Health Informatics*, (pp. 535-542). INSTICC.

Cabitza, F., Locoro, A., & Batini, C. (2015b). A User Study to Assess the Situated Social Value of Open Data in Healthcare. *Procedia Computer Science, 64*, 306–313. doi:10.1016/j.procs.2015.08.494

Cabitza, F., Locoro, A., Fogli, D., & Giacomin, M. (2016). Valuable Visualization of Healthcare Information: From the Quantified Self Data to Conversations. In *Proceedings of the International Working Conference on Advanced Visual Interfaces* (pp. 376-380). ACM. doi:10.1145/2909132.2927474

Cabitza, F., & Simone, C. (2012). Affording Mechanisms: An Integrated View of Coordination and Knowledge Management. *CSCW*, *21*(2), 227–260.

Cabitza, F., Simone, C., & De Michelis, G. (2015a). User-driven prioritization of features for a prospective InterPersonal Health Record: Perceptions from the Italian context. *Computers in Biology and Medicine*, *59*, 202–210. doi:10.1016/j.compbiomed.2014.03.009 PMID:24768267

Cafaro, F. (2012). Using embodied allegories to design gesture suites for human-data interaction. In *Proceedings of the 2012 ACM Conference on Ubiquitous Computing, UbiComp 2012*, (pp. 560–563). ACM. doi:10.1145/2370216.2370309

Crabtree, A., & Mortier, R. (2015). Human data interaction: Historical lessons from social studies and CSCW. In *ECSCW 2015*. Springer. doi:10.1007/978-3-319-20499-4_1

Elmqvist, N. (2011). Embodied human-data interaction. ACM CHI 2011 Workshop "Embodied Interaction: Theory and Practice in HCI", 104–107.

Fitzpatrick, G. (2004). Integrated care and the working record. *Health Informatics Journal*, *10*(4), 291–302. doi:10.1177/1460458204048507

Fitzpatrick, G., & Ellingsen, G. (2013). A review of 25 years of CSCW research in healthcare: Contributions, challenges and future agendas. *CSCW*, *22*(4-6), 609–665.

Gitelman, L. (2013). *Raw data is an oxymoron*. MIT Press.

Gregory, J., Mattison, J. E., & Linde, C. (1995). Naming notes: Transitions from free text to structured entry. *MIM*, *34*(1-2), 57–67. PMID:9082139

Hoffrage, U., Gigerenzer, G., Krauss, S., & Martignon, L. (2002). Representation facilitates reasoning: What natural frequencies are and what they are not. *Cognition*, *84*(3), 343–352. doi:10.1016/S0010-0277(02)00050-1 PMID:12044739

Hornung, H., Pereira, R., Baranauskas, M. C. C., & Liu, K. (2015). Challenges for Human-Data Interaction–A Semiotic Perspective. In *International Conference on Human-Computer Interaction* (pp. 37-48). Springer International Publishing.

Inselberg, A. (2009). Parallel coordinates. In L. Liu & T. Ozsu (Eds.), *Encyclopedia of Database Systems* (pp. 2018–2024). Springer.

Kennedy, J. B., Mitchell, K. J., & Barclay, P. J. (1996). A framework for information visualisation. *SIGMOD Record*, *25*(4), 30–34. doi:10.1145/245882.245895

Liaw, S. T., Rahimi, A., Ray, P., Taggart, J., Dennis, S., de Lusignan, S., & Talaei-Khoei, A. et al. (2013). Towards an ontology for data quality in integrated chronic disease management: A realist review of the literature. *IJMI*, *82*(1), 10–24. PMID:23122633

Lieberman, H., Paternò, F., Klann, M., & Wulf, V. (2006). End-User Development: An Emerging Paradigm. EUD, 9, 1–8.

Locoro, A. (2016). A Map is worth a Thousand Data: Requirements in Tertiary Human-Data Interaction to Foster Participation.*CEUR Workshop Procs of CoPDA 2015*.

Locoro, A., Grignani, D., & Mascardi, V. (2011). MANENT: An infrastructure for integrating, structuring and searching digital libraries. *Studies in Computational Intelligence, Springer, 375*, 315–341.

Longhurst, C. A., Palma, J. P., Grisim, L. M., Widen, E., Chan, M., & Sharek, P. J. (2013). Using an Evidence-Based Approach to EMR Implementation to Optimize Outcomes and Avoid Unintended Consequences. *Journal of Healthcare Information Management, 27*(3), 79. PMID:24771994

Murdoch, T. B., & Detsky, A. S. (2013). The inevitable application of big data to health care. *Journal of the American Medical Association, 309*(13), 1351–1352. doi:10.1001/jama.2013.393 PMID:23549579

Parasuraman, R., & Manzey, D. H. (2010). Complacency and bias in human use of automation: An attentional integration. *Human Factors: Hum. Factors, 52*(3), 381–410. doi:10.1177/0018720810376055 PMID:21077562

Pipino, L., & Lee, Y. W. (2011). Medical Errors and Information Quality: A Review and Research Agenda.AMCIS.

Pipino, L., Lee, Y. W., & Wang, R. Y. (2002). Data quality assessment. *Communications of the ACM, 45*(4), 211–218. doi:10.1145/505248.506010

Rigby, , & Ammenwerth, , Beuscart-Zephir, Brender, Hypponen, Melia, … de Keizer. (2013). Evidence Based Health Informatics: 10 years of efforts to promote the principle. *Yearbook of Medical Informatics, 8*(1), 34–46. PMID:23974546

Roberts, A., Gaizauskas, R., Hepple, M., & Guo, Y. (2008). Mining clinical relationships from patient narratives. *BMC Bioinformatics, 9*(11), S3. doi:10.1186/1471-2105-9-S11-S3 PMID:19025689

Sauleau, E. A., Paumier, J.-P., & Buemi, A. (2005). Medical record linkage in health information systems by approximate string matching and clustering. *BMC Medical Informatics and Decision Making, 5*(1), 32. doi:10.1186/1472-6947-5-32 PMID:16219102

Shankaranarayan, G., Ziad, M., & Wang, R. Y. (2003). Managing data quality in dynamic decision environments: An information product approach. *Journal of Database Management, 14*(4), 14–32. doi:10.4018/jdm.2003100102

Shortliffe, E. H., Perreault, L. E., Wiederhold, G., & Fagan, L. M. (Eds.). (1990). *Medical Informatics: Computer Applications in Health Care and Biomedicine*. Addison-Wesley.

Smith, P. C., Araya-Guerra, R., Bublitz, C., Parnes, B., Dickinson, L. M., Van Vorst, R., & Pace, W. D. (2005). Missing clinical information during primary care visits. *Journal of the American Medical Association, 293*(5), 565–571. doi:10.1001/jama.293.5.565 PMID:15687311

Solomon, J., Scherer, A. M., Exe, N. L., Witteman, H. O., Fagerlin, A., & Zikmund-Fisher, B. J. (2016). Is This Good or Bad? Redesigning Visual Displays of Medical Test Results in Patient Portals to Provide Context and Meaning. In *Proceedings of the 2016 CHI Conference Extended Abstracts on Human Factors in Computing Systems* (pp. 2314-2320). ACM. doi:10.1145/2851581.2892523

Strong, D. M., Lee, Y. W., & Wang, R. Y. (1997). Data quality in context. *Communications of the ACM, 40*(5), 103–110. doi:10.1145/253769.253804

Swinglehurst, D., Greenhalgh, T., & Roberts, C. (2012). Computer templates in chronic disease management: Ethnographic case study in general practice. *BMJ Open*, *2*(6), e001754. doi:10.1136/bmjopen-2012-001754 PMID:23192245

Timmermans, S., & Berg, M. (2003). *The gold standard: the challenge of evidence-based medicine and standardization in health care*. Temple University Press.

Wang, R. Y. (1998). A product perspective on total data quality management. *Communications of the ACM*, *41*(2), 58–65. doi:10.1145/269012.269022

Wang, R. Y., & Strong, D. M. (1996). Beyond accuracy: What data quality means to data consumers. *JMIS*, 5-33.

## ADDITIONAL READING

Coiera, E. (2004). Four rules for the reinvention of health care. *BMJ: British Medical Journal*, *328*(7449), 1197–1199. doi:10.1136/bmj.328.7449.1197 PMID:15142933

Goetz, T. (2010). *The decision tree: taking control of your health in the new era of personalized medicine*. Rodale.

Greenhalgh, T., Howick, J., & Maskrey, N. (2014). Evidence based medicine: A movement in crisis? *BMJ (Clinical Research Ed.)*, *348*, g3725. PMID:24927763

Munzner, T. (2009). A nested model for visualization design and validation. *IEEE Transactions on Visualization and Computer Graphics*, *15*(6), 921–928. doi:10.1109/TVCG.2009.111 PMID:19834155

Shneiderman, B., Plaisant, C., & Hesse, B. W. (2013). Improving healthcare with interactive visualization. *Computer*, *46*(5), 58–66. doi:10.1109/MC.2013.38

## KEY TERMS AND DEFINITIONS

**Data Visualization:** A visual representation of a (subset of) dataset. Also, the scholarly discipline addressing how to design, implement and deploy this kind of representations.

**Data Work:** A class of working activities that regard the production, arrangement, management and interpretaton of data to perform other work tasks adequately.

**Evidence-Based Design:** A design approach that integrates the empirical and user-centered validation of alternative solutions to choose which ones to implement and how to, in order to increase the odds that the overall final system will be found to be usable (efficient, effective, satisfactory) by the users and be appropriated in their practices.

**Human-Data Interaction:** a discipline that addresses the phenomenon of how users make value out of datasets by interacting (i.e., querying, filtering, zooming, etc.) with an either textual or visual representation of those data.

**Open Data:** Those non-personal data that, made available by some institution, organization or association, anyone can freely access, use, modify, and share for any purpose, subject, at most, to requirements that preserve attribution and openness.

## ENDNOTES

[1]   We concur with Hornung et al. (2015) that data are "artifact-mediated representations of phenomena that need to be given meaning by people and that serve some purpose".

[2]   To this respect, datafication is a process of both dis-closure of the representable reality, as well as the closure of what is (willingly or unaware) left tacit behind. Datification constructs facts, but it can also entail the (irreversible) destruction of context, through the emergence of text out of human experience.

[3]   Obviously we are aware that the value of something, and hence also data, can be appraised differently than by adopting a consumer-oriented perspective, which regards what in classical political economy is denoted as "use value". Value can be a function of the resources involved or consumed to get the data (mainly by primary users), to verify and cleanse them, and make them fit to interoperable formats typically in secondary processes); or, simply, a function of how much someone is going to pay to obtain them (cf. the idea of economic value, that is so common in this age of splendour of online advertising). These different perspectives reflect different conceptions of the idea of value, as it has been formulated in centuries of economic and theoretical speculation (see (Dobb, 1975) for a classic review of those conceptions).

[4]   Other interesting cases regard the failure to detect relations between either right data or inconsistent ones; the failure to get the right implication from right data or, the other way round, success in detecting right relations and inferring right implications from wrong data. It is important to distinguish between all of these cases in understanding the root causes of information failures and understand how to minimize the odds of their occurrence.

# Section 3
# Smart Technology and Education

# Chapter 10
# Children Using Social Media to Connect with Others and With Consumer Brands

**Katharine Jones**
*AUT University, New Zealand*

**Mark S. Glynn**
*AUT University, New Zealand*

## ABSTRACT

*Children's use of social media affects their interactions with consumer brands. Because children's social media use is a part of people's increasing use of social platforms to communicate and share content with each other, it is important to understand how children are using such platforms as sources of market-related information. This is because children's socialisation as consumers depends upon their accessing a range of market-related information sources, and social media platforms are envisaged to facilitate such access. Children's interactions with consumer brands are governed by interaction processes, and such processes shape the relationships that children may form with brands. Understanding these interaction processes will provide insights for parents, educators, and business marketers seeking information as to how the next generation of consumers use social media for market-related activities.*

## INTRODUCTION

Children connect with others in their social relationships, and this is how children build their identities and gain social skills (Oyserman, Elmore et al. 2012). Such social connections enable conversations about aspects of the world, and this in turn enables children to actively construct their world (Gergen 2009). Because social connections involve constant communication, within this connecting are possibilities for people including children to change how others think about the world (Gergen 2009).

Social media technologies offer people easy ways of communicating globally with each other (Schultz and Peltier 2013), and the speed of uptake of such technologies is unprecedented. The growth in the numbers and the scale of social media networking sites as ways for people to communicate and share

DOI: 10.4018/978-1-5225-2492-2.ch010

their lives is demonstrated by examples such as "more video uploaded to YouTube in one month than the three major networks in the USA created in 60 years" (Hoffman and Novak 2012; pg.69).

Clustering social media sites into three groups provides a more systematic way of envisaging how people engage with social media; so for example Facebook is a social network; Twitter and tumblr are both microblogging sites; and YouTube is a content community (Smith, Fischer et al. 2012). There are continuing new entrants to the social media space, so it is far from saturated, and such entrants seem to attract large numbers of users quickly, e.g. the site Zynga with the social game known as "CityVille" achieved status as the fastest growing game of all time, moving from zero to 100 million users in a mere 43 days (Hoffman and Novak 2012). Internet websites such as Disney's Club Penguin, offered to very young children and that offer limited social experiences, have been available for some time. However, other websites that are part of the social media ecosystem (Hanna, Rohm and Crittenden 2011) e.g. such as YouTube, have only recently focused on spaces for children to consume content and to socialise.

So people's social media use can be envisaged as actively shaping their social connections, and such use has relevance to how children connect socially with each other too. Additionally, children's consumer development relies upon their acquisition of social, cognitive, and physical skills (John, 1999) so their social media use can be conceptualised as influential upon their consumer development too. This is because social media technologies allow the breakdown of communication barriers between geographically and socially dispersed communities (Barber 2013), and the breaking of these barriers facilitates much easier social interaction, social influence and idea exchanges between people.

This Chapter offers a perspective on children's use of social media to connect with each other, and to form relationships with brands such as celebrity or person brands. The topic is an important part of the technology conversation about how such use relates to children's acquisition of market-place knowledge and skills.

This Chapter is divided into four parts. Part one identifies important issues and discusses how children use social media to connect with others and with consumer brands for their identity development projects. Part two takes a uses and gratifications perspective to show how children make personal gains by using social media. Part three draws the discussion together from Parts one and two and proposes some solutions including an interaction typology for children's brand interactions using social media.

The final part of this Chapter discusses the implications of children's use of social media for such purposes, discussing how children's brand interactions on social media begin to shape their subsequent brand relationships.

## BACKGROUND

The possibility of enabling brands to be involved in pathways of influence between consumers networking on social media is an attractive idea for consumer brand marketers, because of the potential for increasing consumer-brand engagement (Hollebeek, Glynn et al. 2014). However, managing brands in the social media space is a key challenge for marketers, because of the constantly evolving, real-time interactions among consumers that might involve brands, and over which brand marketers have little control (Gensler, Volckner, Liu-Thompkins and Wiertz 2013). Thus, because people's social media interactions are known to involve consumer brands, such interactions should be envisaged as collective, co-creation activities among people involving many brand authors of a brand's story, and some of these authors are consumers (Gensler, Volckner et al. 2013). Further, because children's development as consumers is so socially-directed (Hayta 2008), then it is envisaged that children's social media interactions with consumer brands may also involve co-creation activities, such as sharing and commenting upon a brand to their Facebook friends, or appropriating brand materials for generating content (Christodoulides, Jevons et al. 2012).

Academic researchers already know that children participate as users on social media sites (Dunne, Lawlor et al. 2010), and that such participation involves behaviours such as creating an online identity, for example, which provides children with a social outcome, acceptance by peers. However, nothing much is known about children's other, quite specific social media behaviours such as liking, following, commenting on, or creating particular content, and what is known has been drawn from studies involving college students (Park, Kee and Valenzuela 2009), or young adults (Joinson 2008).

Children's access to various internet tools has increased too, particularly since schools are also fostering technology skills. However of the many studies undertaken of internet participation, most were notable for the heavy use of the internet by university students. For example, of all internet usage by 92% of adult New Zealanders in 2013 (World Internet Project, AUT University, 2013), four out of ten stated that social networking sites are important to their daily lives. Thus children's social media participation is a relatively new area of inquiry, and is an important topic because of how the Internet and the associated Web 2.0 developments (including social media sites) are available for children's use, and because children are growing up in an online environment (Dunne, Lawlor et al. 2010).

## MAIN FOCUS OF THE CHAPTER

### Issues, Controversies and Problems

Children's development as consumers relies upon their acquisition of a constellation of attitudes and skills (John, 1999) and much is known about this process in "offline" contexts. Not much is known about how children's use of social media might facilitate such attitudes and skills acquisition, and what might motivate children to engage in such use.

In a recent study (Jones, 2015) interviewed children (ranging in age from 11 to 14 years) about their social media use for connecting with friends and with brands. The children's experiences provide the context for the following discussion focusing on children's use of social media for identity construction. Links are drawn between these personal identity development projects as motivating factors for children's use of social media.

### Children Use Social Media for Identity Construction: An Important Aspect of Their Consumer Development

The larger notion of "identity" refers to the traits, characteristics, social roles and social relationships that a person has, plus that individual's social group memberships; all these things taken together define "who a person is" (Oyserman, Elmore et al. 2012). Considering the terms 'identity,' 'self,' and 'self-concept' as nested elements (Oyserman, Elmore et al. 2012) helps when thinking about how children are using social media to connect with others and with brands, doing work to reflect their self-concepts (Hollenbeck and Kaikati 2012). The notion of self-concept is derived from identity, and can be described as the complex of identities (people possess more than one "identity"), that comes to mind when a person thinks about her or himself (Oyserman, Elmore et al. 2012).

Developing a concept of oneself relies upon access to connections with others (such as friendships) and access to materials that are easily appropriated and used to display one's identity (such as aspects of brands e.g. photos of favourite fashion items). Children's social connections with others contain significant social interactions that shape their notions of self-concept. Children's adeptness at using digital tools enables them to form friendships and to gain information (Ahn 2013) in market-related contexts (Nairn, Griffin and Wicks 2008), and such behaviour helps reinforce already existing social relationships. For pre-teen and early teenage children, creating and maintaining such relationships is important, because friendships are more important than family relationships (Antheunis, Schouten et al. 2014). So, it is expected that children in this age group will be using the tools available on e.g. Facebook that help them maintain their friendships. In a recent study (Jones 2015) investigating 11 to 14 year old children's social media use, Facebook use is described by a child user below in such "keeping up with friends" terms:

*...Seeing what other people are doing...It keeps you up kind of...I suppose after you've gotten a friend on Facebook it's like you do almost have a connection like...I suppose it's almost like you know them, like you see what they've done and stuff, like photos and it's kind of like you do know them...Most of them have a Facebook, like one friend has only recently just got one, but the only reason she did it was so that she could try and get more votes for a competition she was entered in...*

Keeping up with friends on Facebook probably demands more of the child than just "seeing what other people are doing", and it is expected that children in this age group (11 to 14 years) will be using the tools on Facebook for more interactive tasks. For example, undertaking activities such as influencing others via posting "likes" of friend's posted content, such interactions signifying more importance for children than adults because of the importance of peers' opinions in children's social networks (Antheunis, Schouten et al. 2014).

Children's social media participation could be facilitating the continual renewal of their identities, because of the way in which content is easily appropriated for use in identity formation, and the opportunities that social media provides for children to interact with and think about content that could be relevant to their current identity. Such participation activities would include doing things such as belonging to a particular group (e.g. belonging to a brand fan group on Facebook such as being a fan of Coca-Cola), liking particular brand pages, or posting photos or other information about themselves that includes branded content for example, to show aspects of their identity. The following quote shows how a young social media user constructs an aspect of her identity (hairstyle) by copying the style of a celebrity:

*...but you know also like you know, I keep using like Cara Delevingne always wearing her hair like this, which is why I always bring my hair down because Cara Delevingne doesn't wear her hair up, you know I wear headbands because Cara Delevingne wears headbands that's cool...*

Such identity-forming activities of children can be envisaged as the child being influenced because of the links being constantly established between her or himself and the consumer brand (Hollenbeck and Kaikati 2012). So what the brand stands for symbolically (Charon 1998), is appropriated by children to indicate aspects of identity, and this development task continues through adolescence (Hughes and Morrison 2013). Therefore, some aspects of brands that children are interacting with when participating on social media such as following grunge fashion, or copying Cara Delevingne could be helping them to form a self-concept. Since older social media users are known to use brands and products as cues

(Hollenbeck and Kaikati 2012) to present themselves socially on e.g. Facebook, then it is expected that children will participate in social media in this way too. So since children appropriate aspects of consumer brands to help them form a sense of identity, and since children's learning about brands develops in social relationship contexts (Diamond, Sherry et al. 2009), then the social relationship contexts characterising social media should provide another medium through which children can perform the identity formation tasks that are part of becoming a consumer (Chaplin and John 2005).

Finally, such social media participation might be giving the children much more agency (or freedom) in constructing their identities (Hughes and Morrison 2013), and this could be motivating for children, encouraging them to keep using social media platforms such as Facebook. The social aspect of identity development is important too, because identity is formed in social contexts (Oyserman, Elmore et al. 2012), and social media could be offering children ideal social contexts. Such contexts include relationships such as group memberships (e.g. ethnicity, gender, or a member of a Facebook group), family roles such as being the oldest child, or being a sporty person or a "massive nerd", such as someone who likes Dr. Who, and shares this on Facebook. Such social contexts of identity formation can also be seen in how online brand communities form, in order to bring brand users into a social group so they can share product (or service) information, knowledge and experiences, and to foster identity among group members (Wang, Butt and Wei 2011).

Children connecting with brands by using social media, then, forms the other side of their consumer development, so what follows next shows how such connections are forged.

## Children Use Social Media to Connect with Brands: An Important Aspect of Their Identity and Consumer Development

Social media offers children many more opportunities to connect with brands (Antheunis, Schouten and Krahmer 2014), so understanding how children interact with brands in this environment provides rich insight helping our understanding of children's consumer socialisation (John 1999). Understanding how children are using social media to connect with brands is important as their experiences may give insight into the ways that they behave with consumer brands in the future.

Such interactions can be characterised by their evaluative or descriptive qualities which relate to the level of complexity that children engage in when interacting with brands on social media. More complex interactions that children engage in tend to involve consumer brands in more evaluative and relational ways, shown by the quote below from a recent study (Jones, 2015) on children's social media use asking who the children like and follow on Facebook:

*...I love Taylor Swift. I like her music. She's like really inspirational. I reckon like her songs tell a story and they have a learning behind them kind of thing, like a lot of songs do, but they are just different. I like how she does the whole country thing, quite pitchy...*

The quote shows how the relationship the child has with the singer is shaped. An evaluative statement is made first about her relationship with the singer by saying "I love Taylor Swift". For children to make these kinds of evaluative statements about e.g. person brands a basic level of internalised brand knowledge must exist, showing that a person brand such as a singer can be "loved" as a celebrity in an objectified way. Such internalised brand knowledge could be acquired from a range of sources, and signifies successful brand learning which is a necessary part of children's socialisation as consumers

(Achenreiner and John 2003). In the example shown previously, the child's interaction tendencies with the brand 'Taylor Swift' show how children relate to consumer brands by making certain decisions about a brand and the potential interactions with it. For children to relate to consumer brands on social media then, their internalised brand knowledge needs activating so that they can evaluate the brand and how closely it might "fit" with, for example, their developing self-concepts (Chaplin and John 2005).

Social media users actively generating content for posting and sharing online are known to utilise brand-related materials ((Christodoulides, Jevons et al. 2012). Such content, known as UGC (user-generated content) offers a way for people to participate online, but not much is known if children participate on social media sites in this way. It is not known which factors could encourage such participation, or what the outcomes could be for the children creating such content, or for their relationship with a brand.

What is known is that teenagers and young adults (aged 16 to 25 years), can be inspired to create content and share stories using social media if such topics are made manageable, relevant to them (such as climate change), easy to check-in with, and visually interesting (Greenhow 2008). There are four main groups of general factors thought to be relevant in motivating social media users to create brand-related UGC; co-creation, empowerment, community, and self-concept (Christodoulides, Jevons et al. 2012), but the social factors of self-concept, self-expression, identity shaping and creativity are probably the most relevant motivators for children's participation in this type of activity.

Because of children's participation in using internet technology tools such as social media platforms, and the resultant gains in new media literacy skills fostered by such use (Ahn 2013), it is expected that children would have the capabilities to create UGC if they wished, but whether such material would be brand-related, and positive for the brand, is not known. So while UGC may offer possibilities for encouraging children's social media participation, nothing is known about what benefits children might derive from participating on social media in this way, or of any reciprocal benefits to consumer brands of being used in this way. What follows next is a discussion of children's social media use from a "uses and gratifications" perspective (Dunne, Lawlor et al. 2010), to explain some of the personal gains that children make from using social media platforms.

## Children Use Social Media for Personal Gratifications: A Uses and Gratifications Perspective

This perspective, also known as U and G theory, focuses on the gratifications, or benefits that attract audiences to various types of media, and then hold their attention (Dunne, Lawlor et al. 2010). The perspective takes account of the type of content that is likely to satisfy an audience's social and psychological needs. Essentially, the uses and gratifications theory focuses on what people actually do with media. U and G theory has been used across a range of research settings, especially in the study of mass media and media content, such as the study of radio, television, and print media for example (Dunne, Lawlor et al. 2010), but until the reviewed studies, not in a social media context. Of the six domains commonly assessed within U and G theory, the most useful in the social media context are likely to be the domains that build understanding of children's motivations for using social media, and that offer a way to measure the gratifications that children obtain from such use. Previous research from the perspective of U and G theory (Park, Kee et al. 2009), found that college students (university age; 18 to 29 years) used Facebook (and joined Facebook groups) primarily to find information and to socialise with friends. Adding to their self-status and wanting entertainment were the other uses (or motivations) that students said they had for joining a Facebook group. Some of these reasons should be similar motivators then for children to use social media platforms, but because children are still forming relationships with friends and have strong needs for peer acceptance (Antheunis, Schouten et al. 2014), socialising and communicating with friends are expected to be the primary reason for use. Popular communication topics amongst children are expected to be discussions about celebrities (person brands) because such topics enable children to maintain their friendships in less risky ways. That is, discussing a celebrity with friends on social media enables children to maintain "declarative distance" in their conversations by reading what friends are saying and agreeing, or by simply "watching" a celebrity on platforms designed for this (e.g. tumblr or YouTube). The following quote shows a young user's motivations for watching celebrity activity on tumblr. Such "watching" activity enables her to learn more about the celebrities (person brands) by following them through other links in the social media ecosystem:

*...My favourites would be my two, of my OTP\* (\*one true pairing) my favourite ship, it would be Tyler Oakley and Troy Sivan...It's not like you know, refresh my feed so you get a post. You know, just like you know you can tell if he's in Australia, you can tell, and they'll post, if like their new video is up, it'll be on YouTube, it'll be on tumblr, I'll see that he's got a new video up, I'm like oh cool...*

Children's participation on social media by using the "following" tool available on social media platforms such as tumblr or Facebook provides a practical way by which children can indicate their affinity for someone or something (such as a consumer brand). Such following behaviour constitutes influence (Goggins and Petakovic 2014), because it shows childrens' affiliations with either people or content. So, for children to behave in this way, there must be some link with either improving the quality of their friendships (Antheunis, Schouten et al. 2014), or with portraying their self-concepts, because there are risks attached to publicly show that one is following someone or something. In these situations, children are likely to portray themselves as positively as they can (Dunne, Lawlor et al. 2010), following people or content known to be acceptable to their reference group, or that helps them express who they are (Clarke 2009).

However, some of what is known about adult's use of social media from the U and G perspective (Karnik, Oakley, Venkatanathan, Spiliotopoulos and Nisi 2013) shows that adults' reasons for joining Facebook groups (e.g. such as a music sharing group), are more diverse than those found in the children's study (Dunne, Lawlor et al. 2010). Girls in the Dunne, Lawlor et al. (2010) study used Bebo primarily for communicating with their friends, for creating an identity, and for entertainment. In contrast, the adults in the Karnik, Oakley et al (2013) study were primarily using the Facebook group to discover new content and cultures; to interact socially, use content by listening, and for nostalgia reasons (pg.823). Some of the adult reasons for use could be classified as entertainment, such as watching and consuming content, and this use is similar to what the girls in the Bebo study reported (Dunne, Lawlor et al. 2010).

Watching social media content (such as person brands' fashion) was found to be a more prominent characteristic of social media use for children who tend to be more passive social media users (Jones 2015). That is, such children obtain gratifications from watching specific celebrity content, as depicted in the quote below:

*...I suppose I kind of do, like everyone, I suppose over in America now it's winter kind of like fall and they are all kind of into leather pants and stuff at the moment, like the Kardashians and stuff, they are all wearing leather pants and, yeah I suppose...*

So, social media reasons for use (or gratifications) can be diverse, and such diversity would be expected between children and adults. However, because children are more engaged in formative tasks such as making friends and identity creation, their uses of social media may be more complex than adults in terms of what they want to obtain. For example, creating and managing identity is potentially a more complex task for children than for adults, especially with children's need for peer acceptance, so it could be that children's use of social media reflects their preoccupation with one or two formative tasks that adults have already negotiated. If this is so, then the gratifications that children obtain from such uses of social media could be more difficult for them to achieve. Nothing is known about this, although the study of girls using Bebo did report that they obtained peer acceptance (Dunne, Lawlor et al. 2010) and that this social outcome was linked to the use of Bebo for identity creation and management (pg.54).

In summary, the uses and gratifications perspective (U and G Theory) involves three uses; achievement, enjoyment, and social interaction (or gratifications sought; Dunne, Lawlor et al. 2010). Whether or not such gratifications are obtained is not reported (e.g. Chuang 2015), but the social interaction gratification/use makes sense, and reflects other work using the U and G perspective to argue for people's motivations to use social media. The U and G perspective makes visible children's and young people's motivations for using social media, framing these in a gratifications sought and obtained perspective (Dunne, Lawlor et al. 2010). The perspective is helpful in extending understanding of the reasons why children might be motivated to use social media, and for providing a framework to evaluate the outcome of such use.

Drawing together the preceding perspectives of children's use of social media for identity construction, for connecting with brands to help their identity projects, and for uses and to obtain gratifications, an interaction typology is proposed next. The interaction typology depicts processes by which children engage in brand interactions and how such interactions shape their brand relationships, whilst at the same time connecting with others.

## Children Using Social Media: An Interaction Typology

The modes of interaction that characterise children's brand interactions on social media shape children's brand relationships. That is, such modes provide pathways of influence for children with consumer brands, and such influence can be seen in a typology of relationships (Fournier 1998) that children construct with consumer brands (Jones 2015). For example, children who interact with brands in more evaluative ways (e.g. making decisions to appropriate brand materials for identity formation), form brand friendships that can be described as "compartmentalized" (Fournier 1998; pg.362). Such friendships offer lower intimacy conditions but high socio-emotional rewards, and can be entered into or exited from easily. Such a friendship type with a consumer brand makes sense in the social media context explained here, when seen from the perspective of how easily children will follow or unfollow a person brand on social media especially if the brand has violated some internal criteria the child might be using (Jones 2015).

Direct interactions that children have with brands such as person brands are increased with the integration of social media and new formats for television, such as reality television shows (Tingstad 2007). With these new media formats, developments in advanced viewer connectivity with the celebrity person brand are made possible because of social media platforms, so children have the opportunity to interact directly with a favourite celebrity on a real-time basis. Such interactions are easily seen with television shows such as The X-Factor in New Zealand, where audience members easily interact with the show and its pop star hopefuls using Twitter during the performances, or posting to the show's Facebook page. Practical experience suggests that such direct interactions quickly build interest and foster high levels of emotion among audience members at the time, and this can be evidenced by comments made to Twitter by audience members when things go wrong on a reality show, such as dissatisfaction with a judge's decision. Such integrated use of social media with reality television may increase the speed at which some children are willing to interact directly with e.g. a celebrity brand. Other children will use social media sites as part of a larger brand community to communicate their dissatisfaction with brand activities as this young social media user demonstrates:

*…No, but what I did was I made a Reddit account just to post that, and so I like posted it on like Artemis Fowl like discussion page and I just posted it on there and I haven't looked at it since or posted anything else on Reddit, I just wanted to get it out there…*

So, new media formats such as reality television such as "Pop Idol" (Tingstad 2007), or the more recent X-Factor reality shows in New Zealand, offer children social interaction opportunities, enabling them to directly experience the idol brand.

Such social interactions with brands move beyond treating children as passive receptors of advertising information, into a much more active dialogue offering children many opportunities to build links with brands.

However, children also use social media to watch consumer brands and this implies a passive, or distant orientation, but such watching activity provides children with social learning opportunities. Using social media to watch consumer brands can be influential too (Jones 2015) as depicted in the following quote from a young YouTube user:

*…Well I get quite some influence from just someone I watch who does video games, and I've gotten some views from him, some point views and yeah so he influences me, yeah, to do…*

Watching even a minor celebrity on YouTube helps children learn about aspects of the brand (in the quote above, the young user is learning about how a video game developer creates and promotes his games), and from such watching, increases his knowledge of gaming promotion.

So, children's interactions with person brands on social media by watching such brands can be influential, prompting some children into relating with these brands. Such outcomes are achieved because some children use a "watching with purpose" mode for their social media brand interactions (Jones 2015). These are the children for whom watching with purpose translates into relating to a brand. These are also the children who tend to approach their brand interactions by simultaneous interactions of describing and then evaluating brands for their usefulness to the child. Such mixed interaction modes prompt children to move past just watching brands for e.g. entertainment, towards more relational interactions with them. So, children using "watching with purpose" interactions tend to transform their watching more easily into relating to brands. Watching consumer brands on social media is influential in itself, and the children who tend to move easily from watching to relating are those using a wider range of social platforms, illustrated by the following quote from a young social media user:

*Um I didn't find them on tumblr first, I found them on Youtube and they make really, really funny videos and I like their videos a lot. And then I found they had tumblr and I'm like great I can stalk them now and blog them on tumblr and Facebook and Twitter and those...*

For children who watch brands without relating, such interactions imply passivity. However, watching brands alone still provides social learning opportunities, and the results from a recent study (Jones 2015) show that such children may need to learn more about brands before they are prompted into more relational interactions. That is, more explicit watching with learning might be necessary to prompt children to relate to brands more easily.

More complex brand interactions that children engage in using social media involving evaluative elements, and "watching with purpose" (Jones 2015), show that children using such modes of interaction are testing brand relationship possibilities. Watching with purpose can be described as a form of courtship (Fournier 1998), enabling children to test out the relationship provisions using a trial period of brand watching, e.g. on YouTube. Such watching, if proven satisfactory to the child, will translate into a more committed brand relationship characterised by more influence wielded by the brand to shaping the child's responses to brand-related content (Jones 2015).

Therefore, an interaction typology for children's use of social media for brand interactions can be depicted as consisting of several elements. The micro-element of brand evaluation for it's usefulness to the child is followed by a decision-making element; either to relate to a brand or to "watch a brand with purpose" (Jones, 2015). Both decisions show the nature of children's relationships with brands. That is, these interaction processes are important and not all are used at the same time and also do not occur in a linear fashion.

## SOLUTIONS AND RECOMMENDATIONS

This Chapter helps make visible children's use of social media for interactions with consumer brands. Such interaction processes reflect processes of influence, and these processes can be seen to be shaping children's relationships with consumer brands (Jones 2015). These processes are of interest because of the potential for explaining how children's social media use contributes to the broader processes of children's consumer socialisation (Jones 2015).

Children's interactions with consumer brands are clearly not limited to interacting with brands only within family relationships. The consumer culture that children live within encourages their interactions with brands because of the rapid changes in media technologies, marketing and branding practices towards children, which intensifies their exposure to consumer brands (Nairn, Griffin et al. 2008). Thus, children's experiences in advanced consumer economies enable them to participate in intense relationships with consumer brands for a range of purposes, and this Chapter has discussed how children construct such brand relationships via their use of social media.

## Implications for Parents, Educators, and Policy Makers

Social, educational and public policy matters may be informed by this Chapter. The children who participated in this research represent one of the first consumer groups growing up in a time shaped by their use of the internet. Such use includes social media platforms, and this Chapter shows that children do participate in social media to interact in consumer markets. Such a topic is of interest to parents, educators, and public policy makers because of the way in which consumer brand owners may be informed by the research as to how they can encourage children's increased participation in brand relationships.

Parents have an interest in the research from the perspective of educating their children about consumer markets and branded goods, while educators may be interested in understanding the processes by which children interact with brands on social media. Such understanding may offer educators and policy makers' opportunities to foster social-good projects, such as helping children learn how to manage money in conjunction with a banking brand.

Public policy makers seeking to regulate aspects of the internet may be interested to learn how children actually use web 2.0 social media platforms for brand interactions. Such information may assist policy makers to formulate policy guidelines or codes of practice seeking to provide protection for social media using children. Such guidelines may be adopted by marketers to guide their own codes for operating in children's markets.

## Implications for Technology Marketers

This Chapter discusses the interaction processes that children use to interact with brands on social media. These processes will be of interest to marketers, especially to those offering branded products and services in children's markets. The discussion provides information about how emerging, technologically-literate consumers interact with brands via the use of social media. Such information may have predictive value for marketers, because of the insights offered into how today's emerging consumers expect to interact with brands using new technologies such as social media. This Chapter sheds light on the interaction behaviour of a group of young consumers, and such information provides opportunities for marketers to understand some of the micro-interactions of children with consumer brands.

## FUTURE RESEARCH DIRECTIONS

Children using social media for interactions with consumer brands are part of the first group of young people who have grown up with digital devices, and full access to the Internet. Such freedom of use is envisaged to change how children will relate to consumer brands when they become older consumers, compared to how young people interact with market-related information such as brands now. Understanding and predicting how today's children will expect to interact with consumer brands as they become adult consumers provides an area for further research.

The policy implications of understanding the processes of childrens' interactions with consumer brands using social media provide an alternative research direction. Policy responses at the macro level are needed to guide businesses as to how they may use social media platforms to connect with children. Presently, in many advanced consumer economies, business marketers self-regulate their internet activities with regards to children.

## CONCLUSION

This chapter has shown how social media use is important in identity construction and identity development in children. Social media use is important to children in their development as consumers, allowing them to connect and interact with others. The chapter has provided insights into the childrens' interaction processes with each other as well as the various celebrities and brands in the marketplace. There are several implications outlined at the end of this chapter surrounding the use of social media for parents and educators in terms of their interactions with other children, and for corporates outside childrens' family and friends.

## REFERENCES

Achenreiner, G. B., & John, D. R. (2003). The meaning of brand names to children: A developmental investigation. *Journal of Consumer Psychology*, *13*(3), 205–219. doi:10.1207/S15327663JCP1303_03

Ahn, J. (2013). What can we learn from Facebook activity? Using social learning analytics to observe new media literacy skills.*Proceedings of the Third International Conference on Learning Analytics and Knowledge*, 135-144. doi:10.1145/2460296.2460323

Antheunis, M. L., Schouten, A. P., & Krahmer, E. (2014). The role of social networking sites in early adolescent's lives. *The Journal of Early Adolescence*, 1–24.

Barber, N. A. (2013). Investigating the potential influence of the Internet as a new socialization agent in context with other traditional socialization agents. *Journal of Marketing Theory and Practice*, *21*(2), 179–193. doi:10.2753/MTP1069-6679210204

Chaplin, L. N., & John, D. (2005). The development of self-brand connections in children and adolescents. *The Journal of Consumer Research*, *32*(1), 119–130. doi:10.1086/426622

Charon, J. M. (1998). *Symbolic Interactionism: An Introduction, An Interpretation, An Integration*. Upper Saddle River, NJ: Prentice Hall.

Christodoulides, G., Jevons, C., & Bonhomme, J. (2012). Memo to Marketers: Quantitative Evidence for Change – How User-Generated Content Really Affects Brands. *Journal of Advertising Research*, *52*(1), 53–64. doi:10.2501/JAR-52-1-053-064

Chuang, Y.-W. (2015). Toward an understanding of uses and gratifications theory and the sense of virtual community on knowledge sharing in online game communities. *International Journal of Information and Education Technology*, *5*(6), 472–476. doi:10.7763/IJIET.2015.V5.552

Clarke, B. (2009). Friends forever: How young adolescents use social-networking sites. *IEEE Intelligent Systems, 24*(6), 22–26. doi:10.1109/MIS.2009.114

Diamond, N., Sherry, J. F. Jr, Muniz, A. M. Jr, McGrath, M. A., Kozinets, R. V., & Borghini, S. (2009). American Girl and the Brand Gestalt: Closing the Loop on Sociocultural Branding Research. *Journal of Marketing, 73*(May), 118–134. doi:10.1509/jmkg.73.3.118

Dunne, A., Lawlor, M. A., & Rowley, J. (2010). Young peoples use of online social networking sites – a uses and gratifications perspective. *Journal of Research in Interactive Marketing, 4*(1), 46–58. doi:10.1108/17505931011033551

Fournier, S. (1998). Consumers and their brands: Developing relationship theory in consumer research. *The Journal of Consumer Research, 24*(4), 343–373. doi:10.1086/209515

Gensler, S., Volckner, F., Liu-Thompkins, Y., & Wiertz, C. (2013). Managing brands in the social media environment. *Journal of Interactive Marketing, 27*(4), 242–256. doi:10.1016/j.intmar.2013.09.004

Gergen, K. J. (2009). *An Invitation to Social Construction.* London: Sage Publications Limited.

Goggins, S., & Petakovic, E. (2014). Connecting Theory to Social Technology Platforms: A Framework for Measuring Influence in Context. *The American Behavioral Scientist, 58*(10), 1376–1392. doi:10.1177/0002764214527093

Greenhow, C. (2008). Engaging Youth in Social Media: Is Facebook the New Media Frontier? A NewsCloud – University of Minnesota Research Report Executive Summary. Minneapolis, MN: Institute for Advanced Study, University of Minnesota.

Hanna, R., Rohm, A., & Crittenden, V. (2011). Were all connected: The power of the social media ecosystem. *Business Horizons, 54*(3), 265–273. doi:10.1016/j.bushor.2011.01.007

Hayta, A. B. (2008). Socialization of the child as a consumer. *Family and Consumer Sciences Research Journal, 37*(2), 167–184. doi:10.1177/1077727X08327256

Hoffman, D. L., & Novak, T. P. (2012). Toward a deeper understanding of social media. *Journal of Interactive Marketing, 26*(2), 69–70. doi:10.1016/j.intmar.2012.03.001

Hollebeek, L. D., Glynn, M. S., & Brodie, R. J. (2014). Consumer brand engagement in social media: Conceptualization, scale development, and validation. *Journal of Interactive Marketing, 28*(2), 149–165. doi:10.1016/j.intmar.2013.12.002

Hollenbeck, C. R., & Kaikati, A. M. (2012). Consumers use of brands to reflect their actual and ideal selves on Facebook. *International Journal of Research in Marketing, 29*(4), 395–405. doi:10.1016/j.ijresmar.2012.06.002

Hughes, J., & Morrison, L. (2013). Using Facebook to explore adolescent identities. *International Journal of Social Media and Interactive Learning Environments, 1*(4), 370–386. doi:10.1504/IJSMILE.2013.057464

John, D. (1999). Consumer socialization of children: A retrospective look at twenty-five years of research. *The Journal of Consumer Research, 26*(3), 183–213. doi:10.1086/209559

Joinson, A. N. (2008). 'Looking at', 'looking up' or 'keeping up with' people? Motives and uses of Facebook. CHI 2008 Proceedings, 1027- 1036.

Jones, K. R. (2015). *Brand-Made Children in New Zealand: An Interactionist Perspective on Children's Use of Social Media for Interacting with Consumer Brands* (Unpublished Doctoral Thesis). AUT University, Auckland, New Zealand.

Karnik, M., Oakley, I., Venkatanathan, J., Spiliotopoulos, T., & Nisi, V. (2013). *Uses and gratifications of a Facebook media sharing group.Understanding people's practices in social networks.* CSCW' 13, San Antonio, Texas. doi:10.1145/2441776.2441868

Nairn, A., Griffin, C., & Wicks, P. G. (2008). Childrens use of brand symbolism: A consumer culture theory approach. *European Journal of Marketing, 42*(5/6), 627–640. doi:10.1108/03090560810862543

Oyserman, D., Elmore, K., & Smith, G. (2012). *Self, Self-Concept, and Identity. In Handbook of Self and Identity* (2nd ed.; pp. 69–104). New York: The Guilford Press.

Park, N., Kee, K. F., & Valenzuela, S. (2009). Being immersed in social networking environment: Facebook groups, uses and gratifications and social outcomes. *Cyberpsychology & Behavior, 12*(6), 729–733. doi:10.1089/cpb.2009.0003 PMID:19619037

Schultz, D. E., & And Peltier, J. (2013). Social medias slippery slope: Challenges, opportunities and future research directions. *Journal of Research in Interactive Marketing, 7*(2), 86–99. doi:10.1108/JRIM-12-2012-0054

Smith, A. N., Fischer, E., & Yongjian, C. (2012). How does brand-related user-generated content differ across YouTube, Facebook, and Twitter? *Journal of Interactive Marketing, 26*(2), 102–113. doi:10.1016/j.intmar.2012.01.002

Tingstad, V. (2007). Now its up to you! Children consuming commercial television. *Society and Business Review, 2*(1), 15–36. doi:10.1108/17465680710725254

Wang, Y. J., Butt, O. J., & Wei, J. (2011). My identity is my membership: A longitudinal explanation of online brand community members behavioral characteristics. *Journal of Brand Management, 19*(1), 45–56. doi:10.1057/bm.2011.28

## ADDITIONAL READING

Ballano, S., Uribe, A. C., & Munte-Ramos, R.-A. (2014). Young Users and the Digital Divide: Readers, participants or creators on Internet? *Communicatio Socialis, 27*(4), 147–155.

De Vries, L., Gensler, S., & Leeflang, P. S. H. (2012). Popularity of Brand Posts on Brand Fan Pages: An Investigation of the Effects of Social Media Marketing. *Journal of Interactive Marketing, 26*(2), 83–91. doi:10.1016/j.intmar.2012.01.003

Kucuk, S. U. (2016). Consumerism in the Digital Age. *The Journal of Consumer Affairs, 50*(3), 515–538. doi:10.1111/joca.12101

Lauricella, A. R., Cingel, D. P., Blackwell, C., Wartella, E., & Conway, A. (2014). The Mobile Generation: Youth and Adolescent Ownership and Use of New Media. *Communication Research Reports*, *31*(4), 357–364. doi:10.1080/08824096.2014.963221

Nairn, A., & Clarke, B. (2012). Researching Children: Are we getting it right? A discussion of ethics. *International Journal of Market Research*, *54*(2), 177–198. doi:10.2501/IJMR-54-2-177-198

Valos, M., Polonsky, M. J., Mavondo, F., & Lipscomb, J. (2015). Senior Marketers Insights into the Challenges of Social Media Implementation in Large Organisations: Assessing Generic and Electronic Orientation Models as Potential Solutions. *Journal of Marketing Management*, *31*(7-8), 713–746. doi: 10.1080/0267257X.2014.977931

VanMeter, R. A., Grisaffe, D. B., & Chonko, L. B. (2015). Of Likes and Pins. The Effects of Consumers Attachment to Social Media. *Journal of Interactive Marketing*, *32*, 70–88. doi:10.1016/j.intmar.2015.09.001

## KEY TERMS AND DEFINITIONS

**Blog Page (Tumblr):** The home page with a user's profile, allowing the user to create microblogs and post to their page.

**Comment (Facebook):** Commenting on another's posted content.

**Facebook Friends:** Contacts that a user has added to their own network or responded to invitations to "friend" another user, thus increasing their network.

**Facebook News Feed:** A continuously updated content stream posted by other users in a users network or from pages that a user has "liked". Main way for users to keep up to date with what people in their network are doing, saying, posting, sharing, liking, & who they are following.

**Facebook Page:** User created home page; consists of a profile photo & other details users choose to share.

**Fandom:** Virtual equivalent of a brand community.

**Favourite (Twitter):** Equivalent of the Facebook "like"; a user's followers see content that a user has "favourited".

**Following (Facebook):** Tracking other users or other favourite content.

**Following (Twitter):** People active on Twitter that a user has elected to follow; Followers - the people who are following a specific user.

**Instagram:** Social photo sharing site; users interact with shared photos by "Like", comments, or follow. If a user follows another then the other's photos show up in (your) photo stream. Instagram users have #hashtags and use these in similar ways to Twitter. Instagram is designed for mobile use.

**Like (YouTube):** Viewers can signal their approval of video content in the same way as the Facebook "like".

**Like/s (Facebook):** Signifying agreement with or liking another's posted content.

**Messages (Facebook):** Creating and sending or receiving messages "in-house" using the Messenger app.

**Notifications (Facebook):** Visual reminders of messages or activity by others relevant to a user's network.

**Post (Facebook):** Uploading content to one's own page or posting a comment or message to another page.

**Posts (Tumblr):** Content generated by users and uploaded to their home page. Followers of the user see the posts.

**Promote/d (Twitter):** Users promoting content (possibly commercial) to their network.

**Randoms:** Unknown people inviting a user into their network; invitations are often refused.

**Reblog (Tumblr):** Equivalent of the Facebook share; followers in a user's network will see content that a user has reblogged to her/his home page. The more "reblogs" of content a user gets the greater their influence in the community.

**Reddit:** Social news website and forum whose stories are socially curated and promoted by site members. Reddit uses "threads", storylines relevant to specific topics. Reddit has "subreddits" and these are sub-communities each with their specific topics. Members submit and vote on content before such content is shared to the "front page".

**Reply-to:** Twitter equivalent of a message replying to a user.

**Retweet:** A user's microblog shared by another user to her/his own followers on Twitter.

**Share (Facebook):** Enabling other people in one's network to see content by activating a "share" function.

**Snapchat:** Snapchat is a photo messaging application, designed for mobile, whereby users can take photos, make videos, add their own text and drawings, and then send the content to a "controlled" list of recipients in their social network. Photos sent to a recipient "self-destruct" after about 10 seconds unless the recipient takes a screenshot.

**Tagging (Facebook):** Identifying another user in a photo that has been posted to one's own page.

**Tweet:** The microblog written by a user on Twitter. Limited to 140 characters.

**Twitch:** Twitch is an online social gamers site, created for the gaming community. It is one of the world's largest video streaming platforms, uses live streaming of games, organises competitions, providing "streamers" and "broadcasters" with the opportunity to develop and play video games with others. Has achieved 100 million unique monthly viewers (2014).

**Wiki:** A website or database developed collaboratively by a community of users, allowing any user to add and edit content. The children will refer to "go wiki something", which is the contemporary equivalent of the old "go look something up in the dictionary".

**YouTube Channel:** Content creators pay a fee for their own "channel", to which they upload video content.

**YouTube Subscribers:** Viewers paying a fee to subscribe to a content channel.

**YouTube Views:** Refers to people watching a posted video; the more "views" for a content creators video, the better regarded is the content.

# Chapter 11
# Design of a University Learning Environment for SMART Education

**Nataliia V. Morze**
*Borys Grinchenko Kiev University, Ukraine*

**Eugenia Smyrnova-Trybulska**
*University of Silesia in Katowice, Poland*

**Olena Glazunova**
*National University of Life and Environmental Sciences of Ukraine, Ukraine*

## ABSTRACT

*This chapter discusses theoretical, methodological and practical aspects of a design of a university learning environment for SMART education. Smart technology is analyzed against university background. The authors consider a process of transformation from e-learning to smart education, in particular the VLE objective according to the concept of smart education, formation of individual learning trajectories in a smart environment and a quality university educational environment for smart education. In the second part of chapter, the authors look at the development of teacher ICT competence of teachers in the system of smart education and present their conclusions. The references include more than thirty items: articles, books, chapters, conference proceedings on SMART education, university learning environment, virtual learning environment (VLE).*

## INTRODUCTION

Modern information society is being gradually transformed into Smart Society, as noted by sociologists, philosophers, specialists in IT sector, educational specialists, etc. This concept implies a new quality of society, in which a set of technological means, services and the Internet used by trained people contributes to qualitative changes in the interaction of subjects that allow to receive new effects – social, economic and other benefits for a better life (Tikhomirov 2012).

DOI: 10.4018/978-1-5225-2492-2.ch011

As a result of intensive development of information technologies, in order to replace the solutions that are already familiar and quite limited in their abilities to combine traditional education and e-learning, smart education is gradually being developed. Currently, there is no clearly articulated concept of smart education. Rather, it is an emerging paradigm in education. It is a set of technological, organizational, pedagogical decisions, often contradicting each other, but having a certain potential for innovation.

"Smart" - a property of a system or process that is manifested in its interaction with the environment, and gives the system and\or process the ability to provide an immediate response to changes in the external environment; adapt to the transforming conditions; exercise self-development and self-control; effectively achieve results.

The key in the property of being "smart" is the ability to interact with the environment and adapt to it. This property has an independent meaning and can be applied to categories such as city, university, society and many others. Forty years ago, when the property was devised, the level of technology development did not allow for the property in question to exist in most systems or processes. However, recent advances in ICT have helped build extremely complex systems, such as smart city.

During the Smart Society formation the paradigm of education and educational technology is naturally changing. The tasks of training of the new format specialist, successful and competent to work in the Smart Society rely on new universities – Smart Universities where the integration of technological innovations and the Internet can provide a new quality of educational and scientific processes, the results of training, scientific, innovation, educational, social and other activities.

The conceptual basis of the Smart University is a large number of different scientific sources, and information and educational materials, multimedia resources (audio, graphics, video) that can be easily and quickly designed, assembled as a certain set, adjusted individually for each student's needs and special characteristics of educational activity and the level of educational achievements.

The current situation of the development of higher vocational education is associated with the transition to practical implementation of a new educational paradigm that aims to create an integrated system of lifelong learning, to increase student self-education in learning process by means of information and communication technologies (ICT), which form self-education competence and such skills as self-organization and self- education.

It is obvious that in conditions of development of Smart Society the educational paradigm will also change. Smart Universities will perform new functions. Accordingly, the requirements for an e-learning environment that ensure students' needs in educational resources will change. Our mission is to substantiate theoretically the properties of such an e-learning environment through which students will be able to develop their professional and soft skills according to the conditions of Smart Society.

## SMART TECHNOLOGY AT THE UNIVERSITY, LITERATURE REVIEW, AND BACKGROUND

The use of technological devices has changed the way individuals interact with their university environment. The study (Nuzzaci & Vecchia 2012) examines the use of a smart context as a link between individuals and their university environment through an exemplification of urgent problems deriving from different domains and technological systems, as well as of information and communication devices employed in university teaching-learning contexts, to improve the quality of higher education and individuals' cultural life. When does a university become "smart"? It is not sufficient that universities define themselves as smart places to underline the main challenges they must face in their efforts to become and remain smart. The article recognizes a university as a "smart" institution when it has its roots in the understanding and critical awareness of basic knowledge, in the identification of the more realistic competencies and the search for the meanings of a "smart university community" that pursues high quality. The research concerns the experience of the ICT Centre of the University of Ferrara, which is trying to achieve these goals, implies the adoption of innovative perspectives, and discusses the building of a new culture in the middle a "smart university" and its cultural principles.

This research (Al - Qirim, Nabeel 2016) explores a teaching-faculty's adoption and usage of the Interactive White Board Technology (IWBT) in UAE University (UAEU). The research findings suggested two perspectives concerning IWBT usage by the teaching-faculty in UAEU. The first theme is concerned with IWBT's basic features where the IWBT proved its superiority when compared to other competing technologies in the classroom. The second theme is concerned with the advanced features of the IWBT and the way it is integrated with curricula and course content. This appeared to be yet evolving in institutions around the world in general and in the UAEU more specifically. The research depicts an evolutionary path for the data-show industry across time showing the position of IWBT. The path also shows the direction of the data-show industry along with a depiction of the learning needs across each evolutionary phase. The research discusses theoretical as well as professional contributions and implications emerging from the two perspectives and portrays different research areas in this field.

In the research and paper (Khamayseh et al. 2015), the authors focus on an analysis of the process of enhancing the education process by integrating new tools with teaching environments. This enhancement is part of an emerging concept, called a smart campus. A smart University Campus will come up with a new ubiquitous computing and communication field and change people's lives radically by providing systems and devices supported with smart technologies having the capabilities to rapidly respond to changes and circumstances without human interference, and it will be able to learn from these circumstances. This paper presents a framework architecture for integrating various types of wireless networks into a smart university campus to enhance communication among students, instructors, and administration. Moreover, the authors study two possible applications to utilize the proposed networking framework: smart identification and social collaboration applications. An essential requirement for achieving the main principles of smart university campus is the deployment of smart card technologies for identification and payment. Nowadays, there are several types of smart identification cards that support wireless technologies such as RFIDs and NFC. In both types, a card reader can read card information from a distance. Moreover, in the case of NFC cards, the card is integrated with the user's cellular phone. Social networking services (such as Facebook) facilitate online communication and provide a suitable environment for collaboration among students. As part of future work, the proposed framework is deployed in the authors' university campus to find out the end-end performance and system usability.

The study (Murphy et al., 2011) investigated student adoption of university campus card (UCC) applications. A review of smart cards, technology adoption and Unified Theory of Acceptance and Use of Technology (UTAUT) literature led to the formation of three focus groups and a survey of student perceptions and attitudes towards the university's campus card. Perceptions of 17 UCC components differed significantly across four student variables – international versus domestic, willingness to add funds, gender, and university level – supporting and extending UTAUT. Willingness to add funds to their UCC differed significantly across 16 out of 17 components, followed by domestic versus overseas students differing on 14 components, university level differing on 13 components and gender on 10. Overall, students reported that extra UCC features would enhance the university's image, improve their student experience, and encourage them to use UCCs. The results and managerial implications can help universities select and priorities UCC functions for campus adoption and implementation.

The study (Bomhold 2013) aims to present the results of a survey of undergraduate student use of smart phone applications. Undergraduate students currently enrolled in an information literacy course answered an online survey regarding their use of applications (apps) on their smart phones. However, still a small percentage of most frequently used apps (10.4 percent), search engines, online encyclopedias, and libraries are used by undergraduate students. The apps used most often are familiar to them and allow mobile access to popular web sites available on personal computers. Furthermore, a significant number (76 percent) of undergraduate students also report that they use apps to find academic information. The type of app most frequently used to find academic information is search engines. The research (Bomhold 2013) provides evidence on the actual use of mobile devices by students for library administrators and educators interested in developing integrated mobile academic library applications.

## FROM E-LEARNING TO SMART EDUCATION

If you provide a description of an education system of yesterday's level of development, it is necessary to note that the process of teaching in educational institutions assumed processes of transmission of knowledge from the teacher to the student and the main source of knowledge was the teacher (Figure 1), technology remained beyond class door, for teaching aimed at awarding diplomas was enough, and society was getting ready for professional production.

Today, the situation is slightly different. It is necessary to prepare a specialist, not only to train her/his professional skills, and take into account the fact that the future specialist will work in an open knowledge economy. Teachers not only need to possess professional competence in the subject area, but

*Figure 1. Teacher-student training scheme*

also need to be experts in e-learning technologies. The teaching process is characterized by knowledge being transmitted hierarchically from the teacher to the student, as well as horizontally from student to student, a source of knowledge – becomes group knowledge (Figure 2).

What do we see in the future development of the education system? Firstly, it is necessary to take into account the realities of a new round of information society, which means high dynamism of technological change in the IT industry, the development of social media, e-services and resources, the transition to a new generation of Web 4.0 with the clouds of knowledge and communication, constant opportunity for interaction and exchange. Secondly, the need to take into account today's employers' requirement for hard skills and soft skills. Thirdly, it is necessary to take into account the fact that the role of the teacher in the new environment is changing dramatically. The teacher has ceased to be the exclusive source of knowledge. Changing the paradigm of education in the direction of self-education, motivation to learn, adaptability and flexibility, the presence of large amounts of knowledge and constant generation of new knowledge leads us to a new concept - smart education.

Smart education is an educational paradigm underlying the new type of education, which involves the implementation of an adaptive educational process, perhaps through the use of smart information technology. The implementation of the smart paradigm of education is aimed at the formation of the process of training and education to acquire the knowledge, skills and competencies needed for a flexible and adaptive interaction with a changing social, economic and technological environment. Smart education should provide an opportunity to take advantage of the global information society to meet the educational needs and interests.

The essential principles of smart education include:

1. Use in the educational program of relevant information to solve educational problems. The speed and volume of the flow of information in education and any professional activity is growing rapidly.

*Figure 2. Teacher-student, student-student training scheme*

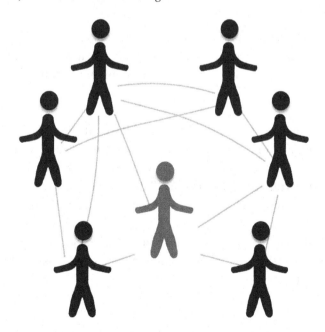

Existing training materials need to be supplemented with information coming in real time, to prepare students to solve practical problems, to work in a real situation and not on training examples and models.

2.  Organization of independent cognitive, research, design activity of students. This principle is the key when preparing specialists who are ready to search for solutions to creative professional problems.

3.  Implementation of the educational process in a distributed learning environment. Educational environment is not limited to the campus, or outside the distance learning system (LMS). Training should be continuous, including learning in a professional environment, with the use of professional activity.

4.  Interaction of students with the professional community. The professional environment is seen not only as a customer in training, but also it becomes an active participant in the learning process. ICTs provide new opportunities for students to participate in the work of professional societies, observation of problem solving professionals.

5.  Flexible educational trajectory, individualized instruction. The education sector is expanding significantly by bringing into the education system working citizens, by frequent change of type of professional activity, and intensive development of technology. Students coming to the University, as a rule, are well aware of and articulate their need for education. The task of the University – is to provide educational services in accordance with the student's needs and capabilities.

6.  Various educational activities require the provision of opportunities for students to study educational programs and courses, the use of tools in the learning process, in accordance with their abilities, material and social conditions.

## SMART UNIVERSITY

Five key characteristics of the Smart University can be distinguished: social orientation, mobility, accessibility, technological effectiveness and openness (Measuring the Information Society 2012).

- **Social Orientation:** Consists in the personalization of education, building of individual education cards (Smart-card), organization of efficient communication and collaboration in education, cooperation, application of design and game techniques, communication via social networks services, etc.

The second, equally important, feature of the Smart University is *mobility*. Mobility should not be understood narrowly - as access to educational content through mobile devices and their use for scientific research, payment transactions, and implementation of feedback with the teacher or the representatives from the dean office or departments, etc. (Traxler 2010). Mobility is important as each student's and teacher's access to the educational services from any place and at any time.

- **Accessibility:** AS a feature of the Smart University is characterized by a single point of entry to e-learning and scientific databases, media library, information kiosks, online resources and access control systems to them, etc.

- **Technological Effectiveness:** Provides a viability of the Smart University IT infrastructure by the means of cloud-technologies, innovative technologies of virtualization, open interfaces, based on the principles of simplicity, modularity, scalability, etc.

An important condition for the effective functioning of electronic informational-educational environment is its transformation into an open system thanks to interaction with the labor market, providing students with more control over the educational process by participating in its planning and evaluation of quality, having self-control and self-assessment. Functioning of an open e-environment in this case will be the basis for academic and scientific mobility of all participants in the educational process as well as a mean of strengthening of the subjective position of students during teaching process. The main requirements for the development and usage of e-environment is understanding its purpose, creation of qualitative content and effectiveness of interaction technologies used by participants in the educational process. During usage of qualitative open e-environment teaching, assessment, curriculum, informational-training platforms, science, management and reporting will be open accordingly. This in turn will enable the exchange of ideas, cooperation between institutions, teachers and students and will have a positive impact on the quality of the educational activity of the university.

*Openness* in the system of the Smart University foresees availability of the open repositories of educational materials for forming e-learning courses and providing training for students, open access to scientific articles and conducted researches and their results (McAuley et al. 2010)

Driven by the different perspectives on openness as discussed in the literature on open education, OER, OCW, and MOOCs, several suggestions can be made as to how "open" should be interpreted (Table 1).

## VLE OBJECTIVE ACCORDING TO THE CONCEPT OF SMART EDUCATION

Given the development of the information society in which conditions exist for effective cooperation, teamwork, sharing and dissemination of knowledge, crowdsourcing, open innovation, universities have to rebuild their approaches to learning. Creation of a virtual learning environment (VLE) University, which will provide support for all the necessary components of modern professional training, can become an effective tool which, combined with the global resources and services, will open the learning environment to provide quality education (Figure 3).

At the present stage of development of information society technologies make possible dissemination of educational, scientific, journalistic nature, which is used both for formal and non-formal education. Open innovation makes it possible to associate in groups, working groups, teams, communities and obtain the latest developments. Progress of society is ensured through effective technologies and services to the organization of cooperation in education, science, of project work. In order to enable students to graduate from universities and to prepare them for successful life in society, an VLE system has been developed, supporting the formation of professional competence, practical and research skills, soft skills, innovation orientation training, development of teachers' professional competencies.

A smart-environment modern university must perform these functions and provide the following services:

*Table 1. Interpretation of the concept of "openness"*

| Component | Description |
|---|---|
| Open learning | Provides understanding into how learners learn in open and networked learning environments and how learners, educators, institutions, and researchers can best support this process (Chatti 2012) |
| Open practice | Gives effect to a participatory culture of creating, sharing, and cooperation |
| Open architectures | Processes, modules, algorithms, tools, techniques, and methods that can be used by following the four R's "Reuse, Redistribute, Revise, Remix" (Hilton et al. 2010). |
| Open access | To learning analytics platforms granted to different stakeholders without any entry requirements in order to promote self-management and creativity |
| Open participation | In the LA process by engaging different stakeholders in the LA exercise. Daniel and Butson (2014) state that in LA, "there is still a divide between those who know how to extract data and what data is available, and those who know what data is required and how it would best be used" (Daniel & Butson 2014, p. 45). Therefore, it is necessary to bring together different stakeholders to work on common LA tasks in order to achieve useful LA results. Further, it is essential to see learners as the central part of the LA practice. |
| Open standards | "To reduce market fragmentation and increase the number of viable products" (Cooper 2014a). Open standards and specifications can help to realize the benefits of better interoperability (Cooper 2014a) |
| Open Research and Open science | (Fry et al. 2009) based on open datasets with legal protection rules that describe how and when the dataset can be used (Verbert et al. 2012). Sclater (2014) points out that datasets "from one environment can be connected to that in another one, not only across the different systems in one institution but potentially with other institutions too" (Sclater 2014) |
| Open learner modeling | Are based on user interfaces that enable refection, planning, attention, and forgetting and that can be accessed by learners to control, edit, update, and manage their models (Kay & Kummerfeld 2011). |
| Open assessment | To help lifelong learners gain recognition of their learning. Open assessment is an agile way of assessment where anyone, anytime, anywhere, can participate towards the assessment goal. |

*Figure 3. Impact of the knowledge society at the university VLE*

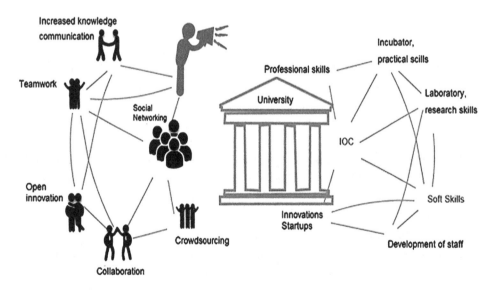

- **Structuring and Systematizing Information:** Database development, cataloging, storing and sharing files, external cloud storage, etc.
- **Implementation of e-Learning and M-Learning Tools:** CLMS system of e-learning courses, dictionaries, media casts, blogs, wikis, repositories, additional resources, massive open online courses.
- **Diagnosis, Evaluation and Monitoring of Educational Resources:** Competence, portfolio, method 360, journals evaluation.
- **Self-Learning Management:** Individual trajectory, organizer training progress
- **Virtual Social Network:** Public profiles, chats, contacts, groups, comments, lists, forums, mail, video conferencing, webinars, etc.
- **Media Environment in Classrooms:** Interactive whiteboards, document camera technology "bring your own device" PC workplaces audio.
- **Campus Network:** Wire, wireless, wide bandwidth channels.
- Integration with scientometric databases of full-text scientific resources;
- Services working together on projects, project management, development of start-ups.

The most popular, convenient and efficient technology of such an environment is the technology of cloud computing. National Institute of Standards and Technology (NIST) defines cloud computing as follows: "Cloud computing is a model to provide a convenient "on demand" access to the Internet so that information resources e.g., networks, servers, storage, applications and services are easily accessible with minimal effort to manage and to interact with the supplier".

There are two main types of cloud infrastructures: internal and external. In an internal cloud, servers and software are used inside the system in order to form a scalable infrastructure that meets the requirements of cloud computing. In an external cloud environments, providers offer services at the request of an educational establishment. IT support, services and experience will be included in the package, which must work only in providing applications and services.

Services for educational cloud computing represent a growing number of relevant services available online, and are the most innovative and fastest growing element of technology and education. They also promise to provide several services, which will be very useful for students, faculty and staff (Bell et al. 2014).

The role of cloud computing in higher education should not be underestimated, as higher educational establishments can benefit in getting direct access to a wide range of different academic resources, research programs and manuals (Glazunova 2015).

Kiran Yadav suggests the following benefits of cloud computing for educational establishments and students (Yadav 2014):

1. The personal approach to learning. Cloud computing allows students to have more options in learning. Using an Internet connected device, students have access to a wide range of resources and software that meet their interests and learning styles.
2. Reduced costs. Cloud services can help educational establishment reduce costs and accelerate new technologies to meet the changing needs of education. Students can use free office applications, install and maintain these programs upgraded on their computers, but at the same time commercial applications are provided too.

3.  Availability. Availability of services is the most important point for users of educational cloud technologies. You can log in and access the necessary information from any place.
4.  The absence of additional infrastructure will increase the number of research centers available for students and will create a global learning environment.

A cloud computing environment provides the necessary foundation to integrate platforms and technologies. It integrates teaching and research resources, which have places, using existing conditions as much as possible to meet the demands of teaching and learning (Rao, Challa 2013).

The term "academic cloud" becomes more and more popular which (Glazunova 2015) defines as information and communication technology of education which is built in the principles of cloud technologies and aims at providing education services at educational establishments. The "academic cloud" of a university is a cloud-oriented environment of an educational establishment which combines technical, software and technological, information resources and services and which functions on the basis of technologies of cloud computing and provides academic process of a university by means of a local network of an educational establishment and Internet.

Higher educational establishments mostly use hybrid cloud environments to organize learning process by integrating internal and external cloud. Thus, hybrid cloud-oriented educational environment of a higher educational establishment is the system that combines the academic cloud of an educational establishment and external academic clouds based on integration of resources into the educational environment of an educational establishment.

The main element of this environment is usually an e-learning course (ELC) (for example, based on CLMS platform Moodle), which places different types of learning resources (Morze 2013). To teach IT specialists using a virtual learning environment it is necessary to upload academic videos, video tutorials, lectures and other resources. To provide students with academic and research activities, the university has institutional knowledge repository that contains full-text electronic academic and research resources. It is available at e-library and can be used by students for self-study. Students have access to a virtual desktop via appropriate links for laboratory or individual work. With virtual desktop DaaS users are able to access necessary applications. All resources, which support every subject, are integrated into a VLE. Efficiency of such an environment is studied in (Glazunova 2015); this research states the efficiency increases by 6%, consent - by 12%, individual work - by 8%, motivation - by 17%.

The incentive of constant practice plays a significant role during the process of training future IT specialists in programming languages and standard algorithms. Therefore, an automated system has been integrated into the VLE of the university, enabling students to receive a significant amount of programming tasks as individual work and thus provides automated assessment of their progress.

A systematic use of external academic clouds such as Microsoft, Cisco, IBM is instrumental in forming professional skills and Soft Skills in a future IT specialist. Students and faculty have access to the Microsoft Office 365 cloud service which gives access to different items of software and services on the Microsoft Office platform, business class email, communication and management functions. Besides, students are advised to use the Microsoft Virtual Academy (MVA), an educational portal, where an interactive academic course is available in programming (Figure 4), software development environments, Windows Server 2012, Windows 8, visualization for HTML5, Windows and Windows Phone, Microsoft Office365, SQL Server, AzureSystem Center and Microsoft Imagine Academy. To provide

*Figure 4. Model of hybrid cloud-oriented environment of a higher educational institution*

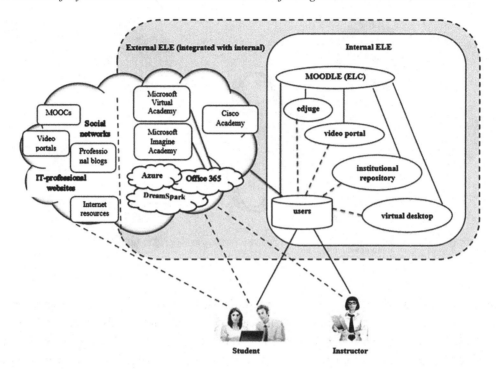

students with learning software we have access to Microsoft DreamSpark, which enables students to get free access to tools to design and develop software. The Microsoft (Windows) Azure platform enables students and faculty to develop software, with data being stored in distributed data servers (Glazunova, Voloshyna 2016).

## DESCRIPTION OF EDUCATIONAL CONTENT OF VLE SMART EDUCATION

Corporate and academic resources (knowledge) in smart environments for education include resources for education, research, innovation. For the effective functioning of these resource components it is necessary to build a management system, which, in addition to the use, exchange and transfer of knowledge will provide search and generate new knowledge (Figure 5).

Educational resources are often generated as e-learning courses. Some scholars define an electronic course as a didactic computer environment that contains classified material from the relevant scientific and practical field of knowledge that is combined by a single software shell, in which the following functional components are selected: information and navigation (meaningful connections, annotation and course structure, information, system of references, the searching system), informative (interrelated informative elements of the course – theory, practice, guidelines, additional materials, information resources, including electronic and open), diagnostic (formative assessment tools in the form of clear evaluation criteria for all types of students activity, including self-assessment and mutual assessment,

*Figure 5. Association of corporate and academic knowledge*

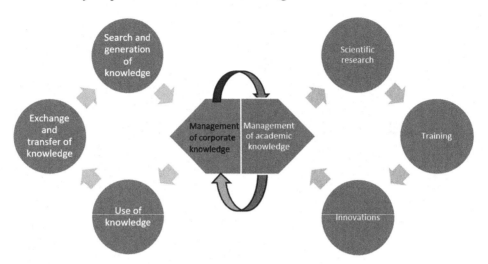

evaluation not only of academic achievements of students, but also evaluation of formation of skills of the 21-st century – to solve problems, work in team, communicate effectively and collaborate, etc., the testing system of current, intermediate and final control). An electronic course for Smart education should provide flexible teaching for students in an interactive learning environment, which allows them to adapt quickly to the environment, to study in any place, at any time on the basis of free access to content all over the world.

In our opinion, an electronic course for Smart Education can be represented as a certain scenario or trajectory of educational events relating to work with electronic resources in the form of a knowledge-map that leads to the achievement of learning effect and has the properties shown in Table 2 (Morze 2013).

The creation of e-learning courses is usually carried out with the help of Content Learning Management Systems. To create an effective e-learning course for Smart education not only available electronic

*Table 2. Properties of electronic course for Smart Education*

| Property | Description |
| --- | --- |
| Flexibility | Enabling rapid resources edition and making adjustments in educational trajectory |
| Availability of individual learning scenario | The possibility to develop an individual educational program for each student from the set of training elements |
| Integration | Integration of training elements with other open information resources |
| Focusing on the learning needs | Personification of content |
| Interactivity | The maximum use of multimedia technologies (video-casts, animation, video tutorials, screencasts, etc. |
| Feedback | Between the teacher and the student in the course |
| Availability of training elements | To ensure communication and cooperation of students between themselves and with the teacher, in particular based on the design technology |
| Gamification learning | Availability of game educational elements |
| Communication | Providing communication through social networks |

resources of information and educational environment of the University should be used, but also open external information resources and Web services that will serve as sources of educational and informational materials for the electronic course and as means of communication and cooperation.

The information and educational environment of a university should be focused on solving the problem of joint creation and use of academic knowledge for the needs of students and teaching staff of the university. On the one hand, the teacher herself/himself adds academic resources to the information and educational environment, such as video clips and video tutorials posted on educational video portal and on the other hand, she/he has the possibility to use available public resources for creating e-learning course. So, to create an electronic course it is sufficient for the teacher to update material that is available from other sources, submit it in accordance with the above mentioned properties and criteria of evaluation of its quality, add the necessary training elements of the course according to the adopted structure and develop an individual learning scenario for each student, consider the individual evaluation criteria of educational achievements of students and developed skills of the 21st century.

A review of papers devoted to the creation and use of e-learning courses (Morze, Glazunova 2009, Deryabina, Losev 2006) leads to the conclusion that in the issue of the course structure focus should be laid on the modular principle of its construction. When structuring the content of an educational subject by the principle of training modules each module should consist of interconnected theoretical, empirical and practical components of the content, each of which would carry out an independent function. Thus, an educational discipline module is an information and didactic unit, in which the approach to structuring the whole into parts is unified. It has a complex structure that includes goal of its integral development, objectives, content and results with the corresponding system of formative assessment.

Furthermore, the structure of the e-course for Smart education should provide availability of: tools to build individual learning trajectory (prior surveys, questionnaires, tests, formative assessment tools, including check-lists and tables of evaluation criteria); multimedia presentations of summarizing character, video resources, interactive electronic manuals, external Web resources with multimedia theoretical material; links to external public resources including articles, conference proceedings, research materials, discussions on the forums, feedback with teacher, webinars and other Web services; intermediate control elements during the lessons and formative evaluation instruments, final control in the form of control tasks and tests, element of reflection.

Each element of the training course must meet certain standards and be evaluated using criteria that are accepted at the level of educational institution.

Approximate structure of Smart course is shown in Figure 6 (Morze 2013, 2014).

Further we will focus in more detail on the features of the e-learning course structure for Smart education.

A special property of the new model electronic course is also the diversity of the theoretical learning resources presentation forms. Besides the fact that theoretical material must be delivered by 60-70% in multimedia interactive form, we also note the necessity to choose the method of material delivery, depending on the level of its teaching. The theoretical material in an electronic course can be delivered on the following four levels: *phenomenological, analytical and synthetic, mathematical, axiomatic* (Deryabina, Losev 2006).

Another feature of an e-course for Smart education is the existence of elements for communication and cooperation between the students in the performance of tasks of mastering theoretical material, practical tasks, research projects, etc. Web 2.0 services, online services, social networks provide tools for organizing discussions, collaboration, and counseling. These elements are embedded in the course

*Figure 6. Structure of an electronic training course for Smart education*

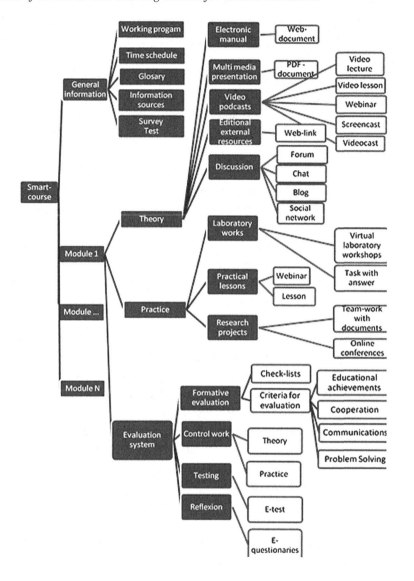

directly through the platform that is used, or by reference to it. While performing tasks students should use modern information and communication technologies effectively. Usually for mastering the theoretical teaching material students (Figure 7) are offered tasks on writing essays, composition of the related bibliography, writing summaries, paraphrasing theoretical information of a small amount in the form of "question-answer", compiling a glossary of terms under the certain topic, performing descriptive works, making instructions for the implementation of various operations, plotting grid plans and schedules.

In order that such tasks become interesting for students it is necessary to use Internet resources, and present the result of the performance in the electronic form using modern information technologies. Tasks on mastering practical skills include solving problems, performance of exercises, graphical works, practical works, calculated works, designing, and modeling, compilation of practical situations from their own experience and on the basis of practical training, performing analysis of enterprise activity.

*Figure 7. Types of tasks to master practical skills*

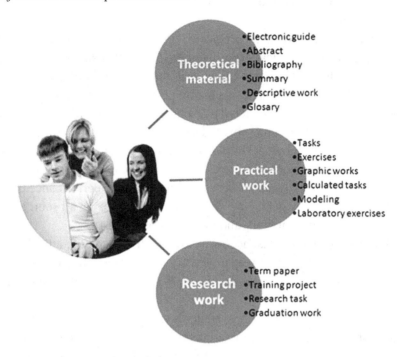

Students should be offered to solve such tasks using virtual laboratory workshops and specialized software. Tasks on forming research activity include implementation of individual research tasks, writing term papers, graduation works, participation in educational projects. Such types of tasks involve creative activity of students, which should be carried out by means of modern computer technologies, teamwork and communication. And one of their special properties is the use of formative assessment tools for their assessment that clearly guide the student to achieve learning goals in all types of educational activity that are presented specifically, clearly and should be achievable for each of them.

Thus, the main features of students' practical work organization using e-course in the Smart education is the availability of tools for collaboration, communication, combination of different information technologies in the performance of tasks. But we should not forget that tasks should have practical significance, and contain detailed information on their implementation, evaluation criteria and support resources.

In the course of the research we proposed a new model of electronic learning course for students of a shortened training period. As a result, after questioning and testing six groups, students were identified who studied in different educational trajectories, successfully completed the training course and demonstrated 13% better academic progress compared to the group of students who studied in one training trajectory. At the same time, the participants of the experimental groups performed a larger volume of tasks on the depth study and worked extra theoretical study material according to the references to the external information resources. In addition, teachers –participating in the experiment, indicated that the presence of the distributed environment of the opened resources in the university allows to create e-learning courses applying much lesser efforts and requires lesser time compared to the case when the course is created from the beginning. Teachers are able to use ready resources for creating elements of the course – presentations, video recordings, electronic versions of manuals and guidelines, a database of scientific publications, etc.

Students of such specialties as "Computer sciences", "Programming Engineering" participated in this pedagogical experiment. The pedagogical experiment envisaged that students of a control group were offered an electronic course to study programming, each theme of this electronic course was presented as a resource "Lesson" which is a structured succession of pages. It is possible to place texts, graphics, video, tests etc. there. Students were also offered a resource "Video lesson" which as (Glazunova 2014) states is the most effective type of resources for students who study IT. This resource was in the form of screen cast of a certain program or practical implementation of software code of scripts with obligatory texting and audio, which is built according to a certain script. The use of this resource enables students to take academic material individually and, if necessary, to revise the performance that is demonstrated in Video Lesson. All this resulted in achieving maximum effect by using all sources of perception and assimilation of information: visual, auditory and kinetic (Morze 2014).

The experimental group had additional access to Microsoft Office 365, attended a distance course in programming at the Microsoft Virtual Academy, Cisco, and had a wide range of professional blogs, communities of IT specialists in social networks, open electronic resources to study programming, different Internet resources.

Courses of the Cisco network academy gave students an opportunity to learn about the functioning of hardware and software components, structure of networks, security problems and methods of solving them, obtain skills to collect and set up a computer, to install operating systems, software, and to identify and correct errors connected with hardware and software (Figures 8 and 9).

Using social networks, IT specialists are able to obtain new knowledge individually because they have open access to professionally-oriented information that is provided in magazines, newspapers, books, videos, blogs, etc., to fast share information with peers being social network users and having common professional interests; to discuss issues on information technology. In addition to social networking

*Figure 8. Course "IT Essentials: PC Hardware and Software"*

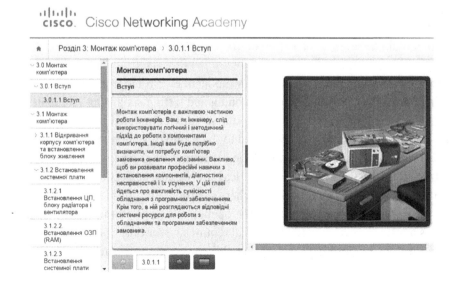

*Figure 9. Course "Introduction to Programming with Python"*

sites, there are special professionally orientated IT sites which contain a large number of manuals, code samples, links for downloading software, discussion forums, blogs, etc.

The outcomes of progress in "Algorithmic and Programming" of the control and experimental groups were measured by means of tests; individual work and motivation was measured by means of observation and surveys. The results of the experiment are presented in Table 3. According to the results of the experiment, individual work increases significantly when students solve problems, fulfill other tasks. Experimental group students are more motivated and ready to solve non-standard tasks.

So, this hybrid cloud oriented environment for students of IT specialties, which combined possibilities of electronic learning environment of the university (internal) and external services of Microsoft and Cisco, where the university gained its part of "academic" cloud (externalities), made it possible to develop Soft Skills together with developing professional skills, namely personal effectiveness, communication skills according, managerial and strategic skills, critical thinking skills and information management skills, which are presented in Figure 10.

The task to identify a number of indicators of students' personal progress, communicative and managerial skills was set as well as the task to identify the ability of managing the information according to the classification of Soft Skills in Figure 10. In particular, in order to determine whether the student is able to manage their time, the groups were given tasks to accurate state the type, beginning time and finish time of the work. In order to identify formal and informal leaders in the group, their abilities to form a group, a sociometric technique developed by J. Moreno was used (Moreno 1958). Students were

*Table 3. The results of the experiment using the system of training of future IT specialists*

| Indicator | Control Group | Experimental Group 2 |
|---|---|---|
| Academic progress (average), maximum – 100 | 64,8 | 79,6 |
| Individual work (high/intermediate/low), % | 17/35/48 | 48/35/17 |
| Motivation (high/intermediate/low), % | 15/55/30 | 44/48/8 |

*Figure 10. Classification of soft skills*

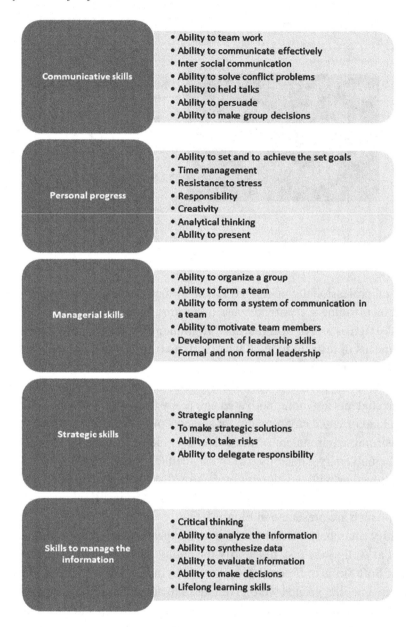

offered to answer some questions of a socio metric card; the number of options was limited. According to these results the index of grouping was identified which revealed internal emotional atmosphere of a group. The students of experimental groups demonstrated qualities to turn the idea into the ability faster than the Control Group. It shows more developed features of personal progress, communication, ability to influence the surrounding people, the ability to foresee the outcome, to manage the process.

## FORMATION OF AN INDIVIDUAL LEARNING TRAJECTORY IN SMART ENVIRONMENT

For the modern student, who has basic IT competences, there is a need not only in access to the resources, but mostly in the navigation knowledge-map, "guidebook" to knowledge, that can be found in information space, as it is important to help the student to find quality resources. And this is a complex task for the untrained student. Smart education using Smart courses of the new model is the most comfortable and modern teaching model for such cyber-students. To build an individual training trajectory of the student in the electronic course you can use several approaches. One of them involves the prior survey and testing of students in terms of competence in the course educational material and the preparation of an educational trajectory on the results of such survey and their identified learning needs (Figure 11). Thus the survey is based on extensive use of formative assessment tools that provide self-assessment and mutual assessment.

During the experimental study of the introduction of e-learning course of the new sample for students of the "Computer Sciences" specialty a survey was conducted for assessing their competencies on the subject according to the scale: "have a good knowledge", "be partially familiar", "heard something", "not familiar". Then each student was offered a test for competence in the training material, which he/she "has a good knowledge of" and "is partially familiar" with. According to the survey and testing results, an individual learning trajectory was built for each student or group of students. In other words, a sequence of learning elements of the course was chosen, which the student should study. The Moodle platform that we used to create the course allows to make each training element available to a particular group of students. Therefore each student or group of students receives an individual set of training elements of the course. The training course is adapted for the personal characteristics of each student that allow to

*Figure 11. Stages of the individual trajectory construction*

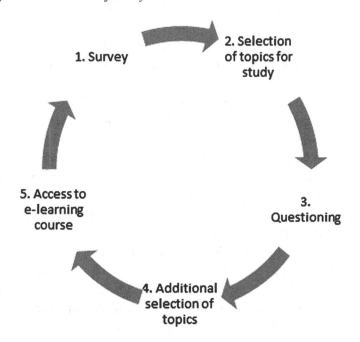

implement a personally oriented approach and to develop an individual training program. At the same time the course itself does not change, but the methods of presentation, set of tasks for performance and the tools, methods of evaluation and control are changed.

## QUALITY UNIVERSITY EDUCATIONAL ENVIRONMENT FOR SMART EDUCATION

To determine the level of educational services and the effectiveness of academic work at the university higher education institution rankings are created – according to indicators of the process and mechanism of performance of such institutions (and / or educational programs), based on certain criteria and factors..

In many Western countries, the rating is one of the tools for evaluation of university activity. The term "rating" (from the Latin "rating") means score, belonging to the class level, group, category (Zimenkovsky 2010). Recently, there has been growing interest in the global rankings of universities that take into account indicators of qualitative education. The definition of the integral index for quality of the university activity is due to the need of mutual recognition of curriculums in combination with the needs of the modern labor market.

The aim of university ratings is:

- To provide information to applicants, students and their parents, investors, employers, university administration;
- To stimulate universities to carry out self-assessment and thus identify the strengths and weaknesses of their activities, and, therefore, enhance their competitiveness through modernization and flexibility of educational programs;
- To form a single unified system of indicators to evaluate the quality of universities.
- The advantage of a rating system is its independence from official state structures that exercise their influence on the assessment of the quality of education.

The key indicators of the quality of educational activity of the university (http://www.euroosvita. net) can serve as indicators of external (world) and internal (university) ratings, objectives of which are reflected in Figure 12.

The leaders among authoritative world rankings are Shanghai (ARWU), THES-QS and Webometrics. Shanghai (Academic Ranking of World Universities - ARWU) ranking of universities is focused solely on the research activities of universities. When a ranking is made, only those universities are selected whose teachers or graduates have a Nobel Prize or Fields Medal. In a methodological aspect, when forming a Shanghai ranking emphasis is laid on easily accessible data sources, including publicly available data on the number of publications, citation indexes etc. The main indicators include: quoting of professors' scientific works listed based on 21 major scientific disciplines according to ISI Highly Cited, number of articles published in Nature and Science for the last 5 years, the number of links to articles in other scientific works (counting based on SCIE - Science Citation Index Expanded, SSCI - Social Sciences Citation Index and AHCI - Arts and Humanities Citation Index). To get into it is necessary to "publish a significant number of works included in the Expanded scientific citation index (SCIE), citation index in Social Sciences (SSCI), citation index in arts and humanities (AHCI)" (http://www.shanghairanking.com).

*Figure 12. The main objectives of rankings usage*

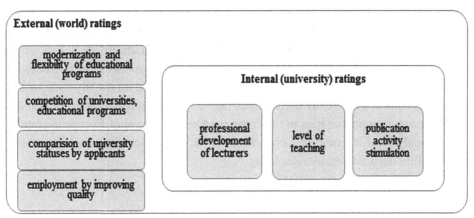

Database developers not only count the number of publications, but also assess effectiveness of research and quality of the scientific publications of researchers in order to create the ranking of scientists of Ukraine. It is believed that "If your papers are not in the databases of ISI - the most famous US scientific database - then you, as a scientist, do not exist..." (Rozhen 1999). The scientists based on this rating are ranked in the index Hirsch (researcher's h-index equals to N if he is the author of at least N items, each of which was cited at least N times, the remaining articles were cited less than N times), and within it by the number of citations. These are the figures excluding self-citation of all co-authors.

The concept of Webometrics ranking of world's universities is explained by Bill Gates: "If you are not in the Internet, then - you do not exist". The University cannot attract talented students and teachers at the global level (and, hence, to prepare high-quality professionals), without being effectively presented in the Internet. Accordingly, an assessment of Internet presence is one possible measure of the university's activity worldwide that is defined by a special methodology, developed in accordance with Berlin Principles on Ranking of Higher Education Institutions, defined by UNESCO.

The integrated rating system of university activity - Webometrics – existing since 2004, accounts for Scientific Publication activity of university scientists exclusively on the basis of Google Scholar. Currently, Google Scholar covers almost all sources of ISI database and additionally includes a large number of collections of scientific publications on various types of web-documents, including the post-Soviet information space. This is important given the fact that, for example, the database ISI indexes only one-third of the 25-thousand peer-reviewed journals, and only 15% of the annual volume of indexed publications presented in an open access.

Webometrics indicator ranking of partner universities within the framework of European IRNet project (www.irnet.us.edu.pl) is described in (Kommers et. al 2015)

The quality of education is the balanced line (as a result, the process of the educational system) between identified needs, goals, requirements, rules (standards). The component requirements of the quality of higher education is to provide training, research and teaching staff, material and technical resources, educational environment, including electronic, educational achievement of students, the system of education management and research results (Slade, Prinsloo 2013).

The European education system - on the contrary, formed under natural choice when quality requirements of education were put forward directly to consumers' educational services - sectors, employers, students. Standards and Guidelines for Quality Assurance in the European Higher Education consists of three aspects: European standards and guidelines for internal quality assurance in higher education, European standards and guidelines for external quality assurance of higher education and European standards and guidelines for agencies external quality assurance (Chatti 2012).

Analyzing the European standards of higher education and the impact of macro trends in the educational system and its transformation we can hypothesize about the need for quality content, component of the educational environment of the University, which includes electronic components. Their consistency and integrity allows modern universities to reach the performance level of European standards.

The results of analysis of international experience show key indicators measuring tools of internal quality standards of modern university education:

1.  University website,
2.  Structural units website,
3.  Teachers' ranking website,
4.  Website of electronic teacher's portfolio,
5.  Website for advanced distance teachers learning,
6.  Institutional repository,
7.  Electronic library resources,
8.  Wiki-portal,
9.  Educational portal LMS based on MOODLE,
10. Specials sections in LMS: e-dean, e-journal, means to assess learning activities of students,
11. A resource for assessing the quality of training content (external experts and employers),
12. A resource for analyzing the results of questioning of students,
13. A resource with information about implementation of ISO 9001.

The case study of smart information and educational environment of the contemporary university, and development of its quality has been described in the publication (Smyrnova-Trybulska 2015).

## THE DEVELOPMENT OF ICT-COMPETENCE OF TEACHERS IN THE SYSTEM OF SMART EDUCATION

Information and communication competence is known as the ability to understand individual autonomy and responsibility in ICT practice to meet individual needs and solving socially important issues, in particular professional tasks in a particular subject area (Figure 13.).

The framework structure of teacher ICT competence is described in UNESCO recommendations which include six modules: understanding the role of ICT in education, curriculum and assessment, pedagogical practices, ICT hardware and software, organization and learning management, professional development, considered as the basis for creating an appropriate model for high school teachers.

Another document which must be taken into account in the establishment of this model is the European ICT competency framework 2.0 (2011).

The framework of ICT competences (The European e-Competence Framework, then e-CF) is a framework describing ICT competencies to be used in business organizations and educational institu-

*Figure 13. Features of teachers in smart environments*

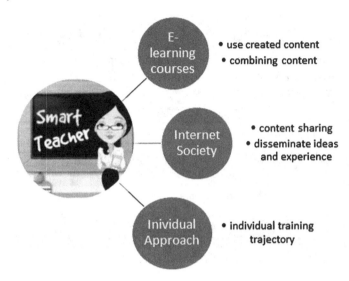

tions in determining the areas of training professionals to the modern labor market and the content of their training. e-CF serves as a tool for international schools for:

- Development, implementation and management of IT projects and processes in schools.
- The use of ICT.
- Decision-making, development strategies.
- Prediction of new learning scenarios and more.

The structure of the ICT competences 2.0 framework consists of 4 descriptors reflecting the different requirements for management staff, and is in addition to the management of employees' duties (see Figure 14).

The model of corporate standard of ICT competence of teaching staff of the modern university is based on UNESCO's relevant recommendations and the European 2.0 ICT competence framework, taking into account the characteristics of scientific-pedagogical employees in the context of the Standards and Guidelines for Quality Assurance in the European Higher Education Area, namely: understanding of the role of ICT in education and their use of ICT use, educational activities, research activities and training.

During the determination of the formation level of ICT competence of teachers it is expedient to take as a basis the standard quality of higher education in Europe and to determine, according to them, the appropriate tools and evaluation criteria. In addition to the basic documents, ISO 9000 is relevant: 2007 and ENQA (European Association for Quality Assurance in Higher Education), which contain commonly required needs or expectations.

The standard ENQA lays special emphasis on the following indicators: teaching (learning process, teaching activities); scientific and teaching staff; educational programs; material base, information and educational environment; students (students, prospective students); educational management; research.

*Figure 14. Structure of the ICT competence 2.0 framework*

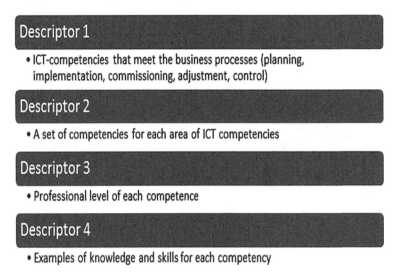

**Descriptor 1**
- ICT-competencies that meet the business processes (planning, implementation, commissioning, adjustment, control)

**Descriptor 2**
- A set of competencies for each area of ICT competencies

**Descriptor 3**
- Professional level of each competence

**Descriptor 4**
- Examples of knowledge and skills for each competency

## CONCLUSION

The Smart-education concept stands for flexibility, suggesting the presence of numerous sources, maximum diversity of media (audio, video, graphics), the ability to quickly and easily adjust to students' level and needs. In addition, Smart-education should be easily manageable when an institution can easily provide the flexibility of the educational process, and its integrated nature that is constantly nourished by external sources.

According to the Smart-education concept, modern curricula take on new features. It must ensure both the quality of education and motivate students to study. To interest modern students, they need to have access to numerous electronic materials, simple text benefits are almost impossible. It is necessary to create a script of all the training activities of the course, which will enthrall students, encouraging them to pursue artistic and scientific activities. Training courses should be integrated, that is, include fragments and multimedia and external electronic resources. Smart-rate should to an 80% extent consist of external sources, developed independently by connections to various channels, allowing students to create content. A modern course - it is the path of action, such as reading a textbook taking no more than 20-30% of the time.

The same requirements (flexibility, integration, individual trajectories and others) must be met by the Smart-textbook. It is a comprehensive teaching material, created and updated through the use of technological innovation and Internet resources, and contains a systematic presentation of knowledge in the subject area. The requirements for technology creating a smart-textbook include the use of cloud technologies in the development and use of smart-tutorial, enhanced use multimedia, interactive educational tools, automatic filtering on the level of development of the material (knowledge rating) subscription to access and use, group work collaborators and viewers in the Internet space, creating content through a personal account of the student.

Flexibility, adaptability, quality indicators, innovation - these requirements must be met by modern universities to keep up with the ongoing changes and students' growing demands.

The smart environment should provide not only high-quality training resources, services but also communications, data storage, integration with external training resources. The conducted research resulted in designing and utilizing a hybrid cloud oriented environment that integrates the components of university academic cloud such as e-learning courses, electronic tools and electronic manuals, video resources, virtual desktop and environment for automated assessment of tasks in programming; with academic components of Microsoft and Cisco clouds and external cloud services. The efficiency of such hybrid clouds in teaching programming to IT students was tested with a pedagogical experiment which showed as effective progress (on average by 14%), so the development of Soft Skills is necessary for career success of future IT specialists.

## ACKNOWLEDGMENT

This research study received, within the framework of the IRNet project, funding from the People Programme (Marie Curie Actions) of the European Union's Seventh Framework Programme FP7/2007-2013/ under REA grant agreement No: PIRSES-GA-2013-612536.

## REFERENCES

Al-Qirim, N. (2016). Smart Board Technology Success in Tertiary Institutions: The Case of the UAE University. *Education and Information Technologies, 21*(2), 265–281. doi:10.1007/s10639-014-9319-7

Bell, J., Sawaya, S., & Cain, W. (2014). Synchromodal classes: Designing for shared learning experiences between face-to-face and online students. *International Journal of Designs for Learning, 5*(1).

Bomhold, C. R. (2013). Educational use of smart phone technology; A survey of mobile phone application use by undergraduate university students. Program: Electronic Library and Information Systems, 47(4), 424-436.

Chatti, M. A., Dyckhoff, A. L., Thüs, H., & Schroeder, U. (2012). A reference model for learning analytics. *International Journal of Technology Enhanced Learning, 4*(5/6), 318–331. doi:10.1504/IJTEL.2012.051815

Cooper, A. (2014). *Open Learning Analytics Network - Summit Europe 2014*. Retrieved October 30, 2016, from http://www.laceproject.eu/open-learning-analytics-network-summit-europe-2014/

Daniel, B., & Butson, R. (2014). Foundations of Big Data and Analytics in Higher Education.*International Conference on Analytics Driven Solutions: ICAS2014*, 39-47.

Deryabina, G.I., & Losev, V.Y. (2006). *Creating e-learning courses: Studies*. Samara. Univers – groups.

Felder, R. M., & Brent, R. (2004). *The abc's of engineering education: abet, bloom's taxonomy, cooperative learning, and so on*. American Society for Engineering Education.

Fry, J., Schroeder, R., & den Besten, M. (2009). Open science in e-science: Contingency or policy? *The Journal of Documentation, 65*(1), 6–32. doi:10.1108/00220410910926103

Glazunova, E. G. (2015). *Theoretical and methodological foundations for the design and use of electronic training future professionals with information technology at universities agricultural profile* (Unpublished doctoral dissertation). National Academy of Pedagogical Sciences of Ukraine Institute of Information Technologies and the studies Kyiv.

Glazunova O.G. (2014). Types of academic internet-resources for it students' individual work management. *Informacijni texnologiyi v osviti, 21*, 78-86.

Glazunova, O. G., & Voloshyna, T. V. (2016). *Hybrid Cloud-Oriented Educational Environment for Training Future IT Specialists. ICT in Education.* Research and Industrial Applications. Retrieved October 30, 2016, from http://ceur-ws.org/Vol-1614/paper_64.pdf

Hilton, J. III, Wiley, D., Stein, J., & Johnson, A. (2010). The Four Rs of Openness and ALMS Analysis: Frameworks for Open Educational Resources. *Open Learning:The Journal of Open and Distance Learning, 25*(1), 37–44. doi:10.1080/02680510903482132

Khamayseh, Y., Mardini, W., Aljawarneh, S., & Yassein, M. (2015). Integration of Wireless Technologies in Smart University Campus Environment: Framework Architecture. *International Journal of Information and Communication Technology Education, 11*(1), 60–74. doi:10.4018/ijicte.2015010104

Kommers, P., Smyrnova-Trybulska, E., Morze, N., Issa, T., & Issa, T. (2015). Conceptual aspects: Analyses law, ethical, human, technical, social factors of Development ICT, e-learning and intercultural development in different countries setting out the previous new theoretical model and preliminary findings. *Int. J. Continuing Engineering Education and Life-long Learning, 25*(4), 365–393. doi:10.1504/IJCEELL.2015.074235

McAuley, A., Stewart, B., Siemens, G., & Cormier, D. (2010). *The MOOC model for digital.* Retrieved October 30, 2016, from http://www.elearnspace.org/Articles/MOOC_Final.pdf

Measuring the Information Society. (2012). *Committed to connecting the world.* Retrieved October 30, 2016, from http://www.itu.int/dms_pub/itu-d/opb/ind/D-IND-ICTOI-2012-SUM-PDF-R.pdf (in Russian)

Moreno J. (1958). *Sociometry. Experimental method and science about society.* Moskwa: "Ynostrannaya literature".

Morze, N. (2013). What Should be E-Learning Course for Smart Education.*ICT in Education, Research and Industrial Applications: Integration, Harmonization and Knowledge Transfer, CEUR Workshop Proceedings*, 411–423. Retrieved October 30, 2016, from http://ceur-ws.org/Vol-1000/ICTERI-2013-MRDL.pdf

Morze, N. (2014). Designing of Electronic Learning Courses For IT Students Considering the Dominant Learning Style. Information and Communication Technologies in Education, Research, and Industrial Applications/Communications in Computer and Information Science (Vol. 469, pp. 261–273). Springer. Retrieved from http://link.springer.com/chapter/10.1007/978-3-319-13206-8

Morze, N. V., & Glazunova, E. G. (2009). Quality Criteria for E-Learning Courses. Informational Technologies in Education, (4), 63-76.

Murphy, J., Lee, R., & Swinger, E. (2011). Student Perceptions and Adoption of University Smart Card Systems. *International Journal of Technology and Human Interaction, 7*(3), 1–15. doi:10.4018/jthi.2011070101

National Institute of Standards and Technology. (n.d.). Retrieved October 30, 2016, from http://www.nist.gov/

Nuzzaci, A., & La Vecchia, L. (2012). A Smart University for a Smart City. *International Journal of Digital Literacy and Digital Competence, 3*(4), 16–32. doi:10.4018/jdldc.2012100102

Rao, S., & Challa, R. K. (2013, October). Adoption of Cloud Computing In Education and Learning. *International Journal of Advanced Research in Computer and Communication Engineering, 2*(10), 4160–4163.

Rozhen, A. (1999). *Say* citation index your articles, and I'll tell you what... you're a scientist. *Zerkalo Nedeli, 45*. (in Russian)

Sclater, N. (2014). *Examining open learning analytics - report from the Lace Project meeting in Amsterdam*. Retrieved October 30, 2016, from http://www.laceproject.eu/blog/examining-open-learninganalytics-report-lace-project-meeting-amsterdam/

Slade, S., & Prinsloo, P. (2013). Learning analytics: ethical issues and dilemmas. American Behavioral Scientist, 57(10), 1509-1528. doi:10.1177/0002764213479366

Smyrnova-Trybulska, E. (2014). Some Results of the Research Conducted at the University of Silesia in the Framework of the International Research Network IRNet. In E. Smyrnova-Trybulska (Ed.), *E-learning and Intercultural Competences Development in Different Countries, Monograph* (pp. 133–144). Katowice, Cieszyn: Studio-Noa for University of Silesia.

Smyrnova-Trybulska, E. (2015). Information and Educational Environment of the University: a Case Study. *High-Tech Educational Informational Environment, Proceedings of the International Scientific Conference*, 25-39.

Tikhomirov, N. V. (2012). *Global strategy for the development of smart-society*. MESI is on a Smart-university. Retrieved October 30, 2016, from http://smartmesi.blogspot.com/2012/03/smart-smart.html (in Russian)

Traxler, J. (2010). *The learner experience of mobiles, mobility and connectedness. Evaluation of Learners' Experiences of e-Learning Special Interest Group*. Retrieved October 30, 2016, from http://www.helenwhitehead.com/elesig/ELESIG%20Mobilities%20ReviewPDF.pdf

Verbert, K., Manouselis, N., Drachsler, H., & Duval, E. (2012). Dataset-Driven Research to Support Learning and Knowledge Analytics. *Journal of Educational Technology & Society, 15*(3), 133–148.

Waldrop, M. (2013, November7). Smart Connections. *Nature, 503*(7474), 22–24. doi:10.1038/503022a PMID:24201264

Yadav K. (2014). Role of Cloud Computing in Education. *International Journal of Innovative Research in Computer and Communication Engineering, 2*(2), 3108-3112.

Zimenkovsky, B. S. (Ed.). (2010). Methodology and ranking multidisciplinary principles of structural units LNMU named Danylo Halytsky: Guidelines. Lvov.

# Chapter 12
# EvalCOMIX®:
## A Web–Based Programme to Support Collaboration in Assessment

**María Soledad Ibarra-Sáiz**
*University of Cadiz, Spain*

**Gregorio Rodríguez-Gómez**
*University of Cadiz, Spain*

## ABSTRACT

*The increasing use of technological tools to support the process of participation in assessment is explained, firstly, by the current tendencies in assessment and learning in Higher Education which encourage the active participation of students as a means to improve their learning; secondly, by the universal presence of technology that makes it impossible to conceive of any educational process that does not contemplate its use and that is leading to ever more courses that are either virtual or require minimal attendance; and, finally, an environment in which there are ever greater numbers of students per class. This chapter presents the results of using the web-based EvalCOMIX® programme in the context of a number of Higher Education training courses. Data has been collected through questionnaires and interviews applied to students, lecturers and academic coordinators. The results illustrate the ease of implementation of EvalCOMIX®, its usefulness in creating and sharing assessment instruments and the opportunity it provides to facilitate student participation in assessment.*

## INTRODUCTION

For many years developments in assessment have focused on ways of integrating assessment and learning by encouraging, among other strategies, the involvement of students in the assessment process. Although there have been some successful innovations, the ongoing challenge is to facilitate the development of models that integrate assessment and learning using technological tools that enable a truly active, collaborative, relevant and systematic participation in the assessment process.

DOI: 10.4018/978-1-5225-2492-2.ch012

Existing Learner Management Systems (LMS) such as Moodle or Blackboard enable certain assessment activities to be delivered in an easy and simple way, but they suffer from two serious deficiencies. Firstly, these platforms do not allow for complex assessment tools to be designed or implemented in ways that enable students' activities or assignments to be assessed in an effective, user-friendly way. Although objective tests with multiple-choice responses or simple rubrics can be created, the platforms do not offer the option of designing the full range of assessment tools, from checklists to complex rubrics. Secondly, these systems are based on a teacher-centred approach to assessment, offering very limited possibilities for involving students in the assessment process through modes of assessment such as self-assessment, peer assessment or co- assessment.

The EvalCOMIX® web-based programme, first devised in 2000, was developed as a direct to response to the limitations of existing LMS. It has subsequently proved to be a valuable tool for facilitating new concepts such as assessment for learning and empowerment and it has demonstrated its usefulness in enabling the collaborative participation of students in the assessment process. Furthermore, it enables assessment to be undertaken using a wide variety of complex assessment instruments. Its ease of use and intuitive nature makes it possible to use it in many different educational contexts and with large numbers of students.

This chapter is divided into three sections. The first section defines the theoretical framework that supports the need and the opportunity to take advantage of technological tools that enable the new concepts of assessment to be employed in the classroom. By this we mean developments that have shifted the focus from simple assessment of learning to the concept of assessment as learning and empowerment, demonstrating the benefits of moving from collaboration in assessment to systematizing student involvement in all aspects of the assessment process and participatory assessment in all its forms. The section concludes with an explanation of the importance of facilitating the implementation of these practices using technology that enhances users' digital literacy.

The main objective of the second section of this chapter is to present and describe experiences following the implementation of the EvalCOMIX® web-based programme. The structure and uses of the tool are explained followed by an analysis and evaluation of its implementation within a university environment and its subsequent evaluation by teachers, students and relevant academics as part of two competitive research projects carried out in an international context.

The chapter concludes with a series of reflections on the results of the research that show the contributions made by the EvalCOMIX® web programme to implementing assessment as learning and empowerment within the classroom. It also proposes future actions and developments that will help to deliver true lifelong learning to students.

## THEORETICAL FRAMEWORK

This section presents the theoretical framework used to validate the study and its results in order to contextualise the importance of the experience and process. It focuses on three key areas:

- Assessment as learning and empowerment.
- Collaborative assessment or co-assessment as means of participative assessment.
- The need to incorporate technological tools in the assessment process to encourage student participation.

## From the Assessment of Learning to Assessment as Learning and Empowerment

Traditionally the assessment of learning has been characterized by maintaining a separation between teaching and learning (Falchikov, 2005, p. 82) and employing a narrow range of systems which do not always reflect the objectives of the curriculum and often fail to specify the marking criteria, therefore giving little or no power to students and missing the opportunity to make them responsible for their own learning process whilst, among other things, causing adverse feelings and lasting negative consequences.

Faced with this situation, common in most educational contexts, many authors with innovative approaches to their practices and contributions are now proposing alternative scenarios that increasingly place the focus of assessment on students' progress and learning rather than on just providing a final grade.

In relation to this we would highlight the contributions of Carless (2007) on learning-oriented assessment; Rodríguez-Gómez & Ibarra-Sáiz (2011) who expand this concept whilst emphasizing the possibilities and importance of electronic forms of assessment; Taras (2010; 2015), who stresses the role of self-assessment; Nicol, Thomson & Breslin (2014) who focus on the value of peer assessment; the concept of sustainable assessment as expressed by Boud (2000) and Boud & Soler (2016); Boud & Molloy (2013) who concentrate on feedback to students or Price, Rust, O'Donovan, Handley & Bryant (2012) with their contributions regarding the need for both tutors and students to receive training in assessment processes.

Against this background, the focus on the development and application of the concept of assessment as learning and empowerment (Rodríguez-Gómez & Ibarra-Sáiz, 2015; Ibarra-Sáiz & Rodríguez-Gómez, 2016) is characterized by three main challenges (Figure 1): achieving the participation of students in the assessment process, incorporating self-assessment, peer assessment and shared assessment; feedforward, understood as strategies that provide proactive information on students' progress and results so that they can participate in their improvement; and high quality tasks, i.e., challenging tasks that are motivational and related to daily life. The implementation of these three challenges allows university students to self-regulate their learning process and delivers empowerment within their personal, professional and working environments.

Assessment as learning and empowerment, then, encompasses strategies that promote students' self-awareness of their own development needs, their self-regulation of the learning process, autonomous

*Figure 1. Assessment as learning and empowerment*
*Rodríguez-Gómez & Ibarra-Sáiz 2015, p. 3.*

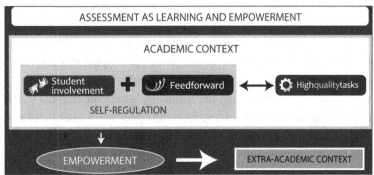

learning that is relevant throughout their lives, self-determination in decision making and their empowerment within both academic and extra-academic contexts in ways that are both ecologically sustainable and socially responsible.

## From Collaboration in Assessment to Collaborative Assessment or Co-Assessment

Collaboration in assessment suggests three possibilities. It may refer to reflections or proposals on aspects of assessment which involve agents within or external to an institution in the decision making process. Alternatively, it could relate to the coordination among a team of lecturers on the planning and development of an assessment (procedures, levels, activities, etc.) to produce a piece of formative assessment that is characterised by being created by the teaching staff, requires their specific involvement, derives from the teaching process and which seeks to produce positive change in students from a position outside the learning process and in which the student's collaboration is merely anecdotal or non-existent. Finally, if the focus is placed on the students' actual participation and collaboration they may be involved in different phases of the assessment process, with different degrees of involvement and responsibility. This latter possibility, despite potentially being viewed initially as simple formative assessment, represents, in fact, a type of formative assessment that is typically initiated as a result of the students' own initiative and reflection on their outputs or performance and which, with the guidance of their tutor, delivers an impact and positive change to the student that emanates from within the learning process.

The collaboration of students in the assessment process comes under the heading of participative assessment, a term used by Reynolds & Trehan (2000) to refer to the assessment community formed by students and teaching staff. Participative assessment is assessment that include strategies for participation that provides all those involved in the learning process with the opportunity to make proposals and collaborate in the development and decision making process of assessment. The quality of a participative assessment process is determined by the following three principles:

- **Transparency:** The assessment is carried out in accordance with procedures, standards and criteria that are published and visible and that are focused on achieving the desired learning outcomes.
- **Shared Responsibility:** Responsibility is shared between students and lecturers and all parties acknowledge, propose and accept the arrangements, decisions and consequences of the assessment.
- **Flexibility:** The ability to reach agreement and capacity to adapt to changes or revisions that result from decisions made about the assessment.

Student participation in assessment can be achieved at all stages of the assessment process. It can occur at the three key points (Ibarra-Sáiz & Rodríguez-Gómez, 2014): a) the initial conception, b) during its implementation, and c) when the results are determined. Consequently, student involvement in assessment can range from their participation in decisions about the outputs or performances to be assessed, weightings in grading, assessment instruments and criteria, the assessment formats to be used so that feedback and feedforward can be delivered and the means by which the outputs will be evaluated. It also includes their active involvement through self-assessment, peer assessment and co-assessment, where co-assessment, collaborative assessment and co-operative assessment are all considered synonymous, as proposed by Dochy, Segers & Sluijmans (1999) and Falchikov (2005).

As shown in Figure 2, the participative assessment methods that can be employed during the implementation and results gathering phases of the process include; self-assessment, which implies a process by which students analyse and evaluate their own outputs and performances; peer assessment, where students analyse and evaluate the outputs or performances other individual or groups of students during their production or on completion; and co-assessment or collaborative assessment, a process by which students and lecturers jointly analyse and evaluate outputs or activities in a way that is collaborative, dialogic, collective and agreed.

This brief narrative has described the progression from collaboration in assessment between a variety of agents to forms of participative assessment in which students play a major role, arriving finally at the implementation of truly collaborative assessment with outcomes being agreed with teaching staff. This form of participative assessment is an improvement on formative assessment and is based on assessment that empowers students as they acquire a fully participative and active role in the assessment process, learning how to assess and improve their own work and performance through self-regulation and harnessing their learning process to the concept of assessment as empowerment introduced previously.

## The Need for Automation and Literacy in the Assessment Process

Various factors support the need for automation of the assessment process. Principal among them is the requirement to manage huge quantities of information, generated in a variety of contexts that extend beyond the physical space of the classroom. Participative forms of assessment generate high volumes of data as observations are not produced solely by the teaching staff. Students also represent a source of information through their self- and peer assessment for example.

*Figure 2. Participative assessment*

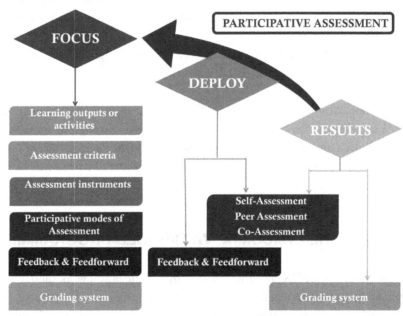

Currently, and for the most part, the process of teaching and learning takes place in classrooms with large numbers of students, despite what recent legislative changes intended to achieve. Furthermore, it covers both knowledge and skills and does not take place only within the classroom but in some cases is developed entirely outside them. These are factors that also imply a change in the conditions and characteristics of the relevant assessment. Within universities, the non-contact nature of some or all subject areas is a fact that demands the use of campus-based or virtual platforms and therefore appropriate and valuable tools are needed to undertake assessment through these platforms and which incorporate the latest thinking on assessment practice, in particular its participative nature.

Assessing skills and knowledge involves using different strategies and undertaking assessment at different times with different objectives and criteria. This entails developments that have produced and continue to produce some unease and insecurity among university tutors, who face a challenging environment and who often do not have the most convincing answers. In this circumstance, technology should be employed to facilitate the assessment process. It should function to support assessment, encouraging the implementation of the advances taking place in the field. Despite this, however, Eyal (2012, p. 44) insists that "teachers in the 21st century prefer to use technologies that advance the assessment methods that emphasize the learning process, enable peer assessment and develop reflective abilities".

According to the concept of assessment as learning and empowerment, technological tools must be integrated with high quality tasks, encourage the participation of students in their own assessment process and provide useful and relevant information on their progress so they can take appropriate decisions in order to improve their work and performance. It is with the express intention of connecting and consolidation these various elements that the EVALfor Research Group[1] has been developing the EvalCOMIX® web-based programme[2] which we introduce in the following sections.

The existence of technological tools and the consequent automation of processes that simplify assessment leads us to consider the need for an appropriate level of digital literacy of students and staff. According to Ibarra-Sáiz & Rodríguez-Gómez (2016b) this should be; a) delivered by experts in the field of assessment; b) have an innovative focus such as assessment as learning and empowerment; c) have skill development as a key aim; and c) exploit the technological resources available in a critical and innovative way (Figure 3).

In essence, as proposed by Eyal (2012) when referring to teaching staff, it would be useful if they had a high level of assessment literacy which:

*… includes the implementation of tests, tasks and projects in a digital environment, the performance indicators for which are determined in cooperation with students; through to implementing advanced estimation approaches based on constructivist-social learning and the development of self-targeted learning, where as part of the assessment teachers must also know how and when to delegate the processes of assessment to the students. (p. 45)*

## EXPERIENCE USING THE EvalCOMIX® WEB-BASED PROGRAMME

This section describes the EvalCOMIX® programme to demonstrate how it works and the potential it offers to enable the simple and intuitive implementation of participative assessment methods (self-assessment, peer assessment and co-assessment) referred to previously. With reference to the DevalSimWeb research

*Figure 3. Key elements for assessment literacy*
*Ibarra-Sáiz & Rodríguez-Gómez, 2016b, p. 28.*

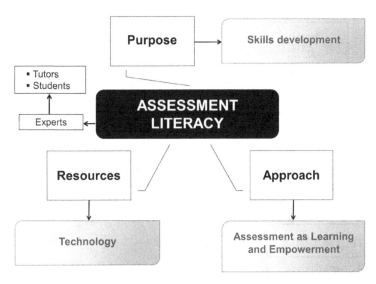

programme[3] – *The development of professional skills through participative assessment and simulation using web tools* and the DevalS Project[4] – *The development of sustainable e-assessment – improving university students' assessment skills using simulations,* the second section presents the results obtained from tutors and students following their use of the EvalCOMIX® programme within their university course, together with the opinions of other relevant academics.

## How Does EvalCOMIX® Work?

EvalCOMIX® is a web-based programme that supports the creation and implementation of assessment tools (rubrics, grading scales, mixed instruments, etc.) and their use in assessment process both by tutors and students. It enables participative assessment methods such as self- or peer assessment to be implemented with relative ease.

The EvalCOMIX® programme is currently available on a Moodle platform, through the API EvalCOMIX_MD®. Figure 4 presents the logical architecture and flow diagram of the possibilities offered by the EvalCOMIX® web programme and illustrates how EvalCOMIX® is a tool that allows for both the design and construction of assessment instruments as well as the implementation of a range of modes of assessment. The results obtained from the assignments and actions of each student assessed by the assessment instruments as designed by the agent(s) concerned (teacher, student or peers) are saved in the Moodle grading book. This process does not require assessors to have any specific computer training only skills at Moodle user level. However, it is advisable to have an understanding and methodological knowledge of both the characteristics of the assessment instruments and the possibilities offered by different modes of assessment. To support the process EvalCOMIX® incorporates a user manual and an online demo.

Below we explain how this programme works once it is installed on a virtual campus platform and we focus on answering the following questions:

*Figure 4. Logical architecture and flow diagram of the EvalCOMIX® web-based programme integrated within Moodle*

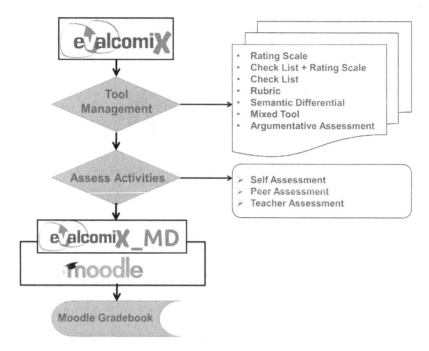

- How can effective assessment instruments be designed?
- How should the roles of assessors be assigned to tutors and students?
- How can the weighted scores of the assessments provided by EvalCOMIX® be interpreted?
- How can the results of the assessments be analysed? (Figure 4).

## Designing Assessment Instruments

Decisions on issues such as the design of assessment instruments, specification of the criteria and the selection of participatory assessment methods are all covered within the programme (Rodríguez-Gómez and Ibarra-Sáiz, 2016). In this section we discuss how to design assessment tools using the EvalCOMIX® programme.

To design appropriate assessment instruments, it is first necessary to access the Tool Management section. From that screen New Instrument is selected (Figure 5). A list of the possible tools that can be built with EvalCOMIX® is then displayed.

EvalCOMIX® guides the process of construction of each instrument by offering options about which decisions must be taken (Figure 6). Before building the tools it is preferable to plan and determine the weighting that each aspect will have within the overall assessment. By default, EvalCOMIX® assigns a pro-rata weighting, but the percentages of all of the elements assessed (dimensions and attributes) can be changed as required. Once a new instrument has been created, it is automatically added to the full list of instruments available to tutors.

*Figure 5. Options and assessment tools provided by EvalCOMIX®*

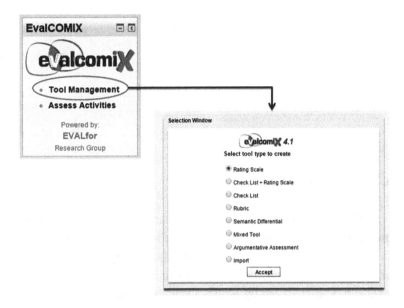

*Figure 6. Interface for the construction of assessment rubrics*

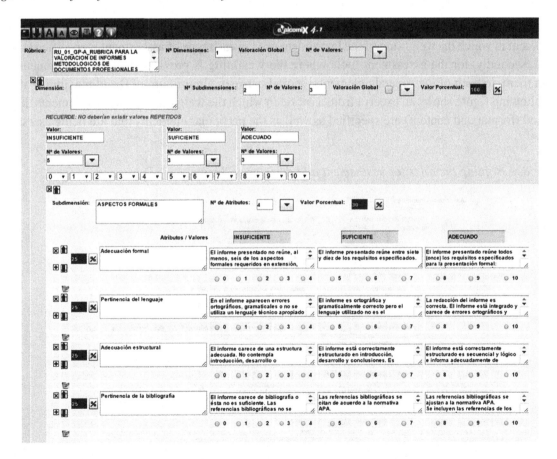

*Figure 7. List of assessment instruments designed by Lecturer X using EvalCOMIX®*

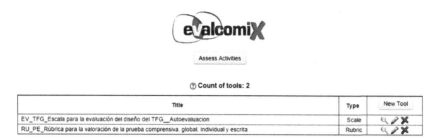

## Assigning the Roles of Assessor

One advantage of EvalCOMIX® is that the role of assessor can be undertaken by both tutors and students, through self-assessment or peer assessment, using some or all of the three modes of assessment. To do this each assessor is assigned the assessment tool they will use (Figure 8). The instrument can be the same or different for each of the assessors. Peer assessment can be anonymous or public. Furthermore, this type of assessment can be carried out by groups or by individual students.

## Considerations on the Issue of Weighting

The weighting of the grades using EvalCOMIX® is achieved by two means. Firstly, for the elements of assessment in which the weighting of the instrument used in each type of assessment is specified (Figure 9) and, secondly, for the assessment tools where the weighting is provided for each component and, within them, to each of the separate elements, scored between a minimum of 0 and maximum of 100. The following figure shows an excerpt from a rubric in which the weighting of the two elements that are assessed (format and content) are specified as well as the particular elements that are being assessed.

*Figure 8. Assigning the roles for assessment and decision making*

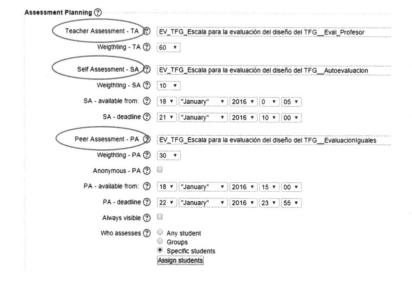

*Figure 9. Examples of weighting for each component and element in a rubric created using EvalCOMIX®*

| RU_02_GP-A_RUBRICA PARA LA VALORACION DE INFORMES METODOLOGICOS DE DOCUMENTOS PROFESIONALES | | | | |
|---|---|---|---|---|
| 100% | | INSUFICIENTE | SUFICIENTE | ADECUADO |
| *30%* | ***ASPECTOS FORMALES*** | | | |
| 25% | Adecuación formal | El informe presentado no reúne, al menos, seis de los aspectos formales requeridos en extensión, formato y entrega. | El informe presentado reúne entre siete y diez de los requisitos especificados. | El informe presentado reúne todos (once) los requisitos especificados para la presentación formal: extensión; identificación, título, índice, desarrollo del informe, referencias bibliográficas, interlineado, márgenes, alineación; entrega en fecha e identificación correcta del archivo. |
| | | 0 1 2 3 4 | 5 6 7 | 8 9 10 |
| 25% | Pertinencia del lenguaje | En el informe aparecen errores ortográficos, gramaticales o no se utiliza un lenguaje técnico apropiado al tema. | El informe es ortográfica y gramaticalmente correcto pero el lenguaje utilizado no es el apropiado, bien por ser repetitivo o por no ser técnico. | La redacción del informe es correcta. El informe está integrado y carece de errores ortográficos y gramaticales. El lenguaje utilizado es adecuado y denota conocimiento del tema. |
| | | 0 1 2 3 4 | 5 6 7 | 8 9 10 |
| 25% | Adecuación estructural | El informe carece de una estructura adecuada. No contempla introducción, desarrollo o conclusiones. No mantiene un desarrollo secuencial adecuado o no comunica suficientemente sobre los apartados. | El informe está correctamente estructurado en introducción, desarrollo y conclusiones. Es secuencial pero no informa suficientemente de uno de esos bloques. | El informe está correctamente estructurado es secuencial y lógico e informa adecuadamente de introducción, desarrollo y conclusiones. |
| | | 0 1 2 3 4 | 5 6 7 | 8 9 10 |
| 25% | Pertinencia de la bibliografía | El informe carece de bibliografía o ésta no es suficiente. Las referencias bibliográficas no se ajustan a la normativa APA. | Las referencias bibliográficas se citan de acuerdo a la normativa APA. Se incluyen las referencias de los informes/artículos analizados. | Las referencias bibliográficas se ajustan a la normativa APA. Se incluyen las referencias de los informes/artículos analizados. Se incluye, al menos, una referencia bibliográfica utilizada por el equipo representativa del tema y que no es de informes/artículos. |
| | | 0 1 2 3 4 | 5 6 7 | 8 9 10 |
| *70%* | ***ASPECTOS DE CONTENIDO*** | | | |
| 25% | Corrección y justificación de las identificaciones | En el informe no se identifican y justifican, al menos, tres aspectos. | El informe identifica todos los apartados del desarrollo y justifica coherentemente un mínimo de cuatro. | El informe identifica y justifica coherentemente los seis apartados del desarrollo: objetivos, responsabilidad, destinatarios, tipo de información, metodología utilizada, proceso de recogida y análisis de datos y resultados. |
| | | 0 1 2 3 4 | 5 6 7 | 8 9 10 |

## Analysis of Results

Once the assessment process is complete (creation of instruments and assessment jointly by the tutors and students) EvalCOMIX® (Figure 10) enables both tutors and students to see all the assessments that have been completed and who has completed each of the different assessment tasks.

Tutors can also get an overview of the gradings in simple diagrams, where the highest, lowest and median scores are shown. Assessment results can be analysed by student group, class and assessment mode used.

## Methodology

The aim of the research is focused on understanding the views of students, lecturers and academic coordinators that have used the EvalCOMIX® programme on different courses. We seek their opinions

*Figure 10. Marks shown by assessment mode and their weighting*

| Modality | Grade | Weighing on final grade |
|---|---|---|
| Teacher Assessment - TA | 80/100 | 60% |
| Self Assessment - SA | 93 / 100 | 10% |
| Peer Assessment - PA | 75/100 99/100 | 30% |

**EvalCOMIX grade: 83.40 / 100**

*Figure 11. Grades achieved by assessment method and weighting and representation using box and whisker plots of scores on self-assessment and peer assessment of a class*

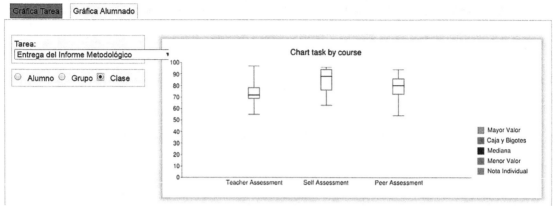

about the usefulness and advantages of using EvalCOMIX®, the opportunities it offers to implement participative assessment methods, deliver relevant information and develop students' assessment skills.

The methodology used has been to apply online questionnaires, aimed at tutors and students, together with interviews with coordinators in their universities. The focus is eclectic as the nature of the data collected is both quantitative, through closed questions, and qualitative, using open questions and responses gained through interviews.

Three online questionnaires were used to gather data. They were applied at different times of the academic year to lecturers taking part in the EVAPES-DevalSimWeb training programme; 1 online questionnaire for students on the APREVAL and EDECOM programmes, 2 online questionnaires for students taking the Project Management module and 3 semi-structured face to face interviews with university coordinators of the Final Dissertation module on the Business Administration and Management (BAM), Finance and Accounting (F&A) and Public Relations (PR) degree courses.

The total sample for the study of 291 participants including tutors and students is shown in the following two tables. Table 1 shows the sample size of lecturers and students and their percentages for each of the five universities where data was collected. Table 2 shows the participants by type and, for the lecturers, their role and, for the students, the course they were taking.

*Table 1. Distribution of participants by university*

|  | **n** | **%** |
|---|---|---|
| PUCESI (Ecuador) | 69 | 19.83 |
| UdeA (Colombia) | 40 | 11.49 |
| UCR (Costa Rica) | 53 | 15.23 |
| UNA (Nicaragua) | 18 | 5.17 |
| UCA (Spain) | 111 | 48.28 |
| Total | 291 | 100 |

*Table 2. Distribution of participants by role and course*

| | n | % | Instrument |
|---|---|---|---|
| **Tutors** | | | |
| Trainers | 5 | 1.72 | Questionnaire |
| Participants | 65 | 22.34 | Questionnaire |
| Coordinators | 3 | 1.03 | Interview |
| **Students** | | | |
| APREVAL | 38 | 13.06 | Questionnaire |
| EDECOM | 72 | 24.74 | Questionnaire |
| BAM, F&A | 108 | 37.11 | Questionnaire |

Descriptive analysis, M (Median) and SD (Standard Deviation), was undertaken only in respect of the items relating to the use of the tool used to incorporate self- and peer assessment. The analysis is provided in the results section. The responses to the interviews are categorised in accordance with the previously established categories.

## Results: What Do Users Think of EvalCOMIX®?

The results of the analysis are presented in three sections relating to the views of the tutors, the university coordinators and the students.

### The Tutors' Views

As part of the DevalSimWeb International Project, during the academic year 2014/2015 a total of 70 tutors from Latin American universities participated in the EVAPES-DevalSimWeb Training Course (*Assessment for Learning in Higher Education*). The tutors chosen to deliver the training course within their own institutions first completed the FEAES-DevalSimWeb Training Course (*Preparation Course for Trainers in Assessment for Learning in Higher Education*). Subsequently, they acted as the tutors on the EVAPES Training Course whilst the remaining 65 tutors all took the course.

Table 3 presents the distribution of the sample according to their role on the training programme (trainer or participant), gender and subject area. A nonparametric tests were used because the items are ordinal level measurements and are not adjusted to a normal distribution (Kolmogorov–Smirnov test, $p<0.01$).

To simplify the interpretation of the results in all the figures the data is grouped into three bands: low (responses 1 & 2), middle (responses 3 & 4) and high (responses 5 & 6).

The responses of tutors to questions about the usefulness and advantages of EvalCOMIX® (Figure 12) are generally positive. They consider it to be a product that simplifies the assessment process for tutors (M=5.50, SD=.95), is applicable to any subject area (M=5.36, SD=1.06), improves tutors' skills in undertaking assessment (M=5.40, SD=1.02), encourages innovation in universities (M=5.56; SD=.91) and they feel it should be more widely used in universities (M=5.47; SD=.91).

*Table 3. Distribution of the simple of tutors by their role, gender, university and subject area*

| | n | % |
|---|---|---|
| **Role** | | |
| Trainer | 5 | 7.1 |
| Participant | 65 | 92.9 |
| **Gender** | | |
| Male | 22 | 31.4 |
| Female | 48 | 68.6 |
| **University** | | |
| PUCESI (Ecuador) | 31 | 44.3 |
| UCR (Costa Rica) | 30 | 42.9 |
| UNA (Nicaragua) | 9 | 12.9 |
| **Subject Area** | | |
| Arts & Humanities | 10 | 14.3 |
| Science | 13 | 18.6 |
| Health Sciences | 10 | 14.3 |
| Social Sciences | 24 | 34.3 |
| Engineering & Architecture | 13 | 18.6 |

*Figure 12. Tutors' responses to the usefulness and advantages of EvalCOMIX®*

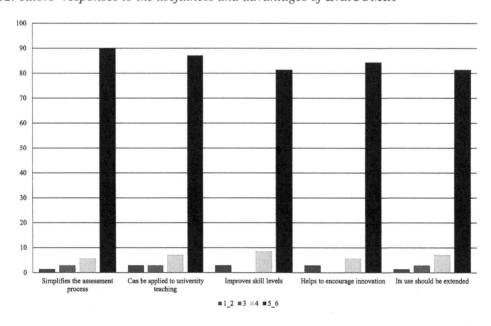

Figure 13 shows that, according to most lecturers, EvalCOMIX® enables instruments to be created easily (M=5.18; DT=1.15), those instruments can be modified (M=5.18; SD=1.12), they can be shared with colleagues (M=5.19; SD=1.12) and that the product simplifies the design and construction of assessment instruments (M=5.14; SD=1.15)

With regard to issues related to collaboration in the assessment process (Figure 14), tutors indicate in the main that EvalCOMIX® is very useful in enabling student participation in assessment (M=5.53, SD=.79), it provides students with information about the results of their assessment (M=5.54, SD=.81) and increases the university students' assessment skills (M=5.53, SD=.83).

A significant majority of lecturers (Figure 15) believe that EvalCOMIX® enables self-assessment (M=5.61, SD=.71) as well as peer assessment (M=5.57, SD=.73) and facilitates both feedback and feedforward (M=5.49, SD=.91).

The open questions in the questionnaires applied to tutors (trainers and participants) that asked about the three most positive aspects of the programme and their overall satisfaction with it, produced the following comments:

1. **Using Technology for Assessment:** "Focused and practical tools to improve assessment", "I now have new tools (technological ones) to deliver assessment as part of the education process"; "The new approach to assessing learning [with] technology based tools I can use for assessment,

2. **Acknowledging the Advantages of EvalCOMIX®:** "Knowledge and use of tools like EvalCOMIX®", "Training in the use of EvalCOMIX®", "Creating more effective and better designed instruments", "A tool [EvalCOMIX®] to implement assessment in the courses I teach" and

*Figure 13. Lecturers' responses to the construction of instruments using EvalCOMIX®*

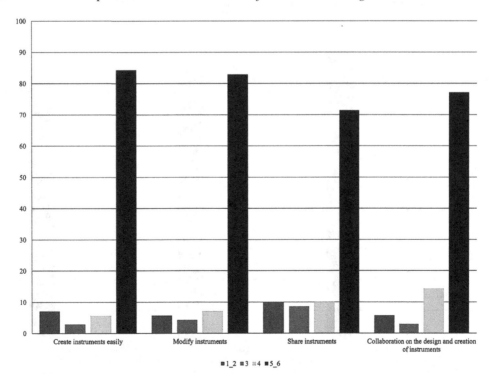

*Figure 14. Tutors' responses about the usefulness of EvalCOMIX®*

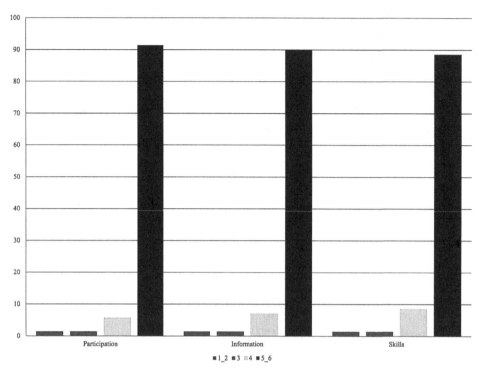

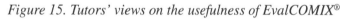

*Figure 15. Tutors' views on the usefulness of EvalCOMIX®*

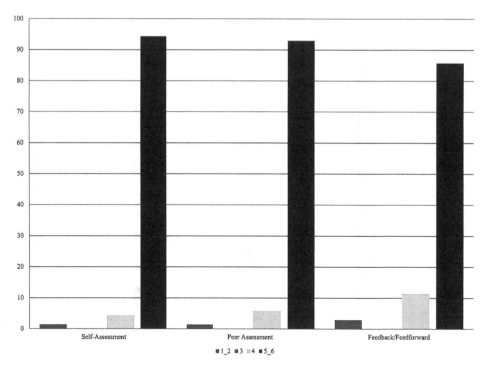

3. **Encouraging the More Participative Forms of Assessment that can be Delivered Using EvalCOMIX®:** "Enabling student participation in the assessment of their learning has been very positive for their academic performance", "The improvements have been in the implementation of self- and peer assessment in the classes I teach, recognising the importance of giving students the chance to participate and take responsibility for their own learning and that of their peers".

In short, using *EvalCOMIX®* "encourages innovation in university teaching" and leads to "innovations in assessment being implemented".

## The Views of the Academic Coordinators

Using semi-structured interviews at the beginning of the 2016-17 academic year the views of 3 academic coordinators were obtained. They are responsible for the Final Dissertations on the Business Administration and Management (BAM), Finance and Accounting (F&A) and Public Relations (PR) degrees.

The views of these coordinators are presented in 6 separate categories according to the statements they made, some of which are transcribed below:

1. **Usefulness of EvalCOMIX®:** "It is a very useful and user-friendly tool", "an easy to use tool"
2. **Advantages of the Rubric Used in the Assessment of the Final Dissertation by the Module Team:** (The Rubric was Developed jointly by the teaching team with advice from experts in assessment and in EvalCOMIX®) "it's a very flexible and adaptable instrument" that enables "coordination between members of the module team" and agreement between the members to "produce a single evaluation that all agree upon". Its availability via the virtual campus means, on the one hand, "it can be used as a communication tool" and, on the other, "all the documentation necessary for the assessment is located in one place, including the evidence and the marks awarded by the module team and the tutors".
3. **Opportunities to Provide Students with Information Using EvalCOMIX®:** "The information provided by the rubric is used to give students information about the assessment of their Final Dissertation", enabling them to "access information about their scores for each separate skill, the results of their learning and each of the criteria applied". Furthermore, the assessment instruments "help and guide the students as well" and as they are made public prior to the starting their Final Dissertations the students know in advance "what their tutor and the module team will be assessing", which helps them self-regulate their learning.
4. **Opportunities for Using Participative Forms of Assessment:** "With EvalCOMIX®, you can use self- and peer assessment though we haven't used them so far", "you can use different modes of assessment, although it does depend on the kind of subject matter you're assessing".
5. **Transferability to Other Contexts:** Advantages in terms of "using it on other modules on the degree course", "we've proposed that EvalCOMIX® should be used to assess the Final Dissertation in degree and masters' courses across the Faculty", "you can produce different instruments for different modules". To ensure all the possibilities offered by EvalCOMIX® are recognised tutors overall highlighted the "importance of disseminating the tool".

6.  **Expressed Needs:** "Lecturers should get training to learn about and practice using EvalCOMIX® in the classes they teach", and "practical workshops should be run so tutors can experience EvalCOMIX®… self- and peer assessment represent a "new assessment mode" that requires training and commitment".

## The Students' Views

In order to illustrate the students' views on EvalCOMIX® the results are presented in two separate sections. Firstly, we present the perceptions of those students at 4 Latin American universities (Ecuador, Colombia, Costa Rica and Nicaragua) who, during the 2013-14 and 2014-15 academic years, completed the APREVAL-DevalSimWeb (Learn Through Assessment in Higher Education) and the EDECOM-DevalSimWeb (Assessment and the Development of Professional Skills) training courses as part of the DevalSimWeb programme. Secondly, we present the views of students who during the 2012-2013 and 2013-2014 academic years used the EvalCOMIX® programme in their Project Management module at a Spanish university. This latter module incorporated the ideas and principles about assessment generated during the DevalS Project undertaken by two groups of students taking the module in two consecutive years. Whilst both the APREVAL and EDECOM projects focused on assessment, the Spanish students used EvalCOMIX® in their normal module (Project Management) as part of their degree course.

## The Views of the Students Who Experienced the APREVAL and EDECOM Training Courses

As part of the DevalSimWeb Project two training courses were developed aimed at undergraduates: the APREVAL course for first year students and the EDECOM course for final year students. The APREVAL course develops students' assessment skills by introducing them to the key principles and aspects of assessment. The main aim of the EDECOM course was to establish a link between university education and the world of work.

On completion of the training courses the students voluntarily responded to a questionnaire about EvalCOMIX®. The questionnaire was designed to obtain the students' overall views on the value of EvalCOMIX® and its use. Table 4 shows the distribution of the 110 respondents of which 38 were first year undergraduates (APREVAL course) and 72 were final year students (EDECOM course).

In terms of the results, the primary focus in this case is on those aspects that relate specifically to the collaborative nature of the assessment. That is, those aspects through which the collaboration or participation of students in the assessment can be inferred.

Figure 16 presents the results based on responses from 110 students. They show that students express a high degree of agreement with the notion that EvalCOMIX® "encourages self-assessment" (M=5.6, SD =1.09) as well as "peer assessment" (M=5.34, SD=1.04). Furthermore, students feel that the EvalCOMIX® programme is very useful for "encouraging student participation in assessment" (M=5.41, SD=0.94), "it provides students with information about the results of their assessment" (M=5.26, SD=1.12) and "it develops students' assessment skills" (M=5.46, SD=0.86).

In order to analyse the differences in views dependent upon the university the students studied at (PUCESI, UdeA, UCR, UNA) or the training course they undertook (APREVAL or EDECOM), various contrastive tests were applied. Non parametric tests were used (Mann-Wihitney and Kruskal–Wallis

*Table 4. Distribution of the sample of students by gender, university and training course*

| | n | % |
|---|---|---|
| **Gender** | | |
| Male | 45 | 40.9 |
| Female | 65 | 59.1 |
| **University** | | |
| PUCESI (Ecuador) | 38 | 34.5 |
| UdeA (Colombia) | 40 | 36.4 |
| UCR (Costa Rica) | 23 | 20.9 |
| UNA (Nicaragua) | 9 | 8.2 |
| **Training Course** | | |
| APREVAL | 38 | 34.5 |
| EDECOM | 72 | 65.5 |

*Figure 16. Students' views on the APREVAL and EDECOM training courses*

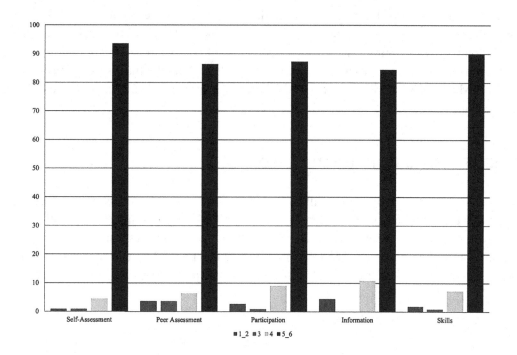

tests) because the items are ordinal level measurements and are not adjusted to a normal distribution (Kolmogorov–Smirnov test, $p<0.01$).

It was found that for the five elements analysed (self-assessment, peer assessment, participation, information and skills) there were no statistically significant differences between the students' opinions in relation to the university they attended, or the training course they had completed.

## The Views of Students Taking Business and Economics Modules

In relation to the application of the focus and strategies as proposed in the DevalS project, the results of the opinions of the 108 students taking the Business Administration and Management and Finance and Accounting degrees at the University of Cádiz are of particular interest. They used the EvalCOMIX® programme in their Project Management module (Rodríguez-Gómez & Ibarra-Sáiz, 2016). Table 5 gives the distribution of results from this particular group by gender and academic year in which the responses were obtained.

The results obtained when asking students on the Business Administration and Management and Finance and Accounting degrees about their experience using the EvalCOMIX® programme for self- and peer assessment are presented in Figure 17. They show that students indicate a high level of agreement that using EvalCOMIX® was "useful for providing in advance information about the assessment instruments and criteria as well as the specific aspects that would be assessed" (M=4.65, SD=1.09). They also say that EvalCOMIX® was "simple and easy to use" (M=4.61; SD=1.10); and "valuable because the information it provides helps to improve subsequent tasks or activities" (M=4.50, SD=1.14); "motivational as you get access to self-assessment, peer assessment and the tutor's assessment rapidly and all together" (M=4.49, SD=1.17) and, finally, it is seen as an environment that is "user-friendly and intuitive" (M=4.24; SD=1.19).

## SOLUTIONS AND RECOMMENDATIONS

The results contained within this chapter all indicate favourable views from lecturers, students and university coordinators on the advantages offered by the EvalCOMIX® programme. Above all they confirm that a key feature is its ease of use. They also highlight its facility for designing and constructing assessment instruments. Furthermore, the responses show it can be used by teachers, tutors and students alike, both individually and in groups, and it also provides for participative assessment methods. It can

*Table 5. Distribution of students by gender and academic year*

|  | n | % |
|---|---|---|
| **Gender** | | |
| Male | 45 | 41.66 |
| Female | 63 | 58.33 |
| **Academic Year** | | |
| 2012-13 | 44 | 40.70 |
| 2013-14 | 64 | 59.25 |

*Figure 17. Students' views on the usefulness of the EvalCOMIX® programme for self- and peer assessment*

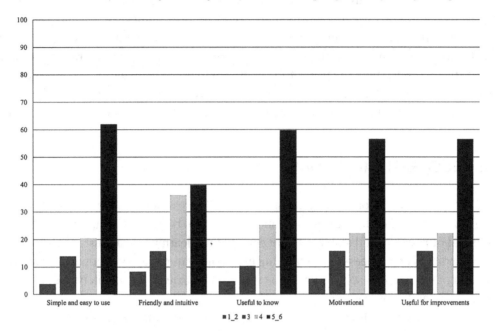

be seen, therefore, that the EvalCOMIX® web-based programme provides information on the results of all aspects of assessment in a useful and rapid manner. Furthermore, these features are consistent with the notion of assessment as learning and empowerment, therefore enabling full student participation in the assessment process and decisions to be taken based on the results obtained.

Increasing numbers of Higher Education institutions are incorporating technology into their courses by way of virtual campuses or learning platforms that enable students to follow their courses in ever simpler and more convenient ways. It is also true that, in many cases, particularly for blended courses where attendance is minimal, virtual campuses represent a repository of materials combined, to a greater or lesser extent, with communication tools. The emphasis within these contexts is primarily on the content, on breaking the traditional constraints of space and time, to enable access by greater numbers of students, etc., but without changing the way the assessment of student work, outputs or products are dealt with, meaning they retain only a passive role in the overall assessment process.

Technology offers many advantages but it is how and for what it is used that really determines whether it represents a help or hindrance to student learning. As suggested above, student learning is enabled through the design and implementation of high quality assessment tasks in which students participate actively, where both feedback and feedforward are provided by the tutors and students alike and in which participative modes of assessment are used, such as self- and peer assessment or co-assessment. Technology should be used to simplify and speed up this process.

Within a university context and in accordance with the parameters of the concept of assessment as learning and empowerment the EvalCOMIX® web programme delivers valuable results and demonstrates its viability and usefulness. The results following its implementation clearly demonstrate the possibilities it offers but certain assessment practices do need to be modified in order to exploit its full potential.

We are now faced with two distinct challenges if we want to make further progress. The first is how to implement current best practice in assessment to provide students with an active and participative role in their assessment that merges learning and assessment. The second challenge concerns encouraging students' active participation using technological tools. Both challenges require training be undertaken by tutors and students alike, both in terms of the approach to assessment and the use of the technology that delivers these assessment methods. In order to fully resolve these issues comprehensive institutional responses that acknowledge the advances being made in the field of assessment are now required.

## FUTURE RESEARCH DIRECTIONS

Boud (2016) proposes, among other things, that the focus of assessment practices needs to change when considering the future. Rather than relying on static data it would be better to focus our efforts on harnessing the potential of assessment that exploits the potential of "learning analytics". We should not think of assessment in terms of a process for identifying excellence but rather for recognising difference and, instead of seeing assessment as something that is isolated or carried out separately, we should conceive it as being an integral part of learning.

In line with the approaches advanced by Ibarra-Sáiz, Rodríguez-Gómez & Olmos-Miguelάñez (In press) one proposal is to develop a package of information about assessment (Unieval) that is created within a Moodle environment (Figure 18). It will be structured in two blocks (EvalCOMIX® and Gescompeval®) through which all the skills to be developed and assessed on any module or degree course will be linked and connected to the assessment instruments to enable the tracking of students' skills development in a fully dynamic way. This would combine the features of EvalCOMIX® with the tracking options provided by Gescompeval®.

A technological development such as the one described above would enable, firstly, tutors to undertake simple, rapid and dynamic monitoring of the students' skills levels. Secondly, it would provide students with feedback and feedforward about their performance in a way that is flexible, rapid and easy to understand. As a result, it would help develop their ability to make value judgements, a key aspect of lifelong learning.

*Figure 18. Diagram of the assessment information package*
*Ibarra-Sáiz, Rodríguez-Gómez & Olmos-Miguelάñez, In press.*

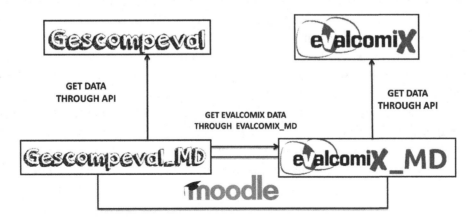

# CONCLUSION

This chapter presents some highly positive results based on the views of tutors and students regarding the use of EvalCOMIX® as part of the assessment process.

Such positive views relate, on the one hand, to its technical features such as ease of use and the user friendly environment it offers. Tutors reinforce this, maintaining the programme is transferable to all subject areas and modules and promotes collaboration in the creation of instruments and their modification to adapt them to different situations. The users' views also highlight that EvalCOMIX® delivers transparency in assessment, making criteria public prior to assessment taking place. This feature provides guidelines for students which help them design and produce their assignments or activities in line with the elements and criteria they will be assessed against. This, in turn, develops their self-regulation of their learning and continual improvements in their work. We would also highlight students' positive views regarding motivation and involvement in assessment which occur as a consequence of the speed with which they gain access to the details of their progress and results. At the same time, and in line with the notion of assessment as learning and empowerment, it is important to acknowledge the value they place on the information they acquire from self- and peer assessment, as well as from their tutors, that enables them to improve their performance.

Based on the results presented here and from other studies, we believe that EvalCOMIX® represents more than just an online assessment package. Its use, on the one hand, promotes student participation in assessment by identifying and defining criteria, creating instruments and participating in self- and peer assessment processes. On the other hand, students receive useful and relevant information about their performance and progress in a way that enables them to improve both their learning process and subsequent results.

EvalCOMIX® is a web-based programme that supports the integration of learning and assessment. But, to achieve this, we must have the right approach to assessment. The full potential of EvalCOMIX® will only be exploited if we are able to introduce real innovation in assessment; making the assessment process more transparent, discussing and agreeing in advance the products and activities to be assessed and the criteria and instruments to be used; encouraging students' engagement in the assessment process; enabling feedback from tutors and students alike on the work they produce; and ensuring high quality tasks are used in assessment.

The EvalCOMIX® programme therefore offers valuable solutions and represents a viable and useful option for implementing coherent modes of assessment, such as assessment for learning and empowerment. It achieves this through the use of enabling technology in the assessment process which addresses two key challenges within the context of assessment.

If the programme is enhanced by adding newly developed applications based on the opportunities offered by learning analytics, as with the proposed assessment information package that integrates Eval-COMIX® and Gescompeval®, we will become fully aligned with the concept of delivering true lifelong learning to students.

# REFERENCES

Boud, D. (2000). Sustainable assessment: Rethinking assessment for the learning society. *Studies in Continuing Education, 22*(2), 151–167. doi:10.1080/713695728

Boud, D. (2016). *Current Influences on Changing Assessment: Implications for Research to Make a Difference*. Keynote presented at 8th Biennial Conference of EARLI SIG1: Assessment & Evaluation. Building bridges between assessment and evaluation. Munchen, Germany. Retrieved from https://goo.gl/1BvvNd

Boud, D., & Molloy, E. (2013). Rethinking models of feedback for learning: The challenge of design. *Assessment & Evaluation in Higher Education, 38*(6), 698–712. doi:10.1080/02602938.2012.691462

Boud, D., & Soler, R. (2016). Sustainable assessment revisited. *Assessment & Evaluation in Higher Education, 41*(3), 400–413. doi:10.1080/02602938.2015.1018133

Carless, D. (2007). Learning-oriented assessment: Conceptual basis and practical implications. *Innovations in Education and Teaching International, 44*(1), 57–66. doi:10.1080/14703290601081332

Dochy, F., Segers, M., & Sluijsmans, D. (1999). The use of self-, peer and co-assessment in higher education: A review. *Studies in Higher Education, 24*(3), 331–350. doi:10.1080/03075079912331379935

Eyal, L. (2012). Digital Assessment Literacy—the Core Role of the Teacher in a Digital Environment. *Journal of Educational Technology & Society, 15*(2), 37–49.

Falchikov, N. (2005). *Improving assessment through student involvement. Practical solutions for aiding learning in higher education and further education*. London: RoutledgeFalmer.

Ibarra-Saiz, M.S., & Rodríguez Gómez, G. (2014). Modalidades participativas de evaluación: Un análisis de la percepción del profesorado y de los estudiantes universitarios. *Revista de Investigación Educativa, 32*(2), 339-361. 10.6018/rie.32.2.172941

Ibarra-Sáiz, M. S., & Rodríguez-Gómez, G. (2016a). *Guía Innovar en evaluación en la Educación Superior*. Producción: EVALfor - Grupo de Investigación. España:Cádiz. Available in: https://dx.doi.org/10.13140/RG.2.1.3925.8488

Ibarra-Sáiz, M. S., & Rodríguez-Gómez, G. (2016b). *Evaluación de competencias en la Educación Superior. El momento de la tecnología y la alfabetización evaluadora. In E. Cano (Coord), Evaluación por competencias: la perspectiva de las primeras promociones de graduados en el EEES* (pp. 17–32). Barcelona: Octaedro.

Ibarra-Sáiz, M. S., Rodríguez-Gómez, G., & Olmos Migueláñez, S. (In press). Monitoring and information on skills development at university: A multiple-case study. In F.J. Garcia-Peñalvo (ed.), *Proceedings TEEM'16 Technological Ecosystems for Enhancing Multiculturality*. doi:10.1145/3012430.3012516

Nicol, D., Thomson, A., & Breslin, C. (2014). Rethinking feedback in higher education: A peer review perspective. *Assessment & Evaluation in Higher Education, 39*(1), 102–122. doi:10.1080/02602938.2013.795518

Price, M., Rust, C., O'Donovan, B., Handley, K., & Bryant, R. (2012). *Assessment literacy. The foundation for improving student learning*. Oxford, UK: Oxford Brookes University.

Reynolds, M., & Trehan, K. (2000). Assessment: A critical perspective. *Studies in Higher Education, 25*(3), 267–278. doi:10.1080/03075070050193406

Rodríguez-Gómez, G., & Ibarra-Saiz, M. S. (Eds.). (2011). e-Evaluación orientada al e-Aprendizaje estratégico en Educación Superior. Madrid: Narcea.

Rodríguez-Gómez, G., & Ibarra-Sáiz, M. S. (2015). Assessment as learning and empowerment: Towards sustainable learning in higher education. In M. Peris-Ortiz & J. M. Merigó Lindahl (Eds.), *Sustainable learning in higher education, innovation, technology, and knowledge management* (pp. 1–20). London: Springer-Verlag; doi:10.1007/978-3-319-10804-9_1

Rodríguez-Gómez, G., & Ibarra-Sáiz, M. S. (2016). *Guía Diseñar procedimientos de evaluación en la Educación Superior*. Producción: EVALfor - Grupo de Investigación. España:Cádiz. Available in: https://dx.doi.org/10.13140/RG.2.1.1844.9524

Taras, M. (2010). Student self-assessment: Processes and consequences. *Teaching in Higher Education, 15*(2), 199–209. doi:10.1080/13562511003620027

Taras, M. (2015). Student self-assessment: what have we learned and what are the challenges. *RELIEVE - E-Journal of educational Research, Assessment and Evaluation, 21*(1), art. ME8. DOI: 10.7203/relieve.21.1.6394

## ADDITIONAL READING

Bain, J. (2010). Integrating Student Voice: Assessment for Empowerment. *Practitioner Research in Higher Education 4* (1): 14–29. (https://goo.gl/p9ZkYt)

Cano, E., & Ion, G. (Eds.). (2016). *Innovative Practices for Higher Education Assessment and Measurement*. IGI Global.

Cubero-Ibáñez, J., Ibarra-Sáiz, M. S., & Rodríguez-Gómez, G. (2014, October). A proposal for skill evaluation via complex tasks in virtual learning environments. In *TEEM'14 Technological Ecosystems for Enhancing Multiculturality* (pp. 429–434). Universidad de Salamanca. España: Salamanca. Disponible en: http://teemconference.eu/2014/

Deneen, C., & Boud, D. (2014). Patterns of Resistance in Managing Assessment Change. *Assessment & Evaluation in Higher Education, 39*(5), 577–591. doi:10.1080/02602938.2013.859654

Hounsell, D., Blair, S., Falchikov, N., Hounsell, J., Huxham, M., Klampfleitner, M., & Thomson, K. (2007). *Innovative Assessment across the Disciplines: An Analytical Review of the Literature*. York: Higher Education Academy; https://goo.gl/se0eZj

Ibarra-Sáiz, M. S., & Rodríguez-Gómez, G. (2013, junio). El servicio web EvalCOMIX. Una herramienta para la retro y proalimentación en contextos de ubicuidad. In *2013 JUTE - XXI Jornadas Universitarias de Tecnología Educativa* (pp. 209–210). España: Valladolid Retrieved from http://www.jute2013.uva.es/Presentacion.html

Ibarra-Sáiz, M. S., & Rodríguez-Gómez, G. (2014). Modalidades participativas de evaluación: Un análisis de la percepción del profesorado y los estudiantes universitarios. *Revista de Investigación Educativa*, *32*(2), 339–361. doi:10.6018/rie.32.2.172941

Ibarra-Sáiz, M. S., & Rodríguez-Gómez, G. (2015, May). Integrating Practices of E-assessment as Learning: Possibilities of EVALCOMIX® Web Service in Higher Education. Paper presented at *The Asian Conference on Technology in the Classroom. ACTC-2015*. Japan: Kobe.

Ibarra-Sáiz, M. S., & Rodríguez-Gómez, G. (2015). Tecnologías para una evaluación participativa. La experiencia de uso de EVALCOMIX® en Ciencias Económicas y Empresariales. *Actas del XVII Congreso Internacional de Investigación Educativa: Investigar con y para la sociedad* (pp. 1889-1895). *AIDIPE 2015*. ISBN: 978-84-686-6906-9 España: Cádiz. Disponible en: http://www.aidipe2015.org

Ibarra-Sáiz, M. S., & Rodríguez-Gómez, G. (2015). *Conceptos básicos en Evaluación como aprendizaje y empoderamiento en la Educación Superior.* Cádiz: EVALfor - Grupo de Investigación. https://dx.doi.org/10.13140/RG.2.1.5070.5686

Ibarra-Sáiz, M. S., & Rodríguez-Gómez, G. (2016). EvalCOMIX®: A web-based programme to support collaboration in assessment. Paper accepted in *the 10th International Conference on E-Learning*. Portugal: Madeira, 1-3 July.

Ibarra-Sáiz, M. S., & Rodríguez-Gómez, G. (2016). *Guía Innovar en evaluación en la Educación Superior.* Cádiz: EVALfor - Grupo de Investigación. ISBN: 978-84-608-4483-9. https://dx.doi.org/10.13140/RG.2.1.3925.8488

Ibarra-Sáiz, M. S., & Rodríguez-Gómez, G. (2016). *Evaluación de competencias en la Educación Superior. El momento de la tecnología y la alfabetización evaluadora. En E. Cano (Coord). Evaluación por competencias: la perspectiva de las primeras promociones de graduados en el EEES* (pp. 17–32). Barcelona: Octaedro.

Kolb, A. Y., & Kolb, D. A. (2005). Learning Styles and Learning Spaces: Enhancing Experiential Learning in Higher Education, *Academy of Management Learning & Education, 4* (2), 193-212. (https://goo.gl/xlMtNe)(18/08/2016)

Mishra, P., & Koehler, M. J. (2006). Technological Pedagogical Content Knowledge: A Framework for Teacher Knowledge. *Teachers College Record*, *108*(6), 1017–1054. doi:10.1111/j.1467-9620.2006.00684.x

Peris-Ortiz, M., Alonso-Gómez, J., Vélez-Torres, F., & Rueda-Armengot, C. (Eds.). (2016). *Education tools for entrepreneurship*. London: Springer International Publishing. doi:10.1007/978-3-319-24657-4

Redecker, C. (2013). *The Use of ICT for Assessment of Key Competences. European Commission. Joint Research Centre.* Luxembourg: Institute for Prospective Tecnological Studies; doi:10.2791/87007

Rodríguez-Gómez, G., & Ibarra-Sáiz, M. S. (Eds.). (2011). e-Evaluación orientada al e-Aprendizaje estratégico en Educación Superior. Madrid: Narcea.

Rodríguez-Gómez, G., & Ibarra-Sáiz, M. S. (2015, August). ICT as a Facilitator of Self- and Peer Assessment: The case of EvalCOMIX®. Paper presented at *The 16th Biennial EARLI Conference for Research on Learning and Instruction*. Cypris: Lymassol.

Rodríguez-Gómez, G., & Ibarra-Sáiz, M. S. (2016). Towards sustainable assessment: ICT as a facilitator of self- and peer assessment. In M. Peris-Ortiz, J. Alonso-Gómez, F. Vélez-Torres, & C. Rueda-Armengot (Eds.), *Education tools for entrepreneurship* (pp. 55–71). Springer International Publishing; doi:10.1007/978-3-319-24657-4_5

Rodríguez Gómez, G., Ibarra Sáiz, M. S., & Cubero Ibáñez, J. (in press). Basic competences related to assessment: A study about university students' perception. *Educación XXI*. ISSN (VERSIÓN ELECTRÓNICA): 2174-5374. Available in: https://goo.gl/X3iC8X

Rodríguez-Gómez, G., Ibarra-Sáiz, M.S., & Gómez-Ruiz, M.A. (2011). e-Autoevaluación en la universidad. Un reto para profesores y estudiantes. Revista de Educación, (365), 401-430. doi: 10-4438/1988-592X-RE-2010-356-045.

Swaffield, S. (2014). Getting to the Heart of Authentic Assessment for Learning. *Assessment & Evaluation in Higher Education*, *18*(4), 433–449. doi:10.1080/0969594X.2011.582838

## ENDNOTES

[1]     EVALfor Research Group – *Assessment in formative contexts*. SEJ509 del Plan Andaluz de Investigación, Desarrollo e Innovación (PAIDI). http://www.evalfor.net/

[2]     EvalCOMIX® - Web Service for e-Assessment. http://evalcomix.uca.es/

[3]     DevalSimWeb Project – *Development of professional skills through participative assessment and simulation using web-based tools*. N° de contrato DCI-ALA/19.09.01/11/21526/264-773/ALFAIII (2011)-10. Programa de cooperación entre la Unión Europea y América Latina en materia de Educación Superior, ALFA III (2007-2013). Comisión Europea, Dirección General de Desarrollo y Cooperación, EuropaAid América Latina y el Caribe. Socios: Universidad de Cádiz (Coordinadora) (España), Durham University (United Kingdom), Pontifica Universidad Católica de Ecuador Sede Ibarra (Ecuador), Universidad de Antioquia (Colombia), Universidad de Costa Rica (Costa Rica) y Universidad Nacional Agraria (Nicaragua).

[4]     DevalS Project. *Development of sustainable e-Assessment – improving university student assessment skills using simulations*. Plan de Nacional de I+D+i. Ministerio de Economía y Competitividad. Ref. EDU2012-31804. Universidad de Cádiz (Coordinadora) (España), Universidad de La Rioja (España), Universidad Rovira i Virgili (España), Universidad de Salamanca (España), Universidad Sevilla (España) y Universidad de Valencia (España).

# Chapter 13
# Transformative Academic Development:
## Complexity and Convergence

**Kuki Singh**
*Edith Cowan University, Australia*

## ABSTRACT

*In a dynamically changing higher education environment, a deep understanding and facilitation of relevant and flexible academic development is vitally important organisationally. A qualitative case study methodology was employed to analyse the organisational positioning and design of academic development as a means of gaining insights into the needs, challenges and evolutionary trends occurring at one university. A non-linear organisational-level data analysis based on triangulation from document study, direct observation, and experiential and reflective knowledge, provided theoretical and practical insights into how academic development is embodied institutionally. A design perspective revealed the characterisation of an expanded remit, as complex, contradictory and complementary. The study concluded that new configurations in the practice of academic development are convergent in nature, integrating a transformative agenda representational of professional learning trends globally. An important implication this study raises is the mounting influence the application of smart technologies can play in the area of training and development within business organisations.*

## 1. INTRODUCTION

For nearly five decades academic development like many other features of university activity has been characterised by phenomenal change. An examination of these shifts provides insights into how the discipline has expanded as it has matured, making visible the variety of ways in which institutions have responded to national and global developments. The current wave of educational transformation establishes academic development as a dynamic area of university activity globally, due to an expanded and rapidly evolving scope of practice. Senior managers and academic developers are challenged to reconfigure organisational structures to reposition academic development and generate adaptive models and

DOI: 10.4018/978-1-5225-2492-2.ch013

innovative designs to operate effectively within internationalised higher education systems. This suggests an interesting relationship between educational transformation, complexity in the positioning and design of academic development, and how the field is evolving. This relationship is explored by linking to the literature variously referred to as educational development, faculty development, instructional development, professional development and academic development (Gosling, 2001), to analyse design and emerging practices contextually, using a case study approach.

Academic development is presented in scholarly literature from many perspectives, including as a profession, a sphere of activity, a leitmotif, a concern, and as an organisational structure. Regardless of perspective, academic development "at best remains elastic and flexible, and at worst, elusive and murky," according to Lebowitz (2014, p. 73). The expanding scope and nature of the field is represented in various definitions, for example, Candy (1996) who suggested it referred to "practices designed to enhance the academic performance of an institution of higher education" (p. 17). Whilst this still holds true many noted scholars have since contributed to this conversation (e.g., Boud, 1999; Boud & Brew, 2013; Gibbs, 2013; Gosling, 2001, 2009) bringing refinement in thinking with consideration of the evolutionary developments and examples that illuminate the variation of activities in terms of target, type, and mode of analysis. This chapter makes a further contribution to that conversation through scholarly analysis of the maturation of academic development at one institution as it has responded to organisational, national and global challenges. This analysis further reinforces the variable nature of academic development activities as it seeks to classify various strategies through the lens of different frameworks representing this sphere of activity as a combination of "old habits" and "disruptive practice" (Märtensson, 2015, p. 303). Through the analysis of one university context, the author shall demonstrate that this combination of traditional and disruptive techniques presents a complex and converging system characteristic of the conditions in which academics work and live in today.

In a higher education environment characterised by dynamic change, a deep understanding and facilitation of timely, relevant and flexible academic development is vitally important. In this chapter the author addresses this issue by characterising the positioning and design of academic development with supporting case examples. First, a structuralist lens is cast to analyse how academic development is embodied institutionally. Second, a design lens is employed to gain insight into the expanded and multifaceted remit contemporary academic development fulfils. Third, an evolutionary lens is adopted to make sense of ways in which academic development is changing in response to global trends. The implications the case raises are then discussed, followed by suggested areas for further research. Finally, speculative conclusions are drawn considering the relative insights gained about an emergent model of academic development.

## 2. BACKGROUND

Recognising that systems and practices differ from one country to another the issue of consistency in terminology deserves clarification. In this chapter, the term 'academic development' is used to refer to the actions planned and undertaken by those working with teaching academics to facilitate their acquisition of new skills and knowledge that can be applied to their teaching, improved performance and development, and in the promotion of scholarship (AITSL, 2014; Gosling, 2001). The term 'higher education' is used to refer to what is otherwise commonly referred to in the literature as tertiary education, post compulsory education and university education. The term 'teacher' is used to refer to academics with responsibility for teaching, otherwise referred to as academic staff, lecturers, tutors, instructors and faculty. The term 'course' is used to refer to what is sometimes referred to as a unit or a subject, offered over a fixed duration (e.g., semester, trimester, etc.) in a university teaching setting.

To properly understand the developments and associated challenges confronting academic development today, it is necessary to draw connections to three influences that have wrought higher education generally, and academic development consequently with changing demands, changing regulatory frameworks, changing modes of organising, and changing modes of practice. These issues, namely massification in education, internationalisation and technological advancements, have meant that education products and services are differentiated to market needs, globally, regionally and locally. Higher education systems have expanded at an unprecedented rate this century. Globally, enrolments increased from 100 million in 2000 to 177.6 million in 2010, and growth to 414.2 million by 2030 is projected, with the majority of enrolments located in developing regions (Calderon, 2012). Massive and rapid increases in growth have meant that universities in some countries are experiencing various levels and cycles of transition and development, supported by diminishing government funding and with emerging private sector funding in some countries (e.g., Brazil and Indonesia). Although most countries have developed national qualifications frameworks and established external quality assurance mechanisms, quality remains a significant concern in the face of unprecedented growth. Both quality enhancement and world rankings are significant drivers for change. A further challenge relates to staffing issues such as shortages in some countries (e.g., China, India), unattractive salaries (e.g., Brazil), and quality and qualification levels of academic staff. Graduate unemployment poses a further challenge in many countries, arguably linked to the economic crisis in the developed economies, and attributable to the education-skill mismatch in some of the developing economies (e.g., India, Indonesia, and Russia). These combined effects of massification in higher education places new demands on institutions and consequently academic development. For instance an expanded role in quality enhancement, knowledge and skills development of teachers aligned to pedagogies associated with mode and scale, and institutional positioning are some of the issues for consideration.

Internationalisation of higher education is notable for the multiple ways in which it has manifested itself globally. Whilst globalisation refers to the broad economic, technological and scientific trends affecting higher education, internationalisation in the higher education context is about the specific policies and programs undertaken by governments, education systems and institutions to deal with globalization (Jarvis, 1999). Although each local, national and regional context presents unique characteristics, several broad internationalisation trends are discernible, including mobility of people, programs, and institutions; growth in collaborative research; evolving curricula and pedagogies; a heightened sense of interconnectedness of higher education; proliferation of internationalisation across institutions; and broadening systems of higher education (Altbach, Reisberg, & Rumbley, 2009). Australia, like United States of America, the UK and other European countries has played a major role in the higher education export industry (Australian Government, 2015; Drew & Klopper, 2014; Marginson, 2011; Universities Australia, 2015). To maintain competitive advantage governments have instituted national quality agendas such as Tertiary Quality Standards Agenda (TEQSA) in Australia, to establish regulatory standards (e.g., Higher Education Standards Framework) for provider organisations about the nature of learning linked to the awarding of qualifications, quality of teaching and learning, quality of research, and quality of information provided to stakeholders (TEQSA, 2011). This move to a standards approach in combination with government funding policies is placing pressure on universities and their quality and service centres, and ultimately on individual teachers to align their quality agendas and their practices, thus signaling ways in which internationalisation is influencing the evolution of academic development.

Whilst the above-mentioned developments in internationalisation have created exciting opportunities in higher education there are risks and challenges inherent in this complex and fluid environment. Institutions are constrained to exercise innovative and strategic thinking to transform themselves and remain competitive and relevant, with consequent effects on academic development strategy and practice organisationally. For instance, international cooperation to assure quality in transnational programs, participation of geographically dispersed teachers with divergent qualifications, educational background and skills in academic development programs, promotion of curriculum and pedagogic innovation in fast-paced competitive programs, and ongoing support for quality teaching across multiple locations, time zones, and modes, with diminishing resources are some of the issues confronting academic development in internationalised higher education systems.

Technological advancements have profoundly changed higher education globally and will continue to do so at a rapid pace. Blended learning approaches are being adopted more widely and significant structural change for institutions is predicted for the next five years (NMC Horizon Report 2016) (Johnson et al., 2016). This industry report further predicts that at all levels, technological change, including the adoption of new technologies in higher education, will continue to be driven by student demand but also by educational leadership, policy change, and changing practices in education. This is evident as many universities worldwide are reshaping themselves to better suit technology- influenced student demands. Alongside these shifts, knowledge of the new affordances provided by ICT in learning environments (e.g., speed, non-linearity, and multimodality) (Conole & Dyke, 2004) has increased the complexity of pedagogical reasoning that teachers need to apply in their teaching, influencing academic development (Day & Lloyd, 2007). In this dynamic environment, the organisational positioning, and foci of academic development is not only expanded but importantly, must assume a transformative mission in keeping with institutional change. Critical opportunities for academic development revolve around advocating and facilitating pedagogic shift through changes in policy and practice (i.e., quality assurance), embedding technology within academic practice itself (i.e., inspiring and modelling cultural change), and supporting and monitoring teaching (i.e., quality enhancement). Resourcing and transitional change are likely concerns in some institutional settings.

In summary, several developments brought by massification, internationalisation and technological advancements, have contributed to evolutionary shifts in academic development, characterised by its positioning organisationally and an expanded range of activities. This extended remit is multifaceted, involving: contributing to policy development, supporting teachers in the enhancement of teaching quality and student learning and engagement; exploring through research how professional development programs inform pedagogic practice; and supporting and monitoring promotion pathways based on teaching quality. Alongside these developments opportunities to tackle a number of tensions have arisen, including perceived barriers to enhancement of teaching, strategic positioning of academic development within university management structures, and role identity of academic developers (Gosling, 2008; Jones & Wisker, 2012). Overall, the significance of academic development within the university sector has been strengthened, despite challenges associated with staffing cuts, redeployment and rationalisation due to funding cuts. Consequently, in some universities academic development centres are still faced with uncertainty in their funding, location, identity and purpose (Drew & Klopper, 2013; Jones & Wisker, 2012). So whilst it is useful to recognise the strengthening potential of recent developments, there remain tough challenges that contradict the current emphasis on the student experience, student engagement and quality learning and teaching, potentially limiting a transformative impact (Drew & Klopper, 2013; Gosling, 2008; Jones & Wisker, 2012).

The developments described above locate academic development within dynamic "socio-material webs" (Stewart, Schifter, & Markaridian Selverian, 2010), implying that it is no longer sufficient, nor helpful to conceive of academic development as a clearly distinguishable, individualised, event-based professional learning activity. In this chapter the author argues that increasingly contemporary academic practice is influenced by multiplicities stemming from regulatory standards, quality indicators, converged university governance, personal agency, emergent knowledge practices arising from technological affordances and rich learning contexts, which are transforming its institutional positioning, location, orientation, purpose, and foci. The thesis this chapter presents is that an expanded academic development remit has ushered evolutionary shifts presently characterised by a set of dualistically principled features making possible highly divergent customisable products. Case study examples are employed to present the characterisation of a new wave of academic development as complex, based on design principles for 21$^{st}$ century learning, and supported by smart technologies.

## 3. SITUATING ACADEMIC DEVELOPMENT IN THE CONTEXT OF GLOBAL TRENDS IN PROFESSIONAL LEARNING

The preceding characterisation of academic development presents professional learning as a significant element within university systems, hence situating it within global trends occurring in professional learning provides a meaningful perspective for understanding not just how it has changed, but also, its complexity. An international study conducted by Innovation Unit on behalf of AITSL (2014), an Australian government funded organisation surmises that a new generation of professional learning is rapidly transforming organisations. Based on an extensive analysis of 50 cases, including universities, this study determined that common features of contemporary professional learning include: collaboration amongst participants; a blended mode of delivery; personalisation; informality; individualised and self-directed learning; incentivisation by the organisation; a culture of high expectations; and close alignment of individual development and organisational goals. This study also found formal programs, mandatory and certified participation were less evident in contemporary professional learning. A synthesis of these features resulted in the determination of five trends (see Table 1) that characterise professional learning and performance and development (AITSL, 2014). The AITSL (2014) study further maps a possible three-tier developmental pathway across the individual criteria, representing existing practice, the next wave of developments and radical innovation on the horizon. it is clear is that the pervasiveness of smart technologies in society and their uptake within business organisations are having a transformative impact on professional learning.

These criteria present an interesting characterisation of modern professional learning. Firstly, features presumed to be in tension with each other (e.g., formal vs informal; self-directed vs facilitated; required vs offered, etc.) emerge as complementary and mutually reinforcing. Secondly, self-directed projects and independent online learning contribute significantly to growing the knowledge base and cultivating a positive cultural climate organisationally. Thirdly, despite the high degree of agency exercised by individuals in pursuing their own needs and motivations, the organisation grows and learns as its people do. Fourthly, with a recognition that professional learning is occurring both inside and outside organisations in unregulated and minimally structured (online) spaces, organisations are beginning to employ

*Table 1. Five trends in professional learning and performance and development*

| Trend | Features |
|---|---|
| Integrated | Professional learning and performance and development are closely connected, and are embedded within organizational culture and practice. |
| Immersive | Intensive, holistic experiences that challenge beliefs and values, and radically alter practice. |
| Design-led | Disciplined, problem-solving processes that require deep understanding of and engagement with users. |
| Market-led | New providers stimulate demand and grow the market for new products and services. |
| Open | Ideas and resources are freely exchanged in unregulated online environments. |

Adapted from AITSL, 2014.

similar principles to host sessions that promote innovation whilst retaining social capital. Principally, this conceptualisation of professional learning is aligned with various ways in which academic development is being conceptualised in recent years – as authentic, practice-based, embedded, experiential, situated, and relational (Boud & Brew, 2013; Loads & Campbell, 2015; Singh, 2014).

The specific ways in which the features of innovative professional learning are harnessed locally within universities will ultimately determine the 'look and feel' of academic professional learning organisationally, and consequently will shape its potential impacts on student learning and teacher development, reinforcing a conceptualisation of academic development as a valued and varied entity.

## 4. ACADEMIC DEVELOPMENT: A VALUED AND VARIED ENTITY

As intimated in the background discussion, several researchers have sought to explain the evolutionary changes in academic development and the implications for practice in modern universities. Systematic reviews conducted by researchers such as Amundsen and Wilson (2012), Boud (1999), Boud and Brew (2013), Brew (1999, 2002), Gibbs (2013), Gosling (2008, 2009), Levinson-Rose and Menges (1981), Steinert et al. (2006), and Stes, Min-Leliveld, Gijbels, & Van Petegem, (2010), amongst others have illuminated a global perspective on academic development. Collectively, the research literature points to the valued status academic development holds within universities currently, evidenced by developments such as recognition of excellence in teaching, introduction of mandatory teacher preparation courses for new staff, formal accreditation of academic development programs, and the advancement of research into teaching and learning in higher education. These relatively recent achievements suggest that academic development has the dual responsibility of effectively supporting the changes that are occurring in teaching and learning, and strategically influencing systemic change to build capacity and advance organisational goals.

The strategic importance and purpose of academic development units has been demonstrated in Gosling's (2008, 2009) research on academic development practice in the UK. Similarly a New Zealand study revealed an extensive provision of teaching development programs that are variable in structure, type and outcomes (Ako Aotearoa, 2010). Likewise in the United States of America, academic development is highly varied incorporating self-directed activities, formal teaching development activities and organisational development strategies targeting change and cultural shift (Caffarella & Zinn, 1999). In Australia, academic development is available at all universities and is highly varied in its organisation, provision, intended audience, institutional support and resourcing (Ling, 2009).

Collectively, the above-mentioned studies have shown significant variation in the positioning and design of academic development within universities. Teaching development activities vary in scope, content, delivery mode, intended outcomes and audience. They can be formal or informal, short or extended, planned or *ad hoc*, and delivered face-to-face or online. Furthermore they may be centrally designed and delivered, decentralised at faculty, school, unit or department level, organised through professional associations or fostered through collaborative peer mentoring or partnership arrangements. Overall, there is a consensus that the advancement of teaching within universities is built upon strong financial provision, supportive policies, flexible structures and a combination of academic development strategies, and is therefore supported or hindered by factors in the four domains that have been hitherto represented – institutional structures, intellectual and psychosocial characteristics, people and interpersonal relationships, and personal considerations and commitments. Previous studies (e.g., Boud, 1999; Brew, 1995; Gibbs, 2013) have thus stressed the need for academic development to be underpinned by research, scholarship and evidence-based practice, as embodied in the current work.

## 5. A TRANSFORMATIONAL ORIENTATION

As discussed in the background section, expansion of a new educational paradigm resultant from the combined effects of massification, internationalisation and accelerated technological advancement is prompting universities and academic developers in particular to rethink the positioning and design of academic development to advance the strategic goals of institutions.

Several interrelated factors characterising educational transformation globally are extending the complex array of knowledge and skills that academic development is challenged to address, whilst also stimulating rethinking around the strategies it employs. First, the expectation that learning carries on throughout life affects teachers as much as their students, potentially accelerating the need for ongoing professional development. Second, massification in higher education has led to extraordinary growth and heterogeneity in students domestically and internationally, contributing to larger classes and greater diversity of learning needs. Third, advancements in information and communication technologies have made content ubiquitous reshaping student expectations about their learning experience. Fourth, technological change has intensified sector growth by enabling varied educational delivery modes (e.g., online, blended and real- time distribution), and expanding national and transnational educational partnerships and programs with varied sources of funding, a complex array of course delivery and quality assurance models and practices, and increased diversity amongst teachers. Fifth, changes in employment practices have resulted in intensification of casualisation and role differentiation in the academic workforce (Percy et al., 2008; Smith & Coombe, 2006). In addition to the three-tier structure of academic appointments (i.e., based on tenure, continuing fractional status, and casual status), the role has been 'unbundled' at a number of universities in Australia and elsewhere (e.g., UK, US and Europe) differentiating 'teaching focused' (also referred to as 'education focused' and 'teaching scholar') and 'research' roles, potentially increasing the expectation for more targeted academic development and often with diminishing resources (Leisyte, 2013; Locke, 2014; Probert, 2013).

The aforementioned trends either explicitly or implicitly is bringing greater urgency and an expanded remit to academic development work, thus impacting the evolution, positioning, and design of academic development, advancing a transformational orientation. For instance, a wider range of programs must be available to assure continual learning and development, and these must be delivered across multiple locations; be available to academics teaching across different sites with vastly different technology infrastructures and facilities; be offered in different modes of delivery and in multiple study cycles throughout the year; and be customised to suit varying academic roles. Furthermore, given the increased diversity amongst teachers, academic development design must be cognisant of highly varied conceptions of teaching and learning and skills. In this dynamic educational climate, the organisational positioning of academic development is complex. It may be located centrally, or dispersed (in transnational sites, faculties, schools, disciplines) or take on a hybrid structure. Intellectually, academic development might be positioned in terms of a focus on content, ongoing professional learning, or a combination of both. Contextually, academic development might position teaching as individual practice, as being socially situated within teaching areas, or as a combination of both. Added to the challenges arising from such complex positioning within institutions, the design of academic development practice can vary considerably as the need to integrate multiple foci (e.g., skills, methods, reflection) increases. The way in which the discipline is responding to these changing conditions is shaping an interesting evolutionary trajectory. To explore these issues contextually a case study analysis follows.

## 6. THE RESEARCH PROCESS

The research question this study sought to address is, 'How is academic development practice evolving within a complex and rapidly changing higher education context?' A qualitative case study methodology was deemed appropriate to analyse the organisational positioning and design of academic development as a means of gaining insights into the evolutionary trends occurring at one university. Case study research serves "the desire that arises out of the desire to understand complex social phenomena" because this strategy allows the investigator to "retain the holistic and meaningful characteristics of real-life events," such as organisational and managerial processes (Yin, 2003, p. 2). It is a preferred method "when the investigator has little control over events", and "when the focus is on a contemporary phenomenon within some real-life context" (p. 5). This research method enabled a contextual focus providing a descriptive case that is analytically generalizable to theoretical propositions.

The boundaries determining the breadth and depth of the study were limited to a study of formal, event-based academic development activities organised centrally and locally, focusing on format, duration, content, and outcomes. Data from multiple sources including documentation, archival records, direct observation, physical artifacts and experiential knowledge (of the author as an academic developer employed at the university) informed the study. Theoretical analysis and reflective practice further strengthened the investigation.

The research process adopted a non-linear organisational-level data analysis technique making it possible to make sense of changes that did not necessarily progress in one direction, and to recognise that the current cycle of change is not an end point but an ongoing process that will continue to be shaped by future developments. A 'researcher-as-practitioner' approach enriched the analysis allowing context-specific and experiential knowledge to guide the study. Data collection and analysis evolved iteratively, whereby qualitative data obtained through multiple sources supported a chain of evidence strategy and facilitated triangulation. Thematic data analysis proceeded by initially categorizing, then tabulating, and recombining evidence. Qualitative content analysis was undertaken using coding, summarizing, explicating, and structuring. These processes supported pattern matching, explanation building, time-series analysis, and cross-case synthesis (Yin, 2003). These analytical techniques led the researcher to establish connections with the theoretical propositions that guided the investigation. Organisation of the data into themes representing their theoretical 'fit' is shown in Tables 2-6.

Whilst the inductive and experiential process employed in this study articulates a pragmatic perspective as a form of personal theory building (Schön, 1987), the relevance of the study and the contribution it makes to the wider community lies in its application of existing theoretical frameworks to make sense of situated practice. The new learning this process has yielded is necessarily iterative, or in Dewey's (1910) words, employs "suspended judgment" (p. 74). Accepting there is no genuine endpoint in case study analysis, the present work is but a snapshot of how things are currently.

## 7. THE CASE STUDY

The case under investigation is an Australian university with an enrolment of 62 000 highly diverse students dispersed over several onshore and offshore sites engaged in face-to-face, blended or fully online course delivery. The university is rapidly modernising the teaching and learning infrastructure to support its strategic transforming learning agenda. Two thousand academics are employed in full-time tenured (59%), part-time ongoing (11%), and casual (30%) appointments, classified as either teaching-focused, teaching-research, or research positions (Curtin University, 2015).

Characterisation of the 'problem' in the case study emerged through a systematic process of content reflection. Historical expansion of the top-down approach to academic development resulted in a proliferation of 2198 centrally and locally organised activities annually, provided by 177 areas within the university (Marks, 2013), creating challenges associated with co-ordination, participation, sustainability, and alignment with current strategic goals. Further, despite demonstrated benefits the dominant event-based academic development model appeared increasingly misaligned with the complexity that characterises the rapidly changing, diverse and dispersed teaching and learning environment described earlier. Also, a lag between organisational structures and academic development policy in relation to the pace of educational transformation and the accompanying urgency for teachers to develop new skills to teach effectively in 21$^{st}$ century learning environments is evident. In an effort to improve co-ordination and reduce costs the university recently brought all centralised academic development services under the control of a newly established unit, which is systematically integrating an experiential learning paradigm to enrich the academic development experience and outcomes. However, this seemingly positive restructure might lack the agility needed to respond to varied and localised needs in a fast-paced, dispersed teaching environment, and the author surmises that more substantial and wide-scale transformation is needed to reinvigorate academic development in this setting.

In summary, the problem is conceptualised as follows. The heavily centralised positioning of academic development only partially addresses the situated nature of academic development (i.e., within Faculties, Schools, departments, within professional organisations, and in informal networks); the embedded nature of professional learning in everyday work is neglected; policy and practice lacks the agility needed to effectively serve a culturally diverse and geographically distributed organisational environment; new technologies are less than optimally leveraged to extend access and flexibility; and perhaps the most critical of all is the perplexing cultural climate increasingly characterised by mostly enthusiastic, but change weary, time poor and employment insecure teachers. These issues are explored as complexities in the characterisation of academic development in this case.

# 8. COMPLEXITIES IN CHARACTERISING TRANSFORMATIVE ACADEMIC DEVELOPMENT

To gain a situated understanding of the nature of academic development the researcher sought to classify academic development along the three dimensions commonly reported in the literature – format (e.g., workshop, seminar, accredited course), outcomes (e.g., self reports of attitudinal change, observed behaviour) and duration (e.g., once off events versus long term events) (see Table 2). The format of academic development activities varied from lectures and information sessions, to workshops, seminars, and practical demonstrations, compounded by further differentiation by delivery mode (i.e., predominantly face-to-face, with some blended, and online elements). Similarly, classification by outcome demonstrated that activities varied from gaining technical skills, to mastering specific techniques and methods, learning that emanated from extended periods of reflection on practice, and action learning. This proved problematic as there was difficulty in separating outcomes from the learning designs in which they are embedded. Classification by duration revealed substantial variation in the number of sessions, contact hours, and length of programs. Hence, none of these classification mechanisms supported meaningful mapping of academic development institutionally because of significant variation in purpose, content, and quality. Consequently, it was determined that differentiation by format, outcome and duration are blunt instruments for describing academic development practice in the case study due to insufficient attention to the situational factors that shape academic development.

Amundsen and Wilson's (2012) theoretical framework of overlapping contrasts was then usefully applied to deepen understanding of academic development organisationally, philosophically and pedagogically. This analytical structure facilitated mapping by "location" (i.e. centralised location or decentralised

*Table 2. Inherent problems in classifying academic development according to format, outcomes and duration*

| Classification criteria | Challenges |
|---|---|
| Format | Activities varied from lectures and information sessions, to workshops, seminars, and practical demonstrations, compounded by further differentiation by delivery mode (i.e., face-to-face, blended, and online). |
| Outcomes | Activities varied from gaining technical skills, to mastering specific techniques and methods, learning that emanated from extended periods of reflection on practice, and action learning. |
| Duration | Variation in the number of sessions, contact hours, and length of programs. |

location), "intellectual orientation" (i.e., focused on content or ongoing professional development), and "practice orientation" (i.e., teaching as individual practice or socially situated practice) (p. 108) (see Table 3).

Recent organisational restructuring and rationalisation of services have reshaped the positioning of academic development resulting in a strengthened central core and diminished peripheral support within faculties and schools. The establishment of a centralised unit with a remit to provide professional learning to improve teaching and learning quality, and promote innovation and student engagement has signalled strategic shifts. For instance, the separation of the professional development function from the broader teaching and learning support unit perhaps indicates the entrenchment of a corporate management style and communicates the perceived significance that professional development of teachers is integral to the educational transformation strategy. Furthermore, with a direct reporting line to the deputy vice chancellor (Teaching and Learning) and representation in the Senior Executive Team and the University Teaching and Learning Committee, the strategic influence of academic developed has been enhanced. Also, the transformation strategy has brought increased short term funding enabling expanded staffing and an increased volume of activity in academic development. Despite the above mentioned early gains in a strengthened central core, several challenges remain, including the existence of a centralised organisational development unit that has responsibility for staff development across the institution (including both academic and professional staff), thus signalling not just pockets of overlapping activity, but also significant paradigmatic differences. Other challenges include limited access to professional development by teachers located in transnational and regional sites, inadequate customisation to support highly varied academic roles, and a traditional pedagogic bias continues to embody academic development in the face of more contemporary approaches. Evidently, localised academic development varies widely in structure, organisation, purpose, audience, target group, and strategic alignment. It is reliant on advocacy by local experts, limited resources and is loosely aligned with other organisational development activities.

Philosophically, or in Amundsen and Wilson's (2012) terms, "intellectually" academic development is predominantly positioned to foster ongoing professional learning, although a content element is integrated in most centralised and decentralised programs to enable incorporation of policy compliance issues. A consequence of the entrenched traditional event-based model means that there is little if any systematic follow-up to assess transfer of learning to drive teaching developments, although there is a substantial evidence-base on participants' professional learning experience, obtained through evaluation surveys. Pedagogically (Amundsen & Wilson, 2012), formal academic development practice is predominantly positioned on a conception of teaching as individual practice. Although a conception of

*Table 3. Theoretical framework of overlapping contrasts to analyse academic development*

| Overlapping dimensions | Distinguishing features |
|---|---|
| Location | Centralised location and/or decentralised location. |
| Intellectual orientation | Focused on specific content and/or ongoing professional development. |
| Practice orientation | Focused on teaching as individual practice and/or as socially situated practice. |

Adapted from Amundsen & Wilson, 2012.

teaching practice as socially situated is emergent at the course team level, this is at best patchy, *ad hoc* and informal, rather than coordinated and strategic.

An analysis of the case study using Amundsen and Wilson's (2012) theoretical framework reveals that academic development has an overlapping rather than a polarised positioning in all three dimensions (see Table 4). The current positioning of academic development in the case study represents a legacy of evolutionary advances that characterise the discipline. The overlapping positioning in location, philosophical and pedagogic orientation highlights the complex and expanded remit that academic development is called upon to address in a rapidly transforming educational environment and signals challenges for contemporary practice.

A deeper understanding of the complexity that underpins contemporary academic development practice can be gained by casting a design perspective. Amundsen and Wilson's (2012) six dimensional (i.e., skills, methods, organisation, reflection, discipline, and action research) design framework offers a new way of thinking about increasingly complex designs that encompass multiple foci. This analytical tool enabled representation of the core characteristics and design coherence of different programs holistically. Programs were categorised as belonging to one of three structures – primary (n=12), occasional (n=1) and other (i.e. mainly self access digitised resource repositories) (n=5). A dual focus on process and outcome was merged into all programs, which individually embraced between four to six foci.

Amundsen and Wilson's (2012) framework was further applied to determine internal consistency and coherence at the program level. A deconstruction of individual programs was undertaken to determine internal consistency and coherence. Figure 1 presents an example showing one program (i.e., Foundations of University Teaching and Learning, *aka* Foundations). Foundations is a two and half day program aimed at academics who are new to the university, many of whom are new to teaching and employed as casual teachers. It is delivered multi-modally and available to academics in geographically dispersed locations.

Analysis of the Foundations program unravelled a complex and interleaving design with a dual focus on both process and outcome, and with characteristics from all six clusters represented to varying degrees (see Figure 1). Outcomes associated with the program are identified and anticipated ahead of time, and learning processes result in different outcomes for individual academics based on changed thinking that over time may lead to strategic teaching improvements. Participants are assessed individually over a period of 12-18 months using a collaborative peer review strategy and an evidence-based teaching portfolio.

*Table 4. Complex positioning of academic development in a contemporary university setting*

| Orientation | Overlapping contrasts in the positioning |
|---|---|
| Location | Centrally funded and located with direct executive responsibility to the vice chancellor (teaching and learning). Aligned to strategic goals. Decentralised management and funding in faculties and schools to meet localised needs. |
| Philosophical | An 'ongoing professional learning' orientation characterises most programs, plus integration of a 'content' orientation to foster policy compliance.<br>A 'content' orientation characterises technology / skills-based programs. |
| Practice | 'Teaching as an individual activity' is the dominant approach.<br>'Teaching as socially situated' is an emergent approach. |

*Figure 1. Internal consistency and coherence of one professional development program*

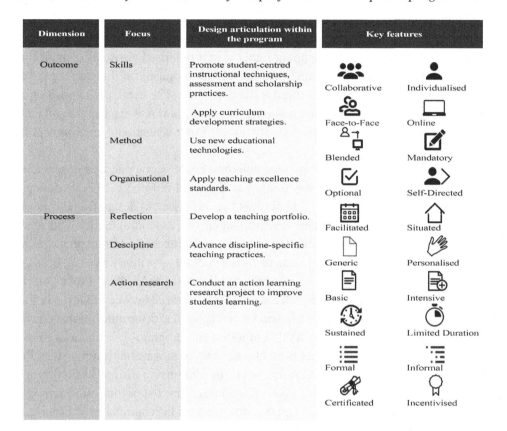

An analysis of one program demonstrates the complexity that typically characterises the design of formal centrally located academic development in the case study. In recent years the desire to extend the reach of centrally positioned academic development has been supplemented with a number of non-traditional academic development strategies, including electronic newsletters, curation of web-based teaching resources, self-access stand alone multimedia resources hosted on a teaching and learning website, online communities of practice to promote teaching excellence and innovation, faculty collaborations with early adopters of new technologies, and grants / scholarships to support 'lighthouse' projects (Singh, Schrape, & Kelly, 2012). An analysis of these emergent strategies similarly reflects complex and strategically aligned design principles (see Figure 1), but importantly also shines a light on the increased role academic developers are required to adopt in facilitating individual and organisational change (Smyth, 2003).

The above analysis reveals an evolutionary approach to academic development characterised by overlapping contrasts and a complex interleaving design with multiple foci customised to suit particular purposes, contexts, and target groups, representative of its maturational stage. Reflective of "a sub-set of change mechanisms in use" (Gibbs, 2013, p. 5), the present analysis reinforces Gibbs' argument that academic development evolves within an institution rather than simply continuing to grow and do more of the same kinds of activities. The expanded and diverse range of academic development activities evidences the progressive shifts onto different kinds of activities that have emerged with maturation.

The recent strategic shifts in location, philosophy and practice are representative of the trends proposed by Gibbs (2013), namely:

- A focus on the classroom to a focus on the learning environment.
- A focus on individual teachers to a focus on course teams, departments and leadership of teaching.
- A focus on teaching to a focus on learning.
- A focus on small, single, separate tactics to large, complex, integrated, aligned multiple tactics.
- A focus on change tactics to change strategies.
- A focus on quality assurance to quality enhancement.
- A focus on fine-tuning of current practice to transforming practice in new directions.

Whilst the above mentioned trends are visible, deeper critical analysis is necessary to determine the assuredness of the underpinning reasoning in this case scenario, in order to determine their 'fit' with the shifts suggested by Gibbs (2013), namely:

- A shift from a psychological to a sociological perspective.
- A shift from an atheoretical to a theoretical perspective.
- A shift from an experiential and reflective basis to a conceptual and empirical basis.
- A shift from unscholarly to scholarly practice.
- A shift from amateur practitioners to professionals.
- A shift from the organisational periphery to the central core.
- A shift from context neutral (blind) to context-and discipline sensitive.

From a pragmatic point of view, the combination of traditional and non-traditional academic development strategies has generated much support from teachers illuminating several practical benefits. Continuity in traditional formal, event-based, individual and collaborative professional development and long-standing informal strategies (e.g., informal professional practice conversations with colleagues) has reinforced "what is already known about [what works in] academic professional development" (Ferman, 2002, p. 147). Anecdotal reports and survey data has consistently shown that teachers value the networking, confidence-building and sharing practice opportunities that event-based academic development offers, despite regular criticism that such programs remain generic and lack sufficient contextualisation to foster transfer of learning easily, particularly amongst new to teaching and early career academics. It is proving challenging to manage this dual tension in centrally located academic development. Additionally, teachers have found the emergent academic development practices valuable for their flexibility, 'just-in-time', and 'information push' features, because they are suited to the increasingly complex routines that characterise the workplace, situating academic development as "authentic, practice-based,... transformative,... and a space for disruption" (Loads & Campbell, 2015, p. 355).

Based on escalating participation rates, it appears that teachers in this setting value technology mediated strategies that resonate with the way people 'interact, connect, create, and share' using social media. A recent study by McPherson, Budge and Lemon (2014) showed that the use of social media platforms such as Twitter can be a powerful force in building informal learning processes and social networks as part of academic development practices in a university setting. The informal technology based strategies used in the case study are proving powerful in engaging the diverse geographically dispersed cohort, free of the logistical constraints associated with event scheduling and less than satisfactory attendance in some

*Figure 2. Evolving approaches to professional development*

| Academic development strategies | Description | Orientation | Focus | Features customised to suit purpose, context, and target group |
|---|---|---|---|---|
| eNewsletters | Published monthly in a university blog as well as via a broadcast email to all staff. Topics on emerging educational technologies and their pedagogical applications are strategically selected to raise awareness and stimulate interest and influence practice. | Outcome Process | Skills, Method Reflection | Collaborative |
| Digitally Curated resources (Scoop.it) | Cloud-based content aggregation tools are used to provide new opportunities to quickly and easily organise, summarise and share (republish) information on topics of interest. | Outcome Process | Skills, Method Reflection, Discipline | Face-to-Face |
| Web resources | The centre's website is an information hub where staff can access multimedia resources and information, including good practice guides. | Outcome Process | Skills, Method Organisational, Reflection | Blended |
| Workshops | An extensive program focusing on the use of technologies & teaching strategies. | Outcome Process | Skills, Method Organisational, Reflection | Optional |
| Peer Learning Program | Work-embedded and situated mentoring partnerships involving observation and peer review of teaching. | Outcome Process | Skills, Method Reflection, Organisational Discipline | Facilitated |
| Open Door Teacher Program | Work-embedded and situated learning to model good teaching and share expertise within and across disciplines. | Process | Skills, Method Reflection, Organisational Discipline | Generic |
| Communities of practice | The iPad, eLReps and Peer Learning groups provide forums for collective informal learning. | Outcome Process | Skills, Method Reflection, Action learning | Basic |
| eScholars program | A strategic competitive grants scheme to advance the university's flexible learning goals, including innovation projects. | Outcome Process | Skills, Method Reflection, Action Research | Sustained |
| Teaching and Learning development projects | A strategic competitive grants scheme to advance the university's Transforming Learning strategic goals. | Outcome Process | Skills, Method Reflection Action Research | Formal |
| Cross department partnership projects | Co-hosted information sessions and demonstrations to promote innovation and enhance student experience. | Outcome | Organisational | Certificated |
| MakerSpace | Networking to foster innovation, collaboration and informal peer learning. | Outcome Process | Skills, Method Reflection Discipline | Individualised |
| Coffee Conversations | Informal discussions, networking and capacity building sponsored by experts/ leaders. | Process | Skills, Method Reflection, Discipline | Online |
| Social networking | Interest groups on specific topics are set up private and or 'public' social networks using the enterprise system Yammer as an instant messaging channel. | Process | Skills, Method Reflection, Discipline | Mandatory |
| Symposia | Opportunities for sharing best practice within faculties and university wide. | Outcome Process | Skills, Method Reflection, Discipline Organisational | Self-Directed |
| Teaching awards | Incentivised scheme for recognising and rewarding excellence, operating at faculty and university levels. Winners of university awards are nominated for the national award scheme. | Outcome Process | Skills, Method Reflection, Discipline Action research Organisational | Situated |
| National teaching and learning grants | Applications for national grants are processed. | Outcome Process | Skills, Method Reflection, Discipline Action research Organisational | Personalised |
| Hosted sessions led by enterprise technology vendors | Information and support sessions aimed to speed the adoption and migration of core and advanced learning technologies. | Process | Skills Organisational | Intensive |

Limited Duration

Informal

Incentivised

Fixed term

Continues

Self paced

Participatory

situations. Early career academics that are typically younger as well as their more experienced peers who are regular users of social media value these dynamic academic development strategies, and non-regular users of social media, are embracing the opportunity to develop their skill set. The incremental and situated nature of these strategies is leveraging opportunities to extend access to academic development in ways that are flexible and responsive to the specific needs of individual teachers and their students, without the constraints of location-based boundaries, and with the affordance of sustainability in a work intensive, diminishing resource climate, and importantly the fluidity of networked informal learning is proving to be a valuable learning space for inspiring transformative teaching and learning practices.

The combined academic development strategies employed in the case study context have increased the opportunities for teachers to regularly engage in professional development activity, consequently advancing an integrated transformative organisational strategy. Not only is the increased participation in academic development activity supporting staff employment confirmation and promotion require-ments (Chalmers, 2010; Drew & Klopper, 2013; Ferman, 2002), it is significantly generating a cultural shift towards adoption of modern approaches to teaching and learning as a means for improved student engagement. The combination of traditional and non-traditional academic development strategies reso-nates with the five-point transformative teacher professional development strategy recommended by Knowledge Delivery Systems – (1) Follow the research; (2) Go online; (3) But not online exclusively; (4) Allow self-pacing and collaboration; and Start right now (Crawford, 2015). The characteristics embedded in Crawford's strategy are seen in the extent to which the case study employs an approach to teacher professional development that is focused, based on colleagial learning, intensive, sustained and continuous, and analytical (i.e., informed currently by participation data and increasingly on outcomes data, with future plans to utlise learning analytics).

The developments described above signal a theoretical shift from an andragogical approach (Knowles, 1975, 1984; Kearsley, 2010) towards a heutagogical approach (Hase & Kenyon, 2000). In academic development andragogy has shaped conventional practice by determining '*what*' academics as learners need to know and '*how*' the knowledge and skills should be taught. This approach is no longer sufficient in a rapidly changing academic environment where information is easily accessible; nowadays 'academics as learners' must take a more active role in determining *what* and *how* their learning should take place. Heutagogy extends self-determined learning by recognising the intuitive, incidental and non-linear nature of learning, arguably generating a progression in the evolution of academic development in the case study. For example, the academic development designs that characterise the emergent strategies support the development of learner generated content, learner self-directedness in information discovery, peer information sharing and support, and individually determined learning pathways. Analytically, these strategies exhibit a set of core heutagogical features including, flexibility, activation of interest to learn in a novel way, reflection on *what* and *how* learning has occurred in relation to pre-existing beliefs and assumptions (i.e., double-loop learning), environmental scanning to situate practice, action learning and valuing experience and interaction with peers. Such non-linear learning designs facilitate a strengthen-ing of individual capabilities, support capacity building, and stimulate creativity and proactivity, thus, collectively representing a more fundamental shift towards holistic development of the individual that is both transformative, and strategically aligned with institutional goals.

The emergent academic development trends occurring in the case study represent an evolutionary shift that Boud (1999) proposed. Arguing that formalised academic development is located primar-ily in sites of academic practice where academic identity is formed and most powerfully influenced, Boud identifies six developmental phases: (1) development as embedded; (2) development as a moral imperative; (3) development as corporate policy; (4) development as multidimensional and distributed; (5) development as localised practice; and (6) development as reciprocal peer learning (see Table 5). These developmental phases are represented in the case study respectively by the following shifts: the incidental occurrence of academic development in day-to-day academic practice; the establishment of formal programs to support professional development of staff; advancement in human resource policy and practice to assure quality enhancement through centralised teaching development; co-existence of centralised and decentralised academic development based on the recognition of diverse needs at multiple organisational levels; and integration of hybrid approaches to flexibly address increasingly complex needs across a dispersed system.

The legacy of earlier developmental phases co-exists with the current developmental phase (i.e., reciprocal peer learning), shaping the positioning and design of academic development institutionally. The reciprocal peer learning evolutionary phase is characterised by cooperative and collaborative learning with a distinct shift from a teaching-focus to a learning-focus, and is supported by flexibility in teaching and learning roles, and a spontaneous and informal culture where academics become agents in their own learning (Boud, 1999). In this developmental stage the role of the academic developer shifts to facilitating the learning process by providing guidance and resources, whilst relinquishing ownership of the learning path and process to the 'learner' (i.e., teachers), who must negotiate what will be learned and how it will be learned (Whitchurch, 2008). There are several examples in the case study representing this phase of academic development, including the peer learning program, the open-door teacher program, and teaching excellence development fund grants, e-scholarships, and the various communities of practice.

*Table 5. Evolutionary shifts in academic development*

| Developmental phases | Key features |
|---|---|
| Development as embedded | Academic development occurs incidentally in day-to-day practice. |
| Development as a moral imperative | Formal programs established to support professional development of staff. |
| Development as corporate policy | Human resource policy and practice implemented to assure quality enhancement through centralised teaching development. |
| Development as multidimensional and distributed | Co-existence of centralised and decentralised academic development based on the recognition of diverse needs at multiple organisational levels. |
| Development as localised practice | Integration of hybrid approaches to flexibly address increasingly complex needs across a dispersed system. |
| Development as reciprocal peer learning | Cooperative and collaborative learning with a distinct shift from a teaching-focus to a learning-focus, and is supported by flexibility in teaching and learning roles, and a spontaneous and informal culture where academics become agents in their own learning. |

Adapted from Boud, 1999.

## 9. DISCUSSION

Premise reflection has revealed an overarching tension towards greater convergence in academic development practice on the one hand, and greater flexibility to accommodate diverse and multifaceted professional learning needs, on the other hand. This tension is represented in four ways. First, academic development is dualistically positioned, with a number of hybrid offerings emerging out of 'cross institutional' collaborations. Second, rapid pedagogical change is prompting converged designs adaptive to multiple foci, consequently reshaping traditional approaches and integrating non-traditional approaches. Third, the complex range of opportunities for group and individual self-learning is prompting design flexibility with multiple entry points and self-determined learning pathways. Fourth, centrally located programs are strategically leveraging opportunities for situated and informal learning to strengthen strategic educational transformation goals. Representation of the tension characterised by convergence and flexibility demonstrates a complex and changing face of academic development. To continue to provide effective support and leadership in academic practice organisationally, the field has necessarily extended beyond a quality assurance agenda in active pursuit of quality enhancement and educational transformation, and the role of the academic developer as a change agent is further intensified (Cordiner, 2014; Ellis, 2014; Griffiths, 2014; Hicks, 2005; Smyth, 2003).

Responsiveness to the overarching tension described above will assist in resolving the challenges previously identified. The emergent academic development practices are likely to substantially improve the potential to embed professional learning in everyday work and to situate it in multiple sites of practice (Jarvis, 1999). Greater organisational agility including policy shifts is needed to respond proactively to the changes shaping the discipline and its practice. Although gradual at present, technology enhanced academic development strategies have the potential to extend participation and engagement amongst diverse groups of teachers dispersed in internationalised higher education settings and working in vastly different educational environments. Collectively, these developments are likely to cultivate a supportive cultural climate and reduce the inherent bias amongst a large sector of the population who favour an event-based academic development paradigm.

Moreover, recent developments in the positioning and practice of academic development in the case study provide encouraging evidence that demonstrates advancement towards global trends in professional learning (AITSL, 2014). For instance, university systems have become increasingly *integrated* by connecting professional development activity, with teaching performance and career progression, thereby strengthening academic development within the organizational culture and practice. Similarly, the introduction of more flexible, self-directed, optional, participatory, personalised and continuous professional learning pathways provides scope for intensive, holistic experiences bringing an *immersive* quality to academic development. Self-paced, incentivised, situated activities, with options for personalisation and or collaboration facilitate problem-solving and enable *design-led* professional learning. Non-traditional offerings such as informal interest oriented groups engaged both on and offline, enable sharing of ideas and resources in minimally regulated environments, giving academic development an *open* quality. Increasingly, the growth of enterprise systems within the university is positioning them as possible external partners in academic development activity, adding a *market-led* quality.

The issues raised in this discussion activate a broadening of the conception of academic development. In adopting an openness in stance about what academic development is likely to look like in the future, the author is guided by Golding's (2014) comment, "if we have very set ideas about what academic development might be, we deprive ourselves of the opportunity to think differently about what it could be, and thus think and strategise in a blinkered manner" (p. 151). Consequently, the disruptive nature of social media in academic development in the context of issues and challenges presented by massification, internationalisation and rapid technological advancements, create spaces for transformative professional learning.

## 10. IMPLICATIONS FOR TRAINING AND DEVELOPMENT WITHIN BUSINESS ORGANISATIONS

The social, economic and technology changes shown to add complexity to the case study raise some considerations about similar impacts for large business organisations. Firstly, the characterisation of academic development as "socio-material webs" (Stewart, Schifter, & Markaridian Selverian, 2010), is equally relevant to how training and development functions in modern businesses where organisational, societal and individual needs coalesce. Secondly, studies have shown that globally a new generation of workplace learning is transforming business organisations (AITSL, 2014). These trends (i.e., integrated, immersion, design-led, market-led, and open), suggest that increasingly approaches to training and development require collaboration amongst employees, is delivered multi-modally, is personalised, informal, and self-directed. Simultaneously, businesses are incentivising training and development to assure that a culture of high expectations is fostered amongst their employees, and that alignment of individual development with organisational goals is stengthened. However, unlike the field of academic development, in businesses mandatory programs and certification of employee skills is still dominant to meet heightened regulatory standards. However, in common with shifts in academic development, greater variety in the format, outcomes and duration of training activities is occurring. Thirdly, it could be argued that like academic development, the remit of training and development in businesses has expanded in tandem with socio-economic growth and technological developments, bringing greater complexity and variety to training and development. Finally, it could be argued that the evolutionary phases of academic development (see Table 5) has synergy with developments that have shaped training and development. Workplace training also has evolved through the six developmental phases, noting its early beginnings in incidental on-the-job training, to the establishment of formal training programs, followed by regulatory developments to establish clear organisational policies and practices, leading to distributed training at multiple levels to meet the needs of rapid growth, to increased flexibility in training to meet complex needs in large multi-site systems, and finally to the contemporary dynamic and spontaneous training options that give employees greater agency for their personal development.

The parallels between the trends in academic development and business organisations are evidenced in data reporting that companies are increasing their budgets for training and development, using mobile learning solutions for training, and leveraging social learning activities (Wentworth, 2014). The remit of training and development has significantly expanded to include for example: IT training, sales training, Crew Resource Management (CRM) training, management / leadership training, team building training, project management training, customer service training, health and safety training, and regulatory training (Musgrove, 2014). Traditional in-person, instructor-led training continues to be offered alongside newer options that include adopting mobile technologies, embracing social media, integrating adaptive learning models, aligning with business objectives, and measuring effectiveness (Wentworth, 2014). Some examples that demonstrate these shifts include the move to using mirco-learning apps and websites to deliver on-demand training, using enterprise online systems to host and or outsource training, and expanding the range of training options available to employees (Kolodny, 2016). For instance, online training encompasses desktop and mobile options that deploy 3-D technology, digital storytelling, simulations, augmented and virtual reality software, social media, and serious games. Multimedia interactive training delivered in bite-sized chunks (e.g., under five minutes) incorporates testing and allows employees flexible access. Online training is also expanding to new and complex areas, for example language learning, competency training, and virtual assistants to name a few (Sharma, 2010).

## 11. FUTURE RESEARCH DIRECTIONS

Whilst the preceding analysis has provided insights into current and future practice, it has raised considerations for further research. The first relates to the tensions that arise when legacy and contemporary practices exist side-by-side, due to their divergent values and philosophies of practice. Accordingly, the development of effective strategies for dealing with cultural issues associated with evolutionary transitions is identified as an interesting area for future research in the case study context. A specific issue in this regard encompasses an investigation of effective approaches for unifying institutional priorities, the needs for development at faculty / school level, the needs of individual teachers, and the specific interests and expertise of academic developers to provide a range of programs, activities and resources. The second challenge relates to complexities arising from cultural lag associated with negotiating systemic change occurring simultaneously at multiple levels (e.g., educational, disciplinary, organisational, and individual). Exploration of models other than centre-periphery co-ordination provides a further direction for future research, such that convergence of cross-institution activity can be effectively harnessed to drive academic development activity in a dynamically transformative educational climate. A third possible direction for future research relates to the disruptive and transformative effects of non-traditional academic development strategies, namely investigation of *how* teachers engage in learning that makes a difference to student learning engagement and outcomes, and *when* and *where* these development opportunities occur. Such an investigation will bring further insights into what combinations of design elements are most effective for particular groups.

## 12. CONCLUSION

The preceding analysis has brought insights about the complexity that characterises academic development globally, and the case study has revealed how a rapidly changing higher education environment is influencing the positioning of academic development institutionally and how programs are designed to meet a complex and expanding range of needs.

This chapter has demonstrated that although the field of academic development is a developing one, there are useful analytical frameworks (e.g., Amundsen & Wilson, 2012; Boud, 1999, Gibbs' 2013) that capture the agility of higher education and provide a prism for the construction of explanations of current practice locally and globally. In employing these existing theoretical frameworks, together with experiential and reflective knowledge, the present work builds upon earlier research by deepening understanding of emergent directions in professional learning in university contexts. The present work further articulates a call for greater flexibility and situatedness in the positioning of academic development within institutions and for expanded opportunities for self-directedness in the design of academic development programs.

To effectively engage a diverse community in ways that are potentially impactful on quality enhancement of student learning, academic development must be dynamic and relevant. This requires embracing the rapid technological and cultural changes that are influencing how we live, communicate, work and 'play.' The strategies and activities must be authentic, situated in practice, collaborative, flexible, customisable, and future oriented.

This study concludes that the deployment of innovative strategies to meet the rapidly evolving needs of diverse, geographically dispersed teachers is representative of new configurations that have emerged from design features drawn from both traditional and non-traditional adult and professional learning approaches. Furthermore, the complex array of features provides for interesting 'remixing' to create customisable academic development activities suited to purpose, context, and target group, reinforcing some of modern trends in professional learning (i.e., integrated, immersive, design-led, open). These hybrid strategies offer potentially exciting and rich opportunities for academic development. Together such developments are likely to assure responsive, relevant and sustainable practice in a complex and rapidly evolving higher education landscape. These insights about the design and practice of academic development provide a basis for thinking about ways in which societal changes and smart technologies are influencing training and development within businesses.

## REFERENCES

Albach, P. G., Reisberg, L., & Rumbley, L. E. (2009). Trends in global higher education: Tracking an academic revolution.*UNESCO 2009 World Conference on Higher Education*. Paris: UNESCO.

Amundsen, C., & Wilson, M. (2012). Are we asking the right questions: A conceptual review of the educational development literature in higher education. *Review of Educational Research*, *82*(1), 90–126. doi:10.3102/0034654312438409

Aotearoa, A. (2010). Tertiary practitioner education training and support: Taking stock. Ako Aotearoa. Wellington, NZ: The National Centre for Tertiary Teaching Excellence. Retrieved from http://akoaotearoa. ac.nz/download/ng/file/group-4/taking-stock---tertiary-practitioner-education-training-and-support.pdf

Australian Government: Department of Education and Training. (2015). *Research snapshot series: Export income to Australia from international education activity in 2014-15.* Retrieved from https://internationaleducation.gov.au/research/Research-Snapshots/Documents/Export%20Income%20FY2014-5.pdf

Australian Institute for Teaching and School Leadership. (2014). *Global trends in professional learning and performance and development: Some implications and ideas for the Australian education system.* Innovation Unit & AITSL.

Boud, D. (1999). Situating academic development in professional work: Using peer learning. *The International Journal for Academic Development, 4*(1), 3–10. doi:10.1080/1360144990040102

Boud, D., & Brew, A. (2013). Reconceptualising academic work as professional practice: Implications for academic development. *The International Journal for Academic Development, 18*(3), 208–221. doi:10.1080/1360144X.2012.671771

Brew, A. (1999). Research and Teaching: Changing Relationships in a Changing Context. *Studies in Higher Education, 24*(3), 291–301. doi:10.1080/03075079912331379905

Brew, A. (2002). Editorial: The changing face of academic development. *The International Journal for Academic Development, 7*(1), 5–6. doi:10.1080/13601440210156420

Cafarella, R. S., & Zinn, L. F. (1999). Professional development for faculty: A conceptual framework of barriers and supports. *Innovative Higher Education, 23*(4), 241–254. doi:10.1023/A:1022978806131

Calderon, A. (2012, Sept 03). Massification continues to transform higher education. *University World News, 237.* Retrieved from http://www.universityworldnews.com/article.php?story=20120831155341147

Candy, P. (1996). Promoting life-long learning: Academic developers and the university as a learning organization. *The International Journal for Academic Development, 1*(1), 7–19. doi:10.1080/1360144960010102

Chalmers, D. (2010). Progress and challenges to the recognition and reward of scholarship of teaching in higher education. *Higher Education Research & Development, 30*(1), 25–38. doi:10.1080/07294360.2011.536970

Conole, G., & Dyke, M. (2004). Understandign and using technological affordances: A response to Boyle and Cook. *ALT-J. Research in Learning Technology, 12*(3), 301–308. doi:10.1080/0968776042000259609

Cordiner, M. (2014). Academic developers as change agents improving quality in a large interprofessional undergraduate subject. *The International Journal for Academic Development, 19*(3), 199–211. doi:10.1080/1360144X.2013.825618

Crawford, A. (2015, March 28). *5 Steps to effective and transformative professional development.* Blog series: Deeper learning, leadership, mission-driven work. Retrieved April 15, 2015 from http://gettingsmart.com/2015/03/5-steps-to-effective-and-transformative-professional-development/

Curtin University. (2015). *2011-2013 Key metrics summary.* Office of Strategy and Planning. Retrieved from https://planning.curtin.edu.au/mir/download.cfm

Day, D., & Lloyd, M. M. (2007). Affordances of online technologies: More than the properties of the technology. *Australian Educational Computing, 22*(2), 17–21.

Dewey, J. (1910). How we think. Lexington, MA: DC Heath. doi:10.1037/10903-000

Drew, S., & Klopper, C. (2013). Evaluating faculty pedagogic practices to inform strategic academic professional development: A case of cases. *The International Journal of Higher Education Research*, *67*, 349–367. doi:10.1007/s10734-013-9657-1

Ellis, R. (2014). Quality assurance for university teaching: Issues and approaches. In R. Ellis (Ed.), *Quality assurance for university teaching* (pp. 3–15). London: SRHE and Open University Press.

Ferman, T. (2002). Academic professional development practice: What lecturers find valuable. *The International Journal for Academic Development*, *7*(2), 146–158. doi:10.1080/1360144032000071305

Gibbs, G. (2013). Reflections on the changing nature of educational development. *The International Journal for Academic Development*, *18*(1), 4–14. doi:10.1080/1360144X.2013.751691

Golding, C. (2014). Blinkered conceptions of academic development. *The International Journal for Academic Development*, *19*(2), 150–152. doi:10.1080/1360144X.2013.855935

Gosling, D. (2001). What educational developments units do - Five years on. *The International Journal for Academic Development*, *6*, 74–92. doi:10.1080/13601440110043039

Gosling, D. (2008). *Educational development in the United Kingdom. Report for The Heads Of Educational Development Group*. London: Heads Of Educational Development Group (HEDG) UK. Retrieved from http://www.hedg.ac.uk/documents/HEDG_Report_final.pdf

Gosling, D. (2009). Educational development in the UK: A complex and contradictory reality. *The International Journal for Academic Development*, *14*(1), 5–18. doi:10.1080/13601440802659122

Griffiths, S. (2014). Staff development and quality assurance. In R. Ellis (Ed.), *Quality assurance for university teaching* (pp. 248–269). London: SRHE and Open University Press.

Hase, S., & Kenyon, C. (2000). *From andragogy to heutagogy*. Retrieved from http://ultibase.rmit.edu.au/Articles/dec00/hase2.htm

Hicks, M. (2005). Academic developers as change agents: Caught in the middle. In A. Brew & C. Asmar (Eds.), *Higher education in a changing world. Research and Development in Higher Education, 28.Proceedings of the 2005 HERDSA Annual Conference* (pp. 175-182). Sydney: HERDSA.

Jarvis, P. (1999). Global trends in lifelong learning and the response of the universities. *Comparative Education*, *35*(2), 249–257. doi:10.1080/03050069928017

Johnson, L., Adams Becker, S., Cummins, M., Estrada, V., & Freeman, A. (2016). *NMC Horizon Report: 2016 Higher Education Edition*. Austin, TX: The New Media Consortium.

Jones, J., & Wisker, G. (2012). *Report for the Heads of Educational Development Group (HEDG)*. Centre for Learning and Teaching. University of Brighton.

Kearsley, G. (2010). Andragogy (M. Knowles). *The theory into practice database*. Retrieved from http://tip.psychology.org

Knowles, M. S. (1975). *Self-directed learning*. Chicago: Follet.

Knowles, M. S. (1984). *The adult learner: A neglected species* (3rd ed.). Houston, TX: Gulf Publishing.

Kolodny, L. (2016, March 13). The latest approach to employee training. *The Wall Street Journal*. Retrieved from http://www.wsj.com/articles/the-latest-approach-to-employee-training-1457921560

Leibowitz, B. (2014). Academic development – no fixed recipes. *The International Journal for Academic Development, 19*(2), 73–75. doi:10.1080/1360144X.2014.912375

Leisyte, L. (2013). Being an academic in Europe and the U.S.: Role differentiation, shifting identities and protected spaces. *Belgium University Foundation Ethical Forum 2013, The academic's burden – University professors under perverse pressure.*

Levinson-Rose, J., & Menges, R. J. (1981). Improving college teaching: A critical review of research. *Review of Educational Research, 51*(3), 403–434. doi:10.3102/00346543051003403

Ling, P. (2009). *Development of academics and higher education futures* (Vol. 1). Sydney: Australian Learning and Teaching Council.

Loads, D., & Campbell, F. (2015). Fresh thinking about academic development: Authentic, transformative, disruptive? *The International Journal for Academic Development, 20*(4), 355–369. doi:10.1080/1360144X.2015.1083866

Locke, W. (2014). *Shifting academic careers: Implications for enhancing professionalism in teaching and supporting learning*. York, UK: The Higher Education Academy.

Marginson, S. (2011). Global position and position-taking in higher education: The case of Australia. In S. Marginson, S. Kaur, & E. Sawir (Eds.), *Higher education in Asia Pacific: Strategic responses to globalization* (Vol. 36, pp. 375–392). Netherlands: Springer. doi:10.1007/978-94-007-1500-4_20

Marks, L. (2013). *Curtin Learning Institute: Mapping professional development activities across Curtin*. Unpublished Report. Curtin University, Perth.

Märtensson, K. (2015). Academic development – old habits or disruptive practice? *The International Journal for Academic Development, 20*(4), 303–305. doi:10.1080/1360144X.2015.1096572

McPherson, M., Budge, K., & Lemon, N. (2015). New practices in doing academic development: Twitter as an informal learning space. *The International Journal for Academic Development, 20*(2), 126–136. doi:10.1080/1360144X.2015.1029485

Musgrove, J. (2014, December 14). 9 crucial competencies for your staff training program. *Saxons Blog*. Retrieved from http://www.saxonsgroup.com.au/blog/human-resources/9-crucial-competencies-for-your-staff-training-program/

Percy, A., et al. (2008). *The RED report: Recognition, enhancement, development. The contribution of sessional teachers to higher education*. Support for the original work was provided by the Australian Learning and Teaching Council, An Initiative of the Australian Government Department of Education, Employment and Workplace Relations.

Probert, B. (2013). *Teaching-focused academic appointments in Australian universities: Recognition, specialisation, or stratification*. Office of Learning and Teaching. Commonwealth of Australia.

Schön, D. (1987). *Educating the reflective practitioner*. San Francisco, CA: Jossey-Bass.

Sharma, R. (2010, September 23). 10 great new ideas for employee training. *Bright Hub*. Retrieved from http://www.brighthub.com/office/human-resources/articles/88251.aspx

Singh, K. (2014). Blended professional learning- modelling the paradigm shift. In B. Hegarty, J. Mc-Donald, & S.-K. Loke (Eds.), *Rhetoric and reality: Critical perspectives on educational technology. Proceedings ascilite* (pp. 404–409). Dunedin.

Singh, K., Schrape, J., & Kelly, J. (2012). Emerging strategies for a sustainable approach to professional development. In M. Brown, M. Hartnett, & T. Stewart (Eds.), *Future challenges, sustainable futures. Proceedings ascilite* (pp. 833–842).

Smith, E., & Coombe, K. (2006). Quality and qualms in the marking of university assignments by sessional staff: An exploratory study. *Higher Education*, *51*(1), 45–69. doi:10.1007/s10734-004-6376-7

Smyth, R. (2003). Concepts of change: Enhancing the practice of academic staff development in higher education. *The International Journal for Academic Development*, *8*(1-2), 51–60. doi:10.1080/1360144042000277937

Steinert, Y., Mann, K., Centeno, A., Dolmans, D., Spencer, J., Gelula, M., & Prideaux, D. (2006). A systematic review of faculty development initiatives designed to improve teaching effectiveness in medical education: BEME Guide No. 8. *Medical Teacher*, *28*(6), 497–526. doi:10.1080/01421590600902976 PMID:17074699

Stes, A., Min-Leliveld, M., Gijbels, D., & Van Petegem, P. (2010). The impact of instructional development in higher education: The state-of-the-art of the research. *Educational Research Review*, *5*(1), 25–49. doi:10.1016/j.edurev.2009.07.001

Stewart, C. M., Schifter, C. C., & Markaridian Selverian, M. E. (Eds.). (2010). *Teaching and learning with technology: Beyond constructivism*. Oxon, UK: Routledge.

TEQSA. (2011). *Higher education standards framework*. Tertiary Education Quality and Standards Agency.

Universities Australia. (2015). *Key facts and data*. Retrieved from https://www.universitiesaustralia.edu.au/australias-universities/key-facts-and-data#.Vxb52T-yBBw

Wentworth, D. (2014, August 28). 5 trends for the future of learning and development. *Training*. Retrieved from https://trainingmag.com/5-trends-future-learning-and-development

Whitchurch, C. (2008). Shifting Identities and blurring boundaries: The emergence of third space professionals in UK higher education. *Higher Education Quarterly*, *62*(4), 377–396. doi:10.1111/j.1468-2273.2008.00387.x

Yin, R. K. (2003). *Case study research: Design and methods* (3rd ed.). Thousand Oaks, CA: Sage.

## ADDITIONAL READING

Argyris, C. (2008). *Teaching smart people how to learn*. Boston: Harvard Business Press.

Brew, A. (2007). Evaluating academic development in a time of perplexity. *The International Journal for Academic Development, 12*(1), 69–72. doi:10.1080/13601440701604823

Clegg, S. (2012). Conceptualising higher education research and/or academic development as fields.. *Higher Education Research & Development, 31*(5), 667–678. doi:10.1080/07294360.2012.690369

Edwards, H., Webb, G., & Murphy, D. (2010). Modelling practice – Academic development for flexible learning. *The International Journal for Academic Development, 5*(2), 149–155. doi:10.1080/13601440050200752

Fraser, K., Gosling, D., & Sorcinelli, M. D. (2010). Conceptualising evolving models of educational development. *New Directions for Teaching and Learning, 122*(122), 49–58. doi:10.1002/tl.397

Fraser, K., & Ling, P. (2014). How academic is academic development? *The International Journal for Academic Development, 19*(3), 226–241. doi:10.1080/1360144X.2013.837827

Ginns, P., Kitay, J., & Prosser, M. (2010). Transfer of academic staff learning in a research-intensive university. *Teaching in Higher Education, 15*(3), 235–246. doi:10.1080/13562511003740783

Kennedy, A. (2005). Models of continuing professional development: A framework for analysis. *Journal of In-service Education, 31*(2), 235–250. doi:10.1080/13674580500200277

Lave, J. (1991). Situating learning in communities of practice. *Perspectives on Socially Shared Cognition, 2*, 63–82. doi:10.1037/10096-003

Lee, A., & McWilliam, E. (2008). What game are we in? Living with academic development. *The International Journal for Academic Development, 13*(1), 67–77. doi:10.1080/13601440701860284

Loads, D. (2014). Re-imagining academic staff development: Spaces for disruption. *The International Journal for Academic Development, 20*(1), 93–104.

Lupton, D. (2014). *Feeling better connected: Academics' use of social media*. Canberra: News & Media Research Centre, University of Canberra.

Lyons, N. (2006). Reflective engagement as professional development in the lives of university teachers. *Teachers and Teaching, 12*(2), 151–168. doi:10.1080/13450600500467324

Making sense of academic development. (2006). Editorial. *International Journal for Academic Development, 11(2), 73-77.*

McAlpine, L. (2006). Coming of age in a time of super-complexity (with apologies to both Mead and Barnett). *The International Journal for Academic Development, 11*(2), 123–128. doi:10.1080/13601440600924488

McAlpine, L., & Akerlind, G. S. (2010). *Becoming an academic: International perspectives*. Hampshire: Palgrave MacMillan. doi:10.1007/978-0-230-36509-4

McKenna, C., & Hughes, J. (2013). Values, digital texts, and open practices – A changing scholarly landscape in higher education. In R. Goodfellow & M. R. Lea (Eds.), *Literacy in the digital university: Learning as social practice in a digital world* (pp. 15–26). Abingdon: Routledge.

McKenna, S. (2012). Interrogating the academic project. In L. Quinn (Ed.). Reimagining academic staff development: Spaces for disruption (pp. 15-26). Stellenbosch: SUN MeDIA.

Quinn, L. (2012). Understanding resistance: An analysis of discourses in academic staff development. *Studies in Higher Education, 37*(1), 68–83. doi:10.1080/03075079.2010.497837

Quinn, L. (Ed.). (2012). Reimagining academic staff development: Spaces for disruption. Stellenbosch: SUN MeDIA. doi:10.18820/9781920338879

Schön, D. A. (1983). *The reflective practitioner: How professionals think in action.* New York: Basic Books.

Shay, S. (2012). Educational development as a field: Are we there yet? *Higher Education Research & Development, 31*(3), 311–323. doi:10.1080/07294360.2011.631520

Taylor, P. G. (1999). *Making sense of academic life: academics, universities and change.* Buckingham, UK: Society for Research into Higher Education and Open University Press.

# Chapter 14

# University Students' Perceptions of Personal Mobile Devices in the Classroom and Policies

**Ieda M. Santos**
*Emirates College for Advanced Education, UAE*

**Otávio Bocheco**
*Federal Institute Catarinense – Rio do Sul, Brazil*

## ABSTRACT

*This chapter discussed the results of a study that explored students' perceptions of personal mobile devices in the classroom and suggestions for policies. Thirty-four students enrolled in two undergraduate courses taught at a Brazilian higher education institution took part in the study. Data collection consisted of a survey and focus group interview. Quantitative data suggested an overall tendency to rare use of the devices for content and non-content activities. Qualitative results, however, showed that students may have used more often their devices in class. The results discussed several policies recommended by the students ranging from allowing the devices for content and emergency to not using social media for off- task activities. The study suggested that inappropriate use of mobile technology in the classroom may be minimized if students participate in the development of policies, and instructors integrate the devices in class to promote engagement and interest among students. Recommendations for practice and future research are discussed.*

## INTRODUCTION

Mobile technology ownership among university students continues to grow, with more students owning smartphones (Dahlstrom & Bichsel, 2014). Students are increasingly bringing their personal devices to the classrooms. This trend known as "bringing your own device" or BYOD is expected to be progressively adopted by higher education institutions (Johnson, Adams Becker, Estrada, & Freeman, 2015). Institutions adopting a BYOD model will allow students to use their own devices for learning (Kobus, Rietveld, & Van Ommeren, 2013). Research has discussed the educational benefits of a BYOD model in

DOI: 10.4018/978-1-5225-2492-2.ch014

the classroom (e.g. Al-Okaily, 2015; Kong & Song, 2015; Lundin, Lymer, Holmquist, Brown, & Rost, 2010). It is common knowledge, however, that students' devices can potentially disrupt lectures (Sharples, 2002), which is a wide shared concern by many instructors (Graham & Gillies, 2016; Kuznekoff & Titsworth, 2013). Common disruptions discussed in the literature include, for example, phone ringing or vibrating, use of social media such as WhatsApp, and sending or receiving messages (Santos, 2015).

Approaches to manage mobile devices in the classroom are varied ranging from adding guidelines to course syllabus to banning the devices (Bayless, Clipson, & Wilson, 2013; Langmia & Glass, 2014). In addition, many universities may not have a campus-wide BYOD policy (Fulbright, 2013). Without clear policies, students may be uncertain about the appropriate in-class use of their devices (Jackson, 2013). Researchers have investigated BYOD in the classroom with the purpose of understanding disruptions, and exploring policies for appropriate practices (e.g. Jackson, 2013; Tindell & Bohlander, 2012). More research is needed to examine the combination of BYOD usage and policies (Jackson, 2013) to advance knowledge in this field of inquiry. In addition, researchers recommended policy development that considers student and instructor viewpoints (Synnott, 2013).

This book chapter aims to discuss the results of a study that explored students' perceptions of classroom use of mobile devices and recommendations for policies. The study is based on two undergraduate courses taught at a Brazilian higher education institution in the academic year of 2015-2016, and builds on previous work by Santos and Bocheco (2014a). The chapter expects to make a contribution towards the development of BYOD policies for the classroom.

## BACKGROUND LITERATURE

Although the BYOD concept can have different meanings (Sharples et al., 2014), this chapter refers to the practice of students using their own mobile devices to support teaching and learning (Johnson et al., 2015). A BYOD model encompasses smartphones, digital media players, personal digital assistants and tablet computers. These smaller devices are distinct from computer laptops for their high flexibility and mobility (Pegrum, Oakley, & Faulkner, 2013). BYOD can potentially support new forms of learning and teaching opportunities (Sharples et al., 2014). It enables:

*...students and educators to leverage the tools that make them most efficient. In many cases, their devices are already populated with productivity apps...helping them to better organize their notes, syllabi, and schedules on campus and beyond. Furthermore, instructors can leverage this mobile device use by implementing polling and other interactive features during class. (Johnson et al., 2015, p. 37)*

Despite the learning opportunities afforded by a BYOD model, it also brings challenges to institutions and classrooms that can hinder its effective implementation. It is out of the scope of this chapter to discuss all the challenges. The reader can refer to Santos (2015) who presented a comprehensive review of the challenges while discussing potential solutions. Other researchers like Graham and Gillies (2016), Traxler (2016) and Dahlstrom and diFilipo (2013) further discussed BYOD issues and concerns. This chapter is concerned with students' personal devices that can threaten the "carefully managed environment of the classroom" (Sharples et al., 2014, p.19). Research has shown that students use their devices in the classroom to perform non-content related activities. For example, they can send or receive text messages (Burns & Lohenry, 2010; Baker, Lusk, & Neuhauser, 2012; Pettijohn et al., 2015), browse social networking sites, web sites or check emails (Aagaard, 2015; McCoy, 2013), although the frequency with which students engaged in these activities may vary.

When the devices are used inappropriately, they can disrupt lectures and learning. A survey by Campbell (2006), for instance, reported that both students and instructors agreed that phone ringing in class was a source of disruption. Langmia and Glass (2014, p.21) further suggested that most of the instructors complained about distractions caused by smartphones. The authors reported that "Different forms of distractions were ascertained during the interviews... when the ring tones go off, there is disruption. This disruption...creates unpleasant distractions...the classroom environment becomes noisy and uncomfortable for instruction." In addition to disrupting lectures, research showed that the devices can distract students from learning (Froese et al., 2012).

Researchers like Tindell & Bohlander (2012) surveyed students across different disciplines to investigate mobile phone usage in the classroom and policies. The majority of the students acknowledged sending or receiving text messages once or twice a week, with some performing this activity every day. The authors reported students' reluctance to support a policy completely banning the devices. Similarly, McCoy (2013) found that the majority of the students opposed bans of mobile devices. However, this finding disagrees with Campbell's (2006) study that found support for policies restricting in-class use of mobile phones. Banning the devices may not be the solution considering the educational benefits afforded by a BYOD model, which have been discussed in the literature (see for example, Kong & Song, 2015; Lundin et al., 2010).

A study by Baker et al. (2012) surveyed instructors and students from three public American universities to explore their perceptions of mobile devices usage and policies. Findings revealed significant differences in perceptions between students and instructors. For example, students considered mobile devices to be more appropriate and less disruptive than instructors did. In addition, most of the students did not favour top-down approaches for policy development, while instructors indicated a preference for a university-wide policy. Baker et al. recommended administrators to taking into account both students' and instructors' views when developing BYOD policies. In the same vein, Jackson (2013) reported students' recommendations for instructors to consider their opinions when developing BYOD classroom policies. The study also showed that students' most frequent responses regarding effective policies included allowing them to decide to use or not the devices and have clear policies. Similar to others (e.g. Baker et al., 2012), the majority of the students did not agree with complete bans of their devices in class. Another study by Bayless et al. (2013) surveyed instructors' perceptions regarding BYOD policies for the classroom. Results suggested mixed results, with some instructors banning the devices, ignoring it, adding statements to the course syllabus or using it to support teaching and learning. Langmia and Glass (2014) reported similar results. They also found that the majority of the instructors preferred a uniform smartphone policy at their university.

The above studies have certainly contributed to advance understanding on how students use their devices in the classroom and provided useful information to guide policy development. Further research is needed to continue exploring usage and policies (e.g. Jackson, 2013; Froese et al., 2012) to maximize the educational benefits of a BYOD model. The objective of this chapter is to report findings from a study that examined students' perceptions of mobile devices usage in the classroom and recommendations for BYOD policies. The following sections explain the methodology, present the results followed by a discussion of the results and conclusions.

## STUDY PARTICIPANTS

The study was conducted at a higher education institution in the South region of Brazil in 2015-2016 academic year. All students enrolled in the Pedagogy (n=34) and Physics (n=16) undergraduate courses were invited to participate. These two courses were chosen because the authors had easy access to the instructors and students. A total of 34 students gave their consent to participate (18 from Pedagogy; 16 from Physics). Students signed a consent form, and were explained that their participation was voluntary. The students' mother language was Portuguese. The sample consisted of female (53%) and male (47%). About 30% were under 20 years old, while 33% were within the 20-25 age group. The remaining students were in the 26-30 (6%), 31-35 (18%), 41-45 (6%), and over 46 (6%) age groups. Upon completion of the survey, the second author of this chapter sent an invitation, via WhatsApp, to all students who completed the survey, asking for volunteers to take part in a focus group interview. Five students (one female, and four males), all enrolled in the Physics course, replied to the invitation and gave their consent to participate in the interview.

## DATA COLLECTION

Data collection consisted of an anonymous survey and focus group interview with a sample of students who completed the survey. A survey developed by Santos and Bocheco (2014a), in both English and Portuguese languages, was used; however, one section was changed to include policy statements using a 5-point Likert scale instead of multiple choices, and two sections were merged and improved for clarity. The adapted survey consisted of ticking boxes, yes/no type of questions, a 4-point rating scaling ranging from frequently used (1) to never (4), a 5-point Likert scale ranging from strongly agree (1) to strongly disagree (5), and open-ended questions. The changes were translated into Portuguese. Main themes covered in the survey were 1) mobile device usage for content and non-content activities, 2) perceptions of usage and policy, 3) advantages and disadvantages of mobile technology in the classroom. The survey was administered face-to-face. A total of 34 students completed and returned the survey.

To complement the information gathered from the survey and explore further the issues, a focus group interview with five students was conducted. The interview protocol developed by Santos and Bocheco (2014b) was used and translated into Portuguese. Main themes covered in the focus group included 1) use of mobile device in class, 2) policy recommendation, 3) disruption, and 4) advantages and disadvantages of mobile devices in the classroom. The translation of the interview and survey questions was verified by a colleague for accuracy. The focus group interview was conducted face-to-face, using the Portuguese language, and was audio taped.

## DATA ANALYSIS

The returned surveys were examined for completion of all questions and accuracy. Analysis of the closed questions consisted of giving a code to each question (e.g. yes=1; no=2). On an Excel Spreadsheet, one column included participants' coded names, and another column was used for each question where the coded information was added. Descriptive statistics consisted of frequency, percentages, and means and standard deviation related to questions/statements on a 4 and 5-point scale.

Qualitative data followed a thematic analysis technique. Analysis was done inductively and codes were created by reading the data. The first author analysed the qualitative data assisted by the second author. The focus group interview was transcribed using a word document. The responses from the open-ended questions from the surveys were typed to a word document. The two documents were uploaded to NVivo qualitative software. The open questions were analysed first by reading the students' responses and making notes of key ideas. After re-reading the responses and key ideas, a list of codes and sub-codes was created (see Appendix, Table 5), and data were later assigned to the respective codes. By analysing the information inside and across categories, two main themes emerged (policy recommendations; advantages and disadvantages). Analysis of the focus group followed a similar procedure described for the open-ended questions. A list of codes was generated (see Appendix, Table 6), and data were coded accordingly. Three main themes emerged from the analysis and were reported in the findings.

Finally, the focus group interview transcript was verified by the second author, who listened to the audio recording. Some corrections were made to the original transcript to ensure accuracy. In addition, the two authors discussed the list of codes for the interview and open questions, and samples of coding to validate the interpretations. Some codes were revised or deleted, and a few themes merged. The results were translated to Portuguese and back translated to English to ensure accuracy; the translation were discussed and verified by the two authors who are bilingual. The quantitative and qualitative data enabled triangulation to enhance the results. Students' quotes were used to illustrate the results.

## RESULTS

This section presents the quantitative results followed by the qualitative analysis.

### Quantitative

Students were asked to state in the survey which mobile device they usually brought to the classroom. Results suggest that 59% of the students brought a mobile phone, 38% brought a smartphone and one student brought another device. About 68% had Internet connection on the devices they brought to class. During lectures, 56% had their devices on silence mode, 26% on vibrating, 15% had it turned-off, and one student (3%) had on ringing mode. Table 1 shows how frequent students used their devices to engage in content related activities in the classroom. There is a trend to rare use of the applications, and a slight tendency to occasional use of the devices to surf the Internet (Table 1).

Table 2 indicates a tendency to rare use of some applications such as WhatsApp or similar application, and Internet to perform non-content activities. There is a trend to never sending or receiving phone calls and other activities. Tables 1 and 2 show low responses for the statement "other activities." It may be that students did not understand the statement in the survey, which needs future revision.

Table 3 suggests a slight tendency to agreement about observing peers sending or receiving text messages, using social media and hearing phone ringing during class time. Students tended to neutral opinions regarding being distracted by their own use or others' use of the devices in class. Table 3 shows, however, agreement that the use mobile technology for non-content is generally disruptive to learning.

With regard to BYOD policy recommendations for the classroom, Table 4 suggests clear agreement with policies allowing the use of the devices for content, emergency, and that phone calls should be answered outside the class. There is also a clear agreement about considering students' opinions when

*Table 1. In-class use of mobile devices for content*

| How often do you use your mobile device in class for course content related activities? (Scale 1-4)[a] | Frequency (n=34) | Mean | Standard Deviation |
|---|---|---|---|
| Send and receive phone calls | 33 | 3.61 | 0.56 |
| Send and receive text message (SMS) | 33 | 3.55 | 0.67 |
| Send and receive phone emails | 33 | 3.15 | 1.05 |
| Access WhatsApp or similar software | 33 | 3.09 | 1.01 |
| Access Twitter or Facebook | 33 | 3.48 | 0.83 |
| Surf the Internet | 33 | 2.79 | 1.19 |
| Other Activities | 15 | 3.40 | 1.12 |

[a]Scale - Frequently (1), Occasionally (2), Rarely (3), and Never Used (4)

*Table 2. In-class use of mobile devices for non-content*

| How often do you use your mobile in class for non-course content related activities? (Scale 1-4)[a] | Frequency (n=34) | Mean | Standard Deviation |
|---|---|---|---|
| Send and receive phone calls | 33 | 3.79 | 0.42 |
| Send and receive text message (SMS) | 32 | 3.56 | 0.72 |
| Send and receive phone emails | 32 | 3.47 | 0.88 |
| Access WhatsApp or similar software | 34 | 3.00 | 1.21 |
| Access Twitter or Facebook | 33 | 3.39 | 0.93 |
| Surf the Internet | 32 | 3.13 | 1.13 |
| Other Activities | 16 | 3.75 | 0.77 |

*Table 3. Perceptions of in-class use of mobile devices*

| Student perceptions of the use of mobile devices in the classroom (Scale 1-5)[b] | Frequency (n=34) | Mean | Standard Deviation |
|---|---|---|---|
| 1. I have seen other students sending or receiving phone text messages | 34 | 2.59 | 0.86 |
| 2. I have heard mobile phones ringing or vibrating | 34 | 2.65 | 1.04 |
| 3. I have seen other students using social media (e.g. Twitter, Facebook, WhatsApp) | 34 | 2.76 | 1.21 |
| 4. I have been distracted by my own use of a mobile device in the classroom | 32 | 3.47 | 1.26 |
| 5. I have been distracted by other students' use of mobile devices in the classroom | 34 | 3.31 | 1.06 |
| 6. The use of mobile devices in the class for non-content is generally disruptive to learning | 34 | 2.21 | 1.12 |

[b]Scale - Strongly Agree (1), Agree (2), Neutral (3), Disagree (4), Strongly Disagree (5)

*Table 4. Policy recommendations*

| | Policy statement (Scale 1-5)[b] | Frequency (n=34) | Mean | Standard Deviation |
|---|---|---|---|---|
| 1. | Instructors should allow the use of mobile devices in class as long as the devices are on silence mode | 34 | 2.35 | 1.04 |
| 2. | Students should be able to answer a phone call as long as they leave the classroom | 34 | 2.00 | 0.98 |
| 3. | Mobile devices must be turned-off during class time | 34 | 3.26 | 0.99 |
| 4. | Mobile devices may be used to send and receive text messages during class as long as the devices do not distract other students | 34 | 2.56 | 1.02 |
| 5. | Instructors should collect students' mobile devices during class time | 32 | 3.91 | 1.06 |
| 6. | Students should be allowed to use the devices in class in emergency situations (e.g. illness) | 34 | 1.65 | 0.77 |
| 7. | Students should be allowed to use their mobile devices in class for content related activities | 33 | 1.94 | 1.00 |
| 8. | Mobile devices must <u>not</u> be used to access social media during class to discuss non-content related activities | 34 | 2.32 | 1.20 |
| 9. | Mobile devices should <u>not</u> be permitted in the classroom under any circumstances | 34 | 3.85 | 1.10 |
| 10. | Instructors should consider student opinions when creating policies about the use of mobile devices in the classroom | 34 | 2.00 | 0.78 |

creating policies regarding mobile technology in the classroom. Table 4 shows a tendency to agreement with a policy that allows the devices in class, phone text message, and non-use of social for off-task activities during lectures. There is a trend to disagreement with a policy that collects the devices, and does not allow their use under any circumstances. As seen in Table 4, students tended to neutral opinion regarding whether mobile devices should be turned-off during class teaching.

In addition to the policy statements described in Table 4, students were asked to indicate a policy that an instructor should adopt in case a student disturbed the class by using her/his mobile device to engage in social activities. About half (52%) felt the instructor should speak to the student in private (52%), 27% were in favour of asking the student to leave the class (27%) and 21% said to switch off the device.

## Qualitative

Results from the open-ended questions are described first followed by the focus group interview. Two main themes emerged from the open-questions, described next.

## Policy Recommendation

Eight students recommended allowing the devices in the classroom for emergency only, while two suggested for both emergency and content. One student, in particular, stressed the devices should be used for emergency but following the instructor's given guidelines. Seven students suggested allowing the devices to support content such as to "research content being studied." Four favoured a policy asking students to set their devices on silence because of "emergency" or "you can use it whenever needed." One suggested turning-off the devices, and another believed it should be either turned-off or on silence mode.

Three students felt the devices should be allowed subject to some conditions such as" using the phone as long as it does not disturb peers." Other recommendations included 1) block social media during lectures, 2) use the devices during break time or before class, and 3) make the rules clear to the students.

## Advantages and Disadvantages

Nine students saw mobile devices as creating opportunities to search information during lectures. Among these, four highlighted quick search "using the Internet." Six mentioned more specifically that mobile technology enables searching information related to content. Student A31 said, "Access to information about the content in a broad and "unlimited" way." Other advantages included 1) use of the devices when needed to complete a task or discuss a topic, 2) interact with others, and 3) useful in case of emergency.

With regard to the disadvantages, eleven students said the devices could affect student concentration to lectures. A further student felt the devices could disturb both student and instructor concentration, and as a consequence, the "student does not learn the lesson proposed by the instructors." Nine students saw mobile devices as a distraction, and three said the devices could disrupt others, "If used incorrectly."

Analysis from the focus group interview revealed three main themes discussed next.

## Classroom Use

All students said in the focus group they brought a mobile device to the classroom. They had their devices on silence mode, and connected to the institution network. While four brought the devices to class every day, student 1 mentioned he purposefully did not bring his device to the class, at least twice a week, because he wanted to "concentrate and study."

Three interviewees (2, 3 and 4) confirmed they used their devices to search information related to content during lectures. Student 2 exemplified:

*...there is an exercise...and you do not remember the equation. Then you do a quick search and look at the equation, and solve the exercise. Quick search, right! You do not have to go to the library to get a book. It's all here in our hands.*

In addition, students 3, 5 and 2 used mobile applications (apps) for content. For example, student 2 said, "if you have the video...image is much easier to clarify and understand what the instructor is talking about." On the other hand, student 1 rarely used apps. He only used when he did not understand the content being covered in class, or when he felt he was falling behind peers.

Analysis also revealed that all five students used WhatsApp during class to discuss issues not related to content. Student 3 stressed using for personal matters but also to discuss a project done in another subject. In addition, although student 1 used WhatsApp for non-content, he purposefully left the phone on silence to avoid the temptation. He said, "If I leave to vibrate, it will draw my attention. Even unconsciously I'll get the phone to see what was sent." However, when the subject is more demanding and requires attention, students 2 and 4 said they "forget the phone, and pay attention." All interviewees suggested they had put their devices away when the lecture was good or attractive. For example, student 5 believed that "When the instructor draws students' attention [to the lecture], the phone will not take that attention away." Student 2 noted, however, that in subjects like Physics and Calculus, independently of the lecture being good or not, he leaves the phone aside as he wants to pass these subjects.

With regard observing peers using their devices in class, three students confirmed they did. Student 1 said that "you notice that people are, for example, on WhatsApp." However, although student 1 had observed peers using WhatsApp and believed it can cause distraction, it rarely disturbed him. Further, student 3 stressed that the use of mobile devices in class increase after the break. He said that students "start a discussion during the break, go back to class and end the discussion there or start planning what they will do after class." He also mentioned "There's always someone...using the phone... regardless of the discipline." While two students could not tell whether peers were using their devices to engage in off-task activities, two others did. Student 3 said the majority use the phone not related to the subject. He said, "in my class, we have a group in WhatsApp...my phone is on my desk. I pick up the phone to look, only...the notifications. I then see the group talking about something not related to the discipline."

## Policy Recommendation

During the interview, students first discussed some of their current institution and instructor policies regarding BYOD. The institution had a policy that limited access to Facebook during classes. Three students (1, 3 and 4) agreed with limiting Facebook as it can cause more distractions than WhatsApp. Student 1 said that "Facebook gives you limitless opportunities to explore...we can totally disappear from class." In contrast, student 2 did not see any problem with Facebook. He said, "...provided it does not make noise, and does not bother others, it should be allowed." Nevertheless, according to student 3, and based on instructors' request, YouTube was now allowed in class.

Three students (1, 2 and 3) had instructors who did not allow the use of mobile devices in class. Student 2 said the instructor "was totally against the use of mobile phones. He did not allow it." Student 3 also mentioned another instructor who recommended not using the phone and leaving it on silence to avoid disturbing the class. In this case, if students wanted to use it, that would be their problem. Student 4 said that one of the instructors did not ban the devices; however, he recommended not using them. She noted that "still, there were students who used it."

Four students recommended a policy allowing the devices in class as long as they do not make noises or disturb others. Students 2 and 3 stressed that students know what they are doing, while student 5 believed each one is responsible for his or her actions. Student 5 also noted that in the world we are living now, it is difficult to ban the devices in class. Similarly, interviewee 3 suggested that, instead of banning the devices, students should be made aware of appropriate practices. He said, "...if all instructors use the devices correctly in the classroom, this will help diminish incorrect use." All interviewees agreed that instructors should consider students' opinions when developing BYOD policies for the classroom. Student 5 stated, "If you create policies together with the class, none of the students will be able to question later why this is being prohibited..."

## Advantages and Disadvantages

A main advantage discussed by three interviewees referred to mobile devices allowing them search information related to content. Student 2 said, "I use a lot if I have doubt about a basic concept. I then look at the phone because the instructor had [already] explained that concept and I should know."

When referring to disadvantages, four students felt the devices disturb when they make noises. For example, student 5 said the device "disrupt the class when it is not left on silence mode. It rings and then draws everyone's attention." A further student (participant 2) did not see a problem if the device distracts the person who is using it, as long as he or she does not "disturb others in the class." Student 4 felt the devices disturb class when a student misses the explanation, because he or she was using the phone, and asks the instructor to repeat. This disrupts the class as the instructor has to explain again the same content to the student. Other disadvantages noted by the interviewees included 1) distracting students' attention from lectures, and 2) disrupting the instructor. On the other hand, student 3 said:

*In my opinion, I see the use of the devices as having more advantages than disadvantages. The disadvantage is its incorrect use. If a person knows how to use the device, it works well. Its incorrect use disturbs oneself and the others.*

## DISCUSSION AND RECOMMENDATIONS

Similar to previous studies (e.g. Kobus et al., 2013), all students brought a mobile device to the classroom in which many had access to the Internet. Quantitative results suggest an overall tendency to rare in-class use of the devices for content and non-content activities (Tables 1-2). There is, however, a slight trend to occasional use of the Internet for content. Qualitative data support this trend where some used their devices to search information related to the lectures, which they considered an advantage. Based on the focus group interview, students may have used more often their devices to engage in content and off-task activities. This is supported by quantitative data that show a slight trend to occasional observations of phone ringing or vibrating, peers using social media or texting. A study by Santos and Bocheco (2014a) also found that qualitative data indicated more in-class use of the devices compared to the quantitative results. In the current study, despite students' observations of others using the devices, and, perhaps, more usage, they tended to neutral opinion regarding being distracted by own or others' use of the devices (Table 3). Students, however, demonstrated awareness of disruptions and distractions when discussing disadvantages of mobile technology in class, and bans of Facebook at their institution; they even agreed that off-task activities could be disruptive to learning (Table 3), and most had their devices either on silence or vibrating mode, possibly to avoid disrupting others.

With regard to BYOD policies, students clearly agreed with a policy that allows the devices for emergency and content. This is supported by qualitative data. Santos and Bocheco's (2014a) findings also showed support for a policy permitting the devices for content. In the current study, data suggest that some students were, to some degree, already using their devices for academic purposes such as search information or access a few apps. In addition, qualitative data indicate that many saw advantages in using their devices for learning. However, and similar to other findings (e.g. Bayless, et al., 2013), the focus group revealed that some instructors recommended or banned the devices in class. As student 5 said, it may be difficult to ban the devices if we consider the world we live now. This echoes Ally and

Palalas (2011) who observed that we are now living in a mobile age where mobile technology is part of students' daily lives. Therefore, as noted by Bayless et al. (2013), at some point, instructors may need to find strategies to adopt the devices in teaching because these devices will not go away.

In addition, overall, students tended to agree with policies allowing the devices in the classroom including texting, and not using social media for off-task activities, and answering phone calls outside the class (Table 4). Students remained neutral on whether the devices should be turned-off during class; however, in case a student caused a disruption by using her/or his device, 27% of the students agreed it should be turned-off. McCoy (2013) reported similar results where students tended to disagree with policies collecting or banning the devices.

Qualitative data suggest that students would put away their devices if the lecture was good or attractive. This may be true; the implication here is that instructors could also make lectures attractive and interesting by using mobile-based activities. In this regard, Bayless et al. (2013, p. 134) recommended instructors to "develop new activities that rely on personal technology to increase student interest as well as engagement." Imazeki (2014, p. 245) further noted:

*I am convinced that the best weapon against any of these distractions is to make sure students are fully engaged in the class. Students who are engrossed in a relevant example or discussing ideas with classmates or puzzling out problems are rarely using their phones for extracurricular texting or surfing. If I see too many students on their phones when I think they should not be, it is a signal to me that I must do something to re-engage their attention. From this perspective, the fact that students have their devices out already for use as clickers becomes an advantage because they tend to feel that they do not need to hide their device...*

Furthermore, when considering participant 3's remark about students being made aware of appropriate use of mobile technology in class, one could argue students could benefit from attending workshops or similar events on appropriate practices.

Concurrent with Jackson (2013), students agreed that instructors should take their opinions into account when developing policies concerning mobile technology in the classroom. This is supported by qualitative data. This finding agrees with Synnott's (2013) observation to consider different perspectives on policy development.

The current study has discussed policies that extend and complement other studies (e.g. Jackson, 2013; McCoy, 2013; Santos & Bocheco, 2014a). The results may be useful to guide policy development regarding mobile technology in the classroom. Based on the results, suggestions for instructors and educational institutions are discussed next.

1. Instructors should plan and integrate mobile-based activities that encourage engagement and learning in the classroom. Also, students should be allowed to use their devices informally and when needed, as illustrated in the results (e.g. clarify a concept).
2. Institutions should provide instructors with opportunities to develop teaching practices to facilitate effective planning and integration of the devices in the classroom.
3. Include students in the discussions regarding BYOD policies for the classroom to avoid top down decided policies.
4. Encourage students to attend workshops to develop more awareness of how to use the devices in class. As noted by Burns and Lohenry (2010, p.5), "awareness and understanding of how cell

phones disturb faculty and fellow students offer initial efforts to ensure an academic environment that fosters learning."

5.  Encourage students to explore other educational applications and activities beyond the ones mentioned in the current study to support their studies.

## LIMITATIONS AND FUTURE RESEARCH DIRECTIONS

Despite the positive outcomes, this study needs to acknowledge some limitations. It is based on a small sample size and a single context. Future research could consider larger samples, multiple subjects, and conduct cross country analysis to assess different perspectives to validate the findings. It is also important to investigate instructors' perspectives on policies, usage and integration of the devices to support learning. Research could also conduct individual interviews to explore more in-depth the issues investigated in this study. In addition, more demographic information about the participants could have been helpful to interpret the results. Future studies could investigate correlations between participants' demographic data and perceptions of policies and usage to inform practice.

Further, technology is constantly evolving. The BYOD concept will develop and, as observed by Roberts and Rees (2014), the range of mobile technology will expand as well as software and hardware supporting these devices. As a consequence, students' habits, behaviours and interests will change which will impact instruction. Therefore, research is needed to continue investigating usage, update policies and learning activities inside and outside the classroom.

There will be a progression from BYOD to wearable devices such as smart watches and Google Glass in teaching and learning. Johnson et al. (2015, p.42-43) noted that:

*Wearable technology is poised to see significant growth in the coming years, spurring experimentation in higher education because of the demand for wearables is seen to be coming in large part from college-aged students...Google Glass 'ability to display information in a hands-free, enable communication via voice command, and broadcast and record student training activities is giving medical school leaders the confidence to begin integrating it into their degree programs...The higher education sector is just beginning to experiment with wearable technologies...*

The BYOD concept has presented many opportunities and challenges to higher education (Santos, 2015). It is likely that when these wearable devices reach the classroom, they will add some more challenges that instructors will need to deal with. These devices will impact interactions among students and instructors, and probably the way we teach and learn. The research agenda will need to advance to study students' usage of wearable devices in the classroom and beyond the classroom walls to inform policies for appropriate practices.

## CONCLUSION

This chapter presented the results of students' perceptions of personal mobile technology usage in the classroom and recommendations for policies within the Brazilian context. The survey results indicated an overall tendency to rare use of mobile technology to perform content and non-content related activities. Qualitative results, however, suggested that students might have used more often their devices in class. The study discussed several BYOD policies recommended by the students. Results suggested that inappropriate use of mobile technology in the classroom may be minimized if students participate in the development of BYOD policies, and instructors integrate the devices in teaching and learning to promote engagement and interest. The study discussed recommendations for practice and future research.

## REFERENCES

Aagaard, J. (2015). Drawn to distraction: A qualitative study of off-task use of educational technology. *Computers & Education*, *87*, 90–97. doi:10.1016/j.compedu.2015.03.010

Al-Okaily, R. (2015) Mobile learning BYOD: Implementation in an intensive English program. In M. Ally, & B. H. Khan (Eds.), International handbook of e-learning, volume 2: Implementation and case studies (pp. 311-323). Routledge.

Ally, M., & Palalas, A. (2011). *State of mobile learning in Canada and future directions*. Retrieved from http://www.rogersbizresources.com/files/308/Mobile_Learning_in_Canada_Final_Report_EN.pdf (2011)

Baker, W. M., Lusk, E. J., & Neuhauser, K. L. (2012). On the use of cell phones and other electronic devices in the classroom: Evidence from a survey of faculty and students. *Journal of Education for Business*, *87*(5), 275–289. doi:10.1080/08832323.2011.622814

Bayless, M. L., Clipson, T. C., & Wilson, S. A. (2013). Faculty perceptions of policies of students' use of personal technology in the classroom. *Faculty Publications*, *32*, 119–136.

Burns, S. M., & Lohenry, K. (2010). Cellular phone use in class: Implications for teaching and learning a pilot study. *College Student Journal*, *44*(3), 805–810.

Campbell, S. W. (2006). Perceptions of mobile phones in college classrooms: Ring, cheating, and classroom policies. *Communication Education*, *55*(3), 280–294. doi:10.1080/03634520600748573

Dahlstrom, E., & Bichsel, J. (2014). *ECAR study of undergraduate students and information technology, 2014*. Research report. Louisville, CO: ECAR. Retrieved from http://www.educause.edu/ecar

Dahlstrom, E., & diFilipo, S. (2013). *The consumerization of technology and the bringing your own everything (BYOT) era of higher education* (Education Report). Retrieved from http://net.educause.edu/ir/library/pdf/ERS1301/ers1301.pdf

Froese, A. D. et al. (2012). Effects of classroom cell phone use on expected and actual learning. *College Student Journal, 46*(2), 323–332.

Fulbright, S. (2013). *Cell phones in the classroom: What's your policy?* Retrieved from http://www.facultyfocus.com/articles/effective-classroom-management/cell-phones-in-the-classroom-whats-your-policy/

Graham, C., & Gillies, M. (2016). To BYOD or not to BYOD: Factors affecting academic acceptance of student mobile devices in the classroom. *Research in Learning Technology, 24*. doi:10.3402/rlt.v24.30357

Imazeki, J. (2014). Bring-your-own-device: Turning cell phones into forces for good. *The Journal of Economic Education, 45*(3), 240–250. doi:10.1080/00220485.2014.917898

Jackson, L. D. (2013). Is mobile technology in the classroom a helpful tool or a distraction? A report of university students' attitudes, usage practices, and suggestions for policies. *The International Journal of Technology. Knowledge in Society, 8*(5), 129–140.

Johnson, L., Adams Becker, S., Estrada, V., & Freeman, A. (2015). *NMC Horizon Report: 2015 Higher Education Edition.* Austin, TX: The New Media Consortium.

Kobus, M. B. W., Rietveld, P., & van Ommeren, J. N. (2013). Ownership versus on-campus use of mobile IT devices by university students. *Computers & Education, 68*, 29–41. doi:10.1016/j.compedu.2013.04.003

Kong, S. C., & Song, Y. (2015). An experience of personalized learning hub initiative embedding BYOD for reflective engagement in higher education. *Computers & Education, 88*, 227–240. doi:10.1016/j.compedu.2015.06.003

Kuznekoff, J. H., & Titsworth, S. (2013). The impact of mobile phone usage on student learning. *Communication Education, 61*(3), 233–252. doi:10.1080/03634523.2013.767917

Langmia, K., & Glass, A. (2014). Coping with Smartphone distractions in a college classroom. *Teaching Journalism and Mass Communication, 4*(1), 13–23.

Lundin, J., Lymer, G., Holmquist, L. E., Brown, B., & Rost, M. (2010). Integrating students mobile technology in higher education. *International Journal of Mobile Learning and Organisation, 4*(1), 1–14. doi:10.1504/IJMLO.2010.029951

McCoy, B. (2013). *Digital distractions in the classroom: Student classroom use of digital devices for non-class related purposes.* Retrieved from http://digitalcommons.unl.edu/journalismfacpub/71

Pegrum, M., Oakley, G., & Faulkner, R. (2014). Schools going mobile: A study of the adoption of mobile handheld technologies in Western Australian independent schools. *Australasian Journal of Educational Technology, 29*(1), 66–81.

Pettijohn, T. F., Frazier, E., Rieser, E., Vaughn, N., & Hupp-Wilds, B. (2015). Classroom texting on college students. *College Student Journal, 49*(4), 513–516.

Roberts, N., & Ress, M. (2014). Student use of mobile devices in university lectures. *Australasian Journal of Educational Technology, 30*(4), 415–426. doi:10.14742/ajet.589

Santos, I. M. (2015). Mobile devices in higher education classrooms: Challenges and opportunities. In J. Keengwe (Ed.), *Promoting active learning through the integration of mobile and ubiquitous technologies* (pp. 37–54). IGI Global; doi:10.4018/978-1-4666-6343-5.ch003

Santos, I. M., & Bocheco, O. (2014a). Students' mobile devices usage during class and policy suggestions for appropriate practices. In M. Kalz, Y. Bayyurt, & M. Specht (Eds.), *Mobile as mainstream: Towards future challenges in mobile learning*. Springer. doi:10.1007/978-3-319-13416-1_9

Santos, I. M., & Bocheco, O. (2014b). Mobile devices in the classroom: Emirati students' perceptions of usage and policies. In *IEEE Proceedings of the Interactive Collaborative Learning* (ICL) (pp. 956-962). IEEE. doi:10.1109/ICL.2014.7017905

Sharples, M. (2002). *Disruptive devices: Mobile technology for conversational learning*. Retrieved from https://www.tlu.ee/~kpata/haridustehnoloogiaTLU/mobilesharples.pdf

Sharples, M. (2014). *Innovating pedagogy 2014: Open University Innovation Report 3*. Milton Keynes, UK: The Open University.

Synnott, K. C. (2013). Smartphones in the classroom: University faculty members' experiences. *Journal of Higher Education Management*, *28*(1), 119–130.

Tindell, D. R., & Bohlander, R. W. (2012). The use and abuse of cell phones and text messaging in the classroom: A survey of college students. *College Teaching*, *60*(1), 1–9. doi:10.1080/87567555.2011.604802

Traxler, J. (2016). Inclusion in an age of mobility. *Research in Learning Technology*, *24*(1), 1–17. doi:10.3402/rlt.v24.31372

## ADDITIONAL READING

Alsadoon, E., & Alsadoon, H. (2015). The current use of cell phone in education. *Communications in Computer and Information Science*, *529*, 224–229. doi:10.1007/978-3-319-21383-5_38

Campbell, W. et al.. (2013). The wild-card character of "bring your own:" A panel discussion. *EDU-CAUSE Review*, *48*(2), 10–12.

Cheung, S. K. S. (2015). Students' typical usage of mobile devices in learning activities. Technology in education. In J. Lam et al. (Eds.), *Technology in education. Technology-mediated proactive learning* (pp. 63–72). Berlin, Heidelberg: Springer. doi:10.1007/978-3-662-48978-9_6

Cochrane, T., Antonczak, L., Keegan, H., & Narayan, V. (2014). Riding the wave of BYOD: Developing a framework for creative pedagogies. *Research in Learning Technology*, *22*(1), 24637. doi:10.3402/rlt.v22.24637

Crompton, H. (2013). A historical overview of m-learning. In Z. L. Berge & L. Y. Muilenburg (Eds.), *Handbook of mobile learning* (pp. 3–14). London: Routledge.

de Waard, I. I. (2014). Using BYOD, mobile social media, apps, and sensors for meaningful mobile learning. In M. Ally, & A. Tsinakos (Eds.), Increasing access through mobile learning (pp. 113-124). Vancouver: Commonwealth of Learning and Athabasca University.

Fang, B. (2009). From distraction to engagement: Wireless devices in the classroom. Retrieved from http://er.educause.edu/articles/2009/12/from-distraction-to-engagement-wireless-devices-in-the-classroom

Gan, C. L., & Balakrishnan, V. (2016). An empirical study of factors affecting mobile wireless technology adoption for promoting interactive lectures in higher education. *International Review of Research in Open and Distance Learning*, *17*(1), 214–216. doi:10.19173/irrodl.v17i1.2111

Geist, E. (2011). The Game changer: Using iPads in college teacher education classes. *College Student Journal*, *45*(4), 758–768.

Hanson, T. L., Drumheller, K., Mallard, J., McKee, C., & Schlegel, P. (2014). Cell phones, text messaging, and Facebook: Competing time demands of todays college students. *College Teaching*, *59*(1), 23–30. doi:10.1080/87567555.2010.489078

Hwang, G. J., & Wu, P. H. (2014). Applications, impacts and trends of mobile technology-enhanced learning: A review of 2008–2012 publications in selected SSCI journals. *International Journal of Mobile Learning and Organisation*, *8*(2), 83–95. doi:10.1504/IJMLO.2014.062346

Karnad, A. (2014). *Trends in educational technologies*. London, UK: The London School of Economics and Political Science.

Kuznekoff, J. H. (2015). Mobile phone behavior in the college classroom: Effects on student learning and implications for students and teachers. In Z. Yan (Ed.), *Encyclopedia of mobile phone behavior* (pp. 648–657). Hershey, PA: Information Science Reference; doi:10.4018/978-1-4666-8239-9.ch054

LaMaster, J., & Ferries-Rowe, J. D. (2013). So we had this idea: Bring your own device technology at Brebeuf Jesuit. In Z. L. Berge & L. Y. Muilenburg (Eds.), *Handbook of mobile learning* (pp. 395–404). London: Routledge.

Looi, C., Seow, P., Zhang, B., So, H., Chen, W., & Wong, L.-H. (2010). Leveraging mobile technology for sustainable seamless learning: A research agenda. *British Journal of Educational Technology*, *41*(2), 154–169. doi:10.1111/j.1467-8535.2008.00912.x

Mueller, J., Wood, E., De Pasquale, D., & Cruikshank, R. (2012). Examining mobile technology in higher education: Handheld devices in and out of the classroom. *International Journal of Higher Education*, *1*(2), 43–53. doi:10.5430/ijhe.v1n2p43

Murphy, A. et al.. (2014). Mobile learning anytime, anywhere: What are our student doing? *Australasian Journal of Information Systems*, *14*(3), 331–341.

Park, Y. (2011). A pedagogical framework for mobile learning: Categorizing educational applications of mobile technologies into four types. *International Review of Research in Open and Distance Learning*, *12*(2), 78–102. doi:10.19173/irrodl.v12i2.791

Parsons, D. (2014). The future of mobile learning and implications for education and training. In M. Ally & A. Tsinakos (Eds), Increasing access through mobile learning (pp. 217-229). Vancouver: Commonwealth of Learning and Athabasca University.

Shelton, J. T., Elliott, E. M., Eaves, S. D. M., & Exner, A. (2009). The distracting effects of a ringing cell phone: An investigation of the laboratory and the classroom setting. *Journal of Environmental Psychology, 29*(4), 513–521. doi:10.1016/j.jenvp.2009.03.001 PMID:21234286

Tal, H. M., & Kurtz, G. (2014). The Laptop, the tablet, and the smartphone attend lectures. J. Keengwe (Ed), Promoting active learning through the integration of mobile and ubiquitous technologies (pp. 183-193). US: IGI Global.

Thomas, K., & OBannon, B. (2013). Cell phones in the classroom: Pre service teachers perceptions. *Journal of Digital Learning in Teacher Education, 30*(1), 11–20. doi:10.1080/21532974.2013.10784721

Traxler, J. (2010). Students and mobile devices. *ALT-J-. Research in Learning Technology, 18*(2), 149–160. doi:10.1080/09687769.2010.492847

Traxler, J. (2010). Will student devices deliver innovation, inclusion, and transformation? *Journal of Research Center for Educational Technology, 6*(1), 3–15.

Yasemin, G., Jacobs, C., & Andreas, K. (2015). Mobile learning in higher education: Current status and future possibilities. In M. Ally & B. Khan (Eds). International handbook of e-learning. Volume 2: Implication and case studies (pp. 33-42). US: Routledge.

## KEY TERMS AND DEFINITIONS

**Bring Your Own Device (BYOD):** The practice that permits students to use their personal mobile devices to support teaching and learning. In this case, instead of universities providing students with the technology, students use their own.

**Disruption:** Inappropriate use of mobile technology such as phone vibrating or ringing, or the use of social media in the classroom that disturbs lectures, peers and learning.

**Mobile Applications (Apps):** Software applications such as WhatsApp and Skype that are installed and run on mobile devices.

**Non-Content Related Activities:** Students use their mobile devices during lectures to engage in activities not related to the subject or content.

**Policies:** A set of guidelines developed by the classroom instructors or educational institutions to outline expectations regarding appropriate practices of mobile devices usage.

**Wearable Devices (or Wearable Technologies):** Refer to technologies that are embedded into items and accessories that individuals wear such as smart watch and glasses. These devices will allow access to information and some sort of communication; they are portable, flexible, ease to access and seamless.

# APPENDIX

*Table 5. Coding scheme survey open questions*

**Codes and sub-codes from open questions**

| *Policy* | *Advantages* |
|---|---|
| • Emergency | • Search information |
|    o  Only emergency | • Search content |
|    o  Content & emergency | • Other Advantages |
| • Status of Devices | *Disadvantages* |
|    o  Silence | • Affect concentration |
|    o  Other modes | • Distraction |
| • Content | • Disturbance |
| • Specific rules | • Other |
| • Other | |

*Table 6. Coding scheme focus group interview*

**Codes and sub-codes from the focus group interview**

| *Device usage* | *Policy* |
|---|---|
| • Status | • Current institution & instructor policy |
| • Content | • Suggestions |
|    o  Search | *Advantages* |
|    o  Apps | *Disadvantages* |
|    o  Other | |
| • Non-content | |
|    o  Apps | |
|    o  Discipline | |
| • Observing device use | |

# Section 4
# Smart Technology in the Information Society

# Chapter 15
# CRM 2.0 and Mobile CRM:
## A Framework Proposal and Study in European Recruitment Agencies

**Tânia Isabel Gregório**
*University of Lisbon, Portugal*

**Pedro Isaías**
*The University of Queensland, Australia*

## ABSTRACT

*Companies are becoming more focused on customers and on new ways to approach them individually. Mobile technologies and Web 2.0 have been pushing companies to evolve in this area. This research is focused on the way Customer Relationship Management (CRM) systems are used, on a European level, by recruiting companies to assist candidates in finding a satisfactory job. A framework is presented to identify how CRM 2.0 and mCRM (mobile CRM) can help candidates to find jobs in a personalized way. A set of four hypotheses have been defined. To gain a better understanding of these CRM systems, the methodology used in the exploratory study was quantitative, employing a non-probabilistic sampling technique, with 35 recruiting agencies being studied. Results showed that the use of software in recruiting agencies is quite common and that CRM 2.0 is present in the vast majority of the studied companies. When it comes to mobile CRM, there's still much to be explored in this channel, as agencies focus their resources on Web 2.0, leaving this channel's great potential of mobile CRM unused.*

## 1. INTRODUCTION

The subject of this chapter lies within the field of customer relationship management (CRM), and deals with customer relationship management in European recruitment companies. This research explores how CRM systems, combined with the recruitment companies' use of email, the Web, social media, applications and SMS, help candidates to find jobs in a personalized way. It aims, thus, to understand the means by which the job offers reach people, and whether these are in accordance with the candidate's profile.

DOI: 10.4018/978-1-5225-2492-2.ch015

Eurostat (2016) data shows that Portugal was the country with the fifth highest unemployment rate (12.6%) in the EU28 in 2015. The highest values were recorded in Greece and Spain, with 24.9% and 22.1%, respectively. The member states with the lowest unemployment rates were Germany, with a rate of unemployment of 4.6%, the Czech Republic with (5.1%), and the United Kingdom with a rate of 5.3%. There have been large variations in unemployment rates over the years. From 2005 to the first quarter of 2008 the unemployment rates in EU28 had been declining, reaching then 6.8%. After that, with the worsening of the economic crisis the numbers for unemployment rose until mid 2010, when they experienced a decrease up until the second quarter of 2011 only to rise again to a record of 11% in the second quarter of 2013. After that period, the numbers have been declining, having reached 9% in 2015 (Eurostat, 2016).

Because of these numbers it becomes important to explore the theme of CRM in recruitment agencies. This chapter's main research question is: How can the CRM systems used by European Union (EU) recruitment agencies help their candidates to find jobs through the personalization of offers according to their profile?

Therefore, this chapter has the overall objective of examining how CRM systems used by EU recruitment agencies help candidates to find jobs through offers customized according to the candidates' profile.

More specifically, this chapter aims to: (1) analyze how CRM 2.0 assists candidates in their job hunt, by providing an understanding of how Web 2.0 and social media are used by the recruitment agencies, the advantages that the agencies offer to the candidates, and the advantages of using CRM 2.0 to the agency; (2) understand how mobile CRM assists the candidates in their job search, by analyzing the advantages of mobile CRM for the agencies and the benefits that the agencies present to their candidates; (3) and analyze how the CRM system can be improved.

## 2. CRM

In order to provide a deeper understanding of CRM, this section begins by presenting a brief description of CRM, a concise historical perspective and some of CRM's concepts. This is followed by the presentation of Critical Success Factors for CRM Implementation in section 3.1. Sections 3.2 and 3.3 are about CRM 2.0 and mobile CRM, respectively. Finally, section 3.4 will briefly discuss the relationship between CRM and the methods of recruitment of agencies.

The origin of CRM derived from the concept of relationship marketing (RM), which RM aims to form long-term relationships with customers by repudiating approaches that focus on products rather than the clients (Debnath, Datta & Mukhopadhyay, 2016). An organisation's success is greatly influenced by its understanding of its clients' needs (King & Burgess, 2008), which is CRM's main concern. It represents a strategic shift that invests in the creation of added value for the customer. CRM has been evolving to incorporate more recent technology, namely Web 2.0 (Orenga-Roglá, Chalmeta, 2016).

Because of the complexity of the concept of CRM and the multitude of authors who, over time, have defined the concept, it becomes difficult to offer a simple and single definition. To Gummesson (2002), CRM represents the values and strategies of RM which emphasize customer relations and which are transformed into practical applications. To Payne and Frow (2005), CRM is a strategic approach that aims to create value for shareholders through the development of appropriate relationships with key customers and key customer segments. Thus, CRM combines the potential of RM strategies with information technology (IT) to create profitable long-term relationships with customers and other stakeholders. Payne and Frow (2005) also focus on the importance of CRM in regard to the method it employs to use information to understand and create value for customers. This requires a multifunctional integration of processes, people, operations and marketing resources which are enabled through information technology and applications. Only the companies that accumulate data about their customers and keep direct contact with them have the ability to enjoy the advantages of CRM (Faase et al., 2011). Despite the multiplicity of and differences between existing CRM definitions, there is a common aspect, which is CRM's objective: customer satisfaction and subsequent customer retention.

CRM involves four key stages. The first stage is the behavioral analysis of the customer, or more specifically the analysis of the customer's needs. The second phase involves the collection of data through the use of IT and is intended to create a more personal interaction with the customer. The third stage concerns market segmentation and is one of the objectives of CRM: the segmentation of the market according to the customers' needs in order to deal with them in an individual and specific manner. Finally, the last phase is to ensure that the customers keep their interest and involvement with the company (Faase et al., 2011).

## 2.1 Critical Success Factors for CRM Implementation

Before introducing the critical success factors (CSFs) of CRM, it is important to understand the concept of critical success factors. According to Caralli (2004), CSFs are key performance areas which are essential for an organization to fulfill its mission. The implementation of a CRM system in a company is a process that requires a set of features and elements that can increase the impact of the existing resources. Therefore, to ensure the success of its implementation it is necessary to understand aspects of the company, such as its culture, people, processes and technology, and to perceive CRM as more than an acquisition of software (Finnegan & Currie, 2010).

Firstly, the strategy of CRM implementation must consider the cultural factor. Finnegan and Currie (2010) argue that a model that focuses on the customer requires a change in the culture of information sharing. Management should train all the employees in the company. Also it should bring together the different departments, with their own subcultures, and communicate the strategies that are to be implemented, so that everyone is equally motivated to work toward the same objectives. Almotairi (2008) adds that to ensure the successful accomplishment of the objectives it is necessary to develop a culture where all employees are encouraged to share and learn the new, customer-oriented work structure.

Secondly, Finnegan and Currie (2010) consider that the implementation of a CRM strategy also involves a wide variety of people, including marketing professionals, IT staff and managers. All employees should be equally involved in the process. For convenience, senior executives should coordinate the entire project and ensure that the entire organization shares the same philosophy. Almotairi (2008) believes that the role of management is crucial in the implementation process, to ensure the financing of the project, and above all to put the project into action. Additionally, it is important to have a framework of qualified and skilled personnel to make the best use of the software (Ranjan & Bhatnagar, 2008).

Thirdly, the processes are also fundamental in the adoption of a CRM strategy. The strategy should therefore be customer-centric rather than product-based (Finnegan & Currie, 2010).

Finally, CRM's strategies exploit technological innovation as a way of collecting and analyzing data about customer patterns. This stage aims to analyze and interpret the customers' behavior and provide responses through personalized communications, and therefore deliver the value of the product or service to individual customers. At a technological level, it is essential to ensure the unification of all customer data, remove duplicate entries and guarantee that customer data are accurately presented throughout the organization (Finnegan & Currie, 2010).

## 2.2 CRM 2.0

The swift advances in technology-based systems, especially those related to the Internet, have led to fundamental changes in the way companies interact with each other and with consumers (Parasuraman & Zinkhan, 2002). There are increasing numbers of people using smartphones, tablets and the Internet every day to obtain information swiftly from wherever they are. In this sense, it is important that companies rethink the best way to reach customers that are becoming increasingly interactive (Hart & Gamal, 2012).

The emergence of Web 2.0 and the growing use of its applications have increased the resources of CRM for businesses. Web 2.0, a concept originally defined by Tim O'Reilly, is the second generation of the Web, which includes wikis and community portals. Its emphasis is placed on cooperation and information sharing (O'Reilly, 2007). With this evolution of Web 1.0 to Web 2.0 there is increasing participation by users. According to Greenberg (2010), social customers are in constant contact with the Internet and mobile devices. They share information and they demand the highest levels of transparency and authenticity.

The main difference between CRM 2.0 and CRM lies in the concept of transparency and the demands of customers. CRM is a philosophy and a business strategy supported by a CRM system, which is designed to improve human interactions in a business environment. CRM 2.0, on the other hand, is seen as a business strategy supported by a technological platform, business rules, processes and social characteristics. It aims to engage the customer in a collaborative conversation and thus benefit the business environment, through trust and transparency (Greenberg, 2010).

The primary concern of CRM is the focus on targets and the delivery of information. In terms of CRM 2.0, special attention is paid to the observation of customers' activities and the conversations that happen among them. It is also important to participate in these conversations (Greenberg, 2010).

CRM 2.0 exploits social media as a CRM strategy. Kaplan and Haenlein (2010) state that social media represent a set of applications that are based on the technological foundations of Web 2.0 and that allow the creation and exchange of user-generated content. Reinhold and Alt (2012) claim that CRM 2.0, also known as Social CRM (SCRM), takes advantage of this CRM strategy, which focuses on interaction (information between different parties), communication (exchange of information between the parties) and cooperation (collective creation). Social media are used to support CRM processes. They act as a communication channel for marketing campaigns and they are a key factor in providing information about the brand or the product. Moreover, they have an analytic function of discovering and evaluating new market perspectives, in which they analyse both the users and the content. They are also used as channels for transactions or sales and as a way to maintain contact with the customer.

According to Reinhold and Alt (2012), social media are an important resource for SCRM, because they provide five types of content: (1) the contents of posts, which can be analyzed by keyword or opinions; (2) data about the source, i.e. detailed information about the author; (3) the data provided by the users' profiles, which include information about e-mail, hobbies and interests; (4) information from the users' profiles about their friends and their activities; and (5) the connections that are established between posts and profiles, which provide information about the influence particular people.

Greenberg (2010) asserts that profiles on social networks have become essential for companies seeking information about the customer and what he/she wants. There is a growing need for companies to be where people are. Facebook, MySpace, Twitter, LinkedIn and Ning are the most popular social networks worldwide (Isaías, Pifano & Miranda, 2011).

With the growing interest in segmentation, profile analysis and the examination of clients' data to understand their lifestyle, social networks like Facebook and LinkedIn have increasingly assumed a role in selecting and predicting future behavior. There are specific tools that extract this type of information from social networks (Greenberg, 2010).

Technological advances can be observed not only on the Web, but also in mobile technology. It therefore becomes pertinent to talk about mobile CRM (mCRM).

## 2.3 Mobile CRM (mCRM)

The business of the mobile industry is evolving rapidly, thanks to a set of technologies that facilitate the development of a wide variety of innovative services. In recent years, a large increase in the use of value-added services available via mobile phones, such as games, GPS, MSN and information services, has been evident. This stresses the great potential of the mobile channel for companies in providing consumers with more complete services and in complementing the company's products (Hsu & Lin, 2008).

Camponovo, Pigneur, Rangone and Renga (2005) define mobile CRM as a set of services that intend to nurture the relationships with clients: the acquisition or maintenance of clients, marketing support, and sales or service processes via wireless networks as a means of delivery to customers. The formats used in mobile marketing include SMS (Short Message Service), MMS (MultiMedia Service) and WAP (Wireless Application Protocol). These formats have a lower cost in comparison to traditional media and they reach their target more easily (Al-alak & Alnawas, 2010).

However, not all authors agree with this definition. Sinisalo et al. (2007) find that, although this definition is useful, it is inadequate. Firstly, it does not sufficiently emphasize the critical role that communication plays in the acquisition and maintenance of profitable customers. Secondly, there is confusion around the concepts of "mobile" and "wireless". Wireless doesn't necessarily mean mobile, since wireless access only allows a limited mobility within the access space. Kumar (2004) also argues that the terms "mobile" and "wireless" have their own specific meanings. The term "mobile" refers to an ability to access devices on the go, whereas "wireless" refers to the ability to have access to a device when it is not physically plugged in. Thus Sinisalo et al. (2007) argue that mCRM can be seen as a specific type of CRM. MCRM can be defined as a type of CRM that works through mobile platforms. It is an interactive or one-way communication method, which is related to sales, marketing and customer service. It works through mobile devices with the aim of maintaining the relationship between the customers and the company.

When analyzing CRM, we can highlight some core features: personalized communication, interaction with clients and a great flexibility in communication (Sinisalo et al., 2007). The mobile and personal nature of mobile and wireless devices, combined with voice and data transmission capabilities, provides a set of unique features, such as ubiquity, 24-hour accessibility, location, personalization and convenience. These features are considered to be the most valuable and distinctive advantages of mobile services and they can build their own proposition of value (Camponovo et al., 2005).

Shankar and Balasubramanian (2009) claim that all mobile devices incorporate features such as text, audio/ data and video. Also, they have particular characteristics such as the specificity of the user's location, portability, cost and ease of response measurement.

One of the advantages of knowing the physical location of users is having the opportunity to direct them to promotional offers. Another great advantage is the portability of mobile devices. These wireless capabilities allow them to be used in any location, thereby creating more opportunities for the transmission of messages. These devices are used continuously and there which is an easier way to get message through. Their main disadvantage is that the fact that they do not allow the delivery of long messages (Shankar & Balasubramanian, 2009).

On the basis of these characteristics, we can make a comparison between the more traditional style of marketing, which uses media such as television, print and radio to get its messages across, and mobile marketing. Mass communication reaches all types of customers, both existing and potential ones, in contrast to mobile marketing, which is more restricted and reaches only those owners of mobile devices that choose to receive marketing communications. With mobile marketing, it is possible to reach customers at a specific place and time, the communication costs are lower than with the traditional channels, and it is easier to reach the target (Shankar & Balasubramanian, 2009).

## 2.4 CRM for Recruitment and Selection

Information technologies have caused changes in recruitment processes in recent decades. The Internet has begun to act as a channel of communication between employers and candidates. Technology has enabled corporate websites and job seekers to become more sophisticated and interactive (Barber, 2006).

The Internet and electronic communication systems, currently, facilitate the recruitment of candidates, who can now use computer applications to fill in their personal data online and submit them automatically. The techniques of e-recruitment (online recruitment) have a key role in storing CVs in a database for future job applications (Correia, 2010).

*Table 1. Differences between mass marketing and mobile marketing*

| Dimension | Mass Marketing | Mobile Marketing |
|---|---|---|
| Audience | All existing and potential users of the product. | All potential users who use mobile devices and who have chosen to receive marketing communications. |
| Communication Potential | Text, voice and video in substantially rich formats. | Text, voice, video and very limited visual space with limitations in the speed of transmission. |
| Communication Process | Marketeer to client | Interactive between the marketeer and the client |
| Ability to deliver the message by destination location | Low | High |
| Ability to measure and monitor the response | Low | High |
| Targeting capacity | Low | Medium |
| Cost per target audience | High | Low |

Source: Adapted from Shankar and Balasubramanian (2009, pp. 119).

Currently, the online recruitment sector is expanding, and it is a useful application of information technology for people. On the one hand, it facilitates the job searches of interested candidates. On the other hand, it facilitates the work of the recruitment professionals, who use their database to search for candidates. In short, online recruitment or e-recruitment has considerable advantages for recruiting agencies, such as the low cost of their online publications, the simplicity of candidates' segmentation by searching the candidates' database, and the fact that it reaches a population which is distinct from that of traditional media such as newspapers. On the other hand, online recruitment also offers advantages for applicants: the receipt of offers appropriate to the candidate's profile and interests; the possibility of doing their job search from home and at any time; and the availability of their CV with professional information on a 24/7 basis and without space limitations (Peretti, 2007).

Online recruitment involves not only the communication of job offers through the Internet but also a set of technological tools capable of selecting appropriate CVs and of maintaining an updated and efficient database to find people with specific characteristics (Mitter & Orlandini, 2005).

## 3. FRAMEWORK AND HYPOTHESES

This section presents a framework to identify how CRM 2.0 and mCRM can help candidates to find jobs in a personalized way. Also, it explores the advantages of using CRM 2.0 and mCRM for both the recruitment agencies and the candidates. For the recruitment agencies, CRM 2.0 promotes the participation, trust, costs reduction, interactivity with candidates and a better segmentation. For the candidates, we also can verify advantages, such as time and space availability to access to the information on a swiftness, personalized and economic way. Mobile CRM could also facilitate the job search process, through the advantages for the recruitment agencies, as the personalized communication, targeting facilities, omnipresence and accessibility. And for the candidates it provides personalized offers, option to decide what to receive and the location. On the basis of the literature review, various dimensions used in several studies to characterize CRM 2.0 and mCRM were identified. The proposed framework is a combination of the most important concepts.

Based on the framework proposed in Figure 1, a set of four hypotheses have been defined as described in the following paragraphs.

### 3.1 Personalization of Job Offers

The literature review allows us to conclude that online recruitment has advantages for applicants, in the sense that it is currently possible to receive job offers that are appropriate to the profile and interest of each candidate (Peretti, 2007). To this end the e-recruitment techniques have a key role in allowing the storage of CVs in a database for future job opportunities (Correia, 2010). This is the principal role of CRM software in data storage and the subsequent selection of candidates according to their characteristics. That said, the following hypothesis was constructed:

**Hypothesis 1:** The delivery of customized job offers is influenced by the use of CRM software by enterprises.

*Figure 1. Framework proposal*
Source: Authors.

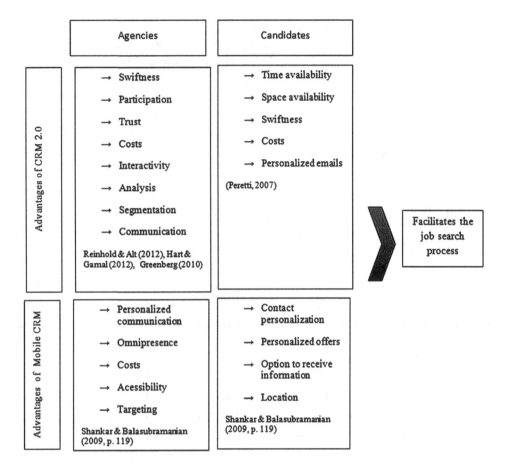

## 3.2 CRM 2.0 and Social Media

The literature review shows that CRM 2.0 exploits social media as a CRM strategy (Reinhold & Alt, 2012), by focusing on interaction, communication and cooperation. According to Reinhold and Alt (2012), there is an analysis' component associated with social media, because they provide different types of content: the content of a post, the data about the source, and the information provided in the profiles about email, hobbies and interests.

Thus, by combining all these benefits of CRM 2.0 and applying them to the reality of recruitment agencies and their use of social networks, the following hypotheses were created:

**Hypothesis 2:** Companies that use CRM software have increased awareness of the importance of CRM 2.0 for companies and candidates.

**Hypothesis 3:** Most recruitment agencies use social networks regularly.

## 3.3 Use of Mobile CRM

As for mobile CRM, it is important to identify communication, location, and targeting costs per contact, based on the characteristics presented by Shankar and Balasubramanian (2009, p. 119). It is also important to note the ubiquity, accessibility and interactivity highlighted by Camponovo et al. (2005).

The combination of all these features of mobile CRM identified in the literature review has led to the following hypothesis:

**Hypothesis 4:** Companies that use CRM software have increased awareness of the importance of mobile CRM for companies and candidates.

## 4. METHODOLOGY

## 4.1 Type of Study

This study is considered an exploratory study, as it aims to understand and examine an under-researched subject, the use of CRM in job selection and recruitment agencies. An exploratory study constitutes a valuable method of uncovering current and new knowledge (Robson, cited by Saunders et al., 2007).

## 4.2 Sampling Method and Sample

The sampling technique that was used is non-probabilistic sampling based on judgment, a technique where the elements of the population are defined according to the judgment of the investigator, in order to provide a better answer to the research questions and achieve the research objectives (Saunders et al, 2007). In this particular case, the selected recruitment agencies were those that were particularly informative and in conformity with the objectives of the study. The agencies were found on business listings from each country of the European Union. This type of sample, based on judgment, does not offer the same guarantees that probability samples do, but its use is justified in exploratory studies, as a first approach to the knowledge of the contours of a particular problem or a certain universe of study. This form of sample is often used when working with very small samples such as in case study research and when you wish to select cases that are particularly informative (Saunders et al, 2007).

The choice of this method is based mainly on the wealth of the information that can be obtained with the selection of particular cases.

The sample consists of 35 agencies from various European countries (mostly from EU) and USA. Most of them are based in Portugal (22.9%), the Netherlands (11.4%) and Belgium (8.6%). Most agencies in this study are private (91.4%), they have between 1 and 10 employees (34.3%) and they use CRM software (68.6%). The majority of respondents are between 25 and 34 years old (45.7%) and are female (71.4%).

*Table 2. Profile of the sample*

| | | | Total | Percentage |
|---|---|---|---|---|
| Enterprise data | Number of employees | 1-10 | 12 | 34.4% |
| | | 11-50 | 9 | 25.7% |
| | | 51-250 | 10 | 28.6% |
| | | >250 | 4 | 11.4% |
| | | **Total** | **35** | **100.0%** |
| | Company classification | Public | 3 | 8.6% |
| | | Private | 32 | 91.4% |
| | | **Total** | **35** | **100.0%** |
| | Company's Head Office | Austria | 2 | 5.7% |
| | | Belgium | 3 | 8.6% |
| | | Bulgaria | 1 | 2.9% |
| | | Germany | 1 | 2.9% |
| | | Ireland | 2 | 5.7% |
| | | Luxembourg | 2 | 5.7% |
| | | Netherlands | 4 | 11.4% |
| | | Portugal | 8 | 22.9% |
| | | Romania | 1 | 2.9% |
| | | Slovakia | 1 | 2.9% |
| | | Spain | 2 | 5.7% |
| | | Sweden | 1 | 2.9% |
| | | Switzerland | 2 | 5.7% |
| | | England | 4 | 11.4% |
| | | USA | 1 | 2.9% |
| | | **Total** | **35** | **100.0%** |
| Personal data | Age | 19-24 | 5 | 14.3% |
| | | 25-34 | 16 | 45.7% |
| | | 35-44 | 10 | 28.6% |
| | | 45-54 | 2 | 5.7% |
| | | 55-64 | 2 | 5.7% |
| | | **Total** | **35** | **100.0%** |
| | Gender | Male | 10 | 28.6% |
| | | Female | 25 | 71.4% |
| | | **Total** | **35** | **100.0%** |
| | Position in the Company | CEO | 6 | 17.1% |
| | | Head of Communication Dept. | 1 | 2.9% |
| | | Head of IT Dept. | 1 | 2.9% |
| | | Head of Marketing Dept. | 2 | 5.7% |
| | | Head of HR Dept. | 5 | 14.3% |
| | | Recruiting and Psychological Evaluation Dept. | 7 | 20.0% |
| | | Other | 13 | 37.1% |
| | | **Total** | **35** | **100.0%** |

## 5. DATA COLLECTION

For the collection of the data, we used an online questionnaire with a Portuguese version and an English version that was hosted by Qualtrics' platform and distributed by email to pre-selected contacts. The online questionnaire is a research method with rapid diffusion and reduced costs.

Before the questionnaire was sent, a pre-test was conducted among 14 people, which resulted in an adjustment to the wording of certain questions and the exclusion of one question. The pre-test has the objective of assessing the adequacy of the questionnaire, i.e. the formulation of the questions and their general disposition in the questionnaire. The questionnaire was available online during the last two weeks of July and the entire month of August. In total, 400 questionnaires were sent and 44 responses were obtained. From those, 35 were considered, since the incomplete questionnaires were eliminated. A follow-up was done to obtain a higher number of responses.

After collection, the data were analyzed quantitatively in a univariate and multivariate statistical analysis with the assistance of SPSS (Statistical Package for Social Sciences) software.

## 6. RESULTS

### 6.1 CRM 2.0

#### 6.1.1 Personalization

The majority of the agencies that were part of this study use CRM software (68.6%) and send job offers on a daily or weekly basis to the candidates via email (65.7%). Among the agencies that send jobs, 83.3% customize the offers according to the preferences of the applicants who previously selected them when they registered on the website/platform. Most of these agencies take into account the "areas of interest" of the candidates (32.1%), their "academic qualifications" (25%) and their "location" (23.2%).

In order to test hypothesis 1 - "The delivery of customized job offers is influenced by the use of CRM software by enterprises" - we used a chi-square test. The data showed that, out of all the agencies that use CRM software (68.6%), most of them (85%) opt for delivery of personalized job offers to the candidates. However, the differences between the agencies that use CRM software and the agencies that do not use the software are not statistically significant ($X^2(1) = 0,624; p > 0.05$), which prevents us from accepting the hypothesis that is being studied. This result may be justified by the sample size, so it becomes necessary to develop this issue in further studies by using a larger sample.

#### 6.1.2 The Importance of CRM 2.0

To evaluate the importance of CRM 2.0, we proceeded to create two synthetic indexes to encompass the perception of the benefits of CRM 2.0 for the companies and for the candidates. In order to test Hypothesis 2, "Companies that use CRM software have increased awareness of the importance of CRM 2.0 for companies and candidates", the Kolmogorov-Smirnov test was performed. It became possible to see that the data did not follow a normal distribution ($p = 0.000$) and for this reason we opted for the application of the non-parametric Mann-Withney (M-W) test to make inferences about the differences between the averages of the companies using CRM software and the averages of the agencies that don't use the software.

We began by testing the reliability of the indexes via Cronbach's Alpha, which has a value of 0.765 and 0.879 for the overall index of perceived advantage of CRM 2.0 for companies and candidates, respectively. These values ensure a good reliability.

According to the results that were obtained from the descriptive statistics (Table 3), it is possible to observe some differences in terms of the averages between the agencies that use and the agencies that do not use CRM software. The agencies that use CRM software have an increased awareness of the benefits that CRM represents for the agencies (Table 4). The average of ordinances is higher in the agencies that are using the software (ascending scale). However, the differences are not statistically significant (M-W = 89.500; $p = 0.133$).

It is also possible to observe that the agencies that use CRM software have a higher perception of the advantages of CRM for the candidates. The ordinance average is superior in the agencies that use the software (ascending scale). Nonetheless, the differences are not statistically significant (M-W = 89.000; $p = 0.133$).

These results do not allow us to accept hypothesis 2: "Companies that use CRM software have increased awareness of the importance of CRM 2.0 for companies and candidates".

## 6.1.3 Use of Social Networks

In order to verify hypothesis 3, "Most recruitment agencies use social networks regularly", firstly there was an assessment of the number of agencies that use social networks. The data showed that 100% of the agencies used social networks. Secondly, there was an analysis of the dimensions related to the manner

*Table 3. Descriptive statistics*

| | Users of CRM Software (N=24) | | Non-users of CRM Software (N=11) | |
| --- | --- | --- | --- | --- |
| | **Mean (N=24)** | **Std. Deviation** | **Mean (N=11)** | **Std. Deviation** |
| Index for the perception of the advantages of CRM for the agencies | 4.04 | 0.310 | 3.74 | 0.550 |
| Index for the perception of the advantages of CRM for the candidates | 4.11 | 0.670 | 3.73 | 0.65 |

Scale: 1 = Totally disagree; 5 = Totally agree.

*Table 4. Mann-Whitney Test*

| | Mean Rank | | |
| --- | --- | --- | --- |
| | **Mann-Whitney** | **Users of CRM Software (N=24)** | **Non-Users of CRM Software (N=11)** |
| Index for the perception of the advantages of CRM 2.0 for the agencies | 89.500 | 19.77 | 14.14 |
| Index for the perception of the advantages of CRM 2.0 for the candidates | 89.000 | 19.79 | 14.09 |

and the frequency of use of social networks. To allow this analysis, a synthetic index was created for the use of social networks that included the dissemination of job offers, the contact point with the client, and analysis of profiles, posts, keywords and opinions. The reliability and the consistency of the index are acceptable (Cronbach's Alpha = 0.648). The global average of the index is 3.19 points, which indicates that, on average, the use is positive. The average is slightly higher than 3 on the scale, thus allowing the confirmation of hypothesis 3.

The analysis of the statements that constitute the index showed that the dissemination of job offers had an average response of 3.91 (on a scale from 1 to 5, where 1 means "never" and 5 stands for "always"). A total of 74.3% of the agencies use social networks "very often" or "always" as a method to disseminate the job offers. With regard to the use of social networks as a point of contact with the candidate, the average does not present positive values: 2.74. A total of 34.4% answered "sometimes" and 28.6% chose "a few times". The analysis of the profiles and the analysis of the posts and opinions for recruitment purposes have an average of 3.03 and 3.09 respectively.

It was equally important to analyse the social networks that were most frequently used by the recruitment agencies. LinkedIn is the most used (37.4%), followed by Facebook (35.2%) and Twitter (19.8%).

## 6.2 Mobile CRM and Its Advantages

A total of 77.1% of the recruitment agencies use mobile technology to contact the candidates. On a scale of 1 to 5, where 1 corresponds to "never" and 5 corresponds to "always", the average score for SMS as a way of contacting candidates was 3.59, whereas email scored 4.41. Nonetheless, there was an inferior average in terms of the use of MMS, Apps and QR Codes. In regard to the use of MMS, 96.3% chose

*Figure 2. Use of social networks by the recruitment agencies*
*Scale: 1 = Never; 5 = Always.*

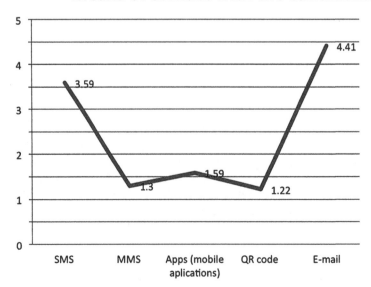

## Means of contact with the candidates

*Figure 3. Means of contact with the candidates used by the recruitment agencies*
*Scale: 1= Never; 5=Always.*

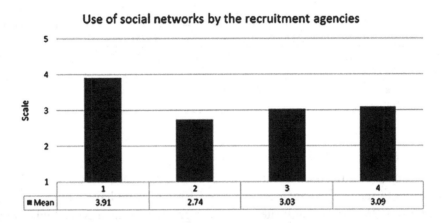

"never" or "a few times". With regard to the use of Apps and QR Codes, the scores of the agencies that replied "never" were 66.7% and 81.5% respectively.

In order to test hypothesis 4 - "Companies that use CRM software have increased awareness of the importance of mobile CRM for companies and candidates" – two synthetic indexes were created to include the perceptions of the advantages of mobile CRM for the companies and for the candidates.

Firstly, the reliability was tested through Cronbach's Alpha, which gave a value of 0.751 for the global index of the perception of the advantages of mobile CRM for the agencies. This means that there is a good reliability score. For the global index of the perception of the advantages of mobile CRM for the candidates, there was a reasonable score of 0.576.

It had already been concluded from the Kolmogorov-Smirnov test that the data did not follow a normal distribution (p = 0.000). Again, we chose to conduct a non-parametric Mann-Withney (M-W) test to make inferences about the differences between the averages of the agencies that use the software and the agencies that do not use it.

According to the results of the descriptive statistics (Table 5), it is possible to see some differences between the averages of the agencies that use the CRM software and the averages of those that do not use it. The agencies that use CRM software have a higher perception of the advantages of mobile CRM

*Table 5. Descriptive statistics*

| | Users of CRM Software (N=24) | | Non-users of CRM Software (N=11) | |
|---|---|---|---|---|
| | Mean (N=24) | Std. Deviation | Mean (N=11) | Std. Deviation |
| Index for the perception of the advantages of mobile CRM for the agencies | 4.04 | 0.450 | 3.96 | 0.450 |
| Index for the perception of the advantages of mobile CRM for the candidates | 4.09 | 0.540 | 4.00 | 0.400 |

Scale: 1 = Totally disagree; 5 = Totally agree

*Table 6. Mann-Whitney Test*

| | Mean Rank | | |
|---|---|---|---|
| | **Mann-Whitney** | **Users of CRM Software (N=24)** | **Non-users of CRM Software (N=11)** |
| Index for the perception of the advantages of mobile CRM for the agencies | 116.500 | 18.65 | 16.59 |
| Index for the perception of the advantages of mobile CRM for the candidates | 109.000 | 18.96 | 15.91 |

for the companies. The average of the ordinances is higher in the agencies that use the software (ascending scale). Nonetheless, the differences are not statistically significant (M-W = 116.500; $p = 0.587$).

It is also possible to see that the agencies that use CRM software have a higher perception of the advantages of mobile CRM for the candidates. The average of the ordinances is higher in the agencies that use the software (ascending scale). Nonetheless, the differences are not statistically significant (M-W = 109.000; $p = 0.430$).

The results allow the rejection of hypothesis 4, "Companies that use CRM software have increased awareness of the importance of mobile CRM for companies and candidates", even though the differences are not statistically significant

## 6.3 Improvements to the CRM system

Among the agencies that stated that there have been improvements in the last year with regard to the agency's processes (74.3%), the changes most frequently reported related to the software that they use (20.9%), to the maximization of the website (18.6%) and to foster the use of mobile channels (18.6%).

Most agencies, 54.3%, stated that they expect to make some modifications to the CRM system, in the short or long term. Among these modifications, it is possible to highlight changes to the software that is used (25.3%), exploring the website's potential (21.5%), and the interconnection of platforms of contact and an increase in the use of social media (16.5%).

*Table 7. Implemented improvements and planned improvements*

| | Implemented Improvements | | Planned Improvements | |
|---|---|---|---|---|
| | **N** | **%** | **N** | **%** |
| Software | 9 | 20.90 | 20 | 25.30 |
| Increased use of the company's database | 6 | 14.00 | 12 | 15.20 |
| Exploring the potential of the website | 8 | 18.60 | 17 | 21.50 |
| Interconnection of platforms of contact (website, social media, mobile) | 5 | 11.60 | 13 | 16.50 |
| Mobile channel maximisation | 8 | 18.60 | 4 | 5.10 |
| More frequent use of social media | 7 | 16.30 | 13 | 16.50 |

## 7. DISCUSSION AND CONCLUSION

The results demonstrate that the use of CRM software and the personalization of the contact processes is increasing among recruitment agencies. The sample that was studied reiterates this conclusion: 68.6% of the agencies use CRM software and the vast majority of them send job offers via email and customize the content for the candidates. Generally speaking, it is possible to highlight that CRM 2.0 has a significant presence in the agencies that not only use the CRM system but also combine it with the development of their own website and a strong presence in social networks such as LinkedIn. In terms of mobile CRM, the developments in this area are not as evident. Despite the fact that the majority of the agencies use mobile technologies in their contact with the candidates, the most noticeable methods of communication are SMS and emails.

When they are properly employed by the recruitment agencies, CRM systems can be essential tools to facilitate both the work of the agency and the job search of the applicant. This study concluded that the agencies that use software that is appropriate for CRM send customized offers to the applicants more often.

The results allow the conclusion that the agencies that use CRM software have a wider awareness of the advantages of CRM 2.0 for the candidates and for their own agency.

This study also concluded that the recruitment agencies have a strong presence in social networks, especially in networks such as LinkedIn and Facebook. They are used mainly for the dissemination of job offers. Also, there is an analytical component that can be explored, which consists in analyzing the posts and the profiles of the candidates. Most agencies claimed that they "sometimes" use social networks for this purpose.

One important conclusion that the results allow is that the agencies that use CRM software have a higher perception of the advantages of mobile CRM for their own agency as well as for the candidates; this is similar to what was concluded in the case of CRM 2.0.

The highlight of this study was that 77.1% of agencies use mobile technologies to contact the candidates, but only frequently use SMS and email, and rarely or never use MMS, Apps or QR codes. It was expected that the agencies that plan to make improvements in software in the short term would have the development of mobile channels as a priority. However, out of the 54.2% of the agencies that expected to make short-term improvements, only 5.1% mention improvements in their mobile channels. This warrants a recommendation to the agencies in terms of the maximization of their mobile channels, namely through mobile applications with job offers, in an era of growing use of smartphones.

Among the recently implemented improvements in the CRM system, it is possible to underline the concern of the agencies with the software they use, which reflects a rising preoccupation of the agencies with focusing on the client, and, in this particular case, the candidate. The improvements made by the agencies in terms of the maximization of their website and their mobile channels were also visible. When it comes to improvements that are planned for the short term, software, the maximization of the websites, the interconnection of the platforms of contact and a more frequent use of social media are the most cited. With respect to these improvements, it becomes important to underline the growing use of CRM software and the interconnection of the platforms of contact, which have the ability to provide more information on the client and to assist the dissemination of job offers.

## REFERENCES

Al-alak, A., & Alnawas, I. (2010). Mobile Marketing: Examining the Impact of Trust, Privacy Concern and Consumers Attitudes on Intention to Purchase. *International Journal of Business and Management, 5*(3), 28–41. doi:10.5539/ijbm.v5n3p28

Almotairi, M. (2008). CRM Success Factors Taxonomy. *European and Mediterranean Conference on Information Systems*, Dubai, UAE.

Barber, L. (2006). E-recruitment Developments. In *HR Network Paper MP63* (1st ed.). Brighton, UK: The Institute for Employment Studies.

Camponovo, G., Pigneur, Y., Rangone, A., & Renga, F. (2005). *Mobile customer relationship management: an explorative investigation of the Italian consumer market.* Paper presented in the 4th International Conference on Mobile Business, Sydney, Australia. doi:10.1109/ICMB.2005.63

Caralli, R. (2004). *The Critical Success Factor Method: Establishing a Foundation for Enterprise Security Management.* Software Engineering Institute.

Correia, C. (2010). *Encontrar um emprego através da internet: modelo de portal de recrutamento online para a Administração Pública Local Autárquica* (Master Dissertation). Instituto Superior de Ciências do Trabalho e da Empresa, Instituto Universitário de Lisboa, Portugal.

Debnath, R., Datta, B., & Mukhopadhyay, S. (2016). Customer Relationship Management Theory and Research in the New Millennium: Directions for Future Research. *Journal of Relationship Marketing, 15*(4), 299–325. doi:10.1080/15332667.2016.1209053

Eurostat. (2016). Unemployment statistics. *Statistics Explained.* Available: http://ec.europa.eu/eurostat/statistics-explained/index.php/Unemployment_statistics#Main_statistical_findings

Faase, R., Helms, R., & Spruit, M. (2011). Web 2.0 in the CRM domain: Defining social CRM. *Int. J. Electronic Customer Relationship Management, 5*(1), 1–22. doi:10.1504/IJECRM.2011.039797

Finnegan, J., & Currie, L. (2010). A multi-layered approach to CRM implementation: An integration perspective. *European Management Journal, 28*(2), 153–167. doi:10.1016/j.emj.2009.04.010

Greenberg, P. (2010). The impact of CRM 2.0 on customer insight. *Journal of Business & Industrial Marketing,Vol., 25*(6), 410–419. doi:10.1108/08858621011066008

Gummesson, E. (2002). *Total Relationship Marketing* (2nd ed.). Oxford, UK: Butterworth-Heinemann.

Hart, S., & Kassem, G. (2012). *Social customer relationship management – from customer to friend.* Presented at European and Mediterranean Conference on Information System, Munich, Germany.

Hsu, F., & Lin, S. (2008). mCRM's New Opportunities of Customer Satisfaction. *World Academy of Science, Engineering and Technology, 40*.

Isaías, P., Pífano, S., & Miranda, P. (2011). Social Network Sites: Modeling the New Business-Customer Relationship. In M. Safar & K. Mahdi (Eds.), *Social Networking and Community Behavior Modeling: Qualitative and Quantitative Measures.* Hershey, PA: IGI Global.

Kaplan, A. M., & Haenlein, M. (2010). Users of the world, unite! The challenges and opportunities of social media. *Business Horizons, 53*(1), 59–68. doi:10.1016/j.bushor.2009.09.003

King, S. F., & Burgess, T. F. (2008). Understanding success and failure in customer relationship management. *Industrial Marketing Management, 37*(4), 421–431. doi:10.1016/j.indmarman.2007.02.005

Kumar, S. (2004). Mobile communications: Global trends in the 21st century. *Int. J. Mobile Communication, 2*(1), 67–86. doi:10.1504/IJMC.2004.004488

Mitter, G. & Orlandini, J. (2005). Recrutamento online/internet. *Maringá Management: Revista de Ciências Empresariais, 2*(2), 19-34.

O'Reilly, T. (2007). What Is Web 2.0: Design Patterns and Business Models for the Next Generation of Software. *International Journal of Digital Economics, 65*, 17-37.

Orenga-Roglá, S., & Chalmeta, R. (2016). Social customer relationship management: Taking advantage of Web 2.0 and Big Data technologies. *SpringerPlus, 5*(1), 1462. doi:10.1186/s40064-016-3128-y PMID:27652037

Parasuraman, A., & Zinkhan, G. (2002). Marketing to and serving customers through the internet: An overview and research agenda. *Journal of the Academy of Marketing Science, 30*(4), 286–295. doi:10.1177/009207002236906

Payne, A., & Frow, P. (2005). A Strategic Framework for Customer Relationship Management. *Journal of Marketing, 69*(4), 167–176. doi:10.1509/jmkg.2005.69.4.167

Peretti, J. (2007). *Recursos Humanos (3rd ed.)*. Lisboa: Edições Sílabo.

Ranjan, J. & Bhatnagar V. (2008). Critical Success Factors For Implementing CRM Using Data Mining. *Journal of Knowledge Management Practice, 9*(3).

Reinhold, O. & Alt, R. (2012). Social Customer Relationship Management: State of the Art and Learnings from Current Projects. *BLED 2012 Proceedings*.

Ryals, L., & Payne, A. (2001). Customer Relationship Management in Financial Services: Towards Information-Enabled Relationship Marketing. *Journal of Strategic Marketing, 9*(1), 3–27. doi:10.1080/713775725

Saunders, M., Lewis, P., & Thornhill, A. (2007). *Research Methods for Business Students* (4th ed.). Prentice Hall.

Shankar, V., & Balasubramanian, S. (2009). Mobile Marketing: A Synthesis and Prognosis. *Journal of Interactive Marketing, 23*(2), 118–129. doi:10.1016/j.intmar.2009.02.002

Sinisalo, J., Salo, J., Karjaluoto, H., & Matti, L. (2007). Mobile customer relationship management: Underlying issues and challenges. *Business Process Management Journal, 13*(6), 771–787. doi:10.1108/14637150710834541

## ADDITIONAL READING

Acker, O., Gröne, F., Akkad, F., Pötscher, F., & Yazbek, R. (2011). Social CRM: How companies can link into the social web of consumers. Journal of Direct. *Data and Digital Marketing Practice, 13*(1), 3–10. doi:10.1057/dddmp.2011.17

Allden, N., & Harris, L. (2013). Building a positive candidate experience: Towards a networked model of e-recruitment. *The Journal of Business Strategy, 34*(5), 36–47. doi:10.1108/JBS-11-2012-0072

Ang, L. (2011). Community relationship management and social media. *The Journal of Database Marketing & Customer Strategy Management, 18*(1), 31–38. doi:10.1057/dbm.2011.3

Berry, L. (1983). Relationship Marketing of Services – Growing Interest, Emerging Perspectives. *Journal of the Academy of Marketing Science, 23*(4), 236–245. doi:10.1177/009207039502300402

Chen, I., & Popvich, K. (2003). Understanding customer relationship management (CRM): People, process and technology. *Business Process Management Journal, 9*(5), 672–688. doi:10.1108/14637150310496758

El Ouirdi, M., El Ouirdi, A., Segers, J., & Henderickx, E. (2014, July). Social recruiting: towards a state-of-the-art synthesis. In *Proceedings of the European conference on social Media university of Brighton* (pp. 734-736).

El Ouirdi, M., Pais, I., Segers, J., & El Ouirdi, A. (2016). The relationship between recruiter characteristics and applicant assessment on social media. *Computers in Human Behavior, 62*, 415–422. doi:10.1016/j.chb.2016.04.012

Furtmüller, E., Wilderom, C., & Van Dick, R. (2010). Sustainable e-Recruiting portals: How to motivate applicants to stay connected throughout their careers?[IJTHI]. *International Journal of Technology and Human Interaction, 6*(3), 1–20. doi:10.4018/jthi.2010070101

Gummerus, J., Liljander, V., Weman, E., & Pihlström, M. (2012). Customer engagement in a Facebook brand community. *Management Research Review, 35*(9), 857–877. doi:10.1108/01409171211256578

Heller Baird, C., & Parasnis, G. (2011). From social media to social customer relationship management. *Strategy and Leadership, 39*(5), 30–37. doi:10.1108/10878571111161507

Hoffman, D. L., & Fodor, M. (2010). Can you measure the ROI of your social media marketing? *MIT Sloan Management Review, 52*(1), 41.

Holm, A. B. (2012). E-recruitment: Towards an ubiquitous recruitment process and candidate relationship management. German Journal of Human Resource Management. *Zeitschrift für Personalforschung, 26*(3), 241–259.

Kim, C., Lee, I.-S., Wang, T., & Mirusmonov, M. (2015). Evaluating effects of mobile CRM on employees performance. *Industrial Management & Data Systems, 115*(4), 740–764. doi:10.1108/IMDS-08-2014-0245

Liang, X., Zhang, J., & Tang, B. (2010). Developing a Mobile Service-Based Customer Relationship Management System Using Fuzzy Logic. *International Journal of Computational Intelligence Systems, 3*(6), 805–814. doi:10.1080/18756891.2010.9727743

Lin, R. J., Chen, R. H., & Kuan-Shun Chiu, K. (2010). Customer relationship management and innovation capability: An empirical study. *Industrial Management & Data Systems*, *110*(1), 111–133. doi:10.1108/02635571011008434

Löffler, C., & Hettich, M. (2010). Enabling Mobile Customer Relationship Management for Small and Medium-Sized Enterprises. In S. Krishnamurthy, & G. Singh (Eds.), *Proceedings of the IADIS International Conference–E-Commerce*, Freiburg (pp. 155-159).

Malthouse, E. C., Haenlein, M., Skiera, B., Wege, E., & Zhang, M. (2013). Managing customer relationships in the social media era: Introducing the social CRM house. *Journal of Interactive Marketing*, *27*(4), 270–280. doi:10.1016/j.intmar.2013.09.008

Melanthiou, Y., Pavlou, F., & Constantinou, E. (2015). The use of social network sites as an e-recruitment tool. *Journal of Transnational Management*, *20*(1), 31–49. doi:10.1080/15475778.2015.998141

Moreira, C. (2007). *Teoria e Práticas de Investigação*. Universidade Técnica de Lisboa, Instituto Superior de Ciências Sociais e Políticas.

Nguyen, B., & Mutum, D. S. (2012). A review of customer relationship management: Successes, advances, pitfalls and futures. *Business Process Management Journal*, *18*(3), 400–419. doi:10.1108/14637151211232614

Sashi, C. M. (2012). Customer engagement, buyer-seller relationships, and social media. *Management Decision*, *50*(2), 253–272. doi:10.1108/00251741211203551

Silberer, G., & Schulz, S. (2010). Mobile customer relationship management (mCRM): constraints and challenges. Handbook of Research on Mobile Marketing Management, 173-189.

Trainor, K. J., Andzulis, J. M., Rapp, A., & Agnihotri, R. (2014). Social media technology usage and customer relationship performance: A capabilities-based examination of social CRM. *Journal of Business Research*, *67*(6), 1201–1208. doi:10.1016/j.jbusres.2013.05.002

Zheng, V. (2011). The value proposition of adopting mCRM strategy in UK SMEs. *Journal of Systems and Information Technology*, *13*(2), 223–245. doi:10.1108/13287261111136025

Zide, J., Elman, B., & Shahani-Denning, C. (2014). LinkedIn and recruitment: How profiles differ across occupations. *Employee Relations*, *36*(5), 583–604. doi:10.1108/ER-07-2013-0086

## KEY TERMS AND DEFINITIONS

**CRM:** Customer Relationship Management represents a strategy that is used for managing a company's current and future clients. It uses customers' data and a variety of processes to enhance the relationship with the clients and promote retention and sales.

**CSF:** Critical Success Factors concern a series of vital factors from which success can be derived. They can represent precepts, activities or any other elements that are required to accomplish a specific mission with success.

**CV:** Curriculum Vitae constitutes a depiction of an individual's academic background and previous professional experiences. It is normally an essential requirement for job applications and it traditionally has a written form, but it is also possible to record audio or video CVs.

**eRecruitment:** Electronic recruitment stands for the use of electronic resources, mostly web-based, for recruitment purposes. It uses technology to perform the several tasks pertaining to the recruitment process, namely candidate selection, interviewing and hiring.

**IT:** Information Technology refers to the use of computers and their associated technology to create, store, process and share any form of electronic data. It also includes multimedia and telecommunications.

**mCRM:** Concerns the use of mobile technology and devices, such as smartphones and tablets to deploy CRM strategies. It represents an adaptation of CRM to the real-time and anywhere requirements of conducting business.

**RM:** A marketing strategy that focuses on the development of long-term relationships with customers. It goes beyond single purchase marketing approaches and it emphasises the need to create client loyalty, by providing superior services and products.

**SCRM:** Represents the use of social media to deliver CRM strategies. It is facet of CRM that focuses on engaging with clients via social media platforms such as Facebook, YouTube or Twitter.

**SPSS:** Currently denominated IBM SPSS Statistics and it is a software package that is used for statistical analysis. Its advanced features enable the user to gain a deeper and more precise understanding from data.

# Chapter 16

# The Complexities of Digital Storytelling:
## Factors Affecting Performance, Production, and Project Completion

**Peter Gobel**
*Kyoto Sangyo University, Japan*

**Makimi Kano**
*Kyoto Sangyo University, Japan*

## ABSTRACT

*This chapter describes a pair of studies investigating factors involved in task-based learning using digital storytelling. In Study 1, the stories were analyzed using the factors of topic, time, medium, and reported technological proficiency. Student attitudes towards the tasks were gauged using a questionnaire that measured perceived task cost and value, engagement with the task, and expectancy for success on future tasks. In Study 2, three mid-task planning conditions were introduced and a questionnaire was administered to see student attitudes towards various modes of mid-task planning. The results of Study 1 suggest that digital storytelling can be incorporated into EFL classes to reduce foreign language anxiety, to provide greater opportunities to use English, and to foster ICT skills. The results of Study 2 suggest that students favor a teacher-led planning condition, and that this planning condition had a positive effect on student attitudes towards the project (value and cost).*

## INTRODUCTION

In early Computer Assisted Language Learning (CALL) programs the stimulus was in the form of text presented on a screen, and the only way in which the learner could respond was by entering an answer at the keyboard. However, more recent approaches to CALL emphasize more learner-centered explorative approaches, in contrast to teacher-centered drill-based approaches (Davies, 2000). For example, Ho and Savignon (2013) expound on the advantages of employing face-to-face peer reviewing (FFPR)

DOI: 10.4018/978-1-5225-2492-2.ch016

and computer-mediated peer review (CMPR) for academic writing contexts in CALL settings. Another example of recent approaches to CALL is digital storytelling. Project work using digital storytelling allows for a variety of opportunities to engage in language learning and provides options for the foreign language classroom. However, using digital storytelling with language students can create a number of challenges for both pedagogy and technology.

The Center for Digital Storytelling defines a digital story as a short story containing digital images, text, recorded audio narration, and/or music. It allows computer users to be creative storytellers through the process of selecting a suitable topic, writing a script, and developing interesting stories based either on their own experience or the course subject matter. By telling stories with the aid of digital media, students are engaged in learner-centered, authentic tasks. In a digital storytelling project, creating an end product (the digital story) is clearly goal-oriented, and the process itself helps students develop a deeper connection with the subject matter. Robin (2008) suggests that digital storytelling projects provide a strong foundation in many different types of literacy such as digital literacy, global literacy, technology literacy and information literacy. Indeed, the digital storytelling process is an example of a 'multiliteracy' approach. Due to the simultaneous use of a foreign language and technology, students not only are asked to cope with an increasingly globalized society, communicating with other cultures through language, but also are asked to develop communicative competence through new communication technologies.

Digital storytelling (DST) has the potential to help students gain "21st century literacy skills," providing a unique opportunity to acquire new media literacy and ICT skills as well as the standard four skills covered in most language classes. Morgan (2014) reported that digital story projects were beneficial for motivating and helping students to improve their writing and reading, because the projects encouraged students to think about how their stories were created. In addition, Kim (2014) suggested that participants in her study were able to develop their oral proficiency. Yang and Wu (2012) have suggested that DST has an effect on both receptive and productive language competences, serving as a transformative technology-supported pedagogy that combines both English language learning in a constructivist/collaborative context, and self-production of authentic materials.

## BACKGROUND OF THE PRESENT STUDIES

Regarding the educational framework of our studies, English as a foreign language (EFL) in Japan, a number of studies have been implemented. Susono (2011) instigated a digital storytelling project at a junior high school for second grade students, finding benefits of the project included a greater understanding of their peers, as well as significant 'knowledge reformation' while writing and rewriting the scripts. Enokida (2015) had students make digital stories about books they had read in an extensive reading assignment and suggested that the stories had a great effect on students' understanding of the content and promoted awareness of story structure. Ono (2014) found that higher proficiency students in his study seemed to feel that their Project Based Learning (PBL) skills such as computer use, data collection, problem solving, discussion and presentation in the field of foreign language teaching, greatly improved after the project, while the lower proficiency students in the study felt that the main benefit of the project was a reduction in their foreign language anxiety.

Many of the above studies dealt with digital stories as projects within a set curriculum. One of the aspects of this kind of project is the amount of time used for planning the task prior to execution. With regard to planning and its effects on production, pre-task planning has received considerable attention from second language researchers (e.g., Foster & Skehan, 1999; Ortega, 2005) with findings suggesting that proper planning can positively affect oral production. Examining and understanding how pre-task planning affects task and project performance has a number of pedagogical benefits. First, pre-task planning helps learners to prepare to achieve project goals, and it can motivate learners to actively engage in the task regardless of their background knowledge (Bui, 2014). The primary purpose of Study 2 was to investigate what kind of pre-task planning improves learners' completion of the digital story project.

## Previous Studies of Pre-Task Planning Types

Past research has investigated the effectiveness of various planning conditions. Although the majority of these studies were undertaken with solitary speaking tasks, the theories and results of these studies are relevant to PBL as well, since PBL involves a series of tasks culminating in a final product. For this reason, a review of previous research on pre-task planning is deemed relevant. In an early study, Foster and Skehan (1999) focused on three types of strategic planning (Teacher-led, Solitary, and Group-based planning, and a control variable) to see how the three different conditions affected learners' speaking performance in decision-making tasks. Their results suggested that that Solitary planning and Teacher-led planning positively affected oral production (in terms of complexity, accuracy, and fluency). The Solitary planning condition led to greater complexity than the control (No-planning) condition and the Teacher-led condition led to greater accuracy than the other conditions. Foster and Skehan believed the Teacher-led condition helped learners attain better levels of complexity and fluency, resulting in an overall superior performance. They noted that the Group planning condition did not seem as effective, perhaps because the students in their study had very little experience working in groups.

Mochizuki and Ortega (2008) looked at the effect of guided and unguided planning on Japanese high school students' oral story-retelling task performance. They compared three planning conditions: Unguided planning; Teacher-guided planning; and Guided planning in the form of a checklist of task-related grammar points. No significant differences were found between Guided and Unguided planning conditions, but the Teacher-guided planning condition enhanced accuracy of the task.

Kawauchi (2005) investigated three types of Solitary planning in which the learners used writing, rehearsing, and reading to aid project completion. Prior to engaging in a speaking task, participants were asked to complete one of three planning conditions: using 10 minutes to write what they wanted to say when they performed the task; rehearsing the task for 10 minutes by talking aloud; and reading a model passage for 10 minutes prior to performance. Analysis revealed that the participants who used the reading planning made use of vocabulary and phrases from the reading passages. Kawauchi felt that lower-proficiency learners would benefit from pre-task reading because of this. On the other hand, the participants who used writing and rehearsing planning conditions focused more on meaning than form.

With the results of previous studies in mind, we set out to explore the design and use of DST projects in a content-based framework at the university level. In Study 1 we focused on the complexity of the projects and the demands of the tasks and how this affected task performance and student perceptions of the task. In Study 2 the focus was on the addition of a planning stage in each project. The addition of a planning stage to each digital story project was influenced by previous research on pre-task planning and its positive effect on task performance. From this previous research it seems that pre-task planning is a reasonable option for stand-alone tasks as well as PBL. In implementing a planning stage into PBL, the researchers were interested in student attitudes towards the pre-task planning methods and whether these planning conditions had any effect on their attitudes (cost and value) towards the projects. Student attitude is important in this regard as it is directly related to perceived efficacy of the planning method and as a result student motivation to successfully complete the project and their attitudes towards further projects.

## STUDY 1 AND STUDY 2

Study 1 is concerned with the design and implementation of presentation projects for EFL university students majoring in cultural studies. The students were expected to create digital stories/presentations on topics covered in the course texts, and to present them to the class for discussion. It was felt that the digital story projects would allow students to deeply explore the cultural content presented in the course while using English in a focused and purposeful way. The story projects reflect the Content-Based Instruction (CBI) goals of helping students connect meaningful content with language instruction, in an effort to improve their cultural knowledge and language and literacy skills. This approach to language learning is still viewed as uncommon in Japanese EFL classes, where the focus is often on grammar and vocabulary, the dissection of texts, and the translation of meaning. Classes often use textbooks that do not require long-term attention to one topic and very little use of critical thinking in analyzing issues. It was felt that the use of content-based projects would be one way to introduce critical thinking into the Japanese EFL classroom.

Project-based learning tends to be more complicated in nature than more directed forms of task-based learning. Digital storytelling, when used in a project-based learning approach, is an inherently messy process, with the product not always in sync with the original task (Thorne & Black, 2007). Due to the number of steps involved in creating a digital story, and the technical skills necessary, task design is of utmost importance. The researchers are interested in what factors contribute to a successful digital story experience for students. The present research explores the question of task design in digital storytelling, taking into account the context of the task, and the four elements of good task design—purpose, content, activity, and completion—and how they were perceived by the participants. Since task complexity is an important factor to consider in design, both the complexity of the task (in terms of familiarity with the topic and cognitive demands of the task) and required technological proficiency are considered. It is hypothesized that more unfamiliar topics will lead to perceptions of higher cost and less engagement on the part of the participants (Hypothesis 1), and that experience and familiarity with technology needed for task completion will lead to perceptions of those tasks as having greater value and a higher expectancy for success (Hypothesis 2). Also to be considered are the limitations of both technology and technological proficiency when designing a task, since previous research in this area has shown that perceived proficiency has an impact on both product and process (Gobel & Kano, 2013; 2014a; 2014b). To this end, the following research questions were formulated for Study 1:

1. How do students perceive their technological proficiency?
2. To what extent does project design affect perceived complexity of each project?
3. What were student attitudes towards the individual tasks?

For Study 2 the focus was on which kind of pre-task planning and evaluation activities would be perceived as beneficial to the completion of the story projects. Previously, the effects of pre-task planning types have varied widely and focused solely on language accuracy and complexity (e.g., Foster & Skehan, 1999; Kawauchi, 2005; Mochizuki & Ortega, 2008). The purpose of this study is to examine student attitudes towards, and the effects of three planning types—Solo planning, Group planning, and Teacher-led planning—on digital story completion. Specifically, Study 2 is guided by the following research questions:

1. Which of the three planning conditions—Solo planning, Group-work, or Teacher-led planning—was seen as more beneficial by the students?
2. To what extent do three planning conditions—Solo planning, Group-work, and Teacher-led planning—affect students' perceived cost and value of each project?

## METHODS AND MATERIALS

### Study 1: Research Design

The participants were 18 third-year non-English major university students, studying in the Faculty of Cultural Studies. Their English proficiency, as measured by the TOEFL ITP ranged from 437-515. The participants were enrolled in a compulsory oral skills presentation class that met for 90 minutes a week. All participants had completed a required information technology course in the first year of their studies at university, so all were familiar with using PowerPoint and the school LMS (Moodle).

The course goals centered around developing presentation skills, but as a content-based course the subjects covered in the text and readings focused on the following topics: problems in urban areas; how products are marketed; describing a process, such as how to perform Japanese tea ceremony; comparing cultural differences. Each topic was covered for three weeks, with outside readings provided to supplement the textbook. While studying the text and topic in class, students were asked to prepare a presentation on the topic. This preparation included choosing a topic based on required readings, writing the story, choosing the media, and creating the final product. Students were given 20-30 minutes each week to work with groups to finalize and present their ideas. Table 1 summarizes the topic, style, and requirements of the projects.

At the end of each topic, students were asked to present a 1-2 minute digital story on their topic, meant to stimulate a final discussion on the topic. As a result, the projects themselves had a focus on meaning and a non-linguistic outcome. The projects themselves were manipulated to emphasize either familiarity with the topic (topics 1 and 3) or technological and process demands (group work versus individual work, and audio recording versus live presentation, and online submission and online feedback). For most of the students, this kind of class and the activities it entailed was a new experience. The majority of EFL

*Table 1. Project topic, style, and requirements*

| Project | Topic | Presentation Style | ICT Requirements |
|---------|-------|--------------------|------------------|
| 1 | city problems | group - in class | visual media, voice recording |
| 2 | marketing tricks | group - in class | visual media, voice recording, auto play |
| 3 | how to ... | individual - in class | visual media, project sent to instructor as file |
| 4 | cultural comparison | individual - watch and respond on LMS | visual media, voice recording, auto play, upload to LMS |

and culture-based courses were either lecture-based and teacher-centered, or dealt with topics on a very cursory level for the purposes of vocabulary and grammar development in the L2.

At the end of each project, students were given a questionnaire (cf. Appendix). The questionnaire was created with 20 Likert scale items meant to measure perceptions of project design and difficulty (5 questions covering perceived purpose of the project, difficulty of content and project), self-efficacy (6 questions covering perceived performance and perceived technological proficiency), and perceived cost and value of each project (9 questions dealing with actual and expected difficulty of the project, amount of time and effort involved, interest in the project, and expectation for success in future tasks). It was hypothesized that unfamiliar topics would lead to higher cost and less engagement with the project, and that familiarity with technology would lead to greater value and higher expectancy for success in future tasks (Gobel & Kano, 2013; 2014b).

## Study 2: Research Design

The participants in this study were 40 non-English major university students, studying in the Faculty of Cultural Studies. Their English proficiency was similar to that of the students in Study 1 (TOEFL 437-515). The participants were enrolled in three separate classes: a compulsory oral skills presentation class (22); an intercultural communication class (9); and a third-year seminar class (9). All classes met for 90 minutes a week. As with the students in Study 1, all participants were familiar with using PowerPoint and the school LMS (Moodle).

The course goals of each course were different, but all were content-based courses where similar (though not identical) subjects could be covered in the projects. Each course was divided into four-week modules covering one topic. At the end of each module students were asked to prepare a 1-2 minute digital presentation on the topic. As with Study 1, this preparation included choosing a topic based on material covered in class, writing the story, choosing the media, and creating the final product. Planning time was factored into the project, with students in each class performing Solo planning in one project, Group work in another, and Teacher-led planning in yet another. Once students had completed their final product, a recorded digital story in movie form, it was uploaded to the Moodle, where students would watch them and respond to their peers' work. Unlike Study 1, in this study the complexity of the project and technical demands of the project did not vary. That is to say, the only differences between the three projects were the topics and the planning conditions.

At the end of each project, students were given a questionnaire specific to the planning type (cf. Appendix). Each of the three questionnaires was created with 20 four-point Likert scale items meant to measure perceptions of planning type, project design and difficulty (5 questions covering perceived purpose of the project, planning type, difficulty of content and project), self-efficacy (6 questions covering perceived performance and perceived technological proficiency), and perceived cost and value of each project (9 questions dealing with actual and expected difficulty of the project, amount of time and effort involved, interest in the project, and expectation for success in future tasks). The questionnaires were identical to each other in all respects other than the items questioning planning type.

The focus of this study was planning condition, and a randomized model was chosen to test the three planning conditions. With three classes and three planning conditions, the researchers needed to control for the intervening variables of time and practice effect. A Latin-squares design was employed in this study to create a randomized assignation of planning type to class. Table 2 shows the data collection schedule for Study 2.

*Table 2. Classes and planning type*

| Class | DST 1 | DST 2 | DST 3 |
|-------|-------|-------|-------|
| 1 | teacher | solo | group |
| 2 | group | teacher | solo |
| 3 | solo | group | teacher |

## Planning Conditions

Three planning conditions were used in this study: Solo planning, Group-work, and Teacher-led planning. The participants in the Solo planning condition, which was designed to help the participants think of appropriate structure for the digital story, were given a checklist of things they should consider when creating their final digital story. This checklist was similar to the grading rubric used, focusing on organization (introduction, body, conclusion), contents of the story (explanation of the topic, background information, importance of the topic), and use of media (pictures and audio). Students were given the checklist and asked to match their first draft with the items on the checklist. If their first draft of the story did not match the checklist they had the opportunity to rewrite and add information to make a more complete digital story. In this condition the teacher played a small role in helping students navigate the checklist, but other than that students worked on their own.

The participants in the Group planning condition talked about the topic of their story and explained what they were going to do. The teacher separated the students into small groups (3-4 students each) and asked them to describe their stories to each other using storyboards and notes as support. Their group would then give feedback on the topic and approach the student was planning to use. To help in their discussion a series of prompts and example questions was given to group members prior to discussion. These questions and prompts were similar to the checklist in the Solo planning condition (covering content, organization, and media), but were framed as questions group members could ask each other about their respective digital story drafts. The teacher simply observed the group discussions during this condition. The Group-work condition was expected to help the participants think about the concept of audience and better understand what would be helpful or interesting for listeners. One of the key points in creating successful stories and presentations is the concept of an audience, something that is often missing in student-created product.

The participants in the Teacher-led planning condition watched a teacher-produced digital story, silently listening while the teacher explained what s/he had done and points the students should consider in their own stories. The digital story was played once without interruption. Following this, the story was played slide by slide, with the teacher pointing out: how the story structure was developed; how media was effectively used in the story to get the message across; and the use of proper audio, voice inflection, and sound effects to enhance the story and increase audience interest. The aim of this condition was to provide the participants with examples of good digital stories and efficient ways to express their ideas. All three planning conditions were performed during class time with 15 minutes given to each planning condition.

# RESULTS

## Study 1

The projects were assessed based on the ratings given by the instructor and the impressions of the participants using questionnaires. Instructor's ratings for the four projects resulted in the following: Topic 1 (city problems) showed a better use of media and a better presentation of material. There were problems with recording sound, such as poor sound quality, narrative that did not accurately match the slides, and stories with no sound at all; Topic 2 (marketing tricks) displayed less coherence in all stories, with less critical thinking involved, and problems with sound and automatic play functions (many students had trouble creating stories that would play automatically from beginning to end); Topic 3 (how to) showed a better use of pictures and visual media, clearer story structure, and better presentation of material; Topic 4 (cultural comparison) showed coherent presentations, less critical thinking (a focus on impact rather than logical thought), problems with sound and automatic play functions similar to those mentioned above, and a number of students had trouble uploading to Moodle and completing forum posts.

After each project, the same questionnaire was administered to elicit participant impressions in four different aspects of the projects: self-efficacy, project design, cost/value of the projects, and presentation and requirement preference. Below are some interesting points we found from the questionnaire results, matched with our research questions.

**Research Question 1:** How do students perceive their technological proficiency?

In general, student use of computers was rather limited (4 hours per week in average). Students reported using computers mostly for school work (homework and reports) and searching for information. They reported a mild dissatisfaction with their PC and PowerPoint proficiency, which stayed stable over the projects.

**Research Question 2:** To what extent does project design affect perceived complexity of each project?

Students were generally satisfied with the projects and what they learned from them, and they felt the projects' purpose became clearer over time (from project 1 through project 4). The group work was viewed as being more difficult than the individual work. They found that the presentation demands and use of computer and PowerPoint became more difficult over time. The recording was the most difficult part of the project for the students, especially in the last project.

**Research Question 3:** What were student attitudes towards the individual tasks?

Student actual and expected difficulties were similar, and the time and effort they put into the projects remained the same, even though they felt the difficulty level of the projects rose over time. As a result, their evaluation of their final product decreased over time, and expectation for success in future projects also slightly decreased.

On the whole, they preferred individual work to group work, and live narration to recording. Manual/auto play preference changed over time. They also preferred Moodle upload to class presentation, responding that they did not have difficulty viewing assignments and commenting on the LMS forum.

## Study 2

Study 2 concentrated on planning conditions and the possibility that different planning conditions would not only be preferred, but would influence perception of the projects (expectancy for success, cost and value of the projects). Data for this study was gathered through means of a survey, and with such a small *N* size statistical analysis of the results would be difficult to interpret. Nevertheless, there were clear differences based on planning condition for a number of the items on the questionnaire. It must be noted that the results presented below represent correlations between planning conditions, attitudes and motivation, and as such do not suggest causation. Without further data it would be difficult to say for certain that a specific planning condition caused a certain motivation. Nevertheless, the findings presented below offer insights into how planning conditions may interact with perceptions and motivations.

**Research Question 1:** Which of the three planning conditions—Solo planning, Group-work, or Teacher-led planning—was seen as more beneficial by the students?

Student attitudes towards all three planning conditions were generally favorable, with Solo planning being seen as the least favorable (mean 2.76). The Group-work and Teacher-led planning conditions had means that seemed not to differ very much (2.91 for Teacher and 3.1 for Group).

**Research Question 2:** To what extent do three planning conditions—Solo planning, Group-work, and Teacher-led planning—affect students' perceived cost and value of each project?

The items in this part of the questionnaire provided insights into how the planning condition might have affected student perceptions of expectancy for success and perceived cost and value of the projects. Items dealing with expectancy for success on the project received slightly more favorable evaluation under the Teacher-led planning condition than under other planning conditions. However, actual difficulty of the project, amount of time to complete the project, and the amount of effort expended on the project differed greatly. This is perhaps due to the difference in topic from project to project.

Regarding interest in the task, students had a somewhat unfavorable impression for the project undertaken under the Group-work condition, with Teacher-led and Solo conditions resulting in identical scores. As for interest in each of the planning conditions, students felt that the projects performed under the Teacher-led condition were the most interesting, followed by Solo planning and Group-work conditions, in that order.

Although students generally had a favorable view of the DST projects as a good way to study, the project undertaken with the Solo planning condition had a slightly lower value. For items dealing with both perceived success on the present task and in future tasks, projects completed under the Teacher-led planning condition were deemed by the students as the most favorable.

## Discussion

The results of Study 1 show that more familiar topics showed a clearer presentation of material. This makes sense since the topic is familiar to the students both in concept and in structure. In addition, the first topic was discussed and produced in groups, allowing for a strong negotiation of meaning which might have led to a more coherent story line. When the topic shifted to a less personal and more critical stance, student presentations faltered slightly. This may be due to the fact that the students have little experience criticizing values or viewpoints, and very little practice at critical thinking. There has been a great deal of criticism regarding this (e.g., McVeigh, 2002) with many educators calling for more chances for students to practice critical thinking in their classes. Related to this is the argument that critical thinking in education may have a cultural bias (Matsuda & Nisbett, 2001), which may be one reason it is not emphasized in Japanese education, but this exploration lies outside of the scope of this chapter. Once the stories moved back to personal experience (Topics 3) the presentations regained some coherence, but the general nature of Topic 4 (cultural comparison) led the stories back towards standard cultural differences and stereotypes, rather than promoting critical thinking, as was the intention.

It seemed clear from the results of Study 1 that the students were not ready to expand their technological proficiency beyond what they had already learned. Despite training in the use of PowerPoint, a plethora of "how to" videos on YouTube (in their L1) and chances to teach each other the skills necessary for the projects, many of them seemed determined to plow ahead with the knowledge they had, without improving their technological skills. This observation was somewhat supported by their reluctance to use computers more than a few hours a week. This reluctance continued into Study 2, where students were able to access PowerPoint on their smartphones if they wished (this feature is provided by the university for all students). Although the majority of students created the DST on their computers at home, a few did so on their phones, but with limited and very basic results. These results speak to a reluctance on the part of some Japanese students to embrace digital technology, a tendency noted by Gobel and Kano (2014b) and Cotes and Milliner (2016). Although this tendency may be specific to the Japanese learning environment, teachers involved in DST and PBL with technology must take these factors into account when designing and implementing tasks and projects.

In line with previous findings, Study 2 suggests that pre-task planning is seen as beneficial, and projects completed under the Teacher-led planning condition produced a greater expectancy for success (both on the project and on future projects) and a higher perceived success on the project than the other two conditions. There are a number of possible explanations for this. First, the Teacher-led condition gave the learners opportunities to think about developing their story using the teacher's model. By giving the students a model that they could use as a goal (something that many students are used to doing), student perhaps felt they understood the task more clearly, or at least understood what was required of them. In addition, the model was a teacher-generated one (in stead of peer-generated), which is something many of the students are used to (though not usually in the form of a digital story) and which may have reduced performance anxiety. Receiving model input allowed students to access and retrieve topic-related lexis more easily when creating their own stories. In other words, teacher-led input allowed the students to produce a product similar to that presented in the Teacher-led planning condition. Second, Teacher-led planning allowed learners to monitor how to say things and helped learners notice useful lexical chunks (e.g., *The first slide will show...* and *In conclusion I would like to say...*). Students could then recycle language from the teacher input (input-mining), which would have improved the quality of their digital stories. This allowed the learners to produce more syntactically complex utterances and a more cohesive narrative. In fact, both the Teacher-led and Group-work planning conditions involve forms of input-mining. The Group-work condition allowed the speakers to use the language and comments produced by their peers, but the results of the questionnaire suggest that students found less value in peer input than in teacher input. Future analysis of the data may show that the Teacher-led condition provides more accurate and richer models for students to mine, which might lead to better project completion.

In the Group-work planning condition, participants were helped by their peers to make a more complex and coherent story structure because the Group-word condition functioned as a kind of rehearsing for their own stories. The participants in the Group-work condition asked each other questions about the story topic and format of the stories they were going to create, so that they could develop ideas that they could talk about and use in their digital stories. As noted by Kawauchi (2005), a rehearsing planning condition may help learners to think about the contents of their narrative. This, in turn, may have allowed the students to create more coherent digital stories.

On the other hand, projects completed under the Solo planning condition seemed to be perceived as the least beneficial. This could be because learners were not being directed to pay attention to certain features of the story. Rather, the onus of story structure and coherence was on the learners themselves.

Finally, this study has raised another important issue about project-based learning: the role of the teacher in a project-based classroom. Project-based learning is generally learner-centered, meaning-focused, and goal-oriented. However, one criticism voiced by researchers and educators against project-based learning is that attention to form is limited. Certainly in classrooms and situations where the students are used to a focus on form, a lack of attention to form may leave students feeling the activity was inadequate. To address this issue one could add form-focused instruction to the projects. Students' systematic use of language mined from the teacher's model input could help provide some examples which would lead students' attention to the useful formulaic language and story structure which would benefit their final products. Study 2 suggests that teachers' input enhancement might play an important role in a project-based classroom.

In addition to the above points, it seems clear that the students involved in Study 2 benefitted from teacher input and felt that teacher input was more valuable than personal insight and peer input, leading to a more favorable view of the project and the effort needed to produce the digital story (value and cost). This is perhaps the area where the teacher may play the most important role. Although the projects themselves are student-centered, depending on student insight and effort to create a final product, the teacher as facilitator (i.e., presenting models, providing lexis, and producing secondary assessment tools) is still very much valued by students. Student autonomy was offered and encouraged in all projects, but teacher support seemed to be both expected and desired by the participants in this study.

## CONCLUSION

In conclusion, the results of Study 1 show that Hypothesis 1 (unfamiliar topic/cost and engagement) was not supported, while Hypothesis 2 (familiarity with technology/value and expectancy for success) was found to be inconclusive. The results suggest that the more familiar/personal topics resulted in a marginally better product (from the instructor's viewpoint). Students' view of their own skills remained stable throughout the entire study, despite the fact that project demands increased over time. Finally, it seemed that the participants had very little motivation to learn new aspects of technology (auto play function, recoding their voice, Moodle forum). In other words, although the DST projects offered opportunities to learn new skills and master old ones, the students saw the completion of the project (the product) as more important than the creation of the story (the process).

This suggests that, at least with these participants, more support regarding the technical aspects of the DST projects is warranted. Although the students were familiar with most aspects of PowerPoint and the Moodle LMS, it might have been beneficial to review technology and skills throughout the projects, in an effort to build up students' technology skills. Although support was provided in the form of video tutorials and links to 'how to' web pages, it seems that students were not that interested in accessing them or improving their skills.

Study 2 explored the effects of pre-task planning types on student perception of the projects and their attitude toward the project regarding cost and value. The findings indicated that all planning conditions were seen as positive by the students, but there seemed to be a greater positive influence from the Teacher-led condition than from the other two conditions. What Study 2 did not investigate was the effect of planning on the quality of the completed projects. A future study is planned that will look at the effect of planning conditions on the quality of final projects, namely accuracy, fluency, narrative story structure, and DST mechanics. This future study will help researchers understand which planning conditions are more beneficial to students involved in PBL.

There are a number of limitations that must be acknowledged regarding both studies. As with any small-scale intact study, the limitations of sample size ($N=18$, $N=40$) meant that meaningful statistical analysis of the data was difficult to perform. With such a small sample size it is difficult to generalize the results in any meaningful way, and the lack of statistical power in the results creates a situation where the findings must be viewed with caution. A future study with a larger population, allowing proper statistical analysis, should provide more robust results that will add to the body of knowledge in this area. Second, the findings may still not be sufficient to understand how the participants use the planning tools and input given to them. For future research, the inclusion of a more in-depth qualitative analysis would be beneficial in terms of finding out what the participants are actually doing during the planning stages. Post-task interviews, retrospective interviews, and even think-aloud protocols or more open-ended questionnaires may help researchers gain a fuller understanding of actual student behavior during the planning stage.

In spite of these limitations, the findings of these two studies have provided some implications for project-based learning. First, pre-task planning helps learners to produce a better final product. In particular, the Teacher-led conditions might play an important role in increasing the quality of students' output, as in previous studies (e.g., Mochizuki & Ortega, 2008). One explanation for this is that the Teacher-led condition helps learners by modeling a final product prior to student completion of their own projects. A second reason is that Teacher-led planning can helps to activate, extend and refine what the students already know and can produce. Thus, Teacher-led pre-task planning highlights and contributes to student knowledge by creating a model story that can be considered input to encourage students' development toward better communication. Hence, teachers retain an important role as a facilitator in a project-based classroom by providing students some input-enhancements to maximize opportunities for the noticing language form and use. More importantly, the study has suggested a number of areas for future research. Among them are the efficacy of interactive presentations, projects using a variety of formats (movie, chat, Google Maps, etc.), projects using mobile devices, online peer feedback at each step, and the effects of recursive training sessions (teacher or peer-led).

# REFERENCES

Bui, G. (2014). Task readiness. In P. Skehan (Ed.), *Processing perspectives on task performance*. Amsterdam: Benjamins.

Cotes, T., & Milliner, B. (2016). *Preparing Japanese students' digital literacy for study abroad: How much CALL training is needed?* Presentation given at Eurocall 2016.

Deci, E. L., & Ryan, R. M. (1985). *Intrinsic motivation and self-determination in human behavior*. New York: Plenum. doi:10.1007/978-1-4899-2271-7

Ellis, R. (2009a). Task-based language teaching: Sorting out the misunderstandings. *International Journal of Applied Linguistics*, *19*(3), 221–246. doi:10.1111/j.1473-4192.2009.00231.x

Ellis, R. (2009b). The differential effects of three types of task planning on the fluency, complexity, and accuracy in L2 oral production. *Applied Linguistics*, *30*(4), 474–509. doi:10.1093/applin/amp042

Foster, P. (1996). Doing the task better: How planning time influences students' performance. In J. Willis & D. Willis (Eds.), *Challenge and change in language teaching* (pp. 126–135). Oxford, UK: MacMillan Heinemann.

Foster, P., & Skehan, P. (1999). The influence of source of planning and focus of planning on task-based performance. *Language Teaching Research*, *3*(3), 215–247. doi:10.1191/136216899672186140

Gobel, P., & Kano, M. (2013). Implementing a Year-long Reading While Listening Program for Japanese University EFL Students. *Computer Assisted Language Learning*, *27*(4), 279–293. doi:10.1080/09588221.2013.864314

Gobel, P., & Kano, M. (2014a). *Japanese teachers' use of technology at the university level. Attitudes to technology in ESL/EFL pedagogy*. Arabia TESOL Publications.

Gobel, P., & Kano, M. (2014b). Mobile natives: Japanese university students' use of digital technology. APACALL Book III. Cambridge Scholars Publishing.

Ho, M. C., & Savignon, S. J. (2013). Face-to-face and computer-mediated peer review in EFL writing. *CALICO Journal*, *24*(2), 269–290.

Kawauchi, C. (2005). The effects of strategic planning on the oral narratives of learners with low and high intermediate proficiency. In R. Ellis (Ed.), *Planning and task-performance in a second language* (pp. 143–166). Amsterdam: Benjamins. doi:10.1075/lllt.11.09kaw

Kim, S. (2014). Developing autonomous learning for oral proficiency using digital storytelling. *Language Learning & Technology*, *18*(2), 20–35.

Matsuda, T., & Nesbitt, R. (2001). Attending holistically vs. analytically: Comparing the context sensitivity of Japanese and Americans. *Journal of Personality and Social Psychology*, *81*(5), 922–934. doi:10.1037/0022-3514.81.5.922 PMID:11708567

McVeigh, B. J. (2002). *Japanese Higher Education as Myth*. New York: East Gate Book.

Mochizuki, N., & Ortega, L. (2008). Balancing communication and grammar in beginning- level foreign language classrooms: A study of guided planning and relativization. *Language Teaching Research*, *12*(1), 11–37. doi:10.1177/1362168807084492

Morgan, H. (2014). Using digital story projects to help students improve in reading and writing. *Reading Improvement*, *51*(1), 20–26.

Ono, Y. (2014). Motivational Effects of Digital Storytelling on Japanese EFL Learners. *Proceedings of CLaSIC*, *2014*, 414–431.

Razmi, M., Pourali, S., & Nozad, S. (2014). Digital Storytelling in EFL Classroom (Oral Presentation of the Story): A Pathway to Improve Oral Production. *Procedia: Social and Behavioral Sciences*, *98*, 1541–1544. doi:10.1016/j.sbspro.2014.03.576

Robin, B. R. (2008). Digital storytelling: A powerful technology tool for the 21st century classroom. *Theory into Practice*, *47*(3), 220–228. doi:10.1080/00405840802153916

Susono, H., Ikawa, T., Kagami, A., & Shimomura, T. (2011). Digital Storytelling "Tegami (A Letter to My Future Myself)" Project by Japanese Junior High Students. In *World Conference on Educational Multimedia, Hypermedia and Telecommunications* (Vol. 2011, No. 1, pp. 2324-2327).

The Center for Digital Storytelling. (n.d.). Retrieved from http://digitalstorytelling.coe.uh.edu/index.cfm

Thorne, S., & Black, R. (2007). Language and literacy development in computer-mediated contexts and communities. *Annual Review of Applied Linguistics*, *27*, 1–28. doi:10.1017/S0267190508070074

Willis, D., & Willis, J. (2007). *Doing Task-based Teaching*. Oxford, UK: Oxford University Press.

Yang, Y. T. C., & Wu, W. C. I. (2012). Digital storytelling for enhancing student academic achievement, critical thinking, and learning motivation: A year-long experimental study. *Computers & Education*, *59*(2), 339–352. doi:10.1016/j.compedu.2011.12.012

## ADDITIONAL READING

Abrahamson, C. E. (1998). Storytelling as a pedagogical tool in higher education. *Education*, *118*(3), 440–451.

Ayas, C. (2006). An examination of the relationship between the integration of technology into social studies and constructivist pedagogies. *The Turkish Online Journal of Educational Technology*, *5*(1), 14–25.

Benmayor, R. (2008). Digital storytelling as a signature pedagogy for the new humanities. *Arts and Humanities in Higher Education*, *7*(2), 188–204. doi:10.1177/1474022208088648

Betoret, F. D. (2007). The influence of students and teachers thinking styles on student course satisfaction and on their learning process. *Educational Psychology*, *27*(2), 219–234. doi:10.1080/01443410601066701

Brinkley, E., Leneway, R., Webb, A., & Harbaugh, C. (2002) Preparing for Digital Story Telling. http://t3.preservice.org/wmu/Preparing%20for%20Digital%20Story%20Telling.htm

Chung, S. K. (2006). Digital storytelling in integrated arts education. *The International Journal of Arts Education, 4*(1), 33–50.

Davis, A. (2005). Co-authoring identity: Digital storytelling in an urban middle school. *THEN, 1.* Retrieved from http:// thenjournal.org/

Dodge, B. (1995). Webquests: A technique for internet-based learning. *Distance Education, 1*(2), 10–13.

EDUCAUSE Learning Initiative. (2007). 7 things you should know about digital storytelling. Retrieved November 1, 2011, from. http://www.educause.edu/ir/library/pdf/ELI7021.pdf

Freidus, N., & Hlubinka, M. (2002). Digital storytelling for reflective practice in communities of learners. *SIGGROUP Bulletin, 23*(2), 24–26. doi:10.1145/962185.962195

Gere, J. (2002). Storytelling tools for the classroom. In J. Gere, B.-A. Kozlovich, & D. A. I. Kelin (Eds.), *By word of mouth: A storytelling guide for the classroom* (pp. 1–8). Hawaii: Pacific Resources for Education and Learning.

Hartley, J., & McWilliam, K. (2009). *Story circle: Digital storytelling around the world*. Maldon, MA: Blackwell. doi:10.1002/9781444310580

Hughes, J. (2005). The role of teacher knowledge and learning experiences in forming technology-integrated pedagogy. *Journal of Technology and Teacher Education, 13*(2), 277–302.

Koohang, A., Riley, L., Smith, T., & Schreurs, J. (2009). E-learning and constructivism: From theory to application. *Interdisciplinary Journal of Knowledge and Learning Objects, 5*, 91–109.

Lambert, J. (2009). *Digital storytelling: Capturing lives, creating community* (3rd ed.). Berkeley, CA: Digital Diner Press.

Lundby, K. (2008). Introduction: Digital storytelling, mediatized stories. In K. Lundby (Ed.), *Digital storytelling, mediatized stories: Self-representations in new media* (pp. 1–17). New York, NY: Peter Lang.

Maier, R. B., & Fisher, M. (2006). Strategies for digital storytelling via tabletop video: Building decision making skills in middle school students in marginalized communities. *Journal of Educational Technology Systems, 35*(2), 175–192. doi:10.2190/5T21-43G4-4415-4MW5

Malita, L., & Martin, C. (2010). Digital storytelling as web passport to success in the 21st century. *Procedia: Social and Behavioral Sciences, 2*(2), 3060–3064. doi:10.1016/j.sbspro.2010.03.465

Mellon, C. A. (1999). Digital Storytelling: Effective learning through the internet. *Educational Technology, 39*(2), 46–50.

Mergendoller, J., & Thomas, J. (2004) Managing Project-Based Learning: Principles from the Field. Buck Institute for Education. http://www.bie.org/research/pbl/index.php

Nelson, M. E., & Hull, G. A. (2008). Self-presentation through multimedia: A Bakhtinian perspective on digital storytelling. In K. Lundby (Ed.), *Digital storytelling, mediatized stories: Self- representations in new media* (pp. 123–141). New York, NY: Peter Lang.

Neo, M., & Neo, T. K. (2010). Students' perceptions in developing a multimedia project within a constructivist learning environment: A Malaysian experience. *The Turkish Online Journal of Educational Technology*, *9*(1), 176–184.

Ohler, J. (2005). The world of digital storytelling. *Educational Leadership*, *63*(4), 44–47.

Ohler, J. (2008). *Digital storytelling in the classroom: New media pathways to literacy, learning, and creativity*. Thousand Oaks, CA: Corwin.

Porter, B. (2005). *Digitales: The art of telling digital stories*. Denver, Colorado, USA: Bernajean Porter Consulting.

Rance-Roney, J. (2008). Digital storytelling for language and culture learning. *Essential Teacher*, *5*(1), 29–31.

Robin, B. R. (2008). Digital storytelling: A powerful technology tool for the 21st century classroom. *Theory into Practice*, *47*(3), 220–228. doi:10.1080/00405840802153916

Sadik, A. (2008). Digital storytelling: A meaningful technology-integrated approach for engaged student learning. *Educational Technology Research and Development*, *56*(4), 487–506. doi:10.1007/s11423-008-9091-8

Salpeter, J. (2005). Telling tales with technology. *Technology and Learning*, *25*(7), 18–24.

Schank, R. C. (1990). *Tell me a story: A new look at real and artificial memory*. New York: Charles Scribner.

Tsou, W., Wang, W., & Tzeng, Y. (2006). Applying a multimedia storytelling website in foreign language learning. *Computers & Education*, *47*(1), 17–28. doi:10.1016/j.compedu.2004.08.013

Verdugo, D. R., & Belmonte, I. A. (2007). Using digital stories to improve listening comprehension with Spanish young learners of English. *Language Learning & Technology*, *11*(1), 87–101.

Vinogradova, P. (2008). Digital stories in an ESL classroom: Giving voice to cultural identity. *LLC Review*, *8*(2), 56–70.

## KEY TERMS AND DEFINITIONS

**CALL:** Computer-assisted language learning. The application of computers in language teaching and learning.

**Digital Storytelling:** Telling stories through a range of digital media such as web-based stories, interactive stories, and presentation software.

**Learning Management System:** A software application for the administration, documentation, tracking, reporting and delivery of electronic educational technology courses.

**Project:** An assignment which generally requires students to undertake a series of tasks to gather and analyze information.

**Project-Based Learning:** A student-centered pedagogy that involves a dynamic classroom approach and active exploration of specific topics.

**Task:** A language activity that has a focus on pragmatic meaning, some kind of gap (either in knowledge, reasoning, or opinion) and a clearly defined linguistic outcome.

**Task-Based Learning:** A form of communicative language teaching focusing on the use of authentic language and on asking students to do meaningful tasks using the target language.

## APPENDIX

## Digital Story Questionnaire Items (Most Set on a Four-Point Likert Scale)

- **Task Design Questions (Don't Agree → Agree)**
  - The purpose of the group presentation was clear to me.
  - I learned things from the project.
  - The topic made the task easy.
  - The task steps were easy to understand.
  - The suggested planning process was easy to follow. (Question for Study 2).
  - Rank the difficulty of each part of the task.
    - Working with others.
    - Difficulty of the topic.
    - Finding information for the presentation.
    - Writing or creating the presentation.
    - Using computers.
    - Using PowerPoint or Prezi.
    - Recording the presentation.
    - Finding digital images.
- **Self-Efficacy Questions (Don't Agree → Agree)**
  - I was able to complete the digital story satisfactorily.
  - I am proficient at using PowerPoint.
  - I am proficient at using a computer.
  - I have a computer at home.
  - How many hours a week do you use a computer?
  - What do you mainly use it for?
- **Cost/Value Questions (Not at All/None → Very/a Lot)**
  - Before starting how difficult did you think the task would be?
  - How difficult was the task to actually complete?
  - Did the task take a lot of time?
  - Did the task take a lot of effort?
  - Was the task interesting?
  - Was working in groups interesting?
  - Did you learn a lot from the task?
  - Was this task a good way to study?
  - Do you think you did well on the task?
  - Do you think you will do well on future tasks?

# Chapter 17

# Our Future:
## With the Good, the Bad, or the Ugly eServices? Case Finland

**Maija R. Korhonen**
*Mikkeli University of Applied Sciences, Finland*

## ABSTRACT

*We live in an ever-changing world. Despite that many new and excellent reforms are achieved, this period of time is also very confusing when many things that were regarded as concrete are becoming virtual. In spite of all this incompleteness, our common goal should be a good information society and the purpose of this chapter is to find out some factors that reveal the steps toward it. The question we ask is how to find a balance between a good life and eServices from the human point of view. The key findings pointed to issues in the needs of structural changes in the society. Another challenge that can be observed and which will be in the most essential role in the future, is the ownership and control over My Data. Agreements are a common practice in the business and when the subject is eServices in the future, we cannot avoid discussion of the end-user agreements, too.*

## INTRODUCTION

The world is in a great structural change and it seems that the economic growth will be based more and more on services in the future. (European Comission, 2015; Jungner, 2015; Koch, 2015) ICT has played a significant role for decades and this trend still seems to continue, however, in a changing world, the role of ICT has also had to change from a technical role to a more user-oriented role (Digitalization, 2016; Jungner, 2015; Koch, 2015). At the same time as we are encountering so many economic challenges, our common objective should still be the steps towards a good life and good information society (Liideri, 2015). But what does good life mean to us? Very different things, of course, depending on your perspective. The Finnish government has a vision that by the year 2030 Finland is a good place to live a meaningful and dignified life for everyone. The starting point is an individual's dignity and right to live a good and dignified life. Firstly the aim is to take each of us as an individual personality and secondly

DOI: 10.4018/978-1-5225-2492-2.ch017

to emphasize self-determination, while, on the other hand, carrying responsibility for ourselves as well. (Korhonen, 2016; Valtioneuvosto, 2016)

Today, knowledge is the raw material and one of the factors of production. Thinking about business life, it can be said that companies are implementing good life by doing profitable business with knowledge. In practice this means that good eServices are established for the people, other companies and the society. Furthermore, when considering good life from the perspective of the society, the main purpose of eServices is to help and motivate people to take care of themselves as well as possible (Korhonen, 2016). To some, it means health and wellbeing services, some others are motivated by hobbies, entertainment or gaming, while for many contacts with the family, neighbours and friends are the most important. In addition the world is undergoing a dramatic demographic transformation: the trend is toward an older population.

As people are living longer, according to many studies these elderly people are suffering from loneliness to a greater extent. Here eServices, and especially platform technology, can offer an opportunity to solve the problem by helping the elderly people to increase interaction with other people (Marcelino et al., 2005). More often than not the elderly also want to live at their homes as long as possible and digital services can help them to live independently and to feel themselves dignified. The working life is also undergoing great changes. In Finland work has traditionally played a very important role in an individual's life, to the extence that sometimes individual's value is measured by one's work or position. Digital services allow new forms of work, as well as different combinations of work and life. Because of that role, eServices are important also in the working life and digital services can be said to be a contribution toward a good life in that sense, too.

The eServices and related matters are reviewed and considered in this chapter. First some background issues are presented while, the next section provides a brief description of digitalization in general and eServices are introduced via three Finnish application examples widely adopted by users: Firstbeat, OnniBus.com, and 112 Suomi. However generally stated and unfortunately, all eServices are not good ones. It can be said that there are way too many bad eServices, even ugly ones and that is why we will study and analyse the features of eServices. Users should demand more and better applications and one key to promote this is try to create awareness of possibilities of applications and enhance the understanding and knowledge of the users. When we discuss eServices one important topic is the end-user agreements and this is, of course, a subject of consideration of that cannot be avoided in this chapter. Personal data and My Data are closely linked to eServices. Therefore, the possibilities of these topics are also discussed. Who owns and controls personal data in the future? The service providers or the person her/himself? What will be the roles of the service provider and the user?

Summarily, the purpose of this chapter is to find out some factors that reveal the steps toward the good information society. It seems that, after all, digital services are the most important building blocks of a good life in the future. However, there are also several significant challenges.

## BACKGROUND

In order to understand what eServices really are or mean, we have to study the nature of digitalization in general first. Swedish professor Gulliksen (2016) unfurled the concept of "digitality" in his conference speeches by the words "digitization" and "digitalization". As a product of digitization a file stored in a digital form is created. There are many different formats and the one to be used is determined by the requirements of the application. For example, files meant to be electronically distributed are normally stored in a packed format. Hence, an average person sees digitization just as a simple process in which a digital picture of any readable material is created by using a smart-phone, computer or scanner. However, in practice, the process is much more complicated, since the quality of the copy, the storage file format, the intended use and the questions related to archiving of the file have to be determined. Gulliksen (2016) described the term digitalization as meaning the renovation of the ways of acting by utilising modern information technology. In a broader sense, it can be said that in addition to the renovation of the ways of acting, digitality also means the digitalization of internal processes and electrifying of services i.e. providing eServices.

In the previous paragraph digitalization was defined as a process of moving to a digital business model, and not just some investigation of software or device. What is more, Gartner (2016) links digitalization with different ages of IT. The first phase was the age of IT manufacturing when the focus was on the technology. The age of IT industrialization can be seen as the second phase when the production was heavily developed. Digitalization is the third age in the development of IT and currently the focus is on the business models where the customer is in the central point, in other words, companies want to establish good eServices to the customers.

Thinking ahead, we all want to have a good life, but who can define what good life really means? Should this question be dealt with the possibility of obtaining information, as well as a function of time? Probably. What comes to the Nordic countries, it can be said that in the not so distant past, it were the authorities and specialists who told and, to a major extent, also decided what was best for the people. This was enforced by the fact that it was difficult to gather information and that the expertise and knowledge truly were in the hands of a small academic or otherwise educated elite. It can be rightfully said that during those days information meant power and it was carefully protected in the fear of loss of that power. Companies and organizations were hierarchical and management was practiced one-way only, top-down (source). On the other hand, power also meant concrete responsibility that could not be delegated or avoided. It is obvious that, at the time, life was not fair to everyone, but it should also be noted that according to the hierarchy of needs, from the perspective of an individual, their focus was mainly on the lower levels of that hierarchy as nowadays. That is why for the most the elements of good life meant satisfying the needs for nutrition and a place to live. Opposite to this, the situation today is quite different. The technical development is playing a big role, since Internet and digital services have changed it all: nowadays Internet gives almost every person on the planet equal means to acquire the same information. Information has become real-time and global: News published in Finland is available and accessible simultaneously also in America and Asia. Furthermore, a future trend is an ever increasing emphasis on individuality. People want individual, tailor-made, high quality services that can be accessed independent of time or place as the building blocks for a good life and the digital services are a good solution for that need.

According to several surveys (Digibarometri, 2016; Digibarometri, 2015; SME barometer, 2015) Finland has excellent technical prerequisities for digitalization, but contradictory to that, they had not been widely been applied in the business life. Even though we have some fresh examples of success, such as in the gaming technology, our predominant ways of acting date back to the industrial age, a fact that also applies to the management practices. It can be seen that we have not yet taken benefit of the possibilities offered by these technical preconditions (Korhonen 2015). In addition to this, the rigid structure of the Finnish society that lacks flexibility has been criticized by many. Gartner's (2016) definition for digitalization is following: "*Digitalization is the use of digital technologies to change a business model and provide new revenue and value-producing opportunities; it is the process of moving to a digital business*". This definition supports the opinion that the Finns have not yet stepped into the era of digitalization.

October 2016 Finnish MIT professor Bengt Holmström was awarded with the Nobel Prize in economics together with professor Oliver Hart for their insights into modern contract theory. Among many others, Holmström (HS, 2015) pointed out that the structures of our working life are too rigid. He manifests that Finland should pay more attention to the changes in the global economy and courageously renew the working life, because the technological development has profoundly changed the nature of work and respectively this calls for large structural reforms respectively. What is more, according to recent studies the new rules in the working life can have a very favourable effect on the economic growth (HS, 2015). Contrary to this, the Finnish labour market institutions have highlighted the problems in the business management. According to the Finnish research (TIVIA, 2016) digitalization, so far, means to Finnish companies more or less electrification of the current processes whereas the possibilities of creating new digital business for international markets have not been utilized yet, and the pioneers of digitalization are low in numbers. Additionally, only 30 per cent of the IT and business managers report that digitalization has evoked interest in the top-level management towards global business opportunities. Stated in this way, the number perhaps does not sound so alarming, but when you look at it from the percpective that 70 per cent of the top-level management is not interested in the utilisation of digitalization, the future outlook raises doubts and worry. According to Kolesnik (2016) the actual roadblock is the lack of leadership. In Finnish organizations, digitalization is, in a way, everybody's and nobody's matter. Even though, digitalization is becoming part of every process and function, the real pioneers of digital business and new business models are missing. Helenius (2016) adds that in Finnish companies, for the time being, the real ownership of the development of digital business is missing and siloed. As a summary, could it be said that according to the made study the managers of digitalization are missing in the Finnish companies and because the digitalization is siloed and nobody's matter, the need for structural reforms becomes inevitable also in the light of this study?

What is more, both the number of ICT equipment and the very essence of ICT has increased continuously in our lives during the last two decades. Among the first digital services that touched the entire Finnish society were the digital banking services introduced by the Finnish banks in the early 90's. It can be said, that closing down of the branch offices and steering the customers into the net to use the new digital services equally involved individuals, companies and authorities. This transition has also been one of the most remarkable structural changes in the society. Furthermore, with the advancements in technology we have started to utilize eservices in our other everyday routines, too. Therefore, it can be said that eservices have creeped in to our lives little by little and this development is one of the reasons why we have not paid enough attention to their quality, but rather have embraced all sorts without much of objection. The development of the majority of eservices has started with the technology, the organizational or financial benefits first in mind whereas the customer or user-friendliness have often been neglected totally. Fortunately, we are slowly heading into a better direction and the successful companies are developing their digital businesses from the basis of customer satisfaction. According to Li & Suomi (2009) the 8 key-elements of the quality of eServices are presented in Table 1: website design, reliability, responsiveness, security, fulfillment, personalization, information and empathy.

Agreements are a common practice in the business life and when the subject turns to eServices, we cannot avoid discussion of agreements, too. According to the Business dictionary (2016) the concept of agreement means negotiated and usually legally enforceable understanding between two or more

*Table 1. The eight dimensions of eService quality*

| Dimension of eService Quality | Description |
|---|---|
| Website design | • Appealing and well organized website<br>• Consistent and standardized navigation<br>• Well-organized appearance of user interface<br>• Quickly downloading<br>• Ease use of the online transaction |
| Reliability | • Accurate delivery service<br>• Complete order service<br>• Company being truthful about it offering<br>• The online service always correct<br>• Keeping service promise<br>• Accurate online booking records<br>• Website always available |
| Responsiveness | • Adequate contact information and performance<br>• Prompt responses to customers<br>• Timely responses to customers<br>• Adequate response time<br>• Quickly solve problems |
| Security | • Protect the financial data of customers<br>• Protect the personal data of customers<br>• Terms on payment and delivery<br>• Good reputation |
| Fulfillment | • Information on products or services available when purchasing<br>• Systems runs smoothly in the transaction process.<br>• Accurate promises about delivery service in purchasing process<br>• Available to modify and/or defer the purchasing process at any time without commitment |
| Personalization | • Personalized<br>• Products and services<br>• Payment terms<br>• Delivery terms<br>• Design |
| Information | • Updated information<br>• Information current and timely<br>• Information accurate and relevant<br>• Information easy to understand |
| Empathy | • Good personal attention<br>• Adequate contacts<br>• Address complaints friendly<br>• Consistently courteous |

Li & Suomi, 2009.

legally competent parties. In this context we are interested in the end-users and it can be said that those are persons or organizations who actually use a product, opposite to the persons or organizations who authorize, order, procure, or pay for it. So, today nearly everyone is an end-user. What about the status of our end-user agreements then? We made a quick and restricted empirical research related to the end-user agreements with a target group selected from consumers who use eServices. The results of the survey were shocking. We will return to these results later in paragraph the "Agreements and contracts" paragraph.

We mentioned earlier that personalization (Li & Suomi, 2009) is an important dimension of the quality of eService, because it could improve customer's satisfaction. On the other hand interactivity between customers and enterprises offers opportunities for enterprises to obtain valuable information on the customer, her/his needs, residence, her/his purchasing habits etc. Collecting customer data has grown exponentially in a relatively short period of time. Nowadays all of our actions on the internet will leave a digital footprint and all data are typically collected by different kinds of companies and organizations. Earlier they were usually big multinational companies, but today "all parties", not just commercial ones, collect relevant, but unfortunately, also irrelevant data about us for their own purposes. We ourselves do not control that data, and generally even know nothing of the nature or contents these collected and recorded contents of data. It is fair to say that the situation is somewhat complicated. In order to offer good eServices companies have to know their customers. However, the data collected needs to be limited to the purposes and use of the eService provided. Warma (2016) presented a good example of this issue in a public lecture held at the Internet Forum organized by Aalto University. In a research test carried out in Germany a candid camera was hidden in a confectionery and when receiving payments from the customers, the shop assistant also asked for their personal information, such as phone number, home address etc. The same customers, who, when using eServices, happily give all the information requested without questioning, were surprised, displeased, angry or even refused to provide the information. In this situation a person wanted to know why the irrelevant information is collected and how that information relates to the purchase of bread. Exactly same questions should be asked when using the eServices, too. This naturally raises the question: Why don't we?

## ESERVICES: THE BUILDING BLOCKS OF A GOOD LIFE

### Eservices in General

The world is really changing now: we had transferred via industrial revolution to the information revolution and are now rushing fast toward the digital world where information is the raw material. (Korhonen, 2015; Liideri, 2015; Porter, 2001) It can be said that in the 19th century gold and other metals were mined, whereas in the 20th century enormous amounts of products were produced in factories to the "market" and now in the 21st century it will be the data mining that brings revenue to most companies and the economic growth will be increasingly based on eServices. Hofacker et al. (2007) defined the concept of eService as "an act or performance that creates value and provides benefits for customers through a process that is stored as an algorithm and typically implemented by networked software." Already entirely new opportunities exist already for the use of the existing information and archives for the creation of innovative digital services by enriching, reformulating and combining digitally stored information. Therefore it seems that eServices will have a lot to give to us as the building blocks of a good life.

In the Finnish government's vision our country is described as a good place to live a meaningful and dignified life for everyone. Thus, the starting point for this vision is the individual's dignity and right to live a good and dignified life. On the other hand the aim is to take each one of us as a unique personality and also to emphasize one's self-determination. The community is written into this vision too - everyone can be her/himself and is accepted by the society. The above mentioned description also directly applies to the characterization of a good digital service. The basis is the customer need, where customer experience data is gathered and analyzed and finally the user-friendly service is personalized based on that data. A service is also available as needed, independent of time and place, in the form and in a channel desired by the user. The aim and purpose of an eService is to make users' life easier and better. Communication with the near-ones and interaction with the known and unknown persons is made possible. Furthermore, the eServices are also entertaining and promote the sense of community. In summary, all of these are essential elements of a good quality of life. (Korhonen, 2016) The next three applications are a couple of examples of how ones's everyday life can be made easier. These examples demonstrate well the needs for structural change in the society, too.

The first example describes a person's own activities to improve her/his own health. A company called Firstbeat Technologies Ltd has developed heart rate analysis technology and their mission is to bring the actual measurement data as the basis for the analysis and decisions to be made related to the personal wellbeing and physical performance. The application transforms heartbeat data into personalized insights on stress-level, exercise and sleep. It can be said that invisible things become visible and, because of that, you really become aware of your own situation and can choose the optimal level of nutrition, exercise and rest to improve your health and wellbeing. Subsequently in the future we will be increasingly measuring and monitoring our own health ourselves by the means of new applications and eServices. Consequently, this development calls for reform of the society, especially of those public organizations that provide health and social services. (Firstbeat Technologies, 2016)

The second example is related to travel and mobility. OnniBus.com is an innovative inter-city express bus service that is based on a new customer-oriented business model. Tickets are priced dynamically starting from one Euros, so that the earlier you purchase your ticket, the cheaper it becomes, which underlies OnniBus.com's philosophy: "An empty seat is the most expensive seat". The company operates modern, fuel efficient coaches which are equipped with air conditioning, toilets, free Wi-Fi and limited mobility access. With the excellent service, new routes and flexible pricing it has proved to be a new alternative to air, train and car travel in Finland. The company was established in 2014 and just after one year of operation, significant changes throughout to entire travel business segment could be observed. The state railways monopoly, as well as other bus companies, had to react on the altered behavior and demands of the customers. This resulted in a more customer-oriented operation, more friendly service, lower prices and better routes throughout the country. (OnniBus.com, 2016)

The third example, 112 Suomi, is a public, free-of-charge smartphone application which makes it easier and more secure to get aid and help in the case of emergency. Surprising many, the citizens immediately adopted the service after it was made available free for download. The application enables automatic delivery of the caller's location information to the emergency service dispatcher (in Finland). The service is especially valuable in places where the determination of the exact location is difficult, such as on streets with the same names in cities or on a traffic accident scene on a highway. The application uses phone's data network connection to transmit the GPS location information. In addition to this, the application also shows the GPS location information on the phone screen and by reading location coordinates aloud the user can forward her/his location to the emergency service dispatcher even without phone's data network connection. 112 Suomi application is a positive example of the trend that we are heading for a good information society. (112 Suomi, 2016)

## Good, Bad or Ugly?

In the previous paragraph an eService was defined from the user and customer perspective. Today, the customer must be placed in the center of action. A successful service is personalized, easy to use and affordable (Lakaniemi, 2014). Unfortunately, in addition to good digital services, there are a lot of not-so-good-services too and when the goal is a good information society and further a good life, it is important to recognize a good eService, which is not always an easy task. Our research is based on user-orientation and we have considered how to help and encourage users to identify differences in eServices. In general, there is a lot of discussion on digitalization, its benefits and threats, but it seems that the debate often takes place on a too abstract level, and we have also found out that many users are tired of the continuous grinding on the subject, which does not get a grip. One useful way has proven to be to illustrate the difference between a bad and an ugly eService. As an example, words good, bad and ugly are described below simply using a dictionary (Table 2.). It is amazing how well the meaning of words also correlates with the features of an eService, including the importance of visibility and owner-ship of your personal data. Again, the world has changed: in the industrial era literacy was an essential skill and the transition to a knowledge society gave birth to a need for media literacy, do we need digital information literacy today, i.e. special skills to be able to read digital information, since it is no longer possible to get by with the means of traditional literacy?

## Eservices and End-User Agreements: Do We Accept the End-User Agreements Just Because We Feel that we Have no Choice?

Contracts and agreements are an integral part of any business. According to the Business dictionary (2016) end-users can be described as persons or organizations that actually use a product, contrary to persons or organizations that authorize, order, procure, or pay for it. Naturally, when discussing eServices, end-user agreements are of main interest to us.

As we noted earlier today, one way or another, most of us are users of digital services and at the same time we can be called end-users, too. Although all kinds of agreements and contracts, as well as

*Table 2. Explanations of words good, bad and ugly, and their correlation with features of eService*

| Term/Word | Good | Bad | Ugly |
|---|---|---|---|
| Explanation and correlation with features of eService | • morally excellent; virtuous; righteous; pious:<br>• satisfactory in quality, quantity, or degree<br>• of high quality; excellent<br>• right, proper, fit, well-behaved<br>• kind, beneficent, or friendly: to do a good deed<br>• honorable or worthy; in good standing<br>• profit or advantage; worth; benefit: What good will that do?<br>• excellence or merit; kindness: to do good<br>• moral righteousness; virtue: to be a power for good<br>• having admirable, pleasing, superior, or positive qualities; not negative, bad or mediocre<br>• suitable or efficient for a purpose<br>• pleasant, enjoyable, interesting<br>• healthy<br>• successful<br>• positive, suitable, satisfaction | • not good in any manner or degree<br>• having a wicked or evil character; morally reprehensible<br>• of poor or inferior quality; defective; deficient<br>• inadequate or below standard; not satisfactory for use<br>• inaccurate, incorrect, or faulty<br>• invalid, unsound, or false: a bad insurance claim; bad judgment<br>• causing or liable to cause sickness or ill health; injurious or harmful<br>• a bad condition, character or quality<br>• not good; of poor quality; inadequate; inferior: bad workmanship, bad soil, bad light for reading<br>• (often foll by at) lacking skill or talent; incompetent: a bad painter, bad at sports<br>• (often foll by for) harmful: bad air, smoking is bad for you | • very unattractive or unpleasant to look at; offensive to the sense of beauty; displeasing in appearance.<br>• disagreeable; unpleasant; objectionable: ugly tricks; ugly discords.<br>• morally revolting: ugly crime.<br>• threatening trouble or danger: ugly symptoms<br>• mean; hostile; quarrelsome:<br>• an ugly mood; an ugly frame of mind.<br>• (especially of natural phenomena) unpleasant or dangerous<br>• ill-favored<br>• hard-featured<br>• unsightly<br>• unlovely<br>• heinous, vile, monstrous<br>• corrupt<br>• disadvantageous<br>• ominous<br>• spiteful, stormy, tempestuous |

Cambridge dictionary, 2016.

their problems are presented daily by press, governments, European Union, companies etc. no extensive general or public discussion, or debate on the end-user agreements related to eServices has taken place. Why not? Are we just happy and satisfied with the current situation? The question awoke our interest, whether there really is nothing to complain or to disagree. So, before a broader planning and conduct of research, we made a quick empirical pilot survey related to the end-user agreements. The objective of a survey was to find out the level of knowledge of users by means of three questions:

- Do you know, what is an end-user agreement?
- Do you read the end-user agreement before accepting it?
- Do you understand terms and conditions of the end-user agreement?

The target group selected were consumers who had used different kinds of eServices at least two years (Table 3). First, we defined a small 10 person (5 women and 5 men) target group consisting of a student, managing director (administration, academic degree), older person, younger person, middle-aged person, ICT consultant (multinational company), entrepreneur (SME, tourism), public servant, trade worker and teacher (lecturer, health care). In this pilot survey we did not select any experts in law to the target group.

Our expectation was that the responses of participants would disperse: some would know and understand the end-user agreements while others would not know anything about the whole issue. However, the results we got were quite shocking. None of participants understood the end-user agreement (terms and conditions) related to the eServices she/he is using. Only 1 out of 10 read the end-user agreement before accepting it (but still did not understand its content). One of the participants sometimes eyed the text of the end-user agreement trying to find out if some collection of data is involved. 8 out of 10 just accepted the end-user agreement straight away in order gain access to the desired application. The general comment was that they have no option but accept the terms.

Summarily, the result of our empirical pilot survey was:

The participants accepted the end-user agreements when using eServices, even though

- They do not understand the "end-user agreement language".
- They do not understand the contents or terms.
- They do not recognize that an end-user agreement is a legal agreement.

*Table 3. Participants of pilot survey in which the familiarity with end-user agreements and their terms and conditions was examined. Consumers had used eServices at least two years.*

| Participants of Pilot Survey (Consumers, 5 Women and 5 Men) |
|---|
| • Student |
| • Managing director (administration, academic degree) |
| • Older person |
| • Younger person |
| • Middle-aged person |
| • ICT consultant (multinational company) |
| • Entrepreneur (SME, tourism) |
| • Public servant |
| • Trade worker |
| • Teacher (lecturer, health care) |

The extent of the pilot survey was limited and that is why broader conclusions should not be drawn. However, the results were so uniform and confusing that we dare to say that this cannot be our future with eServices.

Because the results of study were so surprising, we decided to explore further the contents of the end-user agreements of some applications. Here the focus was specifically on the content, terms, wordings etc. and not on the characteristics or a quality of the application. First of all, if you just read an end-user agreement, you can quickly note that end-user agreements are legal texts and when somebody uses the application, at the same time, she/he will enter into a legal agreement, as well as agrees to all of the listed terms which usually means many pages of obscure legal text. Quite often the next thing the user finds is the adoption of privacy policy which covers how the provider may collect, use, share, and store your personal information. Some agreements are strictly declared that the provider has the ownership of all the data, but there are also cases in which users owns all of the content, feedback, and personal information she/he provides, but even in those cases the users have to grant the provider a non-exclusive license to her/his data. As a rule, the provider announces that they have the right to change or discontinue part or all of the eServices and due to that they do not promise to store user's content or data, but that it is the user's sole responsibility. In those agreements in which the text is clearer there are sometimes lists of matters the user can and cannot do. For example, in the user-agreement of LinkedIn (2016) there are lists of "You agree that you will" and, on contrary, "You agree you will not". However, how a user should react when "you will" –list consist of 4 bullets and "you will not"-list has 44 bullets?

When one thinks about the current end-user agreements described above, it inevitably raises the question whether the situation could be reversed: would any eService provider accept an agreement in which the terms and conditions were not understandable and they were unilaterally dictated by user and, in addition to this, the terms could change during the contract period? Not very likely. Then, why do we accept this as users?

For a very long time it has been said that competition is hard in the business world. However, considering the current situation of end-user agreements of eServices, it is not easy to believe the claim. At the moment, the eService provider can offer an agreement with terms and conditions that only the provider her/him/itself understands and is aware of all the contents. Perhaps this current digital revolution leads to a completely new situation in which companies and organizations really have to compete for customers and the agreement with its terms will be a real means of improving customer satisfaction and further an essential key to a success in business. Most likely, increased transparency in the contractual matters would also increase consumer awareness of the contracts and their contents in each sector. Subsequently, this would make the comparison of the alternatives possible, which in turn would lead to a real competition for the customers. Additionally, that kind of situation would create a real opportunity for the companies to also acquire a competitive advantage and succeed in the global market.

## CHALLENGES

### Personal Data and My Data

The term My Data can be described as a human-centric approach to the management and processing of personal data, in which people are given permission and access to the data gathered on them while they have been using digital service channels. Therefore My Data includes one's shopping history, phone logs, traffic data, health records and other data accumulated into the records of different internet service providers. Subsequently, it can be concluded that, what becomes essential over time, is the ability and possibility for the users of these services to migrate this data either to her/himself or into some other authorized service in a, for them, more reusable form. (Poikola et al., 2014)

However, with the ever expanding and wider use of the personal data, more and more uncertainty and doubt is arising among people regarding the possible loss of privacy (Asp, 2014). It is a common perception among private persons that companies and governments already know too much of them, which in turn makes them feel uncomfortable. On the other hand, people do not understand the various advanced ways and methods in which their personal data is used in promoting goods and services in the social media, and in general, directed and personalized marketing in the web. Furthermore, they have no idea of what kind of personal data and how much of it each individual service provider possesses of them. Related to this, we can again talk about the bad and ugly eServices, because it is important for the users of the services to be able to distinguish and understand whether their personal data is used for executing business, crime or other illegal activity or if the method of data collection is just a clumsy one but the collected data will eventually turn into benefit of the user or, in some cases, for the common good in the form of statistical data or via general research.

Related to this, Poikola et al. (2014) point out that the traditional perspective to the protection of privacy is such that, the less personal data is collected, the better. This point of view, however, neglects the value of accumulated data to the person her/himself and is in contradiction with the megatrend of the increasing collection of and usage of personal data. The goal should be enabling the collection and usage of personal data in such a way that the benefits are maximized and the threat of the exposure of the personal data is minimized. The key to reaching this is to enforce individual's role, rights and practical means in the management of the data related to them.

Big data and open data are concepts often discussed in conjunction with the digitalization and they are naturally and closely related to eServices. When interviewing companies and public authorities, it was revealed that, as the most important factors in the usage of big data were regarded the usability of the data, abundance and real-time nature of the collection points, enhanced forecasting potential created by the accumulated amount of data and, finally, the utilization of the combination of dissimilar datatypes and the user experience. On the other hand, as the obstacles for the utilization of this data were seen, for example, the vast quantity of data, questions related to the cost i.e. free vs. chargeable access to the data, issues with the ownership of and access to the data, risks involving possible abuse and loss of the data and, last but not least, the vague status of the rights of the parties handing over their data. (Valtioneuvosto, 2016)

When considering open data and My Data, common characteristics can be observed. Both call for an agreement on common principles, wise regulation and machine-readable interfaces, standards and services for a managed transfer of data, storage, processing and analysis. According to the definition of open data, anyone is technically and juridically free to use, reuse and share it. Correspondingly, My Data could be defined as data owner of which is technically and juridically free to use, reuse and share it. (Poikola et al., 2014)

Furthermore, almost any mass data can contain aspects of My Data i.e. "my-own-data" and, therefore, it plays a critical role in the development of the mass data ecosystem. As an example, a growing group of services are related to the personal health combining data from several separate sources together. In order to solve the issues related to My Data, it is obvious that we need new practices in which the emphasis shifts from the jurisdiction to the tools for managing the data. It is estimated that one of the most promising means for the creation of tools for managing My Data are the so called blockchain technologies which are well suited to distributed data backup, processing and security and, further, to sharing of a value or resources. (Valtioneuvosto, 2016)

## The Structural Changes of Society

Already twenty years ago, in 1995, Tapscott (2016) painted a picture where people are beginning to ask, "Will the smaller world our children inherit be a better one?" The question is very essential at the moment: changes have touched all of us and transformations can be seen in governments, organizations and companies, as well as, in the relationships between people. Digitalization has changed and is changing our everyday lives. Tapscott also pointed out signs by which a new economy has not led to a better life, but on the contrary, our privacy is vanishing, for example.

The existing laws and norms, structures and practices do not work in the new situation. Our information society is built on the foundation of administration and, therefore, the change takes place very slowly. Although we are well aware of that major reforms in the structures are needed, all parties want to hold on to the benefits achieved, and therefore any changes in the laws, norms and practices are difficult to execute. In addition, this rapidly changing world does not accept preparation times that last years or months. Governments are not adequately equipped to meet the new public expectations, as was also judged by the Governance Committee (2013). According to the survey, many governments are following a logic of simply and directly converting existing processes into their online versions. Some improvements can be observed, but mostly the governments spend their time and resources in digitalizing existing models and practices instead of rethinking the whole system by the requirements of the digital age (Tapscott, 2016). In short, one can say that it has been more digitization than real digitilization (Gulliksen, 2016; HS 2016).

What is more, Finnish society is currently undergoing a large structural reform. The existing methods and practices are being questioned with the aim of making them more effective and flexible. Several studies show that the digital skills of Finns are on a high level and, therefore, the prerequisites for the utilization of digitalization are excellent, when, paradoxically, at the same time we are unable to turn this knowledge into practice. (Digile, 2015; Digile 2016; Korhonen, 2015) However, important background work has been done in several projects: National Service Architecture Programme 2014-2017, eServices and eDemocracy Acceleration Programme 2009-2015 and The Finnish Open Data Programme 2013-2015 (Valtioneuvosto, 2016).

According to Pöysti (2016) the ongoing National Provincial Reform is the most extensive reform of the administration and practices in the history of Finland. It has an impact on every citizens' public services, as well as, on hundreds of thousands of jobs and workplaces. The provinces will be responsible for arranging and managing the social and health-care services, general administration and other essential public services in their domain. In this reform, digitalization plays a vital role and it is also a centric tool when implementing it. Heinonen (2016) says that in Finland we are creating something entirely new, since provinces have never before existed in Finland as independent administrative areas as meant by the Finnish constitution. Along with the National Provincial Reform, duties and tasks of over 400 different organizations will be handed over to the 18 provinces as to be arranged by them in the future. This responsibility of the arrangement of the mentioned services will be effective as of 1.1.2019. As of writing the text, the new provinces' own opinion of the task a ahead is best described as a Mission

Impossible (Mäkinen & Korhonen, 2016) and it is clear that successful execution of this reform requires the involvement of every Finnish individual and organization and that this is also our common goal as a nation i.e. we need to transform it in to a Mission Accomplished by 2019.

## FUTURE RESEARCH DIRECTIONS

We are going through an interesting time of a digital revolution and it can be seen that this period is very different from the previous decades, since changes are taking place so quickly, globally, simultaneously at different levels and in different sizes, whereas before, the changes took place as in a row of a process, locally, and most often as a function of time. Thinking about eServices, a future direction of research could be divided into two entities: human-company-society (Figure 1) and human intelligence-technology (i.e. machine/automation/robots)-artificial intelligence (Figure 2).

### Human-Company-Society

When we think about service business, a direction in the future will be toward more and more customer-oriented and user-centric digital services. From a human point of view, one interesting topic of further research will be the personal data. As mentioned earlier, any mass data can contain aspects of My Data and, therefore, it will play a critical role in the development of the mass data ecosystems (Poikola et al., 2014). Personal health data is a good example: already today there are services that combine data from several sources together. In the future new tools will be needed for managing that combined data rather than a law to control the situation. Along with My Data, we can move from the organization centric ways of organazing personal data into more human centric methods by placing the individual in the center of the data management (Open Knowledge Finland, 2016). This means that the service provider offers back the information it has collected on the individual, in its plain or in an enriched form, which the individual

*Figure 1. The first future direction of research concerning eServices: human-company-society*

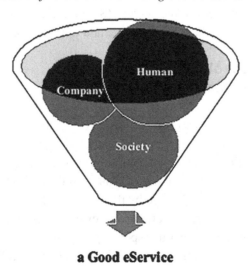

**a Good eService**

*Figure 2. The second direction of research concerning eServices: human intelligence-technology-artificial intelligence*

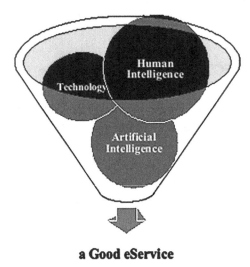

**a Good eService**

can then utilize him/herself or share, trade or sell further to other services. Whether My Data will be the future solution and, unlike today, will we have complete ownership of our personal data in the future?

Further, what comes to services, mobile payment or mobile wallet are important from a company's point of view. Nowadays, instead of paying with cash or a credit card, a consumer can use a mobile phone to pay for services or goods. These payment services are operated under financial regulation, but what about the future? The banking world is also undergoing a rapid evolution, maybe even a revolution. It can be asked if there are any banks at all in the future. Do we have virtual money, bitcoin or a similar form of currency or payment? Will the blockchain technology be the future solution and, unlike today, we have complete ownership of our money in the future?

According to the futurists, health technology is expected to proliferate. There are already several applications which allow for anybody the possibility to figure out the status of her/his daily health. From the society's point of view, this self-measurement will be very interesting and also a significant development that will cause structural changes in the society (Social Affairs and Health), and its implications should be further examined, both on the administrative and operative levels.

## Human Intelligence -Technology (Machine/ Automation/Robot) - Artificial Intelligence

In this chapter we have considered how to find a balance between eServices and a good life. It can be said that a basis for the digital services is a technology and "a source of ideas", as well "a designer" is the human intelligence. As mentioned earlier, a technology-centric eService could usually be named as a bad or ugly eService and according to several international studies, a user-centric, as well as, consumer-oriented eService is considered a good eService by the customers.

Nowadays, researchers generally agree that there are several types of intelligence, including analytic, emotional and linguistic intelligence. Generally speaking, it can be said that human intelligence is the ability to achieve goals in different environments, or as Legg & Hutter (2007) say, intelligence measures the human's ability to achieve goals in different contexts. Contrary to this, artificial intelligence (A.I.) is exhibited by machines. The difference between the human intelligence and A.I. is in the level of capacities: memory, processing power, learning ability and adaptability. (Russell & Norvik, 2013) When simplifying the elements of a eService design, it can be separated in to three issues:

- Goal,
- Challenges that must be crossed to reach the goal,
- Designer, who aims to overcome the challenges has the needed capabilities.

When thinking about the mentioned elements and eServices as the building blocks of a good life in the future i.e. our needs of good eServices, could it be so that artificial intelligence can also be used as a designer of an eService, and not only as an effective calculator or in decision support such as today?

## CONCLUSION

We live in an ever changing world. Although many new and excellent reforms have been achieved, this period of time is also very confusing, when many things which were regarded as concrete and permanent, are becoming virtual. In spite of all this incompleteness, our common goal should be the good information society. As for the economic growth, it seems that eServices are a response to the growth objectives in the near future. The question we ask in this chapter is, how to find a balance between a good life and eServices.

As a conclusion, it seems that digital services will be the most important building blocks of good life in the future. The main purpose of eServices is to help and motivate people to take care of themselves as well as possible. To some, it means health and wellbeing services, some others are motivated by hobbies, entertainment or gaming, while for many contacts with the family, neighbors and friends are the most important. Digital services also allow new forms of work, as well as different combinations of work and living.

On the other hand, also challenges have been identified. The major issue seems to be the need for a structural reform in the society. In Finland the National Provincial Reform (Pöysti, 2016), is going on which means that significant changes in the structure of the society can be expected. These reforms are full of possibilities and, as of writing this text, we believe them to be steps towards a good life, as well as, towards a good information society. However, in order to succeed in this reform, a lot of work, changes in the old attitudes and, especially, cooperation between individuals, companies and organizations is needed.

Digital services can be regarded as information-driven service processes because of the absence of a physical element. Relevant digital information is vital for the customers in their decision making when many things are taking place in the virtual environment and a customer cannot physically examine "what they want or which one to choose". From the human point of view, we need special skills to be able to read and comprehend the digital information, since it is no longer possible to get by with the means of traditional literacy: it certainly can be said that, at the moment, we cannot see the forest from the trees.

There is a lot of discussion of the digitalization and eServices in general, its benefits and threats, but it seems that the debate often takes place on a too abstract level, and we have found that many users are tired of the continuous grinding on the subject. A useful way has proven to be to practically illustrate the differences between a good, a bad and an ugly eService. Another challenge that can be observed and which will be in the most essential role in the future, is the ownership and control over My Data. (Poikola et al., 2014). Furthermore, the end-user agreements are one of the main issues that need to be transformed in to a more user-friendly form. Everyone should understand that they are legally binding agreements that should be taken seriously. It sounds quite absurd that we are willing to accept the terms and conditions that we do not comprehend. This cannot be the right way, and the current practice cannot continue in the future.

In summary we must have courage and determination to demand better and improved eServices, as well as fair agreement terms. Successful companies take the customer experience into account and continuously develop their businesses based on this information and feedback. Tapscott (2016) says that, when you look last twenty years back i.e. the period between 1995 and 2015, it can be detected that the technology alone does not create prosperity, good democracy or justice, but the involvement of the humans is required, too. So, when we set our sight twenty years ahead, it is only the very choices of each one of us that can make a good life possible.

## REFERENCES

Asp, E. (2014). *My Data – johdatus ihmiskeskeiseen henkilötiedon hyödyntämiseen.* Lahti: Markprint.

Business Dictionary. (2016). *Definition of word agreement.* Retrieved October 6, 2016 from http://www.businessdictionary.com/definition/agreement.html

Cambridge Dictionary. (2016). *Definition of words good, bad, ugly.* Retrieved September 29, 2016 from http://dictionary.cambridge.org/dictionary/english/good; http://dictionary.cambridge.org/dictionary/english/bad; http://dictionary.cambridge.org/dictionary/english/ugly

DIGILE. Liikenne- ja viestintäministeriö, Tekes, Teknologiateollisuus ja Verkkoteollisuus. (2015). Digibarometri 2015. Helsinki: Taloustieto Oy.

DIGILE. Liikenne- ja viestintäministeriö, Tekes, Teknologiateollisuus ja Verkkoteollisuus. (2016). Digibarometri 2016. Helsinki: Taloustieto Oy.

Digitalization. (2016). *Valtionvarainministeriö.* Retrieved September 29, 2016 from: http://vm.fi/digitalisaatio?p_p_id=56_INSTANCE_SSKDNE5ODInk&p_p_lifecycle=0&p_p_state=normal&p_p_mode=view&p_p_col_id=column-2&p_p_col_count=1&_56_INSTANCE_SSKDNE5ODInk_languageId=fi_FI

European Commission. (2015). *A Digital Single Market for Europe: Commission sets out 16 initiatives to make it happen.* Press release 6 May 2015. Retrieved September 28, 2016 from http://europa.eu/rapid/press-release_IP-15-4919_en.htm

Firstbeat Technologies. (2016). *Company information.* Retrieved September 29, 2016 from www.firstbeat.com

Governance Committee OECD. (2013). *Public Governance and Territorial Development Directorate Public Committee OECD. E-Government Project Draft OECD Principles on Digital Government Strategies.* Bringing Governments Closer to Citizens and Businesses.

Gulliksen, J. (2016, July). *Human Computer Interaction and societal impact – Can HCI influence public policy making and IT politics?* Keynote in Multi Conference on Computer Science and Information Systems. Madeira.

Heinonen, O. P. (2016). Valtakunnan vaativin johtamistehtävä. *ICT-Newsletter October 20, 2016*. Ministry of Finance. Retrieved October 24, 2016 from http://www.emaileri.fi/g/l/190770/37636482/124013 9/3243/1168/3#bm1

Helenius, M. (2016). In Tietohallintojen johtaminen Suomessa tutkimus 2016. *Tivia julkaisut, tutkimusraportti 2016*. Retrieved October 19, 2016 from http://www.tivia.fi/sites/tivia.fi/files/tivia/Julkaisut/tutkimukset/THJ/Sofigate_tutkimusraportti_2016.pdf

Hofacker, C. F., Goldsmith, R. E., Bridges, E., & Swilley, E. (2007). *E-services: A Synthesis and Research Agenda*. Retrieved October 3, 2016 from: http://myweb.fsu.edu/chofacker/pubs/Hofacker_Goldsmith_Bridges_Swilley_2007.pdf

HS. (2015). Taloustieteilijä Holmström. *Helsingin Sanomat*. Retrieved October 24, 2016 from http://www.hs.fi/talous/a1439870365925

Jungner, M. (2015). Otetaan digiloikka – Suomi digikehityksen kärkeen. Elinkeinoelämän keskusliitto.

Knight, W. (2016). What happens when you give an AI a working memory? *MIT Technology Review*. Retrieved October 25, 2016 from: https://www.technologyreview.com/s/602615/what-happens-when-you-give-an-ai-a-working-memory/

Koch, V. (2015). *Industry 4.0 - Opportunities and challenges of the industrial internet*. Retrieved October 3, 2016 from: http://www.strategyand.pwc.com/media/file/Industry-4-0.pdf

Kolesnik, K. (2016). In Tietohallintojen johtaminen Suomessa tutkimus 2016. *Tivia julkaisut, tutkimusraportti 2016*. Retrieved October 19, 2016 from http://www.tivia.fi/sites/tivia.fi/files/tivia/Julkaisut/tutkimukset/THJ/Sofigate_tutkimusraportti_2016.pdf

Korhonen, M. (2015, July). *Hidden Opportunities - Ecommerce in Finland*. Paper in MCCSIS E-commerce and Digital Marketing.

Korhonen, M. (2016). Sujuvampaa arkea digitaalisuudella. ReAD verkkolehti huhtikuu 2016. Mikkelin ammattikorkeakoulu. Mikkeli.

Lakaniemi, I. (2014). *Taitojen puute yritysten suurin haaste digitalisaatiossa*. The Finnish Chamber Commerce Publication. Retrieved September 29, 2016 from http://kauppakamari.fi/wp-content/uploads/2014/09/kauppakamarin-yritysjohtajakysely-digitalisaatiosta.pdf

Legg, S., & Hutter, M. (2007). Universal Intelligence: A definition of machine intelligence. *Minds and Machines, 17*(4), 391-444.

Li, H., & Suomi, R. (2009). A Proposed Scale for Measuring E-service Quality. *International Journal of u- and e-Service. Science and Technology, 2*(1), 2009.

Liideri. (n.d.). *Business, Productivity and Joy at Work Programme 2012-2018*. Tekes – the Finnish Funding Agency for Technology and Innovation.

LinkedIn. (2016). *User agreement*. Retrieved October 13, 2016 from https://www.linkedin.com/legal/user-agreement

Marcelino, I., Lopes, D., Reis, M., Silva, F., Laza, R., & Pereira, A. (2005). *Using the eServices Platform for Detecting Behavior Patterns Deviation in the Elderly Assisted Living: A Case Study*. Hindawi Publishing Corporation. *BioMed Research International*. doi:10.1155/2015/530828

Onnibus.com. (2016). *Company information*. Retrieved October 3, 2016 from http://www.onnibus.com/fi/tietoa-yrityksesta.htm

Open Knowledge Finland. (2016). *Visiot ja arvot*. Retrieved October 3, 2016 from http://fi.okfn.org/about/visiojaarvot/

Poikola, A., Kuikkaniemi, K., & Kuittinen, O. (2014). *My Data – johdatus ihmiskeskeiseen henkilötiedon hyödyntämiseen*. Lahti: Markprint.

Porter, M. E. (2001, March). Strategy and the Internet. *Hayward Business Review*.

Pöysti, T. (2016). *Sote- ja maakuntauudistuksen toimeenpano*. Retrieved October 19, 2016 from http://alueuudistus.fi/documents/1477425/1892966/Sote-+ja+maakuntauudistus+toimeenpano+22.8.2016.pdf/bc3093ef-d165-4c3c-84bf-26ea77cc17fe

Russell, S., & Norvik, P. (1995). *Articial Intelligence A Modern Approach*. Englewood Cliffs, NJ: Prentice Hall Inc.

Tapscott, D. (2016). After 20 years its harder to ignore the digital economy's dark side. *Harvard Business Review*. Retrieved September 28, 2016 from https://hbr.org/2016/03/after-20-years-its-harder-to-ignore-the-digital-economys-dark-side

TIVIA. (2016). Tietohallintojen johtaminen Suomessa tutkimus 2016. *Tivia julkaisut, tutkimusraportti 2016*. Retrieved October 19, 2016 from http://www.tivia.fi/sites/tivia.fi/files/tivia/Julkaisut/tutkimukset/THJ/Sofigate_tutkimusraportti_2016.pdf

Valtioneuvosto. (2016). Massadatan tehokkaampi käyttö vaatii ymmärrystä sen potentiaalista ja panostusta osaamiseen. *Valtioneuvoston selvitys- ja tutkimustoiminnan julkaisusarja 16/2016*. Retrieved October, 2016 from: http://valtioneuvosto.fi/artikkeli/-/asset_publisher/tutkimus-massadatan-tehokkaampi-kaytto-vaatii-ymmarrysta-sen-potentiaalista-ja-panostusta-osaamiseen?_101_INSTANCE_3wyslLo1Z0ni_groupId=10616

Warma, E. (2016, October). *Presentation My Data (and the EU Data) in Internet Forum*. Aalto University.

## ADDITIONAL READING

Albergotti, R. (2014). After Facebook Deal, Moves App Changes Privacy Policy. *Wall Street Journal May 5, 2016*. Retrieved October 6, 2016 from http://blogs.wsj.com/digits/2014/05/05/after-facebook-deal-moves-app-changes-privacy-policy/

Arina, T. (2016). *Biohacking*. Retrieved October 5, 2016 from http://biohackingbook.com/

Binns, R. (2013). *5 Stars of Personal Data Access*. Retrieved October 3, 2016 from http://www.reuben-binns.com/blog/5-stars-of-personal-data-access/

Bostrom, N., & Yudkowsky, E. (2011). The Ethics of Artificial Intelligence. Retrieved October 19, 2016 from http://www.nickbostrom.com/ethics/artificial-intelligence.pdf

Cristoal, E., Flavian, C., & Guinaliu, M. (2007). Perceived e-service quality: Measurement validity and effects on consumer satisfaction and web site loyalty. Managing Service Quality, Vol. 17 No. 3, pp (317-340).

DIGILE. Liikenne- ja viestintäministeriö, Tekes, Teknologiateollisuus ja Verkkoteollisuus. (2016). Digibarometri 2016. Helsinki: Taloustieto Oy.

Gulliksen, J. (2015). Human–Computer Interaction and International Public Policymaking: A Framework for Understanding and Taking Future Actions. Foundations and Trends R in Human-Computer Interaction Vol. 9, No. 2. pp (69–149).

Jun, M. & Cai, S. (2001). The key determinants of Internet banking service quality: A content analysis. *International Journal of Bank Marketing, Vol 19 No. 7*, pp (276-291).

Karnouskos, S. (2004). Mobile Payment: A journey through existing procedures and standardization initiatives. *IEEE Communications Surveys and Tutorials, 6*(4), 2004. doi:10.1109/COMST.2004.5342298

Legg, S. & Hutter, M.. (2007). Universal Intelligence: A definition of machine intelligence. *Minds and Machines 17 (4)*. pp (391-444).

Poikola, A., Kuikkaniemi, K., & Kuittinen, O. (2014). *My Data – johdatus ihmiskeskeiseen henkilötiedon hyödyntämiseen*. Lahti: Markprint.

White house. (2014). *Big Data: Seizing opportunities, preserving values*. Retrieved October 6, 2016. https://www.whitehouse.gov/sites/default/files/docs/big_data_privacy_report_may_1_2014.pdf

World Economic Forum. (2013). *Unlocking the Value of Personal Data*. Retrieved September 28, 2016 from https://www.weforum.org/reports/unlocking-value-personal-data-collection-usage/

# Compilation of References

Aagaard, J. (2015). Drawn to distraction: A qualitative study of off-task use of educational technology. *Computers & Education, 87,* 90–97. doi:10.1016/j.compedu.2015.03.010

Abdelhak, M., Grostick, S., & Hanken, M. A. (Eds.). (2012). *Health information* (4th ed.). Elsevier.

Abioye, A. O., Prior, S. D., Thomas, G. T., & Saddington, P. (2016). The Multimodal Edge of Human Aerobotic Interaction. In K. Blashki & Y. Xiao (Eds.), *International Conferences Interfaces and Human Computer Interaction* (pp. 243–248). Madeira, Portugal: IADIS Press.

Abiteboul, S. et al.. (2000). *Data on the Web: From Relations to Semistructured Data and XML.* San Francisco, CA: Morgan Kaufmann Publishers.

Abouelfarag, A., Elshenawy, M., & Khattab, E. (2016). High Speed Edge Detection Implementation Using Compressor Cells over RSDA. *Proceedings of the International Conferences Interfaces and Human Computer Interaction 2016, Game and Entertainment Technologies and Computer Graphics, Visualization, Computer Vision and Image Processing 2016,* 229-237.

Absar, R., & Guastavino, C. (2008). Usability of non-speech sounds in user interfaces.*Proceedings of the 14th International Conference on Auditory Display.* Paris France.

ACAPO - Associação dos Cegos e Amblíopes de Portugal. (2016). Retrieved October 23, 2016, from http://www.acapo.pt/

Achenreiner, G. B., & John, D. R. (2003). The meaning of brand names to children: A developmental investigation. *Journal of Consumer Psychology, 13*(3), 205–219. doi:10.1207/S15327663JCP1303_03

ACM/IEEE Association for Computing Machinery (ACM) IEEE Computer Society. (2008). Information Technology 2008 Curriculum Guidelines for Undergraduate Degree Programs in Information Technology. Retrieved from http://www.acm.org//education/curricula/IT2008%20Curriculum.pdf

ACM/IEEE Joint Task Force on Computing Curricula. (2015). Software Engineering 2014 Curriculum Guidelines for Undergraduate Degree Programs in Software Engineering. Retrieved fromhttp://www.acm.org/binaries/content/assets/education/se2014.pdf

ACM/IEEE Joint Task Force on Computing Curricula. (2016). Computer Engineering Curricula 2016 Curriculum Guidelines for Undergraduate Degree Programs in Computer Engineering. Retrieved from http://www.acm.org/binaries/content/assets/education/ce2016-final-report.pdf

ACM/IEEE-CS Joint Task Force on Computing Curricula. (2013). ACM/IEEE Computing Curricula 2013 Final Report. Retrieved from https://www.acm.org/education/CS2013-final-report.pdf

Adame, M. R., Jing, Yu., Moller, K., & Seemann, E. (2013). A wearable navigation aid for blind people using a vibrotactile information transfer system. *Proceedings of the2013 ICME International Conference on Complex Medical Engineering* (pp. 13–18). IEEE. http://doi.org/ doi:10.1109/ICCME.2013.6548203

Adida, B., Birbeck, M., McCarron, S., & Pemberton, S. (2008). RDFa in XHTML: Syntax and processing. Recommendation. *W3C.*

Ahn, J. (2013). What can we learn from Facebook activity? Using social learning analytics to observe new media literacy skills.*Proceedings of the Third International Conference on Learning Analytics and Knowledge,* 135-144. doi:10.1145/2460296.2460323

Al-alak, A., & Alnawas, I. (2010). Mobile Marketing: Examining the Impact of Trust, Privacy Concern and Consumers Attitudes on Intention to Purchase. *International Journal of Business and Management, 5*(3), 28–41. doi:10.5539/ijbm.v5n3p28

Albach, P. G., Reisberg, L., & Rumbley, L. E. (2009). Trends in global higher education: Tracking an academic revolution.*UNESCO 2009 World Conference on Higher Education.* Paris: UNESCO.

Alcorn, A. M., Good, J., & Pain, H. (2013). Deliberate system-side errors as a potential pedagogic strategy for exploratory virtual learning environments. *Proceedings of theInternational Conference on Artificial Intelligence in Education.* doi:10.1007/978-3-642-39112-5_49

Alessandri, M., Thorp, D., Mundy, P., & Tuchman, R. F. (2005). ¿ Podemos curar el autismo? Del desenlace clínico a la intervención. *Revista de Neurologia, 40*(1), 131–136.

Ally, M., & Palalas, A. (2011). *State of mobile learning in Canada and future directions.* Retrieved from http://www.rogersbizresources.com/files/308/Mobile_Learning_in_Canada_Final_Report_EN.pdf (2011)

Almotairi, M. (2008). CRM Success Factors Taxonomy. *European and Mediterranean Conference on Information Systems,* Dubai, UAE.

Al-Okaily, R. (2015) Mobile learning BYOD: Implementation in an intensive English program. In M. Ally, & B. H. Khan (Eds.), International handbook of e-learning, volume 2: Implementation and case studies (pp. 311-323). Routledge.

Al-Qirim, N. (2016). Smart Board Technology Success in Tertiary Institutions: The Case of the UAE University. *Education and Information Technologies, 21*(2), 265–281. doi:10.1007/s10639-014-9319-7

American Psychiatric Association. (2014). Guía de consulta de los criterios diagnósticos del DSM-5 [Desk Reference to the Diagnostic Criteria From DSM-5]. American Psychiatric Pub.

Ammenwerth, E., & Rigby, M. (Eds.). (2016). *Evidence-Based Health Informatics: Promoting Safety and Efficiency Through Scientific Methods and Ethical Policy* (Vol. 222). IOS Press.

Amundsen, C., & Wilson, M. (2012). Are we asking the right questions: A conceptual review of the educational development literature in higher education. *Review of Educational Research, 82*(1), 90–126. doi:10.3102/0034654312438409

Antheunis, M. L., Schouten, A. P., & Krahmer, E. (2014). The role of social networking sites in early adolescent's lives. *The Journal of Early Adolescence,* 1–24.

Anusha, G., Prasad, T. J., & Narayana, D. S. (2012). Implementation of SOBEL Edge Detection on FPGA. *International Journal of Computer Trends and Technology, 3*(3).

Aotearoa, A. (2010). Tertiary practitioner education training and support: Taking stock. Ako Aotearoa. Wellington, NZ: The National Centre for Tertiary Teaching Excellence. Retrieved from http://akoaotearoa.ac.nz/download/ng/file/group-4/taking-stock---tertiary-practitioner-education-training-and-support.pdf

Arantes, P. (2005). Arte e Mídia. São Paulo, Brazil: Senac.

Asanovic, K., Bodik, R., Catanzaro, B. C., Gebis, J. J., Husbands, P., Keutzer, K., & Yelick, K. (2006). The Landscape of Parallel Computing Research: A View from Berkeley. Retrieved from http://www2.eecs.berkeley.edu/Pubs/TechRpts/2006/EECS-2006-183.html

Asp, E. (2014). *My Data – johdatus ihmiskeskeiseen henkilötiedon hyödyntämiseen.* Lahti: Markprint.

Australian Government: Department of Education and Training. (2015). *Research snapshot series: Export income to Australia from international education activity in 2014-15.* Retrieved from https://internationaleducation.gov.au/research/Research-Snapshots/Documents/Export%20Income%20FY2014-5.pdf

Australian Institute for Teaching and School Leadership. (2014). *Global trends in professional learning and performance and development: Some implications and ideas for the Australian education system.* Innovation Unit & AITSL.

Authors, V. (1992). Evidence-based medicine. A new approach to teaching the practice of medicine. *Journal of the American Medical Association, 268*(17), 2420. doi:10.1001/jama.1992.03490170092032 PMID:1404801

Baig, E. C. (2016, January 2). CES 2016 will be virtual reality showcase. *USA Today.* Retrieved from http://www.usatoday.com/story/tech/columnist/baig/2015/12/31/ces-2016-virtual-reality-showcase/77564238/

Bailey, R., Hillman, C., Arent, S., & Petitpas, A. (2013). Physical Activity: An Underestimated Investment in Human Capital? Richard Bailey, Charles Hillman, Shawn Arent, and Albert Petitpas. *Journal of Physical Activity & Health, 10*(3), 289–308. doi:10.1123/jpah.10.3.289 PMID:23620387

Baker, W. M., Lusk, E. J., & Neuhauser, K. L. (2012). On the use of cell phones and other electronic devices in the classroom: Evidence from a survey of faculty and students. *Journal of Education for Business, 87*(5), 275–289. doi:10.1080/08832323.2011.622814

Balan, O., Moldoveanu, A., & Moldoveanu, F. (2014). Navigational 3D audio-based game-training towards rich auditory spatial representation of the environment. *Proceedings of the 18th International Conference on System Theory, Control and Computing (ICSTCC)* (pp. 682–687). http://doi.org/ doi:10.1109/ICSTCC.2014.6982496

Balan, O., Moldoveanu, A., Moldoveanu, F., & Dascalu, M. I. (2014). Audio Games – A novel approach towards effective learning in the case of visually-impaired people. *Proceedings of the7th International Conference of Education, Research and InnovationICERI '14* (pp. 6542–6548). IATED.

Barber, L. (2006). E-recruitment Developments. In *HR Network Paper MP63* (1st ed.). Brighton, UK: The Institute for Employment Studies.

Barber, N. A. (2013). Investigating the potential influence of the Internet as a new socialization agent in context with other traditional socialization agents. *Journal of Marketing Theory and Practice, 21*(2), 179–193. doi:10.2753/MTP1069-6679210204

Bastianelli, E., Nardi, D., Aiello, L. C., Giacomelli, F., & Manes, N. (2015). Speaky for robots: The development of vocal interfaces for robotic applications. *Applied Intelligence.* doi:10.1007/s10489-015-0695-5

Batchelor, D., Wood, P., & Fer, B. (1998). Realismo, Racionalismo, Surrealismo: a arte no entre-guerras. São Paulo: Cosac & Naify.

Bayless, M. L., Clipson, T. C., & Wilson, S. A. (2013). Faculty perceptions of policies of students' use of personal technology in the classroom. *Faculty Publications, 32,* 119–136.

Bell, J., Sawaya, S., & Cain, W. (2014). Synchromodal classes: Designing for shared learning experiences between face-to-face and online students. *International Journal of Designs for Learning, 5*(1).

Berg, M. (1999). Accumulating and coordinating: Occasions for information technologies in medical work. *Computer Supported Cooperative Work, 8*(4), 373–401. doi:10.1023/A:1008757115404

Berg, M., & Goorman, E. (1999). The Contextual Nature of Medical Information. *IJMI, 56,* 51–60. PMID:10659934

Berg, M., & Toussaint, P. (2002). The mantra of modeling and the forgotten powers of paper: A sociotechnical view on the development of process-oriented ICT in health care. *JMI, 69*(2-3), 223–234. PMID:12810126

Bertoli, S., Petroni, M. L., Pagliato, E., Mora, S., Weber, G., Chiumello, G., & Testolin, G. (2005). Validation of food frequency questionnaire for assessing dietary macronutrients and calcium intake in Italian children and adolescents. *Journal of Pediatric Gastroenterology and Nutrition, 40*(5), 555–560. doi:10.1097/01.MPG.0000153004.53610.0E PMID:15861015

Best, K., & Butler, S. (2013). Second life avatars as extensions of social and physical bodies in people with Myalgic Encephalomyelitis/Chronic Fatigue Syndrome. *Continuum, 27*(6), 837–849. doi:10.1080/10304312.2013.794190

Bhurosy, T., & Jeewon, R. (2014). Overweight and Obesity Epidemic in Developing Countries: A Problem with Diet, Physical Activity, or Socioeconomic Status? *TheScientificWorldJournal.* doi:10.1155/2014/964236 PMID:25379554

Bianco, A., Jemni, M., Ramos, J., Thomas, E., & Tabacchi, G. (2015a). A systematic review to determine reliability and usefulness of the field-based test battery for the assessment of physical fitness in adolescents. The ASSO project. *International Journal of Occupational Medicine and Environmental Health, 28*(3), 445–478. doi:10.13075/ijomeh.1896.00393 PMID:26190724

Bianco, A., Palma, A., Jemni, M., Filippi, A. R., Patti, A., Thomas, E., & Tabacchi, G. et al. (2015b). A fitness index model for Italian adolescents living in Southern Italy. The ASSO project. *The Journal of Sports Medicine and Physical Fitness,* (Oct), 16. PMID:26472604

Blanz, V. (2007). A learning-based high-level human computer interface for face modeling and animation. *Proceedings of the20th International Joint Conference on Artificial Intelligence, IJCAI 2007 - Workshop on Artificial Intelligence for Human Computing,LNAI (Vol. 4451,* pp. 296–315). Hyderabad, India: Springer Verlag. doi:10.1007/978-3-540-72348-6_15

Bleich, S.N., Ku, R., & Wang, Y.C. (2011). Relative contribution of energy intake and energy expenditure to childhood obesity: a review of the literature and directions for future research. *International Journal of Obesity, 35*(1), 1–15. doi: pmid:2111966910.1038/ijo.2010.252

Bolas, M. (2011). Keynote remixed: what happened to virtual reality. *Proceedings of ISMAR.* Retrieved from http://projects.ict.usc.edu/mxr/blog/keynote-remixed-what-happened-to-virtual-reality/

Bolt, R.a. (1980). Put-that-there: Voice and Gesture at the Graphics Interface. *Proceedings of the 7th Annual Conference on Computer Graphics and Interactive Techniques - SIGGRAPH '80* (pp. 262–270). doi:10.1145/800250.807503

Bomhold, C. R. (2013). Educational use of smart phone technology; A survey of mobile phone application use by undergraduate university students. Program: Electronic Library and Information Systems, 47(4), 424-436.

Borowski, D. (2015). Create a Virtual Reality Game For Google Cardboard. *Daniel Borowski.* Retrieved from http://danielborowski.com/posts/create-a-virtual-reality-game-for-google-cardboard/

Bossen, C. (2016). Data-work in Healthcare: The New Work Ecologies of Healthcare Infrastructures.*ACM International Conference on Computer-Supported Cooperative Work and Social Computing, CSCW 2016.* doi:10.1145/2818052.2855505

Boud, D. (2016). *Current Influences on Changing Assessment: Implications for Research to Make a Difference.* Keynote presented at 8th Biennial Conference of EARLI SIG1: Assessment & Evaluation. Building bridges between assessment and evaluation. Munchen, Germany. Retrieved from https://goo.gl/1BvvNd

Boud, D. (1999). Situating academic development in professional work: Using peer learning. *The International Journal for Academic Development, 4*(1), 3–10. doi:10.1080/1360144990040102

Boud, D. (2000). Sustainable assessment: Rethinking assessment for the learning society. *Studies in Continuing Education, 22*(2), 151–167. doi:10.1080/713695728

Boud, D., & Brew, A. (2013). Reconceptualising academic work as professional practice: Implications for academic development. *The International Journal for Academic Development, 18*(3), 208–221. doi:10.1080/1360144X.2012.671771

Boud, D., & Molloy, E. (2013). Rethinking models of feedback for learning: The challenge of design. *Assessment & Evaluation in Higher Education, 38*(6), 698–712. doi:10.1080/02602938.2012.691462

Boud, D., & Soler, R. (2016). Sustainable assessment revisited. *Assessment & Evaluation in Higher Education, 41*(3), 400–413. doi:10.1080/02602938.2015.1018133

Bradski, G., & Kaehler, A. (2008). Learning OpenCV: Computer Vision with the OpenCV Library. O'Reilly Media.

Branca, F., Nikogosian, H., & Lobstein, T. (Eds.). (2007). *The Challenge of Obesity in the WHO European Region and the Strategies for Response.* Copenhagen, Denmark: World Health Organization Regional Office for Europe.

Brener, N., Kann, L., Shanklin, S., Kinchen, S., Eaton, D. K., Hawkins, J., & Flint, K. H. (2013). Methodology of the Youth Risk Behavior Surveillance System -. *MMWR. Recommendations and Reports, 62*(1). Retrieved from http://www.cdc.gov/mmwr/pdf/rr/rr6201.pdf PMID:23446553

Brew, A. (1999). Research and Teaching: Changing Relationships in a Changing Context. *Studies in Higher Education, 24*(3), 291–301. doi:10.1080/03075079912331379905

Brew, A. (2002). Editorial: The changing face of academic development. *The International Journal for Academic Development, 7*(1), 5–6. doi:10.1080/13601440210156420

Brewster, S. A. (1997). Using Non-Speech Sound to Overcome Information Overload. *Displays, 17*(3), 179–189. Retrieved from http://eprints.gla.ac.uk/3249/ doi:10.1016/S0141-9382(96)01034-7

Brickley, D., & Miller, L. (2012). FOAF vocabulary specification 0.98. Namespace document, 9.

Broekstra, J., Kampman, A., & Van Harmelen, F. (2002, June). Sesame: A generic architecture for storing and querying rdf and rdf schema. *Proceedings of theInternational semantic web conference* (pp. 54-68). Springer.

Buchanan, R. (1992). Wicked Problems in Design Thinking. *Design Issues, 8*(2), 5–21. doi:10.2307/1511637

Buehler, J. W. (1998). Surveillance. In K. J. Rothman & S. Greenland (Eds.), *Modern epidemiology* (2nd ed.). Philadelphia, PA: Lippencott-Raven.

Bugnariu, N., Young, C., Rockenbach, K., Patterson, R. M., Garver, C., Ranatunga, I., . . . Popa, D. (2013). Human-robot interaction as a tool to evaluate and quantify motor imitation behavior in children with Autism Spectrum Disorders. *Proceedings of the 2013 International Conference on Virtual Rehabilitation (ICVR)* (pp. 57-62). doi:10.1109/ICVR.2013.6662088

Bui, G. (2014). Task readiness. In P. Skehan (Ed.), *Processing perspectives on task performance.* Amsterdam: Benjamins.

Buijs, G. (2009). Better schools through health: Networking for health promoting schools in Europe. *European Journal of Education*, *44*(4), 507–520. doi:10.1111/j.1465-3435.2009.01410.x

Burns, S. M., & Lohenry, K. (2010). Cellular phone use in class: Implications for teaching and learning a pilot study. *College Student Journal*, *44*(3), 805–810.

Business Dictionary. (2016). *Definition of word agreement*. Retrieved October 6, 2016 from http://www.businessdictionary.com/definition/agreement.html

Cabitza, F., & Batini, C. (2016). Information Quality in Healthcare. In Data and Information Quality, (pp. 421–438). Springer. doi:10.1007/978-3-319-24106-7_13

Cabitza, F., Del Zotti, F., & Misericordia, P. (2014). Electronic Records for General Practice – Where we Are, Where we should Head to Improve Them. In *Healthinf'14:Proceedings of the International Conference on Health Informatics*, (pp. 535-542). INSTICC.

Cabitza, F., Locoro, A., & Batini, C. (2015b). A User Study to Assess the Situated Social Value of Open Data in Healthcare. *Procedia Computer Science*, *64*, 306–313. doi:10.1016/j.procs.2015.08.494

Cabitza, F., Locoro, A., Fogli, D., & Giacomin, M. (2016). Valuable Visualization of Healthcare Information: From the Quantified Self Data to Conversations. In *Proceedings of the International Working Conference on Advanced Visual Interfaces* (pp. 376-380). ACM. doi:10.1145/2909132.2927474

Cabitza, F., & Simone, C. (2012). Affording Mechanisms: An Integrated View of Coordination and Knowledge Management. *CSCW*, *21*(2), 227–260.

Cabitza, F., Simone, C., & De Michelis, G. (2015a). User-driven prioritization of features for a prospective InterPersonal Health Record: Perceptions from the Italian context. *Computers in Biology and Medicine*, *59*, 202–210. doi:10.1016/j.compbiomed.2014.03.009 PMID:24768267

Cacace, J., Finzi, A., & Lippiello, V. (2016). Multimodal Interaction with Multiple Co-located Drones in Search and Rescue Missions. CoRR, abs/1605.0

Cafarella, R. S., & Zinn, L. F. (1999). Professional development for faculty: A conceptual framework of barriers and supports. *Innovative Higher Education*, *23*(4), 241–254. doi:10.1023/A:1022978806131

Cafaro, F. (2012). Using embodied allegories to design gesture suites for human-data interaction. In *Proceedings of the 2012 ACM Conference on Ubiquitous Computing, UbiComp 2012*, (pp. 560–563). ACM. doi:10.1145/2370216.2370309

Calderon, A. (2012, Sept 03). Massification continues to transform higher education. *University World News, 237*. Retrieved from http://www.universityworldnews.com/article.php?story=20120831155341147

Calella, J. C., Ortega, F. R., Rishe, N., Bernal, J. F., & Barreto, A. (2016). HandMagic: Towards User Interaction with Inertial Measuring Units. Proceedings of the IEEE Sensors 2016, Orlando, FL, USA. IEEE. doi:10.1109/ICSENS.2016.7808524

Cambridge Dictionary. (2016). *Definition of words good, bad, ugly*. Retrieved September 29, 2016 from http://dictionary.cambridge.org/dictionary/english/good; http://dictionary.cambridge.org/dictionary/english/bad; http://dictionary.cambridge.org/dictionary/english/ugly

Campbell, S. W. (2006). Perceptions of mobile phones in college classrooms: Ring, cheating, and classroom policies. *Communication Education*, *55*(3), 280–294. doi:10.1080/03634520600748573

Camponovo, G., Pigneur, Y., Rangone, A., & Renga, F. (2005). *Mobile customer relationship management: an explorative investigation of the Italian consumer market*. Paper presented in the 4th International Conference on Mobile Business, Sydney, Australia. doi:10.1109/ICMB.2005.63

Candy, P. (1996). Promoting life-long learning: Academic developers and the university as a learning organization. *The International Journal for Academic Development*, *1*(1), 7–19. doi:10.1080/1360144960010102

Cantoni, R.C.A. (2001). Realidade virtual: uma história de imersão interativa. Programa de Pós-graduação em Comunicação e Semiótica da PUC-SP.

Caralli, R. (2004). *The Critical Success Factor Method: Establishing a Foundation for Enterprise Security Management*. Software Engineering Institute.

Carless, D. (2007). Learning-oriented assessment: Conceptual basis and practical implications. *Innovations in Education and Teaching International*, *44*(1), 57–66. doi:10.1080/14703290601081332

Cavett, D., Coker, M., Jimenez, R., & Yaacoubi, B. (2007). Human-computer interface for control of unmanned aerial vehicles. *Proceedings of the 2007 IEEE Systems and Information Engineering Design Symposium, SIEDS,* Charlottesville, VA, USA. IEEE. doi:10.1109/SIEDS.2007.4374014

CDC. (2016). Facts about Autism Spectrum Disorders. Retrieved from http://www.cdc.gov/ncbddd/autism/data.html

Centers for Disease Control and Prevention. (1997). Guidelines for School and Community Programs to Promote Life-long Physical Activity Among Young People. *Morbidity and Mortality Weekly Report*, *46*(RR-6), 1–36. PMID:9072670

Centers for Disease Control and Prevention. (2011). School Health Guidelines to Promote Healthy Eating and Physical Activity. *MMWR*, *60*(5), 1–80. PMID:21918496

Cesário, I. (2015). O Projeto Sala de Estar como Estímulo ao Acesso à Arte e à Cultura. *Proceedings of the 2nd Congresso de Extensão da Associação das Universidades do Grupo de Montevideo (AUGM)*.

Chalmers, D. (2010). Progress and challenges to the recognition and reward of scholarship of teaching in higher education. *Higher Education Research & Development*, *30*(1), 25–38. doi:10.1080/07294360.2011.536970

Chao, G. (2009, March 8-10). Human-computer interaction: Process and principles of human-computer interface design. In *2009 International Conference on Computer and Automation Engineering ICCAE '09*, Bangkok, Thailand (pp. 230–233). IEEE. doi:10.1109/ICCAE.2009.23

Chaomin, L., Yue, C., Krishnan, M., & Paulik, M. (2012). The magic glove: A gesture-based remote controller for intelligent mobile robots.*Proceedings of the SPIE - The International Society for Optical Engineering*. doi:<ALIGNMENT.qj></ALIGNMENT>10.1117/12.912186

Chaplin, L. N., & John, D. (2005). The development of self-brand connections in children and adolescents. *The Journal of Consumer Research*, *32*(1), 119–130. doi:10.1086/426622

Charon, J. M. (1998). *Symbolic Interactionism: An Introduction, An Interpretation, An Integration*. Upper Saddle River, NJ: Prentice Hall.

Chatti, M. A., Dyckhoff, A. L., Thüs, H., & Schroeder, U. (2012). A reference model for learning analytics. *International Journal of Technology Enhanced Learning*, *4*(5/6), 318–331. doi:10.1504/IJTEL.2012.051815

Chilana, P. K., Ko, A. J., & Wobbrock, J. (2015). From User-Centered to Adoption-Centered Design: A Case Study of an HCI Research Innovation Becoming a Product. In *Proceedings of the 33rd Annual ACM Conference on Human Factors in Computing Systems* (pp. 1749–1758). New York: ACM. doi:10.1145/2702123.2702412

Chin, J. P., Diehl, V. A., & Norman, L. K. (1988). Development of an instrument measuring user satisfaction of the human-computer interface.*Proceedings of the SIGCHI conference on Human factors in computing systems CHI '88* (pp. 213–218). New York, USA: ACM Press. doi:10.1145/57167.57203

Chiti, S., & Leporini, B. (2012). *Accessibility of Android-Based Mobile Devices: A Prototype to Investigate Interaction with Blind Users* (pp. 607–614). Springer. doi:10.1007/978-3-642-31534-3_89

Christodoulides, G., Jevons, C., & Bonhomme, J. (2012). Memo to Marketers: Quantitative Evidence for Change – How User-Generated Content Really Affects Brands. *Journal of Advertising Research, 52*(1), 53–64. doi:10.2501/JAR-52-1-053-064

Chuang, Y.-W. (2015). Toward an understanding of uses and gratifications theory and the sense of virtual community on knowledge sharing in online game communities. *International Journal of Information and Education Technology, 5*(6), 472–476. doi:10.7763/IJIET.2015.V5.552

Clarke, B. (2009). Friends forever: How young adolescents use social-networking sites. *IEEE Intelligent Systems, 24*(6), 22–26. doi:10.1109/MIS.2009.114

Clough, B. T. (2002). Metrics, schmetrics! How the heck do you determine a UAV's autonomy anyway? *Proceedings of the 2002 Performance Metrics for Intelligent Systems Workshop,* Gaithersburg, MD, USA (pp. 313–319).

CNA. (2016). Evaluation criteria for the accreditation of professional careers with bachelor's degree and bachelor's degree programs. National Accreditation Commission. Retrieved from https://www.cnachile.cl/Paginas/Acreditacion-Pregrado.aspx

Conole, G., & Dyke, M. (2004). Understandign and using technological affordances: A response to Boyle and Cook. *ALT-J. Research in Learning Technology, 12*(3), 301–308. doi:10.1080/0968776042000259609

Cooper, A. (2014). *Open Learning Analytics Network - Summit Europe 2014*. Retrieved October 30, 2016, from http://www.laceproject.eu/open-learning-analytics-network-summit-europe-2014/

Cordiner, M. (2014). Academic developers as change agents improving quality in a large interprofessional undergraduate subject. *The International Journal for Academic Development, 19*(3), 199–211. doi:10.1080/1360144X.2013.825618

Correia, C. (2010). *Encontrar um emprego através da internet: modelo de portal de recrutamento online para a Administração Pública Local Autárquica* (Master Dissertation). Instituto Superior de Ciências do Trabalho e da Empresa, Instituto Universitário de Lisboa, Portugal.

Cotes, T., & Milliner, B. (2016). *Preparing Japanese students' digital literacy for study abroad: How much CALL training is needed?* Presentation given at Eurocall 2016.

Crabtree, A., & Mortier, R. (2015). Human data interaction: Historical lessons from social studies and CSCW. In *ECSCW 2015*. Springer. doi:10.1007/978-3-319-20499-4_1

Crawford, A. (2015, March 28). *5 Steps to effective and transformative professional development.* Blog series: Deeper learning, leadership, mission-driven work. Retrieved April 15, 2015 from http://gettingsmart.com/2015/03/5-steps-to-effective-and-transformative-professional-development/

Crawley, E., Malmqvist, J., Östlund, S., & Brodeur, D. (2014). *Rethinking engineering education: The CDIO Approach.* Cham, New York: Springer. doi:10.1007/978-3-319-05561-9

Crawley, E., & Sterne, J. C. (2009). Association between school absence and physical function in paediatric chronic fatigue syndrome/myalgic encephalopathy. *Archives of Disease in Childhood, 94*(10), 752–756. doi:10.1136/adc.2008.143537 PMID:19001477

Csapó, Á., Wersényi, G., Nagy, H., & Stockman, T. (2015). A survey of assistive technologies and applications for blind users on mobile platforms: A review and foundation for research. *Journal on Multimodal User Interfaces, 9*(4), 275–286. doi:10.1007/s12193-015-0182-7

Culén, A. L., & Karpova, A. (2014). A Researcher's Perspective: Design for and with Children with Impairments. In Human-Computer Interfaces and Interactivity: Emergent Research and Applications Book (pp. 118–136). IGI Global.

Culén, A. L. (2015). Later Life: Living Alone, Social Connectedness and ICT.*International Conference on Digital Human Modeling and Applications in Health, Safety, Ergonomics and Risk Management.* (pp. 401–412). Springer International Publishing. doi:10.1007/978-3-319-21070-4_40

Culén, A. L., & Gasparini, A. (2012). Situated Techno-Cools: Factors that contribute to making technology cool and the study case of iPad in education. *PsychNology Journal, 10*(2), 117–139.

Culén, A. L., & van der Velden, M. (2013). The Digital Life of Vulnerable Users: Designing with Children, Patients, and Elderly. In M. Aanestad & T. Bratteteig (Eds.), *Nordic Contributions in IS Research* (pp. 53–71). Springer Berlin Heidelberg. doi:10.1007/978-3-642-39832-2_4

Currie, C., Nic Gabhainn, S., & Godeau, E.International HBSC Network Coordinating Committee. (2009). The Health Behaviour in School-aged Children: WHO Collaborative Cross-National (HBSC) Study: origins, concept, history and development 1982–2008. *International Journal of Public Health, 54*(2), 131–139. doi:10.1007/s00038-009-5404-x PMID:19639260

Curtin University. (2015). *2011-2013 Key metrics summary*. Office of Strategy and Planning. Retrieved from https://planning.curtin.edu.au/mir/download.cfm

Cvejić, D. P. T., & Ostojić, S. (2013). Assessment of physical fitness in children and adolescents. *Physical Education and Sport, 11*(2), 135–145.

Dahlstrom, E., & Bichsel, J. (2014). *ECAR study of undergraduate students and information technology, 2014*. Research report. Louisville, CO: ECAR. Retrieved from http://www.educause.edu/ecar

Dahlstrom, E., & diFilipo, S. (2013). *The consumerization of technology and the bringing your own everything (BYOT) era of higher education* (Education Report). Retrieved from http://net.educause.edu/ir/library/pdf/ERS1301/ers1301.pdf

Dalsgaard, P. (2016). Experimental Systems in Research Through Design. In *Proceedings of the 2016 CHI Conference on Human Factors in Computing Systems* (pp. 4991–4996). New York, NY: ACM. doi:10.1145/2858036.2858310

Daniel, B., & Butson, R. (2014). Foundations of Big Data and Analytics in Higher Education.*International Conference on Analytics Driven Solutions: ICAS2014*, 39-47.

Darin, T., Sánchez, J., & Andrade, R. M. C. (2015). Dimensions to Analyze the Design of Multimodal Videogames for the Cognition of People Who Are Blind. Proceedings of the XIV Simpósio Brasileiro sobre Fatores Humanos em Sistemas Computacionais Conference (IHC '15), Salvador Baia, Brasil. Doi:10.13140/RG.2.1.1749.9287

Day, D., & Lloyd, M. M. (2007). Affordances of online technologies: More than the properties of the technology. *Australian Educational Computing, 22*(2), 17–21.

De Bourdeaudhuij, I., van Cauwenberghe, E., Spittaels, H., Oppert, J. M., Rostami, C., Brug, J., & Maes, L. et al. (2010). School-based interventions promoting both physical activity and healthy eating in Europe: A systematic review within the HOPE project. *Obesity Reviews, 12*(3), 205–216. doi:10.1111/j.1467-789X.2009.00711.x PMID:20122137

Debnath, R., Datta, B., & Mukhopadhyay, S. (2016). Customer Relationship Management Theory and Research in the New Millennium: Directions for Future Research. *Journal of Relationship Marketing*, *15*(4), 299–325. doi:10.1080/15 332667.2016.1209053

Deci, E. L., & Ryan, R. M. (1985). *Intrinsic motivation and self-determination in human behavior*. New York: Plenum. doi:10.1007/978-1-4899-2271-7

Deryabina, G.I., & Losev, V.Y. (2006). *Creating e-learning courses: Studies*. Samara. Univers – groups.

Dewey, J. (1910). How we think. Lexington, MA: DC Heath. doi:10.1037/10903-000

Diamond, N., Sherry, J. F. Jr, Muniz, A. M. Jr, McGrath, M. A., Kozinets, R. V., & Borghini, S. (2009). American Girl and the Brand Gestalt: Closing the Loop on Sociocultural Branding Research. *Journal of Marketing*, *73*(May), 118–134. doi:10.1509/jmkg.73.3.118

DIGILE. Liikenne- ja viestintäministeriö, Tekes, Teknologiateollisuus ja Verkkoteollisuus. (2015). Digibarometri 2015. Helsinki: Taloustieto Oy.

DIGILE. Liikenne- ja viestintäministeriö, Tekes, Teknologiateollisuus ja Verkkoteollisuus. (2016). Digibarometri 2016. Helsinki: Taloustieto Oy.

Digitalization. (2016). *Valtionvarainministeriö*. Retrieved September 29, 2016 from: http://vm.fi/digitalisaatio?p_p_id=56_INSTANCE_SSKDNE5ODInk&p_p_lifecycle=0&p_p_state=normal&p_p_mode=view&p_p_col_id=column-2&p_p_col_count=1&_56_INSTANCE_SSKDNE5ODInk_languageId=fi_FI

Dochy, F., Segers, M., & Sluijsmans, D. (1999). The use of self-, peer and co-assessment in higher education: A review. *Studies in Higher Education*, *24*(3), 331–350. doi:10.1080/03075079912331379935

Drew, S., & Klopper, C. (2013). Evaluating faculty pedagogic practices to inform strategic academic professional development: A case of cases. *The International Journal of Higher Education Research*, *67*, 349–367. doi:10.1007/s10734-013-9657-1

Dumas, J., & Redish, J. (1999). *A Practical Guide to Usability Testing*. Portland.

Dunne, A., Lawlor, M. A., & Rowley, J. (2010). Young peoples use of online social networking sites – a uses and gratifications perspective. *Journal of Research in Interactive Marketing*, *4*(1), 46–58. doi:10.1108/17505931011033551

Ellis, R. (2009a). Task-based language teaching: Sorting out the misunderstandings. *International Journal of Applied Linguistics*, *19*(3), 221–246. doi:10.1111/j.1473-4192.2009.00231.x

Ellis, R. (2009b). The differential effects of three types of task planning on the fluency, complexity, and accuracy in L2 oral production. *Applied Linguistics*, *30*(4), 474–509. doi:10.1093/applin/amp042

Ellis, R. (2014). Quality assurance for university teaching: Issues and approaches. In R. Ellis (Ed.), *Quality assurance for university teaching* (pp. 3–15). London: SRHE and Open University Press.

Elmqvist, N. (2011). Embodied human-data interaction. ACM CHI 2011 Workshop "Embodied Interaction: Theory and Practice in HCI", 104–107.

Emotiv. (2014). Wearables for your brain. Retrieved from https://emotiv.com/

European Centre for Disease Prevention and Control. (2008). *Surveillance of communicable diseases in the European Union. A long-term strategy: 2008–2013*. Stockholm: ECDC.

European Centre for Disease Prevention and Control. (2014). *Data quality monitoring and surveillance system evaluation – A handbook of methods and applications.* Stockholm: ECDC.

European Commission. (2015). *A Digital Single Market for Europe: Commission sets out 16 initiatives to make it happen.* Press release 6 May 2015. Retrieved September 28, 2016 from http://europa.eu/rapid/press-release_IP-15-4919_en.htm

European Food Safety Authority. (2011). Evaluation of the FoodEx, the food classification system applied to the development of the EFSA Comprehensive European Food Consumption Database. *EFSA Journal, 9*(3), 1970. doi:10.2903/j.efsa.2011.1970

European Union (EU). (2014). *EU Action Plan on Childhood Obesity 2014–2020.* Online.

European Union. (2014). Special Eurobarometer 412. Sport and physical activity (Report). Retrieved from http://ec.europa.eu/health/nutrition_physical_activity/docs/ebs_412_en.pdf

Eurostat. (2016). Unemployment statistics. *Statistics Explained.* Available: http://ec.europa.eu/eurostat/statistics-explained/index.php/Unemployment_statistics#Main_statistical_findings

Eyal, L. (2012). Digital Assessment Literacy—the Core Role of the Teacher in a Digital Environment. *Journal of Educational Technology & Society, 15*(2), 37–49.

Faase, R., Helms, R., & Spruit, M. (2011). Web 2.0 in the CRM domain: Defining social CRM. *Int. J. Electronic Customer Relationship Management, 5*(1), 1–22. doi:10.1504/IJECRM.2011.039797

Falchikov, N. (2005). *Improving assessment through student involvement. Practical solutions for aiding learning in higher education and further education.* London: RoutledgeFalmer.

Farmer, A., Fowler, T., Scourfield, J., & Thapar, A. (2004). Prevalence of chronic disabling fatigue in children and adolescents. *The British Journal of Psychiatry, 184*(6), 477–481. doi:10.1192/bjp.184.6.477 PMID:15172940

Felder, R. M., & Brent, R. (2004). *The abc's of engineering education: abet, bloom's taxonomy, cooperative learning, and so on.* American Society for Engineering Education.

Ferman, T. (2002). Academic professional development practice: What lecturers find valuable. *The International Journal for Academic Development, 7*(2), 146–158. doi:10.1080/1360144032000071305

Filippi, A., Amodio, E., Napoli, G., Breda, J., Bianco, A., Jemni, M., & Tabacchi, G. et al. (2014). The web-based ASSO-food frequency questionnaire for adolescents: Relative and absolute reproducibility assessment.[Internet]. *Nutrition Journal, 13*(1), 119. Retrieved from http://nutritionj.biomedcentral.com/articles/10.1186/1475-2891-13-119 doi:10.1186/1475-2891-13-119 PMID:25518876

Finnegan, J., & Currie, L. (2010). A multi-layered approach to CRM implementation: An integration perspective. *European Management Journal, 28*(2), 153–167. doi:10.1016/j.emj.2009.04.010

Firstbeat Technologies. (2016). *Company information.* Retrieved September 29, 2016 from www.firstbeat.com

Fitton, D., Horton, M., Read, J. C., Little, L., & Toth, N. (2012). *Climbing the cool wall: exploring teenage preferences of cool.* ACM Press. doi:10.1145/2212776.2223758

Fitzpatrick, G. (2004). Integrated care and the working record. *Health Informatics Journal, 10*(4), 291–302. doi:10.1177/1460458204048507

Fitzpatrick, G., & Ellingsen, G. (2013). A review of 25 years of CSCW research in healthcare: Contributions, challenges and future agendas. *CSCW, 22*(4-6), 609–665.

Fong, T., & Nourbakhsh, I. (2000). Interaction challenges in human-robot space exploration. *Proceedings of the Fourth International Conference and Exposition on Robotics for Challenging Situations and Environments* (pp. 340–346). http://doi.org/ doi:<ALIGNMENT.qj></ALIGNMENT>10.1145/1052438.1052462

Foster, P. (1996). Doing the task better: How planning time influences students' performance. In J. Willis & D. Willis (Eds.), *Challenge and change in language teaching* (pp. 126–135). Oxford, UK: MacMillan Heinemann.

Foster, P., & Skehan, P. (1999). The influence of source of planning and focus of planning on task-based performance. *Language Teaching Research*, *3*(3), 215–247. doi:10.1191/136216899672186140

Fournier, S. (1998). Consumers and their brands: Developing relationship theory in consumer research. *The Journal of Consumer Research*, *24*(4), 343–373. doi:10.1086/209515

Frank, L. D., Andresen, M. A., & Schmid, T. L. (2004). Obesity relationships with community design, physical activity, and time spent in cars. *American Journal of Preventive Medicine*, *27*(2), 87–96. Retrieved from http://www.ajpmonline.org/article/S0749-3797(04)00087-X/pdf doi:10.1016/j.amepre.2004.04.011 PMID:15261894

Freedman, D. S., Khan, L. K., Serdula, M. K., Dietz, W. H., Srinivasan, S. R., & Berenson, G. S. (2005). The relation of childhood BMI to adult adiposity: The Bogalusa Heart Study. *Pediatrics*, *115*(1), 22–27. doi:10.1542/peds.2004-0220 PMID:15629977

Froese, A. D. et al. (2012). Effects of classroom cell phone use on expected and actual learning. *College Student Journal*, *46*(2), 323–332.

Fry, J., & Finley, W. (2005). The prevalence and costs of obesity in the EU. *The Proceedings of the Nutrition Society*, *64*(3), 359–362. doi:10.1079/PNS2005443 PMID:16048669

Fry, J., Schroeder, R., & den Besten, M. (2009). Open science in e-science: Contingency or policy? *The Journal of Documentation*, *65*(1), 6–32. doi:10.1108/00220410910926103

Fulbright, S. (2013). *Cell phones in the classroom: What's your policy?* Retrieved from http://www.facultyfocus.com/articles/effective-classroom-management/cell-phones-in-the-classroom-whats-your-policy/

Galinhas, B. (2011). Developing an accessible interaction model for touch screen mobile devices: preliminary results. *Proceedings of the 10th Brazilian Symposium on Human Factors in Computing Systems and the 5th Latin American Conference on Human-Computer Interaction* (pp. 222–226). Brazilian Computer Society.

Gaver, W. (1986). Auditory Icons: Using Sound in Computer Interfaces. *Human-Computer Interaction*, *2*(2), 167–177. doi:10.1207/s15327051hci0202_3

Gaver, W. (2012). What Should We Expect from Research Through Design? In *Proceedings of the SIGCHI Conference on Human Factors in Computing Systems* (pp. 937–946). New York, NY: ACM. doi:10.1145/2207676.2208538

Gensler, S., Volckner, F., Liu-Thompkins, Y., & Wiertz, C. (2013). Managing brands in the social media environment. *Journal of Interactive Marketing*, *27*(4), 242–256. doi:10.1016/j.intmar.2013.09.004

Gergen, K. J. (2009). *An Invitation to Social Construction*. London: Sage Publications Limited.

German, R.R., Lee, L.M., Horan, J.M., Milstein, R.L., Pertowski, C.A., & Waller, M.N. (2001). Guidelines Working Group Centers for Disease Control and Prevention (CDC). Updated guidelines for evaluating public health surveillance systems: recommendations from the Guidelines Working Group.

Giannetti, C. (2006). *Estética Digital. Sintopia da Arte, a Ciência e a Tecnologia*. Belo Horizonte: C/Arte.

Gibbs, G. (2013). Reflections on the changing nature of educational development. *The International Journal for Academic Development, 18*(1), 4–14. doi:10.1080/1360144X.2013.751691

Giffinger, R. (2007). *Smart Cities: Ranking of European Medium Sized Cities*. Retrieved from http://www.smart-cities. eu/download/smart_cities_final_report.pdf

Gitelman, L. (2013). *Raw data is an oxymoron*. MIT Press.

Glazunova O.G. (2014). Types of academic internet-resources for it students' individual work management. *Informacijni texnologiyi v osviti, 21*, 78-86.

Glazunova, E. G. (2015). *Theoretical and methodological foundations for the design and use of electronic training future professionals with information technology at universities agricultural profile* (Unpublished doctoral dissertation). National Academy of Pedagogical Sciences of Ukraine Institute of Information Technologies and the studies Kyiv.

Glazunova, O. G., & Voloshyna, T. V. (2016). *Hybrid Cloud-Oriented Educational Environment for Training Future IT Specialists. ICT in Education.* Research and Industrial Applications. Retrieved October 30, 2016, from http://ceur-ws. org/Vol-1614/paper_64.pdf

Gobel, P., & Kano, M. (2014a). *Japanese teachers' use of technology at the university level. Attitudes to technology in ESL/EFL pedagogy.* Arabia TESOL Publications.

Gobel, P., & Kano, M. (2014b). Mobile natives: Japanese university students' use of digital technology. APACALL Book III. Cambridge Scholars Publishing.

Gobel, P., & Kano, M. (2013). Implementing a Year-long Reading While Listening Program for Japanese University EFL Students. *Computer Assisted Language Learning, 27*(4), 279–293. doi:10.1080/09588221.2013.864314

Goggins, S., & Petakovic, E. (2014). Connecting Theory to Social Technology Platforms: A Framework for Measuring Influence in Context. *The American Behavioral Scientist, 58*(10), 1376–1392. doi:10.1177/0002764214527093

Golding, C. (2014). Blinkered conceptions of academic development. *The International Journal for Academic Development, 19*(2), 150–152. doi:10.1080/1360144X.2013.855935

Google. (2014). Google Project Soli: Your Hands Are the Only Interface You Will Need. Retrieved from https://atap. google.com/soli/

Gortmaker, S. L., Peterson, K., Wiecha, J., Sobol, A. M., Dixit, S., Fox, M. K., & Laird, N. (1999). Reducing Obesity via a School-Based Interdisciplinary Intervention Among Youth: Planet Health. *Archives of Pediatrics & Adolescent Medicine, 153*(4), 409–418. doi:10.1001/archpedi.153.4.409 PMID:10201726

Gortmaker, S. L., Swinburn, B. A., Levy, D., Carter, R., Mabry, P. L., Finegood, D. T., & Moodie, M. L. et al. (2011). Changing the future of obesity: Science, policy, and action. *Lancet, 378*(9793), 838–847. doi:10.1016/S0140-6736(11)60815-5 PMID:21872752

Gosling, D. (2008). *Educational development in the United Kingdom. Report for The Heads Of Educational Development Group.* London: Heads Of Educational Development Group (HEDG) UK. Retrieved from http://www.hedg.ac.uk/ documents/HEDG_Report_final.pdf

Gosling, D. (2001). What educational developments units do - Five years on. *The International Journal for Academic Development, 6*, 74–92. doi:10.1080/13601440110043039

Gosling, D. (2009). Educational development in the UK: A complex and contradictory reality. *The International Journal for Academic Development, 14*(1), 5–18. doi:10.1080/13601440802659122

Governance Committee OECD. (2013). *Public Governance and Territorial Development Directorate Public Committee OECD. E-Government Project Draft OECD Principles on Digital Government Strategies.* Bringing Governments Closer to Citizens and Businesses.

Grabski, A., Toni, T., Zigrand, T., Weller, R., & Zachmann, G. (2016). Kinaptic - Techniques and insights for creating competitive accessible 3D games for sighted and visually impaired users. *Proceedings of the2016 IEEE Haptics Symposium (HAPTICS)* (pp. 325–331). IEEE. http://doi.org/ doi:10.1109/HAPTICS.2016.7463198

Graham, C., & Gillies, M. (2016). To BYOD or not to BYOD: Factors affecting academic acceptance of student mobile devices in the classroom. *Research in Learning Technology, 24.* doi:10.3402/rlt.v24.30357

Grajales, F. J. III, Sheps, S., Ho, K., Novak-Lauscher, H., & Eysenbach, G. (2014). Social Media: A Review and Tutorial of Applications in Medicine and Health Care. *Journal of Medical Internet Research, 16*(2), e13. doi:10.2196/jmir.2912 PMID:24518354

Greenberg, P. (2010). The impact of CRM 2.0 on customer insight. *Journal of Business & Industrial Marketing,Vol., 25*(6), 410–419. doi:10.1108/08858621011066008

Greenhow, C. (2008). Engaging Youth in Social Media: Is Facebook the New Media Frontier? A NewsCloud – University of Minnesota Research Report Executive Summary. Minneapolis, MN: Institute for Advanced Study, University of Minnesota.

Green, S., Chen, X., Billinnghurst, M., & Chase, J. G. (2007). Human Robot Collaboration: An Augmented Reality Approach a Literature Review and Analysis. *Mechatronics, 5*(1), 1–10. doi:10.1115/DETC2007-34227

Gregory, J., Mattison, J. E., & Linde, C. (1995). Naming notes: Transitions from free text to structured entry. *MIM, 34*(1-2), 57–67. PMID:9082139

Griffiths, S. (2014). Staff development and quality assurance. In R. Ellis (Ed.), *Quality assurance for university teaching* (pp. 248–269). London: SRHE and Open University Press.

Guan, Z., Lee, S., Cuddihy, E., & Ramey, J. (n. d.). *The Validity of the Stimulated Retrospective Think-Aloud Method as Measured by Eye Tracking.*

Gulliksen, J. (2016, July). *Human Computer Interaction and societal impact – Can HCI influence public policy making and IT politics?* Keynote in Multi Conference on Computer Science and Information Systems. Madeira.

Gummesson, E. (2002). *Total Relationship Marketing* (2nd ed.). Oxford, UK: Butterworth-Heinemann.

Gupta, L., & Ma, S. (2001). Gesture-based interaction and communication: Automated classification of hand gesture contours. *IEEE Transactions on Systems, Man and Cybernetics. Part C, Applications and Reviews, 31*(1), 114–120. doi:10.1109/5326.923274

Hammacher Schlemmer. (2015). The Mind Controlled UFO. Retrieved from http://www.hammacher.com/Product/Default.aspx?sku=84249&promo=Toys-Games-Remote-Control-Toys&catid=247

Hanna, R., Rohm, A., & Crittenden, V. (2011). Were all connected: The power of the social media ecosystem. *Business Horizons, 54*(3), 265–273. doi:10.1016/j.bushor.2011.01.007

Harris, J., & Barber, D. (2014). Speech and Gesture Interfaces for Squad Level Human Robot Teaming. In R. E. Karlsen, D. W. Gage, C. M. Shoemaker, & G. R. Gerhart (Eds.), *Unmanned Systems Technology Xvi,* SPIE (Vol. 9084). doi:10.1117/12.2052961

Hart, S., & Kassem, G. (2012). *Social customer relationship management – from customer to friend*. Presented at European and Mediterranean Conference on Information System, Munich, Germany.

Hase, S., & Kenyon, C. (2000). *From andragogy to heutagogy*. Retrieved from http://ultibase.rmit.edu.au/Articles/dec00/hase2.htm

Hayes, G. R., Hirano, S., Marcu, G., Monibi, M., Nguyen, D. H., & Yeganyan, M. (2010). Interactive visual supports for children with autism. *Personal and Ubiquitous Computing, 14*(7), 663–680. doi:10.1007/s00779-010-0294-8

Hayta, A. B. (2008). Socialization of the child as a consumer. *Family and Consumer Sciences Research Journal, 37*(2), 167–184. doi:10.1177/1077727X08327256

HBSC (2016b). Growing up unequal: gender and socioeconomic differences in young people's health and well-being (International Report from the 2013/2014 Survey). Health Policy for children and adolescents.

HBSC. (2016a). *4th Italian report from the international study HBSC* (F. Cavallo, P. Lemma, P. Dalmasso, A. Vieno, G. Lazzeri, & D. Galeone, Eds.).

Heilig, M. (n.d.). *Morton Heilig Website*. Retrieved from http://www.mortonheilig.com/InventorVR.html

Heinonen, O. P. (2016). Valtakunnan vaativin johtamistehtävä. *ICT-Newsletter October 20, 2016*. Ministry of Finance. Retrieved October 24, 2016 from http://www.emaileri.fi/g/l/190770/37636482/1240139/3243/1168/3#bm1

Helenius, M. (2016). In Tietohallintojen johtaminen Suomessa tutkimus 2016. *Tivia julkaisut, tutkimusraportti 2016*. Retrieved October 19, 2016 from http://www.tivia.fi/sites/tivia.fi/files/tivia/Julkaisut/tutkimukset/THJ/Sofigate_tutkimusraportti_2016.pdf

Hernandez Jose, L., Kyriakopoulos, N., & Lindeman, R. (2002). The AcceleGlove a Hole-Hand Input Device for Virtual Reality. In *ACM SIGGRAPH Conference Abstracts and Applications*, 259.

Herrera, O., Lévano, M., Mellado, A., Schindler, M., Donoso, G., & Contreras, G. (2009). *Profile of the Civil Engineering Degree in Computer Science. UCT*. Temuco: School of Computer Engineering.

Hicks, M. (2005). Academic developers as change agents: Caught in the middle. In A. Brew & C. Asmar (Eds.), *Higher education in a changing world. Research and Development in Higher Education, 28.Proceedings of the 2005 HERDSA Annual Conference* (pp. 175-182). Sydney: HERDSA.

Hill, A. F., Cayzer, F., & Wilkinson, P. R. (2007). Effective Operator Engagement with Variable Autonomy. *Proceedings of the2nd SEAS DTC Technical Conference* (p. 7).

Hills, A. P., King, N. A., & Armstrong, T. P. (2007). The contribution of physical activity and sedentary behaviours to the growth and development of children and adolescents: Implications for overweight and obesity. *Sports Medicine, 37*(6), 533–545. doi:10.2165/00007256-200737060-00006 PMID:17503878

Hilton, J. III, Wiley, D., Stein, J., & Johnson, A. (2010). The Four Rs of Openness and ALMS Analysis: Frameworks for Open Educational Resources. *Open Learning:The Journal of Open and Distance Learning, 25*(1), 37–44. doi:10.1080/02680510903482132

HobbyKing & Turnigy. (2015). Turnigy TGY-i10 10ch 2.4GHz Digital Proportional RC System with Telemetry (Mode 2). Retrieved from http://www.hobbyking.com/hobbyking/store/__58455__Turnigy_TGY_i10_10ch_2_4GHz_Digital_Proportional_RC_System_with_Telemetry_Mode_2_.html

Hoelscher, D. M., Day, R. S., Kelder, S. H., & Ward, J. L. (2003). Reproducibility and validity of the secondary level School-Based Nutrition Monitoring student questionnaire. *Journal of the American Dietetic Association, 103*(2), 186–194. doi:10.1053/jada.2003.50031 PMID:12589324

Hofacker, C. F., Goldsmith, R. E., Bridges, E., & Swilley, E. (2007). *E-services: A Synthesis and Research Agenda.* Retrieved October 3, 2016 from: http://myweb.fsu.edu/chofacker/pubs/Hofacker_Goldsmith_Bridges_Swilley_2007.pdf

Hoffman, D. L., & Novak, T. P. (2012). Toward a deeper understanding of social media. *Journal of Interactive Marketing, 26*(2), 69–70. doi:10.1016/j.intmar.2012.03.001

Hoffrage, U., Gigerenzer, G., Krauss, S., & Martignon, L. (2002). Representation facilitates reasoning: What natural frequencies are and what they are not. *Cognition, 84*(3), 343–352. doi:10.1016/S0010-0277(02)00050-1 PMID:12044739

Hollebeek, L. D., Glynn, M. S., & Brodie, R. J. (2014). Consumer brand engagement in social media: Conceptualization, scale development, and validation. *Journal of Interactive Marketing, 28*(2), 149–165. doi:10.1016/j.intmar.2013.12.002

Hollenbeck, C. R., & Kaikati, A. M. (2012). Consumers use of brands to reflect their actual and ideal selves on Facebook. *International Journal of Research in Marketing, 29*(4), 395–405. doi:10.1016/j.ijresmar.2012.06.002

Holtzblatt, K., Wendell, J. B., & Wood, S. (2005). *Rapid contextual design : a how-to guide to key techniques for user-centered design.* Elsevier/Morgan Kaufmann.

Ho, M. C., & Savignon, S. J. (2013). Face-to-face and computer-mediated peer review in EFL writing. *CALICO Journal, 24*(2), 269–290.

Hong, T. K., Dibley, M. J., & Sibbritt, D. (2010). Validity and reliability of an FFQ for use with adolescents in Ho Chi Minh City, Vietnam. *Public Health Nutrition, 13*(3), 368–375. Retrieved from http://www.ncbi.nlm.nih.gov/pubmed/19706213 doi:10.1017/S136898000999125X PMID:19706213

Höök, K., Dalsgaard, P., Reeves, S., Bardzell, J., Löwgren, J., Stolterman, E., & Rogers, Y. (2015). Knowledge Production in Interaction Design. In *Proceedings of the 33rd Annual ACM Conference Extended Abstracts on Human Factors in Computing Systems* (pp. 2429–2432). New York, NY: ACM.

Hornung, H., Pereira, R., Baranauskas, M. C. C., & Liu, K. (2015). Challenges for Human-Data Interaction–A Semiotic Perspective. In *International Conference on Human-Computer Interaction* (pp. 37-48). Springer International Publishing.

Horrigan, F. A.ONR's Committee. (2000). *Review of ONR's Uninhabited Combat Air Vehicles Program.* Washington, D.C.: National Academy press.

Hötting, K., & Röder, B. (2009). Auditory and auditory-tactile processing in congenitally blind humans. *Hearing Research, 258*(1–2), 165–174. doi:10.1016/j.heares.2009.07.012 PMID:19651199

HS. (2015). Taloustieteilijä Holmström. *Helsingin Sanomat.* Retrieved October 24, 2016 from http://www.hs.fi/talous/a1439870365925

Hsu, F., & Lin, S. (2008). mCRM's New Opportunities of Customer Satisfaction. *World Academy of Science, Engineering and Technology, 40.*

Huang, C.-L., & Chung, C.-Y. (2004). A real-time model-based human motion tracking and analysis for human-computer interface systems. *EURASIP Journal on Applied Signal Processing, 2004*(11), 1648–1662. doi:10.1155/S1110865704401206

Hughes, J., & Morrison, L. (2013). Using Facebook to explore adolescent identities. *International Journal of Social Media and Interactive Learning Environments, 1*(4), 370–386. doi:10.1504/IJSMILE.2013.057464

Huhn, K., & Haewon, S. (2014). Evaluation of the safety and usability of touch gestures in operating in-vehicle information systems with visual occlusion. *Applied Ergonomics*, *45*(3), 789–798. doi:10.1016/j.apergo.2013.10.013 PMID:24231034

Human Computer Interaction - ESEC. (2016). Retrieved from https://www.esec.pt/pagina.php?id=429

Humphrey, A. S. (2005). SWOT Analysis for Management Consulting. *SRI Alumni Assoc Newsletters*, *7*, 8. Retrieved from http://www.sri.com/sites/default/files/brochures/dec-05.pdf

Ibarra-Sáiz, M. S., & Rodríguez-Gómez, G. (2016a). *Guía Innovar en evaluación en la Educación Superior*. Producción: EVALfor - Grupo de Investigación. España:Cádiz. Available in: https://dx.doi.org/10.13140/RG.2.1.3925.8488

Ibarra-Saiz, M.S., & Rodríguez Gómez, G. (2014). Modalidades participativas de evaluación: Un análisis de la percepción del profesorado y de los estudiantes universitarios. *Revista de Investigación Educativa, 32*(2), 339-361. 10.6018/rie.32.2.172941

Ibarra-Sáiz, M. S., & Rodríguez-Gómez, G. (2016b). *Evaluación de competencias en la Educación Superior. El momento de la tecnología y la alfabetización evaluadora. In E. Cano (Coord), Evaluación por competencias: la perspectiva de las primeras promociones de graduados en el EEES* (pp. 17–32). Barcelona: Octaedro.

Ibarra-Sáiz, M. S., Rodríguez-Gómez, G., & Olmos Migueláñez, S. (In press). Monitoring and information on skills development at university: A multiple-case study. In F.J. Garcia-Peñalvo (ed.), *Proceedings TEEM´16 Technological Ecosystems for Enhancing Multiculturality*. doi:10.1145/3012430.3012516

Ibrahim, A. A. A., & Embug, A. J. (2014). Sonification of 3D body movement using parameter mapping technique. *Proceedings of the 6th International Conference on Information Technology and Multimedia* (pp. 385–389). IEEE. http://doi.org/ doi:10.1109/ICIMU.2014.7066664

Iglesias, R., Casado, S., Gutierrez, T., Barbero, J. I., Avizzano, C. A., Marcheschi, S., & Bergamasco, M. (n.d.). Computer graphics access for blind people through a haptic and audio virtual environment. *Proceedings. Second International Conference on Creating, Connecting and Collaborating through Computing* (pp. 13–18). IEEE. http://doi.org/ doi:<ALIGNMENT.qj></ALIGNMENT>10.1109/HAVE.2004.1391874

Illner, A. K., Freisling, H., Boeing, H., Huybrechts, I., Crispim, S. P., & Slimani, N. (2012). Review and evaluation of innovative technologies for measuring diet in nutritional epidemiology. *International Journal of Epidemiology*, *41*(4), 1187–1203. doi:10.1093/ije/dys105 PMID:22933652

Imazeki, J. (2014). Bring-your-own-device: Turning cell phones into forces for good. *The Journal of Economic Education*, *45*(3), 240–250. doi:10.1080/00220485.2014.917898

Inselberg, A. (2009). Parallel coordinates. In L. Liu & T. Ozsu (Eds.), *Encyclopedia of Database Systems* (pp. 2018–2024). Springer.

Iroju, O., Soriyan, A., & Gambo, I. (2012). Ontology matching: An ultimate solution for semantic interoperability in healthcare. *International Journal of Computers and Applications*, *51*(21).

Isaías, P., Pífano, S., & Miranda, P. (2011). Social Network Sites: Modeling the New Business-Customer Relationship. In M. Safar & K. Mahdi (Eds.), *Social Networking and Community Behavior Modeling: Qualitative and Quantitative Measures*. Hershey, PA: IGI Global.

Ischinger, B., & Alba, P. (Eds.). (2009). *Higher education in Chile. OCDE Chile*. París: Banco Mundial.

Italia, H. B. S. C. (2011). Stili di vita e salute dei giovani in età scolare - Rapporto sui dati regionali HBSC 2009 -2010. Istituto Superiore di Sanità. Retrieved from http://www.hbsc.unito.it/it/images/pdf/hbsc/sicilia_report_hbsc_2010.pdf

Jackson, L. D. (2013). Is mobile technology in the classroom a helpful tool or a distraction? A report of university students' attitudes, usage practices, and suggestions for policies. *The International Journal of Technology. Knowledge in Society, 8*(5), 129–140.

Jain, R., Kasturi, R., & Schunck, B. (1995). *Machine Vision*. New York: McGraw-Hill, Inc.

Jarvis, P. (1999). Global trends in lifelong learning and the response of the universities. *Comparative Education, 35*(2), 249–257. doi:10.1080/03050069928017

Jason, L., Benton, M., Torres-Harding, S., & Muldowney, K. (2009). The impact of energy modulation on physical functioning and fatigue severity among patients with ME/CFS. *Patient Education and Counseling, 77*(2), 237–241. doi:10.1016/j.pec.2009.02.015 PMID:19356884

John, D. (1999). Consumer socialization of children: A retrospective look at twenty-five years of research. *The Journal of Consumer Research, 26*(3), 183–213. doi:10.1086/209559

Johnson, L., Adams Becker, S., Cummins, M., Estrada, V., & Freeman, A. (2016). *NMC Horizon Report: 2016 Higher Education Edition*. Austin, TX: The New Media Consortium.

Johnson, L., Adams Becker, S., Estrada, V., & Freeman, A. (2015). *NMC Horizon Report: 2015 Higher Education Edition*. Austin, TX: The New Media Consortium.

Johnston, T. C., Bailey, D. G., & Gribbon, K. (2004). Implementing image processing algorithms on FPGAs. *Proc. Elev. Electron New Zealand ENZCon, 04*, 119–123.

Joinson, A. N. (2008). 'Looking at', 'looking up' or 'keeping up with' people? Motives and uses of Facebook. CHI 2008 Proceedings, 1027- 1036.

Jones, D. H., Powell, A., Bouganis, C.-S., & Cheung, P. (2010). GPU versus FPGA for High Productivity Computing. *Proceedings of theInternational Conference on Field Programmable Logic and Applications*, 119-124. doi:10.1109/FPL.2010.32

Jones, K. R. (2015). *Brand-Made Children in New Zealand: An Interactionist Perspective on Children's Use of Social Media for Interacting with Consumer Brands* (Unpublished Doctoral Thesis). AUT University, Auckland, New Zealand.

Jones, J., & Wisker, G. (2012). *Report for the Heads of Educational Development Group (HEDG)*. Centre for Learning and Teaching. University of Brighton.

Judy, M. V., Krishnakumar, U., & Narayanan, A. H. (2012). Constructing a personalized e-learning system for students with autism based on soft semantic web technologies. *Proceedings of the2012 IEEE International Conference on Technology Enhanced Education (ICTEE)*. doi:10.1109/ICTEE.2012.6208625

Jungner, M. (2015). Otetaan digiloikka – Suomi digikehityksen kärkeen. Elinkeinoelämän keskusliitto.

Kane, S. K., Wobbrock, J. O., & Ladner, R. E. (2011). Usable gestures for blind people.*Proceedings of the 2011 annual conference on Human factors in computing systems - CHI'11* (p. 413). New York, New York, USA: ACM Press. doi:10.1145/1978942.1979001

Kaplan, A. M., & Haenlein, M. (2010). Users of the world, unite! The challenges and opportunities of social media. *Business Horizons, 53*(1), 59–68. doi:10.1016/j.bushor.2009.09.003

Karnik, M., Oakley, I., Venkatanathan, J., Spiliotopoulos, T., & Nisi, V. (2013). *Uses and gratifications of a Facebook media sharing group.Understanding people's practices in social networks*. CSCW' 13, San Antonio, Texas. doi:10.1145/2441776.2441868

Kawauchi, C. (2005). The effects of strategic planning on the oral narratives of learners with low and high intermediate proficiency. In R. Ellis (Ed.), *Planning and task-performance in a second language* (pp. 143–166). Amsterdam: Benjamins. doi:10.1075/lllt.11.09kaw

Kearsley, G. (2010). Andragogy (M. Knowles). *The theory into practice database*. Retrieved from http://tip.psychology.org

Kennedy, J. B., Mitchell, K. J., & Barclay, P. J. (1996). A framework for information visualisation. *SIGMOD Record, 25*(4), 30–34. doi:10.1145/245882.245895

Khamayseh, Y., Mardini, W., Aljawarneh, S., & Yassein, M. (2015). Integration of Wireless Technologies in Smart University Campus Environment: Framework Architecture. *International Journal of Information and Communication Technology Education, 11*(1), 60–74. doi:10.4018/ijicte.2015010104

Khidhir, A. M., & Abdullah, N. Y. (2013, June-July). FPGA Based Edge Detection Using Modified Sobel Filter. *International Journal for Research and Development in Engineering, 2*(1), 22–32.

Kim, S., Lee, K., & Nam, T.-J. (2016). Sonic-Badminton. *Proceedings of the 2016 CHI Conference Extended Abstracts on Human Factors in Computing Systems - CHI EA '16* (pp. 1922–1929). New York, USA: ACM Press. http://doi.org/ doi:10.1145/2851581.2892510

Kim, S. (2014). Developing autonomous learning for oral proficiency using digital storytelling. *Language Learning & Technology, 18*(2), 20–35.

Kim, S., Seo, H., Choi, S., & Kim, H. J. (2016). Vision-guided aerial manipulation using a multirotor with a robotic arm. *IEEE/ASME Transactions on Mechatronics, 4435*(c), 1–1. doi:10.1109/TMECH.2016.2523602

King, S. F., & Burgess, T. F. (2008). Understanding success and failure in customer relationship management. *Industrial Marketing Management, 37*(4), 421–431. doi:10.1016/j.indmarman.2007.02.005

Kirner, C. (2008). Evolução da Realidade Virtual no Brasil. *Procedings of X Symposium on Virtual and Augmented Reality,* 1-11.

Knight, W. (2016). What happens when you give an AI a working memory? *MIT Technology Review.* Retrieved October 25, 2016 from: https://www.technologyreview.com/s/602615/what-happens-when-you-give-an-ai-a-working-memory/

Knowles, M. S. (1975). *Self-directed learning.* Chicago: Follet.

Knowles, M. S. (1984). *The adult learner: A neglected species* (3rd ed.). Houston, TX: Gulf Publishing.

Kobus, M. B. W., Rietveld, P., & van Ommeren, J. N. (2013). Ownership versus on-campus use of mobile IT devices by university students. *Computers & Education, 68*, 29–41. doi:10.1016/j.compedu.2013.04.003

Koch, V. (2015). *Industry 4.0 - Opportunities and challenges of the industrial internet.* Retrieved October 3, 2016 from: http://www.strategyand.pwc.com/media/file/Industry-4-0.pdf

Kolb, D. A. (1984). *Experiential learning: Experience as the source of learning and development.* Englewood Cliffs, NJ: Prentice-Hall.

Kolesnik, K. (2016). In Tietohallintojen johtaminen Suomessa tutkimus 2016. *Tivia julkaisut, tutkimusraportti 2016.* Retrieved October 19, 2016 from http://www.tivia.fi/sites/tivia.fi/files/tivia/Julkaisut/tutkimukset/THJ/Sofigate_tutkimusraportti_2016.pdf

Kolodny, L. (2016, March 13). The latest approach to employee training. *The Wall Street Journal.* Retrieved from http://www.wsj.com/articles/the-latest-approach-to-employee-training-1457921560

Kommers, P., Smyrnova-Trybulska, E., Morze, N., Issa, T., & Issa, T. (2015). Conceptual aspects: Analyses law, ethical, human, technical, social factors of Development ICT, e-learning and intercultural development in different countries setting out the previous new theoretical model and preliminary findings. *Int. J. Continuing Engineering Education and Life-long Learning*, *25*(4), 365–393. doi:10.1504/IJCEELL.2015.074235

Kong, S. C., & Song, Y. (2015). An experience of personalized learning hub initiative embedding BYOD for reflective engagement in higher education. *Computers & Education*, *88*, 227–240. doi:10.1016/j.compedu.2015.06.003

Korhonen, M. (2015, July). *Hidden Opportunities - Ecommerce in Finland*. Paper in MCCSIS E-commerce and Digital Marketing.

Korhonen, M. (2016). Sujuvampaa arkea digitaalisuudella. ReAD verkkolehti huhtikuu 2016. Mikkelin ammattikorkeakoulu. Mikkeli.

Koskinen, I., Zimmerman, J., Binder, T., Redstrom, J., & Wensveen, S. (2011). *Design Research Through Practice: From the Lab, Field, and Showroom* (1st ed.). Waltham, MA: Morgan Kaufmann.

Krajnc, E., Feiner, J., & Schmidt, S. (2010). *User Centered Interaction Design for Mobile Applications Focused on Visually Impaired and Blind People* (pp. 195–202). Springer Berlin Heidelberg; doi:10.1007/978-3-642-16607-5_12

Krogh, P. G., Markussen, T., & Bang, A. L. (2015). Ways of Drifting—Five Methods of Experimentation in Research Through Design. In *ICoRD'15 – Research into Design Across Boundaries* (Vol. 1, pp. 39–50). New Delhi: Springer. doi:10.1007/978-81-322-2232-3_4

Kumar, V., Sbirlea, A., Jayaraj, A., Budimlic, Z., Majeti, D., & Sarkar, V. (2015). Heterogeneous work-stealing across CPU and DSP cores. *Proceedings of theHigh Performance Extreme Computing Conference (HPEC)*. IEEE. doi:10.1109/HPEC.2015.7322452

Kumar, S. (2004). Mobile communications: Global trends in the 21st century. *Int. J. Mobile Communication*, *2*(1), 67–86. doi:10.1504/IJMC.2004.004488

Kuznekoff, J. H., & Titsworth, S. (2013). The impact of mobile phone usage on student learning. *Communication Education*, *61*(3), 233–252. doi:10.1080/03634523.2013.767917

Lackey, S., Barber, D., Reinerman, L., Badler, N. I., & Hudson, I. (2011). Defining Next-Generation Multi-Modal Communication in Human Robot Interaction. *Proceedings of the Human Factors and Ergonomics Society Annual Meeting*, *55*(1), 461–464. http://doi.org/ doi:10.1177/1071181311551095

Lafleur, K., Cassady, K., Doud, A., Shades, K., Rogin, E., & He, B. (2013). Quadcopter control in three-dimensional space using a noninvasive motor imagery-based brain-computer interface. *Journal of Neural Engineering*, *10*(4), 046003. doi:10.1088/1741-2560/10/4/046003 PMID:23735712

Lakaniemi, I. (2014). *Taitojen puute yritysten suurin haaste digitalisaatiossa*. The Finnish Chamber Commerce Publication. Retrieved September 29, 2016 from http://kauppakamari.fi/wp-content/uploads/2014/09/kauppakamarin-yritysjohtajakysely-digitalisaatiosta.pdf

Lang, A. R., Martin, J. L., Sharples, S., Crowe, J. A., & Murphy, E. (2012). Not a minor problem: Involving adolescents in medical device design research. *Theoretical Issues in Ergonomics Science*, 1–12.

Langmia, K., & Glass, A. (2014). Coping with Smartphone distractions in a college classroom. *Teaching Journalism and Mass Communication*, *4*(1), 13–23.

Lavars, N. (2016). Thumbsteered drone leaves you with a free hand. Retrieved from http://newatlas.com/shift-drone-thumb/46188/

Le Dantec, C. A., Poole, E. S., & Wyche, S. P. (2009). Values As Lived Experience: Evolving Value Sensitive Design in Support of Value Discovery. In *Proceedings of the SIGCHI Conference on Human Factors in Computing Systems* (pp. 1141–1150). New York, NY: ACM. doi:10.1145/1518701.1518875

Leap Motion Inc. (2010). Leap Motion Controller. Retrieved from https://www.leapmotion.com/

Lee, Y.-C., Yao, C.-Y., Hsieh, C.-Y., Wu, J.-Y., Hsieh, Y.-H., & Chen, C.-H., … Chen, Y.-S. (2013). Egg Pair — A hearing game for the visually impaired people using RFID. *Proceedings of the2013 IEEE International Symposium on Consumer Electronics (ISCE)* (pp. 3–4). IEEE. http://doi.org/ doi:10.1109/ISCE.2013.6570237

Lee, H., & Hyun, E. (2015). The intelligent robot contents for children with speech-language disorder. *Journal of Educational Technology & Society*, *18*(3), 100–113.

Lee, T., Meng, H., Lo, W. K., & Ching, P. C. (2003). The State of the Art in Human-computer Speech-based Interface Technologies. *HKIE Transactions Hong Kong Institution of Engineers*, *10*(4), 50–61.

Legg, S., & Hutter, M. (2007). Universal Intelligence: A definition of machine intelligence. *Minds and Machines, 17*(4), 391-444.

Leibowitz, B. (2014). Academic development – no fixed recipes. *The International Journal for Academic Development*, *19*(2), 73–75. doi:10.1080/1360144X.2014.912375

Leisyte, L. (2013). Being an academic in Europe and the U.S.: Role differentiation, shifting identities and protected spaces. *Belgium University Foundation Ethical Forum 2013, The academic's burden – University professors under perverse pressure.*

Lévano, M., & Albornoz, A. (2016). Findings in profesional training: computer engineering Science program. In J. Björkqvist, K. Edström, R.J. Hugo et al. (Eds.), *Proceedings of the 12th International CDIO Conference: CDIO Implementation* (pp. 528-537). Turku AMK: Turku University of Applied Sciences.

Lévano, M., & Herrera, O. (2012). Validation Strategies of Competences in a Computer Science Curriculum. *Proceedings of the31st International Conference of the Chilean Computer Science Society* (pp. 9-11). Valparaíso: Pontificia Universidad Católica de Valparaíso. doi:10.1109/SCCC.2012.8

Lévano, M., Herrera, O., Mellado, A., Rojas, J., Contreras, G., Peralta, B., & Caro, L. (2016). *Profile of the Civil Engineering Degree in Computer Science*. Chile, Temuco: School of Computer Engineering UCTemuco.

Lévano, M., & Fernández, C. (2015). A model for a Physical and Virtual Environment for Extreme Feedback in the Development of the Metacognition Supported by TICS: The Computer Engineer Career as Case of Study. *Lecture Notes in Electrical Engineering*, *330*, 1345–1352. doi:10.1007/978-3-662-45402-2_187

Levinson-Rose, J., & Menges, R. J. (1981). Improving college teaching: A critical review of research. *Review of Educational Research*, *51*(3), 403–434. doi:10.3102/00346543051003403

Liaw, S. T., Rahimi, A., Ray, P., Taggart, J., Dennis, S., de Lusignan, S., & Talaei-Khoei, A. et al. (2013). Towards an ontology for data quality in integrated chronic disease management: A realist review of the literature. *IJMI*, *82*(1), 10–24. PMID:23122633

Lieberman, H., Paternò, F., Klann, M., & Wulf, V. (2006). End-User Development: An Emerging Paradigm. EUD, 9, 1–8.

Li, H., & Suomi, R. (2009). A Proposed Scale for Measuring E-service Quality. *International Journal of u- and e-Service. Science and Technology*, *2*(1), 2009.

Liideri. (n.d.). *Business, Productivity and Joy at Work Programme 2012-2018*. Tekes – the Finnish Funding Agency for Technology and Innovation.

Liimatainen, J., Häkkinen, M., Nousiainen, T., Kankaanranta, M., & Neittaanmäki, P. (2012). *A Mobile Application Concept to Encourage Independent Mobility for Blind and Visually Impaired Students* (pp. 552–559). Springer. doi:10.1007/978-3-642-31534-3_81

Likert, R. (1932). A technique for the measurement of attitudes. *Archives of Psychology*.

Lim, Y.-K., Stolterman, E., & Tenenberg, J. (2008). The Anatomy of Prototypes: Prototypes As Filters, Prototypes As Manifestations of Design Ideas. *ACM Trans. Comput.-Hum. Interact., 15*(2), 7:1–7:27.

Lindquist, T. E. (1985). Assessing the usability of human-computer interfaces. *IEEE Software, 2*(1), 74–82. doi:10.1109/MS.1985.230052

Ling, P. (2009). *Development of academics and higher education futures* (Vol. 1). Sydney: Australian Learning and Teaching Council.

LinkedIn. (2016). *User agreement*. Retrieved October 13, 2016 from https://www.linkedin.com/legal/user-agreement

Lissner, L., Wijnhoven, T. M. A., Mehlig, K., Sjöberg, A., Kunesova, M., Yngve, A., & Breda, J. et al. (2016). Socio-economic inequalities in childhood overweight: Heterogeneity across five countries in the WHO European Childhood Obesity Surveillance Initiative (COSI–2008). *International Journal of Obesity, 40*(5), 796–802. doi:10.1038/ijo.2016.12 PMID:27136760

Little, L., Fitton, D., Bell, B. T., & Toth, N. (Eds.). (2016). *Perspectives on HCI Research with Teenagers*. Cham: Springer International Publishing. doi:10.1007/978-3-319-33450-9

Loads, D., & Campbell, F. (2015). Fresh thinking about academic development: Authentic, transformative, disruptive? *The International Journal for Academic Development, 20*(4), 355–369. doi:10.1080/1360144X.2015.1083866

Locke, W. (2014). *Shifting academic careers: Implications for enhancing professionalism in teaching and supporting learning*. York, UK: The Higher Education Academy.

Locoro, A. (2016). A Map is worth a Thousand Data: Requirements in Tertiary Human-Data Interaction to Foster Participation.*CEUR Workshop Procs of CoPDA 2015*.

Locoro, A., Grignani, D., & Mascardi, V. (2011). MANENT: An infrastructure for integrating, structuring and searching digital libraries. *Studies in Computational Intelligence, Springer, 375*, 315–341.

Longhurst, C. A., Palma, J. P., Grisim, L. M., Widen, E., Chan, M., & Sharek, P. J. (2013). Using an Evidence-Based Approach to EMR Implementation to Optimize Outcomes and Avoid Unintended Consequences. *Journal of Healthcare Information Management, 27*(3), 79. PMID:24771994

Lundin, J., Lymer, G., Holmquist, L. E., Brown, B., & Rost, M. (2010). Integrating students mobile technology in higher education. *International Journal of Mobile Learning and Organisation, 4*(1), 1–14. doi:10.1504/IJMLO.2010.029951

Ma, Y., Mao, Z.-H., Jia, W., Li, C., Yang, J., & Sun, M. (2010, May 9-12). Magnetic hand tracking for human-computer interface. *Proceedings of the14th Biennial IEEE Conference on Electromagnetic Field Computation CEFC '10*, Chicago, IL, USA. IEEE. Doi:<ALIGNMENT.qj></ALIGNMENT>10.1109/CEFC.2010.5481499

Makey Makey | Buy Direct (Official Site). (2016). Retrieved from http://www.makeymakey.com/

Malaika, Y. (2015). Interaction Design in VR: The Rules Have Changed (Again). *Proceedings of Game Developers Conference Europe*. Retrieved from http://www.gdcvault.com/play/1022810/Interaction-Design-in-VR-The

Mangiron, C., & Zhang, X. (2016). Game Accessibility for the Blind: Current Overview and the Potential Application of Audio Description as the Way Forward. In Researching Audio Description (pp. 75–95). London: Palgrave Macmillan UK. doi:10.1057/978-1-137-56917-2_5

Marcelino, I., Lopes, D., Reis, M., Silva, F., Laza, R., & Pereira, A. (2005). *Using the eServices Platform for Detecting Behavior Patterns Deviation in the Elderly Assisted Living: A Case Study. Hindawi Publishing Corporation. BioMed Research International*. doi:10.1155/2015/530828

Marginson, S. (2011). Global position and position-taking in higher education: The case of Australia. In S. Marginson, S. Kaur, & E. Sawir (Eds.), *Higher education in Asia Pacific: Strategic responses to globalization* (Vol. 36, pp. 375–392). Netherlands: Springer. doi:10.1007/978-94-007-1500-4_20

Marks, L. (2013). *Curtin Learning Institute: Mapping professional development activities across Curtin*. Unpublished Report. Curtin University, Perth.

Märtensson, K. (2015). Academic development – old habits or disruptive practice? *The International Journal for Academic Development, 20*(4), 303–305. doi:10.1080/1360144X.2015.1096572

Martinovic, I., Davies, D., Frank, M., Perito, D., Ros, T., & Song, D. (2012). On the Feasibility of Side-Channel Attacks with Brain-Computer Interfaces. *Usenixorg*, 1–16.

MASTERMIND | Toys for Kids | Hasbro Games. (n. d.). Retrieved from http://www.hasbro.com/en-ca/product/mastermind:93765D16-6D40-1014-8BF0-9EFBF894F9D4

Matsuda, T., & Nesbitt, R. (2001). Attending holistically vs. analytically: Comparing the context sensitivity of Japanese and Americans. *Journal of Personality and Social Psychology, 81*(5), 922–934. doi:10.1037/0022-3514.81.5.922 PMID:11708567

Matthys, C., Pynaert, I., De Keyzer, W., & De Henauw, S. (2007). Validity and reproducibility of an adolescent web-based food frequency questionnaire. *Journal of the American Dietetic Association, 107*(4), 605–610. Retrieved from http://www.sciencedirect.com/science/article/pii/S0002822307000247 doi:10.1016/j.jada.2007.01.005 PMID:17383266

Mazé, R., & Redström, J. (2005). Form and the computational object. *Digital Creativity, 16*(1), 7–18. doi:10.1080/14626260500147736

McAuley, A., Stewart, B., Siemens, G., & Cormier, D. (2010). *The MOOC model for digital*. Retrieved October 30, 2016, from http://www.elearnspace.org/Articles/MOOC_Final.pdf

Mccool, M. (2008). Signal Processing And General-Purpose Computing And GPUs. *IEEE Signal Processing Magazine, 24*(3), 109–114. doi:10.1109/MSP.2007.361608

McCoy, B. (2013). *Digital distractions in the classroom: Student classroom use of digital devices for non-class related purposes*. Retrieved from http://digitalcommons.unl.edu/journalismfacpub/71

McCray, A. T., Trevvett, P., & Frost, H. R. (2014). Modeling the autism spectrum disorder phenotype. *Neuroinformatics, 12*(2), 291–305. doi:10.1007/s12021-013-9211-4 PMID:24163114

McPherson, M., Budge, K., & Lemon, N. (2015). New practices in doing academic development: Twitter as an informal learning space. *The International Journal for Academic Development, 20*(2), 126–136. doi:10.1080/136014 4X.2015.1029485

McVeigh, B. J. (2002). *Japanese Higher Education as Myth*. New York: East Gate Book.

Measuring the Information Society. (2012). *Committed to connecting the world.* Retrieved October 30, 2016, from http://www.itu.int/dms_pub/itu-d/opb/ind/D-IND-ICTOI-2012-SUM-PDF-R.pdf (in Russian)

Milanova, M., & Sirakov, N. (2008, December 16-19). Recognition of emotional states in natural human-computer interaction. *Proceedings of the8th IEEE International Symposium on Signal Processing and Information Technology ISSPIT '08* (pp. 186–191). IEEE. doi:10.1109/ISSPIT.2008.4775663

Miller, D., Parecki, A., & Douglas, S. A. (2007). Finger dance. *Proceedings of the 9th international ACM SIGAC-CESS conference on Computers and accessibility - Assets '07* (p. 253). New York, USA: ACM Press. http://doi.org/doi:10.1145/1296843.1296898

Milne, L. R., Bennett, C. L., & Ladner, R. E. (2013). VBGhost. *Proceedings of the 15th International ACM SIGAC-CESS Conference on Computers and Accessibility - ASSETS '13* (pp. 1–2). New York, USA: ACM Press. http://doi.org/doi:10.1145/2513383.2513396

Milne, L. R., Bennett, C. L., Ladner, R. E., & Azenkot, S. (2014). BraillePlay. *Proceedings of the 16th international ACM SIGACCESS conference on Computers & accessibility - ASSETS '14* (pp. 137–144). New York, USA: ACM Press. http://doi.org/ doi:10.1145/2661334.2661377

Minshew, N. J., & Goldstein, G. (1998). Autism as a disorder of complex information processing. *Mental Retardation and Developmental Disabilities Research Reviews, 4*(2), 129–136. doi:10.1002/(SICI)1098-2779(1998)4:2<129::AID-MRDD10>3.0.CO;2-X

Mitter, G. & Orlandini, J. (2005). Recrutamento online/internet. *Maringá Management: Revista de Ciências Empresariais, 2*(2), 19-34.

Mochizuki, N., & Ortega, L. (2008). Balancing communication and grammar in beginning-level foreign language classrooms: A study of guided planning and relativization. *Language Teaching Research, 12*(1), 11–37. doi:10.1177/1362168807084492

Moore, H. J., Ells, L. J., McLure, S. A., Crooks, S., Cumbor, D., Summerbell, C. D., & Batterham, A. M. (2008). The development and evaluation of a novel computer program to assess previous-day dietary and physical activity behaviours in school children: The Synchronised Nutrition and Activity ProgramTM (SNAPTM). *The British Journal of Nutrition, 99*(06), 1266–1274. doi:10.1017/S0007114507862428 PMID:18042307

Morbidity and Mortality Weekly Report (MMWR). (2011). School Health Guidelines to Promote Healthy Eating and Physical Activity. *Recommendations and Reports, 60*(RR05), 1-71.

Morelli, T., & Folmer, E. (2014). Real-time sensory substitution to enable players who are blind to play video games using whole body gestures. *Entertainment Computing, 5*(1), 83–90. doi:10.1016/j.entcom.2013.08.003

Moreno J. (1958). *Sociometry. Experimental method and science about society.* Moskwa: "Ynostrannaya literature".

Moreno, L. A., Joyanes, M., Mesana, M. I., González-Gross, M., Gil, C. M., Sarría, A., & Marcos, A. et al.AVENA Study Group. (2003). Harmonization of anthropometric measurements for a multicenter nutrition survey in Spanish adolescents. *Nutrition (Burbank, Los Angeles County, Calif.), 19*(6), 481–486. doi:10.1016/S0899-9007(03)00040-6 PMID:12781845

Morgan, H. (2014). Using digital story projects to help students improve in reading and writing. *Reading Improvement, 51*(1), 20–26.

Morris, G., Snider, D., & Katz, M. (1996). Integrating public health information and surveillance systems. *Journal of Public Health Management and Practice, 2*(4), 24–27. doi:10.1097/00124784-199623000-00007 PMID:10186689

Morris, T., Blenkhorn, P., & Zaidi, F. (2002). Blink Detection for Real-time Eye Tracking. *Journal of Network and Computer Applications, 25*(2), 129–143. doi:10.1016/S1084-8045(02)90130-X

Morze, N. (2013). What Should be E-Learning Course for Smart Education. *ICT in Education, Research and Industrial Applications: Integration, Harmonization and Knowledge Transfer, CEUR Workshop Proceedings*, 411–423. Retrieved October 30, 2016, from http://ceur-ws.org/Vol-1000/ICTERI-2013-MRDL.pdf

Morze, N. (2014). Designing of Electronic Learning Courses For IT Students Considering the Dominant Learning Style. Information and Communication Technologies in Education, Research, and Industrial Applications/Communications in Computer and Information Science (Vol. 469, pp. 261–273). Springer. Retrieved from http://link.springer.com/chapter/10.1007/978-3-319-13206-8

Morze, N. V., & Glazunova, E. G. (2009). Quality Criteria for E-Learning Courses. Informational Technologies in Education, (4), 63-76.

Mu-Chun, S., & Ming-Tsang, C. (2001). Voice-controlled human-computer interface for the disabled. *Computing & Control Engineering Journal, 12*(5), 225–230. doi:10.1049/cce:20010504

Mulas, F., Ros-Cervera, G., Millá, M. G., Etchepareborda, M. C., Abad, L., & Téllez de Meneses, M. (2010). Modelos de intervención en niños con autismo. *Revista de Neurologia, 50*(3), 77–84. PMID:20112215

Munster, A. (2006). *Materializing New Media: Embodiment in Information Aesthetics*. Dartmouth College Press.

Murdoch, T. B., & Detsky, A. S. (2013). The inevitable application of big data to health care. *Journal of the American Medical Association, 309*(13), 1351–1352. doi:10.1001/jama.2013.393 PMID:23549579

Murphy, J., Lee, R., & Swinger, E. (2011). Student Perceptions and Adoption of University Smart Card Systems. *International Journal of Technology and Human Interaction, 7*(3), 1–15. doi:10.4018/jthi.2011070101

Murphy, R., Shell, D., Guerin, A., Duncan, B., Fine, B., Pratt, K., & Zourntos, T. (2011). A Midsummer Nights Dream (with flying robots). *Autonomous Robots, 30*(2), 143–156. doi:10.1007/s10514-010-9210-3

Muscio, G., Pierri, F., Trujillo, M. A., Cataldi, E., Giglio, G., & Antonelli, G., … Ollero, A. (2016). Experiments on coordinated motion of aerial robotic manipulators. *Proceedings of theIEEE International Conference on Robotics and Automation (ICRA),* Stockholm, Sweden (pp. 1224–1229). doi:10.1109/ICRA.2016.7487252

Musgrove, J. (2014, December 14). 9 crucial competencies for your staff training program. *Saxons Blog*. Retrieved from http://www.saxonsgroup.com.au/blog/human-resources/9-crucial-competencies-for-your-staff-training-program/

Mynatt, E. D. (1994). Designing with auditory icons - how well do we identify auditory cues? Proceedings of the Conference companion on Human factors in computing systems CHI '94 (pp. 269–270). New York, USA: ACM Press; doi:10.1145/259963.260483

Nagar, A., & Xu, Z. (2015). Gesture control by wrist surface electromyography. *Proceedings of the2015 IEEE International Conference on Pervasive Computing and Communication Workshops* (pp. 556–561). doi:<ALIGNMENT.qj></ALIGNMENT>10.1109/percomw.2015.7134098

Nairn, A., Griffin, C., & Wicks, P. G. (2008). Childrens use of brand symbolism: A consumer culture theory approach. *European Journal of Marketing, 42*(5/6), 627–640. doi:10.1108/03090560810862543

National Institute of Standards and Technology. (n.d.). Retrieved October 30, 2016, from http://www.nist.gov/

Nayak, S., Pujari, S., & Dash, P. (2014). Implementation of Edge Detection Using FPGA and Model Based Approach. *Proceedings oftheInternationalConferenceonInformationCommunicationandEmbeddedSystems(ICICES).* doi:10.1109/ICICES.2014.7033990

NeuroSky. (2011). Brainwaves. Not Thoughts. Retrieved from http://neurosky.com/biosensors/eeg-sensor/

Ng, M., Fleming, T., Robinson, M., Thomson, B., Graetz, N., & Margono, C. et al.. (2014). Global, regional and national prevalence of overweight and obesity in children and adults 19802013: A systematic analysis. *Lancet*, *384*(9945), 766–781. Retrieved from https://www.ncbi.nlm.nih.gov/pmc/articles/PMC4624264/ doi:10.1016/S0140-6736(14)60460-8 PMID:24880830

Nicol, D., Thomson, A., & Breslin, C. (2014). Rethinking feedback in higher education: A peer review perspective. *Assessment & Evaluation in Higher Education*, *39*(1), 102–122. doi:10.1080/02602938.2013.795518

Nimble VR. (2012). Nimble VR is joining Oculus. Retrieved from http://nimblevr.com/index.html

No Isolation. (2015). Retrieved March 2, 2016, from http://www.noisolation.com/en/

Norman, D. A. (2006). *O Design do dia-a-dia*. Rio de Janeiro: Rocco.

Norwegian M. E. Association. (2016). Retrieved from http://me-foreningen.com/

Nuzzaci, A., & La Vecchia, L. (2012). A Smart University for a Smart City. *International Journal of Digital Literacy and Digital Competence*, *3*(4), 16–32. doi:10.4018/jdldc.2012100102

Nwana, H. S. (1996). Software Agents : An Overview. *The Knowledge Engineering Review*, *11*(3), 205–244. doi:10.1017/S026988890000789X

O'Reilly, T. (2007). What Is Web 2.0: Design Patterns and Business Models for the Next Generation of Software. *International Journal of Digital Economics*, *65*, 17-37.

Odom, W., Wakkary, R., Lim, Y., Desjardins, A., Hengeveld, B., & Banks, R. (2016). From Research Prototype to Research Product. In *Proceedings of the 2016 CHI Conference on Human Factors in Computing Systems* (pp. 2549–2561). New York, NY: ACM. doi:10.1145/2858036.2858447

Onnibus.com. (2016). *Company information*. Retrieved October 3, 2016 from http://www.onnibus.com/fi/tietoa-yrityksesta.htm

Ono, Y. (2014). Motivational Effects of Digital Storytelling on Japanese EFL Learners. *Proceedings of CLaSIC, 2014*, 414–431.

Open Knowledge Finland. (2016). *Visiot ja arvot*. Retrieved October 3, 2016 from http://fi.okfn.org/about/visiojaarvot/

OpenCV. (2016). Retrieved from http://opencv.org/

Orenga-Roglá, S., & Chalmeta, R. (2016). Social customer relationship management: Taking advantage of Web 2.0 and Big Data technologies. *SpringerPlus*, *5*(1), 1462. doi:10.1186/s40064-016-3128-y PMID:27652037

Oviatt, S. (2003). Multimodal interfaces. In J. A. Jacko & A. Sears (Eds.), The Human-Computer Interaction Handbook: Fundamentals, Evolving Technologies, and Emerging Applications (pp. 286–304). London: Lawrence Erlbaum Associates, Incorporated.

Oviatt, S. (2002). Breaking the robustness barrier: Recent progress on the design of robust multimodal systems. *Advances in Computers*, *56*(C), 305–341. doi:10.1016/S0065-2458(02)80009-2

Owen, C. (2007). Design thinking: Notes on its nature and use. *Design Research Quarterly*, *2*(1), 16–27.

Oyserman, D., Elmore, K., & Smith, G. (2012). *Self, Self-Concept, and Identity. In Handbook of Self and Identity* (2nd ed.; pp. 69–104). New York: The Guilford Press.

Pangburn, D. J. (2016). This Guy Just Spent 48hours in virtual reality. *In The Creators Project*. Retrieved from http://thecreatorsproject.vice.com/blog/48-hours-in-vr

Parasuraman, A., & Zinkhan, G. (2002). Marketing to and serving customers through the internet: An overview and research agenda. *Journal of the Academy of Marketing Science, 30*(4), 286–295. doi:10.1177/009207002236906

Parasuraman, R., & Manzey, D. H. (2010). Complacency and bias in human use of automation: An attentional integration. *Human Factors: Hum. Factors, 52*(3), 381–410. doi:10.1177/0018720810376055 PMID:21077562

Park, N., Kee, K. F., & Valenzuela, S. (2009). Being immersed in social networking environment: Facebook groups, uses and gratifications and social outcomes. *Cyberpsychology & Behavior, 12*(6), 729–733. doi:10.1089/cpb.2009.0003 PMID:19619037

Pasqualotto, A., Lam, J. S. Y., & Proulx, M. J. (2013). Congenital blindness improves semantic and episodic memory. *Behavioural Brain Research, 244*, 162–165. doi:10.1016/j.bbr.2013.02.005 PMID:23416237

Payne, A., & Frow, P. (2005). A Strategic Framework for Customer Relationship Management. *Journal of Marketing, 69*(4), 167–176. doi:10.1509/jmkg.2005.69.4.167

Payne, K. (2007). *Autonomy - Proposal for a UK Route Map*. United Kingdom: BAE Systems.

Pegrum, M., Oakley, G., & Faulkner, R. (2014). Schools going mobile: A study of the adoption of mobile handheld technologies in Western Australian independent schools. *Australasian Journal of Educational Technology, 29*(1), 66–81.

Percy, A., et al. (2008). *The RED report: Recognition, enhancement, development. The contribution of sessional teachers to higher education*. Support for the original work was provided by the Australian Learning and Teaching Council, An Initiative of the Australian Government Department of Education, Employment and Workplace Relations.

Peretti, J. (2007). *Recursos Humanos (3ʳᵈ ed.)*. Lisboa: Edições Sílabo.

Perrin, J. M., Anderson, L. E., & Van Cleave, J. (2014). The Rise In Chronic Conditions Among Infants, Children, And Youth Can Be Met With Continued Health System Innovations. *Health Affairs, 33*(12), 2099–2105. doi:10.1377/hlthaff.2014.0832 PMID:25489027

Pettijohn, T. F., Frazier, E., Rieser, E., Vaughn, N., & Hupp-Wilds, B. (2015). Classroom texting on college students. *College Student Journal, 49*(4), 513–516.

Pfeifer, R., & Scheier, C. (1999). Embodied Cognitive Science: Basic Concepts. In R. Pfeifer & C. Scheier (Eds.), *Understanding Intelligence* (pp. 81–138). MIT Press.

Pipino, L., & Lee, Y. W. (2011). Medical Errors and Information Quality: A Review and Research Agenda.AMCIS.

Pipino, L., Lee, Y. W., & Wang, R. Y. (2002). Data quality assessment. *Communications of the ACM, 45*(4), 211–218. doi:10.1145/505248.506010

Plos, O., & Buisine, S. (2006). Universal design for mobile phones. In *CHI '06 extended abstracts on Human factors in computing systems - CHI EA '06* (p. 1229). New York, New York, USA: ACM Press; doi:10.1145/1125451.1125681

Poikola, A., Kuikkaniemi, K., & Kuittinen, O. (2014). *My Data – johdatus ihmiskeskeiseen henkilötiedon hyödyntämiseen*. Lahti: Markprint.

Poole, E. S., & Peyton, T. (2013). Interaction Design Research with Adolescents: Methodological Challenges and Best Practices. In *Proceedings of the 12th International Conference on Interaction Design and Children* (pp. 211–217). New York, NY: ACM. doi:10.1145/2485760.2485766

Popkin, B. M., Adair, L. S., & Ng, S. W. (2012). Now and then: The Global Nutrition Transition: The Pandemic of Obesity in Developing Countries. *Nutrition Reviews, 70*(1), 3–21. doi:10.1111/j.1753-4887.2011.00456.x PMID:22221213

Porter, M. E. (2001, March). Strategy and the Internet. *Hayward Business Review*.

Pöysti, T. (2016). *Sote- ja maakuntauudistuksen toimeenpano*. Retrieved October 19, 2016 from http://alueuudistus.fi/documents/1477425/1892966/Sote-+ja+maakuntauudistus+toimeenpano+22.8.2016.pdf/bc3093ef-d165-4c3c-84bf-26ea77cc17fe

Preece, J., & Rogers, Y. (2005). *Design de Interação: além da interacao homem-computador*. Porto Alegre: Bookman.

Price, M., Rust, C., O'Donovan, B., Handley, K., & Bryant, R. (2012). *Assessment literacy. The foundation for improving student learning*. Oxford, UK: Oxford Brookes University.

Probert, B. (2013). *Teaching-focused academic appointments in Australian universities: Recognition, specialisation, or stratification*. Office of Learning and Teaching. Commonwealth of Australia.

Qing, C., Cordea, M. D., Petriu, E. M., Whalen, T. E., Rudas, I. J., & Varkonyi-Koczy, A. (2008). Hand-Gesture and Facial-Expression Human-Computer Interfaces for Intelligent Space Applications. *Proceedings of the IEEE International Workshop on Medical Measurements and Applications MeMeA '08* (pp. 1–6). doi:<ALIGNMENT.qj></ALIGNMENT>10.1109/MEMEA.2008.4542987

Ranjan, J. & Bhatnagar V. (2008). Critical Success Factors For Implementing CRM Using Data Mining. *Journal of Knowledge Management Practice*, *9*(3).

Rao, S. M., & Gagie, B. (2006). Learning through seeing and doing: Visual supports for children with autism. *Teaching Exceptional Children*, *38*(6), 26–33. doi:10.1177/004005990603800604

Rao, S., & Challa, R. K. (2013, October). Adoption of Cloud Computing In Education and Learning. *International Journal of Advanced Research in Computer and Communication Engineering*, *2*(10), 4160–4163.

Razmi, M., Pourali, S., & Nozad, S. (2014). Digital Storytelling in EFL Classroom (Oral Presentation of the Story): A Pathway to Improve Oral Production. *Procedia: Social and Behavioral Sciences*, *98*, 1541–1544. doi:10.1016/j.sbspro.2014.03.576

Raz, N., Striem, E., Pundak, G., Orlov, T., & Zohary, E. (2007). Superior serial memory in the blind: A case of cognitive compensatory adjustment. *Current Biology*, *17*(13), 1129–1133. doi:10.1016/j.cub.2007.05.060 PMID:17583507

Read, J., Fitton, D., Cowan, B., Beale, R., Guo, Y., & Horton, M. (2011). Understanding and designing cool technologies for teenagers. In *Proceedings of the 2011 annual conference extended abstracts on Human factors in computing systems* (pp. 1567–1572). New York, NY: ACM. doi:10.1145/1979742.1979809

Reeves, L. M., Martin, J.-C., McTear, M., Raman, T., Stanney, K. M., Su, H., & Kraal, B. et al. (2004). Guidelines for multimodal user interface design. *Communications of the ACM*, *47*(1), 57. doi:10.1145/962081.962106

Reinhold, O. & Alt, R. (2012). Social Customer Relationship Management: State of the Art and Learnings from Current Projects. *BLED 2012 Proceedings*.

Ren, H. (2014). A Brief Introduction on Contemporary High-Level Synthesis. *Proceedings of the IEEE International Conference on IC Design & Technology (ICICDT 2014)*. doi:10.1109/ICICDT.2014.6838614

Renitto, J. E., & Thomas, N. K. (2014). A Survey on Gesture Recognition Technology. *International Journal for Technological Research in Engineering*, *1*(10), 1058–1060.

Reuters. (2015). Using The Force? No, it's an Apple Watch flying this drone. Retrieved from http://www.reuters.com/article/us-apple-watch-drone-idUSKBN0UE14Q20160101

Reynolds, M., & Trehan, K. (2000). Assessment: A critical perspective. *Studies in Higher Education*, *25*(3), 267–278. doi:10.1080/03075070050193406

Riaño, D., Real, F., López-Vallverdú, J. A., Campana, F., Ercolani, S., Mecocci, P., & Caltagirone, C. et al. (2012). An ontology-based personalization of health-care knowledge to support clinical decisions for chronically ill patients. *Journal of Biomedical Informatics*, *45*(3), 429–446. doi:10.1016/j.jbi.2011.12.008 PMID:22269224

Rigby, , & Ammenwerth, , Beuscart-Zephir, Brender, Hypponen, Melia, … de Keizer. (2013). Evidence Based Health Informatics: 10 years of efforts to promote the principle. *Yearbook of Medical Informatics*, *8*(1), 34–46. PMID:23974546

Rittel, H. W. J., & Webber, M. M. (1973). Dilemmas in a general theory of planning. *Policy Sciences*, *4*(2), 155–169. doi:10.1007/BF01405730

Roberts, A., Gaizauskas, R., Hepple, M., & Guo, Y. (2008). Mining clinical relationships from patient narratives. *BMC Bioinformatics*, *9*(11), S3. doi:10.1186/1471-2105-9-S11-S3 PMID:19025689

Roberts, N., & Ress, M. (2014). Student use of mobile devices in university lectures. *Australasian Journal of Educational Technology*, *30*(4), 415–426. doi:10.14742/ajet.589

Robin, B. R. (2008). Digital storytelling: A powerful technology tool for the 21st century classroom. *Theory into Practice*, *47*(3), 220–228. doi:10.1080/00405840802153916

Robinson, T. N. (1999). Reducing Children's Television Viewing to Prevent Obesity: A Randomized Controlled Trial. *Journal of the American Medical Association*, *282*(16), 1561–1567. doi:10.1001/jama.282.16.1561 PMID:10546696

Rocha, C. (2010). Três concepções de ciberespaço. Proceedings of 9° Encontro Internacional de Arte e Tecnologia.

Rocha, C. (2010). *Três concepções de ciberespaço. Proceedings of the 9th Encontro Internacional de Arte e Tecnologia*. Brasília: PPG Arte/IdA/UnB.

Rodríguez-Gómez, G., & Ibarra-Sáiz, M. S. (2016). *Guía Diseñar procedimientos de evaluación en la Educación Superior*. Producción: EVALfor - Grupo de Investigación. España:Cádiz. Available in: https://dx.doi.org/10.13140/RG.2.1.1844.9524

Rodríguez-Gómez, G., & Ibarra-Saiz, M. S. (Eds.). (2011). e-Evaluación orientada al e-Aprendizaje estratégico en Educación Superior. Madrid: Narcea.

Rodríguez-Gómez, G., & Ibarra-Sáiz, M. S. (2015). Assessment as learning and empowerment: Towards sustainable learning in higher education. In M. Peris-Ortiz & J. M. Merigó Lindahl (Eds.), *Sustainable learning in higher education, innovation, technology, and knowledge management* (pp. 1–20). London: Springer-Verlag; doi:10.1007/978-3-319-10804-9_1

Rozhen, A. (1999). *Say* citation index your articles, and I'll tell you what … you're a scientist. *Zerkalo Nedeli, 45*. (in Russian)

Russell, S., & Norvik, P. (1995). *Articial Intelligence A Modern Approach*. Englewood Cliffs, NJ: Prentice Hall Inc.

Ryals, L., & Payne, A. (2001). Customer Relationship Management in Financial Services: Towards Information-Enabled Relationship Marketing. *Journal of Strategic Marketing*, *9*(1), 3–27. doi:10.1080/713775725

Sánchez, J., Darin, T., & Andrade, R. (2015). *Multimodal Videogames for the Cognition of People Who Are Blind: Trends and Issues*. Springer International Publishing. doi:10.1007/978-3-319-20684-4_52

Sanchez, J., & Hassler, T. (2007). AudioMUD: A Multiuser Virtual Environment for Blind People. *IEEE Transactions on Neural Systems and Rehabilitation Engineering*, *15*(1), 16–22. doi:10.1109/TNSRE.2007.891404 PMID:17436871

Sánchez, T. (2005). *Educational Model of the UC Temuco*. Temuco, Chile: Universidad Católica de Temuco.

Santos, I. M., & Bocheco, O. (2014b). Mobile devices in the classroom: Emirati students' perceptions of usage and policies. In *IEEE Proceedings of the Interactive Collaborative Learning* (ICL) (pp. 956-962). IEEE. doi:10.1109/ICL.2014.7017905

Santos, I. M. (2015). Mobile devices in higher education classrooms: Challenges and opportunities. In J. Keengwe (Ed.), *Promoting active learning through the integration of mobile and ubiquitous technologies* (pp. 37–54). IGI Global; doi:10.4018/978-1-4666-6343-5.ch003

Santos, I. M., & Bocheco, O. (2014a). Students' mobile devices usage during class and policy suggestions for appropriate practices. In M. Kalz, Y. Bayyurt, & M. Specht (Eds.), *Mobile as mainstream: Towards future challenges in mobile learning*. Springer. doi:10.1007/978-3-319-13416-1_9

Sanz, P., Mezcua, B., Pena, J., & Walker, B. (2014). Scenes and Images into Sounds: A Taxonomy of Image Sonification Methods for Mobility Applications. *Journal of the Audio Engineering Society, 62*(3), 161–171. doi:10.17743/jaes.2014.0009

Saponara, C., Casula, M., & Fanucci, L. (2008). ASIP-based reconfigurable architectures for power-efficient and real-time image/video processing. *Journal of Real-Time Image Processing, 3*(3), 201–216. doi:10.1007/s11554-008-0084-y

Sauleau, E. A., Paumier, J.-P., & Buemi, A. (2005). Medical record linkage in health information systems by approximate string matching and clustering. *BMC Medical Informatics and Decision Making, 5*(1), 32. doi:10.1186/1472-6947-5-32 PMID:16219102

Saunders, M., Lewis, P., & Thornhill, A. (2007). *Research Methods for Business Students* (4th ed.). Prentice Hall.

Schiel, J., & Bainbridge-Smith, A. (2015). *Efficient Edge Detection on Low Cost FPGAs*. Academic Press.

Schnipper, M. (2014). The Rise and Fall and Rise of Virtual Reality: coming Monday - An Oculus Rift in every home? *The Verge*. Retrieved from http://www.theverge.com/a/virtual-reality/>

Schön, D. (1987). *Educating the reflective practitioner*. San Francisco, CA: Jossey-Bass.

Schultz, D. E., & And Peltier, J. (2013). Social medias slippery slope: Challenges, opportunities and future research directions. *Journal of Research in Interactive Marketing, 7*(2), 86–99. doi:10.1108/JRIM-12-2012-0054

Sclater, N. (2014). *Examining open learning analytics - report from the Lace Project meeting in Amsterdam*. Retrieved October 30, 2016, from http://www.laceproject.eu/blog/examining-open-learninganalytics-report-lace-project-meeting-amsterdam/

Scratch - Imagine. Program, Share. (n. d.). Retrieved from https://scratch.mit.edu/

Sellen, A., Rogers, Y., Harper, R., & Rodden, T. (2009). Reflecting Human Values in the Digital Age. *Communications of the ACM, 52*(3), 58–66. doi:10.1145/1467247.1467265

Shah, J., & Breazeal, C. (2010). An Empirical Analysis of Team Coordination Behaviors and Action Planning With Application to Human-Robot Teaming. *Human Factors: The Journal of the Human Factors and Ergonomics Society, 52*(2), 234–245. doi:10.1177/0018720809350882 PMID:20942253

Shankaranarayan, G., Ziad, M., & Wang, R. Y. (2003). Managing data quality in dynamic decision environments: An information product approach. *Journal of Database Management, 14*(4), 14–32. doi:10.4018/jdm.2003100102

Shankar, V., & Balasubramanian, S. (2009). Mobile Marketing: A Synthesis and Prognosis. *Journal of Interactive Marketing, 23*(2), 118–129. doi:10.1016/j.intmar.2009.02.002

Sharma, R. (2010, September 23). 10 great new ideas for employee training. *Bright Hub*. Retrieved from http://www.brighthub.com/office/human-resources/articles/88251.aspx

Sharma, R., Pavlovic, V. I., & Huang, T. S. (1998). Toward multimodal human-computer interface. *Proceedings of the IEEE, 86*(5 pt 1), 853–869. doi:10.1109/5.664275

Sharples, M. (2002). *Disruptive devices: Mobile technology for conversational learning*. Retrieved from https://www.tlu.ee/~kpata/haridustehnoloogiaTLU/mobilesharples.pdf

Sharples, M. (2014). *Innovating pedagogy 2014: Open University Innovation Report 3*. Milton Keynes, UK: The Open University.

Shatenstein, B., Amre, D., Jabbour, M., & Feguery, H. (2010). Examining the relative validity of an adult food frequency questionnaire in children and adolescents. *Journal of Pediatric Gastroenterology and Nutrition, 51*(5), 645–652. doi:10.1097/MPG.0b013e3181eb6881 PMID:20871415

Sheridan, A. K., Scott, L., MacDonald, N., Murray, L., Holt, S., & Allen, K.Scottish Cross Party Working Group: Education of Children & Young People with M.E. (2013). Exploring E-learning provision for Children with ME in Scotland. *Other Education: The Journal of Educational Alternatives, 2*(1), 78–80.

Sholes, E. (2007). Evolution of a UAV autonomy classification taxonomy. *Proceedings of theIEEE Aerospace Conference Proceedings*. doi:10.1109/AERO.2007.352738

Shortliffe, E. H., Perreault, L. E., Wiederhold, G., & Fagan, L. M. (Eds.). (1990). *Medical Informatics: Computer Applications in Health Care and Biomedicine*. Addison-Wesley.

Simovska, V., Dadaczynski, K., & Woynarowska, B. (2012). Healthy eating and physical activity in schools in Europe: A toolkit for policy development and its implementation. *Health Education, 112*(6), 513–524. doi:10.1108/09654281211275863

Singh, K. (2014). Blended professional learning- modelling the paradigm shift. In B. Hegarty, J. McDonald, & S.-K. Loke (Eds.), *Rhetoric and reality: Critical perspectives on educational technology. Proceedings ascilite* (pp. 404–409). Dunedin.

Singh, K., Schrape, J., & Kelly, J. (2012). Emerging strategies for a sustainable approach to professional development. In M. Brown, M. Hartnett, & T. Stewart (Eds.), *Future challenges, sustainable futures. Proceedings ascilite* (pp. 833–842).

Sinisalo, J., Salo, J., Karjaluoto, H., & Matti, L. (2007). Mobile customer relationship management: Underlying issues and challenges. *Business Process Management Journal, 13*(6), 771–787. doi:10.1108/14637150710834541

Slade, S., & Prinsloo, P. (2013). Learning analytics: ethical issues and dilemmas. American Behavioral Scientist, 57(10), 1509-1528. doi:10.1177/0002764213479366

SlashGear. (2016). *Iris camera concept reinvents blink detection*. Retrieved from http://www.slashgear.com/iris-camera-concept-reinvents-blink-detection-01236626/

Smith, A. N., Fischer, E., & Yongjian, C. (2012). How does brand-related user-generated content differ across YouTube, Facebook, and Twitter? *Journal of Interactive Marketing, 26*(2), 102–113. doi:10.1016/j.intmar.2012.01.002

Smith, E., & Coombe, K. (2006). Quality and qualms in the marking of university assignments by sessional staff: An exploratory study. *Higher Education, 51*(1), 45–69. doi:10.1007/s10734-004-6376-7

Smith, P. C., Araya-Guerra, R., Bublitz, C., Parnes, B., Dickinson, L. M., Van Vorst, R., & Pace, W. D. (2005). Missing clinical information during primary care visits. *Journal of the American Medical Association, 293*(5), 565–571. doi:10.1001/jama.293.5.565 PMID:15687311

Smyrnova-Trybulska, E. (2015). Information and Educational Environment of the University: a Case Study. *High-Tech Educational Informational Environment,Proceedings of the International Scientific Conference*, 25-39.

Smyrnova-Trybulska, E. (2014). Some Results of the Research Conducted at the University of Silesia in the Framework of the International Research Network IRNet. In E. Smyrnova-Trybulska (Ed.), *E-learning and Intercultural Competences Development in Different Countries, Monograph* (pp. 133–144). Katowice, Cieszyn: Studio-Noa for University of Silesia.

Smyth, R. (2003). Concepts of change: Enhancing the practice of academic staff development in higher education. *The International Journal for Academic Development, 8*(1-2), 51–60. doi:10.1080/1360144042000277937

Solomon, J., Scherer, A. M., Exe, N. L., Witteman, H. O., Fagerlin, A., & Zikmund-Fisher, B. J. (2016). Is This Good or Bad? Redesigning Visual Displays of Medical Test Results in Patient Portals to Provide Context and Meaning. In *Proceedings of the 2016 CHI Conference Extended Abstracts on Human Factors in Computing Systems* (pp. 2314-2320). ACM. doi:10.1145/2851581.2892523

Soto-Gerrero, D., & Ramrez-Torres, J. G. (2013). A human-machine interface with unmanned aerial vehicles. *Proceedings of the 2013 10th International Conference Electrical Engineering, Computing Science and Automatic Control,* Mexico City, Mexico (Vol. 37, pp. 307–312). IEEE. http://doi.org/ doi:10.1109/ICEEE.2013.6676045

Steinert, Y., Mann, K., Centeno, A., Dolmans, D., Spencer, J., Gelula, M., & Prideaux, D. (2006). A systematic review of faculty development initiatives designed to improve teaching effectiveness in medical education: BEME Guide No. 8. *Medical Teacher, 28*(6), 497–526. doi:10.1080/01421590600902976 PMID:17074699

Stes, A., Min-Leliveld, M., Gijbels, D., & Van Petegem, P. (2010). The impact of instructional development in higher education: The state-of-the-art of the research. *Educational Research Review, 5*(1), 25–49. doi:10.1016/j.edurev.2009.07.001

Stewart, C. M., Schifter, C. C., & Markaridian Selverian, M. E. (Eds.). (2010). *Teaching and learning with technology: Beyond constructivism.* Oxon, UK: Routledge.

Storey, K. E. (2015). A changing landscape: Web-based methods for dietary assessment in adolescents. *Current Opinion in Clinical Nutrition and Metabolic Care, 18*(5), 437–445. doi:10.1097/MCO.0000000000000198 PMID:26125112

Strong, D. M., Lee, Y. W., & Wang, R. Y. (1997). Data quality in context. *Communications of the ACM, 40*(5), 103–110. doi:10.1145/253769.253804

Stuart, K. (2014, November 20). What a virtual reality art show could say about the future of games. *The Guardian.* Retrieved from http://www.theguardian.com/technology/2014/nov/20/virtual-reality-art-future-games

Sujatha, P., & Sudha, K. (2015). Performance Analysis of Different Edge Detection Techniques for Image Segmentation. *Indian Journal of Science and Technology, 8*(14). doi:10.17485/ijst/2015/v8i14/72946

Susono, H., Ikawa, T., Kagami, A., & Shimomura, T. (2011). Digital Storytelling "Tegami (A Letter to My Future Myself)" Project by Japanese Junior High Students. In *World Conference on Educational Multimedia, Hypermedia and Telecommunications* (Vol. 2011, No. 1, pp. 2324-2327).

Svensson, A. (2014). *Assessment of dietary intake in young populations using new approaches and technologies.* Umeå, Sweden: Print & Media. Retrieved from http://umu.diva-portal.org/

Swinburn, B. A., Sacks, G., Hall, K. D., McPherson, K., Finegood, D. T., Moodie, M. L., & Gortmaker, S. L. (2011). The global obesity pandemic: Shaped by global drivers and local environments. *Lancet, 378*(9793), 804–814. doi:10.1016/S0140-6736(11)60813-1 PMID:21872749

Swinglehurst, D., Greenhalgh, T., & Roberts, C. (2012). Computer templates in chronic disease management: Ethnographic case study in general practice. *BMJ Open, 2*(6), e001754. doi:10.1136/bmjopen-2012-001754 PMID:23192245

Synnott, K. C. (2013). Smartphones in the classroom: University faculty members' experiences. *Journal of Higher Education Management, 28*(1), 119–130.

Tabacchi, G., Amodio, E., Di Pasquale, M., Bianco, A., Jemni, M., & Mammina, C. (2014). Validation and reproducibility of dietary assessment methods in adolescents: A systematic literature review. *Public Health Nutrition, 17*(12), 2700–2714. doi:10.1017/S1368980013003157 PMID:24476625

Tabacchi, G., Filippi, A. R., Breda, J., Censi, L., Amodio, E., Napoli, G., & Mammina, C. et al. (2015). Comparative validity of the ASSO Food Frequency Questionnaire for the web-based assessment of food and nutrients intake in adolescents. *Food Nutrition Research, 59*(1), 26216. doi:10.3402/fnr.v59.26216 PMID:25882537

Tabacchi, G., Filippi, A., Amodio, E., Jemni, M., Bianco, A., Firenze, A., & Mammina, C. (2015). A meta-analysis of the validity of food frequency questionnaires targeted to adolescents. *Public Health Nutrition, 19*(7), 1168–1183. doi:10.1017/S1368980015002505 PMID:26354204

Talsma, D., Doty, T. J., & Woldorff, M. G. (2006). Selective Attention and Audiovisual Integration: Is Attending to Both Modalities a Prerequisite for Early Integration? *Cerebral Cortex, 17*(3), 679–690. doi:10.1093/cercor/bhk016 PMID:16707740

Tamarit, J. (2005). Autismo: Modelos educativos para una vida de calidad. *Revista de Neurologia, 40*(1), 181–186.

Tang, J. (2015). A new RFID-based and ontological recreation system for blind people. *International Journal of Radio Frequency Identification Technology and Applications, 4*(4), 291. doi:10.1504/IJRFITA.2015.070548

Tapscott, D. (2016). After 20 years its harder to ignore the digital economy's dark side. *Harvard Business Review*. Retrieved September 28, 2016 from https://hbr.org/2016/03/after-20-years-its-harder-to-ignore-the-digital-economys-dark-side

Taras, M. (2015). Student self-assessment: what have we learned and what are the challenges. *RELIEVE - E-Journal of educational Research, Assessment and Evaluation, 21*(1), art. ME8. DOI: 10.7203/relieve.21.1.6394

Taras, M. (2010). Student self-assessment: Processes and consequences. *Teaching in Higher Education, 15*(2), 199–209. doi:10.1080/13562511003620027

Targett, S., & Fernstrom, M. (2003). Audio games: Fun for all? All for fun! Tayebi, A., Islas Sedano, C., Tayebi, A., & Islas Sedano, C. (2014). What can your ears do? A systematic literature review regarding the role of non-speech audio. *Proceedings of EdMedia: World Conference on Educational Media and Technology, 2014*, 2653–2663.

TEACCH, Y. (2012). Modelos de intervención terapéutica educativa en autismo: ABA y TEACCH. *Revista Chilena de Psiquiatría y Neurología de la Infancia y Adolescencia, 23*(1), 50.

TEQSA. (2011). *Higher education standards framework*. Tertiary Education Quality and Standards Agency.

Teutsch, S. M., & Thacker, S. B. (1995). Planning a public health surveillance system. *Epidemiological Bulletin: Pan American Health Organization, 16*, 1–6. PMID:7794696

Thalmic Labs. (2013). Homepage - Gesture Control Has Arrived. Retrieved from https://www.myo.com/

Thalmic Labs. (2015). Myo - Real Life Applications of the Myo Armband. Retrieved from https://www.youtube.com/watch?v=te1RBQQlHz4

The Center for Digital Storytelling. (n.d.). Retrieved from http://digitalstorytelling.coe.uh.edu/index.cfm

Thorne, S., & Black, R. (2007). Language and literacy development in computer-mediated contexts and communities. *Annual Review of Applied Linguistics, 27*, 1–28. doi:10.1017/S0267190508070074

Tikhomirov, N. V. (2012). *Global strategy for the development of smart-society*. MESI is on a Smart-university. Retrieved October 30, 2016, from http://smartmesi.blogspot.com/2012/03/smart-smart.html (in Russian)

Timmermans, S., & Berg, M. (2003). *The gold standard: the challenge of evidence-based medicine and standardization in health care.* Temple University Press.

Tindell, D. R., & Bohlander, R. W. (2012). The use and abuse of cell phones and text messaging in the classroom: A survey of college students. *College Teaching, 60*(1), 1–9. doi:10.1080/87567555.2011.604802

Tingstad, V. (2007). Now its up to you! Children consuming commercial television. *Society and Business Review, 2*(1), 15–36. doi:10.1108/17465680710725254

TIVIA. (2016). Tietohallintojen johtaminen Suomessa tutkimus 2016. *Tivia julkaisut, tutkimusraportti 2016.* Retrieved October 19, 2016 from http://www.tivia.fi/sites/tivia.fi/files/tivia/Julkaisut/tutkimukset/THJ/Sofigate_tutkimusraportti_2016.pdf

Tobón, S. (2007). *Metodología sistémica de diseño curricular por competencias.* Bogotá: Grupo cife.ws.

Traxler, J. (2010). *The learner experience of mobiles, mobility and connectedness. Evaluation of Learners' Experiences of e-Learning Special Interest Group.* Retrieved October 30, 2016, from http://www.helenwhitehead.com/elesig/ELE-SIG%20Mobilities% 20ReviewPDF.pdf

Traxler, J. (2016). Inclusion in an age of mobility. *Research in Learning Technology, 24*(1), 1–17. doi:10.3402/rlt.v24.31372

Tsui, K. M., & Yanco, H. A. (2013). Design Challenges and Guidelines for Social Interaction Using Mobile Telepresence Robots. *Reviews of Human Factors and Ergonomics, 9*(1), 227–301. doi:10.1177/1557234X13502462

Turk, M. (2014). Multimodal interaction: A review. *Pattern Recognition Letters, 36*(1), 189–195. doi:10.1016/j.patrec.2013.07.003

UCT (Ed.). (2008). *Generic competences for the integral formation of socially responsible citizens.* Temuco, Chile: Universidad Católica de Temuco.

UNICEF, WHO, World Bank. (2015). *Levels and trends in child malnutrition: UNICEF-WHO-World Bank joint child malnutrition estimates.* Washington, DC: World Bank.

Universities Australia. (2015). *Key facts and data.* Retrieved from https://www.universitiesaustralia.edu.au/australias-universities/key-facts-and-data#.Vxb52T-yBBw

Valtioneuvosto. (2016). Massadatan tehokkaampi käyttö vaatii ymmärrystä sen potentiaalista ja panostusta osaamiseen. *Valtioneuvoston selvitys- ja tutkimustoiminnan julkaisusarja 16/2016.* Retrieved October, 2016 from: http://valtioneuvosto.fi/artikkeli/-/asset_publisher/tutkimus-massadatan-tehokkaampi-kaytto-vaatii-ymmarrysta-sen-potentiaalista-ja-panostusta-osaamiseen?_101_INSTANCE_3wyslLo1Z0ni_groupId=10616

van der Velden, M., Sommervold, M. M., Culén, A., & Nakstad, B. (2016). Designing Interactive Technologies with Teenagers in a Hospital Setting. In L. Little, D. Fitton, B. T. Bell, & N. Toth (Eds.), *Perspectives on HCI Research with Teenagers* (pp. 103–131). Springer International Publishing. doi:10.1007/978-3-319-33450-9_5

Venkatesan, K., Nelaturu, S., Vullamparthi, A. J., & Rao, S. 2013. Hybrid ontology based e-Learning expert system for children with Autism. *Proceedings of the2013 International Conference of Information and Communication Technology (ICoICT).* doi:10.1109/ICoICT.2013.6574555

Verbert, K., Manouselis, N., Drachsler, H., & Duval, E. (2012). Dataset-Driven Research to Support Learning and Knowledge Analytics. *Journal of Educational Technology & Society, 15*(3), 133–148.

Vereecken, C. A., Covents, M., Matthys, C., & Maes, L. (2005). Young adolescents' nutrition assessment on computer (YANA-C). *European Journal of Clinical Nutrition, 59*(5), 658–667. doi:10.1038/sj.ejcn.1602124 PMID:15741983

Vereecken, C. A., Covents, M., Sichert-Hellert, W., Alvira, J. M., Le Donne, C., De Henauw, S., & Moreno, L. A. et al. HELENA Study Group. (2008). Development and evaluation of a self-administered computerized 24-h dietary recall method for adolescents in Europe. *International Journal of Obesity*, *32*(5), S26–S34. doi:10.1038/ijo.2008.180 PMID:19011650

Vereecken, C. A., De Bourdeaudhuij, I., & Maes, L. (2010). The HELENA online food frequency questionnaire: Reproducibility and comparison with four 24-hour recalls in Belgian-Flemish adolescents. *European Journal of Clinical Nutrition*, *64*(5), 541–548. doi:10.1038/ejcn.2010.24 PMID:20216566

Vereecken, C. A., & Maes, L. (2006). Comparison of a computer administered and paper-and-pencil administered questionnaire on health and lifestyle behaviors. *The Journal of Adolescent Health*, *38*(4), 426–432. doi:10.1016/j.jadohealth.2004.10.010 PMID:16549304

Verma, P. (2016). Flying User Interface. *Adjunct Proceedings of the 29th Annual Symposium on User Interface Software and Technology UIST '16,* Tokyo, Japan (pp. 203–204). ACM. doi:10.1145/2984751.2984770

Wadley, G., Vetere, F., Hopkins, L., Green, J., & Kulik, L. (2014). Exploring ambient technology for connecting hospitalised children with school and home. *International Journal of Human-Computer Studies*, *72*(8–9), 640–653. doi:10.1016/j.ijhcs.2014.04.003

Wainer, J., Robins, B., Amirabdollahian, F., & Dautenhahn, K. 2014. Using the Humanoid Robot KASPAR to Autonomously Play Triadic Games and Facilitate Collaborative Play Among Children With Autism. IEEE Transactions on Autonomous Mental Development, 6(3), 183-199. doi:10.1109/TAMD.2014.2303116

Waldrop, M. (2013, November7). Smart Connections. *Nature*, *503*(7474), 22–24. doi:10.1038/503022a PMID:24201264

Wang, R. Y., & Strong, D. M. (1996). Beyond accuracy: What data quality means to data consumers. *JMIS*, 5-33.

Wang, R. Y. (1998). A product perspective on total data quality management. *Communications of the ACM*, *41*(2), 58–65. doi:10.1145/269012.269022

Wang, Y. J., Butt, O. J., & Wei, J. (2011). My identity is my membership: A longitudinal explanation of online brand community members behavioral characteristics. *Journal of Brand Management*, *19*(1), 45–56. doi:10.1057/bm.2011.28

Warma, E. (2016, October). *Presentation My Data (and the EU Data) in Internet Forum*. Aalto University.

Watanabe, M., Yamaoka, K., Yokotsuka, M., Adachi, M., & Tango, T. (2011). Validity and reproducibility of the FFQ (FFQW82) for dietary assessment in female adolescents. *Public Health Nutrition*, *14*(2), 297–305. doi:10.1017/S1368980010001618 PMID:20537215

Wentworth, D. (2014, August 28). 5 trends for the future of learning and development. *Training*. Retrieved from https://trainingmag.com/5-trends-future-learning-and-development

Whitchurch, C. (2008). Shifting Identities and blurring boundaries: The emergence of third space professionals in UK higher education. *Higher Education Quarterly*, *62*(4), 377–396. doi:10.1111/j.1468-2273.2008.00387.x

WHO Regional Office for Europe. (2006, November 15–17). European charter on counteracting obesity (document EUR/06/5062700/8).

Willett, W. C. (2012). Overview of Nutritional Epidemiology. In W. C. Willett (Ed.), *Nutritional Epidemiology*. Oxford Scholar Online. doi:10.1093/acprof:oso/9780199754038.003.0001

Willis, D., & Willis, J. (2007). *Doing Task-based Teaching*. Oxford, UK: Oxford University Press.

World Health Organization. (2014). Global status report on noncommunicable diseases.

World Health Organization. (2016). WHO Library Cataloguing-in-Publication Data Report of the commission on ending childhood obesity.

World Health Organization. 2016. Autism spectrum disorders. Retrieved from http://www.who.int/mediacentre/factsheets/autism-spectrum-disorders/en/

Xbee, OEM. (2012). OEM RF Modules by MaxStream. Inc. Specifications. *ZigBee, 802*(15), 4.

Xilinx.com. (2016). *Vivado High Level Synthesis*. Retrieved from https://www.xilinx.com/products/design-tools/vivado/integration/esl-design.html

Yadav K. (2014). Role of Cloud Computing in Education. *International Journal of Innovative Research in Computer and Communication Engineering, 2*(2), 3108-3112.

Yang, Y. T. C., & Wu, W. C. I. (2012). Digital storytelling for enhancing student academic achievement, critical thinking, and learning motivation: A year-long experimental study. *Computers & Education, 59*(2), 339–352. doi:10.1016/j.compedu.2011.12.012

Yániz, C. & Villardón, L. (2006). Planificar desde competencias para promover el aprendizaje. *Cuadernos Monográficos del ICE*, 12.

Yinghong, M., Zhi-Hong, M., Wenyan, J., Chengliu, L., Jiawei, Y., & Mingui, S. (2011). Magnetic Hand Tracking for Human-Computer Interface. *IEEE Transactions on* Magnetics, *47*(5), 970–973. doi:10.1109/TMAG.2010.2076401

Yin, R. K. (2003). *Case study research: Design and methods* (3rd ed.). Thousand Oaks, CA: Sage.

Yuan, B., & Folmer, E. (2008). Blind hero. *Proceedings of the 10th international ACM SIGACCESS conference on Computers and accessibility - Assets '08* (p. 169). New York, USA: ACM Press. http://doi.org/ doi:10.1145/1414471.1414503

ZedBoard. (2016). Retrieved from http://zedboard.org/product/zedboard

Zhen-tao, L., Tao, L., & Jun-gang, H. (2013). A novel reconfigurable data-flow architecture for real time video processing. *Journal of shanghai Jiaotong University (Science), 18*(3), 348-359.

Zimenkovsky, B. S. (Ed.). (2010). Methodology and ranking multidisciplinary principles of structural units LNMU named Danylo Halytsky: Guidelines. Lvov.

Zimmerman, J., & Forlizzi, J. (2014). Research Through Design in HCI. In J. S. Olson & W. A. Kellogg (Eds.), *Ways of Knowing in HCI* (pp. 167–189). Springer New York. doi:10.1007/978-1-4939-0378-8_8

# About the Contributors

**Tomayess Issa** is a senior lecturer at the School of Information Systems at Curtin University, Australia. Tomayess completed her doctoral research in Web development and Human Factors. As an academic, she is also interested in establishing teaching methods and styles to enhance the students' learning experiences and resolve problems that students face. Tomayess Issa Conference and Program Co-Chair of the IADIS International Conference on Internet Technologies and Society and ADIS International Conference on International Higher Education. Furthermore, she initiated the IADIS conference for Sustainability, Green IT and Education. Currently, she conducts research locally and globally in information systems, Human-Computer Interaction, Usability, Social Networking, Teaching and Learning, Sustainability, Green IT and Cloud Computing. Tomayess participated in a couple of conferences and published her work in several peer-reviewed journals, books, book chapters, papers and research reports Tomayess Issa is a Project leader in the International research network (IRNet-EU (Jan2014 – Dec 2017)) to study and develop new tools and methods for advanced pedagogical science in the field of ICT instruments, e-learning and intercultural competences and she is a senior research member of ISRLAb (Information Society Research Lab) from International Association for Development of the Information Society.

**Piet Kommers** focused his teaching and research on the topic Media, Education and Communication. His study Pedagogy and School Education at the University of Utrecht was dedicated to find out how learning dialogues can be made adaptive to the actual state in the learner's mind. As minor he built an experimental setup in order to detect hemispheric asymmetry in the detection of a simple figure in the larger visual context. He received the academic reward for excellent research achievement. The University of Utrecht offered Piet Kommers the appointment of junior researcher at the topic of "Small group learning through collaborative problem solving". A computer-based observation system was developed and led to the conclusion that the more heterogeneous group composition triggered a wider elicitation of prior concepts and reflection during joint problem solving. During the episode 1982-2015 Piet Kommers was appointed by the University of Twente that made him elaborate further research into educational technology, new media like hypertext, concept mapping and virtual spaces for surgical training. He was elected to lead the Nato Advanced Research Workshops into "Cognitive Learning Tools" and instigated quite many international European research projects. As associate professor he became responsible for the courses "Designing New Media Applications", "Visual Communication" and "Social Media for Communication." Fontys University for Applied Sciences welcomed his part-time position as professor at the aspect of "Didactic Integration of ICT" (2003-2005). In this function he conveyed teacher trainers in the new media prospects like mobile- and networked learning. Piet Kommers is renown keynote speaker at international conferences around the world and was elected as overall chairman of the IADIS conferences on Societal Impact of ICT. He is Associate- en Executive Editor of the respective journals "International Journal of Continuous Engineering Education and Life-long Learning" and the "International Journal for Web-based Communities". As professor Educational Technologies for UNESCO, Piet Kommers wrote numerous reports for authorities in Eastern European- and Asian countries on how ICT and new media increasingly work catalytic on the continuous evolution of education, training and lifelong learning. From November 2014 Piet Kommers joins the scientific staff at the University of Utrecht for supervising Master level students in Educational Science.

**Theodora Issa** is a Senior Lecturer in the School of Management at Curtin University. She is the recipient of the Emerald/European Fund for Management Development 2010 Outstanding Research Award for her PhD thesis under the title 'Ethical mindsets, aesthetics and spirituality: a mixed-methods approach analysis of the Australian services sector'. Theodora holds the title of Curtin Business School's 'New Researcher of the Year' that was bestowed on her in 2010. Theodora is the recipient of multi awards and grants from the faculty, university and external bodies. She has published and continues to publish research work on business ethics, sustainability, technology, social media, corporate social responsibility, and higher education. Currently, Theodora is conducting her post-doctoral research on ethical mindsets, spirituality and aesthetics and currently working on a manuscript for a book on 'Ethical Mindsets: A Comparative Study' for publication with Springer, Switzerland. Theodora is a co-researcher in projects on sustainable development and business strategies, cloud computing, green IT and sustainability, corruption resistance, misconduct, social media and social awareness. Theodora is a member of the 'Sustainability and Leadership Research Network (SLRN)'. Theodora is also a member in the International research network (IRNet) for study and development of new tools and methods for advanced pedagogical science in the field of ICT instruments, e-learning and intercultural competences with some twenty scholars from Europe. Theodora is an Associate Editor, and a member of editorial committees of international journals and a member of organising committees of international conferences, also a reviewer of journals such as the Journal of Business Ethics. Theodora holds memberships in several local and international bodies including Australia and New Zealand Academy of Management (ANZAM), American Academy of Management (AOM), and European Business Ethics Network, UK (EBEN-UK). Theodora is one of the webmasters of her community's website http://soca.cjb.net (since 1995) and is one of the editors of the weekly bulletin since 1995 that is currently available online under URL http://noohro.cjb.net. In 2012 Theodora was appointed a delegate to the 10th Assembly, Busan, South Korea, of the World Council of Churches (WCC) representing her Syrian Orthodox Church. In November 2013, and during this assembly's sessions, Dr Theodora Issa was elected a member of the Central Committee of the WCC representing the Syrian Orthodox Patriarchate of Antioch and all the East. It is worthwhile noting that this is the first time a female member has been elected to this position on behalf of the Syrian Orthodox Church. In July 2014 Theodora was nominated by the church and later voted as a member of the 'Education and Ecumenical Formation (EEF) Commission of the WCC. In June 2016 Theodora was nominated by the church and later voted as a member of the Permanent Committee on Consensus and Collaboration (PCCC).

**Pedro Isaías** is an associate professor at The University of Queensland, Brisbane, Australia. Previously he was associate professor at the Universidade Aberta (Portuguese Open University) in Lisbon, Portugal, responsible for several courses and director of the master degree program in Management / MBA. Was director of master degree program in Electronic Commerce and Internet for 10 years. He holds a PhD in Information Management (in the specialty of information and decision systems) from the New University of Lisbon. Author of several books, book chapters, papers and research reports, all in the information systems area, he has headed several conferences and workshops within the mentioned area. He has also been responsible for the scientific coordination of several EU funded research projects. He is also member of the editorial board of several journals and program committee member of several conferences and workshops. At the moment he conducts research activity related to E-Commerce and E-Business, E-Learning, Information Systems in general, and WWW related areas.

**Touma B. Issa** holds Ph.D. from Murdoch University, Western Australia. He is an Adjunct Research Associate at Murdoch University. He has an over twenty-five years' experience in academia and industry in chemistry. Between 2009 and 2014, he presented lectures on Energy Storage to post graduate students. His research interests include: analytical chemistry particularly relating to atmospheric pollution, electrochemistry as applied to batteries where he was involved in planning and conducting research and development activities to optimize the smart flow battery chemistry technologies, surface modified electrodes, waste water purification and remediation of ground drinking water. Touma is a member of The Royal Australian Chemical Institute since 1993, and a member of The Electrochemical Society since 2006.

* * *

**Ayodeji O. Abioye** is a PhD research student with the Aeronautic, Astronautic, and Computational Engineering (AACE) academic unit of the Faculty of Engineering and the Environment (FEE), University of Southampton, UK.

**Antonino Bianco** since 2008 to present is working as assistant Professor at University of Palermo, Italy (http://portale.unipa.it/persone/docenti/b/antonino.bianco). Of interest, in January 2011, he becomes member of TEG (Technical Expert Group) on EHFA project. The European Health and Fitness Association (EHFA) is a UE initiative with the aim to standardize and disseminate standards on fitness vocational education training. EHFA Standards are developed by the EHFA Standards Council which is an independent body responsible for the direction and strategic thinking for developing the regulatory framework, which underpins public confidence in the work and development of the European Health and Fitness industry, and in a complex environment of European dimensions. It works closely with the European Commission, especially in support of its Lifelong Learning Programme. In January 2012, he becomes Scientific Consultant of the ASSO Project (2012-2014). A national project supported by the Italian Ministry of Health and managed by the Principal Investigator Dr. Garden Tabacchi (Ministero della Salute / Age.na.s – CUP: I85J10000500001). From 2013 up to 2016. Scientific Advisor UNIPA Team for LISTANet consortium-European Project. "A Healthy Diet for a Healthy Life (JPI HDHL), first joint action: the Knowledge Hub on the DEterminants of DIet and Physical Activity (DEDIPAC–HK)". Since 2013 to present, he is the Deputy Dean for International Relations of Sport and Exercise Sciences

Degree Courses at University of Palermo. From 2005 to present, he published 80 Peer-Reviewed Research Papers and 145 Proceedings and participated as Speaker and Keynote Speaker at National invited presentations and International invited presentation.

**Otávio Bocheco** holds a Master's degree in Scientific and Technological Education from the Federal University of Santa Catarina, Brazil. He is a lecturer at the Federal Institute Catarinense, Campus Rio do Sul. He teacher undergraduate courses in Physics and Teaching of Physics. Bocheco is also a coordinator for the Institutional Program Initiation Teaching Grant. He is involved in research and professional development of teachers in public schools.

**Jorun Børsting** is a Ph.D. candidate at the University of Oslo, with particular interests in the design of health information technology. Her current research address how technology could support children and teens suffering from Myalgic Encephalomyelitis (ME) in their everyday lives.

**Federico Cabitza** received his Master in IT Engineering from the Politecnico of Milan in 2001. Since then, he has worked as a Requirement Engineer in the private sector, specialising in health informatics. In 2007, he received his PhD in Informatics. Currently, he is an Assistant Professor at the University of Milano-Bicocca (Milan, Italy) where he teaches human-computer interaction. His current research interests regard requirement social settings in general. He is an author of more than 120 research publications to date, in international conference proceedings, edited books and scientific journals.

**Verónica Cevallos León Wong** is a clinical psychologist, currently developing research projects in Universidad Politécnica Salesiana, in Cuenca Ecuador, addressed to support vulnerable population through technology. In addition, she offers psychological services at the Ecuadorian Social Ensurance Institute, and private consulting has complemented her professional exercise. Her career has focused on child psychology, as she collaborated with the foster care institution, Mensajeros de la Paz. Psychologist Cevallos was also immersed in education, since she worked at the psychology department of Bell Academy elementary school.

**Alma Leora Culén** is the associate professor at the Institute of Informatics, University of Oslo. Her teaching and research interests are in the field of interaction design. One of the research directions that she likes is on use and design of technology for people at risk (elderly, children and adolescents).

**Olena Glazunova** (Doctor sciences in Pedagogic, specialty: Information Communication Technologies in Education) possesses an expertise in the development and use of information technologies in educational process, design and development of e-learning environment, e-learning courses. She has experience in creating educational cluster University, development of managing procedures of electronic educational environment based on ISO 9001, integration of Microsoft's cloud services with e-learning environment, guidelines of creating e-learning courses, provision of attestation e-learning courses. She also initiated three International conferences in the field of e-education. She took part in three research projects commissioned by the Ministry Education and Science of Ukraine (Models of Distance Learning (2008-2010), Certification of e-learning courses (2010-2012), Creating a hybrid cloud-based information and educational environment of the university of agrarian profile (2016-2017)) and three international TEMPUS projects. She has more then 90 publications, 3 of them – in Scopus DB.

**Mark S. Glynn** is an Associate Professor in the Faculty of Business and Law at the Auckland University of Technology, Auckland, New Zealand. He has a PhD in Marketing from the University of Auckland and won an Emerald/EFMD Best Thesis Award for outstanding doctoral research in Marketing Strategy. His research areas include branding, business-to-business marketing, private labels and buyer-seller relationships. Mark's research has been published in many international journals including the European Journal of Marketing, Industrial Marketing Management, Journal of Business Research, Journal of Business & Industrial Marketing and Marketing Theory. He recently coedited a special issue on resource management for the Australasian Marketing Journal.

**Peter Gobel** is a professor in the Faculty of Cultural Studies. His research interests include communication strategies, learning strategies, motivation, individual differences in language learning, extensive reading/listening and digital storytelling.

**Pablo Gobira** is a Professor Doctor at Escola Guignard (UEMG, Brazil), artist, curator and researcher. He is a research fellow and manager of Digital Promotion Services of the Brazilian Network at IBICT/Brazil Ministry of Science, Technology, Innovation and Communication (MCTI). Member of the National Institute of Science and Technology INCT-Acqua (CNPq). Writer and editor of the books: "Post-digital configurations" (Forthcoming UEMG Press, 2017); "Games and Society" (Crisálida Press, 2012); Walter Benjamin "B-side" (Crisálida Press, 2011) among others books and writings. He works in curatorship, creation and production in the field of culture and digital arts and also creative economy. He is coordinating the Laboratory of Front Poetics (http://labfront.tk).

**Anabela de Jesus Gomes** (born 1971) concluded her PhD, MSc and BSc ("Licenciatura" - 5 years), all in Informatics Engineering at the University of Coimbra, in 2010, 2000 and 1995, respectively. She is a Professor at the Department of Informatics Engineering of the Polytechnic Institute of Coimbra (DEIS-IPC) since 1997 where she has been teaching Digital Systems, Operating Systems, Informatics Technology, Computer Architecture, Multimedia, Programming and Human Computer Interaction. She has led various projects and internships within the various degrees offered in the DEIS-IPC, as well as under the Erasmus program. She has been member of the jury panel for several projects and internships of the different degrees taught in DEIS-IPC. She has over 50 scientific articles in prestigious international journals and conferences, as exemplified by the FIE-"Frontiers in Education Conference", ITiCSE-"Conference on Innovation and Technology in Computer Science Education", SIGCSE- "Association for Computing Machinery's Special Interest Group on Computer Science Education", PPIG-"Psychology of Programming Interest Group", Journal of Universal Computer Science or the Journal of Algorithms. She is a member of the Cognitive and Media Systems research group at the Centre for Informatics and Systems of the University of Coimbra (CISUC) and of the Applied Research Institute of IPC. Her research work focuses mostly in the area of Programming Teaching and Learning, Learning Styles, Learning Taxonomies, Learning Theories, Psychology of Programming and E-learning. Her work has been referenced in publications of other authors. She has participated in the organisation of several national and international scientific meetings, as a member of the Organising and Scientific Committees, chair of sessions and reviewer of scientific papers. She has also participated in several professional development courses, especially focusing on their areas of interest and integrated various working groups in the DEIS-IPC.

**María Soledad Ibarra-Sáiz** is a professor of Educational Assessment at the University of Cadiz, and Director of EVALfor Research Group. Her research interests include e-assessment, self- and peer-assessment in Higher Education.

**Monèm Jemni** is a well-established and World leading authorities in Sport and Exercise Science. Following 22 years of professional career between, France, the USA and the UK, he joined Qatar University as Qatar Olympic Committee Professorial Chair in Sport Science Programme since late 2014. An exercise physiologist by training, his research focuses on the optimization of human performance tackled with a cross-disciplinary orientated approach, in sports and in health related conditions (obesity, type 2 diabetes, heart diseases...). His research background was in coaching and fitness training regimes in high-level athletes. He was one of the European Commission's reviewers for Health related research projects set between several EU countries (consortiums). He was appointed as an International Expert in several health, exercise, diet and life style projects, such as the ASSO project, funded by the Italian Ministry of Health and with support of the World Health organisation. Dr Jemni is still an active member within the Diabetes working group of the South Asians Health Foundation, a stakeholder of NICE at the UK's Health Government. His key skills are: strong interpersonal, tactfulness and managerial skills with strategically thinking and work collaboratively to developing and delivering quality controlled programs in order to reach all key stakeholders. He has experience in planning, budgeting and leading of small to big international projects from conception to socially and academically impacting deliveries. Dr. Monèm Jemni sits in several journal editorial boards as Associate Chief Editor, such as the British Journal of sport medicine. He published one textbook, was invited as keynote speaker in 25 World stages/conferences, edited 5 International conference proceedings and 115 original manuscripts. He also led a dozen of postgraduate students to success, including MS Research and PhDs.

**Katharine Jones** teaches marketing communications at AUT University in Auckland, New Zealand, and is actively researching in the area of social media use, especially looking at how children use social media to connect with brands. Other areas of research interest involve the development of social policy for the protection of vulnerable children, with a special focus on children's online protection.

**Makimi Kano** is an associate professor in the Faculty of Cultural Studies. She is a corpus linguist, carrying out lexical research on loanwords, metaphors, and language change. Her other research interests include extensive reading/listening, vocabulary acquisition, and lexicography.

**Esraa Khattab** received her computer engineering degree in 2014 with a GPA 3.94. Just after graduating, she started her Masters studies and submitted the thesis entitled "High Performance Implementation for Blink Detection Using FPGAs" in November 2014.

**Maija Korhonen** is a Licentiate of Science (Technology) graduated from Helsinki University of Technology (since 2010 called Aalto University) with studies in Industrial Engineering and Management, Chemistry, Business Law and additional studies in Communication at Helsinki University. She has also conducted studies on Human Resource Management at Jyväskylä University School of Business and Economics. She has especially concentrated on Digitalization, and the aspects of and issues in the Finnish leadership, both on the public and private sectors, an area she sees as a major obstacle for future success of Finland as a nation. Currently she is a Research Manager at Mikkeli University of Applied

Sciences where her main areas of research include eServices, e-commerce, My Data, Business models, Management and Leadership. During the years 2011 to 2014 she worked as a senior advisor in Tekes – the Finnish Funding Agency for Innovation, where she acquired extensive experience and knowledge on R&D funding and had the opportunity to work together with several Finnish high-tech companies and innovative organizations. In addition to this, for over 20 years she has held board memberships in several small and middle sized enterprises. Previously, she also stayed 5 years as a research scientist at Helsinki University of Technology, in the Laboratory of Polymers Science Technology, a unit that was nominated Centre of Excellence by Academy of Finland. Maija Korhonen has several publication published in international conference proceedings and academic journals as well as on national publications. She is also an Aalto University Alumni.

**Marcos Lévano** received his Bachelor's degree in Computer Science in 2001. In 2002 he graduated from Computer Engineering Program at Universidad Nacional de Trujillo, Peru. In 2005 he received the Master degree in Computer Engineering Science at Universidad de Santiago de Chile. Since 2006 he has worked as a teacher in the Computer Engineering Science Program in Universidad Católica de Temuco. Currently, he is the Head Master of the program. His main research areas are education, media, communication & education and pattern recognition in clustering. Professor Lévano is the chief responsible for updating the curriculum of studies of the Civil Engineering Computer Science at the Universidad Católica de Temuco based on the agenda of improvement plan by the accreditation agency sent by CNA Chile.

**Angela Locoro** holds an MA in Modern Literatures, BSc in Computer Science and PhD in Information Engineering. She is currently a research fellow at Università degli Studi di Milano-Bicocca. She has eight years of experience in knowledge representation, natural language processing and semantic web technologies, and two years experience in knowledge artefacts theory and design. She is in the organisation committee of the EUSSET Summer School on Computer Supported Cooperative Work. Her recent works focused on human-data interaction, collaborative and semantic annotation tools, and knowledge artefacts. She has a strong research interest for science and technologies studies, and feminist studies.

**Martín López-Nores** received the Ph.D. degree in computer science from the University of Vigo in 2006. He is currently an Associate Professor with the Department of Telematics Engineering of the University, and a member of the Services for Information Society Research Group. His research interests touch all areas of semantic knowledge modelling and reasoning, mobile information services and expert system applications.

**Nataliia Morze** is a professor, Vice-Rector on Informational Technologies of Borys Grinchenko Kyiv University. She is a Corresponding Member of the National Academy of Pedagogical Sciences of Ukraine. Her professional and scientific interests are in the areas of distance learning technologies, education for adults, implementation of information and communication technologies into education process of secondary and higher educational institutions, creation of teaching and scientific e-learning environment, development of teachers information competence. She is an author more than 300 scientific articles and monographs.

**Antônio Mozelli** has a Degree in Computer Science and a Degree in Fine Arts at the Escola Guignard (UEMG). He is a member of Laboratory of Front Poetics (http://labfront.tk).

**Jose J. Pazos-Arias** received his degree in Telecommunications Engineering from the Technical University of Madrid (Spain-UPM) in 1987, and his Ph.D. degree in Computer Science at the same University in 1995. Nowadays, he is a Professor at the Department of Telematics Engineering at the University of Vigo. He is the director and founder of the Services for Information Society Research Group (http://gssi.det.uvigo.es) in the University of Vigo, which is currently involved with national and international projects for the development of services and applications in the Information Society field, receiving funds from both public institutions and industry. He has written more than 190 papers on international journals, books, conferences and workshops. He has been the advisor of seven PhD and more than 30 Master thesis. He was the head of the Department of Telematics Engineering from its foundation to July 2004. In the last few years, his research interests have dealt with transversal technologies that reach far beyond the purposes of any specific media. Thus, he has achieved relevant results in the area of personalization, recommendation and adaptation of contents grounded on semantic technologies. In this field, he has participated in several pilot projects involved with the construction of personalized tourist experiences, with the recommendation of audiovisual contents, with personalized mobile TV services, with a platform of contextualized and non-intrusive advertising, with residential gateways for ambient intelligence, and with e-learning services, among others. Most recently, with the aim of combining the power of semantic reasoning technologies and the participation phenomena arising in the knowledge society, he is exploring the interest of social-semantic technologies to assist the users when it comes to facing complex decision takings in the cloud.

**Diego Quisi-Peralta** was born in Cuenca, Ecuador in 1989. He received the engineering degree in computer systems from the Universidad Politécnica Salesiana, Cuenca, Ecuador in 2013. He continued his studies in area of advanced computer technologies and obtained the Master degree from University of Catilla-La Mancha(Spain) in 2015. Nowadays, he is a member of the research group in artificial intelligence, and assistive technologies at the Universidad Politécnica Salesiana, where collaborates as full-time teacher-technical. His research interests include artificial intelligence, assistive technologies, data mining, ontologies, computer vision and development web and mobile.

**Vladimir Robles-Bykbaev** was born in Azogues, Ecuador in 1980. He received the engineering degree in computer systems from the Universidad Politécnica Salesiana, Cuenca, Ecuador in 2006. He continued his studies in area of artificial intelligence and obtained the Master degree from Universidad Politécnica de Valencia (Spain) in 2010. In 2016 year he has obtained the PhD degree from University of Vigo (Spain). Nowadays, he is in charge of the research group in artificial intelligence, and assistive technologies at the Universidad Politécnica Salesiana, where collaborates as full-time teacher. His research interests include artificial intelligence, assistive technologies, data mining, and computer vision.

**Gregorio Rodríguez-Gómez** is a professor of Educational Research Methods at the University of Cadiz, and member of EVALfor Research Group. His research interests include e-assessment, self- and peer-assessment in Higher Education.

**Peter Saddington** is an experienced software engineer who has worked on a broad range of technical and market domains during his employment at TEKEVER and previously at Roke Manor Research Ltd. Peter has developed software solutions ranging from simple command-line applications to highly complex multi-threaded multi-application developments. His work spans a variety of technical domains including 2G & 3G mobile telephone technologies, Ultra-wideband, millimetre-wave passive radar, phase array radar data capture platforms and data analysis tools, and latterly, a significant number of diverse 2D & 3D image processing applications. A large part of the image processing applications involve the processing of live data to provide near real-time capabilities for mobile platforms. Peter holds a Ph.D. in Artificial Intelligence from the University of Surrey, complimented by a B.Eng in Information Systems Engineering with French.

**Ieda M. Santos** holds a PhD in Education. She is an Associate Professor at Emirates College for Advanced Education. She teaches educational technology courses and research methods courses at undergraduate and graduate level. Her research interests include mobile learning, social network, technology integration in the classroom, mobile learning and bring your own device (BYOD).

**Kuki Singh** has taught in undergraduate and graduate education in a variety of settings, for over three decades. Her work has included course design and development, as well as staff and student development. In recent years her research and practice has included strategic academic development projects encompassing innovations in elearning, improving student engagement and teaching quality.

**Eugenia Smyrnova-Trybulska** is an Associate Professor at the University of Silesia in Katowice, Poland. She is Head of the Department of Humanistic Education and Auxiliary Sciences of Pedagogy, Faculty of Ethnology and Sciences of Education at the University's Cieszyn Branch. She is Coordinator of the Faculty Distance Learning Platform (http://el.us.edu.pl/weinoe) and of the Theoretical and Practical Aspects of Distance Learning Conference (http://www.dlcc.us.edu.pl) as well as a coordinator for the European IRNet project (www.irnet.us.edu.pl) and other scientific and education projects. She has written more than 150 scholarly papers and monographs in the field of e-learning methodology, ICT in education, multimedia, teacher training in the area of ICT and e-learning and has been a teaching methodology consultant for more than 160 distance learning courses.

**Garden Tabacchi** received her degree in Biology from the University of Palermo in 1998. She continues her academic career working on research in the field of human nutrition, obtaining the specialization title as nutritionist, the PhD in Human food science and nutrition, and a Master title in Clinical Nutrition and Dietetics. She acquires skills in nutritional surveillance, prevention of obesity and chronic diseases in adults and especially in youth at the Italian Institute of Human Nutrition and at the Regional Office for Europe, Nutrition section of the World Health Organization in Copenhagen. She is Principal Investigator of the ASSO Project funded by the Italian Ministry of Health, and collaborates in different other projects funded by other Institutions and EC. She is temporary professor of three disciplines at the University of Palermo (Hygiene, Epidemiologic methodology, and Health prevention and promotion in youth). She is author of numerous international and national publications and communications.

**Ana Rita Assunção Teixeira** (born 1981) has a Graduation in Mathematics applied to Technology, Porto University; a Master in Electronic Engineering and Telecommunications, Aveiro University and a PhD in Electronic Engineering, Aveiro University (17/02/2011). She did a Postdoctoral researcher at the University of Aveiro with a FCT grant during one year in computer science. She is Professor at the Department of Informatics of the Polytechnic Institute of Coimbra (ESEC-IPC) since 2009. She has been member of the jury panel for several projects and internships of the different degrees taught in ESEC-IPC and in Aveiro University. She is a professor in Human Computer Interaction (HCI) Master in ESEC/IPC where already supervised several master thesis. She has over 65 scientific articles in prestigious international journals and conferences. She is a member of the Processing Signal research group at the Institute of Electronic Engineering of the University of Aveiro (IEETA) and of the Applied Research Institute of IPC. She has participated in the organisation of several national and international scientific meetings.

**João Viana** is the Director of the Research Center in Sports Sciences, Health Sciences and Human Development at the University Institute of Maia, Portugal.

# Index

## A

## B

## C

## D

## E

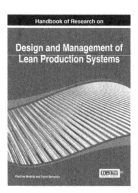
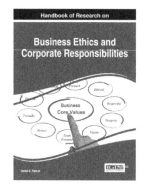

Printed in the United States
By Bookmasters